⬠ **W9-BYZ-361**

FEDERAL RULES OF EVIDENCE

2019–2020 Edition

Prepared by Professor Daniel J. Capra

Reed Professor of Law, Fordham Law School
Reporter to the Advisory Committee on Evidence Rules

Including

1. Reporter's Comments on Restyled Rules
effective December 1, 2011
2. Notes by the Federal Judicial Center on Changes made
by Congress to the Advisory Committee's proposals
3. New Amendments to Rules 803 and 902,
which took effect on December 1, 2017
4. New Amendment to Rule 807, with Committee Note,
scheduled to take effect on December 1, 2019
5. Pertinent Advisory Committee Notes
6. Relevant Legislative History
7. Deleted and Superseded Materials

also

UNIFORM RULES OF EVIDENCE

CALIFORNIA EVIDENCE CODE

REPORT ON CASE LAW DIVERGENCE FROM FEDERAL
RULES OF EVIDENCE BY DANIEL J. CAPRA

BEST PRACTICES FOR AUTHENTICATING DIGITAL EVIDENCE
BY HON. PAUL W. GRIMM, DANIEL J. CAPRA,
AND GREGORY P. JOSEPH

WEST
ACADEMIC
PUBLISHING

© West, a Thomson business, 1997–2002, 2004–2008
© 2009–2012 Thomson Reuters
© 2013 LEG, Inc. d/b/a West Academic Publishing
© 2014–2018 LEG, Inc. d/b/a West Academic
© 2019 LEG, Inc. d/b/a West Academic
    444 Cedar Street, Suite 700
    St. Paul, MN 55101
    1-877-888-1330

Printed in the United States of America

ISBN: 978-1-64242-916-9

SUMMARY OF CONTENTS

FEDERAL RULES OF EVIDENCE
FOR UNITED STATES COURTS

ARTICLE I. GENERAL PROVISIONS

ARTICLE II. JUDICIAL NOTICE

ARTICLE III. PRESUMPTIONS IN CIVIL CASES

ARTICLE IV. RELEVANCY AND ITS LIMITS

ARTICLE V. PRIVILEGES

ARTICLE VI. WITNESSES

SUMMARY OF CONTENTS

ARTICLE VII. OPINIONS AND EXPERT TESTIMONY

ARTICLE VIII. HEARSAY

ARTICLE IX. AUTHENTICATION AND IDENTIFICATION

ARTICLE X. CONTENTS OF WRITINGS, RECORDINGS, AND PHOTOGRAPHS

SUMMARY OF CONTENTS

SUMMARY OF CONTENTS

FEDERAL RULES OF EVIDENCE FOR UNITED STATES COURTS*

PUBLIC LAW 93–595; 88 STAT. 1926

Approved Jan. 2, 1975

[H.R. 5463]

An Act to establish rules of evidence for certain courts and proceedings.

Be it enacted by the Senate and House of Representatives of the United States of America in Congress assembled, That:

The following rules shall take effect on the one hundred and eightieth day beginning after the date of the enactment of this Act. These rules apply to actions, cases, and proceedings brought after the rules take effect. These rules also apply to further procedure in actions, cases, and proceedings then pending, except to the extent that application of the rules would not be feasible, or would work injustice, in which event former evidentiary principles apply.

SUPREME COURT ORDERS AUTHORIZING PROPOSED AMENDMENTS TO THE FEDERAL RULES OF EVIDENCE TO BE TRANSMITTED TO CONGRESS[1]

ORDER OF APRIL 30, 1979

1.   That Rule 410 of the Federal Rules of Evidence be, and it hereby is, amended to read as follows:

2.   That the foregoing amendment to the Federal Rules of Evidence shall take effect on November 1, 1979, and shall be applicable to all proceedings then pending except to the extent that in the opinion of the court

---

* Each rule of the original Federal Rules of Evidence enacted in 1975 also includes a Note by the Federal Judicial Center setting forth any change that was made by Congress to the Advisory Committee's proposed rule.

[1] The process of amending the Federal Rules of Evidence, and the respective roles of the Supreme Court and Congress, are set forth in 28 U.S.C. § 2074:

§ 2074. **Rules of procedure and evidence; submission to Congress; effective date**

(a) The Supreme Court shall transmit to the Congress not later than May 1 of the year in which a rule prescribed under section 2072 is to become effective a copy of the proposed rule. Such rule shall take effect no earlier than December 1 of the year in which such rule is so transmitted unless otherwise provided by law. The Supreme Court may fix the extent such rule shall apply to proceedings then pending, except that the Supreme Court shall not require the application of such rule to further proceedings then pending to the extent that, in the opinion of the court in which such proceedings are pending, the application of such rule in such proceedings would not be feasible or would work injustice, in which event the former rule applies.

(b) Any such rule creating, abolishing, or modifying an evidentiary privilege shall have no force or effect unless approved by Act of Congress.

The amendments referred to in the orders can be found under each rule, post.—Ed.

the application of the amended rule in a particular proceeding would not be feasible or would work injustice.

3.   That THE CHIEF JUSTICE be, and he hereby is, authorized to transmit to the Congress the foregoing amendment to the Federal Rules of Evidence in accordance with the provisions of 28 U.S.C. § 2076.

CONGRESSIONAL ACTION ON AMENDMENT
PROPOSED APRIL 30, 1979

Pub.L. 96–42, July 31, 1979, 93 Stat. 326, provided that the amendment proposed and transmitted to the Federal Rules of Evidence affecting rule 410, shall not take effect until Dec. 1, 1980, or until and then only to the extent approved by Act of Congress, whichever is earlier.

ORDER OF MARCH 2, 1987

1.   That the Federal Rules of Evidence be, and they hereby are, amended by including therein amendments to Rules 101, 104, 106, 404, 405, 411, 602, 603, 604, 606, 607, 608, 609, 610, 611, 612, 613, 615, 701, 703, 705, 706, 801, 803, 804, 806, 902, 1004, 1007 and 1101, as hereinafter set forth:

2.   That the foregoing changes in the Federal Rules of Evidence shall take effect on October 1, 1987.

3.   That THE CHIEF JUSTICE be, and he hereby is, authorized to transmit to the Congress the foregoing changes in the rules of evidence in accordance with the provisions of Section 2076 of Title 28, United States Code.

ORDER OF APRIL 25, 1988

1.   That the Federal Rules of Evidence be, and they hereby are, amended by including therein amendments to Rules 101, 602, 608, 613, 615, 902, and 1101, as hereinafter set forth:

2.   That the foregoing changes in the Federal Rules of Evidence shall take effect on November 1, 1988.

3.   That THE CHIEF JUSTICE be, and he hereby is, authorized to transmit to the Congress the foregoing changes in the rules of evidence in accordance with the provisions of Section 2076 of Title 28, United States Code.

ORDER OF JANUARY 26, 1990

1.   That the Federal Rules of Evidence be, and they hereby are, amended by including therein amendments to Rule 609(a)(1) and (2), as hereinafter set forth:

2.   That the foregoing changes in the Federal Rules of Evidence shall take effect on December 1, 1990.

3.   That THE CHIEF JUSTICE be, and he hereby is, authorized to transmit to the Congress the foregoing changes in the rules of evidence in accordance with the provisions of Section 2074 of Title 28, United States Code.

FEDERAL RULES OF EVIDENCE

ORDER OF APRIL 30, 1991

1.   That the Federal Rules of Evidence for the United States District Courts be, and they hereby are, amended by including therein amendments to Evidence Rules 404(b) and 1102.

2.   That the foregoing amendments to the Federal Rules of Evidence shall take effect on December 1, 1991, and shall govern in all proceedings thereafter commenced and, insofar as just and practicable, all proceedings then pending.

3.   That THE CHIEF JUSTICE be, and he hereby is, authorized to transmit to the Congress the foregoing amendments to the Federal Rules of Evidence in accordance with the provisions of Section 2072 of Title 28, United States Code.

ORDER OF APRIL 22, 1993

1.   That the Federal Rules of Evidence for the United States District Courts be, and they hereby are, amended by including therein amendments to Evidence Rules 101, 705, and 1101.

2.   That the foregoing amendments to the Federal Rules of Evidence shall take effect on December 1, 1993, and shall govern in all proceedings thereafter commenced and, insofar as just and practicable, all proceedings then pending.

3.   That THE CHIEF JUSTICE be, and he hereby is, authorized to transmit to the Congress the foregoing amendments to the Federal Rules of Evidence in accordance with the provisions of Section 2072 of Title 28, United States Code.

ORDER OF APRIL 29, 1994

1.   That the Federal Rules of Evidence for the United States District Courts be, and they hereby are, amended by including therein amendments to Evidence Rule 412.

2.   That the foregoing amendments to the Federal Rules of Evidence shall take effect on December 1, 1994, and shall govern in all proceedings thereafter commenced and, insofar as just and practicable, all proceedings then pending.

3.   That THE CHIEF JUSTICE be, and he hereby is, authorized to transmit to the Congress the foregoing amendments to the Federal Rules of Evidence in accordance with the provisions of Section 2072 of Title 28, United States Code.

ORDER OF APRIL 11, 1997

ORDERED:

1.   That the Federal Rules of Evidence be, and they hereby are, amended by including therein amendments to Evidence Rules 407, 801, 803(24), 804(b)(5), and 806, and new Rules 804(b)(6) and 807.

2.   That the foregoing amendments to the Federal Rules of Evidence shall take effect on December 1, 1997, and shall govern in all proceedings thereafter commenced and, insofar as just and practicable, all proceedings then pending.

FEDERAL RULES OF EVIDENCE

3.   That THE CHIEF JUSTICE be, and hereby is, authorized to transmit to the Congress the foregoing amendments to the Federal Rules of Evidence in accordance with the provisions of Section 2072 of Title 28, United States Code.

ORDER OF APRIL 24, 1998

ORDERED:

1.   That the Federal Rules of Evidence be, and they hereby are, amended by including therein an amendment to Evidence Rule 615.

2.   That the foregoing amendment to the Federal Rules of Evidence shall take effect on December 1, 1998, and shall govern in all proceedings thereafter commenced and, insofar as just and practicable, all proceedings then pending.

3.   That THE CHIEF JUSTICE be, and hereby is, authorized to transmit to the Congress the foregoing amendments to the Federal Rules of Evidence in accordance with the provisions of Section 2072 of Title 28, United States Code.

ORDER OF APRIL 17, 2000

ORDERED:

1.   That the Federal Rules of Evidence for the United States District Courts be, and they hereby are, amended by including therein amendments to Evidence Rules 103, 404, 702, 703, 803(b) and 902.

2.   That the foregoing amendments to the Federal Rules of Evidence shall take effect on December 1, 2000, and shall govern in all proceedings thereafter commenced and, insofar as just and practicable, all proceedings then pending.

3.   That THE CHIEF JUSTICE be, and hereby is, authorized to transmit to the Congress the foregoing amendments to the Federal Rules of Evidence in accordance with the provisions of Section 2072 of Title 28, United States Code.

ORDER OF MARCH 27, 2003

ORDERED:

1.   That the Federal Rules of Evidence for the United States District Courts be, and they hereby are, amended by including therein an amendment to Evidence Rule 608(b).

2.   That the foregoing amendment to the Federal Rules of Evidence shall take effect on December 1, 2003, and shall govern in all proceedings thereafter commenced and, insofar as just and practicable, all proceedings then pending.

3.   That THE CHIEF JUSTICE be, and hereby is, authorized to transmit to the Congress the foregoing amendments to the Federal Rules of Evidence in accordance with the provisions of Section 2072 of Title 28, United States Code.

FEDERAL RULES OF EVIDENCE

ORDER OF APRIL 12, 2006

ORDERED:

1. That the Federal Rules of Evidence be, and they hereby are, amended by including therein the amendments to Evidence Rules 404, 408, 606 and 609.

2. That the foregoing amendments to the Federal Rules of Evidence shall take effect on December 1, 2006, and shall govern in all proceedings thereafter commenced and, insofar as just and practicable, all proceedings then pending.

3. That the CHIEF JUSTICE be, and hereby is, authorized to transmit to the Congress the foregoing amendments to the Federal Rules of Evidence in accordance with the provisions of Section 2072 of Title 28, United States Code.

CONGRESSIONAL ACTION ON PROPOSED RULE 502

Pub.L. 110–322, September 19, 2008, 122 Stat. 3537, added Rule 502 to the Federal Rules of Evidence and inserted it in the Table of Contents. The amendments apply in all proceedings commenced after September 19, 2008, and, insofar as is just and practicable, in all proceedings pending on that date.[2]

ORDER OF APRIL 28, 2010

ORDERED:

1. That the Federal Rules of Evidence be, and they hereby are, amended by including therein the amendment to Evidence Rule 804.

2. That the foregoing amendment to the Federal Rules of Evidence shall take effect on December 1, 2010, and shall govern in all proceedings thereafter commenced and, insofar as just and practicable, all proceedings then pending.

3. That the CHIEF JUSTICE be, and hereby is, authorized to transmit to the Congress the foregoing amendments to the Federal Rules of Evidence in accordance with the provisions of Section 2072 of Title 28, United States Code.

ORDER OF APRIL 26, 2011

ORDERED:

1. That the Federal Rules of Evidence be, and they hereby are, amended by including the amendments to Evidence Rules 101–1103.

2. That the foregoing amendments to the Federal Rules of Evidence shall take effect on December 1, 2011, and shall govern in all proceedings thereafter commenced and, insofar as just and practicable, all proceedings then pending.

3. That the CHIEF JUSTICE be, and hereby is, authorized to transmit to the Congress the foregoing amendments to the Federal Rules of

---

[2] There is no Supreme Court order for Rule 502 because rules on privilege must be directly enacted by Congress. 28 U.S.C. § 2074(b).—Ed.

FEDERAL RULES OF EVIDENCE

Evidence in accordance with the provisions of Section 2072 of Title 28, United States Code.

ORDER OF APRIL 16, 2013

ORDERED:

1. That the Federal Rules of Evidence be, and they hereby are, amended by including therein an amendment to Evidence Rule 803.

2. That the foregoing amendment to the Federal Rules of Evidence shall take effect on December 1, 2013, and shall govern in all proceedings thereafter commenced and, insofar as just and practicable, all proceedings then pending.

3. That the CHIEF JUSTICE be, and hereby is, authorized to transmit to the Congress the foregoing amendment to the Federal Rules of Evidence in accordance with the provisions of Section 2072 of Title 28, United States Code.

ORDER OF APRIL 25, 2014

ORDERED:

1. That the Federal Rules of Evidence be, and they hereby are, amended by including therein amendments to Evidence Rules 801(d)(1)(B) and 803(6)–(8).

2. That the foregoing amendments to the Federal Rules of Evidence shall take effect on December 1, 2014, and shall govern in all proceedings thereafter commenced and, insofar as just and practicable, all proceedings then pending.

3. That the CHIEF JUSTICE be, and hereby is, authorized to transmit to the Congress the foregoing amendments to the Federal Rules of Evidence in accordance with the provisions of Section 2072 of Title 28, United States Code.

ORDER OF APRIL 27, 2017

ORDERED:

1. That the Federal Rules of Evidence be, and they hereby are, amended by including therein amendments to Evidence Rules 803 and 902.

2. That the foregoing amendments to the Federal Rules of Evidence shall take effect on December 1, 2017, and shall govern in all proceedings thereafter commenced and, insofar as just and practicable, all proceedings then pending.

3. That THE CHIEF JUSTICE be, and hereby is, authorized to transmit to the Congress the foregoing amendments to the Federal Rules of Evidence in accordance with the provisions of Section 2074 of Title 28, United States Code.

FEDERAL RULES
OF EVIDENCE

With Restyling Committee Note immediately after the Rule, followed in some rules with Commentary by Professor Daniel J. Capra, Reporter to the Restyling Project.

ARTICLE I. GENERAL PROVISIONS

Rule 101. Scope; Definitions

(a) Scope. These rules apply to proceedings in United States courts. The specific courts and proceedings to which the rules apply, along with exceptions, are set out in Rule 1101.

(b) Definitions. In these rules:

(1) "civil case" means a civil action or proceeding;

(2) "criminal case" includes a criminal proceeding;

(3) "public office" includes a public agency;

(4) "record" includes a memorandum, report, or data compilation;

(5) a "rule prescribed by the Supreme Court" means a rule adopted by the Supreme Court under statutory authority; and

(6) a reference to any kind of written material or any other medium includes electronically stored information.

(As amended Mar. 2, 1987, eff. Oct. 1, 1987; Apr. 25, 1988, eff. Nov. 1, 1988; Apr. 22, 1993, eff. Dec. 1, 1993; Apr. 26, 2011, eff. Dec. 1, 2011.)

RESTYLED RULES COMMITTEE NOTE
FOR RESTYLED RULES OF EVIDENCE
EFFECTIVE DECEMBER 1, 2011

The language of Rule 101 has been amended, and definitions have been added, as part of the general restyling of the Evidence Rules to make them more easily understood and to make style and terminology consistent throughout the rules. These changes are intended to be stylistic only. There is no intent to change any result in any ruling on evidence admissibility.

The reference to electronically stored information is intended to track the language of Fed. R. Civ. P. 34.

The Style Project

The Evidence Rules are the fourth set of national procedural rules to be restyled. The restyled Rules of Appellate Procedure took effect in 1998. The restyled Rules of Criminal Procedure took effect in 2002. The restyled Rules of Civil Procedure took effect in 2007. The restyled Rules of Evidence apply the same general drafting guidelines and principles used in restyling the Appellate, Criminal, and Civil Rules.

1.   General Guidelines

Guidance in drafting, usage, and style was provided by Bryan Garner, *Guidelines for Drafting and Editing Court Rules,* Administrative Office of the

United States Courts (1969) and Bryan Garner, *Dictionary of Modern Legal Usage* (2d ed. 1995). *See also* Joseph Kimble, *Guiding Principles for Restyling the Civil Rules,* in *Preliminary Draft of Proposed Style Revision of the Federal Rules of Civil Procedure,* at page x (Feb. 2005); Joseph Kimble, *Lessons in Drafting from the New Federal Rules of Civil Procedure,* 12 Scribes J. Legal Writing 25 (2008–2009). For specific commentary on the Evidence restyling project, see Joseph Kimble, *Drafting Examples from the Proposed New Federal Rules of Evidence,* 88 Mich. B.J. 52 (Aug. 2009); 88 Mich. B.J. 46 (Sept. 2009); 88 Mich. B.J. 54 (Oct. 2009); 88 Mich. B.J. 50 (Nov. 2009).

2.   *Formatting Changes*

Many of the changes in the restyled Evidence Rules result from using format to achieve clearer presentations. The rules are broken down into constituent parts, using progressively indented subparagraphs with headings and substituting vertical for horizontal lists. "Hanging indents" are used throughout. These formatting changes make the structure of the rules graphic and make the restyled rules easier to read and understand even when the words are not changed. Rules 103, 404(b), 606(b), and 612 illustrate the benefits of formatting changes.

3.   *Changes to Reduce Inconsistent, Ambiguous, Redundant, Repetitive, or Archaic Words*

The restyled rules reduce the use of inconsistent terms that say the same thing in different ways. Because different words are presumed to have different meanings, such inconsistencies can result in confusion. The restyled rules reduce inconsistencies by using the same words to express the same meaning. For example, consistent expression is achieved by not switching between "accused" and "defendant" or between "party opponent" and "opposing party" or between the various formulations of civil and criminal action/case/proceeding.

The restyled rules minimize the use of inherently ambiguous words. For example, the word "shall" can mean "must," "may," or something else, depending on context. The potential for confusion is exacerbated by the fact the word "shall" is no longer generally used in spoken or clearly written English. The restyled rules replace "shall" with "must," "may," or "should," depending on which one the context and established interpretation make correct in each rule.

The restyled rules minimize the use of redundant "intensifiers." These are expressions that attempt to add emphasis, but instead state the obvious and create negative implications for other rules. The absence of intensifiers in the restyled rules does not change their substantive meaning. *See, e.g.,* Rule 104(c) (omitting "in all cases"); Rule 602 (omitting "but need not"); Rule 611(b) (omitting "in the exercise of discretion").

The restyled rules also remove words and concepts that are outdated or redundant.

4.   *Rule Numbers*

The restyled rules keep the same numbers to minimize the effect on research. Subdivisions have been rearranged within some rules to achieve greater clarity and simplicity.

5.   *No Substantive Change*

The Committee made special efforts to reject any purported style improvement that might result in a substantive change in the application of a rule. The Committee considered a change to be "substantive" if any of the following conditions were met:

    a.   Under the existing practice in any circuit, the change could lead to a different result on a question of admissibility (*e.g.,* a change that requires a court to provide either a less or more stringent standard in evaluating the admissibility of particular evidence);

b.   Under the existing practice in any circuit, it could lead to a change in the procedure by which an admissibility decision is made (*e.g.*, a change in the time in which an objection must be made, or a change in whether a court must hold a hearing on an admissibility question);

c.   The change would restructure a rule in a way that would alter the approach that courts and litigants have used to think about, and argue about, questions of admissibility (*e.g.*, merging Rules 104(a) and 104(b) into a single subdivision); or

d.   The amendment would change a "sacred phrase"—one that has become so familiar in practice that to alter it would be unduly disruptive to practice and expectations. Examples in the Evidence Rules include "unfair prejudice" and "truth of the matter asserted."

REPORTER'S COMMENT ON RESTYLED RULES

The Restyled Rules of Evidence represent the last chapter in the decades-long effort to make the national rules of procedure more clear, concise, and easier to use. The Judicial Conference Standing Committee on Rules of Practice and Procedure has led a decades-long effort to adopt clear and consistent style conventions for all of the national rules of procedure. The rules had been enacted without consistent style conventions, so there were differences from one set of rules to another, and even from one rule to another within the same set. Different rules expressed the same thought in different ways, leading to a risk that they would be interpreted differently. Different rules sometimes used the same word or phrase to mean different things, again leading to a risk of misinterpretation. Drafters made no effort to write the rules in plain English.

Despite some initial opposition, each of the restyling projects has proved successful—substantially assisting lawyers, judges and law students in understanding and applying the rules. The Restyled Evidence Rules have won legal writing awards, including a Clear Mark award for plain language and the Burton Award for Legal Reform. A number of states—such as Maine, Pennsylvania, and Texas—have restyled their Evidence Rules in general accordance with the Federal restyling.

The Restyled Rules became effective on December 1, 2011. Subsequently, substantive amendments to four rules (Rules 801(d)(1)(B) and Rules 803(6)–(8)) took effect on December 1, 2014 and of course they were written consistently with the Restyling. The same goes for the amendment to Rule 803(16) and new Rules 902(13) and (14), which became effective on December 1, 2017.

The Process for Restyling the Evidence Rules

With the approval of the Chief Justice of the United States—the Chair of the Judicial Conference—the Advisory Committee on Evidence Rules undertook its restyling project beginning in the Fall of 2007. The Committee established a step-by-step process for restyling in compliance with previous restyling projects and with the Rules Enabling Act. Those steps involved multiple levels of drafting and review by the Evidence Rules Committee, the Style Subcommittee of the Standing Committee, as well as substantial input from judges, lawyers and academics.

Professor Capra, the editor of this book, served as the Reporter for the restyling. Professor Joseph Kimble, a legal writing professor, served as the principal restylist.

The restyling protocol was as follows:

1.   The restylist prepared a first draft. The Reporter commented on the draft, pointing out where the proposals would make a substantive change and

also suggesting style improvements. The restylist then prepared a second draft for review by the Advisory Committee as a whole.

2.   The Advisory Committee reviewed the second draft to determine whether proposed changes were substantive and to provide style suggestions. If the Advisory Committee determined that a change was substantive—see the definition of "substantive" below—then the change was not implemented. If the Advisory Committee determined that the proposed change was one of style—but disagreed with the change—then the Style Subcommittee of the Standing Committee on Rules of Practice and Procedure would have the last word.

No Substantive Change

The most challenging part of the restyling process was to improve the style of the Evidence Rules *without changing the substance*. The Advisory Committee established a working definition of a substantive change—a proposed change is "substantive" if:

- under the existing practice in any circuit, it could lead to a different result on a question of admissibility;

- under the existing practice in any circuit, it could lead to a change in the procedure by which an admissibility decision is made; or

- it changes the structure of a rule or method of analysis in a manner that would fundamentally alter how courts and litigants have thought about, or argued about, the rule—for example, changing or intermixing the concepts of admissibility, *e.g.*, Rule 104(a) and conditional relevance (Rule 104(b)); or

- it changes a "sacred phrase"—phrases that have become so familiar to courts and litigators that to change them would result in substantial dislocation costs.

Goals of Restyling

The restyling effort provides consistent terminology, plain language, and generally makes the Evidence Rules more user-friendly. That end-product results from many specific techniques applied consistently throughout the rules.

First, the Restyled Evidence Rules use a special format to achieve clearer presentations. The rules are broken down into constituent parts, using progressively indented subparagraphs with headings and substituting vertical for horizontal lists. "Hanging indents" are used throughout. These formatting changes make the structure of the rules graphic and make the restyled rules easier to read and understand even when the words are not changed.

Second, the Restyled Rules reduce the use of inconsistent terms that say the same thing in different ways. Because different words are presumed to have different meanings, such inconsistencies can result in confusion. The restyled rules reduce inconsistencies by using the same words to express the same meaning. For example, consistent expression is achieved by not switching between "accused" and "defendant" or between "party opponent" and "opposing party" or between the various formulations of civil and criminal action/case/ proceeding.

Third, the Restyled Rules minimize the use of inherently ambiguous words. For example, the word "shall" can mean "must," "may," or something else, depending on context. The potential for confusion is exacerbated by the fact the word "shall" is no longer generally used in spoken or clearly written English. The restyled rules replace "shall" with "must," "may," or "should," depending on which one the context and established interpretation make correct in each rule. (Though it is interesting to note that the Supreme Court's Order referring the Restyled Rules to Congress uses "shall" multiple times.)

Fourth, the Restyled Rules minimize the use of redundant "intensifiers." These are expressions that attempt to add emphasis, but instead state the obvious and create negative implications for other rules. For example, phrases like "in the interests of justice" have been largely eliminated because presumably everything that a court does in ruling on evidence must be in the interests of justice.

Fifth, the Restyled Rules improve the drafting of the Evidence Rules by changing passive to active voice whenever possible; eliminating unnecessary, vague, or redundant language; and correcting inadvertent errors in the original rules.

Sixth, the Restyled Rules seek to accommodate technological advances in the presentation of evidence by including, in a new definitions section, language that defines written material to include material stored in electronic form. The definitions are set forth in Rule 101.

Seventh, the Restyled Rules streamline the rules by placing recurring terms in the definition section so that those terms do not have to be fully stated in each rule. See Rule 101.

Note by Federal Judicial Center

The rule enacted by the Congress is the rule prescribed by the Supreme Court without change.

Advisory Committee's Note

56 F.R.D. 183, 194

Rule 1101 specifies in detail the courts, proceedings, questions, and stages of proceedings to which the rules apply in whole or in part.

1987 Amendment

United States bankruptcy judges are added to conform this rule with Rule 1101(b) and Bankruptcy Rule 9017.

1988 Amendment

The amendment is technical. No substantive change is intended.

1993 Amendment

This revision is made to conform the rule to changes made by the Judicial Improvements Act of 1990.

———————

Rule 102. Purpose

These rules should be construed so as to administer every proceeding fairly, eliminate unjustifiable expense and delay, and promote the development of evidence law, to the end of ascertaining the truth and securing a just determination.

(As amended Apr. 26, 2011, eff. Dec. 1, 2011.)

RESTYLED RULE 102 COMMITTEE NOTE

The language of Rule 102 has been amended as part of the restyling of the Evidence Rules to make them more easily understood and to make style and terminology consistent throughout the rules. These changes are intended to be stylistic only. There is no intent to change any result in any ruling on evidence admissibility.

Note by Federal Judicial Center

The rule enacted by the Congress is the rule prescribed by the Supreme Court without change.

Advisory Committee's Note

56 F.R.D. 183, 194

For similar provisions see Rule 2 of the Federal Rules of Criminal Procedure, Rule 1 of the Federal Rules of Civil Procedure, California Evidence Code § 2, and New Jersey Evidence Rule 5.

"question and answer form"

Rule 103. Rulings on Evidence

(a) **Preserving a Claim of Error.** A party may claim error in a ruling to admit or exclude evidence only if the error affects a substantial right of the party and:

    (1) if the ruling admits evidence, a party, on the record:

        (A) timely objects or moves to strike and

        (B) states the specific ground, unless it was apparent from the context; or

    (2) if the ruling excludes evidence, a party informs the court of its substance by an offer of proof, unless the substance was apparent from the context.

(b) **Not Needing to Renew an Objection or Offer of Proof.** Once the court rules definitively on the record—either before or at trial—a party need not renew an objection or offer of proof to preserve a claim of error for appeal.

(c) **Court's Statement About the Ruling; Directing an Offer of Proof.** The court may make any statement about the character or form of the evidence, the objection made, and the ruling. The court may direct that an offer of proof be made in question-and-answer form.

(d) **Preventing the Jury from Hearing Inadmissible Evidence.** To the extent practicable, the court must conduct a jury trial so that inadmissible evidence is not suggested to the jury by any means.

(e) **Taking Notice of Plain Error.** A court may take notice of a plain error affecting a substantial right, even if the claim of error was not properly preserved.

(As amended Apr. 17, 2000, eff. Dec. 1, 2000; Apr. 26, 2011, eff. Dec. 1, 2011.)

RESTYLED RULE 103 COMMITTEE NOTE

The language of Rule 103 has been amended as part of the restyling of the Evidence Rules to make them more easily understood and to make style and terminology consistent throughout the rules. These changes are intended to be stylistic only. There is no intent to change any result in any ruling on evidence admissibility.

REPORTER'S COMMENT ON RESTYLED RULE 103

Rule 103 is one of a handful of Restyled Rules in which the internal subdivisions were restructured. For example, the plain error provision is subdivision (d) in the original, subdivision (e) restyled. The reason for this particular restructuring is that restylists hate hanging indent paragraphs. They believe that everything should be a numbered or lettered subdivision if possible, as it is more user-friendly and also easier to cite. Thus, the hanging paragraph in old subdivision (a) has been turned into a new subdivision (b).

Of course there is a cost to restructuring subdivisions—anyone engaged in an electronic search for cases involving the provision about preserving error from an in limine determination will now be looking under Rule 103(b). For all cases decided before December 1, 2011, the search will be problematic in two respects: 1) it won't uncover any cases on point; and 2) it will uncover cases off point, *i.e.*, those dealing with old Rule 103(b).

For this reason, the Advisory Committee resolved to keep the restructuring of subdivisions to a minimum. The restylist had to make a compelling case for it.

With respect to Rule 103, the Advisory Committee determined that the benefits of restructuring outweighed the costs.

It should also be noted that the Advisory Committee prohibited any change to rule numbers themselves. That is, it forestalled all efforts to reorganize or combine the numbered rules. That was considered too disruptive.

Section references, McCormick 7th ed.

§§ 51–55

Note by Federal Judicial Center

The rule enacted by the Congress is the rule prescribed by the Supreme Court, amended by substituting "court" in place of "judge," with appropriate pronominal change.

Advisory Committee's Note

56 F.R.D. 183, 195

Subdivision (a) states the law as generally accepted today. Rulings on evidence cannot be assigned as error unless (1) a substantial right is affected, and (2) the nature of the error was called to the attention of the judge, so as to alert him to the proper course of action and enable opposing counsel to take proper corrective measures. The objection and the offer of proof are the techniques for accomplishing these objectives. For similar provisions see Uniform Rules 4 and 5; California Evidence Code §§ 353 and 354; Kansas Code of Civil Procedure §§ 60–404 and 60–405. The rule does not purport to change the law with respect to harmless error. See 28 U.S.C. § 2111, F.R.Civ.P. 61, F.R.Crim.P. 52, and decisions construing them. The status of constitutional error as harmless or not is treated in Chapman v. California, 386 U.S. 18, 87 S.Ct. 824, 17 L.Ed.2d 705 (1967), reh. denied *id.* 987, 87 S.Ct. 1283, 18 L.Ed.2d 241.

Subdivision (b). [Restyled as (c).—Ed.] The first sentence is the third sentence of Rule 43(c) of the Federal Rules of Civil Procedure[3] virtually verbatim. Its purpose is to reproduce for an appellate court, insofar as possible, a true reflection of what occurred in the trial court. The second sentence is in part derived from the final sentence of Rule 43(c). It is designed to resolve doubts as to what testimony the witness would have in fact given, and, in nonjury cases, to provide the appellate court with material for a possible final disposition of the case in the event of reversal of a ruling which excluded evidence. See 5 Moore's Federal Practice § 43.11 (2d ed. 1968). Application is made discretionary in view of the practical impossibility of formulating a satisfactory rule in mandatory terms.

Subdivision (c). [Restyled as (d).—Ed.] This subdivision proceeds on the supposition that a ruling which excludes evidence in a jury case is likely to be a pointless procedure if the excluded evidence nevertheless comes to the attention of the jury. Bruton v. United States, 389 U.S. 818, 88 S.Ct. 126, 19 L.Ed.2d 70 (1968). Rule 43(c) of the Federal Rules of Civil Procedure provides: "The court may require the offer to be made out of the hearing of the jury." In re McConnell, 370 U.S. 230, 82 S.Ct. 1288, 8 L.Ed.2d 434 (1962), left some doubt whether questions on which an offer is based must first be asked in the presence of the jury. The subdivision answers in the negative. The judge can foreclose a particular line of testimony and counsel can protect his record without a series of questions

---

[3] Rule 43(c) of the Federal Rules of Civil Procedure was deleted by order of the Supreme Court entered on November 20, 1972, 93 S.Ct. 3073, 3075, 3076, 3077, 34 L.Ed.2d lxv, ccv, ccviii, which action was affirmed by the Congress in P.L. 93–595 § 3 (January 2, 1975).—Federal Judicial Center.

before the jury, designed at best to waste time and at worst "to waft into the jury box" the very matter sought to be excluded.

    Subdivision (d). [Restyled as (e).—Ed.] This wording of the plain error principle is from Rule 52(b) of the Federal Rules of Criminal Procedure. While judicial unwillingness to be constricted by mechanical breakdowns of the adversary system has been more pronounced in criminal cases, there is no scarcity of decisions to the same effect in civil cases. In general, see Campbell, Extent to Which Courts of Review Will Consider Questions Not Properly Raised and Preserved, 7 Wis.L.Rev. 91, 160 (1932); Vestal, Sua Sponte Consideration in Appellate Review, 27 Fordham L.Rev. 477 (1958–59); 64 Harv.L.Rev. 652 (1951). In the nature of things the application of the plain error rule will be more likely with respect to the admission of evidence than to exclusion, since failure to comply with normal requirements of offers of proof is likely to produce a record which simply does not disclose the error.

2000 Amendment Committee Note

    The amendment applies to all rulings on evidence whether they occur at or before trial, including so-called "*in limine*" rulings. One of the most difficult questions arising from *in limine* and other evidentiary rulings is whether a losing party must renew an objection or offer of proof when the evidence is or would be offered at trial, in order to preserve a claim of error on appeal. Courts have taken differing approaches to this question. Some courts have held that a renewal at the time the evidence is to be offered at trial is always required. *See, e.g., Collins v. Wayne Corp.*, 621 F.2d 777 (5th Cir. 1980). Some courts have taken a more flexible approach, holding that renewal is not required if the issue decided is one that (1) was fairly presented to the trial court for an initial ruling, (2) may be decided as a final matter before the evidence is actually offered, and (3) was ruled on definitively by the trial judge, *See, e.g., Rosenfeld v. Basquiat*, 78 F.3d 84 (2d Cir. 1996) (admissibility of former testimony under the Dead Man's Statute; renewal not required). Other courts have distinguished between objections to evidence, which must be renewed when evidence is offered, and offers of proof, which need not be renewed after a definitive determination is made that the evidence is inadmissible. *See, e.g., Fusco v. General Motors Corp.*, 11 F.3d 259 (1st Cir. 1993). Another court, aware of this Committee's proposed amendment, has adopted its approach. *Wilson v. Williams*, 182 F. 3d 562 (7th Cir. 1999) (en banc). Differing views on this question create uncertainty for litigants and unnecessary work for the appellate courts.

    The amendment provides that a claim of error with respect to a definitive ruling is preserved for review when the party has otherwise satisfied the objection or offer of proof requirements of Rule 103(a). When the ruling is definitive, a renewed objection or offer of proof at the time the evidence is to be offered is more a formalism than a necessity. *See* Fed.R.Civ.P. 46 (formal exceptions unnecessary); Fed.R.Cr.P. 51 (same); *United States v. Mejia-Alarcon*, 995 F.2d 982, 986 (10th Cir. 1993) ("Requiring a party to renew an objection when the district court has issued a definitive ruling on a matter that can be fairly decided before trial would be in the nature of a formal exception and therefore unnecessary."). On the other hand, when the trial court appears to have reserved its ruling or to have indicated that the ruling is provisional, it makes sense to require the party to bring the issue to the court's attention subsequently. *See, e.g., United States v. Vest*, 116 F.3d 1179, 1188 (7th Cir. 1997) (where the trial court ruled n limine that testimony from defense witnesses could not be admitted, but allowed the defendant to seek leave at trial to call the witnesses should their testimony turn out to be relevant, the defendant's failure to seek such leave at trial meant that it was "too late to reopen the issue now on appeal"); *United States v. Valenti*, 60 F.3d 941 (2d Cir. 1995) (failure to proffer evidence at trial waives any claim of error where the trial judge had stated that he would reserve judgment on the *in limine* motion until he had heard the trial evidence).

The amendment imposes the obligation on counsel to clarify whether an *in limine* or other evidentiary ruling is definitive when there is doubt on that point. *See, e.g., Walden v. Georgia-Pacific Corp.*, 126 F.3d 506, 520 (3d Cir. 1997) (although "the district court told plaintiffs' counsel not to reargue every ruling, it did not countermand its clear opening statement that all of its rulings were tentative, and counsel never requested clarification, as he might have done.").

Even where the court's ruling is definitive, nothing in the amendment prohibits the court from revisiting its decision when the evidence is to be offered. If the court changes its initial ruling, or if the opposing party violates the terms of the initial ruling, objection must be made when the evidence is offered to preserve the claim of error for appeal. The error, if any, in such a situation occurs only when the evidence is offered and admitted. *United States Aviation Underwriters, Inc. v. Olympia Wings, Inc.*, 896 F.2d 949, 956 (5th Cir. 1990) ("objection is required to preserve error when an opponent, or the court itself, violates a motion *in limine* that was granted"); *United States v. Roenigk*, 810 F.2d 809 (8th Cir. 1987) (claim of error was not preserved where the defendant failed to object at trial to secure the benefit of a favorable advance ruling).

A definitive advance ruling is reviewed in light of the facts and circumstances before the trial court at the time of the ruling. If the relevant facts and circumstances change materially after the advance ruling has been made, those facts and circumstances cannot be relied upon on appeal unless they have been brought to the attention of the trial court by way of a renewed, and timely, objection, offer of proof, or motion to strike. *See Old Chief v. United States*, 519 U.S. 172, 182, n.6 (1997) ("It is important that a reviewing court evaluate the trial court's decision from its perspective when it had to rule and not indulge in review by hindsight."). Similarly, if the court decides in an advance ruling that proffered evidence is admissible subject to the eventual introduction by the proponent of a foundation for the evidence, and that foundation is never provided, the opponent cannot claim error based on the failure to establish the foundation unless the opponent calls that failure to the court's attention by a timely motion to strike or other suitable motion. *See Huddleston v. United States*, 485 U.S. 681, 690, n.7 (1988) ("It is, of course, not the responsibility of the judge *sua sponte* to ensure that the foundation evidence is offered; the objector must move to strike the evidence if at the close of the trial the offeror has failed to satisfy the condition.").

Nothing in the amendment is intended to affect the provisions of Fed.R.Civ.P. 72(a) or 28 U.S.C. § 636(b)(1) pertaining to nondispositive pretrial rulings by magistrate judges in proceedings that are not before a magistrate judge by consent of the parties. Fed.R.Civ.P. 72(a) provides that a party who fails to file a written objection to a magistrate judge's nondispositive order within ten days of receiving a copy "may not thereafter assign as error a defect" in the order. 28 U.S.C. § 636(b)(1) provides that any party "may serve and file written objections to such proposed findings and recommendations as provided by rules of court" within ten days of receiving a copy of the order. Several courts have held that a party must comply with this statutory provision in order to preserve a claim of error. *See, e.g., Wells v. Shriners Hospital*, 109 F.3d 198, 200 (4th Cir. 1997) ("[i]n this circuit, as in others, a party 'may' file objections within ten days or he may not, as he chooses, but he 'shall' do so if he wishes further consideration."). When Fed.R.Civ.P. 72(a) or 28 U.S.C. § 636(b)(1) is operative, its requirement must be satisfied in order for a party to preserve a claim of error on appeal, even where Evidence Rule 103(a) would not require a subsequent objection or offer of proof.

Nothing in the amendment is intended to affect the rule set forth in *Luce v. United States*, 469 U.S. 38 (1984), and its progeny. The amendment provides that an objection or offer of proof need not be renewed to preserve a claim of error with respect to a definitive pretrial ruling. *Luce* answers affirmatively a separate question: whether a criminal defendant must testify at trial in order to preserve a claim of error predicated upon a trial court's decision to admit the defendant's prior convictions for impeachment. The *Luce* principle has been extended by many lower courts to other situations. *See United States v. DiMatteo*, 759 F.2d 831 (11th Cir. 1985) (applying *Luce* where the defendant's witness would be impeached with evidence offered under Rule 608). *See also United States v. Goldman*, 41 F.3d 785, 788 (1st Cir. 1994) ("Although *Luce* involved impeachment by conviction under Rule 609, the reasons given by the Supreme Court for requiring the defendant to testify apply with full force to the kind of Rule 403 and 404 objections that are advanced by Goldman in this case."); *Palmieri v. DeFaria*, 88 F.3d 136 (2d Cir. 1996) (where the plaintiff decided to take an adverse judgment rather than challenge an advance ruling by putting on evidence at trial, the *in limine* ruling would not be reviewed on appeal); *United States v. Ortiz*, 857 F.2d 900 (2d Cir. 1988) (where uncharged misconduct is ruled admissible if the defendant pursues a certain defense, the defendant must actually pursue that defense at trial in order to preserve a claim of error on appeal); *United States v. Bond*, 87 F.3d 695 (5th Cir. 1996) (where the trial court rules *in limine* that the defendant would waive his fifth amendment privilege were he to testify, the defendant must take the stand and testify in order to challenge that ruling on appeal).

The amendment does not purport to answer whether a party who objects to evidence that the court finds admissible in a definitive ruling, and who then offers the evidence to "remove the sting" of its anticipated prejudicial effect, thereby waives the right to appeal the trial court's ruling. *See, e.g., United States v. Fisher*, 106 F.3d 622 (5th Cir. 1997) (where the trial judge ruled *in limine* that the government could use a prior conviction to impeach the defendant if he testified, the defendant did not waive his right to appeal by introducing the conviction on direct examination); *Judd v. Rodman*, 105 F.3d 1339 (11th Cir. 1997) (an objection made *in limine* is sufficient to preserve a claim of error when the movant, as a matter of trial strategy, presents the objectionable evidence herself on direct examination to minimize its prejudicial effect); *Gill v. Thomas*, 83 F.3d 537, 540 (1st Cir. 1996) ("by offering the misdemeanor evidence himself, Gill waived his opportunity to object and thus did not preserve the issue for appeal"); *United States v. Williams*, 939 F.2d 721 (9th Cir. 1991) (objection to impeachment evidence was waived where the defendant was impeached on direct examination).

Rule 104. Preliminary Questions

(a) **In General.** The court must decide any preliminary question about whether a witness is qualified, a privilege exists, or evidence is admissible. In so deciding, the court is not bound by evidence rules, except those on privilege.

(b) **Relevance That Depends on a Fact.** When the relevance of evidence depends on whether a fact exists, proof must be introduced sufficient to support a finding that the fact does exist. The court may admit the proposed evidence on the condition that the proof be introduced later.

(c) **Conducting a Hearing So That the Jury Cannot Hear It.** The court must conduct any hearing on a preliminary question so that the jury cannot hear it if:

    (1) the hearing involves the admissibility of a confession;

    (2) a defendant in a criminal case is a witness and so requests; or

    (3) justice so requires.

(d) **Cross-Examining a Defendant in a Criminal Case.** By testifying on a preliminary question, a defendant in a criminal case does not become subject to cross-examination on other issues in the case.

(e) **Evidence Relevant to Weight and Credibility.** This rule does not limit a party's right to introduce before the jury evidence that is relevant to the weight or credibility of other evidence.

(As amended Mar. 2, 1987, eff. Oct. 1, 1987; Apr. 26, 2011, eff. Dec. 1, 2011.)

RESTYLED RULE 104 COMMITTEE NOTE

The language of Rule 104 has been amended as part of the restyling of the Evidence Rules to make them more easily understood and to make style and terminology consistent throughout the rules. These changes are intended to be stylistic only. There is no intent to change any result in any ruling on evidence admissibility.

Section references, McCormick 7th ed.

§ 53, § 59

Note by Federal Judicial Center

The rule enacted by the Congress is the rule prescribed by the Supreme Court, amended by substituting "court" in place of "judge," with appropriate pronominal change, and by adding to subdivision (c) the concluding phrase, "or when an accused is a witness, if he so requests."[4]

Advisory Committee's Note

56 F.R.D. 183, 196

Subdivision (a). The applicability of a particular rule of evidence often depends upon the existence of a condition. Is the alleged expert a qualified physician? Is a witness whose former testimony is offered unavailable? Was a stranger present during a conversation between attorney and client? In each instance the admissibility of evidence will turn upon the answer to the question of the existence of the condition. Accepted practice, incorporated in the rule,

---

    [4] The effect of the amendment was to restore language included in the 1971 Revised Draft of the Proposed Rules but deleted before the rules were presented to and prescribed by the Supreme Court.—Federal Judicial Center.

places on the judge the responsibility for these determinations. McCormick § 53; Morgan, Basic Problems of Evidence 45–50 (1962).

To the extent that these inquiries are factual, the judge acts as a trier of fact. Often, however, rulings on evidence call for an evaluation in terms of a legally set standard. Thus when a hearsay statement is offered as a declaration against interest, a decision must be made whether it possesses the required against-interest characteristics. These decisions, too, are made by the judge.

In view of these considerations, this subdivision refers to preliminary requirements generally by the broad term "questions," without attempt at specification.

This subdivision is of general application. It must, however, be read as subject to the special provisions for "conditional relevancy" in subdivision (b) and those for confessions in subdivision (c).

If the question is factual in nature, the judge will of necessity receive evidence pro and con on the issue. The rule provides that the rules of evidence in general do not apply to this process. McCormick § 53, p. 123, n. 8, points out that the authorities are "scattered and inconclusive," and observes:

> "Should the exclusionary law of evidence, 'the child of the jury system' in Thayer's phrase, be applied to this hearing before the judge? Sound sense backs the view that it should not, and that the judge should be empowered to hear any relevant evidence, such as affidavits or other reliable hearsay."

This view is reinforced by practical necessity in certain situations. An item, offered and objected to, may itself be considered in ruling on admissibility, though not yet admitted in evidence. Thus the content of an asserted declaration against interest must be considered in ruling whether it is against interest. Again, common practice calls for considering the testimony of a witness, particularly a child, in determining competency. Another example is the requirement of Rule 602 dealing with personal knowledge. In the case of hearsay, it is enough, if the declarant "so far as appears [has] had an opportunity to observe the fact declared." McCormick, § 10, p. 19.

If concern is felt over the use of affidavits by the judge in preliminary hearings on admissibility, attention is directed to the many important judicial determinations made on the basis of affidavits. Rule 47 of the Federal Rules of Criminal Procedure provides:

> "An application to the court for an order shall be by motion. . . . It may be supported by affidavit."

The Rules of Civil Procedure are more detailed. Rule 43(e), dealing with motions generally, provides:

> "When a motion is based on facts not appearing of record the court may hear the matter on affidavits presented by the respective parties, but the court may direct that the matter be heard wholly or partly on oral testimony or depositions."

Rule 4(g) provides for proof of service by affidavit. Rule 56 provides in detail for the entry of summary judgment based on affidavits. Affidavits may supply the foundation for temporary restraining orders under Rule 65(b).

The study made for the California Law Revision Commission recommended an amendment to Uniform Rule 2 as follows: "In the determination of the issue aforesaid [preliminary determination], exclusionary rules shall not apply, subject, however, to Rule 45 and any valid claim of privilege." Tentative Recommendation and a Study Relating to the Uniform Rules of Evidence (Article VIII, Hearsay), Cal.Law Revision Comm'n, Rep., Rec. & Studies, 470 (1962). The proposal was not adopted in the California Evidence Code. The Uniform Rules are likewise silent on the subject. However, New Jersey Evidence Rule 8(1), dealing with preliminary inquiry by the judge, provides: "In his determination the rules of evidence shall not apply except for Rule 4 [exclusion on grounds of confusion, etc.] or a valid claim of privilege."

Subdivision (b). In some situations, the relevancy of an item of evidence, in the large sense, depends upon the existence of a particular preliminary fact. Thus when a spoken statement is relied upon to prove notice to X, it is without probative value unless X heard it. Or if a letter purporting to be from Y is relied upon to establish an admission by him, it has no probative value unless Y wrote or authorized it. Relevance in this sense has been labelled "conditional relevancy." Morgan, Basic Problems of Evidence 45–46 (1962). Problems arising in connection with it are to be distinguished from problems of logical relevancy, *e.g.* evidence in a murder case that accused on the day before purchased a weapon of the kind used in the killing, treated in Rule 401.

If preliminary questions of conditional relevancy were determined solely by the judge, as provided in subdivision (a), the functioning of the jury as a trier of fact would be greatly restricted and in some cases virtually destroyed. These are appropriate questions for juries. Accepted treatment, as provided in the rule, is consistent with that given fact questions generally. The judge makes a preliminary determination whether the foundation evidence is sufficient to support a finding of fulfillment of the condition. If so, the item is admitted. If after all the evidence on the issue is in, pro and con, the jury could reasonably conclude that fulfillment of the condition is not established, the issue is for them. If the evidence is not such as to allow a finding, the judge withdraws the matter from their consideration. Morgan, *supra*; California Evidence Code § 403; New Jersey Rule 8(2). *See also* Uniform Rules 19 and 67.

The order of proof here, as generally, is subject to the control of the judge.

Subdivision (c). Preliminary hearings on the admissibility of confessions must be conducted outside the hearing of the jury. See Jackson v. Denno, 378 U.S. 368, 84 S.Ct. 1774, 12 L.Ed.2d 908 (1964).[5] Otherwise, detailed treatment of when preliminary matters should be heard outside the hearing of the jury is not feasible. The procedure is time consuming. Not infrequently the same evidence which is relevant to the issue of establishment of fulfillment of a condition precedent to admissibility is also relevant to weight or credibility, and time is saved by taking foundation proof in the presence of the jury. Much evidence on preliminary questions, though not relevant to jury issues, may be heard by the jury with no adverse effect. A great deal must be left to the discretion of the judge who will act as the interests of justice require.

Report of the House Committee on the Judiciary on Rule 104(c)

House Comm. on Judiciary, Fed. Rules of Evidence, H.R.Rep. No. 650, 93d Cong., 1st Sess., p. 15 (1973); 1974 U.S.Code Cong. & Ad. News 7075, 7080

Rule 104(c) as submitted to the Congress provided that hearings on the admissibility of confessions shall be conducted outside the presence of the jury and hearings on all other preliminary matters should be so conducted when the interests of justice require. The Committee amended the Rule to provide that where an accused is a witness as to a preliminary matter, he has the right, upon his request, to be heard outside the jury's presence. Although recognizing that in some cases duplication of evidence would occur and that the procedure could be subject to abuse, the Committee believed that a proper regard for the right of an

---

[5]   At this point the Advisory Committee's Note to the 1971 Revised Draft contained the sentence, "Also, due regard for the right of an accused not to testify generally in the case requires that he be given an option to testify out of the presence of the jury upon preliminary matters." The statement was deleted in view of the deletion from the rule, mentioned in the preceding footnote.—Federal Judicial Center.

accused not to testify generally in the case dictates that he be given an option to testify out of the presence of the jury on preliminary matters.

The Committee construes the second sentence of subdivision (c) as applying to civil actions and proceedings as well as to criminal cases, and on this assumption has left the sentence unamended.

Advisory Committee's Note to Subdivision (d)

56 F.R.D. 183, 199

Subdivision (d). The limitation upon cross-examination is designed to encourage participation by the accused in the determination of preliminary matters. He may testify concerning them without exposing himself to cross-examination generally. The provision is necessary because of the breadth of cross-examination [possible] under Rule 611(b).

The rule does not address itself to questions of the subsequent use of testimony given by an accused at a hearing on a preliminary matter. See Walder v. United States, 347 U.S. 62 (1954); Simmons v. United States, 390 U.S. 377 (1968); Harris v. New York, 401 U.S. 222 (1971).

Report of Senate Committee on the Judiciary on Rule 104(d)

Senate Comm. on Judiciary, Fed. Rules of Evidence, S.Rep. No. 1277, 93d Cong., 2d Sess., p. 24 (1974); 1974 U.S.Code Cong. & Ad. News 7051, 7070

Under Rule 104(c) the hearing on a preliminary matter may at times be conducted in front of the jury. Should an accused testify in such a hearing, waiving his privilege against self-incrimination as to the preliminary issue, Rule 104(d) provides that he will not generally be subject to cross-examination as to any other issue. This rule is not, however, intended to immunize the accused from cross-examination where, in testifying about a preliminary issue, he injects other issues into the hearing. If he could not be cross-examined about any issues gratuitously raised by him beyond the scope of the preliminary matters, injustice might result. Accordingly, in order to prevent any such unjust result, the committee intends the rule to be construed to provide that the accused may subject himself to cross-examination as to issues raised by his own testimony upon a preliminary matter before a jury.

Advisory Committee's Note to Subdivision (e)

56 F.R.D. 183, 199

Subdivision (e). For similar provisions see Uniform Rule 8; California Evidence Code § 406; Kansas Code of Civil Procedure § 60–408; New Jersey Evidence Rule 8(1).

1987 Amendment

The amendments are technical. No substantive change is intended.

———————

Rule 105. Limiting Evidence That Is Not Admissible Against Other Parties or for Other Purposes

If the court admits evidence that is admissible against a party or for a purpose—but not against another party or for another purpose—the court, on timely request, must restrict the evidence to its proper scope and instruct the jury accordingly.

(As amended Apr. 26, 2011, eff. Dec. 1, 2011.)

RESTYLED RULE 105 COMMITTEE NOTE

The language of Rule 105 has been amended as part of the restyling of the Evidence Rules to make them more easily understood and to make style and terminology consistent throughout the rules. These changes are intended to be stylistic only. There is no intent to change any result in any ruling on evidence admissibility.

Section references, McCormick 7th ed.

§ 59

Note by Federal Judicial Center

The rule enacted by the Congress is the rule prescribed by the Supreme Court as Rule 106, amended by substituting "court" in place of "judge." Rule 105 as prescribed by the Court was deleted from the rules enacted by the Congress.

[Editor's Note: The initially proposed Rule 105 authorized a judge to sum up and comment on the evidence. That rejected rule—and the reasons given for rejection—can be found in the section on "Deleted and Superseded Materials" in this Book.]

Advisory Committee's Note

56 F.R.D. 183, 200

A close relationship exists between this rule and Rule 403 which requires exclusion when "probative value is substantially outweighed by the danger of unfair prejudice, confusion of the issues, or misleading the jury." The present rule recognizes the practice of admitting evidence for a limited purpose and instructing the jury accordingly. The availability and effectiveness of this practice must be taken into consideration in reaching a decision whether to exclude for unfair prejudice under Rule 403. In Bruton v. United States, 389 U.S. 818, 88 S.Ct. 126, 19 L.Ed.2d 70 (1968), the Court ruled that a limiting instruction did not effectively protect the accused against the prejudicial effect of admitting in evidence the confession of a codefendant which implicated him. The decision does not, however, bar the use of limited admissibility with an instruction where the risk of prejudice is less serious.

Similar provisions are found in Uniform Rule 6; California Evidence Code § 355; Kansas Code of Civil Procedure § 60–406; New Jersey Evidence Rule 6. The wording of the present rule differs, however, in repelling any implication that limiting or curative instructions are sufficient in all situations.

Report of House Committee on the Judiciary

House Comm. on Judiciary, Fed. Rules of Evidence, H.R.Rep. No. 650, 93d Cong., 1st Sess., p. 6 (1973); 1974 U.S.Code Cong. & Ad. News 7075, 7080

Rule 106 as submitted by the Supreme Court (now Rule 105 in the bill) dealt with the subject of evidence which is admissible as to one party or for one purpose but is not admissible against another party or for another purpose. The

Committee adopted this Rule without change on the understanding that it does not affect the authority of a court to order a severance in a multi-defendant case.

Rule 106. Remainder of or Related Writings or Recorded Statements

If a party introduces all or part of a writing or recorded statement, an adverse party may require the introduction, at that time, of any other part—or any other writing or recorded statement—that in fairness ought to be considered at the same time.

(As amended Mar. 2, 1987, eff. Oct. 1, 1987; Apr. 26, 2011, eff. Dec. 1, 2011.)

RESTYLED RULE 106 COMMITTEE NOTE

The language of Rule 106 has been amended as part of the restyling of the Evidence Rules to make them more easily understood and to make style and terminology consistent throughout the rules. These changes are intended to be stylistic only. There is no intent to change any result in any ruling on evidence admissibility.

REPORTER'S COMMENT ON RESTYLED RULE 106

One of the major goals of restyling was to "electrify" the Evidence Rules, *i.e.*, to update the language to accommodate technological changes in the presentation of evidence. When the Rules were adopted in the 1970's, it is understandable that the focus was on the presentation of hardcopy evidence. Rules throughout refer to "writings" and similar paper-based words. Rule 106 is an example. When the restyling effort began, the Reporter was determined to modify every use of the term "writing" to include "in any form" or "including in electronic form." The restylist determined that employing such a solution in every rule referring to a writing would be balky—there are at least 30 evidence rules that refer to paper in some way. So the Reporter and restylist came up with an alternative solution—a provision in the definitions section, Rule 101, stating that any reference to anything in written form includes information in electronic form.

Section references, McCormick 7th ed.

§ 56

Note by Federal Judicial Center

The rule enacted by the Congress is the rule prescribed by the Supreme Court as Rule 107 without change.

Advisory Committee's Note

56 F.R.D. 183, 201

The rule is an expression of the rule of completeness. McCormick § 56. It is manifested as to depositions in Rule 32(a)(4) of the Federal Rules of Civil Procedure, of which the proposed rule is substantially a restatement.

The rule is based on two considerations. The first is the misleading impression created by taking matters out of context. The second is the inadequacy of repair work when delayed to a point later in the trial. See McCormick § 56; California Evidence Code § 356. The rule does not in any way circumscribe the right of the adversary to develop the matter on cross-examination or as part of his own case.

For practical reasons, the rule is limited to writings and recorded statements and does not apply to conversations.

1987 Amendment

The amendments are technical. No substantive change is intended.

ARTICLE II. JUDICIAL NOTICE

Rule 201. Judicial Notice of Adjudicative Facts

(a) Scope. This rule governs judicial notice of an adjudicative fact only, not a legislative fact.

(b) Kinds of Facts That May Be Judicially Noticed. The court may judicially notice a fact that is not subject to reasonable dispute because it:

(1) is generally known within the trial court's territorial jurisdiction; or

(2) can be accurately and readily determined from sources whose accuracy cannot reasonably be questioned.

(c) Taking Notice. The court:

(1) may take judicial notice on its own; or

(2) must take judicial notice if a party requests it and the court is supplied with the necessary information.

(d) Timing. The court may take judicial notice at any stage of the proceeding.

(e) Opportunity to Be Heard. On timely request, a party is entitled to be heard on the propriety of taking judicial notice and the nature of the fact to be noticed. If the court takes judicial notice before notifying a party, the party, on request, is still entitled to be heard.

(f) Instructing the Jury. In a civil case, the court must instruct the jury to accept the noticed fact as conclusive. In a criminal case, the court must instruct the jury that it may or may not accept the noticed fact as conclusive.

(As amended Apr. 26, 2011, eff. Dec. 1, 2011.)

COMMITTEE NOTE TO RESTYLED RULE 201

The language of Rule 201 has been amended as part of the restyling of the Evidence Rules to make them more easily understood and to make style and terminology consistent throughout the rules. These changes are intended to be stylistic only. There is no intent to change any result in any ruling on evidence admissibility.

REPORTER'S COMMENT ON RESTYLED RULE 201

This is another of the handful of rules subject to internal restructuring. The Committee agreed with the restylist that: 1) it made sense to combine the rules on the procedure under which the court takes notice; and 2) it was logical to discuss the time in which notice is taken before discussing a party's opportunity to be heard.

Section references, McCormick 7th ed.

§§ 328–335

Note by Federal Judicial Center

The rule enacted by the Congress is the rule prescribed by the Supreme Court with the following changes:

In subdivisions (c) and (d) the words "judge or" before "court" were deleted.

Subdivision (g) as it is shown was substituted in place of, "The judge shall instruct the jury to accept as established any facts judicially noticed." The substituted language is from the 1969 Preliminary Draft. 46 F.R.D. 161, 195.

Advisory Committee's Note

56 F.R.D. 183, 201

[Editor's Note: Rule 201 was partially restructured in the 2011 restyling. Consequently, some of the references in the Committee Note to particular subdivisions are no longer accurate.]

Subdivision (a). This is the only evidence rule on the subject of judicial notice. It deals only with judicial notice of "adjudicative" facts. No rule deals with judicial notice of "legislative" facts. Judicial notice of matters of foreign law is treated in Rule 44.1 of the Federal Rules of Civil Procedure and Rule 26.1 of the Federal Rules of Criminal Procedure.

The omission of any treatment of legislative facts results from fundamental differences between adjudicative facts and legislative facts. Adjudicative facts are simply the facts of the particular case. Legislative facts, on the other hand, are those which have relevance to legal reasoning and the lawmaking process, whether in the formulation of a legal principle or ruling by a judge or court or in the enactment of a legislative body. The terminology was coined by Professor Kenneth Davis in his article An Approach to Problems of Evidence in the Administrative Process, 55 Harv.L.Rev. 364, 404–407 (1942). The following discussion draws extensively upon his writings. In addition, see the same author's Judicial Notice, 55 Colum.L.Rev. 945 (1955); Administrative Law Treatise, ch. 15 (1958); A System of Judicial Notice Based on Fairness and Convenience, in Perspectives of Law 69 (1964).

The usual method of establishing adjudicative facts is through the introduction of evidence, ordinarily consisting of the testimony of witnesses. If particular facts are outside the area of reasonable controversy, this process is dispensed with as unnecessary. A high degree of indisputability is the essential prerequisite.

Legislative facts are quite different. As Professor Davis says:

> "My opinion is that judge-made law would stop growing if judges, in thinking about questions of law and policy, were forbidden to take into account the facts they believe, as distinguished from facts which are 'clearly . . . within the domain of the indisputable.' Facts most needed in thinking about difficult problems of law and policy have a way of being outside the domain of the clearly indisputable." A System of Judicial Notice Based on Fairness and Convenience, *supra*, at 82.

An illustration is Hawkins v. United States, 358 U.S. 74, 79 S.Ct. 136, 3 L.Ed.2d 125 (1958), in which the Court refused to discard the common law rule that one spouse could not testify against the other, saying, "Adverse testimony given in criminal proceedings would, we think, be likely to destroy almost any marriage." This conclusion has a large intermixture of fact, but the factual aspect is scarcely "indisputable." See Hutchins and Slesinger, Some Observations on the Law of Evidence—Family Relations, 13 Minn.L.Rev. 675 (1929). If the destructive effect of the giving of adverse testimony by a spouse is not indisputable, should the Court have refrained from considering it in the absence of supporting evidence?

> "If the Model Code or the Uniform Rules had been applicable, the Court would have been barred from thinking about the essential factual ingredient of the problems before it, and such a result would be obviously intolerable. What the law needs at its growing points is more, not less, judicial thinking about the factual ingredients of problems of what the law ought to be, and the needed facts are seldom 'clearly' indisputable." Davis, *supra*, at 83.

Professor Morgan gave the following description of the methodology of determining domestic law:

> "In determining the content or applicability of a rule of domestic law, the judge is unrestricted in his investigation and conclusion. He may reject the propositions of either party or of both parties. He may consult the sources of pertinent data to which they refer, or he may refuse to do so. He may make an independent search for persuasive data or rest content with what he has or what the parties present. . . . [T]he parties do no more than to assist; they control no part of the process." Morgan, Judicial Notice, 57 Harv.L.Rev. 269, 270–271 (1944).

This is the view which should govern judicial access to legislative facts. It renders inappropriate any limitation in the form of indisputability, any formal requirements of notice other than those already inherent in affording opportunity to hear and be heard and exchanging briefs, and any requirement of formal findings at any level. It should, however, leave open the possibility of introducing evidence through regular channels in appropriate situations. See Borden's Farm Products Co. v. Baldwin, 293 U.S. 194, 55 S.Ct. 187, 79 L.Ed. 281 (1934), where the cause was remanded for the taking of evidence as to the economic conditions and trade practices underlying the New York Milk Control Law.

Similar considerations govern the judicial use of non-adjudicative facts in ways other than formulating laws and rules. Thayer described them as a part of the judicial reasoning process.

> "In conducting a process of judicial reasoning, as of other reasoning, not a step can be taken without assuming something which has not been proved; and the capacity to do this with competent judgment and efficiency, is imputed to judges and juries as part of their necessary mental outfit." Thayer, Preliminary Treatise on Evidence 279–280 (1898).

As Professor Davis points out, A System of Judicial Notice Based on Fairness and Convenience, in Perspectives of Law 69, 73 (1964), every case involves the use of hundreds or thousands of non-evidence facts. When a witness in an automobile accident case says "car," everyone, judge and jury included, furnishes, from non-evidence sources within himself, the supplementing information that the "car" is an automobile, not a railroad car, that it is self-propelled, probably by an internal combustion engine, that it may be assumed to have four wheels with pneumatic rubber tires, and so on. The judicial process cannot construct every case from scratch, like Descartes creating a world based on the postulate *Cogito, ergo sum*. These items could not possibly be introduced into evidence, and no one suggests that they be. Nor are they appropriate subjects for any formalized treatment of judicial notice of facts. See Levin and Levy, Persuading the Jury with Facts Not in Evidence: The Fiction-Science Spectrum, 105 U.Pa.L.Rev. 139 (1956).

Another aspect of what Thayer had in mind is the use of non-evidence facts to appraise or assess the adjudicative facts of the case. Pairs of cases from two jurisdictions illustrate this use and also the difference between non-evidence facts thus used and adjudicative facts. In People v. Strook, 347 Ill. 460, 179 N.E. 821 (1932), venue in Cook County had been held not established by testimony that the crime was committed at 7956 South Chicago Avenue, since judicial notice would not be taken that the address was in Chicago. However, the same court subsequently ruled that venue in Cook County was established by testimony that a crime occurred at 8900 South Anthony Avenue, since notice would be taken of the common practice of omitting the name of the city when speaking of local addresses, and the witness was testifying in Chicago. People v. Pride, 16 Ill.2d 82, 156 N.E.2d 551 (1951). And in Hughes v. Vestal, 264 N.C. 500, 142 S.E.2d 361 (1965), the Supreme Court of North Carolina disapproved the trial judge's admission in evidence of a state-published table of automobile stopping distances on the basis of judicial notice, though the court itself had referred to the same table in an earlier case in a "rhetorical and illustrative" way in determining that the defendant could not have stopped her car in time to avoid striking a child who suddenly appeared in the highway and that a nonsuit was properly granted. Ennis v. Dupree, 262 N.C. 224, 136 S.E.2d 702 (1964). *See also* Brown v. Hale, 263 N.C. 176, 139 S.E.2d 210 (1964); Clayton v. Rimmer, 262 N.C. 302, 136 S.E.2d 562 (1964). It is apparent that this use of non-evidence facts in evaluating the adjudicative facts of the case is not an appropriate subject for a formalized judicial notice treatment.

In view of these considerations, the regulation of judicial notice of facts by the present rule extends only to adjudicative facts.

What, then, are "adjudicative" facts? Davis refers to them as those "which relate to the parties," or more fully:

"When a court or an agency finds facts concerning the immediate parties—who did what, where, when, how, and with what motive or intent—the court or agency is performing an adjudicative function, and the facts are conveniently called adjudicative facts. . . .

"Stated in other terms, the adjudicative facts are those to which the law is applied in the process of adjudication. They are the facts that normally go to the jury in a jury case. They relate to the parties, their activities, their properties, their businesses." 2 Administrative Law Treatise 353.

Subdivision (b). With respect to judicial notice of adjudicative facts, the tradition has been one of caution in requiring that the matter be beyond reasonable controversy. This tradition of circumspection appears to be soundly based, and no reason to depart from it is apparent. As Professor Davis says:

"The reason we use trial-type procedure, I think, is that we make the practical judgment, on the basis of experience, that taking evidence, subject to cross-examination and rebuttal, is the best way to resolve controversies involving disputes of adjudicative facts, that is, facts pertaining to the parties. The reason we require a determination on the record is that we think fair procedure in resolving disputes of adjudicative facts calls for giving each party a chance to meet in the appropriate fashion the facts that come to the tribunal's attention, and the appropriate fashion for meeting disputed adjudicative facts includes rebuttal evidence, cross-examination, usually confrontation, and argument (either written or oral or both). The key to a fair trial is opportunity to use the appropriate weapons (rebuttal evidence, cross-examination, and argument) to meet adverse materials that come to the tribunal's attention." A System of Judicial Notice Based on Fairness and Convenience, in Perspectives of Law 69, 93 (1964).

The rule proceeds upon the theory that these considerations call for dispensing with traditional methods of proof only in clear cases. Compare Professor Davis' conclusion that judicial notice should be a matter of convenience, subject to requirements of procedural fairness. *Id.*, 94.

This rule is consistent with Uniform Rule 9(1) and (2) which limit judicial notice of facts to those "so universally known that they cannot reasonably be the subject of dispute," those "so generally known or of such common notoriety within the territorial jurisdiction of the court that they cannot reasonably be the subject of dispute," and those "capable of immediate and accurate determination by resort to easily accessible sources of indisputable accuracy." The traditional textbook treatment has included these general categories (matters of common knowledge, facts capable of verification), McCormick §§ 324, 325, and then has passed on into detailed treatment of such specific topics as facts relating to the personnel and records of the court, *id.* § 327, and other governmental facts, *id.* § 328. The California draftsmen, with a background of detailed statutory regulation of judicial notice, followed a somewhat similar pattern. California Evidence Code §§ 451, 452. The Uniform Rules, however, were drafted on the theory that these particular matters are included within the general categories and need no specific mention. This approach is followed in the present rule.

The phrase "propositions of generalized knowledge," found in Uniform Rule 9(1) and (2) is not included in the present rule. It was, it is believed, originally included in Model Code Rules 801 and 802 primarily in order to afford some minimum recognition to the right of the judge in his "legislative" capacity (not acting as the trier of fact) to take judicial notice of very limited categories of generalized knowledge. The limitations thus imposed have been discarded herein as undesirable, unworkable, and contrary to existing practice. What is left, then, to be considered, is the status of a "proposition of generalized knowledge" as an "adjudicative" fact to be noticed judicially and communicated by the judge to the jury. Thus viewed, it is considered to be lacking practical significance. While judges used judicial notice of "propositions of generalized knowledge" in a variety of situations: determining the validity and meaning of statutes, formulating common law rules, deciding whether evidence should be admitted, assessing the sufficiency and effect of evidence, all are essentially nonadjudicative in nature. When judicial notice is seen as a significant vehicle for progress in the law, these are the areas involved, particularly in developing fields of scientific knowledge. See McCormick 712. It is not believed that judges now instruct juries as to "propositions of generalized knowledge" derived from encyclopedias or other sources, or that they are likely to do so, or, indeed, that it is desirable that they do so. There is a vast difference between ruling on the basis of judicial notice that radar evidence of speed is admissible and explaining to the jury its principles and degree of accuracy, or between using a table of stopping distances of automobiles at various speeds in a judicial evaluation of testimony and telling the jury its precise application in the case. For cases raising doubt as to the propriety of the use of medical texts by lay triers of fact in passing on disability claims in administrative proceedings, see Sayers v. Gardner, 380 F.2d 940 (6th Cir. 1967); Ross v. Gardner, 365 F.2d 554 (6th Cir. 1966); Sosna v. Celebrezze, 234 F.Supp. 289 (E.D.Pa. 1964); Glendenning v. Ribicoff, 213 F.Supp. 301 (W.D.Mo. 1962).

Subdivisions (c) and (d). Under subdivision (c) the judge has a discretionary authority to take judicial notice, regardless of whether he is so requested by a party. The taking of judicial notice is mandatory, under subdivision (d), only when a party requests it and the necessary information is supplied. This scheme is believed to reflect existing practice. It is simple and workable. It avoids troublesome distinctions in the many situations in which the process of taking judicial notice is not recognized as such.

Compare Uniform Rule 9 making judicial notice of facts universally known mandatory without request, and making judicial notice of facts generally known in the jurisdiction or capable of determination by resort to accurate sources discretionary in the absence of request but mandatory if request is made and the information furnished. But see Uniform Rule 10(3), which directs the judge to decline to take judicial notice if available information fails to convince him that the matter falls clearly within Uniform Rule 9 or is insufficient to enable him to notice it judicially. Substantially the same approach is found in California Evidence Code §§ 451–453 and in New Jersey Evidence Rule 9. In contrast, the present rule treats alike all adjudicative facts which are subject to judicial notice.

Subdivision (e). Basic considerations of procedural fairness demand an opportunity to be heard on the propriety of taking judicial notice and the tenor of the matter noticed. The rule requires the granting of that opportunity upon request. No formal scheme of giving notice is provided. An adversely affected party may learn in advance that judicial notice is in contemplation, either by virtue of being served with a copy of a request by another party under subdivision (d) that judicial notice be taken, or through an advance indication by the judge.

Or he may have no advance notice at all. The likelihood of the latter is enhanced by the frequent failure to recognize judicial notice as such. And in the absence of advance notice, a request made after the fact could not in fairness be considered untimely. See the provision for hearing on timely request in the Administrative Procedure Act, 5 U.S.C. § 556(e). *See also* Revised Model State Administrative Procedure Act (1961), 9C U.L.A. § 10(4) (Supp. 1967).

Subdivision (f). In accord with the usual view, judicial notice may be taken at any stage of the proceedings, whether in the trial court or on appeal. Uniform Rule 12; California Evidence Code § 459; Kansas Rules of Evidence § 60–412; New Jersey Evidence Rule 12; McCormick § 330, p. 712.

Subdivision (g). Much of the controversy about judicial notice has centered upon the question whether evidence should be admitted in disproof of facts of which judicial notice is taken.

The writers have been divided. Favoring admissibility are Thayer, Preliminary Treatise on Evidence 308 (1898); 9 Wigmore § 2567; Davis, A System of Judicial Notice Based on Fairness and Convenience, in Perspectives of Law, 69, 76–77 (1964). Opposing admissibility are Keeffe, Landis and Shaad, Sense and Nonsense about Judicial Notice, 2 Stan.L.Rev. 664, 668 (1950); McNaughton, Judicial Notice—Excerpts Relating to the Morgan-Whitmore Controversy, 14 Vand.L.Rev. 779 (1961); Morgan, Judicial Notice, 57 Harv.L.Rev. 269, 279 (1944); McCormick 710–711. The Model Code and the Uniform Rules are predicated upon indisputability of judicially noticed facts.

The proponents of admitting evidence in disproof have concentrated largely upon legislative facts. Since the present rule deals only with judicial notice of adjudicative facts, arguments directed to legislative facts lose their relevancy.

Report of House Committee on the Judiciary

House Comm. on Judiciary, Fed. Rules of Evidence, H.R.Rep. No. 650, 93d Cong., 1st Sess., p. 6 (1973); 1974 U.S.Code Cong. & Ad.News 7075, 7080

Rule 201(g) as received from the Supreme Court provided that when judicial notice of a fact is taken, the court shall instruct the jury to accept that fact as established. Being of the view that mandatory instruction to a jury in a criminal case to accept as conclusive any fact judicially noticed is inappropriate because contrary to the spirit of the Sixth Amendment right to a jury trial, the Committee adopted the 1969 Advisory Committee draft of this subsection, allowing a mandatory instruction in civil actions and proceedings and a discretionary instruction in criminal cases.

Advisory Committee's Note (Continued)

[The following portion of the Advisory Committee's Note is from the 1969 Preliminary Draft. 46 F.R.D. 161, 204.—Ed.]

Within its relatively narrow area of adjudicative facts, the rule contemplates there is to be no evidence before the jury in disproof in civil cases. The judge instructs the jury to take judicially noticed facts as conclusive. This position is justified by the undesirable effects of the opposite rule in limiting the rebutting party, though not his opponent, to admissible evidence, in defeating the reasons for judicial notice, and in affecting the substantive law to an extent and in ways largely unforeseeable. Ample protection and flexibility are afforded by the broad provision for opportunity to be heard on request, set forth in subdivision (e).

Criminal cases are treated somewhat differently in the rule. While matters falling within the common fund of information supposed to be possessed by jurors need not be proved, State v. Dunn, 221 Mo. 530, 120 S.W. 1179 (1909), these are not, properly speaking, adjudicative facts but an aspect of legal reasoning. The considerations which underlie the general rule that a verdict cannot be directed against the accused in a criminal case seem to foreclose the judge's directing the jury on the basis of judicial notice to accept as conclusive any adjudicative facts in the case. State v. Main, 91 R.I. 338, 180 A.2d 814 (1962); State v. Lawrence, 120 Utah 323, 234 P.2d 600 (1951). Cf. People v. Mayes, 113 Cal. 618, 45 P. 860 (1896); Ross v. United States, 374 F.2d 97 (8th Cir. 1967). However, this view presents no obstacle to the judge's advising the jury as to a matter judicially noticed, if he instructs them that it need not be taken as conclusive.

Note on Judicial Notice of Law
(by the Advisory Committee)

56 F.R.D. 183, 207

By rules effective July 1, 1966, the method of invoking the law of a foreign country is covered elsewhere. Rule 44.1 of the Federal Rules of Civil Procedure; Rule 26.1 of the Federal Rules of Criminal Procedure. These two new admirably designed rules are founded upon the assumption that the manner in which law is fed into the judicial process is never a proper concern of the rules of evidence but rather of the rules of procedure. The Advisory Committee on Evidence, believing that this assumption is entirely correct, proposes no evidence rule with respect to judicial notice of law, and suggests that those matters of law which, in addition to foreign-country law, have traditionally been treated as requiring pleading and proof and more recently as the subject of judicial notice be left to the Rules of Civil and Criminal Procedure.

ARTICLE III. PRESUMPTIONS IN CIVIL CASES

Rule 301. Presumptions in Civil Cases Generally

In a civil case, unless a federal statute or these rules provide otherwise, the party against whom a presumption is directed has the burden of producing evidence to rebut the presumption. But this rule does not shift the burden of persuasion, which remains on the party who had it originally.

(As amended Apr. 26, 2011, eff. Dec. 1, 2011.)

RESTYLED RULE 301 COMMITTEE NOTE

The language of Rule 301 has been amended as part of the restyling of the Evidence Rules to make them more easily understood and to make style and terminology consistent throughout the rules. These changes are intended to be stylistic only. There is no intent to change any result in any ruling on evidence admissibility.

REPORTER'S COMMENT ON RESTYLED RULE 301

The balky reference to "civil actions and proceedings" has been streamlined to "a civil case." Research indicated that for purposes of the Evidence Rules, there was no distinction between a civil action and a civil proceeding. Just to be safe, the definitions section defines "civil case" to include both civil actions and civil proceedings.

Another innovation is to simplify the original rule's confusingly-put reference to "the burden of proof in the sense of the risk of nonpersuasion." All that was meant by that was the "burden of persuasion"—so the restyled rule uses the more direct term.

Section references, McCormick 7th ed.

§§ 342–348

Note by Federal Judicial Center

The bill passed by the House substituted a substantially different rule in place of that prescribed by the Supreme Court. The Senate bill substituted yet a further version, which was accepted by the House, was enacted by the Congress, and is the rule [ultimately enacted].

Excerpt from Advisory Committee's Note

This rule governs presumptions generally. See Rule 302 for presumptions controlled by state law and Rule 303 for those against an accused in a criminal case. **[Proposed Rule 303 was deleted by Congress. See the section on "Deleted and Superseded Materials"** *infra* **in this Book.—Ed.]**

Presumptions governed by this rule are given the effect of placing upon the opposing party the burden of establishing the nonexistence of the presumed fact, once the party invoking the presumption establishes the basic facts giving rise to it. The same considerations of fairness, policy, and probability which dictate the allocation of the burden of the various elements of a case as between the prima facie case of a plaintiff and affirmative defenses also underlie the creation of presumptions. These considerations are not satisfied by giving a lesser effect to presumptions. Morgan and Maguire, Looking Backward and Forward at Evidence, 50 Harv. L. Rev. 909, 913 (1937); Morgan, Instructing the Jury upon Presumptions and Burden of Proof, 47 Harv. L. Rev. 59, 82 (1933); Cleary, Presuming and Pleading: An Essay on Juristic Immaturity, 12 Stan. L. Rev. 5 (1959). **[This approach was rejected by Congress.—Ed.]**

[For the remainder of the Committee Note, see the section *infra* on "Deleted and Superseded Materials." The Report of the Senate Committee, below, explains the reasons given by Congress for rejecting the Advisory Committee proposal.]

Report of Senate Committee on the Judiciary

Senate Comm. on Judiciary, Fed. Rules of Evidence, S.Rep. No. 1277, 93d Cong., 2d Sess., p. 9 (1974); 1974 U.S.Code Cong. & Ad. News 7051, 7055

This rule governs presumptions in civil cases generally. Rule 302 provides for presumptions in cases controlled by State law.

As submitted by the Supreme Court, presumptions governed by this rule were given the effect of placing upon the opposing party the burden of establishing the nonexistence of the presumed fact, once the party invoking the presumption established the basic facts giving rise to it.

Instead of imposing a burden of persuasion on the party against whom the presumption is directed, the House adopted a provision which shifted the burden of going forward with the evidence. They further provided that "even though met with contradicting evidence, a presumption is sufficient evidence of the fact presumed, to be considered by the trier of fact." The effect of the amendment is that presumptions are to be treated as evidence.

The committee feels the House amendment is ill-advised. As the joint committees (the Standing Committee on Practice and Procedure of the Judicial Conference and the Advisory Committee on the Rules of Evidence) stated: "Presumptions are not evidence, but ways of dealing with evidence."[6] This treatment requires juries to perform the task of considering "as evidence" facts upon which they have no direct evidence and which may confuse them in performance of their duties. California had a rule much like that contained in the House amendment. It was sharply criticized by Justice Traynor in Speck v. Sarver[7] and was repealed after 93 troublesome years.[8]

Professor McCormick gives a concise and compelling critique of the presumption as evidence rule:

* * *

"Another solution, formerly more popular than now, is to instruct the jury that the presumption is 'evidence', to be weighed and considered with the testimony in the case. This avoids the danger that the jury may infer that the presumption is conclusive, but it probably means little to the jury, and certainly runs counter to accepted theories of the nature of evidence.[9]"

For these reasons the committee has deleted that provision of the House-passed rule that treats presumptions as evidence. The effect of the rule as adopted by the committee is to make clear that while evidence of facts giving rise to a presumption shifts the burden of coming forward with evidence to rebut or meet the presumption, it does not shift the burden of persuasion on the existence of the presumed facts. The burden of persuasion remains on the party to whom it is allocated under the rules governing the allocation in the first instance.

The court may instruct the jury that they may infer the existence of the presumed fact from proof of the basic facts giving rise to the presumption. However, it would be inappropriate under this rule to instruct the jury that the inference they are to draw is conclusive.

---

[6]   Hearings Before the Committee on the Judiciary, United States Senate, H.R. 5463, p. 56.—Ed.

[7]   20 Cal.2d 585, 594, 128 P.2d 16, 21 (1942).—Ed.

[8]   Cal.Ev.Code 1965, § 600.—Ed.

[9]   McCormick, Evidence, 669 (1954); *id.* 825 (2d ed. 1972).—Ed.

Conference Report

H.R., Fed. Rules of Evidence, Conf.Rep. No. 1597, 93d Cong., 2d Sess., p. 5 (1974); 1974 U.S. Code Cong. & Ad. News 7098, 7099

The House bill provides that a presumption in civil actions and proceedings shifts to the party against whom it is directed the burden of going forward with evidence to meet or rebut it. Even though evidence contradicting the presumption is offered, a presumption is considered sufficient evidence of the presumed fact to be considered by the jury. The Senate amendment provides that a presumption shifts to the party against whom it is directed the burden of going forward with evidence to meet or rebut the presumption, but it does not shift to that party the burden of persuasion on the existence of the presumed fact.

Under the Senate amendment, a presumption is sufficient to get a party past an adverse party's motion to dismiss made at the end of his case-in-chief. If the adverse party offers no evidence contradicting the presumed fact, the court will instruct the jury that if it finds the basic facts, it may presume the existence of the presumed fact. If the adverse party does offer evidence contradicting the presumed fact, the court cannot instruct the jury that it may *presume* the existence of the presumed fact from proof of the basic facts. The court may, however, instruct the jury that it may infer the existence of the presumed fact from proof of the basic facts.

The Conference adopts the Senate amendment.

_____

Rule 302. Applying State Law to Presumptions in Civil Cases

In a civil case, state law governs the effect of a presumption regarding a claim or defense for which state law supplies the rule of decision.

(As amended Apr. 26, 2011, eff. Dec. 1, 2011.)

RESTYLED RULE 302 COMMITTEE NOTE

The language of Rule 302 has been amended as part of the restyling of the Evidence Rules to make them more easily understood and to make style and terminology consistent throughout the rules. These changes are intended to be stylistic only. There is no intent to change any result in any ruling on evidence admissibility.

Section references, McCormick 7th ed.

§ 349

Note by Federal Judicial Center

The rule enacted by the Congress is the rule prescribed by the Supreme Court, amended by adding "and proceedings" after "actions."

Advisory Committee's Note

56 F.R.D. 183, 211

A series of Supreme Court decisions in diversity cases leaves no doubt of the relevance of Erie Railroad Co. v. Tompkins, 304 U.S. 64, 58 S.Ct. 817, 82 L.Ed. 1188 (1938), to questions of burden of proof. These decisions are Cities Service Oil Co. v. Dunlap, 308 U.S. 208, 60 S.Ct. 201, 84 L.Ed. 196 (1939), Palmer v. Hoffman, 318 U.S. 109, 63 S.Ct. 477, 87 L.Ed. 645 (1943), and Dick v. New York Life Ins. Co., 359 U.S. 437, 79 S.Ct. 921, 3 L.Ed.2d 935 (1959). They involved burden of proof, respectively, as to status as bona fide purchaser, contributory negligence, and nonaccidental death (suicide) of an insured. In each instance the state rule was held to be applicable. It does not follow, however, that all presumptions in diversity cases are governed by state law. In each case cited, the burden of proof question had to do with a substantive element of the claim or defense. Application of the state law is called for only when the presumption operates upon such an element. Accordingly the rule does not apply state law when the presumption operates upon a lesser aspect of the case, *i.e.* "tactical" presumptions.

The situations in which the state law is applied have been tagged for convenience in the preceding discussion as "diversity cases." The designation is not a completely accurate one since *Erie* applies to any claim or issue having its source in state law, regardless of the basis of federal jurisdiction, and does not apply to a federal claim or issue, even though jurisdiction is based on diversity. Vestal, Erie R.R. v. Tompkins: A Projection, 48 Iowa L.Rev. 248, 257 (1963); Hart and Wechsler, The Federal Courts and the Federal System, 697 (1953); 1A Moore, Federal Practice ¶ 0.305[3] (2d ed. 1965); Wright, Federal Courts, 217–218 (1963). Hence the rule employs, as appropriately descriptive, the phrase "as to which state law supplies the rule of decision." See A.L.I. Study of the Division of Jurisdiction Between State and Federal Courts, § 2344(c), p. 40, P.F.D. No. 1 (1965).

ARTICLE IV. RELEVANCY AND ITS LIMITS

Rule 401. Test for Relevant Evidence

Evidence is relevant if:

(a) it has any tendency to make a fact more or less probable than it would be without the evidence; and

(b) the fact is of consequence in determining the action.

(As amended Apr. 26, 2011, eff. Dec. 1, 2011.)

RESTYLED RULE 401 COMMITTEE NOTE

The language of Rule 401 has been amended as part of the restyling of the Evidence Rules to make them more easily understood and to make style and terminology consistent throughout the rules. These changes are intended to be stylistic only. There is no intent to change any result in any ruling on evidence admissibility.

REPORTER'S COMMENT ON RESTYLED RULE 401

This Restyled Rule is an example of the Committee's attempt to "unpack" a rule that, as originally adopted, is a jumble of words and concepts. Rule 401 covers the two traditional concepts of relevance and materiality. The Restyled Rule breaks out the two separate concepts, and also makes the rule visually more approachable.

Section references, McCormick 7th ed.

§ 184

Note by Federal Judicial Center

The rule enacted by the Congress is the rule prescribed by the Supreme Court without change.

Advisory Committee's Note

56 F.R.D. 183, 215

Problems of relevancy call for an answer to the question whether an item of evidence, when tested by the processes of legal reasoning, possesses sufficient probative value to justify receiving it in evidence. Thus, assessment of the probative value of evidence that a person purchased a revolver shortly prior to a fatal shooting with which he is charged is a matter of analysis and reasoning.

The variety of relevancy problems is coextensive with the ingenuity of counsel in using circumstantial evidence as a means of proof. An enormous number of cases fall in no set pattern, and this rule is designed as a guide for handling them. On the other hand, some situations recur with sufficient frequency to create patterns susceptible of treatment by specific rules. Rule 404 and those following it are of that variety; they also serve as illustrations of the application of the present rule as limited by the exclusionary principles of Rule 403.

Passing mention should be made of so-called "conditional" relevancy. Morgan, Basic Problems of Evidence 45–46 (1962). In this situation, probative value depends not only upon satisfying the basic requirement of relevancy as described above but also upon the existence of some matter of fact. For example, if evidence of a spoken statement is relied upon to prove notice, probative value is lacking unless the person sought to be charged heard the statement. The problem is one of fact, and the only rules needed are for the purpose of determining the respective functions of judge and jury. See Rules 104(b) and 901.

The discussion which follows in the present note is concerned with relevancy generally, not with any particular problem of conditional relevancy.

Relevancy is not an inherent characteristic of any item of evidence but exists only as a relation between an item of evidence and a matter properly provable in the case. Does the item of evidence tend to prove the matter sought to be proved? Whether the relationship exists depends upon principles evolved by experience or science, applied logically to the situation at hand. James, Relevancy, Probability and the Law, 29 Calif.L.Rev. 689, 696, n. 15 (1941), in Selected Writings on Evidence and Trial 610, 615, n. 15 (Fryer ed. 1957). The rule summarizes this relationship as a "tendency to make the existence" of the fact to be proved "more probable or less probable." Compare Uniform Rule 1(2) which states the crux of relevancy as "a tendency in reason," thus perhaps emphasizing unduly the logical process and ignoring the need to draw upon experience or science to validate the general principle upon which relevancy in a particular situation depends.

The standard of probability under the rule is "more . . . probable than it would be without the evidence." Any more stringent requirement is unworkable and unrealistic. As McCormick § 152, p. 317, says, "A brick is not a wall," or, as Falknor, Extrinsic Policies Affecting Admissibility, 10 Rutgers L.Rev. 574, 576 (1956), quotes Professor McBaine, " . . . [I]t is not to be supposed that every witness can make a home run." Dealing with probability in the language of the rule has the added virtue of avoiding confusion between questions of admissibility and questions of the sufficiency of the evidence.

The rule uses the phrase "fact that is of consequence to the determination of the action" to describe the kind of fact to which proof may properly be directed. The language is that of California Evidence Code § 210; it has the advantage of avoiding the loosely used and ambiguous word "material." Tentative Recommendation and a Study Relating to the Uniform Rules of Evidence (Art. I. General Provisions), Cal. Law Revision Comm'n, Rep., Rec. & Studies, 10–11 (1964). The fact to be proved may be ultimate, intermediate, or evidentiary; it matters not, so long as it is of consequence in the determination of the action. Cf. Uniform Rule 1(2) which requires that the evidence relate to a "material" fact.

The fact to which the evidence is directed need not be in dispute. While situations will arise which call for the exclusion of evidence offered to prove a point conceded by the opponent, the ruling should be made on the basis of such considerations as waste of time and undue prejudice (see Rule 403), rather than under any general requirement that evidence is admissible only if directed to matters in dispute. Evidence which is essentially background in nature can scarcely be said to involve disputed matter, yet it is universally offered and admitted as an aid to understanding. Charts, photographs, views of real estate, murder weapons, and many other items of evidence fall in this category. A rule limiting admissibility to evidence directed to a controversial point would invite the exclusion of this helpful evidence, or at least the raising of endless questions over its admission. Cf. California Evidence Code § 210, defining relevant evidence in terms of tendency to prove a disputed fact.

Rule 402. General Admissibility of Relevant Evidence

Relevant evidence is admissible unless any of the following provides otherwise:

- the United States Constitution;

- a federal statute;

- these rules; or

- other rules prescribed by the Supreme Court.

Irrelevant evidence is not admissible.

(As amended Apr. 26, 2011, eff. Dec. 1, 2011.)

RESTYLED RULE 402 COMMITTEE NOTE

The language of Rule 402 has been amended as part of the restyling of the Evidence Rules to make them more easily understood and to make style and terminology consistent throughout the rules. These changes are intended to be stylistic only. There is no intent to change any result in any ruling on evidence admissibility.

REPORTER'S COMMENT ON RESTYLED RULE 402

Restyled Rule 402 uses "bullet points" to unpack the Rule and make it easier to approach and apply. The use of bullet points is not without controversy. Some lawyers objected to their use on the ground that a bullet point cannot be cited conveniently. The Committee's response to that criticism was that the concepts that are not bulleted could not have been individually cited under the old rule. Because of the controversy, bullet points are used sparingly in the Restyled Rules—generally speaking only when the original rule sets forth a string of independent concepts in a long-running sentence.

Section references, McCormick 7th ed.

§§ 184–185

Note by Federal Judicial Center

The rule enacted by the Congress is the rule prescribed by the Supreme Court, with the first sentence amended by substituting "prescribed" in place of "adopted", and by adding at the end thereof the phrase "pursuant to statutory authority." **[Editor's Note: The language "pursuant to statutory authority" was dropped in the restyling as superfluous, as the Supreme Court's evidence rulemaking is by definition pursuant to statutory authority.]**

Advisory Committee's Note

56 F.R.D. 183, 216

The provisions that all relevant evidence is admissible, with certain exceptions, and that evidence which is not relevant is not admissible are "a presupposition involved in the very conception of a rational system of evidence." Thayer, Preliminary Treatise on Evidence 264 (1898). They constitute the foundation upon which the structure of admission and exclusion rests. For similar provisions see California Evidence Code §§ 350, 351. Provisions that all relevant evidence is admissible are found in Uniform Rule 7(f); Kansas Code of Civil Procedure § 60–407(f); and New Jersey Evidence Rule 7(f); but the exclusion of evidence which is not relevant is left to implication.

Not all relevant evidence is admissible. The exclusion of relevant evidence occurs in a variety of situations and may be called for by these rules, by the Rules of Civil and Criminal Procedure, by Bankruptcy Rules, by Act of Congress, or by constitutional considerations.

Succeeding rules in the present article, in response to the demands of particular policies, require the exclusion of evidence despite its relevancy. In addition, Article V recognizes a number of privileges **[The Advisory Committee's proposals on privileges were rejected by Congress. See the Advisory Committee Proposals on Privilege in the Section on Deleted and Superseded Materials, *infra*.—Ed.]**; Article VI imposes limitations upon witnesses and the manner of dealing with them; Article VII specifies requirements with respect to opinions and expert testimony; Article VIII excludes hearsay not falling within an exception; Article IX spells out the handling of authentication and identification; and Article X restricts the manner of proving the contents of writings and recordings.

The Rules of Civil and Criminal Procedure in some instances require the exclusion of relevant evidence. For example, Rules 30(b) and 32(a) (3) of the Rules of Civil Procedure, by imposing requirements of notice and unavailability of the deponent, place limits on the use of relevant depositions. Similarly, Rule 15 of the Rules of Criminal Procedure restricts the use of depositions in criminal cases, even though relevant. And the effective enforcement of the command, originally statutory and now found in Rule 5(a) of the Rules of Criminal Procedure, that an arrested person be taken without unnecessary delay before a commissioner or other similar officer is held to require the exclusion of statements elicited during detention in violation thereof. Mallory v. United States, 354 U.S. 449, 77 S.Ct. 1356, 1 L.Ed.2d 1479 (1957); 18 U.S.C. § 3501(c).

While congressional enactments in the field of evidence have generally tended to expand admissibility beyond the scope of the common law rules, in some particular situations they have restricted the admissibility of relevant evidence. Most of this legislation has consisted of the formulation of a privilege or of a prohibition against disclosure. 8 U.S.C. § 1202(f), records of refusal of visas or permits to enter United States confidential, subject to discretion of Secretary of State to make available to court upon certification of need; 10 U.S.C. § 3693, replacement certificate of honorable discharge from Army not admissible in evidence; 10 U.S.C. § 8693, same as to Air Force; 11 U.S.C. § 25(a)(10), testimony given by bankrupt on his examination not admissible in criminal proceedings against him, except that given in hearing upon objection to discharge; 11 U.S.C. § 205(a), railroad reorganization petition, if dismissed, not admissible in evidence; 11 U.S.C. § 403(a), list of creditors filed with municipal composition plan not an admission; 13 U.S.C. § 9(a), census information confidential, retained copies of reports privileged; 47 U.S.C. § 605, interception and divulgence of wire or radio communications prohibited unless authorized by sender. These statutory provisions would remain undisturbed by the rules.

The rule recognizes but makes no attempt to spell out the constitutional considerations which impose basic limitations upon the admissibility of relevant evidence. Examples are evidence obtained by unlawful search and seizure, Weeks v. United States, 232 U.S. 383, 34 S.Ct. 341, 58 L.Ed. 652 (1914); Katz v. United States, 389 U.S. 347, 88 S.Ct. 507, 19 L.Ed.2d 576 (1967); incriminating statement elicited from an accused in violation of right to counsel, Massiah v. United States, 377 U.S. 201, 84 S.Ct. 1199, 12 L.Ed.2d 246 (1964).

Report of House Committee on the Judiciary

House Comm. on Judiciary, Fed Rules of Evidence, H.R. Rep. No. 650, 93d Cong., 1st Sess., p. 7 (1973); 1974 U.S. Code Cong. & Ad. News 7075, 7081

Rule 402 as submitted to the Congress contained the phrase "or by other rules adopted by the Supreme Court". To accommodate the view that the Congress should not appear to acquiesce in the Court's judgment that it has authority under the existing Rules Enabling Acts to promulgate Rules of Evidence, the Committee amended the above phrase to read "or by other rules prescribed by the Supreme Court pursuant to statutory authority" in this and other Rules where the reference appears.

———————

Rule 403. Excluding Relevant Evidence for Prejudice, Confusion, Waste of Time, or Other Reasons

The court may exclude relevant evidence if its probative value is substantially outweighed by a danger of one or more of the following: unfair prejudice, confusing the issues, misleading the jury, undue delay, wasting time, or needlessly presenting cumulative evidence.

(As amended Apr. 26, 2011, eff. Dec. 1, 2011.)

RESTYLED RULE 403 COMMITTEE NOTE

The language of Rule 403 has been amended as part of the restyling of the Evidence Rules to make them more easily understood and to make style and terminology consistent throughout the rules. These changes are intended to be stylistic only. There is no intent to change any result in any ruling on evidence admissibility.

REPORTER'S COMMENT ON RESTYLED RULE 403

Rule 403 is the most important, most frequently invoked, and most cited Evidence Rule. As such, the Committee was very wary about making any changes, even in the name of better style. Style conventions such as bullet points and restructuring were rejected. Restyled Rule 403 is "restyle-lite."

Section references, McCormick 7th ed.

§ 7, §§ 11–13, § 16, § 19, § 26, § 30, §§ 35–36, § 39, §§ 41–42, §§ 44–45, § 47, § 52, §§ 56–59, § 185, § 193, §§ 196–197, §§ 199–200, § 202, § 214, § 250, § 255, § 293, § 322

Note by Federal Judicial Center

The rule enacted by the Congress is the rule prescribed by the Supreme Court without change.

Advisory Committee's Note

56 F.R.D. 183, 218

The case law recognizes that certain circumstances call for the exclusion of evidence which is of unquestioned relevance. These circumstances entail risks which range all the way from inducing decision on a purely emotional basis, at one extreme, to nothing more harmful than merely wasting time, at the other extreme. Situations in this area call for balancing the probative value of and need for the evidence against the harm likely to result from its admission. Slough, Relevancy Unraveled, 5 Kan.L.Rev. 1, 12–15 (1956); Trautman, Logical or Legal Relevancy—A Conflict in Theory, 5 Van.L.Rev. 385, 392 (1952); McCormick § 152, pp. 319–321. The rules which follow in this Article are concrete applications evolved for particular situations. However, they reflect the policies underlying the present rule, which is designed as a guide for the handling of situations for which no specific rules have been formulated.

Exclusion for risk of unfair prejudice, confusion of issues, misleading the jury, or waste of time, all find ample support in the authorities. "Unfair prejudice" within its context means an undue tendency to suggest decision on an improper basis, commonly, though not necessarily, an emotional one.

The rule does not enumerate surprise as a ground for exclusion, in this respect following Wigmore's view of the common law. 6 Wigmore § 1849. Cf. McCormick § 152, p. 320, n. 29, listing unfair surprise as a ground for exclusion but stating that it is usually "coupled with the danger of prejudice and confusion of issues." While Uniform Rule 45 incorporates surprise as a ground and is followed in Kansas Code of Civil Procedure § 60–445, surprise is not included in

California Evidence Code § 352 or New Jersey Rule 4, though both the latter otherwise substantially embody Uniform Rule 45. While it can scarcely be doubted that claims of unfair surprise may still be justified despite procedural requirements of notice and instrumentalities of discovery, the granting of a continuance is a more appropriate remedy than exclusion of the evidence. Tentative Recommendation and a Study Relating to the Uniform Rules of Evidence (Art. VI. Extrinsic Policies Affecting Admissibility), Cal. Law Revision Comm'n, Rep., Rec. & Studies, 612 (1964). Moreover, the impact of a rule excluding evidence on the ground of surprise would be difficult to estimate.

In reaching a decision whether to exclude on grounds of unfair prejudice, consideration should be given to the probable effectiveness or lack of effectiveness of a limiting instruction. See Rule 106 **[now 105—Ed.]** and Advisory Committee's Note thereunder. The availability of other means of proof may also be an appropriate factor.

———————————

Rule 404. Character Evidence; Crimes or Other Acts

(a) Character Evidence.

(1) *Prohibited Uses.* Evidence of a person's character or character trait is not admissible to prove that on a particular occasion the person acted in accordance with the character or trait.

(2) *Exceptions for a Defendant or Victim in a Criminal Case.* The following exceptions apply in a criminal case:

(A) a defendant may offer evidence of the defendant's pertinent trait, and if the evidence is admitted, the prosecutor may offer evidence to rebut it;

(B) subject to the limitations in Rule 412, a defendant may offer evidence of an alleged victim's pertinent trait, and if the evidence is admitted, the prosecutor may:

(i) offer evidence to rebut it; and

(ii) offer evidence of the defendant's same trait; and

(C) in a homicide case, the prosecutor may offer evidence of the alleged victim's trait of peacefulness to rebut evidence that the victim was the first aggressor.

(3) *Exceptions for a Witness.* Evidence of a witness's character may be admitted under Rules 607, 608, and 609.

(b) Crimes, Wrongs, or Other Acts.

(1) *Prohibited Uses.* Evidence of a crime, wrong, or other act is not admissible to prove a person's character in order to show that on a particular occasion the person acted in accordance with the character.

(2) *Permitted Uses; Notice in a Criminal Case.* This evidence may be admissible for another purpose, such as proving motive, opportunity, intent, preparation, plan, knowledge, identity, absence of mistake, or lack of accident. On request by a defendant in a criminal case, the prosecutor must:

(A) provide reasonable notice of the general nature of any such evidence that the prosecutor intends to offer at trial; and

(B) do so before trial—or during trial if the court, for good cause, excuses lack of pretrial notice.

(As amended Mar. 2, 1987, eff. Oct. 1, 1987; Apr. 30, 1991, eff. Dec. 1, 1991; Apr. 17, 2000, eff. Dec. 1, 2000; Apr. 12, 2006, eff. Dec. 1, 2006; Apr. 26, 2011, eff. Dec. 1, 2011.)

RESTYLED RULE 404 COMMITTEE NOTE

The language of Rule 404 has been amended as part of the restyling of the Evidence Rules to make them more easily understood and to make style and terminology consistent throughout the rules. These changes are intended to be stylistic only. There is no intent to change any result in any ruling on evidence admissibility.

REPORTER'S COMMENT ON RESTYLED RULE 404

Rule 404(b) provides that a bad act "may be admissible" to prove not-for-character purposes such as intent, motive, etc. The restyling consultant sought to change it to "the court may admit" for a not-for-character purpose. The consultant's position was that "*may* be admis*sible*" was a potentiality on top of a potentiality. But the Department of Justice objected strenuously to the proposed change, on the ground that it had fought for 40 years to establish the proposition that the phrase "may be admissible" mandates treating Rule 404(b) as a rule of *inclusion,* not exclusion. Given that hard-fought battle, the Department was not about to start over again with a new phrase. In other words, in the Department's view, the phrase "may be admissible" was a sacred phrase that could not be restyled. The Advisory Committee ultimately found it politic to accede to the Department's demand.

In the Reporter's view, the notice provision in Restyled Rule 404(b) contains a possible substantive change. The original rule states that a bad act is admissible for a not-for-character purpose "provided that" in a criminal case the government gives proper notice to the defendant. Thus admissibility is conditioned on the notice. The restyled notice provision requires the government to provide notice but does not specifically say that the evidence is inadmissible if notice is not given. This leaves the government to argue that even if it does not give notice, the evidence should be admitted—the remedy could instead be something like a sanction. Restylists are opposed to legalistic terms such as "provided that"—but stylistic distaste does not justify a substantive change. The Standing Committee of Practice and Procedure approved the change to the notice provision over the objection of the Reporter.

Section references, McCormick 7th ed.

§§ 186–194

Note by Federal Judicial Center

The rule enacted by the Congress is the rule prescribed by the Supreme Court, with the second sentence of subdivision (b) amended by substituting "It may, however, be admissible" in place of "This subdivision does not exclude the evidence when offered."

Advisory Committee's Note

56 F.R.D. 183, 219

Subdivision (a). This subdivision deals with the basic question whether character evidence should be admitted. Once the admissibility of character evidence in some form is established under this rule, reference must then be made to Rule 405, which follows, in order to determine the appropriate method of proof. If the character is that of a witness, see Rules 608 and 610 **[the correct reference is to Rule 609—Ed.]** for methods of proof.

Character questions arise in two fundamentally different ways. (1) Character may itself be an element of a crime, claim, or defense. A situation of this kind is commonly referred to as "character in issue." Illustrations are: the chastity of the victim under a statute specifying her chastity as an element of the crime of seduction, or the competency of the driver in an action for negligently entrusting a motor vehicle to an incompetent driver. No problem of the general relevancy of character evidence is involved, and the present rule therefore has no provision on the subject. The only question relates to allowable methods of proof, as to which see Rule 405, immediately following. (2) Character evidence is susceptible of being used for the purpose of suggesting an inference that the person acted on the occasion in question consistently with his character. This use of character is often described as "circumstantial." Illustrations are: evidence of a violent disposition to prove that person was the aggressor in an affray, or evidence of honesty in disproof of a charge of theft. This circumstantial use of character evidence raises questions of relevancy as well as questions of allowable methods of proof.

In most jurisdictions today, the circumstantial use of character is rejected but with important exceptions: (1) an accused may introduce pertinent evidence of good character (often misleadingly described as "putting his character in issue"), in which event the prosecution may rebut with evidence of bad character; (2) an accused may introduce pertinent evidence of the character of the victim, as in support of a claim of self-defense to a charge of homicide or consent in a case of rape,[10] and the prosecution may introduce similar evidence in rebuttal of the character evidence, or, in a homicide case, to rebut a claim that deceased was the first aggressor, however proved; and (3) the character of a witness may be gone into as bearing on his credibility. McCormick §§ 155–161. This pattern is incorporated in the rule. While its basis lies more in history and experience than in logic an underlying justification can fairly be found in terms of the relative presence and absence of prejudice in the various situations. Falknor, Extrinsic Policies Affecting Admissibility, 10 Rutgers L.Rev. 574, 584 (1956); McCormick § 157. In any event, the criminal rule is so deeply imbedded in our jurisprudence as to assume almost constitutional proportions and to override doubts of the basic relevancy of the evidence.

The limitation to pertinent traits of character, rather than character generally, in paragraphs (1) and (2) is in accordance with the prevailing view. McCormick § 158, p. 334. A similar provision in Rule 608, to which reference is made in paragraph (3), limits character evidence respecting witnesses to the trait of truthfulness or untruthfulness.

The argument is made that circumstantial use of character ought to be allowed in civil cases to the same extent as in criminal cases, *i.e.* evidence of good (nonprejudicial) character would be admissible in the first instance, subject to rebuttal by evidence of bad character. Falknor, Extrinsic Policies Affecting Admissibility, 10 Rutgers L.Rev. 574, 581–583 (1956); Tentative Recommendation and a Study Relating to the Uniform Rules of Evidence (Art. VI. Extrinsic Policies Affecting Admissibility), Cal. Law Revision Comm'n, Rep., Rec. & Studies, 657–658 (1964). Uniform Rule 47 goes farther, in that it assumes that character evidence in general satisfies the conditions of relevancy, except as provided in Uniform Rule 48. The difficulty with expanding the use of character evidence in civil cases is set forth by the California Law Revision Commission in its ultimate rejection of Uniform Rule 47, *id.*, 615:

> "Character evidence is of slight probative value and may be very prejudicial. It tends to distract the trier of fact from the main question of what actually happened on the particular occasion. It subtly permits the trier of fact to reward the good man and to punish the bad man because of their respective characters despite what the evidence in the case shows actually happened."

Much of the force of the position of those favoring greater use of character evidence in civil cases is dissipated by their support of Uniform Rule 48 which excludes the evidence in negligence cases, where it could be expected to achieve its maximum usefulness. Moreover, expanding concepts of "character," which seem of necessity to extend into such areas as psychiatric evaluation and psychological testing, coupled with expanded admissibility, would open up such vistas of mental examinations as caused the Court concern in Schlagenhauf v. Holder, 379 U.S. 104, 85 S.Ct. 234, 13 L.Ed.2d 152 (1964). It is believed that those espousing change have not met the burden of persuasion.

Subdivision (b) deals with a specialized but important application of the general rule excluding circumstantial use of character evidence. Consistently with that rule, evidence of other crimes, wrongs, or acts is not admissible to prove character as a basis for suggesting the inference that conduct on a particular occasion was in conformity with it. However, the evidence may be offered for another purpose, such as proof of motive, opportunity, and so on, which does not

---

[10] But see Rule 412, *infra*, added by Act of Congress in 1978.—Ed.

fall within the prohibition. In this situation the rule does not require that the evidence be excluded. No mechanical solution is offered. The determination must be made whether the danger of undue prejudice outweighs the probative value of the evidence in view of the availability of other means of proof and other factors appropriate for making decisions of this kind under Rule 403. Slough and Knightly, Other Vices, Other Crimes, 41 Iowa L.Rev. 325 (1956).

Report of House Committee on the Judiciary

House Comm. on Judiciary, Fed. Rules of Evidence, H.R. Rep. No. 650, 93d Cong., 1st Sess., p. 7 (1973); 1974 U.S.Code Cong. & Ad. News 7075, 7081

The second sentence of Rule 404(b) as submitted to the Congress began with the words "This subdivision does not exclude the evidence when offered". The Committee amended this language to read "It may, however, be admissible", the words used in the 1971 Advisory Committee draft, on the ground that this formulation properly placed greater emphasis on admissibility than did the final Court version.

Report of Senate Committee on the Judiciary

Senate Comm. on Judiciary, Fed. Rules of Evidence, S. Rep. No. 1277, 93d Cong., 2d Sess., p. 24 (1974); 1974 U.S.Code Cong. & Ad. News 7051, 7071

This rule provides that evidence of other crimes, wrongs, or acts is not admissible to prove character but may be admissible for other specified purposes such as proof of motive.

Although your committee sees no necessity in amending the rule itself, it anticipates that the use of the discretionary word "may" with respect to the admissibility of evidence of crimes, wrongs, or acts is not intended to confer any arbitrary discretion on the trial judge. Rather, it is anticipated that with respect to permissible uses for such evidence, the trial judge may exclude it only on the basis of those considerations set forth in Rule 403, *i.e.* prejudice, confusion or waste of time.

1987 Amendment Committee Note

The amendments are technical. No substantive change is intended.

1991 Amendment Committee Note

Rule 404(b) has emerged as one of the most cited Rules in the Rules of Evidence.

And in many criminal cases evidence of an accused's extrinsic acts is viewed as an important asset in the prosecution's case against an accused. Although there are a few reported decisions on use of such evidence by the defense, *see, e.g., United States v. McClure,* 546 F.2d 670 (5th Cir. 1990) (acts of informant offered in entrapment defense), the overwhelming number of cases involve introduction of that evidence by the prosecution.

The amendment to Rule 404(b) adds a pretrial notice requirement in criminal cases and is intended to reduce surprise and promote early resolution on the issue of admissibility. The notice requirement thus places Rule 404(b) in the mainstream with notice and disclosure provisions in other rules of evidence. *See, e.g.,* Rule 412 (written motion of intent to offer evidence under rule), Rule 609 (written notice of intent to offer conviction older than 10 years), Rule 803(24) and 804(b)(5) (notice of intent to use residual hearsay exceptions).

The Rule expects that counsel for both the defense and the prosecution will submit the necessary request and information in a reasonable and timely fashion. Other than requiring pretrial notice, no specific time limits are stated in recognition that what constitutes a reasonable request or disclosure will depend largely on the circumstances of each case. *Compare* Fla.Stat.Ann. § 90.404(2)(b) (notice must be given at least 10 days before trial) *with* Tex.R.Evid. 404(b) (no time limit).

Likewise, no specific form of notice is required. The Committee considered and rejected a requirement that the notice satisfy the particularity requirements normally required of language used in a charging instrument. *Cf.* Fla.Stat.Ann. § 90.404(2)(b) (written disclosure must describe uncharged misconduct with particularity required of an indictment or information). Instead, the Committee opted for a generalized notice provision which requires the prosecution to apprise the defense of the general nature of the evidence of extrinsic acts. The Committee does not intend that the amendment will supercede other rules of admissibility or disclosure, such as the Jencks Act, 18 U.S.C. § 3500, et seq. nor require the prosecution to disclose directly or indirectly the names and addresses of its witnesses, something it is currently not required to do under Federal Rule of Criminal Procedure 16.

The amendment requires the prosecution to provide notice, regardless of how it intends to use the extrinsic act evidence at trial, *i.e.*, during its case-in-chief, for impeachment, or for possible rebuttal. The court in its discretion may, under the facts, decide that the particular request or notice was not reasonable, either because of the lack of timeliness or completeness. Because the notice requirement serves as condition precedent to admissibility of 404(b) evidence, the offered evidence is inadmissible if the court decides that the notice requirement has not been met.

Nothing in the amendment precludes the court from requiring the government to provide it with an opportunity to rule *in limine* on 404(b) evidence before it is offered or even mentioned during trial. When ruling *in limine,* the court may require the government to disclose to it the specifics of such evidence which the court must consider in determining admissibility.

The amendment does not extend to evidence of acts which are "intrinsic" to the charged offense, *see United States v. Williams,* 900 F.2d 823 (5th Cir. 1990) (noting distinction between 404(b) evidence and intrinsic offense evidence). Nor is the amendment intended to redefine what evidence would otherwise be admissible under Rule 404(b). Finally, the Committee does not intend through the amendment to affect the role of the court and the jury in considering such evidence. *See Huddleston v. United States,* 485 U.S. 681, 108 S.Ct. 1496 (1988).

2000 Amendment Committee Note

Rule 404(a)(1) has been amended to provide that when the accused attacks the character of an alleged victim under subdivision (a)(2) of this Rule, the door is opened to an attack on the same character trait of the accused. Current law does not allow the government to introduce negative character evidence as to the accused unless the accused introduces evidence of good character. *See, e.g., United States v. Fountain*, 768 F.2d 790 (7th Cir. 1985) (when the accused offers proof of self-defense, this permits proof of the alleged victim's character trait for peacefulness, but it does not permit proof of the accused's character trait for violence).

The amendment makes clear that the accused cannot attack the alleged victim's character and yet remain shielded from the disclosure of equally relevant evidence concerning the same character trait of the accused. For example, in a murder case with a claim of self-defense, the accused, to bolster this defense, might offer evidence of the alleged victim's violent disposition. If the government has evidence that the accused has a violent character, but is not allowed to offer this evidence as part of its rebuttal, the jury has only part of the information it needs for an informed assessment of the probabilities as to who was the initial aggressor. This may be the case even if evidence of the accused's prior violent acts is admitted under Rule 404(b), because such evidence can be admitted only for limited purposes and not to show action in conformity with the accused's character on a specific occasion. Thus, the amendment is designed to permit a more balanced presentation of character evidence when an accused chooses to attack the character of the alleged victim.

The amendment does not affect the admissibility of evidence of specific acts of uncharged misconduct offered for a purpose other than proving character under Rule 404(b). Nor does it affect the standards for proof of character by evidence of other sexual behavior or sexual offenses under Rules 412–415. By its placement in Rule 404(a)(1), the amendment covers only proof of character by way of reputation or opinion.

The amendment does not permit proof of the accused's character if the accused merely uses character evidence for a purpose other than to prove the alleged victim's propensity to act in a certain way. *See United States v. Burks*, 470 F.2d 432, 434–5 (D.C.Cir. 1972) (evidence of the alleged victim's violent character, when known by the accused, was admissible "on the issue of whether or not the defendant reasonably feared he was in danger of imminent great bodily harm"). Finally, the amendment does not permit proof of the accused's character when the accused attacks the alleged victim's character as a witness under Rule 608 or 609.

The term "alleged" is inserted before each reference to "victim" in the Rule, in order to provide consistency with Evidence Rule 412.

2006 Amendment Committee Note

The Rule has been amended to clarify that in a civil case evidence of a person's character is never admissible to prove that the person acted in conformity with the character trait. The amendment resolves the dispute in the case law over whether the exceptions in subdivisions (a)(1) and (2) permit the circumstantial use of character evidence in civil cases. Compare *Carson v. Polley*, 689 F.2d 562, 576 (5th Cir. 1982) ("when a central issue in a case is close to one of a criminal nature, the exceptions to the Rule 404(a) ban on character evidence may be invoked"), with *SEC v. Towers Financial Corp.*, 966 F.Supp. 203 (S.D.N.Y. 1997) (relying on the terms "accused" and "prosecution" in Rule 404(a) to conclude that the exceptions in subdivisions (a)(1) and (2) are inapplicable in civil cases). The amendment is consistent with the original intent of the Rule, which was to prohibit the circumstantial use of character evidence in civil cases, even where closely related to criminal charges. See *Ginter v. Northwestern Mut. Life Ins. Co.*, 576 F.Supp. 627, 629–30 (D. Ky. 1984) ("It seems beyond peradventure of doubt that the drafters of F.R.Ev. 404(a) explicitly intended that all character evidence, except where 'character is at issue' was to be excluded" in civil cases).

The circumstantial use of character evidence is generally discouraged because it carries serious risks of prejudice, confusion and delay. See *Michelson v. United States*, 335 U.S. 469, 476 (1948) ("The overriding policy of excluding such evidence, despite its admitted probative value, is the practical experience that its disallowance tends to prevent confusion of issues, unfair surprise and undue prejudice."). In criminal cases, the so-called "mercy rule" permits a criminal defendant to introduce evidence of pertinent character traits of the defendant and the victim. But that is because the accused, whose liberty is at stake, may need "a counterweight against the strong investigative and prosecutorial resources of the government." C. Mueller & L. Kirkpatrick, Evidence: Practice Under the Rules, pp. 264–5 (2d ed. 1999). *See also* Richard Uviller, Evidence of Character to Prove Conduct: Illusion, Illogic, and Injustice in the Courtroom, 130 U.Pa.L.Rev. 845, 855 (1982) (the rule prohibiting circumstantial use of character evidence "was relaxed to allow the criminal defendant with so much at stake and so little available in the way of conventional proof to have special dispensation to tell the factfinder just what sort of person he really is"). Those concerns do not apply to parties in civil cases.

The amendment also clarifies that evidence otherwise admissible under Rule 404(a)(2) may nonetheless be excluded in a criminal case involving sexual misconduct. In such a case, the admissibility of evidence of the victim's sexual behavior and predisposition is governed by the more stringent provisions of Rule 412.

Nothing in the amendment is intended to affect the scope of Rule 404(b). While Rule 404(b) refers to the "accused," the "prosecution," and a "criminal case," it does so only in the context of a notice requirement. The admissibility standards of Rule 404(b) remain fully applicable to both civil and criminal cases.

Rule 405. Methods of Proving Character

(a) **By Reputation or Opinion.** When evidence of a person's character or character trait is admissible, it may be proved by testimony about the person's reputation or by testimony in the form of an opinion. On cross-examination of the character witness, the court may allow an inquiry into relevant specific instances of the person's conduct.

(b) **By Specific Instances of Conduct.** When a person's character or character trait is an essential element of a charge, claim, or defense, the character or trait may also be proved by relevant specific instances of the person's conduct.

(As amended Mar. 2, 1987, eff. Oct. 1, 1987; Apr. 26, 2011, eff. Dec. 1, 2011.)

RESTYLED RULE 405 COMMITTEE NOTE

The language of Rule 405 has been amended as part of the restyling of the Evidence Rules to make them more easily understood and to make style and terminology consistent throughout the rules. These changes are intended to be stylistic only. There is no intent to change any result in any ruling on evidence admissibility.

REPORTER'S COMMENT ON RESTYLED RULE 405

The original Rule 405(a) provided in the second sentence that on cross-examination, inquiry is allowed into specific instances of conduct. But the sentence is confusing because it cannot mean that inquiry is allowed on cross-examination of *any* witness. The Restyled Rule 405(a) clarifies that specific act admissibility arises when it is a *character witness* who is being cross-examined. That cross-examination is permissible to test the character witness's knowledge of the person whose character is being addressed.

Section references, McCormick 7th ed.

Generally § 187, § 191

Note by Federal Judicial Center

The rule enacted by the Congress is the rule prescribed by the Supreme Court without change. The bill reported by the House Committee on the Judiciary deleted the provision in subdivision (a) for making proof by testimony in the form of an opinion, but the provision was reinstated on the floor of the House. [120 Cong.Rec. 2370–73 (1974)]. **[Editor's Note: The reinstatement of the Advisory Committee's proposal of permissible proof by way of opinion was justified on the floor of the House by Representatives by Representative Maine—who stated that proof of character by reputation only was too narrow because "[i]n our modern, increasingly urbanized society today, especially in urban communities, we no longer have the same kind of community knowledge that used to be typical of all America." The Senate adopted the change that the House made on the floor—to add opinion as a permissible basis of proving character.]**

Advisory Committee's Note

56 F.R.D. 183, 222

The rule deals only with allowable methods of proving character, not with the admissibility of character evidence, which is covered in Rule 404.

Of the three methods of proving character provided by the rule, evidence of specific instances of conduct is the most convincing. At the same time it possesses the greatest capacity to arouse prejudice, to confuse, to surprise, and to consume time. Consequently the rule confines the use of evidence of this kind to cases in which character is, in the strict sense, in issue and hence deserving of a searching inquiry. When character is used circumstantially and hence occupies a lesser status in the case, proof may be only by reputation and opinion. These latter methods are also available when character is in issue. This treatment is, with respect to specific instances of conduct and reputation, conventional contemporary common law doctrine. McCormick § 153.

In recognizing opinion as a means of proving character, the rule departs from usual contemporary practice in favor of that of an earlier day. See 7 Wigmore § 1986, pointing out that the earlier practice permitted opinion and arguing strongly for evidence based on personal knowledge and belief as contrasted with "the secondhand, irresponsible product of multiplied guesses and gossip which we term 'reputation'." It seems likely that the persistence of reputation evidence is due to its largely being opinion in disguise. Traditionally character has been regarded primarily in moral overtones of good and bad: chaste, peaceable, truthful, honest. Nevertheless, on occasion nonmoral considerations crop up, as in the case of the incompetent driver, and this seems bound to happen increasingly. If character is defined as the kind of person one is, then account must be taken of varying ways of arriving at the estimate. These may range from the opinion of the employer who has found the man honest to the opinion of the psychiatrist based upon examination and testing. No effective dividing line exists between character and mental capacity, and the latter traditionally has been provable by opinion.

According to the great majority of cases, on cross-examination inquiry is allowable as to whether the reputation witness has heard of particular instances of conduct pertinent to the trait in question. Michelson v. United States, 335 U.S. 469, 69 S.Ct. 213, 93 L.Ed. 168 (1948); Annot., 47 A.L.R.2d 1258. The theory is that, since the reputation witness relates what he has heard, the inquiry tends to shed light on the accuracy of his hearing and reporting. Accordingly, the opinion witness would be asked whether he knew, as well as whether he had heard. The fact is, of course, that these distinctions are of slight if any practical significance, and the second sentence of subdivision (a) eliminates them as a factor in formulating questions. This recognition of the propriety of inquiring into specific instances of conduct does not circumscribe inquiry otherwise into the bases of opinion and reputation testimony.

The express allowance of inquiry into specific instances of conduct on cross-examination in subdivision (a) and the express allowance of it as part of a case in chief when character is actually in issue in subdivision (b) contemplate that testimony of specific instances is not generally permissible on the direct examination of an ordinary opinion witness to character. Similarly as to witnesses to the character of witnesses under Rule 608(b). Opinion testimony on direct in these situations ought in general to correspond to reputation testimony as now given, *i.e.*, be confined to the nature and extent of observation and acquaintance upon which the opinion is based. See Rule 701.

1987 Amendment

The amendment is technical. No substantive change is intended.

---

reputation vs. opinion

exception on (b) – used to prove essential element
look at rule in conjunction w/ 404

Rule 406. Habit; Routine Practice

Evidence of a person's habit or an organization's routine practice may be admitted to prove that on a particular occasion the person or organization acted in accordance with the habit or routine practice. The court may admit this evidence regardless of whether it is corroborated or whether there was an eyewitness.

(As amended Apr. 26, 2011, eff. Dec. 1, 2011.)

RESTYLED RULE 406 COMMITTEE NOTE

The language of Rule 406 has been amended as part of the restyling of the Evidence Rules to make them more easily understood and to make style and terminology consistent throughout the rules. These changes are intended to be stylistic only. There is no intent to change any result in any ruling on evidence admissibility.

REPORTER'S COMMENT ON RESTYLED RULE 406

The original rule stated that habit evidence is "relevant" to prove conduct in conformity. The restylist proposed changing the word "relevant" on the ground that all evidence must be relevant under Rule 401 to be admissible. So to the restylist "is relevant" was superfluous. The Reporter responded that the habit rule has always been superfluous in the sense that it states that relevant evidence is admissible. But the rule is nonetheless important because 1) it emphasizes the distinction between character (which is usually excluded to prove conduct) and habit (which is usually admitted to prove conduct), and 2) it emphasizes that certain common-law conditions on admissibility of habit evidence—corroboration and the absence of an eyewitness—have been lifted. The Reporter argued that the word "relevant" should be retained in order to keep the emphases that animated the original rule. But the Advisory Committee found that the change from "is relevant" to "may be admitted" was one of style only. Under the Restyling Protocol, the Advisory Committee had the final word over substance, while the Rules Committee restylists had the final word over questions of style.

Section references, McCormick 7th ed.

§ 195

Note by Federal Judicial Center

The rule enacted by the Congress is subdivision (a) of the rule prescribed by the Supreme Court. Subdivision (b) of the Court's rule was deleted for reasons stated in the Report of the House Committee on the Judiciary set forth below.

Advisory Committee's Note

56 F.R.D. 183, 223

Subdivision (a). [Editor's Note: As proposed by the Advisory Committee, Rule 406 contained two subdivisions; subdivision (b) was deleted by Congress. See Deleted and Superseded Materials, *infra*.] An oft-quoted paragraph, McCormick § 162, p. 340, describes habit in terms effectively contrasting it with character.

Character and habit are close akin. Character is a generalized description of one's disposition, or of one's disposition in respect to a general trait, such as honesty, temperance, or peacefulness. "Habit," in modern usage, both lay and psychological, is more specific. It describes one's regular response to a repeated specific situation. If we speak of character for care, we think of the person's tendency to act prudently in all the varying situations of life, in business, family life, in handling automobiles and in walking across the street. A habit, on the other hand, is the person's regular practice of meeting a particular kind of situation with a specific type of conduct, such as the habit of going down a particular stairway two stairs at a time, or of giving the hand-signal for a left turn, or of alighting from railway cars while they are moving. The doing of the habitual acts may become semi-automatic.

Equivalent behavior on the part of a group is designated "routine practice of an organization" in the rule.

Agreement is general that habit evidence is highly persuasive as proof of conduct on a particular occasion. Again quoting McCormick § 162, p. 341:

Character may be thought of as the sum of one's habits though doubtless it is more than this. However, unquestionably the uniformity of one's response to habit is far greater than the consistency with which one's conduct conforms to character or disposition. Even though character comes in only exceptionally as evidence of an act, surely any sensible man in investigating whether X did a particular act would be greatly helped in his inquiry by evidence as to whether he was in the habit of doing it.

When disagreement has appeared, its focus has been upon the question what constitutes habit, and the reason for this is readily apparent. The extent to which instances must be multiplied and consistency of behavior maintained in order to rise to the status of habit inevitably gives rise to differences of opinion. Lewan, Rationale of Habit Evidence, 16 Syracuse L. Rev. 39, 49 (1964). While adequacy of sampling and uniformity of response are key factors, precise standards for measuring their sufficiency for evidence purposes cannot be formulated.

The rule is consistent with prevailing views. Much evidence is excluded simply because of failure to achieve the status of habit. Thus, evidence of intemperate "habits" is generally excluded when offered as proof of drunkenness in accident cases, Annot., 46 A.L.R.2d 103, and evidence of other assaults is inadmissible to prove the instant one in a civil assault action, Annot., 66 A.L.R.2d 806. In *Levin v. United States*, 338 F.2d 265, 119 U.S. App. D.C. 156 (1964), testimony as to the religious "habits" of the accused, offered as tending to prove that he was at home observing the Sabbath rather than out obtaining money through larceny by trick, was held properly excluded:

It seems apparent to us that an individual's religious practices would not be the type of activities which would lend themselves to the characterization of "invariable regularity." [1 Wigmore 520.] Certainly the very volitional basis of the activity raises serious questions as to its invariable nature and hence its probative value.

Id. at 272.

These rulings are not inconsistent with the trend towards admitting evidence of business transactions between one of the parties and a third person as tending to prove that he made the same bargain or proposal in the litigated situation. Slough, Relevancy Unraveled, 6 Kan. L. Rev. 38–41 (1957). Nor are they inconsistent with such cases as *Whittemore v. Lockheed Aircraft Corp.*, 65 Cal. App. 2d 737, 151 P.2d 670 (1944), upholding the admission of evidence that plaintiff's intestate had on four other occasions flown planes from defendant's factory for delivery to his employer airline, offered to prove that he was piloting rather than a guest on a plane which crashed and killed all on board while en route for delivery.

A considerable body of authority has required that evidence of the routine practice of an organization be corroborated as a condition precedent to its admission in evidence. Slough, Relevancy Unraveled, 5 Kan. L. Rev. 404–449 (1957). This requirement is specifically rejected by the rule on the ground that it relates to the sufficiency of the evidence rather than admissibility. A similar position is taken in New Jersey Rule 49. The rule also rejects the requirement of the absence of eyewitnesses, sometimes encountered with respect to admitting habit evidence to prove freedom from contributory negligence in wrongful death cases. For comment critical of the requirements see Frank, J., in *Cereste v. New York, N.H. & H.R. Co.*, 231 F.2d 50 (2d Cir. 1956), *cert. denied,* 351 U.S. 951, 76 S.Ct. 848, 100 L.Ed. 1475, 10 Vand. L. Rev. 447 (1957); McCormick § 162, p. 342. The omission of the requirement from the California Evidence Code is said to have effected its elimination. Comment, California Evidence Code § 1105.

Subdivision (b). [Editor's Note: This subdivision—which set forth permissible methods of proving habit—was deleted by Congress. For an explanation of the deletion, see the House Report below. For the proposed rule that was deleted, see Deleted and Superseded Materials, *infra*.] Permissible methods of proving habit or routine conduct include opinion and specific instances sufficient in number to warrant a finding that the habit or routine practice in fact existed. Opinion evidence must be "rationally based on the perception of the witness" and helpful, under the provisions of Rule 701. Proof by specific instances may be controlled by the overriding provisions of Rule 403 for exclusion on grounds of prejudice, confusion, misleading the jury, or waste of time. Thus the illustrations following A.L.I. Model Code of Evidence Rule 307 suggest the possibility of admitting testimony by *W* that on numerous occasions he had been with *X* when *X* crossed a railroad track and that on each occasion *X* had first stopped and looked in both directions, but discretion to exclude offers of 10 witnesses, each testifying to a different occasion.

Similar provisions for proof by opinion or specific instances are found in Uniform Rule 50 and Kansas Code of Civil Procedure § 60–450. New Jersey Rule 50 provides for proof by specific instances but is silent as to opinion. The California Evidence Code is silent as to methods of proving habit, presumably proceeding on the theory that any method is relevant and all relevant evidence is admissible unless otherwise provided. Tentative Recommendation and a Study Relating to the Uniform Rules of Evidence (Art. VI. Extrinsic Policies Affecting Admissibility), Rep., Rec. & Study, Cal. Law Rev. Comm'n, 620 (1964).

Report of House Committee on the Judiciary

House Comm. on Judiciary, Fed. Rules of Evidence, H.R. Rep. No. 650, 93d Cong., 1st Sess., p. 5 (1973); 1974 U.S.Code Cong. & Ad. News 7075, 7079

Rule 406 as submitted to Congress contained a subdivision (b) providing that the method of proof of habit or routine practice could be "in the form of an opinion or by specific instances of conduct sufficient in number to warrant a finding that the habit existed or that the practice was routine." The Committee deleted this subdivision believing that the method of proof of habit and routine practice should be left to the courts to deal with on a case-by-case basis. At the same time, the Committee does not intend that its action be construed as sanctioning a general authorization of opinion evidence in this area.

———————

to when would need to prove ownership?

Rule 407. Subsequent Remedial Measures

When measures are taken that would have made an earlier injury or harm less likely to occur, evidence of the subsequent measures is not admissible to prove:

- negligence;

- culpable conduct;

- a defect in a product or its design; or

- a need for a warning or instruction.

But the court may admit this evidence for another purpose, such as impeachment or—if disputed—proving ownership, control, or the feasibility of precautionary measures.

(As amended Apr. 11, 1997, eff. Dec. 1, 1997; Apr. 26, 2011, eff. Dec. 1, 2011.)

RESTYLED RULE 407 COMMITTEE NOTE

The language of Rule 407 has been amended as part of the general restyling of the Evidence Rules to make them more easily understood and to make style and terminology consistent throughout the rules. These changes are intended to be stylistic only. There is no intent to change any result in any ruling on evidence admissibility.

Rule 407 previously provided that evidence was not excluded if offered for a purpose not explicitly prohibited by the Rule. To improve the language of the Rule, it now provides that the court may admit evidence if offered for a permissible purpose. There is no intent to change the process for admitting evidence covered by the Rule. It remains the case that if offered for an impermissible purpose, it must be excluded, and if offered for a purpose not barred by the Rule, its admissibility remains governed by the general principles of Rules 402, 403, 801, etc.

REPORTER'S COMMENT ON RESTYLED RULE 407

The original Rule 407 was a rule of exclusion—it excluded subsequent remedial measures if offered for certain listed purposes. The second sentence of the original Rule provided that if the evidence is offered for any other purpose, the Rule is simply inapplicable—"This rule does not require the exclusion . . . "

The restylist was of the opinion that the "rule does not require the exclusion" was bad style. He proposed language that "the court may admit" the evidence if offered for a proper purpose. The Reporter disagreed, arguing that the proposed restyling changed the character of the rule—from one that expressed no opinion about evidence offered for a proper purpose, to one that provides an affirmative ground of admissibility for such evidence. The Advisory Committee ultimately determined that the change was one of style rather than substance. But as a compromise, the Reporter was allowed to add to the basic restyling Committee Note a second paragraph to emphasize that when a subsequent remedial measure is offered for a proper purpose, its admissibility is governed not by Rule 407 but by other rules, such as 403.

Note that the opening phrase of the rule is written in the passive voice: "When measures are taken . . ." without saying by whom. The Restylers of the Evidence Rules sought to avoid the use of passive voice. But in this case, passive voice was required to avoid a substantive change in the application of Rule 407 in some courts. Here was the problem: what if the remedial measure was taken by someone who was not a party? For example, what if a purchaser of a product made an alteration that would have made the injury less likely to occur, but the plaintiff is suing the manufacturer, not the distributor? On that question, some courts have found that Rule 407 is not applicable, because it should only apply to measures taken by the defendant. Other courts find that such third party measures are covered by the Rule. So, changing the rule to say "measures taken by the defendant" would change the result in some courts; while changing the rule to say "measures taken by anyone" would have changed the result in others. That is why the rule was left in passive voice. One of the virtues of passive voice is that it leaves wiggle room.

Section references, McCormick 7th ed.

§ 267

Note by Federal Judicial Center

The rule enacted by the Congress is the rule prescribed by the Supreme Court without change.

Advisory Committee's Note

56 F.R.D. 183, 225

The rule incorporates conventional doctrine which excludes evidence of subsequent remedial measures as proof of an admission of fault. The rule rests on two grounds. (1) The conduct is not in fact an admission, since the conduct is equally consistent with injury by mere accident or through contributory negligence. Or, as Baron Bramwell put it, the rule rejects the notion that "because the world gets wiser as it gets older, therefore it was foolish before." Hart v. Lancashire & Yorkshire Ry. Co., 21 L.T.R. N.S. 261, 263 (1869). Under a liberal theory of relevancy this ground alone would not support exclusion as the inference is still a possible one. (2) The other, and more impressive, ground for exclusion rests on a social policy of encouraging people to take, or at least not discouraging them from taking, steps in furtherance of added safety. The courts have applied this principle to exclude evidence of subsequent repairs, installation of safety devices, changes in company rules, and discharge of employees, and the language of the present rule is broad enough to encompass all of them. See Falknor, Extrinsic Policies Affecting Admissibility, 10 Rutgers L.Rev. 574, 590 (1956).

The second sentence of the rule directs attention to the limitations of the rule. **[This was restyled into a second paragraph in 2011.—Ed.]** Exclusion is called for only when the evidence of subsequent remedial measures is offered as proof of negligence or culpable conduct. In effect it rejects the suggested inference that fault is admitted. Other purposes are, however, allowable, including ownership or control, existence of duty, and feasibility of precautionary measures, if controverted, and impeachment. 2 Wigmore § 283; Annot., 64 A.L.R.2d 1296. Two recent federal cases are illustrative. Boeing Airplane Co. v. Brown, 291 F.2d 310 (9th Cir. 1961), an action against an airplane manufacturer for using an allegedly defectively designed alternator shaft which caused a plane crash, upheld the admission of evidence of subsequent design modification for the purpose of showing that design changes and safeguards were feasible. And Powers v. J.B. Michael & Co., 329 F.2d 674 (6th Cir. 1964), an action against a road contractor for negligent failure to put out warning signs, sustained the admission of evidence that defendant subsequently put out signs to show that the portion of the road in question was under defendant's control. The requirement that the other purpose be controverted calls for automatic exclusion unless a genuine issue be present and allows the opposing party to lay the groundwork for exclusion by making an admission. Otherwise the factors of undue prejudice, confusion of issues, misleading the jury, and waste of time remain for consideration under Rule 403.

For comparable rules, see Uniform Rule 51; California Evidence Code § 1151; Kansas Code of Civil Procedure § 60–451; New Jersey Evidence Rule 51.

1997 Amendment Committee Note

The amendment to Rule 407 makes two changes in the rule. First, the words "an injury or harm allegedly caused by" were added to clarify that the rule applies only to changes made after the occurrence that produced the damages giving rise to the action. Evidence of measures taken by the defendant prior to the "event" causing "injury or harm" do not fall within the exclusionary scope of Rule 407 even if they occurred after the manufacture or design of the product. See *Chase v. General Motors Corp.*, 856 F.2d 17, 21–22 (4th Cir. 1988).

Second, Rule 407 has been amended to provide that evidence of subsequent remedial measures may not be used to prove "a defect in a product or its design, or that a warning or instruction should have accompanied a product." This amendment adopts the view of a majority of the circuits that have interpreted Rule 407 to apply to products liability actions. See *Raymond v. Raymond Corp.*, 938 F.2d 1518, 1522 (1st Cir. 1991); *In re Joint Eastern District and Southern District Asbestos Litigation v. Armstrong World Industries, Inc.*, 995 F.2d 343 (2d Cir. 1993); *Cann v. Ford Motor Co.*, 658 F.2d 54, 60 (2d Cir. 1981), *cert. denied*, 456 U.S. 960 (1982); *Kelly v. Crown Equipment Co.*, 970 F.2d 1273, 1275 (3d Cir. 1992); *Werner v. Upjohn, Inc.*, 628 F.2d 848 (4th Cir. 1980), *cert. denied*, 449 U.S. 1080 (1981); *Grenada Steel Industries, Inc. v. Alabama Oxygen Co., Inc.*, 695 F.2d 883 (5th Cir. 1983); *Bauman v. Volkswagenwerk Aktiengesellschaft*, 621 F.2d 230, 232 (6th Cir. 1980); *Flaminio v. Honda Motor Company, Ltd.*, 733 F.2d 463, 469 (7th Cir. 1984); *Gauthier v. AMF, Inc.*, 788 F.2d 634, 636–37 (9th Cir. 1986).

Although this amendment adopts a uniform federal rule, it should be noted that evidence of subsequent remedial measures may be admissible pursuant to the second sentence of Rule 407. **[Restyled into a second paragraph in 2011.—Ed.]** Evidence of subsequent measures that is not barred by Rule 407 may still be subject to exclusion on Rule 403 grounds when the dangers of prejudice or confusion substantially outweigh the probative value of the evidence.

---

settlement offers
offers made
what was said

can be used to
show bad faith

Rule 408. Compromise Offers and Negotiations

(a) **Prohibited Uses.** Evidence of the following is not admissible—on behalf of any party—either to prove or disprove the validity or amount of a disputed claim or to impeach by a prior inconsistent statement or a contradiction:

(1) furnishing, promising, or offering—or accepting, promising to accept, or offering to accept—a valuable consideration in compromising or attempting to compromise the claim; and

(2) conduct or a statement made during compromise negotiations about the claim—except when offered in a criminal case and when the negotiations related to a claim by a public office in the exercise of its regulatory, investigative, or enforcement authority.

(b) **Exceptions.** The court may admit this evidence for another purpose, such as proving a witness's bias or prejudice, negating a contention of undue delay, or proving an effort to obstruct a criminal investigation or prosecution.

(Pub.L. 93–595, § 1, Jan. 2, 1975, 88 Stat. 1933; Apr. 12, 2006, eff. Dec. 1, 2006; Apr. 26, 2011, eff. Dec. 1, 2011.)

RESTYLED RULE 408 COMMITTEE NOTE

The language of Rule 408 has been amended as part of the general restyling of the Evidence Rules to make them more easily understood and to make style and terminology consistent throughout the rules. These changes are intended to be stylistic only. There is no intent to change any result in any ruling on evidence admissibility.

Rule 408 previously provided that evidence was not excluded if offered for a purpose not explicitly prohibited by the Rule. To improve the language of the Rule, it now provides that the court may admit evidence if offered for a permissible purpose. There is no intent to change the process for admitting evidence covered by the Rule. It remains the case that if offered for an impermissible purpose, it must be excluded, and if offered for a purpose not barred by the Rule, its admissibility remains governed by the general principles of Rules 402, 403, 801, etc.

The Committee deleted the reference to "liability" on the ground that the deletion makes the Rule flow better and easier to read, and because "liability" is covered by the broader term "validity." Courts have not made substantive decisions on the basis of any distinction between validity and liability. No change in current practice or in the coverage of the Rule is intended.

REPORTER'S COMMENT ON RESTYLED RULE 408

Restyled Rule 408—like Restyled Rule 407—arguably changes a rule of exclusion to a rule that provides a ground of admissibility for evidence offered for a proper purpose. See the Reporter's Comment on Restyled Rule 407 for a discussion of this point.

The original Rule 408 prohibited compromise evidence when offered to prove "liability for, invalidity of, or amount of a claim." One goal of the restyling was to eliminate unnecessary verbiage. The restylist proposed that "liability" could be deleted because it was sufficiently covered by the term "validity." One public comment questioned whether something would be missed by deleting "liability." The Reporter researched the topic and found no case in which "liability" was treated differently or independently from "validity" for purposes of applicability of Rule 408. But in an excess of caution, the Reporter added language to the

Committee Note to emphasize that no substantive change was intended by deleting the term "liability."

Section references, McCormick 7th ed.

§ 267

Note by Federal Judicial Center

The rule enacted by the Congress is the rule prescribed by the Supreme Court, amended by the insertion of the third sentence. **[That sentence, providing that the rule does not require exclusion of evidence merely because it was presented in the course of compromise negotiations, was struck as superfluous in 2006. See the Committee Note to the 2006 amendment.—Ed.]** Other amendments, proposed by the House bill, were not enacted, for reasons stated in the Report of the Senate Committee on the Judiciary and in the Conference Report. [set forth below]

Advisory Committee's Note

56 F.R.D. 183, 226

As a matter of general agreement, evidence of an offer to compromise a claim is not receivable in evidence as an admission of, as the case may be, the validity or invalidity of the claim. As with evidence of subsequent remedial measures, dealt with in Rule 407, exclusion may be based on two grounds. (1) The evidence is irrelevant, since the offer may be motivated by a desire for peace rather than from any concession of weakness of position. The validity of this position will vary as the amount of the offer varies in relation to the size of the claim and may also be influenced by other circumstances. (2) A more consistently impressive ground is promotion of the public policy favoring the compromise and settlement of disputes. McCormick §§ 76, 251. While the rule is ordinarily phrased in terms of offers of compromise, it is apparent that a similar attitude must be taken with respect to completed compromises when offered against a party thereto. This latter situation will not, of course, ordinarily occur except when a party to the present litigation has compromised with a third person.

The same policy underlies the provision of Rule 68 of the Federal Rules of Civil Procedure that evidence of an unaccepted offer of judgment is not admissible except in a proceeding to determine costs.

The practical value of the common law rule has been greatly diminished by its inapplicability to admissions of fact, even though made in the course of compromise negotiations, unless hypothetical, stated to be "without prejudice," or so connected with the offer as to be inseparable from it. McCormick § 251, pp. 540–541. An inevitable effect is to inhibit freedom of communication with respect to compromise, even among lawyers. Another effect is the generation of controversy over whether a given statement falls within or without the protected area. These considerations account for the expansion of the rule herewith to include evidence of conduct or statements made in compromise negotiations, as well as the offer or completed compromise itself. For similar provisions see California Evidence Code §§ 1152, 1154.

The policy considerations which underlie the rule do not come into play when the effort is to induce a creditor to settle an admittedly due amount for a lesser sum. McCormick § 251, p. 540. Hence the rule requires that the claim be disputed as to either validity or amount.

The final sentence of the rule serves to point out some limitations upon its applicability. Since the rule excludes only when the purpose is proving the validity or invalidity of the claim or its amount, an offer for another purpose is not within the rule. The illustrative situations mentioned in the rule are supported by the authorities. As to proving bias or prejudice of a witness, see

Annot., 161 A.L.R. 395, contra, Fenberg v. Rosenthal, 348 Ill.App. 510, 109 N.E.2d 402 (1952), and negativing a contention of lack of due diligence in presenting a claim, 4 Wigmore § 1061. An effort to "buy off" the prosecution or a prosecuting witness in a criminal case is not within the policy of the rule of exclusion. McCormick § 251, p. 542.

For other rules of similar import, see Uniform Rules 52 and 53; California Evidence Code §§ 1152, 1154; Kansas Code of Civil Procedure §§ 60–452, 60–453; New Jersey Evidence Rules 52 and 53.

Report of House Committee on the Judiciary

House Comm. on Judiciary, Fed.Rules of Evidence, H.R.Rep. No. 650, 93d Cong., 1st Sess., p. 8 (1973); 1974 U.S.Code Cong. & Ad. News 7075, 7081

Under existing federal law evidence of conduct and statements made in compromise negotiations is admissible in subsequent litigation between the parties. The second sentence of Rule 408 as submitted by the Supreme Court proposed to reverse that doctrine in the interest of further promoting non-judicial settlement of disputes. Some agencies of government expressed the view that the Court formulation was likely to impede rather than assist efforts to achieve settlement of disputes. For one thing, it is not always easy to tell when compromise negotiations begin, and informal dealings end. Also, parties dealing with government agencies would be reluctant to furnish factual information at preliminary meetings; they would wait until "compromise negotiations" began and thus hopefully effect an immunity for themselves with respect to the evidence supplied. In light of these considerations, the Committee recast the Rule so that admissions of liability or opinions given during compromise negotiations continue inadmissible, but evidence of unqualified factual assertions is admissible. The latter aspect of the Rule is drafted, however, so as to preserve other possible objections to the introduction of such evidence. The Committee intends no modification of current law whereby a party may protect himself from future use of his statements by couching them in hypothetical conditional form.

Report of Senate Committee on the Judiciary

Senate Comm. on Judiciary, Fed. Rules of Evidence, S.Rep. No. 1277, 93d Cong., 2d Sess., p. 10 (1974); 1974 U.S.Code Cong. & Ad. News 7051, 7056

This rule as reported makes evidence of settlement or attempted settlement of a disputed claim inadmissible when offered as an admission of liability or the amount of liability. The purpose of this rule is to encourage settlements which would be discouraged if such evidence were admissible.

Under present law, in most jurisdictions, statements of fact made during settlement negotiations, however, are excepted from this ban and are admissible. The only escape from admissibility of statements of fact made in a settlement negotiation is if the declarant or his representative expressly states that the statement is hypothetical in nature or is made without prejudice. Rule 408 as submitted by the Court reversed the traditional rule. It would have brought statements of fact within the ban and made them, as well as an offer of settlement, inadmissible.

The House amended the rule and would continue to make evidence of facts disclosed during compromise negotiations admissible. It thus reverted to the traditional rule. The House committee report states that the committee intends to preserve current law under which a party may protect himself by couching his statements in hypothetical form.[11] The real impact of this amendment, however, is to deprive the rule of much of its salutary effect. The exception for factual admissions was believed by the Advisory Committee to hamper free communication between parties and thus to constitute an unjustifiable restraint

---

[11] See Report No. 93–650, dated November 15, 1973.—Ed.

upon efforts to negotiate settlements—the encouragement of which is the purpose of the rule. Further, by protecting hypothetically phrased statements, it constituted a preference for the sophisticated, and a trap for the unwary.

Three States which had adopted rules of evidence patterned after the proposed rules prescribed by the Supreme Court opted for versions of rule 408 identical with the Supreme Court draft with respect to the inadmissibility of conduct or statements made in compromise negotiations.[12]

For these reasons, the committee has deleted the House amendment and restored the rule to the version submitted by the Supreme Court with one additional amendment. This amendment adds a sentence to insure that evidence, such as documents, is not rendered inadmissible merely because it is presented in the course of compromise negotiations if the evidence is otherwise discoverable. A party should not be able to immunize from admissibility documents otherwise discoverable merely by offering them in a compromise negotiation.

Conference Report

H.R., Fed. Rules of Evidence, Conf. Rep. No. 1597, 93d Cong., 2d Sess., p. 6 (1974); 1974 U.S.Code Cong. & Ad. News 7098, 7099

The House bill provides that evidence of admissions of liability or opinions given during compromise negotiations is not admissible, but that evidence of facts disclosed during compromise negotiations is not inadmissible by virtue of having been first disclosed in the compromise negotiations. The Senate amendment provides that evidence of conduct or statements made in compromise negotiations is not admissible. The Senate amendment also provides that the rule does not require the exclusion of any evidence otherwise discoverable merely because it is presented in the course of compromise negotiations.

The House bill was drafted to meet the objection of executive agencies that under the rule as proposed by the Supreme Court, a party could present a fact during compromise negotiations and thereby prevent an opposing party from offering evidence of that fact at trial even though such evidence was obtained from independent sources. The Senate amendment expressly precludes this result.

The Conference adopts the Senate amendment.

2006 Amendment Committee Note

Rule 408 has been amended to settle some questions in the courts about the scope of the Rule, and to make it easier to read. First, the amendment provides that Rule 408 does not prohibit the introduction in a criminal case of statements or conduct during compromise negotiations regarding a civil dispute by a government regulatory, investigative, or enforcement agency. *See, e.g., United States v. Prewitt*, 34 F.3d 436, 439 (7th Cir. 1994) (admissions of fault made in compromise of a civil securities enforcement action were admissible against the accused in a subsequent criminal action for mail fraud). Where an individual makes a statement in the presence of government agents, its subsequent admission in a criminal case should not be unexpected. The individual can seek to protect against subsequent disclosure through negotiation and agreement with the civil regulator or an attorney for the government.

Statements made in compromise negotiations of a claim by a government agency may be excluded in criminal cases where the circumstances so warrant under Rule 403. For example, if an individual was unrepresented at the time the statement was made in a civil enforcement proceeding, its probative value in a

---

[12] Nev.Rev.Stats. § 48.105; N.Mex.Stats.Anno. (1973 Supp.) § 20–4–408; West's Wis.Stats.Anno. (1973 Supp.) § 904.08.—Ed.

subsequent criminal case may be minimal. But there is no absolute exclusion imposed by Rule 408.

In contrast, statements made during compromise negotiations of other disputed claims are not admissible in subsequent criminal litigation, when offered to prove liability for, invalidity of, or amount of those claims. When private parties enter into compromise negotiations they cannot protect against the subsequent use of statements in criminal cases by way of private ordering. The inability to guarantee protection against subsequent use could lead to parties refusing to admit fault, even if by doing so they could favorably settle the private matter. Such a chill on settlement negotiations would be contrary to the policy of Rule 408.

The amendment distinguishes statements and conduct (such as a direct admission of fault) made in compromise negotiations of a civil claim by a government agency from an offer or acceptance of a compromise of such a claim. An offer or acceptance of a compromise of any civil claim is excluded under the Rule if offered against the defendant as an admission of fault. In that case, the predicate for the evidence would be that the defendant, by compromising with the government agency, has admitted the validity and amount of the civil claim, and that this admission has sufficient probative value to be considered as evidence of guilt. But unlike a direct statement of fault, an offer or acceptance of a compromise is not very probative of the defendant's guilt. Moreover, admitting such an offer or acceptance could deter a defendant from settling a civil regulatory action, for fear of evidentiary use in a subsequent criminal action. *See, e.g.,* Fishman, Jones on Evidence, Civil and Criminal, § 22:16 at 199, n.83 (7th ed. 2000) ("A target of a potential criminal investigation may be unwilling to settle civil claims against him if by doing so he increases the risk of prosecution and conviction.").

The amendment retains the language of the original rule that bars compromise evidence only when offered as evidence of the "validity," "invalidity," or "amount" of the disputed claim. The intent is to retain the extensive case law finding Rule 408 inapplicable when compromise evidence is offered for a purpose other than to prove the validity, invalidity, or amount of a disputed claim. *See, e.g., Athey v. Farmers Ins. Exchange,* 234 F.3d 357 (8th Cir. 2000) (evidence of settlement offer by insurer was properly admitted to prove insurer's bad faith); *Coakley & Williams v. Structural Concrete Equip.,* 973 F.2d 349 (4th Cir. 1992) (evidence of settlement is not precluded by Rule 408 where offered to prove a party's intent with respect to the scope of a release); *Cates v. Morgan Portable Bldg. Corp.,* 708 F.2d 683 (7th Cir. 1985) (Rule 408 does not bar evidence of a settlement when offered to prove a breach of the settlement agreement, as the purpose of the evidence is to prove the fact of settlement as opposed to the validity or amount of the underlying claim); *Uforma/Shelby Bus. Forms, Inc. v. NLRB,* 111 F.3d 1284 (6th Cir. 1997) (threats made in settlement negotiations were admissible; Rule 408 is inapplicable when the claim is based upon a wrong that is committed during the course of settlement negotiations). So for example, Rule 408 is inapplicable if offered to show that a party made fraudulent statements in order to settle a litigation.

The amendment does not affect the case law providing that Rule 408 is inapplicable when evidence of the compromise is offered to prove notice. *See, e.g., United States v. Austin,* 54 F.3d 394 (7th Cir. 1995) (no error to admit evidence of the defendant's settlement with the FTC, because it was offered to prove that the defendant was on notice that subsequent similar conduct was wrongful); *Spell v. McDaniel,* 824 F.2d 1380 (4th Cir. 1987) (in a civil rights action alleging that an officer used excessive force, a prior settlement by the City of another brutality claim was properly admitted to prove that the City was on notice of aggressive behavior by police officers).

The amendment prohibits the use of statements made in settlement negotiations when offered to impeach by prior inconsistent statement or through contradiction. Such broad impeachment would tend to swallow the exclusionary rule and would impair the public policy of promoting settlements. See McCormick on Evidence at 186 (5th ed. 1999) ("Use of statements made in compromise negotiations to impeach the testimony of a party, which is not specifically treated in Rule 408, is fraught with danger of misuse of the statements to prove liability, threatens frank interchange of information during negotiations, and generally should not be permitted."). *See also EEOC v. Gear Petroleum, Inc.*, 948 F.2d 1542 (10th Cir. 1991) (letter sent as part of settlement negotiation cannot be used to impeach defense witnesses by way of contradiction or prior inconsistent statement; such broad impeachment would undermine the policy of encouraging uninhibited settlement negotiations).

The amendment makes clear that Rule 408 excludes compromise evidence even when a party seeks to admit its own settlement offer or statements made in settlement negotiations. If a party were to reveal its own statement or offer, this could itself reveal the fact that the adversary entered into settlement negotiations. The protections of Rule 408 cannot be waived unilaterally because the Rule, by definition, protects both parties from having the fact of negotiation disclosed to the jury. Moreover, proof of statements and offers made in settlement would often have to be made through the testimony of attorneys, leading to the risks and costs of disqualification. *See generally, Pierce v. F.R. Tripler & Co.*, 955 F.2d 820, 828 (2d Cir. 1992) (settlement offers are excluded under Rule 408 even if it is the offeror who seeks to admit them; noting that the "widespread admissibility of the substance of settlement offers could bring with it a rash of motions for disqualification of a party's chosen counsel who would likely become a witness at trial").

The sentence of the Rule referring to evidence "otherwise discoverable" has been deleted as superfluous. *See, e.g.,* Advisory Committee Note to Maine Rule of Evidence 408 (refusing to include the sentence in the Maine version of Rule 408 and noting that the sentence "seems to state what the law would be if it were omitted"); Advisory Committee Note to Wyoming Rule of Evidence 408 (refusing to include the sentence in Wyoming Rule 408 on the ground that it was "superfluous"). The intent of the sentence was to prevent a party from trying to immunize admissible information, such as a pre-existing document, through the pretense of disclosing it during compromise negotiations. See *Ramada Development Co. v. Rauch*, 644 F.2d 1097 (5th Cir. 1981). But even without the sentence, the Rule cannot be read to protect pre-existing information simply because it was presented to the adversary in compromise negotiations.

Rule 409. Offers to Pay Medical and Similar Expenses

Evidence of furnishing, promising to pay, or offering to pay medical, hospital, or similar expenses resulting from an injury is not admissible to prove liability for the injury.

(As amended Apr. 26, 2011, eff. Dec. 1, 2011.)

RESTYLED RULE 409 COMMITTEE NOTE

The language of Rule 409 has been amended as part of the restyling of the Evidence Rules to make them more easily understood and to make style and terminology consistent throughout the rules. These changes are intended to be stylistic only. There is no intent to change any result in any ruling on evidence admissibility.

Section references, McCormick 7th ed.

§ 267

Note by Federal Judicial Center

The rule enacted by the Congress is the rule prescribed by the Supreme Court without change.

Advisory Committee's Note

56 F.R.D. 183, 228

The considerations underlying this rule parallel those underlying Rules 407 and 408, which deal respectively with subsequent remedial measures and offers of compromise. As stated in Annot., 20 A.L.R.2d 291, 293:

"[G]enerally, evidence of payment of medical, hospital, or similar expenses of an injured party by the opposing party, is not admissible, the reason often given being that such payment or offer is usually made from humane impulses and not from an admission of liability, and that to hold otherwise would tend to discourage assistance to the injured person."

Contrary to Rule 408, dealing with offers of compromise, the present rule does not extend to conduct or statements not a part of the act of furnishing or offering or promising to pay. This difference in treatment arises from fundamental differences in nature. Communication is essential if compromises are to be effected, and consequently broad protection of statements is needed. This is not so in cases of payments or offers or promises to pay medical expenses, where factual statements may be expected to be incidental in nature.

For rules on the same subject, but phrased in terms of "humanitarian motives," see Uniform Rule 52; California Evidence Code § 1152; Kansas Code of Civil Procedure § 60–452; New Jersey Evidence Rule 52.

Rule 410. Pleas, Plea Discussions, and Related Statements

(a) Prohibited Uses. In a civil or criminal case, evidence of the following is not admissible against the defendant who made the plea or participated in the plea discussions:

(1) a guilty plea that was later withdrawn;

(2) a nolo contendere plea;

(3) a statement made during a proceeding on either of those pleas under Federal Rule of Criminal Procedure 11 or a comparable state procedure; or

(4) a statement made during plea discussions with an attorney for the prosecuting authority if the discussions did not result in a guilty plea or they resulted in a later-withdrawn guilty plea.

(b) Exceptions. The court may admit a statement described in Rule 410(a)(3) or (4):

(1) in any proceeding in which another statement made during the same plea or plea discussions has been introduced, if in fairness the statements ought to be considered together; or

(2) in a criminal proceeding for perjury or false statement, if the defendant made the statement under oath, on the record, and with counsel present.

(As amended by P.L. 94–149, § 1(9), Dec. 12, 1975, 89 Stat. 805; Apr. 30, 1979, eff. Dec. 1, 1980; Apr. 26, 2011, eff. Dec. 1, 2011.)

RESTYLED RULE 410 COMMITTEE NOTE

The language of Rule 410 has been amended as part of the restyling of the Evidence Rules to make them more easily understood and to make style and terminology consistent throughout the rules. These changes are intended to be stylistic only. There is no intent to change any result in any ruling on evidence admissibility.

Section references, McCormick 7th ed.

§ 257, § 266

Rule 410 as originally enacted

Editorial Note

When first enacted together with the other Federal Rules of Evidence, Rule 410 read as follows:

Except as otherwise provided by Act of Congress, evidence of a plea of guilty, later withdrawn, or a plea of nolo contendere, or of an offer to plead guilty or nolo contendere to the crime charged or any other crime, or of statements made in connection with any of the foregoing pleas or offers, is not admissible in any civil or criminal action, case, or proceeding against the person who made the plea or offer. This rule shall not apply to the introduction of voluntary and reliable statements made in court on the record in connection with any of the foregoing pleas or offers where offered for impeachment purposes or in a subsequent prosecution of the declarant for perjury or false statement.

This rule shall not take effect until August 1, 1975, and shall be superseded by any amendment to the Federal Rules of Criminal Procedure which is inconsistent with this rule, and which takes effect after the date of the enactment of the Act establishing these Federal Rules of Evidence.

As prescribed by the Supreme Court, the rule had consisted only of the first sentence, without the clause "Except as otherwise provided by Act of Congress". That clause and the remaining language were added by congressional amendment. The theory of the Supreme Court's rule is explained in the Advisory Committee's Note set forth immediately below, and the reasons for the amendments are stated in the congressional reports which follow it. In addition to these latter reports, see Chairman Hungate's explanation. 120 Cong.Rec. 40890 (1974); 1975 U.S.Code Cong. & Ad.News 7108, 7109.

Advisory Committee's Note

56 F.R.D. 183, 228

Withdrawn pleas of guilty were held inadmissible in federal prosecutions in Kercheval v. United States, 274 U.S. 220, 47 S.Ct. 582, 71 L.Ed. 1009 (1927). The Court pointed out that to admit the withdrawn plea would effectively set at naught the allowance of withdrawal and place the accused in a dilemma utterly inconsistent with the decision to award him a trial. The New York Court of Appeals, in People v. Spitaleri, 9 N.Y.2d 168, 212 N.Y.S.2d 53, 173 N.E.2d 35 (1961), reexamined and overturned its earlier decisions which had allowed admission. In addition to the reasons set forth in Kercheval, which was quoted at length, the court pointed out that the effect of admitting the plea was to compel defendant to take the stand by way of explanation and to open the way for the prosecution to call the lawyer who had represented him at the time of entering the plea. State court decisions for and against admissibility are collected in Annot., 86 A.L.R.2d 326.

Pleas of *nolo contendere* are recognized by Rule 11 of the Rules of Criminal Procedure, although the law of numerous States is to the contrary. The present rule gives effect to the principal traditional characteristic of the *nolo* plea, *i.e.* avoiding the admission of guilt which is inherent in pleas of guilty. This position is consistent with the construction of Section 5 of the Clayton Act, 15 U.S.C. § 16(a), recognizing the inconclusive and compromise nature of judgments based on *nolo* pleas. General Electric Co. v. City of San Antonio, 334 F.2d 480 (5th Cir. 1964); Commonwealth Edison Co. v. Allis-Chalmers Mfg. Co., 323 F.2d 412 (7th Cir. 1963), cert. denied 376 U.S. 939, 84 S.Ct. 794, 11 L.Ed.2d 659; Armco Steel Corp. v. North Dakota, 376 F.2d 206 (8th Cir. 1967); City of Burbank v. General Electric Co., 329 F.2d 825 (9th Cir. 1964). *See also* state court decisions in Annot., 18 A.L.R.2d 1287, 1314.

Exclusion of offers to plead guilty or *nolo* has as its purpose the promotion of disposition of criminal cases by compromise. As pointed out in McCormick § 251, p. 543.

"Effective criminal law administration in many localities would hardly be possible if a large proportion of the charges were not disposed of by such compromises."

See also People v. Hamilton, 60 Cal.2d 105, 32 Cal.Rptr. 4, 383 P.2d 412 (1963), discussing legislation designed to achieve this result. As with compromise offers generally, Rule 408, free communication is needed, and security against having an offer of compromise or related statement admitted in evidence effectively encourages it.

Limiting the exclusionary rule to use against the accused is consistent with the purpose of the rule, since the possibility of use for or against other persons will not impair the effectiveness of withdrawing pleas or the freedom of discussion which the rule is designed to foster. See A.B.A. Standards Relating to Pleas of

Guilty § 2.2 (1968). *See also* the narrower provisions of New Jersey Evidence Rule 52(2) and the unlimited exclusion provided in California Evidence Code § 1153.

Report of House Committee on the Judiciary

House Comm. on Judiciary, Fed. Rules of Evidence, H.R.Rep. No. 650, 93d Cong., 1st Sess., p. 8 (1973); 1974 U.S.Code Cong. & Ad. News 7075, 7082

The Committee added the phrase "Except as otherwise provided by Act of Congress" to Rule 410 as submitted by the Court in order to preserve particular congressional policy judgments as to the effect of a plea of guilty or of nolo contendere. See 15 U.S.C. § 16(a). The Committee intends that its amendment refers to both present statutes and statutes subsequently enacted.

Report of Senate Committee on the Judiciary

Senate Comm. on Judiciary, Fed. Rules of Evidence, S. Rep. No. 1277, 93d Cong., 2d Sess., p. 10 (1974); 1974 U.S.Code Cong. & Ad. News 7051, 7057

As adopted by the House, Rule 410 would make inadmissible pleas of guilty or nolo contendere subsequently withdrawn as well as offers to make such pleas. Such a rule is clearly justified as a means of encouraging pleading. However, the House rule would then go on to render inadmissible for any purpose statements made in connection with these pleas or offers as well.

The committee finds this aspect of the House rule unjustified. Of course, in certain circumstances such statements should be excluded. If, for example, a plea is vitiated because of coercion, statements made in connection with the plea may also have been coerced and should be inadmissible on that basis. In other cases, however, voluntary statements of an accused made in court on the record, in connection with a plea, and determined by a court to be reliable should be admissible even though the plea is subsequently withdrawn. This is particularly true in those cases where, if the House rule were in effect, a defendant would be able to contradict his previous statements and thereby lie with impunity. To prevent such an injustice, the rule has been modified to permit the use of such statements for the limited purposes of impeachment and in subsequent perjury or false statement prosecutions.

Conference Report

H.R., Fed. Rules of Evidence, Conf. Rep. No. 1597, 93d Cong., 2d Sess., p. 6 (1974); 1974 U.S.Code Cong. & Ad. News 7098, 7100

The House bill provides that evidence of a guilty or nolo contendere plea, of an offer of either plea, or of statements made in connection with such pleas or offers of such pleas, is inadmissible in any civil or criminal action, case or proceeding against the person making such plea or offer. The Senate amendment makes the rule inapplicable to a voluntary and reliable statement made in court on the record where the statement is offered in a subsequent prosecution of the declarant for perjury or false statement.

The issues raised by Rule 410 are also raised by proposed Rule 11(e)(6) of the Federal Rules of Criminal Procedure presently pending before Congress. This proposed rule, which deals with the admissibility of pleas of guilty or nolo contendere, offers to make such pleas, and statements made in connection with such pleas, was promulgated by the Supreme Court on April 22, 1974, and in the absence of congressional action will become effective on August 1, 1975. The conferees intend to make no change in the presently-existing case law until that date, leaving the courts free to develop rules in this area on a case-by-case basis.

The Conferees further determined that the issues presented by the use of guilty and nolo contendere pleas, offers of such pleas, and statements made in connection with such pleas or offers, can be explored in greater detail during Congressional consideration of Rule 11(e)(6) of the Federal Rules of Criminal

Procedure. The Conferees believe, therefore, that it is best to defer its effective date until August 1, 1975. The Conferees intend that Rule 410 would be superseded by any subsequent Federal Rule of Criminal Procedure or Act of Congress with which it is inconsistent, if the Federal Rule of Criminal Procedure or Act of Congress takes effect or becomes law after the date of the enactment of the act establishing the rules of evidence.

The conference adopts the Senate amendment with an amendment that expresses the above intentions.

Rule 410 as amended in 1975

Editorial Note

In 1975 Congress amended Rule 11(e)(6) of the Federal Rules of Criminal Procedure, P.L. 94–64, July 31, 1975, 89 Stat. 371, and then amended Evidence Rule 410 to conform to it. Amended Rule 410 read:

> Except as otherwise provided in this rule, evidence of a plea of guilty, later withdrawn, or a plea of nolo contendere, or of an offer to plead guilty or nolo contendere to the crime charged or any other crime, or of statements made in connection with, and relevant to, any of the foregoing pleas or offers, is not admissible in any civil or criminal proceeding against the person who made the plea or offer. However, evidence of a statement made in connection with, and relevant to, a plea of guilty, later withdrawn, a plea of nolo contendere, or an offer to plead guilty or nolo contendere to the crime charged or any other crime, is admissible in a criminal proceeding for perjury or false statement if the statement was made by the defendant under oath, on the record, and in the presence of counsel.

P.L. 94–149, Dec. 12, 1975, 89 Stat. 805.

Report of House Committee on the Judiciary

House Comm. on Judiciary, Fed. Rules of Criminal Procedure, H.R. Rep. No. 247, 94th Cong., 1st Sess. (1975); 1975 U.S.Code Cong. & Ad.News 674, 679

The Committee added an exception to subdivision (e)(6). That subdivision provides:[13]

> Evidence of a plea of guilty, later withdrawn, or a plea of nolo contendere, or of an offer to plead guilty or nolo contendere to the crime charged or any other crime, or of statements made in connection with any of the foregoing pleas or offers, is not admissible in any civil or criminal proceeding against the person who made the plea or offer.

The Committee's exception permits the use of such evidence in a perjury or false statement prosecution where the plea, offer, or related statement was made by the defendant on the record, under oath and in the presence of counsel. The Committee recognizes that even this limited exception may discourage defendants from being completely candid and open during plea negotiations and may even result in discouraging the reaching of plea agreements. However, the Committee believes that, on balance, it is more important to protect the integrity of the judicial process from willful deceit and untruthfulness. [The Committee does not intend its language to be construed as mandating or encouraging the swearing-in of the defendant during proceedings in connection with the disclosure and acceptance or rejection of a plea agreement.] The Committee recast the language of Rule 11(c), which deals with the advice given to a defendant before the court can accept his plea of guilty or nolo contendere. The Committee acted in part because it believed that the warnings given to the defendant ought to include those that Boykin v. Alabama, 395 U.S. 238 (1969), said were constitutionally

---

[13]   As prescribed by the Supreme Court and transmitted to the Congress.—Ed.

required. In addition, and as a result of its change in subdivision (e)(6), the Committee thought it only fair that the defendant be warned that his plea of guilty (later withdrawn) or nolo contendere, or his offer of either plea, or his statements made in connection with such pleas or offers, could later be used against him in a perjury trial if made under oath, on the record, and in the presence of counsel.

Conference Report

H.R., Fed. Rules of Criminal Procedure, Conf. Rep. No. 414, 94th Cong., 1st Sess. (1975); 1976 U.S.Code Cong. & Ad.News 713, 714

Rule 11(e)(6) deals with the use of statements made in connection with plea agreements. The House version permits a limited use of pleas of guilty, later withdrawn, or nolo contendere, offers of such pleas, and statements made in connection with such pleas or offers. Such evidence can be used in a perjury or false statement prosecution if the plea, offer, or related statement was made under oath, on the record, and in the presence of counsel. The Senate version permits evidence of voluntary and reliable statements made in court on the record to be used for the purpose of impeaching the credibility of the declarant or in a perjury or false statement prosecution.

The Conference adopts the House version with changes. The Conference agrees that neither a plea nor the offer of a plea ought to be admissible for any purpose. The Conference-adopted provision, therefore, like the Senate provision, permits only the use of statements made in connection with a plea of guilty, later withdrawn, or a plea of nolo contendere, or in connection with an offer of a guilty or nolo contendere plea.

Rule 410 as revised in 1980

Editorial Note

The Supreme Court adopted and on April 30, 1979, transmitted to the Congress a revision of Rule 11(e)(6) of the Federal Rules of Criminal Procedure, which was to operate also as a revision of Evidence Rule 410. Congress suspended the effective date of the revision to December 1, 1980, absent congressional action otherwise. P.L. 96–42, July 31, 1979, 93 Stat. 326. Congress having taken no action, the rule as revised became effective on December 1, 1980, and is the present Rule 410, though subsequently restyled in 2011.

In 2002, Criminal Rule 11(e)(6) was amended so that it serves only as a cross-reference to Evidence Rule 410. That amendment alleviated the problem of two rules saying the same thing in two separate bodies of rules. Rule 410 alone now controls admissibility of pleas, discussions, and related statements in a criminal case.

Advisory Committee's Note

77 F.R.D. 507, 533

The major objective of the amendment to rule 11(e)(6) transmitted by the Supreme Court on April 30, 1979 is to describe more precisely, consistent with the original purpose of the provision, what evidence relating to pleas or plea discussions is inadmissible. The present language is susceptible to interpretation which would make it applicable to a wide variety of statements made under various circumstances other than within the context of those plea discussions authorized by rule 11(e) and intended to be protected by subdivision (e)(6) of the rule. See United States v. Herman, 544 F.2d 791 (5th Cir. 1977), discussed herein.

Fed.R.Ev. 410, as originally adopted by Pub.L. 93–595, provided in part that "evidence of a plea of guilty, later withdrawn, or a plea of nolo contendere, or of an offer to plead guilty or nolo contendere to the crime charged or any other crime, or of statements made in connection with any of the foregoing pleas or offers, is not admissible in any civil or criminal action, case, or proceeding against the person who made the plea or offer." (This rule was adopted with the proviso that it "shall be superseded by any amendment to the Federal Rules of Criminal Procedure which is inconsistent with this rule.") As the Advisory Committee Note explained: "Exclusion of offers to plead guilty or nolo has as its purpose the promotion of disposition of criminal cases by compromise." The amendment of Fed.R.Crim.P. 11, transmitted to Congress by the Supreme Court in April 1974, contained a subdivision (e)(6) essentially identical to the rule 410 language quoted above, as a part of a substantial revision of rule 11. The most significant feature of this revision was the express recognition given to the fact that the "attorney for the government and the attorney for the defendant or the defendant when acting pro se may engage in discussions with a view toward reaching" a plea agreement. Subdivision (e)(6) was intended to encourage such discussions. As noted in H.R.Rep. No. 94–247, 94th Cong., 1st Sess. 7 (1975), the purpose of subdivision (e)(6) is to not "discourage defendants from being completely candid and open during plea negotiations." Similarly, H.R.Rep. No. 94–414, 94th Cong., 1st Sess. 10 (1975), states that "Rule 11(e)(6) deals with the use of statements made in connection with plea agreements." (Rule 11(e)(6) was thereafter enacted, with the addition of the proviso allowing use of statements in a prosecution for perjury, and with the qualification that the inadmissible statements must also be "relevant to" the inadmissible pleas or offers. Pub.L. 94–64; Fed.R.Ev. 410 was then amended to conform. Pub.L. 94–149.)

While this history shows that the purpose of Fed.R.Ev. 410 and Fed.R.Crim.P. 11(e)(6) is to permit the unrestrained candor which produces effective plea discussions between the "attorney for the government and the attorney for the defendant or the defendant when acting pro se," given visibility and sanction in rule 11(e), a literal reading of the language of these two rules could reasonably lead to the conclusion that a broader rule of inadmissibility obtains. That is, because "statements" are generally inadmissible if "made in connection with, and relevant to" an "offer to plead guilty," it might be thought that an otherwise voluntary admission to law enforcement officials is rendered inadmissible merely because it was made in the hope of obtaining leniency by a plea. Some decisions interpreting rule 11(e)(6) point in this direction. See United States v. Herman, 544 F.2d 791 (5th Cir. 1977) (defendant in custody of two postal inspectors during continuance of removal hearing instigated conversation with them and at some point said he would plead guilty to armed robbery if the murder charge was dropped; one inspector stated they were not "in position" to make any deals in this regard; held, defendant's statement inadmissible under rule 11(e)(6) because the defendant "made the statements during the course of a conversation in which he sought concessions from the government in return for a guilty plea"); United States v. Brooks, 536 F.2d 1137 (6th Cir. 1976) (defendant telephoned postal inspector and offered to plead guilty if he got 2-year maximum; statement inadmissible).

The amendment makes inadmissible statements made "in the course of any proceedings under this rule regarding" either a plea of guilty later withdrawn or a plea of nolo contendere, and also statements "made in the course of plea discussions with an attorney for the government which do not result in a plea of guilty or which result in a plea of guilty later withdrawn." It is not limited to statements by the defendant himself, and thus would cover statements by defense counsel regarding defendant's incriminating admissions to him. It thus fully protects the plea discussion process authorized by rule 11 without attempting to deal with confrontations between suspects and law enforcement agents, which involve problems of quite different dimensions. See, e.g., ALI Model Code of Pre-Arraignment Procedure, art. 140 and § 150.2(8) (Proposed Official Draft, 1975) (latter section requires exclusion if "a law enforcement officer induces any person to make a statement by promising leniency"). This change, it must be emphasized, does not compel the conclusion that statements made to law enforcement agents, especially when the agents purport to have authority to bargain, are inevitably admissible. Rather, the point is that such cases are not covered by the per se rule of 11(e)(6) and thus must be resolved by that body of law dealing with police interrogations.

If there has been a plea of guilty later withdrawn or a plea of nolo contendere, subdivision (e)(6)(C) makes inadmissible statements made "in the course of any proceedings under this rule" regarding such pleas. This includes, for example, admissions by the defendant when he makes his plea in court pursuant to rule 11 and also admissions made to provide the factual basis pursuant to subdivision (f). However, subdivision (e)(6)(C) is not limited to statements made in court. If the court were to defer its decision on a plea agreement pending examination of the presentence report, as authorized by subdivision (e)(2), statements made to the probation officer in connection with the preparation of that report would come within this provision.

This amendment is fully consistent with all recent and major law reform efforts on this subject. ALI Model Code of Pre-Arraignment Procedure § 350.7 (Proposed Official Draft, 1975), and ABA Standards Relating to Pleas of Guilty § 3.4 (Approved Draft, 1968) both provide:

> Unless the defendant subsequently enters a plea of guilty or nolo contendere which is not withdrawn, the fact that the defendant or his counsel and the prosecuting attorney engaged in plea discussions or made a plea agreement should not be received in evidence against or in favor of the defendant in any criminal or civil action or administrative proceedings.

The Commentary to the latter states:

> The above standard is limited to discussions and agreements with the prosecuting attorney. Sometimes defendants will indicate to the police their willingness to bargain, and in such instances these statements are sometimes admitted in court against the defendant. State v. Christian, 245 S.W.2d 895 (Mo. 1952). If the police initiate this kind of discussion, this may have some bearing on the admissibility of the defendant's statement. However, the policy considerations relevant to this issue are better dealt with in the context of standards governing in-custody interrogation by the police.

Similarly, Unif.R.Crim.P. 441(d) (Approved Draft, 1974), provides that except under limited circumstances "no discussion between the parties or statement by the defendant or his lawyer under this Rule," i.e., the rule providing "the parties may meet to discuss the possibility of pretrial diversion . . . or of a plea agreement," are admissible. The amendment is likewise consistent with the typical state provision on this subject; see, e.g., Ill.S.Ct. Rule 402(f).

The language of the amendment identifies with more precision than the present language the necessary relationship between the statements and the plea or discussion. See the dispute between the majority and concurring opinions in United States v. Herman, 544 F.2d 791 (5th Cir. 1977), concerning the meanings and effect of the phrases "connection to" and "relevant to" in the present rule. Moreover, by relating the statements to "plea discussions" rather than "an offer to plead," the amendment ensures "that even an attempt to open plea bargaining [is] covered under the same rule of inadmissibility." United States v. Brooks, 536 F.2d 1137 (6th Cir. 1976).

The last sentence of Rule 11(e)(6) is amended to provide a second exception to the general rule of nonadmissibility of the described statements. Under the amendment, such a statement is also admissible "in any proceeding wherein another statement made in the course of the same plea or plea discussions has been introduced and the statement ought in fairness be considered contemporaneously with it." This change is necessary so that, when evidence of statements made in the course of or as a consequence of a certain plea or plea discussions are introduced under circumstances not prohibited by this rule (*e.g.,* not "against" the person who made the plea), other statements relating to the same plea or plea discussions may also be admitted when relevant to the matter at issue. For example, if a defendant upon a motion to dismiss a prosecution on some ground were able to admit certain statements made in aborted plea discussions in his favor, then other relevant statements made in the same plea discussions should be admissible against the defendant in the interest of determining the truth of the matter at issue. The language of the amendment follows closely that in Fed.R.Evid. 106, as the considerations involved are very similar.

The phrase "in any civil or criminal proceeding" has been moved from its present position, following the word "against" for purposes of clarity. An ambiguity presently exists because the word "against" may be read as referring either to the kind of proceeding in which the evidence is offered or the purpose for which it is offered. The change makes it clear that the latter construction is correct. No change is intended with respect to provisions making evidence rules inapplicable in certain situations. *See, e.g.,* Fed.R.Evid. 104(a) and 1101(d).

Unlike ABA Standards Relating to Pleas of Guilty § 3.4 (Approved Draft, 1968), and ALI Model Code of Pre-Arraignment Procedure § 350.7 (Proposed Official Draft, 1975), rule 11(e)(6) does not also provide that the described evidence is inadmissible "in favor of" the defendant. This is not intended to suggest, however, that such evidence will inevitably be admissible in the defendant's favor. Specifically, no disapproval is intended of such decisions as United States v. Verdoorn, 528 F.2d 103 (8th Cir. 1976), holding that the trial judge properly refused to permit the defendants to put into evidence at their trial the fact the prosecution had attempted to plea bargain with them, as "meaningful dialogue between the parties would, as a practical matter, be impossible if either party had to assume the risk that plea offers would be admissible in evidence."

Rule 411. Liability Insurance

Evidence that a person was or was not insured against liability is not admissible to prove whether the person acted negligently or otherwise wrongfully. But the court may admit this evidence for another purpose, such as proving a witness's bias or prejudice or proving agency, ownership, or control.

(As amended Mar. 2, 1987, eff. Oct. 1, 1987; Apr. 26, 2011, eff. Dec. 1, 2011.)

RESTYLED RULE 411 COMMITTEE NOTE

The language of Rule 411 has been amended as part of the general restyling of the Evidence Rules to make them more easily understood and to make style and terminology consistent throughout the rules. These changes are intended to be stylistic only. There is no intent to change any result in any ruling on evidence admissibility.

Rule 411 previously provided that evidence was not excluded if offered for a purpose not explicitly prohibited by the Rule. To improve the language of the Rule, it now provides that the court may admit evidence if offered for a permissible purpose. There is no intent to change the process for admitting evidence covered by the Rule. It remains the case that if offered for an impermissible purpose, it must be excluded, and if offered for a purpose not barred by the Rule, its admissibility remains governed by the general principles of Rules 402, 403, 801, etc.

REPORTER'S COMMENT ON RESTYLED RULE 411

Restyled Rule 411—like Restyled Rule 407—arguably changes a rule of exclusion to a rule that provides a ground of admissibility for evidence offered for a proper purpose. See the Reporter's Comment on Restyled Rule 407 for a discussion of this point.

Section references, McCormick 7th ed.

§ 201

Note by Federal Judicial Center

The rule enacted by the Congress is the rule prescribed by the Supreme Court without change.

Advisory Committee's Note

56 F.R.D. 183, 230

The courts have with substantial unanimity rejected evidence of liability insurance for the purpose of proving fault, and absence of liability insurance as proof of lack of fault. At best the inference of fault from the fact of insurance coverage is a tenuous one, as is its converse. More important, no doubt, has been the feeling that knowledge of the presence or absence of liability insurance would induce juries to decide cases on improper grounds. McCormick § 168; Annot., 4 A.L.R.2d 761. The rule is drafted in broad terms so as to include contributory negligence or other fault of a plaintiff as well as fault of a defendant.

The second sentence points out the limits of the rule, using well established illustrations. *Id.*

For similar rules see Uniform Rule 54; California Evidence Code § 1155; Kansas Code of Civil Procedure § 60–454; New Jersey Evidence Rule 54.

1987 Amendment Committee Note

The amendment is technical. No substantive change is intended.

———————————

Rule 412. Sex-Offense Cases: The Victim's Sexual Behavior or Predisposition

(a) Prohibited Uses. The following evidence is not admissible in a civil or criminal proceeding involving alleged sexual misconduct:

(1) evidence offered to prove that a victim engaged in other sexual behavior; or

(2) evidence offered to prove a victim's sexual predisposition.

(b) Exceptions.

(1) *Criminal Cases.* The court may admit the following evidence in a criminal case:

(A) evidence of specific instances of a victim's sexual behavior, if offered to prove that someone other than the defendant was the source of semen, injury, or other physical evidence;

(B) evidence of specific instances of a victim's sexual behavior with respect to the person accused of the sexual misconduct, if offered by the defendant to prove consent or if offered by the prosecutor; and

(C) evidence whose exclusion would violate the defendant's constitutional rights.

(2) *Civil Cases.* In a civil case, the court may admit evidence offered to prove a victim's sexual behavior or sexual predisposition if its probative value substantially outweighs the danger of harm to any victim and of unfair prejudice to any party. The court may admit evidence of a victim's reputation only if the victim has placed it in controversy.

(c) Procedure to Determine Admissibility.

(1) *Motion.* If a party intends to offer evidence under Rule 412(b), the party must:

(A) file a motion that specifically describes the evidence and states the purpose for which it is to be offered;

(B) do so at least 14 days before trial unless the court, for good cause, sets a different time;

(C) serve the motion on all parties; and

(D) notify the victim or, when appropriate, the victim's guardian or representative.

(2) *Hearing.* Before admitting evidence under this rule, the court must conduct an in camera hearing and give the victim and parties a right to attend and be heard. Unless the court orders otherwise, the motion, related materials, and the record of the hearing must be and remain sealed.

(d) Definition of "Victim." In this rule, "victim" includes an alleged victim.

(Added Pub.L. 95–540, § 2(a), Oct. 28, 1978, 92 Stat. 2046, and amended Nov. 18, 1988, Pub.L. 100–690, Title VII, § 7046(a), 102 Stat. 4400; Apr. 29, 1994, eff. Dec. 1, 1994; Sept. 13, 1994, Pub.L. 103–322, Title IV, § 40141(b), 108 Stat. 1919; Apr. 26, 2011, eff. Dec. 1, 2011.)

RESTYLED RULE 412 COMMITTEE NOTE

The language of Rule 412 has been amended as part of the restyling of the Evidence Rules to make them more easily understood and to make style and terminology consistent throughout the rules. These changes are intended to be stylistic only. There is no intent to change any result in any ruling on evidence admissibility.

Section references, McCormick 7th ed.

§ 193

Legislative History of Rule 412

[Editor's Note: There is no Advisory Committee Note to the original Rule 412. An amendment to Rule 412 was passed as part of the Violent Crime Control and Law Enforcement Act of 1994. It adopted verbatim the text of a proposal for amendment to Rule 412 that the Advisory Committee had proposed but had been rejected by the Supreme Court. House Conference Report 103–711 states that the "Conferees intend that the Advisory Committee Note on Rule 412, as transmitted by the Judicial Conference of the United States to the Supreme Court on October 25, 1993, applies to Rule 412 as enacted by this section." Thus the Advisory Committee Note—set forth immediately below—is the legislative history of the amended Rule 412 as directly enacted by Congress in 1994.]

1994 Amendment Committee Note

Rule 412 has been revised to diminish some of the confusion engendered by the original rule and to expand the protection afforded alleged victims of sexual misconduct. Rule 412 applies to both civil and criminal proceedings. The rule aims to safeguard the alleged victim against the invasion of privacy, potential embarrassment and sexual stereotyping that is associated with public disclosure of intimate sexual details and the infusion of sexual innuendo into the factfinding process. By affording victims protection in most instances, the rule also encourages victims of sexual misconduct to institute and to participate in legal proceedings against alleged offenders.

Rule 412 seeks to achieve these objectives by barring evidence relating to the alleged victim's sexual behavior or alleged sexual predisposition, whether offered as substantive evidence or for impeachment, except in designated circumstances in which the probative value of the evidence significantly outweighs possible harm to the victim.

The revised rule applies in all cases involving sexual misconduct without regard to whether the alleged victim or person accused is a party to the litigation. Rule 412 extends to "pattern" witnesses in both criminal and civil cases whose testimony about other instances of sexual misconduct by the person accused is otherwise admissible. When the case does not involve alleged sexual misconduct, evidence relating to a third-party witness' alleged sexual activities is not within the ambit of Rule 412. The witness will, however, be protected by other rules such as Rules 404 and 608, as well as Rule 403.

The terminology "alleged victim" is used because there will frequently be a factual dispute as to whether sexual misconduct occurred. It does not connote any requirement that the misconduct be alleged in the pleadings. Rule 412 does not, however, apply unless the person against whom the evidence is offered can reasonably be characterized as a "victim of alleged sexual misconduct." When this is not the case, as for instance in a defamation action involving statements concerning sexual misconduct in which the evidence is offered to show that the alleged defamatory statements were true or did not damage the plaintiff's reputation, neither Rule 404 nor this rule will operate to bar the evidence; Rule [sic] 401 and 403 will continue to control. Rule 412 will, however, apply in a Title VII action in which the plaintiff has alleged sexual harassment.

The reference to a person "accused" is also used in a non-technical sense. **[All references to the "accused" were deleted in the 2011 restyling, in favor of the term "defendant in a criminal case".—Ed.]** There is no requirement that there be a criminal charge pending against the person or even that the misconduct would constitute a criminal offense. Evidence offered to prove allegedly false prior claims by the victim is not barred by Rule 412. However, this evidence is subject to the requirements of Rule 404.

Subdivision (a). As amended, Rule 412 bars evidence offered to prove the victim's sexual behavior and alleged sexual predisposition. Evidence, which might otherwise be admissible under Rules 402, 404(b), 405, 607, 608, 609, or some other evidence rule, must be excluded if Rule 412 so requires. The word "other" is used to suggest some flexibility in admitting evidence "intrinsic" to the alleged sexual misconduct. *Cf.* Committee Note to 1991 amendment to Rule 404(b).

Past sexual behavior connotes all activities that involve actual physical conduct, *i.e.* sexual intercourse and sexual contact, or that imply sexual intercourse or sexual contact. *See, e.g., United States v. Galloway,* 937 F.2d 542 (10th Cir. 1991), *cert. denied,* 113 S.Ct. 418 (1992) (use of contraceptives inadmissible since use implies sexual activity); *United States v. One Feather,* 702 F.2d 736 (8th Cir. 1983) (birth of an illegitimate child inadmissible); *State v. Carmichael,* 727 P.2d 918, 925 (Kan. 1986) (evidence of venereal disease inadmissible). In addition, the word "behavior" should be construed to include activities of the mind, such as fantasies or dreams. *See* 23 C. Wright & K. Graham, Jr., *Federal Practice and Procedure,* § 5384 at p. 548 (1980) ("While there may be some doubt under statutes that require 'conduct,' it would seem that the language of Rule 412 is broad enough to encompass the behavior of the mind.").

The rule has been amended to also exclude all other evidence relating to an alleged victim of sexual misconduct that is offered to prove a sexual predisposition. This amendment is designed to exclude evidence that does not directly refer to sexual activities or thoughts but that the proponent believes may have a sexual connotation for the factfinder. Admission of such evidence would contravene Rule 412's objectives of shielding the alleged victim from potential embarrassment and safeguarding the victim against stereotypical thinking. Consequently, unless the (b)(2) exception is satisfied, evidence such as that relating to the alleged victim's mode of dress, speech, or life-style will not be admissible.

The introductory phrase in subdivision (a) was deleted because it lacked clarity and contained no explicit reference to the other provisions of law that were intended to be overridden. The conditional clause, "except as provided in subdivisions (b) and (c)" is intended to make clear that evidence of the types described in subdivision (a) is admissible only under the strictures of those sections.

The reason for extending the rule to all criminal cases is obvious. The strong social policy of protecting a victim's privacy and encouraging victims to come forward to report criminal acts is not confined to cases that involve a charge of sexual assault. The need to protect the victim is equally great when a defendant is charged with kidnapping, and evidence is offered, either to prove motive or as background, that the defendant sexually assaulted the victim.

The reason for extending Rule 412 to civil cases is equally obvious. The need to protect alleged victims against invasions of privacy, potential embarrassment, and unwarranted sexual stereotyping, and the wish to encourage victims to come forward when they have been sexually molested do not disappear because the context has shifted from a criminal prosecution to a claim for damages or injunctive relief. There is a strong social policy in not only punishing those who engage in sexual misconduct, but in also providing relief to the victim. Thus, Rule 412 applies in any civil case in which a person claims to be the victim of sexual misconduct, such as actions for sexual battery or sexual harassment.

Subdivision (b). Subdivision (b) spells out the specific circumstances in which some evidence may be admissible that would otherwise be barred by the general rule expressed in subdivision (a). As amended, Rule 412 will be virtually unchanged in criminal cases, but will provide protection to any person alleged to be a victim of sexual misconduct regardless of the charge actually brought against an accused. A new exception has been added for civil cases.

In a criminal case, evidence may be admitted under subdivision (b)(1) pursuant to three possible exceptions, provided the evidence also satisfies other requirements for admissibility specified in the Federal Rules of Evidence, including Rule 403. Subdivisions (b)(1)(A) and (b)(1)(B) require proof in the form of specific instances of sexual behavior in recognition of the limited probative value and dubious reliability of evidence of reputation or evidence in the form of an opinion.

Under subdivision (b)(1)(A), evidence of specific instances of sexual behavior with persons other than the person whose sexual misconduct is alleged may be admissible if it is offered to prove that another person was the source of semen, injury or other physical evidence. Where the prosecution has directly or indirectly asserted that the physical evidence originated with the accused, the defendant must be afforded an opportunity to prove that another person was responsible. *See United States v. Begay,* 937 F.2d 515, 523 n. 10 (10th Cir. 1991). Evidence offered for the specific purpose identified in this subdivision may still be excluded if it does not satisfy Rules 401 or 403. *See, e.g., United States v. Azure,* 845 F.2d 1503, 1505–06 (8th Cir. 1988) (10 year old victim's injuries indicated recent use of force; court excluded evidence of consensual sexual activities with witness who testified at *in camera* hearing that he had never hurt victim and failed to establish recent activities).

Under the exception in subdivision (b)(1)(B), evidence of specific instances of sexual behavior with respect to the person whose sexual misconduct is alleged is admissible if offered to prove consent, or offered by the prosecution. Admissible pursuant to this exception might be evidence of prior instances of sexual activities between the alleged victim and the accused, as well as statements in which the alleged victim expressed an intent to engage in sexual intercourse with the accused, or voiced sexual fantasies involving the specific accused. In a prosecution for child sexual abuse, for example, evidence of uncharged sexual activity between the accused and the alleged victim offered by the prosecution may be admissible pursuant to Rule 404(b) to show a pattern of behavior. Evidence relating to the victim's alleged sexual predisposition is not admissible pursuant to this exception.

Under subdivision (b)(1)(C), evidence of specific instances of conduct may not be excluded if the result would be to deny a criminal defendant the protections afforded by the Constitution. For example, statements in which the victim has expressed an intent to have sex with the first person encountered on a particular occasion might not be excluded without violating the due process right of a rape defendant seeking to prove consent. Recognition of this basic principle was expressed in subdivision (b)(1) of the original rule. The United States Supreme Court has recognized that in various circumstances a defendant may have a right to introduce evidence otherwise precluded by an evidence rule under the Confrontation Clause. *See, e.g., Olden v. Kentucky,* 488 U.S. 227 (1988) (defendant in rape cases had right to inquire into alleged victim's cohabitation with another man to show bias).

Subdivision (b)(2) governs the admissibility of otherwise proscribed evidence in civil cases. It employs a balancing test rather than the specific exceptions stated in subdivision (b)(1) in recognition of the difficulty of foreseeing future developments in the law. Greater flexibility is needed to accommodate evolving causes of action such as claims for sexual harassment.

The balancing test requires the proponent of the evidence, whether plaintiff or defendant, to convince the court that the probative value of the proffered evidence "substantially outweighs the danger of harm to any victim and of unfair prejudice of any party." This test for admitting evidence offered to prove sexual behavior or sexual propensity in civil cases differs in three respects from the general rule governing admissibility set forth in Rule 403. First, it reverses the usual procedure spelled out in Rule 403 by shifting the burden to the proponent to demonstrate admissibility rather than making the opponent justify exclusion of the evidence. Second, the standard expressed in subdivision (b)(2) is more stringent than in the original rule; it raises the threshold for admission by requiring that the probative value of the evidence *substantially* outweigh the specified dangers. Finally, the Rule 412 test puts "harm to the victim" on the scale in addition to prejudice to the parties.

Evidence of reputation may be received in a civil case only if the alleged victim has put his or her reputation into controversy. The victim may do so without making a specific allegation in a pleading. *Cf.* Fed.R.Civ.P. 35(a).

Subdivision (c). Amended subdivision (c) is more concise and understandable than the subdivision it replaces. The requirement of a motion before trial is continued in the amended rule, as is the provision that a late motion may be permitted for good cause shown. In deciding whether to permit late filing, the court may take into account the conditions previously included in the rule: namely whether the evidence is newly discovered and could not have been obtained earlier through the existence of due diligence, and whether the issue to which such evidence relates has newly arisen in the case. The rule recognizes that in some instances the circumstances that justify an application to introduce evidence otherwise barred by Rule 412 will not become apparent until trial.

The amended rule provides that before admitting evidence that falls within the prohibition of Rule 412(a), the court must hold a hearing in camera at which the alleged victim and any party must be afforded the right to be present and an opportunity to be heard. All papers connected with the motion and any record of a hearing on the motion must be kept and remain under seal during the course of trial and appellate proceedings unless otherwise ordered. This is to assure that the privacy of the alleged victim is preserved in all cases in which the court rules that proffered evidence is not admissible, and in which the hearing refers to matters that are not received, or are received in another form.

The procedures set forth in subdivision (c) do not apply to discovery of a victim's past sexual conduct or predisposition in civil cases, which will be continued to be governed by Fed.R.Civ.P. 26. In order not to undermine the rationale of Rule 412, however, courts should enter appropriate orders pursuant to Fed.R.Civ.P. 26(c) to protect the victim against unwarranted inquiries and to ensure confidentiality. Courts should presumptively issue protective orders barring discovery unless the party seeking discovery makes a showing that the evidence sought to be discovered would be relevant under the facts and theories of the particular case, and cannot be obtained except through discovery. In an action for sexual harassment, for instance, while some evidence of the alleged victim's sexual behavior and/or predisposition in the workplace may perhaps be relevant, non-work place conduct will usually be irrelevant. *Cf. Burns v. McGregor Electronic Industries, Inc.,* 989 F.2d 959, 962–63 (8th Cir. 1993) (posing for a nude magazine outside work hours is irrelevant to issue of unwelcomeness of sexual advances at work). Confidentiality orders should be presumptively granted as well.

One substantive change made in subdivision (c) is the elimination of the following sentence: "Notwithstanding subdivision (b) of Rule 104, if the relevancy of the evidence which the accused seeks to offer in the trial depends upon the fulfillment of a condition of fact, the court, at the hearing in chambers or at a subsequent hearing in chambers scheduled for such purpose, shall accept evidence on the issue of whether such condition of fact is fulfilled and shall determine such issue." On its face, this language would appear to authorize a trial judge to exclude evidence of past sexual conduct between an alleged victim and an accused or a defendant in a civil case based upon the judge's belief that such past acts did not occur. Such an authorization raises questions of invasion of the right to a jury trial under the Sixth and Seventh Amendments. *See* 1 S. Saltzburg & M. Martin, *Federal Rules of Evidence Manual,* 396–97 (5th ed. 1990).

The Advisory Committee concluded that the amended rule provided adequate protection for all persons claiming to be the victims of sexual misconduct, and that it was inadvisable to continue to include a provision in the rule that has been confusing and that raises substantial constitutional issues.

[Advisory Committee Note adopted by Congressional Conference Report accompanying Pub.L. 103–322. See H.R.Conf.Rep. No. 103–711, 103rd Cong., 2nd Sess., 383 (1994).]

Rule 413. Similar Crimes in Sexual-Assault Cases

(a) Permitted Uses. In a criminal case in which a defendant is accused of a sexual assault, the court may admit evidence that the defendant committed any other sexual assault. The evidence may be considered on any matter to which it is relevant.

(b) Disclosure to the Defendant. If the prosecutor intends to offer this evidence, the prosecutor must disclose it to the defendant, including witnesses' statements or a summary of the expected testimony. The prosecutor must do so at least 15 days before trial or at a later time that the court allows for good cause.

(c) Effect on Other Rules. This rule does not limit the admission or consideration of evidence under any other rule.

(d) Definition of "Sexual Assault." In this rule and Rule 415, "sexual assault" means a crime under federal law or under state law (as "state" is defined in 18 U.S.C. § 513) involving:

    (1) any conduct prohibited by 18 U.S.C. chapter 109A;

    (2) contact, without consent, between any part of the defendant's body—or an object—and another person's genitals or anus;

    (3) contact, without consent, between the defendant's genitals or anus and any part of another person's body;

    (4) deriving sexual pleasure or gratification from inflicting death, bodily injury, or physical pain on another person; or

    (5) an attempt or conspiracy to engage in conduct described in subparagraphs (1)–(4).

(Added Sept. 13, 1994, Pub.L. 103–322, Title XXXII, § 320935(a), 108 Stat. 2135, effective July 9, 1995; as amended Apr. 26, 2011, eff. Dec. 1, 2011.)

RESTYLED RULE 413 COMMITTEE NOTE

The language of Rule 413 has been amended as part of the restyling of the Evidence Rules to make them more easily understood and to make style and terminology consistent throughout the rules. These changes are intended to be stylistic only. There is no intent to change any result in any ruling on evidence admissibility.

REPORTER'S COMMENT ON RESTYLED RULE 413

As drafted and enacted by Congress, Rule 413 provided that evidence of the defendant's commission of "another offense or offenses of sexual assault" is admissible. The restylist thought this language was cumbersome and proposed to change it to "another sexual assault." The Reporter objected that this would be a substantive change because it could be read to allow admissibility of *only one* sexual assault. Thus, a defendant with more than one sexual assault in his past could argue to the court that only one of them could be admitted under the Rule. The restylist argued that there is a restyling convention providing that a reference to the singular automatically includes a reference to the plural. The Reporter responded that proper rulemaking cannot be dependent on obscure restyling conventions. The Advisory Committee agreed with the Reporter that a reference to "another sexual assault" would result in a substantive change to the rule. The Restyled Rule now provides that the court may admit evidence that the defendant committed "any other sexual assault."

Section references, McCormick 7th ed.

§ 190

Legislative History of Rules 413–415

[Editor's Note: Rules 413–15 are not the product of the usual procedure by which Federal Rules of Evidence are enacted. They were added to the Federal Rules of Evidence directly by Congress—Public Law 103–322, the Violent Crime Control and Law Enforcement Act of 1994. Public Law 103–322 was adopted September 13, 1994, and became effective July 9, 1995. There is therefore no Advisory Committee Note to accompany the Rules. There is also no Congressional Committee or Conference Report on the Rules.]

Excerpts from Statements on the Floor of Congress Concerning Rules 413–415

Statement of Congresswoman Molinari:

The new rules will supersede in sex offenses the restrictive aspects of Federal Rule of Evidence 404(b). In contrast to Rule 404(b)'s general prohibition of evidence of character or propensity, the new rules for sex offense cases authorize admission and consideration of an uncharged offense for its bearing "on any matter to which it is relevant." This includes the defendant's propensity to commit sexual assault or child molestation offenses, and assessment of the probability or improbability that the defendant has been falsely or mistakenly accused of such an offense.

In other respects, the general standards of the rules of evidence will continue to apply, including the restrictions on hearsay evidence and the court's authority under Rule 403 to exclude evidence whose probative value is substantially outweighed by its prejudicial effect. . . .

The proposed reform is critical to the protection of the public from rapists and child molesters, and is justified by the distinctive characteristics of the cases it will affect. In child molestation cases, for example, a history of similar acts tends to be exceptionally probative because it shows an unusual disposition of the defendant . . . that simply does not exist in ordinary people. Moreover, such cases require reliance on child victims whose credibility can readily be attacked in the absence of substantial corroboration. In such cases, there is a compelling public interest in admitting all significant evidence that will illuminate the credibility of the charge and any denial by the defense.

. . .

Statement of Senator Dole:

[T]oo often, crucial evidentiary information is thrown out at trial because of technical evidentiary rulings. This amendment is designed to clarify the law and make clear what evidence is admissible, and what evidence is not admissible, in sex crime cases.

The amendment would create a new rule 413 of the Federal Rules of Evidence. This new rule would provide that in a criminal case in which the defendant is accused of assault, evidence of the defendant's commission of another offense or offenses of sexual assault is admissible, and may be considered for its bearing on any matter to which it is relevant.

. . . .

. . . I think if somebody is a repeat offender, if you brought in eight or nine women, for example, . . . and he had one offense after another, it would be probative. If it had not happened for 10 years, it probably would not have any value.

We also provide protection for the defendant because we require the Government to disclose the evidence to the defendant, including a statement of witnesses or a summary of the substance of any testimony expected to be offered at least 15 days before the scheduled date or trial, or at such later time as the court may allow for good cause.

. . . [I]f we are really going to get tough, and if we are really going to try to make certain that justice is provided for the victim as well as the defendant, of course, then I think we ought to look seriously at this.

113 Cong. Rec. S15072–3.

Statement of Senator Biden:

[W]hat the Republican leader is doing is changing 404(b) of the Federal Rules of Criminal Procedure [*sic*]. . . . Right now the rule in a courtroom in a Federal court is you go in and if you wish to introduce evidence of a similar crime . . . you can only do it under very limited circumstances . . . as proof of motive, opportunity, intent, preparation, plan, knowledge, identity, or absence of a mistake or accident. These are the only circumstances in which you can offer this as evidence. . . . There is a reason for that. These rules of relevancy . . . it took essentially 800 years to develop the rules of evidence under our English jurisprudence system. . . . We found out from 800 years of experience that [evidence of prior crimes] tends to blind people [from] looking at the real facts before them and making an independent judgment, at this time, at this circumstance, at this situation, that this defendant did that thing.

113 Cong. Rec. S15072.

———————

Rule 414. Similar Crimes in Child-Molestation Cases

(a) Permitted Uses. In a criminal case in which a defendant is accused of child molestation, the court may admit evidence that the defendant committed any other child molestation. The evidence may be considered on any matter to which it is relevant.

(b) Disclosure to the Defendant. If the prosecutor intends to offer this evidence, the prosecutor must disclose it to the defendant, including witnesses' statements or a summary of the expected testimony. The prosecutor must do so at least 15 days before trial or at a later time that the court allows for good cause.

(c) Effect on Other Rules. This rule does not limit the admission or consideration of evidence under any other rule.

(d) Definition of "Child" and "Child Molestation." In this rule and Rule 415:

    (1) "child" means a person below the age of 14; and

    (2) "child molestation" means a crime under federal law or under state law (as "state" is defined in 18 U.S.C. § 513) involving:

        (A) any conduct prohibited by 18 U.S.C. chapter 109A and committed with a child;

        (B) any conduct prohibited by 18 U.S.C. chapter 110;

        (C) contact between any part of the defendant's body—or an object—and a child's genitals or anus;

        (D) contact between the defendant's genitals or anus and any part of a child's body;

        (E) deriving sexual pleasure or gratification from inflicting death, bodily injury, or physical pain on a child; or

        (F) an attempt or conspiracy to engage in conduct described in subparagraphs (A)–(E).

(Added Sept. 13, 1994, Pub.L. 103–322, Title XXXII, § 320935(a), 108 Stat. 2135, effective July 9, 1995; Apr. 26, 2011, eff. Dec. 1, 2011.)

RESTYLED RULE 414 COMMITTEE NOTE

The language of Rule 414 has been amended as part of the restyling of the Evidence Rules to make them more easily understood and to make style and terminology consistent throughout the rules. These changes are intended to be stylistic only. There is no intent to change any result in any ruling on evidence admissibility.

Section references, McCormick 7th ed.

§ 190

Legislative History

[Editor's Note: Rule 414 was enacted directly by Congress, together with Rules 413 and 415. See Rule 413 for a discussion of the legislative history.]

———————

Rule 415. Similar Acts in Civil Cases Involving Sexual Assault or Child Molestation

(a) Permitted Uses. In a civil case involving a claim for relief based on a party's alleged sexual assault or child molestation, the court may admit evidence that the party committed any other sexual assault or child molestation. The evidence may be considered as provided in Rules 413 and 414.

(b) Disclosure to the Opponent. If a party intends to offer this evidence, the party must disclose it to the party against whom it will be offered, including witnesses' statements or a summary of the expected testimony. The party must do so at least 15 days before trial or at a later time that the court allows for good cause.

(c) Effect on Other Rules. This rule does not limit the admission or consideration of evidence under any other rule.

(Added Sept. 13, 1994, Pub.L. 103–322, Title XXXII, § 320935(a), 108 Stat. 2135, effective July 9, 1995; Apr. 26, 2011, eff. Dec. 1, 2011.)

RESTYLED RULE 415 COMMITTEE NOTE

The language of Rule 415 has been amended as part of the restyling of the Evidence Rules to make them more easily understood and to make style and terminology consistent throughout the rules. These changes are intended to be stylistic only. There is no intent to change any result in any ruling on evidence admissibility.

Section references, McCormick 7th ed.

§ 190

Legislative History

[Editor's Note: Rule 415 was enacted directly by Congress, together with Rules 413 and 414. See Rule 413 for a discussion of the legislative history.]

ARTICLE V. PRIVILEGES

Rule 501. Privilege in General

The common law—as interpreted by United States courts in the light of reason and experience—governs a claim of privilege unless any of the following provides otherwise:

- the United States Constitution;

- a federal statute; or

- rules prescribed by the Supreme Court.

But in a civil case, state law governs privilege regarding a claim or defense for which state law supplies the rule of decision.

(As amended Apr. 26, 2011, eff. Dec. 1, 2011.)

RESTYLED RULE 501 COMMITTEE NOTE

The language of Rule 501 has been amended as part of the restyling of the Evidence Rules to make them more easily understood and to make style and terminology consistent throughout the rules. These changes are intended to be stylistic only. There is no intent to change any result in any ruling on evidence admissibility.

REPORTER'S COMMENT ON RESTYLED RULE 501

The provision concerning applicability of state privilege law does not accurately describe the case law under Rule 501. As originally written and also as restyled, the language provides that state privilege law governs every claim arising under state law that is brought in a federal court. But this is not so when a state claim is joined with a federal claim—either under pendent jurisdiction or independently in diversity when joined with a federal claim. The federal courts have generally held that when state claims are joined with federal claims, the federal rule of privilege prevails and applies to state claims as well. *See, e.g., Hancock v. Dodson,* 958 F.2d 1367 (6th Cir. 1992); *Hancock v. Hobbs,* 967 F.2d 462 (11th Cir. 1992). It could be argued that while restyling the Evidence Rules, the Advisory Committee should have taken the opportunity to conform the Rules to caselaw where there is a divergence. But that would have been a much more massive undertaking, and would have involved substantive changes to the existing rules. Generally speaking, the Restyling Project sought to leave the substantive content of the Rules where it found it.

Section references, McCormick 7th ed.

§§ 72–77

Note by Federal Judicial Center

The rules enacted by the Congress substituted the single Rule 501 in place of the 13 rules dealing with privilege prescribed by the Supreme Court as Article V. . . . The reasons given in support of the congressional action are stated in the Report of the House Committee on the Judiciary, the Report of the Senate Committee on the Judiciary, and Conference Report. [set forth below]

[Editor's Note: The 13 rules on privilege proposed by the Advisory Committee, all rejected by Congress, can be found in the section on "Deleted and Superseded Materials" *infra* **in this Book.]**

Report of House Committee on the Judiciary

House Comm. of Judiciary, Fed. Rules of Evidence, H.R.Rep. No. 650, 93d Cong., 1st Sess., p. 8 (1973); 1974 U.S.Code Cong. & Ad.News 7075, 7082

Article V as submitted to Congress contained thirteen Rules. Nine of those Rules defined specific non-constitutional privileges which the federal courts must recognize (*i.e.* required reports, lawyer-client, psychotherapist-patient, husband-wife, communications to clergymen, political vote, trade secrets, secrets of state and other official information, and identity of informer). Another Rule provided that only those privileges set forth in Article V or in some other Act of Congress could be recognized by the federal courts. The three remaining Rules addressed collateral problems as to waiver of privilege by voluntary disclosure, privileged matter disclosed under compulsion or without opportunity to claim privilege, comment upon or inference from a claim of privilege, and jury instruction with regard thereto.

The Committee amended Article V to eliminate all of the Court's specific Rules on privileges. Instead, the Committee, through a single Rule, 501, left the law of privileges in its present state and further provided that privileges shall continue to be developed by the courts of the United States under a uniform standard applicable both in civil and criminal cases. That standard, derived from Rule 26 of the Federal Rules of Criminal Procedure, mandates the application of the principles of the common law as interpreted by the courts of the United States in the light of reason and experience. The words "person, government, State, or political subdivision thereof" were added by the Committee to the lone term "witnesses" used in Rule 26 to make clear that, as under present law, not only witnesses may have privileges. The Committee also included in its amendment a proviso modeled after Rule 302 and similar to language added by the Committee to Rule 601 relating to the competency of witnesses. The proviso is designed to require the application of State privilege law in civil actions and proceedings governed by Erie R. Co. v. Tompkins, 304 U.S. 64 (1938), a result in accord with current federal court decisions. See Republic Gear Co. v. Borg-Warner Corp., 381 F.2d 551, 555–556 n. 2 (2nd Cir. 1967). The Committee deemed the proviso to be necessary in the light of the Advisory Committee's view (see its note to Court Rule 501) that this result is not mandated under *Erie*.

The rationale underlying the proviso is that federal law should not supersede that of the States in substantive areas such as privilege absent a compelling reason. The Committee believes that in civil cases in the federal courts where an element of a claim or defense is not grounded upon a federal question, there is no federal interest strong enough to justify departure from State policy. In addition, the Committee considered that the Court's proposed Article V would have promoted forum shopping in some civil actions, depending upon differences in the privilege law applied as among the State and federal courts. The Committee's proviso, on the other hand, under which the federal courts are bound to apply the State's privilege law in actions founded upon a State-created right or defense, removes the incentive to "shop".

Report of Senate Committee on the Judiciary

Senate Comm. on Judiciary, Fed. Rules of Evidence, S.Rep. No. 1277, 93d Cong., 2d Sess., p. 11 (1974); 1974 U.S.Code Cong. & Ad.News 7051, 7058

Article V as submitted to Congress contained 13 rules. Nine of those rules defined specific nonconstitutional privileges which the Federal courts must recognize (*i.e.*, required reports, lawyer-client, psychotherapist-patient, husband-wife, communications to clergymen, political vote, trade secrets, secrets of state and other official information, and identity of informer). Many of these rules contained controversial modifications or restrictions upon common law privileges. As noted *supra*, the House amended article V to eliminate all of the Court's specific rules on privileges. Through a single rule, 501, the House provided that privileges shall be governed by the principles of the common law as interpreted by the courts of the United States in the light of reason and experience (a standard derived from rule 26 of the Federal Rules of Criminal Procedure) except in the case of an element of a civil claim or defense as to which State law supplies the rule of decision in which event state privilege law was to govern.

The committee agrees with the main thrust of the House amendment: that a federally developed common law based on modern reason and experience shall apply except where the State nature of the issues renders deference to State privilege law the wiser course, as in the usual diversity case. The committee understands that thrust of the House amendment to require that State privilege law be applied in "diversity" cases (actions on questions of State law between citizens of different States arising under 28 U.S.C. § 1332). The language of the House amendment, however, goes beyond this in some respects, and falls short of it in others: State privilege law applies even in nondiversity, Federal question civil cases, where an issue governed by State substantive law is the object of the evidence (such issues do sometimes arise in such cases); and, in all instances where State privilege law is to be applied, *e.g.*, on proof of a State issue in a diversity case, a close reading reveals that State privilege law is not to be applied unless the matter to be proved is an element of that state claim or defense, as distinguished from a step along the way in the proof of it.

The committee is concerned that the language used in the House amendment could be difficult to apply. It provides that "in civil actions . . . with respect to an element of a claim or defense as to which State law supplies the rule of decision," State law on privilege applies. The question of what is an element of a claim or defense is likely to engender considerable litigation. If the matter in question constitutes an element of a claim, State law supplies the privilege rule; whereas if it is a mere item of proof with respect to a claim, then, even though State law might supply the rule of decision, Federal law on the privilege would apply. Further, disputes will arise as to how the rule should be applied in an antitrust action or in a tax case where the Federal statute is silent as to a particular aspect of the substantive law in question, but Federal cases had incorporated State law by reference to State law. Is a claim (or defense) based on such a reference a claim or defense as to which federal or State law supplies the rule of decision?

Another problem not entirely avoidable is the complexity or difficulty the rule introduces into the trial of a Federal case containing a combination of Federal and State claims and defenses, *e.g.* an action involving Federal antitrust and State unfair competition claims. Two different bodies of privilege law would need to be consulted. It may even develop that the same witness-testimony might be relevant on both counts and privileged as to one but not the other.

The formulation adopted by the House is pregnant with litigious mischief. The committee has, therefore, adopted what we believe will be a clearer and more practical guideline for determining when courts should respect State rules of privilege. Basically, it provides that in criminal and Federal question civil cases, federally evolved rules on privilege should apply since it is Federal policy which is being enforced. Conversely, in diversity cases where the litigation in question turns on a substantive question of State law, and is brought in the Federal courts because the parties reside in different States, the committee believes it is clear that State rules of privilege should apply unless the proof is directed at a claim or defense for which Federal law supplies the rule of decision (a situation which would not commonly arise.) It is intended that the State rules of privilege should apply equally in original diversity actions and diversity actions removed under 28 U.S.C. § 1441(b).

Two other comments on the privilege rule should be made. The committee has received a considerable volume of correspondence from psychiatric organizations and psychiatrists concerning the deletion of rule 504 of the rule submitted by the Supreme Court. It should be clearly understood that, in approving this general rule as to privileges, the action of Congress should not be understood as disapproving any recognition of a psychiatrist-patient, or husband-wife, or any other of the enumerated privileges contained in the Supreme Court rules. Rather, our action should be understood as reflecting the view that the recognition of a privilege based on a confidential relationship and other privileges should be determined on a case-by-case basis.

Further, we would understand that the prohibition against spouses testifying against each other is considered a rule of privilege and covered by this rule and not by rule 601 of the competency of witnesses.

Conference Report

H.R., Fed. Rules of Evidence, Conf.Rep. No. 1597, 93d Cong., 2d Sess., p. 7 (1974); 1974 U.S.Code Cong. & Ad.News 7098, 7100

Rule 501 deals with the privilege of a witness not to testify. Both the House and Senate bills provide that federal privilege law applies in criminal cases. In civil actions and proceedings, the House bill provides that state privilege law applies "to an element of a claim or defense as to which State law supplies the rule of decision." The Senate bill provides that "in civil actions and proceedings arising under 28 U.S.C. § 1332 or 28 U.S.C. § 1335, or between citizens of different States and removed under 28 U.S.C. § 1441(b) the privilege of a witness, person, government, State or political subdivision thereof is determined in accordance with State law, unless with respect to the particular claim or defense, Federal law supplies the rule of decision."

The wording of the House and Senate bills differs in the treatment of civil actions and proceedings. The rule in the House bill applies to evidence that relates to "an element of a claim or defense." If an item of proof tends to support or defeat a claim or defense, or an element of a claim or defense, and if state law supplies the rule of decision for that claim or defense, then state privilege law applies to that item of proof.

Under the provision in the House bill, therefore, state privilege law will usually apply in diversity cases. There may be diversity cases, however, where a claim or defense is based upon federal law. In such instances, federal privilege law will apply to evidence relevant to the federal claim or defense. See Sola Electric Co. v. Jefferson Electric Co., 317 U.S. 173 (1942).

In nondiversity jurisdiction civil cases, federal privilege law will generally apply. In those situations where a federal court adopts or incorporates state law to fill interstices or gaps in federal statutory phrases, the court generally will apply federal privilege law. As Justice Jackson has said:

> A federal court sitting in a non-diversity case such as this does not sit as a local tribunal. In some cases it may see fit for special reasons to give the law of a particular state highly persuasive or even controlling effect, but in the last analysis its decision turns upon the law of the United States, not that of any state.

D'Oench, Duhme & Co. v. Federal Deposit Insurance Corp., 315 U.S. 447, 471 (1942) (Jackson, J., concurring).

When a federal court chooses to absorb state law, it is applying the state law as a matter of federal common law. Thus, state law does not supply the rule of decision (even though the federal court may apply a rule derived from state decisions), and state privilege law would not apply. See C.A. Wright, Federal Courts 251–252 (2d ed. 1970); Holmberg v. Armbrecht, 327 U.S. 392 (1946); DeSylva v. Ballentine, 351 U.S. 570, 581 (1956); 9 Wright & Miller, Federal Rules and Procedure § 2408.

In civil actions and proceedings, where the rule of decision as to a claim or defense or as to an element of a claim or defense is supplied by state law, the House provision requires that state privilege law apply.

The Conference adopts the House provision.

———————

Rule 502. Attorney-Client Privilege and Work Product; Limitations on Waiver

The following provisions apply, in the circumstances set out, to disclosure of a communication or information covered by the attorney-client privilege or work-product protection.

(a) Disclosure Made in a Federal Proceeding or to a Federal Office or Agency; Scope of a Waiver. When the disclosure is made in a federal proceeding or to a federal office or agency and waives the attorney-client privilege or work-product protection, the waiver extends to an undisclosed communication or information in a federal or state proceeding only if:

> **(1)** the waiver is intentional;

> **(2)** the disclosed and undisclosed communications or information concern the same subject matter; and

> **(3)** they ought in fairness to be considered together.

(b) Inadvertent Disclosure. When made in a federal proceeding or to a federal office or agency, the disclosure does not operate as a waiver in a federal or state proceeding if:

> **(1)** the disclosure is inadvertent;

> **(2)** the holder of the privilege or protection took reasonable steps to prevent disclosure; and

> **(3)** the holder promptly took reasonable steps to rectify the error, including (if applicable) following Federal Rule of Civil Procedure 26(b)(5)(B).

(c) Disclosure Made in a State Proceeding. When the disclosure is made in a state proceeding and is not the subject of a state-court order concerning waiver, the disclosure does not operate as a waiver in a federal proceeding if the disclosure:

> **(1)** would not be a waiver under this rule if it had been made in a federal proceeding; or

> **(2)** is not a waiver under the law of the state where the disclosure occurred.

(d) Controlling Effect of a Court Order. A federal court may order that the privilege or protection is not waived by disclosure connected with the litigation pending before the court—in which event the disclosure is also not a waiver in any other federal or state proceeding.

(e) Controlling Effect of a Party Agreement. An agreement on the effect of disclosure in a federal proceeding is binding only on the parties to the agreement, unless it is incorporated into a court order.

(f) Controlling Effect of this Rule. Notwithstanding Rules 101 and 1101, this rule applies to state proceedings and to federal court-annexed and federal court-mandated arbitration proceedings, in the circumstances set out in the rule. And notwithstanding Rule 501, this rule applies even if state law provides the rule of decision.

(g) Definitions. In this rule:

(1) "attorney-client privilege" means the protection that applicable law provides for confidential attorney-client communications; and

(2) "work-product protection" means the protection that applicable law provides for tangible material (or its intangible equivalent) prepared in anticipation of litigation or for trial.

(Added September 19, 2008, Pub.L. 110–322, 122 Stat. 3537; as amended Apr. 26, 2011, eff. Dec. 1, 2011.)

RESTYLED RULE 502 COMMITTEE NOTE

Rule 502 has been amended by changing the initial letter of a few words from uppercase to lowercase as part of the restyling of the Evidence Rules to make style and terminology consistent throughout the rules. There is no intent to change any result in any ruling on evidence admissibility.

REPORTER'S COMMENT ON RESTYLED RULE 502

Under the basic rulemaking procedure established in the Enabling Act, when the amendment is approved by the Supreme Court it is sent to Congress and if Congress *does nothing* within 180 days, the rule becomes law. Usually Congress does exactly that with rules approved by the Supreme Court: nothing. But the process of enacting Rule 502 was more difficult, because it required Congress to directly vote on and enact the Rule. Under the Enabling Act, rules of privilege must be directly enacted by Congress. See 28 U.S.C. § 2074(b).

In the process of enactment of Rule 502, the Advisory Committee encountered not only politics and congressional gridlock, but also attempts by legislators to "restyle" the Rule as it was approved by the Advisory Committee. Congress essentially wanted the Rule to read more like a statute than a rule of procedure. If you've read a statute, you know they are not models of clear drafting. Statutes include "shalls", "heretofore" and all sorts of legalese that make them difficult to read and apply. The Advisory Committee fended off all efforts at legislative restyling by arguing that Rule 502, as drafted, comported with the style conventions used in the rulemaking process.

Rule 502 was enacted in 2008, basically in the middle of the process for restyling all the rules. Somewhat unbelievably, the restylist proposed several new style changes for the freshly-enacted Rule 502 as part of the restyling of all the Rules. Those suggestions were rejected out of hand by the Advisory Committee on the ground that Rule 502 as enacted had already been drafted in accordance with style conventions, and that stylization was retained only after extensive negotiations with Congress. Those conventions could not have changed over the course of a few months. (If style was such a moving target, it raised questions about the value of the Restyling Project itself; and it would undermine the argument made to Congress that Rule 502 was drafted in accordance with standard rulemaking style conventions.) Accordingly, the only changes in Rule 502 as restyled were in the nature of changing capitalizations that had been made by Congress.

Section references, McCormick 7th ed.

§ 93

Committee Note to Rule 502

[Editor's Note: The Enabling Act requires rules of privilege to be directly enacted by Congress. See 28 U.S.C. § 2074(b). Most rule amendments become law without any direct Congressional intervention,

and accordingly the Rules Committee Note takes the place of any legislative history. Rule 502 did not become law in the same way as other amendments to the Evidence Rules. It was directly enacted by Congress, though it was drafted by the Advisory Committee. Importantly, the Rules Committee Note to the proposed Rule was explicitly made part of the legislative history by Congress.

What follows immediately below is the introductory portion of the Rules Committee Note. The rest of the Committee Note is interspersed through the Report of the Senate Judiciary Committee, set forth after the excerpt.]

Advisory Committee Note to Rule 502

This new rule has two major purposes:

1)   It resolves some longstanding disputes in the courts about the effect of certain disclosures of communications or information protected by the attorney-client privilege or as work product—specifically those disputes involving inadvertent disclosure and subject matter waiver.

2)   It responds to the widespread complaint that litigation costs necessary to protect against waiver of attorney-client privilege or work product have become prohibitive due to the concern that any disclosure (however innocent or minimal) will operate as a subject matter waiver of all protected communications or information. This concern is especially troubling in cases involving electronic discovery. *See, e.g., Hopson v. City of Baltimore,* 232 F.R.D. 228, 244 (D.Md. 2005) (electronic discovery may encompass "millions of documents" and to insist upon "record-by-record pre-production privilege review, on pain of subject matter waiver, would impose upon parties costs of production that bear no proportionality to what is at stake in the litigation").

The rule seeks to provide a predictable, uniform set of standards under which parties can determine the consequences of a disclosure of a communication or information covered by the attorney-client privilege or work-product protection. Parties to litigation need to know, for example, that if they exchange privileged information pursuant to a confidentiality order, the court's order will be enforceable. Moreover, if a federal court's confidentiality order is not enforceable in a state court then the burdensome costs of privilege review and retention are unlikely to be reduced.

The rule makes no attempt to alter federal or state law on whether a communication or information is protected under the attorney-client privilege or work-product immunity as an initial matter. Moreover, while establishing some exceptions to waiver, the rule does not purport to supplant applicable waiver doctrine generally.

The rule governs only certain waivers by disclosure. Other common-law waiver doctrines may result in a finding of waiver even where there is no disclosure of privileged information or work product. *See, e.g., Nguyen v. Excel Corp.,* 197 F.3d 200 (5th Cir. 1999) (reliance on an advice of counsel defense waives the privilege with respect to attorney-client communications pertinent to that defense); *Ryers v. Burleson,* 100 F.R.D. 436 (D.D.C. 1983) (allegation of lawyer malpractice constituted a waiver of confidential communications under the circumstances). The rule is not intended to displace or modify federal common law concerning waiver of privilege or work product where no disclosure has been made.

House of Representatives

September 8, 2008, 154 Cong. Rec. H7817–H7819 (2008) (statement offered by Rep. Jackson-Lee)

STATEMENT OF CONGRESSIONAL INTENT REGARDING RULE 502 OF THE FEDERAL RULES OF EVIDENCE

During consideration of this rule in Congress, a number of questions were raised about the scope and contours of the effect of the proposed rule on current law regarding attorney-client privilege and work-product protection. These questions were ultimately answered satisfactorily, without need to revise the text of the rule as submitted to Congress by the Judicial Conference.

In general, these questions are answered by keeping in mind the limited though important purpose and focus of the rule. The rule addresses only the effect of disclosure, under specified circumstances, of a communication that is otherwise protected by attorney-client privilege, or of information that is protected by work-product protection, on whether the disclosure itself operates as a waiver of the privilege or protection for purposes of admissibility of evidence in a federal or state judicial or administrative proceeding.

The rule does not alter the substantive law regarding attorney-client privilege or work-product protection in any other respect, including the burden on the party invoking the privilege (or protection) to prove that the particular information (or communication) qualifies for it. And it is not intended to alter the rules and practices governing use of information outside this evidentiary context.

Some of these questions are addressed more specifically below, in order to help further avoid uncertainty in the interpretation and application of the rule.

Report of Senate Committee on the Judiciary

Senate Comm. on Judiciary, Fed. Rules of Evidence, S.Rep. No. 264, 110th Cong., 2d Sess. (2008); 2008 U.S.Code Cong. & Ad.News 1305–1307

I.   BACKGROUND AND PURPOSE OF THE BILL

A.   BACKGROUND

An efficient and cost-effective discovery process is important to preserving the integrity of our legal system. The costs of discovery have increased dramatically in recent years as the proliferation of email and other forms of electronic record-keeping have multiplied the number of documents litigants must review to protect privileged material. Outdated law affecting inadvertent disclosure coupled with the stark increase in discovery materials has led to dramatic litigation cost increases.

Currently, the inadvertent production of even a single privileged document puts the producing party at significant risk. If a privileged document is disclosed, a court may find that the waiver applies not only to that specific document and case but to all other documents and cases concerning the same subject matter. Furthermore, the privilege can be waived even if the party took reasonable steps to avoid disclosing it.

The increased use of email and other electronic media in today's business environment have exacerbated the problems with the current doctrine on waiver. Electronic information is even more voluminous and dispersed than traditional record-keeping methods, greatly increasing the time needed to review and separate privileged from non-privileged material. As the time spent reviewing documents has increased, so too has the amount of money litigants on all sides must spend to protect against the potential waiver of privilege.

In his floor statement introducing legislation to correct this problem, Senator Leahy observed:

> Billions of dollars are spent each year in litigation to protect against the inadvertent disclosure of privileged materials. With the routine use of email and other electronic media in today's business environment, discovery can encompass millions of documents in a given case, vastly expanding the risks of inadvertent disclosure. The rule proposed by the Standing Committee is aimed at adapting to the new realities that accompany today's modes of communication, and reducing the burdens associated with the conduct of diligent electronic discovery.

In his statement supporting the proposed legislation, co-sponsor Senator Specter remarked:

> Current law on attorney-client privilege and work product is responsible in large part for the rising costs of discovery—especially electronic discovery. Right now, it is far too easy to inadvertently lose—or "waive" the privilege. A single inadvertently disclosed document can result in waiving the privilege not only as to what was produced, but as to all documents on the same subject matter. In some courts, a waiver may be found even if the producing party took reasonable steps to avoid disclosure. Such waivers will not just affect the case in which the accidental disclosure is made, but will also impact other cases filed subsequently in State or Federal courts.

In sum, though most documents produced during discovery have little value, lawyers must nevertheless conduct exhaustive reviews to prevent the inadvertent disclosure of privileged material. In addition to the amount of resources litigants must dedicate to preserving privileged material, the fear of waiver also leads to extravagant claims of privilege, further undermining the purpose of the discovery process. Consequently, the costs of privilege review are often wholly disproportionate to the overall cost of the case.

B.   PURPOSE OF THE BILL

The bill addresses these problems by providing a predictable and consistent standard to govern the waiver of privileged information. It improves the efficiency of the discovery process while preserving accountability. Furthermore, it does not alter federal or state law on whether information is protected by the attorney-client privilege or work product doctrine in the first instance, but merely modifies the consequences of inadvertent disclosure once a privilege is found to exist.

The bill provides a new Federal Rule of Evidence 502 to limit the consequences of inadvertent disclosure, thereby relieving litigants of the burden that a single mistake during the discovery process can cost them the protection of a privilege. It provides that if there is a waiver of privilege, it applies only to the specific information disclosed and not the broader subject matter unless the holder has intentionally used the privileged information in a misleading fashion. An inadvertent disclosure of privileged information does not constitute a waiver as long as the holder took reasonable steps to prevent disclosure and acted promptly to retrieve the mistakenly disclosed information.

The bill provides a new rule to ensure that parties will take advantage of its protections by remaining enforceable in subsequent proceedings. If a federal court enters an order finding that an inadvertent disclosure of privileged information does not constitute a waiver, that order will be enforceable against persons in federal or state proceedings. This protects the rule's ability to limit discovery costs by ensuring that parties in any given case will know they can rely on the new waiver rules in subsequent proceedings.

Importantly, the bill respects federal-state comity. The bill will ensure that if there is a disclosure of privileged information at the federal level then courts must honor Rule 502 in any subsequent state proceedings. If there is a disclosure in a state proceeding, then admissibility in any subsequent federal proceeding will be determined by the law that is most protective against waiver. However, it does not apply to any disclosure made in a state proceeding that is later introduced in a subsequent state proceeding.

Litigants recognize the need to adopt a new waiver doctrine to adapt to the effects of changing technology in the business environment. The bill has attracted widespread support from major legal organizations representing stakeholders on all sides of modern litigation. Among those groups voicing support for the measure are the American Bar Association, American College of Trial Lawyers, U.S. Chamber of Commerce, former Chairs of the Section of Litigation of the American Bar Association, Lawyers for Civil Justice, and several private law firms.

Advisory Committee's Note to Subdivision (a)

Subdivision (a). The rule provides that a voluntary disclosure in a federal proceeding or to a federal office or agency, if a waiver, generally results in a waiver only of the communication or information disclosed; a subject matter waiver (of either privilege or work product) is reserved for those unusual situations in which fairness requires a further disclosure of related, protected information, in order to prevent a selective and misleading presentation of evidence to the disadvantage of the adversary. *See, e.g., In re United Mine Workers of America Employee Benefit Plans Litig.*, 159 F.R.D. 307, 312 (D.D.C. 1994) (waiver of work product limited to materials actually disclosed, because the party did not deliberately disclose documents in an attempt to gain a tactical advantage). Thus, subject matter waiver is limited to situations in which a party intentionally puts protected information into the litigation in a selective, misleading and unfair manner. It follows that an inadvertent disclosure of protected information can never result in a subject matter waiver. *See* Rule 502(b). The rule rejects the result in *In re Sealed Case,* 877 F.2d 976 (D.C.Cir. 1989), which held that inadvertent disclosure of documents during discovery automatically constituted a subject matter waiver.

The language concerning subject matter waiver—"ought in fairness"—is taken from Rule 106, because the animating principle is the same. Under both Rules, a party that makes a selective, misleading presentation that is unfair to the adversary opens itself to a more complete and accurate presentation.

To assure protection and predictability, the rule provides that if a disclosure is made at the federal level, the federal rule on subject matter waiver governs subsequent state court determinations on the scope of the waiver by that disclosure.

House of Representatives

September 8, 2008, 154 Cong. Rec. H7817–H7819 (2008) (statement offered by Rep. Jackson-Lee)

Subdivision (a)—Disclosure vs. Use

This subdivision does not alter the substantive law regarding when a party's strategic use in litigation of otherwise privileged information obliges that party to waive the privilege regarding other information concerning the same subject matter, so that the information being used can be fairly considered in context. One situation in which this issue arises, the assertion as a defense in patent-infringement litigation that a party was relying on advice of counsel, is discussed elsewhere in this Note. In this and similar situations, under subdivision (a)(1) the party using an attorney-client communication to its advantage in the litigation has, in so doing, intentionally waived the privilege as to other communications concerning the same subject matter, regardless of the circumstances in which the communication being so used was initially disclosed.

Subdivisions (a) and (b)—Disclosures to Federal Office or Agency

This rule, as a Federal Rule of Evidence, applies to admissibility of evidence. While subdivisions (a) and (b) are written broadly to apply as appropriate to disclosures of information to a federal office or agency, they do not apply to uses of information—such as routine use in government publications—that fall outside the evidentiary context. Nor do these subdivisions relieve the party seeking to protect the information as privileged from the burden of proving that the privilege applies in the first place.

Report of Senate Committee on the Judiciary

Senate Comm. on Judiciary, Fed. Rules of Evidence, S.Rep. No. 264, 110th Cong., 2d Sess. (2008); 2008 U.S.Code Cong. & Ad.News 1305, 1308

(a)   This section limits the effect of disclosures made in a Federal proceeding or to a Federal officer or agency that waive the attorney-client privilege or the work-product doctrine. The section prevents such a waiver from extending to undisclosed information or information in a State or Federal proceeding unless: the waiver was intentional, the disclosed and undisclosed information concern the same subject matter, and in fairness, the undisclosed and disclosed information should be considered together.

Advisory Committee's Note to Subdivision (b)

Subdivision (b). Courts are in conflict over whether an inadvertent disclosure of a communication or information protected as privileged or work product constitutes a waiver. A few courts find that a disclosure must be intentional to be a waiver. Most courts find a waiver only if the disclosing party acted carelessly in disclosing the communication or information and failed to request its return in a timely manner. And a few courts hold that any inadvertent disclosure of a communication or information protected under the attorney-client privilege or as work product constitutes a waiver without regard to the protections taken to avoid such a disclosure. *See generally, Hopson v. City of Baltimore,* 232 F.R.D. 228 (D.Md. 2005), for a discussion of this case law.

The rule opts for the middle ground: inadvertent disclosure of protected communications or information in connection with a federal proceeding or to a federal office or agency does not constitute a waiver if the holder took reasonable steps to prevent disclosure and also promptly took reasonable steps to rectify the error. This position is in accord with the majority view on whether inadvertent disclosure is a waiver.

Cases such as *Lois Sportswear, U.S.A., Inc. v. Levi Strauss & Co.,* 104 F.R.D. 103, 105 (S.D.N.Y. 1985) and *Hartford Fire Ins. Co. v. Garvey,* 109 F.R.D. 323, 332 (N.D.Cal. 1985), set out a multifactor test for determining whether inadvertent disclosure is a waiver. The stated factors (none of which is dispositive) are the reasonableness of precautions taken, the time taken to rectify the error, the scope of discovery, the extent of disclosure and the overriding issue of fairness. The rule does not explicitly codify that test, because it is really a set of non-determinative guidelines that vary from case to case. The rule is flexible enough to accommodate any of those listed factors. Other considerations bearing on the reasonableness of a producing party's efforts include the number of documents to be reviewed and the time constraints for production. Depending on the circumstances, a party that uses advanced analytical software applications and linguistic tools in screening for privilege and work product may be found to have taken "reasonable steps" to prevent inadvertent disclosure. The implementation of an efficient system of records management before litigation may also be relevant.

The rule does not require the producing party to engage in a post-production review to determine whether any protected communication or information has been produced by mistake. But the rule does require the producing party to follow up on any obvious indications that a protected communication or information has been produced inadvertently.

The rule applies to inadvertent disclosures made to a federal office or agency, including but not limited to an office or agency that is acting in the course of its regulatory, investigative or enforcement authority. The consequences of waiver, and the concomitant costs of pre-production privilege review, can be as great with respect to disclosures to offices and agencies as they are in litigation.

House of Representatives

September 8, 2008, 154 Cong. Rec. H7817–H7819 (2008) (statement offered by Rep. Jackson-Lee)

Subdivision (b)—Fairness Considerations

The standard set forth in this subdivision for determining whether a disclosure operates as a waiver of the privilege or protection is, as explained elsewhere in this Note, the majority rule in the federal courts. The majority rule has simply been distilled here into a standard designed to be predictable in its application. This distillation is not intended to foreclose notions of fairness from continuing to inform application of the standard in all aspects as appropriate in particular cases—for example, as to whether steps taken to rectify an erroneous inadvertent disclosure were sufficiently prompt under subdivision (b)(3) where the receiving party has relied on the information disclosed.

Report of Senate Committee on the Judiciary

Senate Comm. on Judiciary, Fed. Rules of Evidence, S.Rep. No. 264, 110th Cong., 2d Sess. (2008); 2008 U.S.Code Cong. & Ad.News 1305, 1308

(b) This section prevents inadvertent disclosures made in Federal proceedings or to a Federal Officer or agency from operating as a waiver if: the disclosure was inadvertent, the holder of the privilege or protection took reasonable steps to prevent disclosure, and the holder took steps to quickly rectify the disclosure under Federal Rule of Civil Procedure 26(b)(5)(B).

Advisory Committee's Note to Subdivision (c)

Subdivision (c). Difficult questions can arise when 1) a disclosure of a communication or information protected by the attorney-client privilege or as work product is made in a state proceeding, 2) the communication or information is offered in a subsequent federal proceeding on the ground that the disclosure waived the privilege or protection, and 3) the state and federal laws are in conflict on the question of waiver. The Committee determined that the proper solution for the federal court is to apply the law that is most protective of privilege and work product. If the state law is more protective (such as where the state law is that an inadvertent disclosure can never be a waiver), the holder of the privilege or protection may well have relied on that law when making the disclosure in the state proceeding. Moreover, applying a more restrictive federal law of waiver could impair the state objective of preserving the privilege or work-product protection for disclosures made in state proceedings. On the other hand, if the federal law is more protective, applying the state law of waiver to determine admissibility in federal court is likely to undermine the federal objective of limiting the costs of production.

The rule does not address the enforceability of a state court confidentiality order in a federal proceeding, as that question is covered both by statutory law and principles of federalism and comity. See 28 U.S.C. § 1738 (providing that state judicial proceedings "shall have the same full faith and credit in every court within the United States . . . as they have by law or usage in the courts of such State . . . from which they are taken"). See also Tucker v. Ohtsu Tire & Rubber

Co., 191 F.R.D. 495, 499 (D.Md. 2000) (noting that a federal court considering the enforceability of a state confidentiality order is "constrained by principles of comity, courtesy, and ... federalism"). Thus, a state court order finding no waiver in connection with a disclosure made in a state court proceeding is enforceable under existing law in subsequent federal proceedings.

Report of Senate Committee on the Judiciary

Senate Comm. on Judiciary, Fed. Rules of Evidence, S.Rep. No. 264, 110th Cong., 2d Sess. (2008); 2008 U.S.Code Cong. & Ad.News 1305, 1308–09

(c)   This section prevents disclosures made in a State proceeding, which are not the subject of a State-court order concerning waiver, from constituting a waiver in Federal court if: the disclosure would not have been a waiver under this rule if made in Federal court or the disclosure would not be a waiver under the law of the State where the disclosure occurred.

Advisory Committee's Note to Subdivision (d)

Subdivision (d). Confidentiality orders are becoming increasingly important in limiting the costs of privilege review and retention, especially in cases involving electronic discovery. But the utility of a confidentiality order in reducing discovery costs is substantially diminished if it provides no protection outside the particular litigation in which the order is entered. Parties are unlikely to be able to reduce the costs of pre-production review for privilege and work product if the consequence of disclosure is that the communications or information could be used by non-parties to the litigation.

There is some dispute on whether a confidentiality order entered in one case is enforceable in other proceedings. *See generally, Hopson v. City of Baltimore,* 232 F.R.D. 228 (D.Md. 2005), for a discussion of this case law. The rule provides that when a confidentiality order governing the consequences of disclosure in that case is entered in a federal proceeding, its terms are enforceable against non-parties in any federal or state proceeding. For example, the court order may provide for return of documents without waiver irrespective of the care taken by the disclosing party; the rule contemplates enforcement of "claw-back" and "quick peek" arrangements as a way to avoid the excessive costs of pre-production review for privilege and work product. *See Zubulake v. UBS Warburg LLC,* 216 F.R.D. 280, 290 (S.D.N.Y. 2003) (noting that parties may enter into "so-called 'claw-back' agreements that allow the parties to forego privilege review altogether in favor of an agreement to return inadvertently produced privilege documents"). The rule provides a party with a predictable protection from a court order—predictability that is needed to allow the party to plan in advance to limit the prohibitive costs of privilege and work product review and retention.

Under the rule, a confidentiality order is enforceable whether or not it memorializes an agreement among the parties to the litigation. Party agreement should not be a condition of enforceability of a federal court's order.

Under subdivision (d), a federal court may order that disclosure of privileged or protected information "in connection with" a federal proceeding does not result in waiver. But subdivision (d) does not allow the federal court to enter an order determining the waiver effects of a separate disclosure of the same information in other proceedings, state or federal. If a disclosure has been made in a state proceeding (and is not the subject of a state-court order on waiver), then subdivision (d) is inapplicable. Subdivision (c) would govern the federal court's determination whether the state-court disclosure waived the privilege or protection in the federal proceeding.

House of Representatives

September 8, 2008, 154 Cong. Rec. H7817–H7819 (2008) (statement offered by Rep. Jackson-Lee)

Subdivision (d)—Court Orders

This subdivision authorizes a court to enter orders only in the context of litigation pending before the court. And it does not alter the law regarding waiver of privilege resulting from having acquiesced in the use of otherwise privileged information. Therefore, this subdivision does not provide a basis for a court to enable parties to agree to a selective waiver of the privilege, such as to a federal agency conducting an investigation, while preserving the privilege as against other parties seeking the information. This subdivision is designed to enable a court to enter an order, whether on motion of one or more parties or on its own motion, that will allow the parties to conduct and respond to discovery expeditiously, without the need for exhaustive pre-production privilege reviews, while still preserving each party's right to assert the privilege to preclude use in litigation of information disclosed in such discovery.

While the benefits of a court order under this subdivision would be equally available in government enforcement actions as in private actions, acquiescence by the disclosing party in use by the federal agency of information disclosed pursuant to such an order would still be treated as under current law for purposes of determining whether the acquiescence in use of the information, as opposed to its mere disclosure, effects a waiver of the privilege. The same applies to acquiescence in use by another private party.

Moreover, whether the order is entered on motion of one or more parties, or on the court's own motion, the court retains its authority to include the conditions it deems appropriate in the circumstances.

Report of Senate Committee on the Judiciary

Senate Comm. on Judiciary, Fed. Rules of Evidence, S.Rep. No. 264, 110th Cong., 2d Sess. (2008); 2008 U.S.Code Cong. & Ad.News 1305, 1309

(d)   This section allows Federal courts to order that privileged or otherwise protected information is not waived by disclosure connected with the present litigation, and provides that such disclosure is not a waiver in any other Federal or State proceeding.

Advisory Committee's Note to Subdivision (e)

Subdivision (e). Subdivision (e) codifies the well-established proposition that parties can enter an agreement to limit the effect of waiver by disclosure between or among them. Of course such an agreement can bind only the parties to the agreement. The rule makes clear that if parties want protection against non-parties from a finding of waiver by disclosure, the agreement must be made part of a court order.

House of Representatives

September 8, 2008, 154 Cong. Rec. H7817–H7819 (2008) (statement offered by Rep. Jackson-Lee)

Subdivision (e)—Party Agreements

This subdivision simply makes clear that while parties to a case may agree among themselves regarding the effect of disclosures between each other in a federal proceeding, it is not binding on others unless it is incorporated into a court order. This subdivision does not confer any authority on a court to enter any order regarding the effect of disclosures. That authority must be found in subdivision (d), or elsewhere.

Report of Senate Committee on the Judiciary

Senate Comm. on Judiciary, Fed. Rules of Evidence, S.Rep. No. 264, 110th Cong., 2d Sess. (2008); 2008 U.S.Code Cong. & Ad.News 1305, 1309

(e) This section limits agreements made between parties on the effects of disclosure in a Federal proceeding to be binding only on the parties to the agreement unless the agreement is incorporated into a court order.

Advisory Committee's Note to Subdivision (f)

Subdivision (f). The protections against waiver provided by Rule 502 must be applicable when protected communications or information disclosed in federal proceedings are subsequently offered in state proceedings. Otherwise the holders of protected communications and information, and their lawyers, could not rely on the protections provided by the Rule, and the goal of limiting costs in discovery would be substantially undermined. Rule 502(f) is intended to resolve any potential tension between the provisions of Rule 502 that apply to state proceedings and the possible limitations on the applicability of the Federal Rules of Evidence otherwise provided by Rules 101 and 1101.

The rule is intended to apply in all federal court proceedings, including court-annexed and court-ordered arbitrations, without regard to any possible limitations of Rules 101 and 1101. This provision is not intended to raise an inference about the applicability of any other rule of evidence in arbitration proceedings more generally.

The costs of discovery can be equally high for state and federal causes of action, and the rule seeks to limit those costs in all federal proceedings, regardless of whether the claim arises under state or federal law. Accordingly, the rule applies to state law causes of action brought in federal court.

Report of Senate Committee on the Judiciary

Senate Comm. on Judiciary, Fed. Rules of Evidence, S.Rep. No. 264, 110th Cong., 2d Sess. (2008); 2008 U.S.Code Cong. & Ad.News 1305, 1309

(f) This section defines the applicability of this rule, notwithstanding Rules 101 and 1101, to State proceedings and to Federal-court annexed and Federal-court mandated arbitration proceedings, in the circumstances set out in this rule. Notwithstanding Rule 501, this rule applies even if State law provides the rules of decision.

Advisory Committee's Note to Subdivision (g)

Subdivision (g). The rule's coverage is limited to attorney-client privilege and work product. The operation of waiver by disclosure, as applied to other evidentiary privileges, remains a question of federal common law. Nor does the rule purport to apply to the Fifth Amendment privilege against compelled self-incrimination.

The definition of work product "materials" is intended to include both tangible and intangible information. *See In re Cendant Corp. Sec. Litig.*, 343 F.3d 658, 662 (3d Cir. 2003) ("work product protection extends to both tangible and intangible work product").

Report of Senate Committee on the Judiciary

Senate Comm. on Judiciary, Fed. Rules of Evidence, S.Rep. No. 264, 110th Cong., 2d Sess. (2008); 2008 U.S.Code Cong. & Ad.News 1305, 1309

(g) This section defines "attorney-client privilege" as "the protection that applicable law provides for confidential attorney-client communications"; and defines "work-product protection" as "the protection that applicable law provides for tangible material (or its intangible equivalent) prepared in anticipation of litigation or for trial."

ARTICLE VI. WITNESSES

Rule 601. Competency to Testify in General

Every person is competent to be a witness unless these rules provide otherwise. But in a civil case, state law governs the witness's competency regarding a claim or defense for which state law supplies the rule of decision.

(As amended, Apr. 26, 2011, eff. Dec. 1, 2011.)

COMMITTEE NOTE TO RESTYLED RULE 601

The language of Rule 601 has been amended as part of the restyling of the Evidence Rules to make them more easily understood and to make style and terminology consistent throughout the rules. These changes are intended to be stylistic only. There is no intent to change any result in any ruling on evidence admissibility.

Section references, McCormick 7th ed.

§§ 61–71

Note by Federal Judicial Center

The first sentence of the rule enacted by the Congress is the entire rule prescribed by the Supreme Court, without change. The second sentence was added by congressional action.

Advisory Committee's Note

56 F.R.D. 183, 262

This general ground-clearing eliminates all grounds of incompetency not specifically recognized in the succeeding rules of this Article. Included among the grounds thus abolished are religious belief, conviction of crime, and connection with the litigation as a party or interested person or spouse of a party or interested person. With the exception of the so-called Dead Man's Acts, American jurisdictions generally have ceased to recognize these grounds.

The Dead Man's Acts are surviving traces of the common law disqualification of parties and interested persons. They exist in variety too great to convey conviction of their wisdom and effectiveness. These rules contain no provision of this kind. For the reason underlying the decision not to give effect to state statutes in diversity cases, see the Advisory Committee's Note to Rule 501. **[Editor's Note: This proposal by the Advisory Committee, providing that federal rules of competency applied even where state law provided the rule of decision, was subsequently rejected by Congress; and the Committee Note to Rule 501, referred to by the Advisory Committee, was rejected as well. See Deleted and Superseded Materials, *infra*.]**

No mental or moral qualifications for testifying as a witness are specified. Standards of mental capacity have proved elusive in actual application. A leading commentator observes that few witnesses are disqualified on that ground. Weihofen, Testimonial Competence and Credibility, 34 Geo.Wash.L.Rev. 53 (1965). Discretion is regularly exercised in favor of allowing the testimony. A witness wholly without capacity is difficult to imagine. The question is one particularly suited to the jury as one of weight and credibility, subject to judicial authority to review the sufficiency of the evidence. 2 Wigmore §§ 501, 509. Standards of moral qualification in practice consist essentially of evaluating a person's truthfulness in terms of his own answers about it. Their principal utility is in affording an opportunity on voir dire examination to impress upon the witness his moral duty. This result may, however, be accomplished more directly, and without haggling in terms of legal standards, by the manner of administering the oath or affirmation under Rule 603.

Admissibility of religious belief as a ground of impeachment is treated in Rule 610. Conviction of crime as a ground of impeachment is the subject of Rule 609. Marital relationship is the basis for privilege under Rule 505. **[Editor's Note: Proposed Rule 505 was rejected by Congress.]** Interest in the outcome of litigation and mental capacity are, of course, highly relevant to credibility and require no special treatment to render them admissible along with other matters bearing upon the perception, memory, and narration of witnesses.

Report of House Committee on the Judiciary

House Comm. on Judiciary, Fed. Rules of Evidence, H.R.Rep. No. 650, 93d Cong., 1st Sess., p. 9 (1973); 1974 U.S.Code Cong. & Ad.News 7075, 7083

Rule 601 as submitted to the Congress provided that "Every person is competent to be a witness except as otherwise provided in these rules." One effect of the Rule as proposed would have been to abolish age, mental capacity, and other grounds recognized in some State jurisdictions as making a person incompetent as a witness. The greatest controversy centered around the Rule's rendering inapplicable in the federal courts the so-called Dead Man's Statutes which exist in some States. Acknowledging that there is substantial disagreement as to the merit of Dead Man's Statutes, the Committee nevertheless believed that where such statutes have been enacted they represent State policy which should not be overturned in the absence of a compelling federal interest. The Committee therefore amended the Rule to make competency in civil actions determinable in accordance with State law with respect to elements of claims or defenses as to which State law supplies the rule of decision. Cf. Courtland v. Walston & Co., Inc., 340 F.Supp. 1076, 1087–1092 (S.D.N.Y. 1972).

Report of Senate Committee on the Judiciary

Senate Comm. on Judiciary, Fed. Rules of Evidence, S.Rep. No. 1277, 2d Sess., p. 13 (1974); 1974 U.S.Code Cong. & Ad.News 7051, 7059

The amendment to rule 601 parallels the treatment accorded rule 501 discussed immediately above.

Conference Report

H.R., Fed. Rules of Evidence, Conf.Rep. No. 1597, 93d Cong., 2d Sess., p. 8 (1974); 1975 U.S.Code Cong. & Ad.News 7098, 7101

Rule 601 deals with competency of witnesses. Both the House and Senate bills provide that federal competency law applies in criminal cases. In civil actions and proceedings, the House bill provides that state competency law applies "to an element of a claim or defense as to which State law supplies the rule of decision." The Senate bill provides that "in civil actions and proceedings arising under 28 U.S.C. § 1332 or 28 U.S.C. § 1335, or between citizens of different States and removed under 28 U.S.C. § 1441(b) the competency of a witness, person, government, State or political subdivision thereof is determined in accordance with State law, unless with respect to the particular claim or defense, Federal law supplies the rule of decision."

The wording of the House and Senate bills differs in the treatment of civil actions and proceedings. The rule in the House bill applies to evidence that relates to "an element of a claim or defense." If an item of proof tends to support or defeat a claim or defense, or an element of a claim or defense, and if state law supplies the rule of decision for that claim or defense, then state competency law applies to that item of proof.

For reasons similar to those underlying its action on Rule 501, the Conference adopts the House provision.

Rule 602. Need for Personal Knowledge

A witness may testify to a matter only if evidence is introduced sufficient to support a finding that the witness has personal knowledge of the matter. Evidence to prove personal knowledge may consist of the witness's own testimony. This rule does not apply to a witness's expert testimony under Rule 703.

(As amended Mar. 2, 1987, eff. Oct. 1, 1987; Apr. 25, 1988, eff. Nov. 1, 1988; Apr. 26, 2011, eff. Dec. 1, 2011.)

RESTYLED RULE 602 COMMITTEE NOTE

The language of Rule 602 has been amended as part of the restyling of the Evidence Rules to make them more easily understood and to make style and terminology consistent throughout the rules. These changes are intended to be stylistic only. There is no intent to change any result in any ruling on evidence admissibility.

Section references, McCormick 7th ed.

§ 69

Note by Federal Judicial Center

The rule enacted by the Congress is the rule prescribed by the Supreme Court without change.

Advisory Committee's Note

56 F.R.D. 183, 263

"[T]he rule requiring that a witness who testifies to a fact which can be perceived by the senses must have had an opportunity to observe, and must have actually observed the fact" is a "most pervasive manifestation" of the common law insistence upon "the most reliable sources of information." McCormick § 10, p. 19. These foundation requirements may, of course, be furnished by the testimony of the witness himself; hence personal knowledge is not an absolute but may consist of what the witness thinks he knows from personal perception. 2 Wigmore § 650. It will be observed that the rule is in fact a specialized application of the provisions of Rule 104(b) on conditional relevancy.

This rule does not govern the situation of a witness who testifies to a hearsay statement as such, if he has personal knowledge of the making of the statement. Rules 801 and 805 would be applicable. This rule would, however, prevent him from testifying to the subject matter of the hearsay statement, as he has no personal knowledge of it.

The reference to Rule 703 is designed to avoid any question of conflict between the present rule and the provisions of that rule allowing an expert to express opinions based on facts of which he does not have personal knowledge.

1987 Amendment Committee Note

The amendments are technical. No substantive change is intended.

1988 Amendment Committee Note

The amendment is technical. No substantive change is intended.

Rule 603. Oath or Affirmation to Testify Truthfully

Before testifying, a witness must give an oath or affirmation to testify truthfully. It must be in a form designed to impress that duty on the witness's conscience.

(As amended Mar. 2, 1987, eff. Oct. 1, 1987; Apr. 26, 2011, eff. Dec. 1, 2011.)

RESTYLED RULE 603 COMMITTEE NOTE

The language of Rule 603 has been amended as part of the restyling of the Evidence Rules to make them more easily understood and to make style and terminology consistent throughout the rules. These changes are intended to be stylistic only. There is no intent to change any result in any ruling on evidence admissibility.

Section references, McCormick 7th ed.

§ 62

Note by Federal Judicial Center

The rule enacted by the Congress is the rule prescribed by the Supreme Court without change.

Advisory Committee's Note

56 F.R.D. 183, 263

The rule is designed to afford the flexibility required in dealing with religious adults, atheists, conscientious objectors, mental defectives, and children. Affirmation is simply a solemn undertaking to tell the truth; no special verbal formula is required. As is true generally, affirmation is recognized by federal law. "Oath" includes affirmation, 1 U.S.C. § 1; judges and clerks may administer oaths and affirmations, 28 U.S.C. §§ 459, 953; and affirmations are acceptable in lieu of oaths under Rule 43(d) of the Federal Rules of Civil Procedure. Perjury by a witness is a crime, 18 U.S.C. § 1621.

1987 Amendment Committee Note

The amendments are technical. No substantive change is intended.

Rule 604. Interpreter

An interpreter must be qualified and must give an oath or affirmation to make a true translation.

(As amended Apr. 26, 2011; eff. Dec. 1, 2011.)

RESTYLED RULE 604 COMMITTEE NOTE

The language of Rule 604 has been amended as part of the restyling of the Evidence Rules to make them more easily understood and to make style and terminology consistent throughout the rules. These changes are intended to be stylistic only. There is no intent to change any result in any ruling on evidence admissibility.

Section references, McCormick 7th ed.

None

Note by Federal Judicial Center

The rule enacted by the Congress is the rule prescribed by the Supreme Court without change.

Advisory Committee's Note

56 F.R.D. 183, 264

The rule implements Rule 43(f) of the Federal Rules of Civil Procedure and Rule 28(b) of the Federal Rules of Criminal Procedure, both of which contain provisions for the appointment and compensation of interpreters.

1987 Amendment Committee Note

The amendment is technical. No substantive change is intended.

_____

Rule 605. Judge's Competency as a Witness

The presiding judge may not testify as a witness at the trial. A party need not object to preserve the issue.

(As amended Apr. 26, 2011; eff. Dec. 1, 2011.)

RESTYLED RULE 605 COMMITTEE NOTE

The language of Rule 605 has been amended as part of the restyling of the Evidence Rules to make them more easily understood and to make style and terminology consistent throughout the rules. These changes are intended to be stylistic only. There is no intent to change any result in any ruling on evidence admissibility.

REPORTER'S COMMENT ON RESTYLED RULE 605

One of the goals of restyling is to delete excess verbiage. But care must be taken lest the words deleted have a possible substantive importance. In Rule 605, the restylist thought that the phrase "may not testify in that trial as a witness" could be shortened to "may not testify." In other words, the word "witness" was thought duplicative of the word "testify." How else can you testify other than as a witness?

But the Reporter opposed deleting "witness" on the ground that there is a large body of case law concerning the permissibility of judges commenting on the evidence—not as "witnesses" but in their role instructing the jury. It could be argued that a judge in such a situation is "testifying" but not as a witness—and Rule 605 was never intended to apply to judges commenting on the evidence. Thus, cutting out the term "witness" could be argued to expand the scope of Rule 605 to cover judges commenting on the evidence, and this would be a substantive change. The Advisory Committee agreed with the Reporter and disapproved the proposal to delete the phrase "as a witness" from Restyled Rule 605.

Section references, McCormick 7th ed.

§ 68, § 70

Note by Federal Judicial Center

The rule enacted by the Congress is the rule prescribed by the Supreme Court without change.

Advisory Committee's Note

56 F.R.D. 183, 264

In view of the mandate of 28 U.S.C. § 455 that a judge disqualify himself in "any case in which he . . . is or has been a material witness," the likelihood that the presiding judge in a federal court might be called to testify in the trial over which he is presiding is slight. Nevertheless the possibility is not totally eliminated.

The solution here presented is a broad rule of incompetency, rather than such alternatives as incompetency only as to material matters, leaving the matter to the discretion of the judge, or recognizing no incompetency. The choice is the result of inability to evolve satisfactory answers to questions which arise when the judge abandons the bench for the witness stand. Who rules on objections? Who compels him to answer? Can he rule impartially on the weight and admissibility of his own testimony? Can he be impeached or cross-examined effectively? Can he, in a jury trial, avoid conferring his seal of approval on one side in the eyes of the jury? Can he, in a bench trial, avoid an involvement destructive of impartiality? The rule of general incompetency has substantial support. See Report of the Special Committee on the Propriety of Judges Appearing as

Witnesses, 36 A.B.A.J. 630 (1950); cases collected in Annot. 157 A.L.R. 311; McCormick § 68, p. 147; Uniform Rule 42; California Evidence Code § 703; Kansas Code of Civil Procedure § 60–442; New Jersey Evidence Rule 42. Cf. 6 Wigmore § 1909, which advocates leaving the matter to the discretion of the judge, and statutes to that effect collected in Annot., 157 A.L.R. 311.

The rule provides an "automatic" objection. To require an actual objection would confront the opponent with a choice between not objecting, with the result of allowing the testimony, and objecting, with the probable result of excluding the testimony but at the price of continuing the trial before a judge likely to feel that his integrity had been attacked by the objector.

Rule 606. Juror's Competency as a Witness

(a) At the Trial. A juror may not testify as a witness before the other jurors at the trial. If a juror is called to testify, the court must give a party an opportunity to object outside the jury's presence.

(b) During an Inquiry into the Validity of a Verdict or Indictment.

(1) *Prohibited Testimony or Other Evidence.* During an inquiry into the validity of a verdict or indictment, a juror may not testify about any statement made or incident that occurred during the jury's deliberations; the effect of anything on that juror's or another juror's vote; or any juror's mental processes concerning the verdict or indictment. The court may not receive a juror's affidavit or evidence of a juror's statement on these matters.

(2) *Exceptions.* A juror may testify about whether:

(A) extraneous prejudicial information was improperly brought to the jury's attention;

(B) an outside influence was improperly brought to bear on any juror; or

(C) a mistake was made in entering the verdict on the verdict form.

(As amended P.L. 94–149, § 1(10), Dec. 12, 1975, 89 Stat. 805; Mar. 2, 1987, eff. Oct. 1, 1987; Apr. 12, 2006, eff. Dec. 1, 2006; Apr. 26, 2011, eff. Dec. 1, 2011.)

RESTYLED RULE 606 COMMITTEE NOTE

The language of Rule 606 has been amended as part of the restyling of the Evidence Rules to make them more easily understood and to make style and terminology consistent throughout the rules. These changes are intended to be stylistic only. There is no intent to change any result in any ruling on evidence admissibility.

REPORTER'S COMMENT ON RESTYLED RULE 606

Restyled Rule 606(b) is a good example of "unpacking" a rule. The original rule was jammed together with many different concepts, in no particular conceptual order. The Restyled Rule separates the basic rule from the exceptions in two separate subdivisions, and sets forth the exceptions in a way that is easier to read and apply. Because of the use of subdivisions, the Restyled Rule required new numbering, but the Advisory Committee thought that the cost of the possible disruption to electronic searches was outweighed by the benefits in making the rule easier to read and apply.

Section references, McCormick 7th ed.

§ 68

Note by Federal Judicial Center

The rule enacted by the Congress is the rule prescribed by the Supreme Court, amended only by the addition of the concluding phrase "for these purposes." The bill originally passed by the House did not contain in the first sentence the prohibition as to matters or statements during the deliberations or the clause beginning "except."

Advisory Committee's Note

56 F.R.D. 183, 265

Subdivision (a). The considerations which bear upon the permissibility of testimony by a juror in the trial in which he is sitting as juror bear an obvious similarity to those evoked when the judge is called as a witness. See Advisory Committee's Note to Rule 605. The judge is not, however, in this instance so involved as to call for departure from usual principles requiring objection to be made; hence the only provision on objection is that opportunity be afforded for its making out of the presence of the jury. Compare Rule 605.

Subdivision (b). Whether testimony, affidavits, or statements of jurors should be received for the purpose of invalidating or supporting a verdict or indictment, and if so, under what circumstances, has given rise to substantial differences of opinion. The familiar rubric that a juror may not impeach his own verdict, dating from Lord Mansfield's time, is a gross oversimplification. The values sought to be promoted by excluding the evidence include freedom of deliberation, stability and finality of verdicts, and protection of jurors against annoyance and embarrassment. McDonald v. Pless, 238 U.S. 264, 35 S.Ct. 785, 59 L.Ed. 1300 (1915). On the other hand, simply putting verdicts beyond effective reach can only promote irregularity and injustice. The rule offers an accommodation between these competing considerations.

The mental operations and emotional reactions of jurors in arriving at a given result would, if allowed as a subject of inquiry, place every verdict at the mercy of jurors and invite tampering and harassment. See Grenz v. Werre, 129 N.W.2d 681 (N.D. 1964). The authorities are in virtually complete accord in excluding the evidence. Fryer, Note on Disqualification of Witnesses, Selected Writings on Evidence and Trial 345, 347 (Fryer ed. 1957); Maguire, Weinstein, et al., Cases on Evidence 887 (5th ed. 1965); 8 Wigmore § 2349 (McNaughton Rev. 1961). As to matters other than mental operations and emotional reactions of jurors, substantial authority refuses to allow a juror to disclose irregularities which occur in the jury room, but allows his testimony as to irregularities occurring outside and allows outsiders to testify as to occurrences both inside and out. 8 Wigmore § 2354 (McNaughton Rev. 1961). However, the door of the jury room is not necessarily a satisfactory dividing point, and the Supreme Court has refused to accept it for every situation. Mattox v. United States, 146 U.S. 140, 13 S.Ct. 50, 36 L.Ed. 917 (1892).

Under the federal decisions the central focus has been upon insulation of the manner in which the jury reached its verdict, and this protection extends to each of the components of deliberation, including arguments, statements, discussions, mental and emotional reactions, votes, and any other feature of the process. Thus testimony or affidavits of jurors have been held incompetent to show a compromise verdict, Hyde v. United States, 225 U.S. 347, 382 (1912); a quotient verdict, McDonald v. Pless, 238 U.S. 264 (1915); speculation as to insurance coverage, Holden v. Porter, 405 F.2d 878 (10th Cir. 1969), Farmers Coop. Elev. Ass'n v. Strand, 382 F.2d 224, 230 (8th Cir. 1967), cert. denied 389 U.S. 1014; misinterpretation of instructions, Farmers Coop. Elev. Ass'n v. Strand, *supra*; mistake in returning verdict, United States v. Chereton, 309 F.2d 197 (6th Cir. 1962); interpretation of guilty plea by one defendant as implicating others, United States v. Crosby, 294 F.2d 928, 949 (2d Cir. 1961). The policy does not, however, foreclose testimony by jurors as to prejudicial extraneous information or influences injected into or brought to bear upon the deliberative process. Thus a juror is recognized as competent to testify to statements by the bailiff or the introduction of a prejudicial newspaper account into the jury room, Mattox v. United States, 146 U.S. 140 (1892). *See also* Parker v. Gladden, 385 U.S. 363 (1966).

This rule does not purport to specify the substantive grounds for setting aside verdicts for irregularity; it deals only with the competency of jurors to testify concerning those grounds. Allowing them to testify as to matters other than their own inner reactions involves no particular hazard to the values sought to be protected. The rule is based upon this conclusion. It makes no attempt to specify the substantive grounds for setting aside verdicts for irregularity. *See also* Rule 6(e) of the Federal Rules of Criminal Procedure and 18 U.S.C. § 3500, governing the secrecy of grand jury proceedings. The present rule does not relate to secrecy and disclosure but to the competency of certain witnesses and evidence.

Report of House Judiciary Committee

House Comm. on Judiciary, Fed. Rules of Evidence, H.R.Rep. No. 650, 93d Cong., 1st Sess., p. 9 (1973); 1974 U.S.Code Cong. & Ad.News 7075, 7083

As proposed by the Court, Rule 606(b) limited testimony by a juror in the course of an inquiry into the validity of a verdict or indictment. He could testify as to the influence of extraneous prejudicial information brought to the jury's attention (*e.g.* a radio newscast or a newspaper account) or an outside influence which improperly had been brought to bear upon a juror (*e.g.* a threat to the safety of a member of his family), but he could not testify as to other irregularities which occurred in the jury room. Under this formulation a quotient verdict could not be attacked through the testimony of a juror, nor could a juror testify to the drunken condition of a fellow juror which so disabled him that he could not participate in the jury's deliberations.

The 1969 and 1971 Advisory Committee drafts would have permitted a member of the jury to testify concerning these kinds of irregularities in the jury room. The Advisory Committee note in the 1971 draft stated that " . . . the door of the jury room is not a satisfactory dividing point, and the Supreme Court has refused to accept it." The Advisory Committee further commented that—

> The trend has been to draw the dividing line between testimony as to mental processes, on the one hand, and as to the existence of conditions or occurrences of events calculated improperly to influence the verdict, on the other hand, without regard to whether the happening is within or without the jury room. . . . The jurors are the persons who know what really happened. Allowing them to testify as to matters other than their own reactions involves no particular hazard to the values sought to be protected. The rule is based upon this conclusion. It makes no attempt to specify the substantive grounds for setting aside verdicts for irregularity.

Objective jury misconduct may be testified to in California, Florida, Iowa, Kansas, Nebraska, New Jersey, North Dakota, Ohio, Oregon, Tennessee, Texas, and Washington.

Persuaded that the better practice is that provided for in the earlier drafts, the Committee amended subdivision (b) to read in the text of those drafts.

Report of Senate Judiciary Committee

Senate Comm. on Judiciary, Fed. Rules of Evidence, S.Rep. No. 1277, 93d Cong., 2d Sess., p. 13 (1974); 1974 U.S.Code Cong. & Ad.News 7051, 7060

As adopted by the House, this rule would permit the impeachment of verdicts by inquiry into, not the mental processes of the jurors, but what happened in terms of conduct in the jury room. This extension of the ability to impeach a verdict is felt to be unwarranted and ill-advised.

The rule passed by the House embodies a suggestion by the Advisory Committee of the Judicial Conference that is considerably broader than the final version adopted by the Supreme Court, which embodied long-accepted Federal law. Although forbidding the impeachment of verdicts by inquiry into the jurors' mental processes, it deletes from the Supreme Court version the proscription against testimony "as to any matter or statement occurring during the course of the jury's deliberations." This deletion would have the effect of opening verdicts up to challenge on the basis of what happened during the jury's internal deliberations, for example, where a juror alleged that the jury refused to follow the trial judge's instructions or that some of the jurors did not take part in deliberations.

Permitting an individual to attack a jury verdict based upon the jury's internal deliberations has long been recognized as unwise by the Supreme Court. In McDonald v. Pless, the Court stated:

> [L]et it once be established that verdicts solemnly made and publicly returned into court can be attacked and set aside on the testimony of those who took part in their publication and all verdicts could be, and many would be, followed by an inquiry in the hope of discovering something which might invalidate the finding. Jurors would be harassed and beset by the defeated party in an effort to secure from them evidence of facts which might establish misconduct sufficient to set aside a verdict. If evidence thus secured could be thus used, the result would be to make what was intended to be a private deliberation, the constant subject of public investigation—to the destruction of all frankness and freedom of discussion and conference.[14]

As it stands then, the rule would permit the harassment of former jurors by losing parties as well as the possible exploitation of disgruntled or otherwise badly-motivated ex-jurors.

Public policy requires a finality to litigation. And common fairness requires that absolute privacy be preserved for jurors to engage in the full and free debate necessary to the attainment of just verdicts. Jurors will not be able to function effectively if their deliberations are to be scrutinized in post-trial litigation. In the interest of protecting the jury system and the citizens who make it work, rule 606 should not permit any inquiry into the internal deliberations of the jurors.

Conference Report

H.R., Fed.Rules of Evidence, Conf.Rep. No. 1597, 93d Cong., 2d Sess., p. 8 (1974); 1974 U.S.Code Cong. & Ad.News 7098, 7102

Rule 606(b) deals with juror testimony in an inquiry into the validity of a verdict or indictment. The House bill provides that a juror cannot testify about his mental processes or about the effect of anything upon his or another juror's mind as influencing him to assent to or dissent from a verdict or indictment. Thus, the House bill allows a juror to testify about objective matters occurring during the jury's deliberation, such as the misconduct of another juror or the reaching of a quotient verdict. The Senate bill does not permit juror testimony about any matter or statement occurring during the course of the jury's deliberations. The Senate bill does provide, however, that a juror may testify on the question whether extraneous prejudicial information was improperly brought to the jury's attention and on the question whether any outside influence was improperly brought to bear on any juror.

The Conference adopts the Senate amendment. The Conferees believe that jurors should be encouraged to be conscientious in promptly reporting to the court misconduct that occurs during jury deliberations.

1987 Amendment Committee Note

The amendments are technical. No substantive change is intended.

---

[14] 238 U.S. 264, at 267 (1914).—Ed.

2006 Amendment Committee Note

Rule 606(b) has been amended to provide that juror testimony may be used to prove that the verdict reported was the result of a mistake in entering the verdict on the verdict form. The amendment responds to a divergence between the text of the Rule and the case law that has established an exception for proof of clerical errors. *See, e.g., Plummer v. Springfield Term. Ry.*, 5 F.3d 1, 3 (1st Cir. 1993) ("A number of circuits hold, and we agree, that juror testimony regarding an alleged clerical error, such as announcing a verdict different than that agreed upon, does not challenge the validity of the verdict or the deliberation of mental processes, and therefore is not subject to Rule 606(b)."); *Teevee Toons, Inc., v. MP3.Com, Inc.*, 148 F.Supp.2d 276, 278 (S.D.N.Y. 2001) (noting that Rule 606(b) has been silent regarding inquiries designed to confirm the accuracy of a verdict).

In adopting the exception for proof of mistakes in entering the verdict on the verdict form, the amendment specifically rejects the broader exception, adopted by some courts, permitting the use of juror testimony to prove that the jurors were operating under a misunderstanding about the consequences of the result that they agreed upon. *See, e.g., Attridge v. Cencorp Div. of Dover Techs. Int'l, Inc.*, 836 F.2d 113, 116 (2d Cir. 1987); *Eastridge Development Co., v. Halpert Associates, Inc.*, 853 F.2d 772 (10th Cir. 1988). The broader exception is rejected because an inquiry into whether the jury misunderstood or misapplied an instruction goes to the jurors' mental processes underlying the verdict, rather than the verdict's accuracy in capturing what the jurors had agreed upon. *See, e.g., Karl v. Burlington Northern R.R.*, 880 F.2d 68, 74 (8th Cir. 1989) (error to receive juror testimony on whether verdict was the result of jurors' misunderstanding of instructions: "The jurors did not state that the figure written by the foreman was different from that which they agreed upon, but indicated that the figure the foreman wrote down was intended to be a net figure, not a gross figure. Receiving such statements violates Rule 606(b) because the testimony relates to how the jury interpreted the court's instructions, and concerns the jurors' 'mental processes,' which is forbidden by the rule."); *Robles v. Exxon Corp.*, 862 F.2d 1201, 1208 (5th Cir. 1989) ("the alleged error here goes to the substance of what the jury was asked to decide, necessarily implicating the jury's mental processes insofar as it questions the jury's understanding of the court's instructions and application of those instructions to the facts of the case"). Thus, the exception established by the amendment is limited to cases such as "where the jury foreperson wrote down, in response to an interrogatory, a number different from that agreed upon by the jury, or mistakenly stated that the defendant was 'guilty' when the jury had actually agreed that the defendant was not guilty." *Id.*

It should be noted that the possibility of errors in the verdict form will be reduced substantially by polling the jury. Rule 606(b) does not, of course, prevent this precaution. See 8 C. Wigmore, Evidence, § 2350 at 691 (McNaughten ed. 1961) (noting that the reasons for the rule barring juror testimony, "namely, the dangers of uncertainty and of tampering with the jurors to procure testimony, disappear in large part if such investigation as may be desired is made by the judge and takes place before the jurors' discharge and separation") (emphasis in original). Errors that come to light after polling the jury "may be corrected on the spot, or the jury may be sent out to continue deliberations, or, if necessary, a new trial may be ordered." C. Mueller & L. Kirkpatrick, Evidence Under the Rules at 671 (2d ed. 1999) (citing Sincox v. United States, 571 F.2d 876, 878–79 (5th Cir. 1978)).

Rule 607. Who May Impeach a Witness

Any party, including the party that called the witness, may attack the witness's credibility.

(As amended Mar. 2, 1987, eff. Oct. 1, 1987; Apr. 26, 2011, eff. Dec. 1, 2011.)

RESTYLED RULE 607 COMMITTEE NOTE

The language of Rule 607 has been amended as part of the restyling of the Evidence Rules to make them more easily understood and to make style and terminology consistent throughout the rules. These changes are intended to be stylistic only. There is no intent to change any result in any ruling on evidence admissibility.

Section references, McCormick 7th ed.

§ 23, § 39

Note by Federal Judicial Center

The rule enacted by the Congress is the rule prescribed by the Supreme Court without change.

Advisory Committee's Note

56 F.R.D. 183, 266

The traditional rule against impeaching one's own witness is abandoned as based on false premises. A party does not hold out his witnesses as worthy of belief, since he rarely has a free choice in selecting them. Denial of the right leaves the party at the mercy of the witness and the adversary. If the impeachment is by a prior statement, it is free from hearsay dangers and is excluded from the category of hearsay under Rule 801(d)(1). Ladd, Impeachment of One's Own Witness—New Developments, 4 U.Chi.L.Rev. 69 (1936); McCormick § 38; 3 Wigmore §§ 896–918. The substantial inroads into the old rule made over the years by decisions, rules, and statutes are evidence of doubts as to its basic soundness and workability. Cases are collected in 3 Wigmore § 905. Revised Rule 32(a)(1) of the Federal Rules of Civil Procedure allows any party to impeach a witness by means of his deposition, and Rule 43(b) has allowed the calling and impeachment of an adverse party or person identified with him. Illustrative statutes allowing a party to impeach his own witness under varying circumstances are Ill.Rev.Stats. 1967, c. 110, § 60; Mass.Laws Annot. 1959, c. 233 § 23; 20 N.M.Stats. Annot. 1953, § 20–2–4; N.Y. CPLR § 4514 (McKinney 1963); 12 Vt.Stats. Annot. 1959, §§ 1641a, 1642. Complete judicial rejection of the old rule is found in United States v. Freeman, 302 F.2d 347 (2d Cir. 1962). The same result is reached in Uniform Rule 20; California Evidence Code § 785; Kansas Code of Civil Procedure § 60–420. See also New Jersey Evidence Rule 20.

1987 Amendment Committee Note

The amendment is technical. No substantive change is intended.

Rule 608. A Witness's Character for Truthfulness or Untruthfulness

(a) Reputation or Opinion Evidence. A witness's credibility may be attacked or supported by testimony about the witness's reputation for having a character for truthfulness or untruthfulness, or by testimony in the form of an opinion about that character. But evidence of truthful character is admissible only after the witness's character for truthfulness has been attacked.

(b) Specific Instances of Conduct. Except for a criminal conviction under Rule 609, extrinsic evidence is not admissible to prove specific instances of a witness's conduct in order to attack or support the witness's character for truthfulness. But the court may, on cross-examination, allow them to be inquired into if they are probative of the character for truthfulness or untruthfulness of:

(1) the witness; or

(2) another witness whose character the witness being cross-examined has testified about.

By testifying on another matter, a witness does not waive any privilege against self-incrimination for testimony that relates only to the witness's character for truthfulness.

(As amended Mar. 2, 1987, eff. Oct. 1, 1987; Apr. 25, 1988, eff. Nov. 1, 1988; March 27, 2003, eff. Dec. 1, 2003; Apr. 26, 2011, eff. Dec. 1, 2011.)

RESTYLED RULE 608 COMMITTEE NOTE

The language of Rule 608 has been amended as part of the general restyling of the Evidence Rules to make them more easily understood and to make style and terminology consistent throughout the rules. These changes are intended to be stylistic only. There is no intent to change any result in any ruling on evidence admissibility.

The Committee is aware that the Rule's limitation of bad-act impeachment to "cross-examination" is trumped by Rule 607, which allows a party to impeach witnesses on direct examination. Courts have not relied on the term "on cross-examination" to limit impeachment that would otherwise be permissible under Rules 607 and 608. The Committee therefore concluded that no change to the language of the Rule was necessary in the context of a restyling project.

REPORTER'S COMMENT ON RESTYLED RULE 608

Rule 608 by its terms states that bad-act impeachment of a witness must occur on "cross-examination." Yet this is not an accurate statement of the law. Under Rule 607, a party is permitted to impeach witnesses on direct—that may be done either to attack an unfavorable witness or to take the wind out of the sails of the adversary's expected impeachment of a favorable witness. The Advisory Committee considered whether to change the "cross-examination" limitation in the context of the Restyling Project. Reasonable minds can differ on this question. The "cross-examination" limitation has been rightly ignored by courts and litigants, and could be thought to be the kind of unnecessary verbiage that a restyling effort should delete. But ultimately the Committee determined that the restyling effort should have a limited impact—any attempt to bring all of the language of the Evidence Rules in accordance with the case law would constitute a vast project and could lead to a potential substantive overhaul of many of the rules. The Committee compromised by adding a paragraph to the basic restyling Committee Note, as indicated above.

Section references, McCormick 7th ed.

(a). § 43, § 47

(b). § 41

Note by Federal Judicial Center

The rule enacted by the Congress is the rule prescribed by the Supreme Court, changed only by amending the second sentence of subdivision (b). The sentence as prescribed by the Court read: "They may, however, if probative of truthfulness or untruthfulness and not remote in time, be inquired into on cross-examination of the witness himself or on cross-examination of a witness who testifies to his character for truthfulness or untruthfulness." The effect of the amendments was to delete the phrase "and not remote in time," to add the phrase "in the discretion of the court," and otherwise only to clarify the meaning of the sentence. The reasons for the amendments are stated in the Report of the House Committee on the Judiciary. *See also* Note to Rule 405(a) by Federal Judicial Center, *supra.*

Advisory Committee's Note

56 F.R.D. 183, 268

Subdivision (a). In Rule 404(a) the general position is taken that character evidence is not admissible for the purpose of proving that the person acted in conformity therewith, subject, however, to several exceptions, one of which is character evidence of a witness as bearing upon his credibility. The present rule develops that exception.

In accordance with the bulk of judicial authority, the inquiry is strictly limited to character for veracity, rather than allowing evidence as to character generally. The result is to sharpen relevancy, to reduce surprise, waste of time, and confusion, and to make the lot of the witness somewhat less unattractive. McCormick § 44.

The use of opinion and reputation evidence as means of proving the character of witnesses is consistent with Rule 405(a). While the modern practice has purported to exclude opinion, witnesses who testify to reputation seem in fact often to be giving their opinions, disguised somewhat misleadingly as reputation. See McCormick § 44. And even under the modern practice, a common relaxation has allowed inquiry as to whether the witnesses would believe the principal witness under oath. United States v. Walker, 313 F.2d 236 (6th Cir. 1963), and cases cited therein; McCormick § 44, pp. 94–95, n. 3.

Character evidence in support of credibility is admissible under the rule only after the witness' character has first been attacked, as has been the case at common law. Maguire, Weinstein, et al., Cases on Evidence 295 (5th ed. 1965); McCormick § 49, p. 105; 4 Wigmore § 1104. The enormous needless consumption of time which a contrary practice would entail justifies the limitation. Opinion or reputation that the witness is untruthful specifically qualifies as an attack under the rule, and evidence of misconduct, including conviction of crime, and of corruption also fall within this category. Evidence of bias or interest does not. McCormick § 49; 4 Wigmore §§ 1106, 1107. Whether evidence in the form of contradiction is an attack upon the character of the witness must depend upon the circumstances. McCormick § 49. Cf. 4 Wigmore §§ 1108, 1109.

As to the use of specific instances on direct by an opinion witness, see the Advisory Committee's Note to Rule 405, *supra.*

Subdivision (b). In conformity with Rule 405, which forecloses use of evidence of specific incidents as proof in chief of character unless character is an issue in the case, the present rule generally bars evidence of specific instances of conduct of a witness for the purpose of attacking or supporting his credibility. There are, however, two exceptions: (1) specific instances are provable when they have been the subject of criminal conviction, and (2) specific instances may be inquired into on cross-examination of the principal witness or of a witness giving an opinion of his character for truthfulness.

(1)   Conviction of crime as a technique of impeachment is treated in detail in Rule 609, and here is merely recognized as an exception to the general rule excluding evidence of specific incidents for impeachment purposes.

(2)   Particular instances of conduct, though not the subject of criminal conviction, may be inquired into on cross-examination of the principal witness himself or of a witness who testifies concerning his character for truthfulness. Effective cross-examination demands that some allowance be made for going into matters of this kind, but the possibilities of abuse are substantial. Consequently safeguards are erected in the form of specific requirements that the instances inquired into be probative of truthfulness or its opposite and not remote in time. **[Editor's Note: The Advisory Committee's proposal precluded impeachment with bad acts that were remote in time. Congress deleted that provision in favor of a case-by-case balancing of probative value and prejudicial effect.]** Also, the overriding protection of Rule 403 requires that probative value not be outweighed by danger of unfair prejudice, confusion of issues or misleading the jury, and that of Rule 611 bars harassment and undue embarrassment.

The final sentence constitutes a rejection of the doctrine of such cases as People v. Sorge, 301 N.Y. 198, 93 N.E.2d 637 (1950), that any past criminal act relevant to credibility may be inquired into on cross-examination, in apparent disregard of the privilege against self-incrimination. While it is clear that an ordinary witness cannot make a partial disclosure of incriminating matter and then invoke the privilege on cross-examination, no tenable contention can be made that merely by testifying he waives his right to foreclose inquiry on cross-examination into criminal activities for the purpose of attacking his credibility. So to hold would reduce the privilege to a nullity. While it is true that an accused, unlike an ordinary witness, has an option whether to testify, if the option can be exercised only at the price of opening up inquiry as to any and all criminal acts committed during his lifetime, the right to testify could scarcely be said to possess much vitality. In Griffin v. California, 380 U.S. 609, 85 S.Ct. 1229, 14 L.Ed.2d 106 (1965), the Court held that allowing comment on the election of an accused not to testify exacted a constitutionally impermissible price, and so here. While no specific provision in terms confers constitutional status on the right of an accused to take the stand in his own defense, the existence of the right is so completely recognized that a denial of it or substantial infringement upon it would surely be of due process dimensions. See Ferguson v. Georgia, 365 U.S. 570, 81 S.Ct. 756, 5 L.Ed.2d 783 (1961); McCormick § 131; 8 Wigmore § 2276 (McNaughton Rev. 1961). In any event, wholly aside from constitutional considerations, the provision represents a sound policy.

Report of House Committee on the Judiciary

House Comm. on Judiciary, Fed.Rules of Evidence, H.R.Rep. No. 650, 93d Cong., 1st Sess., p. 10 (1973); 1974 U.S.Code Cong. & Ad.News 7075, 7084

The second sentence of Rule 608(b) as submitted by the Court permitted specific instances of misconduct of a witness to be inquired into on cross-examination for the purpose of attacking his credibility, if probative of truthfulness or untruthfulness, "and not remote in time." Such cross-examination could be of the witness himself or of another witness who testifies as to "his" character for truthfulness or untruthfulness.

The Committee amended the Rule to emphasize the discretionary power of the court in permitting such testimony and deleted the reference to remoteness in time as being unnecessary and confusing (remoteness from time of trial or remoteness from the incident involved?). As recast, the Committee amendment also makes clear the antecedent of "his" in the original Court proposal.

1987 Amendment Committee Note

The amendments are technical. No substantive change is intended.

1988 Amendment Committee Note

The amendment is technical. No substantive change is intended.

2003 Amendment Committee Note

The Rule has been amended to clarify that the absolute prohibition on extrinsic evidence applies only when the sole reason for proffering that evidence is to attack or support the witness' character for truthfulness. *See United States v. Abel,* 469 U.S. 45 (1984); *United States v. Fusco,* 748 F.2d 996 (5th Cir. 1984) (Rule 608(b) limits the use of evidence "designed to show that the witness has done things, unrelated to the suit being tried, that make him more or less believable per se"); Ohio R.Evid. 608(b). On occasion the Rule's use of the overbroad term "credibility" has been read "to bar extrinsic evidence for bias, competency and contradiction impeachment since they too deal with credibility." American Bar Association Section of Litigation, *Emerging Problems Under the Federal Rules of Evidence* at 161 (3d ed. 1998). The amendment conforms the language of the Rule to its original intent, which was to impose an absolute bar on extrinsic evidence only if the sole purpose for offering the evidence was to prove the witness' character for veracity. *See* Advisory Committee Note to Rule 608(b) (stating that the Rule is "[i]n conformity with Rule 405, which forecloses use of evidence of specific incidents as proof in chief of character unless character is in issue in the case . . . ").

By limiting the application of the Rule to proof of a witness' character for truthfulness, the amendment leaves the admissibility of extrinsic evidence offered for other grounds of impeachment (such as contradiction, prior inconsistent statement, bias and mental capacity) to Rules 402 and 403. *See, e.g., United States v. Winchenbach,* 197 F.3d 548 (1st Cir. 1999) (admissibility of a prior inconsistent statement offered for impeachment is governed by Rules 402 and 403, not Rule 608(b)); *United States v. Tarantino,* 846 F.2d 1384 (D.C. Cir. 1988) (admissibility of extrinsic evidence offered to contradict a witness is governed by Rules 402 and 403); *United States v. Lindemann,* 85 F.3d 1232 (7th Cir. 1996) (admissibility of extrinsic evidence of bias is governed by Rules 402 and 403).

It should be noted that the extrinsic evidence prohibition of Rule 608(b) bars any reference to the consequences that a witness might have suffered as a result of an alleged bad act. For example, Rule 608(b) prohibits counsel from mentioning that a witness was suspended or disciplined for the conduct that is the subject of impeachment, when that conduct is offered only to prove the character of the witness. *See United States v. Davis,* 183 F.3d 231, 257 n.12 (3d Cir. 1999) (emphasizing that in attacking the defendant's character for truthfulness "the government cannot make reference to Davis's forty-four day suspension or that Internal Affairs found that he lied about" an incident because "[s]uch evidence would not only be hearsay to the extent it contains assertion of fact, it would be inadmissible extrinsic evidence under Rule 608(b)"). *See also* Stephen A. Saltzburg, *Impeaching the Witness: Prior Bad Acts and Extrinsic Evidence,* 7 Crim. Just. 28, 31 (Winter 1993) ("counsel should not be permitted to circumvent the no-extrinsic-evidence provision by tucking a third person's opinion about prior acts into a question asked of the witness who has denied the act").

For purposes of consistency the term "credibility" has been replaced by the term "character for truthfulness" in the last sentence of subdivision (b). The term "credibility" is also used in subdivision (a). But the Committee found it unnecessary to substitute "character for truthfulness" for "credibility" in Rule 608(a), because subdivision (a)(1) already serves to limit impeachment to proof of such character.

Rules 609(a) and 610 also use the term "credibility" when the intent of those Rules is to regulate impeachment of a witness' character for truthfulness. No inference should be derived from the fact that the Committee proposed an amendment to Rule 608(b) but not to Rules 609 and 610.

Rule 609. Impeachment by Evidence of a Criminal Conviction

(a) **In General.** The following rules apply to attacking a witness's character for truthfulness by evidence of a criminal conviction:

(1)   for a crime that, in the convicting jurisdiction, was punishable by death or by imprisonment for more than one year, the evidence:

(A)   must be admitted, subject to Rule 403, in a civil case or in a criminal case in which the witness is not a defendant; and

(B)   must be admitted in a criminal case in which the witness is a defendant, if the probative value of the evidence outweighs its prejudicial effect to that defendant; and

(2)   for any crime regardless of the punishment, the evidence must be admitted if the court can readily determine that establishing the elements of the crime required proving—or the witness's admitting—a dishonest act or false statement.

(b) **Limit on Using the Evidence After 10 Years.** This subdivision (b) applies if more than 10 years have passed since the witness's conviction or release from confinement for it, whichever is later. Evidence of the conviction is admissible only if:

(1)   its probative value, supported by specific facts and circumstances, substantially outweighs its prejudicial effect; and

(2)   the proponent gives an adverse party reasonable written notice of the intent to use it so that the party has a fair opportunity to contest its use.

(c) **Effect of a Pardon, Annulment, or Certificate of Rehabilitation.** Evidence of a conviction is not admissible if:

(1)   the conviction has been the subject of a pardon, annulment, certificate of rehabilitation, or other equivalent procedure based on a finding that the person has been rehabilitated, and the person has not been convicted of a later crime punishable by death or by imprisonment for more than one year; or

(2)   the conviction has been the subject of a pardon, annulment, or other equivalent procedure based on a finding of innocence.

(d) **Juvenile Adjudications.** Evidence of a juvenile adjudication is admissible under this rule only if:

(1)   it is offered in a criminal case;

(2)   the adjudication was of a witness other than the defendant;

(3)   an adult's conviction for that offense would be admissible to attack the adult's credibility; and

(4)   admitting the evidence is necessary to fairly determine guilt or innocence.

(e) **Pendency of an Appeal.** A conviction that satisfies this rule is admissible even if an appeal is pending. Evidence of the pendency is also admissible.

(As amended Mar. 2, 1987, eff. Oct. 1, 1987; Jan. 26, 1990, eff. Dec. 1, 1990; Apr. 12, 2006, eff. Dec. 1, 2006; Apr. 26, 2011, eff. Dec. 1, 2011.)

RESTYLED RULE 609 COMMITTEE NOTE

The language of Rule 609 has been amended as part of the restyling of the Evidence Rules to make them more easily understood and to make style and terminology consistent throughout the rules. These changes are intended to be stylistic only. There is no intent to change any result in any ruling on evidence admissibility.

REPORTER'S COMMENT ON RESTYLED RULE 609

The restylist suggested that the reference to Rule 403 in Rule 609(a)(1) should be deleted because "Rule 403 applies to everything unless the rule says otherwise"—so the reference to Rule 403 was thought to be excess verbiage. But the Reporter argued that the reference to Rule 403 should be kept in the unique circumstances presented by Rule 609(a)(1). Rule 609 contains four separate tests for admitting prior convictions—one for crimes requiring proof of a dishonest act or false statement (automatic admissibility); one for other felonies when offered against a criminal defendant (probative value must outweigh prejudice); one for other felonies when offered against any other witness (admitted unless prejudice substantially outweighs probative value, *i.e.*, the Rule 403 test); and one for old crimes (Rule 609(b), admissible only if the probative value substantially outweighs the prejudicial effect). Given all the different tests for admissibility being thrown about in so short a space, the Reporter argued that it was useful, even necessary, to specify that one of them was the Rule 403 test. Courts and litigants should not have to reason from a failure to specify a balancing test in that forest of other balancing tests. The Advisory Committee agreed with the Reporter.

Section references, McCormick 7th ed.

§ 42

Note by Federal Judicial Center

Subdivision (a) of the rule prescribed by the Supreme Court was revised successively in the House, in the Senate, and in the Conference. The nature of the rule prescribed by the Court, the various amendments, and the reasons therefor are stated in the Report of the House Committee on the Judiciary, the Report of the Senate Committee on the Judiciary, and the Conference Report.

Subdivision (b) of the rule prescribed by the Supreme Court was also revised successively in the House, in the Senate, and in the Conference. The nature of the rule prescribed by the Court, those amendments and the reasons therefor are likewise stated in the Report of the House Committee on the Judiciary, the Report of the Senate Committee on the Judiciary, and the Conference Report.

Subdivision (c) enacted by the Congress is the subdivision prescribed by the Supreme Court, with amendments and reasons therefor stated in the Report of the House Committee on the Judiciary.

Subdivision (d) enacted by the Congress is the subdivision prescribed by the Supreme Court, amended in the second sentence by substituting "court" in place of "judge" and by adding the phrase "in a criminal case."

Subdivision (e) enacted by the Congress is the subdivision prescribed by the Supreme Court without change.

Advisory Committee's Note

56 F.R.D. 183, 270

As a means of impeachment, evidence of conviction of crime is significant only because it stands as proof of the commission of the underlying criminal act. There is little dissent from the general proposition that at least some crimes are relevant to credibility but much disagreement among the cases and commentators about which crimes are usable for this purpose. See McCormick § 43; 2 Wright, Federal Practice and Procedure: Criminal § 416 (1969). The weight of traditional authority has been to allow use of felonies generally, without regard to the nature of the particular offense, and of *crimen falsi* without regard to the grade of the offense. This is the view accepted by Congress in the 1970 amendment of § 14–305 of the District of Columbia Code, P.L. 91–358, 84 Stat. 473. Uniform Rule 21 and Model Code Rule 106 permit only crimes involving "dishonesty or false statement." Others have thought that the trial judge should have discretion to exclude convictions if the probative value of the evidence of the crime is substantially outweighed by the danger of unfair prejudice. Luck v. United States, 121 U.S.App.D.C. 151, 348 F.2d 763 (1965); McGowan, Impeachment of Criminal Defendants by Prior Convictions, 1970 Law & Soc. Order 1. Whatever may be the merits of those views, this rule is drafted to accord with the policy manifested in the 1970 legislation. **[Editor's Note: The rule ultimately adopted by Congress provides for trial court balancing of probative value and prejudicial effect with respect to convictions that do not involve dishonesty or false statement.]**

The proposed rule incorporates certain basic safeguards, in terms applicable to all witnesses but of particular significance to an accused who elects to testify. These protections include the imposition of definite time limitations, giving effect to demonstrated rehabilitation, and generally excluding juvenile adjudications.

Subdivision (a). For purposes of impeachment, crimes are divided into two categories by the rule: (1) those of what is generally regarded as felony grade, without particular regard to the nature of the offense, and (2) those involving dishonesty or false statement, without regard to the grade of the offense. Provable convictions are not limited to violations of federal law. By reason of our constitutional structure, the federal catalog of crimes is far from being a complete one, and resort must be had to the laws of the states for the specification of many crimes. For example, simple theft as compared with theft from interstate commerce. Other instances of borrowing are the Assimilative Crimes Act, making the state law of crimes applicable to the special territorial and maritime jurisdiction of the United States, 18 U.S.C. § 13, and the provision of the Judicial Code disqualifying persons as jurors on the grounds of state as well as federal convictions, 28 U.S.C. § 1865. For evaluation of the crime in terms of seriousness, reference is made to the congressional measurement of felony (subject to imprisonment in excess of one year) rather than adopting state definitions which vary considerably. See 28 U.S.C. § 1865, *supra*, disqualifying jurors for conviction in state or federal court of crime punishable by imprisonment for more than one year.[15]

Report of House Committee on the Judiciary on Rule 609(a)

House Comm. on Judiciary, Fed.Rules of Evidence, H.R.Rep. No. 650, 93d Cong., 1st Sess., p. 11 (1973); 1974 U.S.Code Cong. & Ad.News 7075, 7084

Rule 609(a) as submitted by the Court was modeled after Section 133(a) of Public Law 91–358, 14 D.C.Code 305(b)(1), enacted in 1970. The Rule provided that:

> For the purpose of attacking the credibility of a witness, evidence that he has been convicted of a crime is admissible but only if the crime (1) was punishable by death or imprisonment in excess of one year under the law under which he was convicted or (2) involved dishonesty or false statement regardless of the punishment.

---

[15] The Advisory Note continues after the legislative reports which are particular to Rule 609(a)—and which are extensive.—Ed.

As reported to the Committee by the Subcommittee, Rule 609(a) was amended to read as follows:

For the purpose of attacking the credibility of a witness, evidence that he has been convicted of a crime is admissible only if the crime (1) was punishable by death or imprisonment in excess of one year, unless the court determines that the danger of unfair prejudice outweighs the probative value of the evidence of the conviction, or (2) involved dishonesty or false statement.

In full committee, the provision was amended to permit attack upon the credibility of a witness by prior conviction only if the prior crime involved dishonesty or false statement. While recognizing that the prevailing doctrine in the federal courts and in most States allows a witness to be impeached by evidence of prior felony convictions without restriction as to type, the Committee was of the view that, because of the danger of unfair prejudice in such practice and the deterrent effect upon an accused who might wish to testify, and even upon a witness who was not the accused, cross-examination by evidence of prior conviction should be limited to those kinds of convictions bearing directly on credibility, *i.e.*, crimes involving dishonesty or false statement.

Report of Senate Committee on the Judiciary on Rule 609(a)

Senate Comm. on Judiciary, Fed.Rules of Evidence, S.Rep. No. 1277, 93d Cong., 2d Sess., p. 14 (1974); 1974 U.S.Code Cong. & Ad.News 7051, 7060

As proposed by the Supreme Court, the rule would allow the use of prior convictions to impeach if the crime was a felony or a misdemeanor if the misdemeanor involved dishonesty or false statement. As modified by the House, the rule would admit prior convictions for impeachment purposes only if the offense, whether felony or misdemeanor, involved dishonesty or false statement.

The committee has adopted a modified version of the House-passed rule. In your committee's view, the danger of unfair prejudice is far greater when the accused, as opposed to other witnesses, testifies, because the jury may be prejudiced not merely on the question of credibility but also on the ultimate question of guilt or innocence. Therefore, with respect to defendants, the committee agreed with the House limitation that only offenses involving false statement or dishonesty may be used. By that phrase, the committee means crimes such as perjury or subornation of perjury, false statement, criminal fraud, embezzlement or false pretense, or any other offense, in the nature of crimen falsi the commission of which involves some element of untruthfulness, deceit or falsification bearing on the accused's propensity to testify truthfully.

With respect to other witnesses, in addition to any prior conviction involving false statement or dishonesty, any other felony may be used to impeach if, and only if, the court finds that the probative value of such evidence outweighs its prejudicial effect against the party offering that witness.

Notwithstanding this provision, proof of any prior offense otherwise admissible under rule 404 could still be offered for the purposes sanctioned by that rule. Furthermore, the committee intends that notwithstanding this rule, a defendant's misrepresentation regarding the existence or nature of prior convictions may be met by rebuttal evidence, including the record of such prior convictions. Similarly, such records may be offered to rebut representations made by the defendant regarding his attitude toward or willingness to commit a general category of offense, although denials or other representations by the defendant regarding the specific conduct which forms the basis of the charge against him shall not make prior convictions admissible to rebut such statement.

In regard to either type of representation, of course, prior convictions may be offered in rebuttal only if the defendant's statement is made in response to defense counsel's questions or is made gratuitously in the course of cross-examination. Prior convictions may not be offered as rebuttal evidence if the prosecution has sought to circumvent the purpose of this rule by asking questions which elicit such representations from the defendant.

One other clarifying amendment has been added to this subsection, that is, to provide that the admissibility of evidence of a prior conviction is permitted only upon cross-examination of a witness. It is not admissible if a person does not testify. It is to be understood, however, that a court record of a prior conviction is admissible to prove that conviction if the witness has forgotten or denies its existence.

Conference Report on Rule 609(a)

H.R., Fed.Rules of Evidence, Conf.Rep. No. 1597, 93d Cong., 2d Sess., p. 9 (1974); 1974 U.S.Code Cong. & Ad.News 7098, 7102

Rule 609 defines when a party may use evidence of a prior conviction in order to impeach a witness. The Senate amendments make changes in two subsections of Rule 609.

The House bill provides that the credibility of a witness can be attacked by proof of prior conviction of a crime only if the crime involves dishonesty or false statement. The Senate amendment provides that a witness' credibility may be attacked if the crime (1) was punishable by death or imprisonment in excess of one year under the law under which he was convicted or (2) involves dishonesty or false statement, regardless of the punishment.

The Conference adopts the Senate amendment with an amendment. The Conference amendment provides that the credibility of a witness, whether a defendant or someone else, may be attacked by proof of a prior conviction but only if the crime: (1) was punishable by death or imprisonment in excess of one year under the law under which he was convicted and the court determines that the probative value of the conviction outweighs its prejudicial effect to the defendant; or (2) involved dishonesty or false statement regardless of the punishment.

By the phrase "dishonesty and false statement" the Conference means crimes such as perjury or subornation of perjury, false statement, criminal fraud, embezzlement, or false pretense, or any other offense in the nature of crimen falsi, the commission of which involves some element of deceit, untruthfulness, or falsification bearing on the accused's propensity to testify truthfully.

The admission of prior convictions involving dishonesty and false statement is not within the discretion of the Court. Such convictions are peculiarly probative of credibility and, under this rule, are always to be admitted. Thus, judicial discretion granted with respect to the admissibility of other prior convictions is not applicable to those involving dishonesty or false statement.

With regard to the discretionary standard established by paragraph (1) of rule 609(a), the Conference determined that the prejudicial effect to be weighed against the probative value of the conviction is specifically the prejudicial effect *to the defendant*. The danger of prejudice to a witness other than the defendant (such as injury to the witness' reputation in his community) was considered and rejected by the Conference as an element to be weighed in determining admissibility. It was the judgment of the Conference that the danger of prejudice to a nondefendant witness is outweighed by the need for the trier of fact to have as much relevant evidence on the issue of credibility as possible. Such evidence should only be excluded where it presents a danger of improperly influencing the outcome of the trial by persuading the trier of fact to convict the defendant on the basis of his prior criminal record.

Advisory Committee's Note on Rule 609(b)

56 F.R.D. 183, 271

Subdivision (b). Few statutes recognize a time limit on impeachment by evidence of conviction. However, practical considerations of fairness and relevancy demand that some boundary be recognized. See Ladd, Credibility Tests—Current Trends, 89 U.Pa.L.Rev. 166, 176–177 (1940). This portion of the rule is derived from the proposal advanced in Recommendation Proposing an Evidence Code, § 788(5), p. 142, Cal.Law Rev.Comm'n (1965), though not adopted. See California Evidence Code § 788. **[Editor's Note: The rule ultimately adopted by Congress provides for admissibility of convictions over ten years old, but limits admissibility to convictions as to which the probative value substantially outweighs the prejudicial effect.]**

Report of House Committee on the Judiciary on Rule 609(b)

House Comm. on Judiciary, Fed.Rules of Evidence, H.R.Rep. No. 650, 93d Cong., 1st Sess., p. 11 (1973); 1974 U.S.Code Cong. & Ad.News 7075, 7085

Rule 609(b) as submitted by the Court was modeled after Section 133(a) of Public Law 91–358, 14 D.C.Code 305(b)(2)(B), enacted in 1970. The Rule provided:

> Evidence of a conviction under this rule is not admissible if a period of more than ten years has elapsed since the date of the release of the witness from confinement imposed for his most recent conviction, or the expiration of the period of his parole, probation, or sentence granted or imposed with respect to his most recent conviction, whichever is the later date.

Under this formulation, a witness' entire past record of criminal convictions could be used for impeachment (provided the conviction met the standard of subdivision (a)), if the witness had been most recently released from confinement, or the period of his parole or probation had expired, within ten years of the conviction.

The Committee amended the Rule to read in the text of the 1971 Advisory Committee version to provide that upon the expiration of ten years from the date of a conviction of a witness, or of his release from confinement for that offense, that conviction may no longer be used for impeachment. The Committee was of the view that after ten years following a person's release from confinement (or from the date of his conviction) the probative value of the conviction with respect to that person's credibility diminished to a point where it should no longer be admissible.

Report of Senate Committee on the Judiciary on Rule 609(b)

Senate Comm. on Judiciary, Fed.Rules of Evidence, S.Rep. No. 1277, 93d Cong., 2d Sess., p. 15 (1974); 1974 U.S.Code Cong. & Ad.News 7051, 7061

Although convictions over ten years old generally do not have much probative value, there may be exceptional circumstances under which the conviction substantially bears on the credibility of the witness. Rather than exclude all convictions over 10 years old, the committee adopted an amendment in the form of a final clause to the section granting the court discretion to admit convictions over 10 years old, but only upon a determination by the court that the probative value of the convictions supported by specific facts and circumstances, substantially outweighs its prejudicial effect.

It is intended that convictions over 10 years old will be admitted very rarely and only in exceptional circumstances. The rules provide that the decision be supported by specific facts and circumstances thus requiring the court to make specific findings on the record as to the particular facts and circumstances it has considered in determining that the probative value of the conviction substantially outweighs its prejudicial impact. It is expected that, in fairness, the court will give the party against whom the conviction is introduced a full and adequate opportunity to contest its admission.

Conference Report on Rule 609(b)

H.R., Fed.Rules of Evidence, Conf.Rep. No. 1597, 93d Cong., 2d Sess., p. 10 (1974); 1974 U.S.Code Cong. & Ad.News 7098, 7103

The House bill provides in subsection (b) that evidence of conviction of a crime may not be used for impeachment purposes under subsection (a) if more than ten years have elapsed since the date of the conviction or the date the witness was released from confinement imposed for the conviction, whichever is later. The Senate amendment permits the use of convictions older than ten years, if the court determines, in the interests of justice, that the probative value of the conviction, supported by specific facts and circumstances, substantially outweighs its prejudicial effect.

The Conference adopts the Senate amendment with an amendment requiring notice by a party that he intends to request that the court allow him to use a conviction older than ten years. The Conferees anticipate that a written notice, in order to give the adversary a fair opportunity to contest the use of the evidence, will ordinarily include such information as the date of the conviction, the jurisdiction, and the offense or statute involved. In order to eliminate the possibility that the flexibility of this provision may impair the ability of a party-opponent to prepare for trial, the Conferees intend that the notice provision operate to avoid surprise.

Advisory Committee's Note on Rule 609(c)

56 F.R.D. 183, 271

Subdivision (c). A pardon or its equivalent granted solely for the purpose of restoring civil rights lost by virtue of a conviction has no relevance to an inquiry into character. If, however, the pardon or other proceeding is hinged upon a showing of rehabilitation the situation is otherwise. The result under the rule is to render the conviction inadmissible. The alternative of allowing in evidence both the conviction and the rehabilitation has not been adopted for reasons of policy, economy of time, and difficulties of evaluation.

A similar provision is contained in California Evidence Code § 788. Cf. A.L.I. Model Penal Code, Proposed Official Draft § 306.6(3)(e) (1962), and discussion in A.L.I. Proceedings 310 (1961).

Pardons based on innocence have the effect, of course, of nullifying the conviction *ab initio.*

Report of House Committee on the Judiciary on Rule 609(c)

House Comm. on Judiciary, Fed.Rules of Evidence, H.R.Rep. No. 650, 93d Cong., 1st Sess., p. 12 (1973); 1974 U.S.Code Cong. & Ad.News 7075, 7085

Rule 609(c) as submitted by the Court provided in part that evidence of a witness' prior conviction is not admissible to attack his credibility if the conviction was the subject of a pardon, annulment, or other equivalent procedure, based on a showing of rehabilitation, and the witness has not been convicted of a subsequent crime. The Committee amended the Rule to provide that the "subsequent crime" must have been "punishable by death or imprisonment in excess of one year", on the ground that a subsequent conviction of an offense not a felony is insufficient to rebut the finding that the witness has been rehabilitated. The Committee also intends that the words "based on a finding of the rehabilitation of the person convicted" apply not only to "certificate of rehabilitation, or other equivalent procedure", but also to "pardon" and "annulment."

Advisory Committee's Note on Rule 609(d) and (e)

56 F.R.D. 183, 271

Subdivision (d). The prevailing view has been that a juvenile adjudication is not usable for impeachment. Thomas v. United States, 74 App.D.C. 167, 121 F.2d 905 (1941); Cotton v. United States, 355 F.2d 480 (10th Cir. 1966). This conclusion was based upon a variety of circumstances. By virtue of its informality, frequently diminished quantum of required proof, and other departures from accepted standards for criminal trials under the theory of *parens patriae,* the juvenile adjudication was considered to lack the precision and general probative value of the criminal conviction. While In re Gault, 387 U.S. 1, 87 S.Ct. 1428, 18 L.Ed.2d 527 (1967), no doubt eliminates these characteristics insofar as objectionable, other obstacles remain. Practical problems of administration are raised by the common provisions in juvenile legislation that records be kept confidential and that they be destroyed after a short time. While *Gault* was skeptical as to the realities of confidentiality of juvenile records, it also saw no constitutional obstacles to improvement. 387 U.S. at 25, 87 S.Ct. 1428. *See also* Note, Rights and Rehabilitation in the Juvenile Courts, 67 Colum.L.Rev. 281, 289 (1967). In addition, policy considerations much akin to those which dictate exclusion of adult convictions after rehabilitation has been established strongly suggest a rule of excluding juvenile adjudications. Admittedly, however, the rehabilitative process may in a given case be a demonstrated failure, or the strategic importance of a given witness may be so great as to require the overriding of general policy in the interests of particular justice. See Giles v. Maryland, 386 U.S. 66, 87 S.Ct. 793, 17 L.Ed.2d 737 (1967). Wigmore was outspoken in his condemnation of the disallowance of juvenile adjudications to impeach, especially when the witness is the complainant in a case of molesting a minor. 1 Wigmore § 196; 3 *id.* §§ 924a, 980. The rule recognizes discretion in the judge to effect an accommodation among these various factors by departing from the general principle of exclusion. In deference to the general pattern and policy of juvenile statutes, however, no discretion is accorded when the witness is the accused in a criminal case.

Subdivision (e). The presumption of correctness which ought to attend judicial proceedings supports the position that pendency of an appeal does not preclude use of a conviction for impeachment. United States v. Empire Packing Co., 174 F.2d 16 (7th Cir. 1949), cert. denied 337 U.S. 959, 69 S.Ct. 1534, 93 L.Ed. 1758; Bloch v. United States, 226 F.2d 185 (9th Cir. 1955), cert. denied 350 U.S. 948, 76 S.Ct. 323, 100 L.Ed. 826 and 353 U.S. 959, 77 S.Ct. 868, 1 L.Ed.2d 910; and see Newman v. United States, 331 F.2d 968 (8th Cir. 1964). Contra, Campbell v. United States, 85 U.S.App.D.C. 133, 176 F.2d 45 (1949). The pendency of an appeal is, however, a qualifying circumstance properly considerable.

1987 Amendment Committee Note

The amendments are technical. No substantive change is intended.

1990 Amendment Committee Note

The amendment to Rule 609(a) makes two changes in the rule. The first change removes from the rule the limitation that the conviction may only be elicited during cross-examination, a limitation that virtually every circuit has found to be inapplicable. It is common for witnesses to reveal on direct examination their convictions to "remove the sting" of the impeachment. *See, e.g.,* United States v. Bad Cob, 560 F.2d 877 (8th Cir. 1977). The amendment does not contemplate that a court will necessarily permit proof of prior convictions through testimony, which might be time-consuming and more prejudicial than proof through a written record. Rules 403 and 611(a) provide sufficient authority for the court to protect against unfair or disruptive methods of proof.

The second change effected by the amendment resolves an ambiguity as to the relationship of Rules 609 and 403 with respect to impeachment of witnesses other than the criminal defendant. See, *Green v. Bock Laundry Machine Co.*, 109 S.Ct. 1981, 490 U.S. 504 (1989). The amendment does not disturb the special balancing test for the criminal defendant who chooses to testify. Thus, the rule recognizes that, in virtually every case in which prior convictions are used to impeach the testifying defendant, the defendant faces a unique risk of prejudice— *i.e.*, the danger that convictions that would be excluded under Fed.R.Evid. 404 will be misused by a jury as propensity evidence despite their introduction solely for impeachment purposes. Although the rule does not forbid all use of convictions to impeach a defendant, it requires that the government show that the probative value of convictions as impeachment evidence outweighs their prejudicial effect.

Prior to the amendment, the rule appeared to give the defendant the benefit of the special balancing test when defense witnesses other than the defendant were called to testify. In practice, however, the concern about unfairness to the defendant is most acute when the defendant's own convictions are offered as evidence. Almost all of the decided cases concern this type of impeachment, and the amendment does not deprive the defendant of any meaningful protection, since Rule 403 now clearly protects against unfair impeachment of any defense witness other than the defendant. There are cases in which a defendant might be prejudiced when a defense witness is impeached. Such cases may arise, for example, when the witness bears a special relationship to the defendant such that the defendant is likely to suffer some spill-over effect from impeachment of the witness.

The amendment also protects other litigants from unfair impeachment of their witnesses. The danger of prejudice from the use of prior convictions is not confined to criminal defendants. Although the danger that prior convictions will be misused as character evidence is particularly acute when the defendant is impeached, the danger exists in other situations as well. The amendment reflects the view that it is desirable to protect all litigants from the unfair use of prior convictions, and that the ordinary balancing test of Rule 403, which provides that evidence shall not be excluded unless its prejudicial effect substantially outweighs its probative value, is appropriate for assessing the admissibility of prior convictions for impeachment of any witness other than a criminal defendant.

The amendment reflects a judgment that decisions interpreting Rule 609(a) as requiring a trial court to admit convictions in civil cases that have little, if anything, to do with credibility reach undesirable results. *See, e.g., Diggs v. Lyons, 741 F.2d 577* (3d Cir. 1984), cert. denied, 105 S.Ct. 2157 (1985). The amendment provides the same protection against unfair prejudice arising from prior convictions used for impeachment purposes as the rules provide for other evidence. The amendment finds support in decided cases. *See, e.g., Petty v. Ideco*, 761 F.2d 1146 (5th Cir. 1985); *Czaka v. Hickman,* 703 F.2d 317 (8th Cir. 1983).

Fewer decided cases address the question whether Rule 609(a) provides any protection against unduly prejudicial prior convictions used to impeach government witnesses. Some courts have read Rule 609(a) as giving the government no protection for its witnesses. *See, e.g., United States v. Thorne*, 547 F.2d 56 (8th Cir. 1976); *United States v. Nevitt*, 563 F.2d 406 (9th Cir. 1977), cert. denied, 444 U.S. 847 (1979). This approach also is rejected by the amendment. There are cases in which impeachment of government witnesses with prior convictions that have little, if anything, to do with credibility may result in unfair prejudice to the government's interest in a fair trial and unnecessary embarrassment to a witness. Fed.R.Evid. 412 already recognizes this and excluded certain evidence of past sexual behavior in the context of prosecutions for sexual assaults.

The amendment applies the general balancing test of Rule 403 to protect all litigants against unfair impeachment of witnesses. The balancing test protects civil litigants, the government in criminal cases, and the defendant in a criminal case who calls other witnesses. The amendment addresses prior convictions offered under Rule 609, not for other purposes, and does not run afoul, therefore, of *Davis v. Alaska,* 415 U.S. 308 (1974). Davis involved the use of a prior juvenile adjudication not to prove a past law violation, but to prove bias. The defendant in a criminal case has the right to demonstrate the bias of a witness and to be assured a fair trial, but not to unduly prejudice a trier of fact. *See generally,* Rule 412. In any case in which the trial court believes that confrontation rights require admission of impeachment evidence, obviously the Constitution would take precedence over the rule.

The probability that prior convictions of an ordinary government witness will be unduly prejudicial is low in most criminal cases. Since the behavior of the witness is not the issue in dispute in most cases, there is little chance that the trier of fact will misuse the convictions offered as impeachment evidence as propensity evidence. Thus, trial courts will be skeptical when the government objects to impeachment of its witnesses with prior convictions. Only when the government is able to point to a real danger of prejudice that is sufficient to outweigh substantially the probative value of the conviction for impeachment purposes will the conviction be excluded.

The amendment continues to divide subdivision (a) into subsections (1) and (2) thus facilitating retrieval under current computerized research programs which distinguish the two provisions. The Committee recommended no substantive change in subdivision (a)(2), even though some cases raise a concern about the proper interpretation of the words "dishonesty or false statement." These words were used but not explained in the original Advisory Committee Note accompanying Rule 609. Congress extensively debated the rule, and the Report of the House and Senate Conference Committee states that "[b]y the phrase 'dishonesty and false statement,' the Conference means crimes such as perjury, subornation of perjury, false statement, criminal fraud, embezzlement, or false pretense, or any other offense in the nature of *crimen falsi,* commission of which involves some element of deceit, untruthfulness, or falsification bearing on the accused's propensity to testify truthfully." The Advisory Committee concluded that the Conference Report provides sufficient guidance to trial courts and that no amendment is necessary, notwithstanding some decisions that take an unduly broad view of "dishonesty," admitting convictions such as for bank robbery or bank larceny. Subsection (a)(2) continues to apply to any witness, including a criminal defendant.

Finally, the Committee determined that it was unnecessary to add to the rule language stating that, when a prior conviction is offered under Rule 609, the trial court is to consider the probative value of the prior conviction *for impeachment*, not for other purposes. The Committee concluded that the title of the rule, its first sentence, and its placement among the impeachment rules clearly establish that evidence offered under Rule 609 is offered only for purposes of impeachment.

2006 Amendment Committee Note

The amendment provides that Rule 609(a)(2) mandates the admission of evidence of a conviction only when the conviction required the proof of (or in the case of a guilty plea, the admission of) an act of dishonesty or false statement. Evidence of all other convictions is inadmissible under this subsection, irrespective of whether the witness exhibited dishonesty or made a false statement in the process of the commission of the crime of conviction. Thus, evidence that a witness was convicted for a crime of violence, such as murder, is not admissible under Rule 609(a)(2), even if the witness acted deceitfully in the course of committing the crime.

The amendment is meant to give effect to the legislative intent to limit the convictions that are to be automatically admitted under subdivision (a)(2). The Conference Committee provided that by "dishonesty and false statement" it meant "crimes such as perjury, subornation of perjury, false statement, criminal fraud, embezzlement, or false pretense, or any other offense in the nature of crimen falsi, the commission of which involves some element of deceit, untruthfulness, or falsification bearing on the [witness's] propensity to testify truthfully." Historically, offenses classified as crimina falsi have included only those crimes in which the ultimate criminal act was itself an act of deceit. See Green, *Deceit and the Classification of Crimes: Federal Rule of Evidence 609(a)(2) and the Origins of Crimen Falsi*, 90 J. Crim. L. & Criminology 1087 (2000).

Evidence of crimes in the nature of crimina falsi must be admitted under Rule 609(a)(2), regardless of how such crimes are specifically charged. For example, evidence that a witness was convicted of making a false claim to a federal agent is admissible under this subdivision regardless of whether the crime was charged under a section that expressly references deceit (*e.g.*, 18 U.S.C. § 1001, Material Misrepresentation to the Federal Government) or a section that does not (*e.g.*, 18 U.S.C. § 1503, Obstruction of Justice).

The amendment requires that the proponent have ready proof that the conviction required the factfinder to find, or the defendant to admit, an act of dishonesty or false statement. Ordinarily, the statutory elements of the crime will indicate whether it is one of dishonesty or false statement. Where the deceitful nature of the crime is not apparent from the statute and the face of the judgment—as, for example, where the conviction simply records a finding of guilt for a statutory offense that does not reference deceit expressly—a proponent may offer information such as an indictment, a statement of admitted facts, or jury instructions to show that the factfinder had to find, or the defendant had to admit, an act of dishonesty or false statement in order for the witness to have been convicted. Cf. *Taylor v. United States*, 495 U.S. 575, 602 (1990) (providing that a trial court may look to a charging instrument or jury instructions to ascertain the nature of a prior offense where the statute is insufficiently clear on its face); *Shepard v. United States*, 125 S.Ct. 1254 (2005) (the inquiry to determine whether a guilty plea to a crime defined by a nongeneric statute necessarily admitted elements of the generic offense was limited to the charging document's terms, the terms of a plea agreement or transcript of colloquy between judge and defendant in which the factual basis for the plea was confirmed by the defendant, or a comparable judicial record). But the amendment does not contemplate a "mini-trial" in which the court plumbs the record of the previous proceeding to determine whether the crime was in the nature of crimen falsi.

The amendment also substitutes the term "character for truthfulness" for the term "credibility" in the first sentence of the Rule. The limitations of Rule 609 are not applicable if a conviction is admitted for a purpose other than to prove the witness's character for untruthfulness. *See, e.g., United States v. Lopez*, 979 F.2d 1024 (5th Cir. 1992) (Rule 609 was not applicable where the conviction was offered for purposes of contradiction). The use of the term "credibility" in subdivision (d) is retained, however, as that subdivision is intended to govern the use of a juvenile adjudication for any type of impeachment.

———

Rule 610. Religious Beliefs or Opinions

Evidence of a witness's religious beliefs or opinions is not admissible to attack or support the witness's credibility.

(As amended Mar. 2, 1987, eff. Oct. 1, 1987; Apr. 26, 2011, eff. Dec. 1, 2011.)

RESTYLED RULE 610 COMMITTEE NOTE

The language of Rule 610 has been amended as part of the restyling of the Evidence Rules to make them more easily understood and to make style and terminology consistent throughout the rules. These changes are intended to be stylistic only. There is no intent to change any result in any ruling on evidence admissibility.

Section references, McCormick 7th ed.

§ 46

Note by Federal Judicial Center

The rule enacted by the Congress is the rule prescribed by the Supreme Court without change.

Advisory Committee's Note

56 F.R.D. 183, 272

While the rule forecloses inquiry into the religious beliefs or opinions of a witness for the purpose of showing that his character for truthfulness is affected by their nature, an inquiry for the purpose of showing interest or bias because of them is not within the prohibition. Thus disclosure of affiliation with a church which is a party to the litigation would be allowable under the rule. Cf. Tucker v. Reil, 51 Ariz. 357, 77 P.2d 203 (1938). To the same effect, though less specifically worded, is California Evidence Code § 789. See 3 Wigmore § 936.

1987 Amendment Committee Note

The amendment is technical. No substantive change is intended.

Rule 611. Mode and Order of Examining Witnesses and Presenting Evidence

(a) Control by the Court; Purposes. The court should exercise reasonable control over the mode and order of examining witnesses and presenting evidence so as to:

(1) make those procedures effective for determining the truth;

(2) avoid wasting time; and

(3) protect witnesses from harassment or undue embarrassment.

(b) Scope of Cross-Examination. Cross-examination should not go beyond the subject matter of the direct examination and matters affecting the witness's credibility. The court may allow inquiry into additional matters as if on direct examination.

(c) Leading Questions. Leading questions should not be used on direct examination except as necessary to develop the witness's testimony. Ordinarily, the court should allow leading questions:

(1) on cross-examination; and

(2) when a party calls a hostile witness, an adverse party, or a witness identified with an adverse party.

(As amended Mar. 2, 1987, eff. Oct. 1, 1987; Apr. 26, 2011, eff. Dec. 1, 2011.)

RESTYLED RULE 611 COMMITTEE NOTE

The language of Rule 611 has been amended as part of the restyling of the Evidence Rules to make them more easily understood and to make style and terminology consistent throughout the rules. These changes are intended to be stylistic only. There is no intent to change any result in any ruling on evidence admissibility.

REPORTER'S COMMENT ON RESTYLED RULE 611

One of the goals of the Restyling Project was to eliminate the use of the passive voice. So for example, a phrase like "the evidence may be admissible" should be changed because it doesn't refer to an actor. Use of the active voice would change it to "the court may admit the evidence"—and so forth. But as any drafter knows, the passive voice is sometimes useful—indeed necessary—when it is unclear who if anyone has the responsibility for acting. Rule 611(b) is an example. The original states that "cross-examination should be limited to the subject matter of the direct examination . . . " But by whom? The restylist proposed changing this language to "the court should limit cross-examination" to the subject matter of the direct. But the Advisory Committee thought that the active voice mischaracterized how Rule 611(b) works in practice—it is really a collective effort of the parties and the court to apply a rule of thumb. Moreover, a statement that the court "should" limit the scope of cross-examination creates tension with the second sentence of the rule, which states that the court has discretion to expand the scope of cross-examination. To say the court "should" limit the scope but "may" expand it arguably has the rule working at cross-purposes and micromanages the court. For all these reasons, the Advisory Committee determined that a change to the active voice would actually change the substance of the rule—it would alter the way the rule is applied in the courts. Accordingly, the passive voice is retained in Rule 611(b).

Section references, McCormick 7th ed.

§§ 5–9, §§ 19–32

Note by Federal Judicial Center

Subdivision (a) of the rule enacted by the Congress is the subdivision prescribed by the Supreme Court, amended only by substituting "court" in place of "judge."

Subdivision (b) of the rule enacted by the Congress is substantially different from the subdivision prescribed by the Supreme Court. The nature of the changes and the reasons therefor are stated in the Report of the House Committee on the Judiciary.

The first two sentences of subdivision (c) of the rule enacted by the Congress are the same as prescribed by the Supreme Court. The third sentence has been amended in the manner and for the reasons stated in the Report of the House Committee on the Judiciary.

Advisory Committee's Note

56 F.R.D. 183, 273

Subdivision (a). Spelling out detailed rules to govern the mode and order of interrogating witnesses and presenting evidence is neither desirable nor feasible. The ultimate responsibility for the effective working of the adversary system rests with the judge. The rule sets forth the objectives which he should seek to attain.

Item (1) restates in broad terms the power and obligation of the judge as developed under common law principles. It covers such concerns as whether testimony shall be in the form of a free narrative or responses to specific questions, McCormick § 5, the order of calling witnesses and presenting evidence, 6 Wigmore § 1867, the use of demonstrative evidence, McCormick § 179, and the many other questions arising during the course of a trial which can be solved only by the judge's common sense and fairness in view of the particular circumstances.

Item (2) is addressed to avoidance of needless consumption of time, a matter of daily concern in the disposition of cases. A companion piece is found in the discretion vested in the judge to exclude evidence as a waste of time in Rule 403(b). **[Editor's Note: The reference is to Rule 403. There is no Rule 403(b).]**

Item (3) calls for a judgment under the particular circumstances whether interrogation tactics entail harassment or undue embarrassment. Pertinent circumstances include the importance of the testimony, the nature of the inquiry, its relevance to credibility, waste of time, and confusion. McCormick § 42. In Alford v. United States, 282 U.S. 687, 694, 51 S.Ct. 218, 75 L.Ed. 624 (1931), the Court pointed out that, while the trial judge should protect the witness from questions which "go beyond the bounds of proper cross-examination merely to harass, annoy or humiliate," this protection by no means forecloses efforts to discredit the witness. Reference to the transcript of the prosecutor's cross-examination in Berger v. United States, 295 U.S. 78, 55 S.Ct. 629, 79 L.Ed. 1314 (1935), serves to lay at rest any doubts as to the need for judicial control in this area.

The inquiry into specific instances of conduct of a witness allowed under Rule 608(b) is, of course, subject to this rule.

Subdivision (b). [Editor's Note: The Advisory Committee's version of Rule 611(b) called for wide open cross-examination on any relevant issue. Congress rejected this proposal and adopted a rule limiting the scope of the cross-examination to the subject matter of the direct, with the trial court having discretion to broaden the scope. The Advisory Committee's note makes the case for the Committee's proposal.]

The tradition in the federal courts and in numerous state courts has been to limit the scope of cross-examination to matters testified to on direct, plus matters bearing upon the credibility of the witness. Various reasons have been advanced to justify the rule of limited cross-examination. (1) A party vouches for his own witness but only to the extent of matters elicited on direct. Resurrection Gold Mining Co. v. Fortune Gold Mining Co., 129 Fed. 668, 675 (8th Cir. 1904), quoted in Maguire, Weinstein, et al., Cases on Evidence 277, n. 38 (5th ed. 1965). But the concept of vouching is discredited, and Rule 607 rejects it. (2) A party cannot ask his own witness leading questions. This is a problem properly solved in terms of what is necessary for a proper development of the testimony rather than by a mechanistic formula similar to the vouching concept. See discussion under subdivision (c). (3) A practice of limited cross-examination promotes orderly presentation of the case. Finch v. Weiner, 109 Conn. 616, 145 Atl. 31 (1929). While this latter reason has merit, the matter is essentially one of the order of presentation and not one in which involvement at the appellate level is likely to prove fruitful. See for example, Moyer v. Aetna Life Ins. Co., 126 F.2d 141 (3rd Cir. 1942); Butler v. New York Central R. Co., 253 F.2d 281 (7th Cir. 1958); United States v. Johnson, 285 F.2d 35 (9th Cir. 1960); Union Automobile Indemnity Ass'n v. Capitol Indemnity Ins. Co., 310 F.2d 318 (7th Cir. 1962). In evaluating these considerations, McCormick says:

> The foregoing considerations favoring the wide-open or restrictive rules may well be thought to be fairly evenly balanced. There is another factor, however, which seems to swing the balance overwhelmingly in favor of the wide-open rule. This is the consideration of economy of time and energy. Obviously, the wide-open rule presents little or no opportunity for dispute in its application. The restrictive practice in all its forms, on the other hand, is productive in many court rooms, of continual bickering over the choice of the numerous variations of the 'scope of the direct' criterion, and of their application to particular cross-questions. These controversies are often reventilated on appeal, and reversals for error in their determination are frequent. Observance of these vague and ambiguous restrictions is a matter of constant and hampering concern to the cross-examiner. If these efforts, delays and misprisions were the necessary incidents to the guarding of substantive rights or the fundamentals of fair trial, they might be worth the cost. As the price of the choice of an obviously debatable regulation of the order of evidence, the sacrifice seems misguided. The American Bar Association's Committee for the Improvement of the Law of Evidence for the year 1937–38 said this:

>> "The rule limiting cross-examination to the precise subject of the direct examination is probably the most frequent rule (except the Opinion rule) leading in the trial practice today to refined and technical quibbles which obstruct the progress of the trial, confuse the jury, and give rise to appeal on technical grounds only. Some of the instances in which Supreme Courts have ordered new trials for the mere transgression of this rule about the order of evidence have been astounding.

>> We recommend that the rule allowing questions upon any part of the issue known to the witness . . . be adopted . . . "

McCormick, § 27, p. 51. See also 5 Moore's Federal Practice para. 43.10 (2nd ed. 1964).

The provision of the second sentence, that the judge may in the interests of justice limit inquiry into new matters on cross-examination, is designed for those situations in which the result otherwise would be confusion, complication, or protraction of the case, not as a matter of rule but as demonstrable in the actual development of the particular case. The rule does not purport to determine the extent to which an accused who elects to testify thereby waives his privilege against self-incrimination. The question is a constitutional one, rather than a mere matter of administering the trial. Under Simmons v. United States, 390 U.S. 377 (1968), no general waiver occurs when the accused testifies on such preliminary matters as the validity of a search and seizure or the admissibility of a confession. Rule 1–04(d) [104(d)], *supra.* When he testifies on the merits, however, can he foreclose inquiry into an aspect or element of the crime by avoiding it on direct? The affirmative answer given in Tucker v. United States, 5 F.2d 818 (8th Cir. 1925), is inconsistent with the description of the waiver as extending to "all other relevant facts" in Johnson v. United States, 318 U.S. 189, 195 (1943). *See also* Brown v. United States, 356 U.S. 148 (1958). The situation of an accused who desires to testify on some but not all counts of a multiple-count indictment is one to be approached, in the first instance at least, as a problem of severance under Rule 14 of the Federal Rules of Criminal Procedure. Cross v. United States, 335 F.2d 987 (D.C.Cir. 1964). Cf. United States v. Baker, 262 F.Supp. 657, 686 (D.D.C. 1966). In all events, the extent of the waiver of the privilege against self-incrimination ought not to be determined as a by-product of a rule on scope of cross-examination.

Report of House Committee on the Judiciary on Rule 611(b)

House Comm. on Judiciary, Fed.Rules of Evidence, H.R.Rep. No. 650, 93d Cong., 1st Sess., p. 12 (1973); 1974 U.S.Code Cong. & Ad.News 7075, 7085

As submitted by the Court, Rule 611(b) provided:

A witness may be cross-examined on any matter relevant to any issue in the case, including credibility. In the interests of justice, the judge may limit cross-examination with respect to matters not testified to on direct examination.

The Committee amended this provision to return to the rule which prevails in the federal courts and thirty-nine State jurisdictions. As amended, the Rule is in the text of the 1969 Advisory Committee draft. It limits cross-examination to credibility and to matters testified to on direct examination, unless the judge permits more, in which event the cross-examiner must proceed as if on direct examination. This traditional rule facilitates orderly presentation by each party at trial. Further, in light of existing discovery procedures, there appears to be no need to abandon the traditional rule.

Report of Senate Committee on the Judiciary on Rule 611(b)

Senate Comm. on Judiciary, Fed.Rules of Evidence, S.Rep. No. 1277, 93d Cong., 2d Sess., p. 25 (1974); 1974 U.S.Code Cong. & Ad.News 7051, 7071

Rule 611(b) as submitted by the Supreme Court permitted a broad scope of cross-examination: "cross-examination on any matter relevant to any issue in the case" unless the judge, in the interests of justice, limited the scope of cross-examination.

The House narrowed the Rule to the more traditional practice of limiting cross-examination to the subject matter of direct examination (and credibility), but with discretion in the judge to permit inquiry into additional matters in situations where that would aid in the development of the evidence or otherwise facilitate the conduct of the trial.

The committee agrees with the House amendment. Although there are good arguments in support of broad cross-examination from perspectives of developing all relevant evidence, we believe the factors of insuring an orderly and predictable development of the evidence weigh in favor of the narrower rule, especially when discretion is given to the trial judge to permit inquiry into additional matters. The committee expressly approves this discretion and believes it will permit sufficient flexibility allowing a broader scope of cross-examination whenever appropriate.

The House amendment providing broader discretionary cross-examination permitted inquiry into additional matters only as if on direct examination. As a general rule, we concur with this limitation, however, we would understand that this limitation would not preclude the utilization of leading questions if the conditions of subsection (c) of this rule were met, bearing in mind the judge's discretion in any case to limit the scope of cross-examination.

Further, the committee has received correspondence from Federal judges commenting on the applicability of this rule to section 1407 of title 28. It is the committee's judgment that this rule as reported by the House is flexible enough to provide sufficiently broad cross-examination in appropriate situations in multidistrict litigation.

Advisory Committee's Note on Rule 611(c)

56 F.R.D. 183, 275

Subdivision (c). The rule continues the traditional view that the suggestive powers of the leading question are as a general proposition undesirable. Within this tradition, however, numerous exceptions have achieved recognition: The witness who is hostile, unwilling, or biased; the child witness or the adult with communication problems; the witness whose recollection is exhausted; and undisputed preliminary matters. 3 Wigmore §§ 774–778. An almost total unwillingness to reverse for infractions has been manifested by appellate courts. See cases cited in 3 Wigmore § 770. The matter clearly falls within the area of control by the judge over the mode and order of interrogation and presentation and accordingly is phrased in words of suggestion rather than command.

The rule also conforms to tradition in making the use of leading questions on cross-examination a matter of right. The purpose of the qualification "ordinarily" is to furnish a basis for denying the use of leading questions when the cross-examination is cross-examination in form only and not in fact, as for example the "cross-examination" of a party by his own counsel after being called by the opponent (savoring more of re-direct) or of an insured defendant who proves to be friendly to the plaintiff.

The final sentence deals with categories of witnesses automatically regarded and treated as hostile. Rule 43(b) of the Federal Rules of Civil Procedure has included only "an adverse party or an officer, director, or managing agent of a public or private corporation or of a partnership or association which is an adverse party." This limitation virtually to persons whose statements would stand as admissions is believed to be an unduly narrow concept of those who may safely be regarded as hostile without further demonstration. See, for example, Maryland Casualty Co. v. Kador, 225 F.2d 120 (5th Cir. 1955), and Degelos v. Fidelity and Casualty Co., 313 F.2d 809 (5th Cir. 1963), holding despite the language of Rule 43(b) that an insured fell within it, though not a party in an action under the Louisiana direct action statute. The phrase of the rule, "witness identified with" an adverse party, is designed to enlarge the category of persons thus callable.

Report of House Committee on the Judiciary on Rule 611(c)

House Comm. on Judiciary, Fed.Rules of Evidence, H.R.Rep. No. 650, 93d Cong., 1st Sess., p. 12 (1973); 1974 U.S.Code Cong. & Ad.News 7075, 7086

The third sentence of Rule 611(c) as submitted by the Court provided that:

In civil cases, a party is entitled to call an adverse party or witness identified with him and interrogate by leading questions.

The Committee amended this Rule to permit leading questions to be used with respect to any hostile witness, not only an adverse party or person identified with such adverse party. The Committee also substituted the word "When" for the phrase "In civil cases" to reflect the possibility that in criminal cases a defendant may be entitled to call witnesses identified with the government, in which event the Committee believed the defendant should be permitted to inquire with leading questions.

Report of Senate Committee on the Judiciary on Rule 611(c)

Senate Comm. on Judiciary, Fed.Rules of Evidence, S.Rep. No. 1277, 93d Cong., 2d Sess., p. 25 (1974); 1974 U.S.Code Cong. & Ad.News 7051, 7072

As submitted by the Supreme Court, the rule provided: "In civil cases, a party is entitled to call an adverse party or witness identified with him and interrogate by leading questions."

The final sentence of subsection (c) was amended by the House for the purpose of clarifying the fact that a "hostile witness"—that is a witness who is hostile in fact—could be subject to interrogation by leading questions. The rule as submitted by the Supreme Court declared certain witnesses hostile as a matter of law and thus subject to interrogation by leading questions without any showing of hostility in fact. These were adverse parties or witnesses identified with adverse parties. However, the wording of the first sentence of subsection (c) while generally prohibiting the use of leading questions on direct examination, also provides "except as may be necessary to develop his testimony." Further, the first paragraph of the Advisory Committee note explaining the subsection makes clear that they intended that leading questions could be asked of a hostile witness or a witness who was unwilling or biased and even though that witness was not associated with an adverse party. Thus, we question whether the House amendment was necessary.

However, concluding that it was not intended to affect the meaning of the first sentence of the subsection and was intended solely to clarify the fact that leading questions are permissible in the interrogation of a witness, who is hostile in fact, the committee accepts that House amendment.

The final sentence of this subsection was also amended by the House to cover criminal as well as civil cases. The committee accepts this amendment, but notes that it may be difficult in criminal cases to determine when a witness is "identified with an adverse party," and thus the rule should be applied with caution.

1987 Amendment Committee Note

The amendment is technical. No substantive change is intended.

Rule 612. Writing Used to Refresh a Witness's Memory

(a) Scope. This rule gives an adverse party certain options when a witness uses a writing to refresh memory:

(1) while testifying; or

(2) before testifying, if the court decides that justice requires the party to have those options.

(b) Adverse Party's Options; Deleting Unrelated Matter. Unless 18 U.S.C. § 3500 provides otherwise in a criminal case, an adverse party is entitled to have the writing produced at the hearing, to inspect it, to cross-examine the witness about it, and to introduce in evidence any portion that relates to the witness's testimony. If the producing party claims that the writing includes unrelated matter, the court must examine the writing in camera, delete any unrelated portion, and order that the rest be delivered to the adverse party. Any portion deleted over objection must be preserved for the record.

(c) Failure to Produce or Deliver the Writing. If a writing is not produced or is not delivered as ordered, the court may issue any appropriate order. But if the prosecution does not comply in a criminal case, the court must strike the witness's testimony or—if justice so requires—declare a mistrial.

(As amended Mar. 2, 1987, eff. Oct. 1, 1987; Apr. 26, 2011, eff. Dec. 1, 2011.)

RESTYLED RULE 612 COMMITTEE NOTE

The language of Rule 612 has been amended as part of the restyling of the Evidence Rules to make them more easily understood and to make style and terminology consistent throughout the rules. These changes are intended to be stylistic only. There is no intent to change any result in any ruling on evidence admissibility.

REPORTER'S COMMENT ON RESTYLED RULE 612

Rule 612 is a poster-child for restyling. Just looking at the original version made one reluctant to read it. It was a really long bunch of language. The restylist did a good job of separating out concepts into a logical grouping, and in breaking out the rule so that it is easier to approach and apply. The Advisory Committee readily concluded that a new subdivision structure would provide benefits in reading and applying the Rule that outweighed the cost of disruption in electronic searches.

Section references, McCormick 7th ed.

§ 9, § 93, § 97

Note by Federal Judicial Center

The rule enacted by the Congress is the rule prescribed by the Supreme Court, amended by substituting "court" in place of "judge," with appropriate pronominal change, and in the first sentence, by substituting "the writing" in place of "it" before "produced," and by substituting the phrase "(1) while testifying, or (2) before testifying if the court in its discretion determines it is necessary in the interests of justice" in place of "before or while testifying." The reasons for the latter amendment are stated in the Report of the House Committee on the Judiciary.

Advisory Committee's Note

56 F.R.D. 183, 277

The treatment of writings used to refresh recollection while on the stand is in accord with settled doctrine. McCormick § 9, p. 15. The bulk of the case law has, however, denied the existence of any right to access by the opponent when the writing is used prior to taking the stand, though the judge may have discretion in the matter. Goldman v. United States, 316 U.S. 129, 62 S.Ct. 993, 86 L.Ed. 1322 (1942); Needelman v. United States, 261 F.2d 802 (5th Cir. 1958), cert. dismissed 362 U.S. 600, 80 S.Ct. 960, 4 L.Ed.2d 980, rehearing denied 363 U.S. 858, 80 S.Ct. 1606, 4 L.Ed.2d 1739, Annot., 82 A.L.R.2d 473, 562 and 7 A.L.R.3d 181, 247. An increasing group of cases has repudiated the distinction, People v. Scott, 29 Ill.2d 97, 193 N.E.2d 814 (1963); State v. Mucci, 25 N.J. 423, 136 A.2d 761 (1957); State v. Hunt, 25 N.J. 514, 138 A.2d 1 (1958); State v. Deslovers, 40 R.I. 89, 100 A. 64 (1917), and this position is believed to be correct. As Wigmore put it, "the risk of imposition and the need of safeguard is just as great" in both situations. 3 Wigmore § 762, p. 111. To the same effect is McCormick § 9, p. 17. **[Editor's Note: The Advisory Committee proposal to require disclosure of documents relied on by witnesses before trial was rejected in favor of a provision for disclosure only if the court, in its discretion, finds that it is necessary in the interests of justice.]**

The purpose of the phrase "for the purpose of testifying" is to safeguard against using the rule as a pretext for wholesale exploration of an opposing party's files and to insure that access is limited only to those writings which may fairly be said in fact to have an impact upon the testimony of the witness.

The purpose of the rule is the same as that of the *Jencks* statute, 18 U.S.C. § 3500: to promote the search of credibility and memory. The same sensitivity to disclosure of government files may be involved; hence the rule is expressly made subject to the statute, subdivision (a) of which provides: "In any criminal prosecution brought by the United States, no statement or report in the possession of the United States which was made by a Government witness or prospective Government witness (other than the defendant) shall be the subject of subpena, discovery, or inspection until said witness has testified on direct examination in the trial of the case." Items falling within the purview of the statute are producible only as provided by its terms, Palermo v. United States, 360 U.S. 343, 351 (1959), and disclosure under the rule is limited similarly by the statutory conditions. With this limitation in mind, some differences of application may be noted. The *Jencks* statute applies only to statements of witnesses; the rule is not so limited. The statute applies only to criminal cases; the rule applies to all cases. The statute applies only to government witnesses; the rule applies to all witnesses. The statute contains no requirement that the statement be consulted for purposes of refreshment before or while testifying; the rule so requires. Since many writings would qualify under either statute or rule, a substantial overlap exists, but the identity of procedures makes this of no importance.

The consequences of nonproduction by the government in a criminal case are those of the *Jencks* statute, striking the testimony or in exceptional cases a mistrial. 18 U.S.C. § 3500(d). In other cases these alternatives are unduly limited, and such possibilities as contempt, dismissal, finding issues against the offender, and the like are available. See Rule 16(g) of the Federal Rules of Criminal Procedure and Rule 37(b) of the Federal Rules of Civil Procedure for appropriate sanctions.

Report of House Committee on the Judiciary

House Comm. on Judiciary, Fed.Rules of Evidence, H.R.Rep. No. 650, 93d Cong., 1st Sess., p. 13 (1973); 1974 U.S.Code Cong. & Ad.News 7075, 7086

As submitted to Congress, Rule 612 provided that except as set forth in 18 U.S.C. § 3500, if a witness uses a writing to refresh his memory for the purpose of testifying, "either before or while testifying," an adverse party is entitled to have the writing produced at the hearing, to inspect it, to cross-examine the witness on it, and to introduce in evidence those portions relating to the witness' testimony. The Committee amended the Rule so as still to require the production of writings used by a witness while testifying, but to render the production of writings used by a witness to refresh his memory before testifying discretionary with the court in the interests of justice, as is the case under existing federal law. See Goldman v. United States, 316 U.S. 129 (1942). The Committee considered that permitting an adverse party to require the production of writings used before testifying could result in fishing expeditions among a multitude of papers which a witness may have used in preparing for trial.

The Committee intends that nothing in the Rule be construed as barring the assertion of a privilege with respect to writings used by a witness to refresh his memory.

1987 Amendment Committee Note

The amendment is technical. No substantive change is intended.

Rule 613. Witness's Prior Statement

(a) Showing or Disclosing the Statement During Examination. When examining a witness about the witness's prior statement, a party need not show it or disclose its contents to the witness. But the party must, on request, show it or disclose its contents to an adverse party's attorney.

(b) Extrinsic Evidence of a Prior Inconsistent Statement. Extrinsic evidence of a witness's prior inconsistent statement is admissible only if the witness is given an opportunity to explain or deny the statement and an adverse party is given an opportunity to examine the witness about it, or if justice so requires. This subdivision (b) does not apply to an opposing party's statement under Rule 801(d)(2).

(As amended Mar. 2, 1987, eff. Oct. 1, 1987; Apr. 25, 1988, eff. Nov. 1, 1988; Apr. 26, 2011, eff. Dec. 1, 2011.)

RESTYLED RULE 613 COMMITTEE NOTE

The language of Rule 613 has been amended as part of the restyling of the Evidence Rules to make them more easily understood and to make style and terminology consistent throughout the rules. These changes are intended to be stylistic only. There is no intent to change any result in any ruling on evidence admissibility.

REPORTER'S COMMENT ON RESTYLED RULE 613

The reference in the last sentence of subdivision (b) of the original version to "admissions of a party-opponent" had to be changed because the Evidence Rules no longer call such statements "admissions"—the term "admissions" was found confusing and inaccurate as applied to party-statements. See the Comment to Rule 801.

Section references, McCormick 7th ed.

§§ 34–37

Note by Federal Judicial Center

The rule enacted by the Congress is the rule prescribed by the Supreme Court, amended only by substituting "nor" in the place of "or" in subdivision (a).

Advisory Committee's Note

56 F.R.D. 183, 278

Subdivision (a). The Queen's Case, 2 Br. & B. 284, 129 Eng.Rep. 976 (1820), laid down the requirement that a cross-examiner, prior to questioning the witness about his own prior statement in writing, must first show it to the witness. Abolished by statute in the country of its origin, the requirement nevertheless gained currency in the United States. The rule abolishes this useless impediment, to cross-examination. Ladd, Some Observations on Credibility: Impeachment of Witnesses, 52 Cornell L.Q. 239, 246–247 (1967); McCormick § 28; 4 Wigmore §§ 1259–1260. Both oral and written statements are included.

The provision for disclosure to counsel is designed to protect against unwarranted insinuations that a statement has been made when the fact is to the contrary.

The rule does not defeat the application of Rule 1002 relating to production of the original when the contents of a writing are sought to be proved. Nor does it defeat the application of Rule 26(b)(3) of the Rules of Civil Procedure, as revised, entitling a person on request to a copy of his own statement, though the operation of the latter may be suspended temporarily.

Subdivision (b). The familiar foundation requirement that an impeaching statement first be shown to the witness before it can be proved by extrinsic evidence is preserved but with some modifications. See Ladd, Some Observations on Credibility: Impeachment of Witnesses, 52 Cornell L.Q. 239, 247 (1967). The traditional insistence that the attention of the witness be directed to the statement on cross-examination is relaxed in favor of simply providing the witness an opportunity to explain and the opposite party an opportunity to examine on the statement, with no specification of any particular time or sequence. Under this procedure, several collusive witnesses can be examined before disclosure of a joint prior inconsistent statement. See Comment to California Evidence Code § 770. Also, dangers of oversight are reduced. See McCormick § 37, p. 68.

In order to allow for such eventualities as the witness becoming unavailable by the time the statement is discovered, a measure of discretion is conferred upon the judge. Similar provisions are found in California Evidence Code § 770 and New Jersey Evidence Rule 22(b).

Under principles of *expression unius* the rule does not apply to impeachment by evidence of prior inconsistent conduct. The use of inconsistent statements to impeach a hearsay declaration is treated in Rule 806.

1987 Amendment Committee Note

The amendments are technical. No substantive change is intended.

1988 Amendment Committee Note

The amendment is technical. No substantive change is intended.

Rule 614. Court's Calling or Examining a Witness

(a) Calling. The court may call a witness on its own or at a party's request. Each party is entitled to cross-examine the witness.

(b) Examining. The court may examine a witness regardless of who calls the witness.

(c) Objections. A party may object to the court's calling or examining a witness either at that time or at the next opportunity when the jury is not present.

(As amended Apr. 26, 2011; eff. Dec. 1, 2011.)

RESTYLED RULE 614 COMMITTEE NOTE

The language of Rule 614 has been amended as part of the restyling of the Evidence Rules to make them more easily understood and to make style and terminology consistent throughout the rules. These changes are intended to be stylistic only. There is no intent to change any result in any ruling on evidence admissibility.

Section references, McCormick 7th ed.

§ 8

Note by Federal Judicial Center

The rule enacted by the Congress is the rule prescribed by the Supreme Court, amended only by substituting "court" in place of "judge," with conforming pronominal changes.

Advisory Committee's Note

56 F.R.D. 183, 279

Subdivision (a). While exercised more frequently in criminal than in civil cases, the authority of the judge to call witnesses is well established. McCormick § 8, p. 14; Maguire, Weinstein, et al., Cases on Evidence 303–304 (5th ed. 1965); 9 Wigmore § 2484. One reason for the practice, the old rule against impeaching one's own witness, no longer exists by virtue of Rule 607, *supra*. Other reasons remain, however, to justify the continuation of the practice of calling court's witnesses. The right to cross-examine, with all it implies, is assured. The tendency of juries to associate a witness with the party calling him, regardless of technical aspects of vouching, is avoided. And the judge is not imprisoned within the case as made by the parties.

Subdivision (b). The authority of the judge to question witnesses is also well established. McCormick § 8, pp. 12–13; Maguire, Weinstein, et al., Cases on Evidence 737–739 (5th ed. 1965); 3 Wigmore § 784. The authority is, of course, abused when the judge abandons his proper role and assumes that of advocate, but the manner in which interrogation should be conducted and the proper extent of its exercise are not susceptible of formulation in a rule. The omission in no sense precludes courts of review from continuing to reverse for abuse.

Subdivision (c). The provision relating to objections is designed to relieve counsel of the embarrassment attendant upon objecting to questions by the judge in the presence of the jury, while at the same time assuring that objections are made in apt time to afford the opportunity to take possible corrective measures. Compare the "automatic" objection feature of Rule 605 when the judge is called as a witness.

Rule 615. Excluding Witnesses

At a party's request, the court must order witnesses excluded so that they cannot hear other witnesses' testimony. Or the court may do so on its own. But this rule does not authorize excluding:

> **(a)** a party who is a natural person;

> **(b)** an officer or employee of a party that is not a natural person, after being designated as the party's representative by its attorney;

> **(c)** a person whose presence a party shows to be essential to presenting the party's claim or defense; or

> **(d)** a person authorized by statute to be present.

(As amended Mar. 2, 1987, eff. Oct. 1, 1987; Apr. 25, 1988, eff. Nov. 1, 1988; Nov. 18, 1988, Pub.L. 100–690, Title VII, § 7075(a), 102 Stat. 4405; Apr. 24, 1998, eff. Dec. 1, 1998; Apr. 26, 2011, eff. Dec. 1, 2011.)

RESTYLED RULE 615 COMMITTEE NOTE

The language of Rule 615 has been amended as part of the restyling of the Evidence Rules to make them more easily understood and to make style and terminology consistent throughout the rules. These changes are intended to be stylistic only. There is no intent to change any result in any ruling on evidence admissibility.

REPORTER'S COMMENT ON RESTYLED RULE 615

The restyling changed the original, numbered subdivisions to lettered subdivisions. Why? Because the standard convention in all rulemaking is the following sequence: number, small letter, number, capital letter—*e.g.*, Rule 801(d)(2)(A). Unfortunately, the original rules were numbered haphazardly—*see, e.g.*, this rule and Rule 803, which follows a number with a number. The Restyling Project resolved to apply conventional numbering sequences in the Evidence Rules—at least where that would not be too disruptive to electronic searches and basic understandings. As you will see, the numbering in Rule 803 has not been changed as it was considered to be a significant disruption to an important and oft-cited set of rules.

Section references, McCormick 7th ed.

§ 50

Note by Federal Judicial Center

The rule enacted by the Congress is the rule prescribed by the Supreme Court, amended only by substituting "court," in place of "judge," with conforming pronominal changes.

Advisory Committee's Note

56 F.R.D. 183, 280

The efficacy of excluding or sequestering witnesses has long been recognized as a means of discouraging and exposing fabrication, inaccuracy, and collusion. 6 Wigmore §§ 1837–1838. The authority of the judge is admitted, the only question being whether the matter is committed to his discretion or one of right. The rule takes the latter position. No time is specified for making the request.

Several categories of persons are excepted. (1) Exclusion of persons who are parties would raise serious problems of confrontation and due process. Under accepted practice they are not subject to exclusion. 6 Wigmore § 1841. (2) As the equivalent of the right of a natural-person party to be present, a party which is not a natural person is entitled to have a representative present. Most of the cases have involved allowing a police officer who has been in charge of an investigation to remain in court despite the fact that he will be a witness. United States v. Infanzon, 235 F.2d 318 (2d Cir. 1956); Portomene v. United States, 221 F.2d 582 (5th Cir. 1955); Powell v. United States, 208 F.2d 618 (6th Cir. 1953); Jones v. United States, 252 F.Supp. 781 (W.D.Okl. 1966). Designation of the representative by the attorney rather than by the client may at first glance appear to be an inversion of the attorney-client relationship, but it may be assumed that the attorney will follow the wishes of the client, and the solution is simple and workable. See California Evidence Code § 777. (3) The category contemplates such persons as an agent who handled the transaction being litigated or an expert needed to advise counsel in the management of the litigation. See 6 Wigmore § 1841, n. 4.

Report of Senate Committee on the Judiciary

Senate Comm. on Judiciary, Fed.Rules of Evidence, S.Rep. No. 1277, 93d Cong., 2d Sess., p. 26 (1974); 1974 U.S.Code Cong. & Ad.News 7051, 7072

Many district courts permit government counsel to have an investigative agent at counsel table throughout the trial although the agent is or may be a witness. The practice is permitted as an exception to the rule of exclusion and compares with the situation defense counsel finds himself in—he always has the client with him to consult during the trial. The investigative agent's presence may be extremely important to government counsel, especially when the case is complex or involves some specialized subject matter. The agent, too, having lived with the case for a long time, may be able to assist in meeting trial surprises where the best-prepared counsel would otherwise have difficulty. Yet, it would not seem the Government could often meet the burden under rule 615 of showing that the agent's presence is essential. Furthermore, it could be dangerous to use the agent as a witness as early in the case as possible, so that he might then help counsel as a nonwitness, since the agent's testimony could be needed in rebuttal. Using another, nonwitness agent from the same investigative agency would not generally meet government counsel's needs.

This problem is solved if it is clear that investigative agents are within the group specified under the second exception made in the rule, for "an officer or employee of a party which is not a natural person designated as its representative by its attorney." It is our understanding that this was the intention of the House committee. It is certainly this committee's construction of the rule.

1987 Amendment Committee Note

The amendment is technical. No substantive change is intended.

1988 Amendment Committee Note

The amendment is technical. No substantive change is intended.

1998 Amendment Committee Note

The amendment is in response to: (1) the Victim's Rights and Restitution Act of 1990, 42 U.S.C. § 10606, which guarantees, within certain limits, the right of a crime victim to attend the trial; and (2) the Victim Rights Clarification Act of 1997 (18 U.S.C. § 3510).

ARTICLE VII. OPINIONS AND EXPERT TESTIMONY

Rule 701. Opinion Testimony by Lay Witnesses

If a witness is not testifying as an expert, testimony in the form of an opinion is limited to one that is:

(a) rationally based on the witness's perception;

(b) helpful to clearly understanding the witness's testimony or to determining a fact in issue; and

(c) not based on scientific, technical, or other specialized knowledge within the scope of Rule 702.

(As amended Mar. 2, 1987, eff. Oct. 1, 1987; Apr. 17, 2000, eff. Dec. 1, 2000; Apr. 26, 2011.)

RESTYLED RULE 701 COMMITTEE NOTE

The language of Rule 701 has been amended as part of the general restyling of the Evidence Rules to make them more easily understood and to make style and terminology consistent throughout the rules. These changes are intended to be stylistic only. There is no intent to change any result in any ruling on evidence admissibility.

The Committee deleted all reference to an "inference" on the grounds that the deletion made the Rule flow better and easier to read, and because any "inference" is covered by the broader term "opinion." Courts have not made substantive decisions on the basis of any distinction between an opinion and an inference. No change in current practice is intended.

REPORTER'S COMMENT ON RESTYLED RULE 701

One goal of restyling is to eliminate superfluous language. The references in original Article VII to "opinions" were usually—but not always—accompanied by a reference to "inferences." The restylist proposed eliminating all the references to inferences on the ground that they were superfluous. The Advisory Committee conducted substantial research into whether opinions and inferences are or could be subject to different treatment as evidence. The Committee determined that there is no evidentiary difference between an opinion and an inference, and more importantly that no reported case had distinguished between opinions and inferences in any respect. An inference is defined as "the process of arriving at some *conclusion* that, though it is not logically derivable from the assumed premises, possesses some degree of probability relative to the premises." That's just a flowery way of saying it is an opinion. The term "opinion" is certainly broader than "inference" but there is no inference that is not an opinion. Therefore the Advisory Committee agreed with the proposal to delete all references to inferences in Article VII. In an excess of caution, the Committee Notes to Rules 701, 703, 704 and 705 were expanded to explain the Committee's reasoning for deleting the references to inferences and to note that no change in practice was intended.

Section references, McCormick 7th ed.

§§ 10–12, § 18

Note by Federal Judicial Center

The rule enacted by the Congress is the rule prescribed by the Supreme Court without change.

Advisory Committee's Note

56 F.R.D. 183, 281

The rule retains the traditional objective of putting the trier of fact in possession of an accurate reproduction of the event.

Limitation (a) is the familiar requirement of first-hand knowledge or observation.

Limitation (b) is phrased in terms of requiring testimony to be helpful in resolving issues. Witnesses often find difficulty in expressing themselves in language which is not that of an opinion or conclusion. While the courts have made concessions in certain recurring situations, necessity as a standard for permitting opinions and conclusions has proved too elusive and too unadaptable to particular situations for purposes of satisfactory judicial administration. McCormick § 11. Moreover, the practical impossibility of determining by rule what is a "fact," demonstrated by a century of litigation of the question of what is a fact for purposes of pleading under the Field Code, extends into evidence also. 7 Wigmore § 1919. The rule assumes that the natural characteristics of the adversary system will generally lead to an acceptable result, since the detailed account carries more conviction than the broad assertion, and a lawyer can be expected to display his witness to the best advantage. If he fails to do so, cross-examination and argument will point up the weakness. See Ladd, Expert Testimony, 5 Vand.L.Rev. 414, 415–417 (1952). If, despite these considerations, attempts are made to introduce meaningless assertions which amount to little more than choosing up sides, exclusion for lack of helpfulness is called for by the rule.

The language of the rule is substantially that of Uniform Rule 56(1). Similar provisions are California Evidence Code § 800; Kansas Code of Civil Procedure § 60–456(a); New Jersey Evidence Rule 56(1).

1987 Amendment Committee Note

The amendments are technical. No substantive change is intended.

2000 Amendment Committee Note

Rule 701 has been amended to eliminate the risk that the reliability requirements set forth in Rule 702 will be evaded through the simple expedient of proffering an expert in lay witness clothing. Under the amendment, a witness' testimony must be scrutinized under the rules regulating expert opinion to the extent that the witness is providing testimony based on scientific, technical, or other specialized knowledge within the scope of Rule 702. *See generally, Asplundh Mfg. Div. v. Benton Harbor Eng'g*, 57 F.3d 1190 (3d Cir. 1995). By channeling testimony that is actually expert testimony to Rule 702, the amendment also ensures that a party will not evade the expert witness disclosure requirements set forth in Fed.R.Civ.P. 26 and Fed.R.Crim.P. 16 by simply calling an expert witness in the guise of a layperson. *See* Joseph, *Emerging Expert Issues Under the 1993 Disclosure Amendments to the Federal Rules of Civil Procedure*, 164 F.R.D. 97, 108 (1996) (noting that "there is no good reason to allow what is essentially surprise expert testimony." and that "the Court should be vigilant to preclude manipulative conduct designed to thwart the expert disclosure and discovery process") *See also United States v. Figueroa-Lopez*, 125 F.3d 1241, 1246 (9th Cir. 1997) (law enforcement agents testifying that the defendant's conduct was consistent with that of a drug trafficker could not testify as lay witnesses: to permit such testimony under Rule 701 "subverts the requirements of Federal Rule of Criminal Procedure 16(a)(1)(E)").

The amendment does not distinguish between expert and lay *witnesses*, but rather between expert and lay *testimony*. Certainly it is possible for the same witness to provide both lay and expert testimony in a single case. *See, e.g., United States v. Figueroa-Lopez*, 125 F.3d 1241, 1246 (9th Cir. 1997) (law enforcement agents could testify that the defendant was acting suspiciously, without being qualified as experts; however, the rules on experts were applicable where the agents testified on the basis of extensive experience that the defendant was using code words to refer to drug quantities and prices). The amendment makes clear that any part of a witness' testimony that is based upon scientific, technical, or other specialized knowledge within the scope of Rule 702 is governed by the standards of Rule 702 and the corresponding disclosure requirements of the Civil and Criminal Rules.

The amendment is not intended to affect the "prototypical example[s] of the type of evidence contemplated by the adoption of Rule 701 relat[ing] to the appearance of persons or things, identity, the manner of conduct, competency of a person, degrees of light or darkness, sound, size, weight, distance, and an endless number of items that cannot be described factually in words apart from inferences." *Asplundh Mfg. Div. v. Benton Harbor Eng'g*, 57 F.3d 1190, 1196 (3d Cir. 1995).

For example, most courts have permitted the owner or officer of a business to testify to the value or projected profits of the business. without the necessity of qualifying the witness as an accountant, appraiser, or similar expert. *See, e.g., Lightning Lube, Inc. v. Witco Corp.* 4 F.3d 1153 (3d Cir. 1993) (no abuse of discretion in permitting the plaintiff's owner to give lay opinion testimony as to damages, as it was based on his knowledge and participation in the day-to-day affairs of the business). Such opinion testimony is admitted not because of experience, training or specialized knowledge within the realm of an expert, but because of the particularized knowledge that the witness has by virtue of his or her position in the business. The amendment does not purport to change this analysis. Similarly, courts have permitted lay witnesses to testify that a substance appeared to be a narcotic, so long as a foundation of familiarity with the substance is established. *See, e.g., United States v. Westbrook*, 896 F.2d 330 (8th Cir. 1990) (two lay witnesses who were heavy amphetamine users were properly permitted to testify that a substance was amphetamine; but it was error to permit another witness to make such an identification where she had no experience with amphetamines). Such testimony is not based on specialized knowledge within the scope of Rule 702, but rather is based upon a layperson's personal knowledge. If, however, that witness were to describe how a narcotic was manufactured, or to describe the intricate workings of a narcotic distribution network, then the witness would have to qualify as an expert under Rule 702. *United States v. Figueroa-Lopez, supra.*

The amendment incorporates the distinctions set forth in *State v. Brown*. 836 S.W.2d 530, 549 (1992), a case involving former Tennessee Rule of Evidence 701, a rule that precluded lay witness testimony based on "special knowledge." In *Brown*, the court declared that the distinction between lay and expert witness testimony is that lay testimony "results from a process of reasoning familiar in everyday life," while expert testimony "results from a process of reasoning which can be mastered only by specialists in the field." The court in *Brown* noted that a lay witness with experience could testify that a substance appeared to be blood, but that a witness would have to qualify as an expert before he could testify that bruising around the eyes is indicative of skull trauma. That is the kind of distinction made by the amendment to this Rule.

Rule 702. Testimony by Expert Witnesses

A witness who is qualified as an expert by knowledge, skill, experience, training, or education may testify in the form of an opinion or otherwise if:

 (a) the expert's scientific, technical, or other specialized knowledge will help the trier of fact to understand the evidence or to determine a fact in issue;

 (b) the testimony is based on sufficient facts or data;

 (c) the testimony is the product of reliable principles and methods; and

 (d) the expert has reliably applied the principles and methods to the facts of the case.

(As amended Apr. 17, 2000, eff. Dec. 1, 2000; Apr. 26, 2011, eff. Dec. 1, 2011.)

RESTYLED RULE 702 COMMITTEE NOTE

The language of Rule 702 has been amended as part of the restyling of the Evidence Rules to make them more easily understood and to make style and terminology consistent throughout the rules. These changes are intended to be stylistic only. There is no intent to change any result in any ruling on evidence admissibility.

Section references, McCormick 7th ed.

§§ 12–14, §§ 202–211

Note by Federal Judicial Center

The rule enacted by the Congress is the rule prescribed by the Supreme Court without change.

Advisory Committee's Note

56 F.R.D. 183, 282

An intelligent evaluation of facts is often difficult or impossible without the application of some scientific, technical, or other specialized knowledge. The most common source of this knowledge is the expert witness, although there are other techniques for supplying it.

Most of the literature assumes that experts testify only in the form of opinions. The assumption is logically unfounded. The rule accordingly recognizes that an expert on the stand may give a dissertation or exposition of scientific or other principles relevant to the case, leaving the trier of fact to apply them to the facts. Since much of the criticism of expert testimony has centered upon the hypothetical question, it seems wise to recognize that opinions are not indispensable and to encourage the use of expert testimony in nonopinion form when counsel believes the trier can itself draw the requisite inference. The use of opinions is not abolished by the rule, however. It will continue to be permissible for the expert to take the further step of suggesting the inference which should be drawn from applying the specialized knowledge to the facts. See Rules 703 to 705.

Whether the situation is a proper one for the use of expert testimony is to be determined on the basis of assisting the trier. "There is no more certain test for determining when experts may be used than the common sense inquiry whether the untrained layman would be qualified to determine intelligently and to the best possible degree the particular issue without enlightenment from those having a specialized understanding of the subject involved in the dispute." Ladd, Expert Testimony, 5 Vand.L.Rev. 414, 418 (1952). When opinions are excluded, it is because they are unhelpful and therefore superfluous and a waste of time. 7 Wigmore § 1918.

The rule is broadly phrased. The fields of knowledge which may be drawn upon are not limited merely to the "scientific" and "technical" but extend to all "specialized" knowledge. Similarly, the expert is viewed, not in a narrow sense, but as a person qualified by "knowledge, skill, experience, training, or education." Thus within the scope of the rule are not only experts in the strictest sense of the word, *e.g.* physicians, physicists, and architects, but also the large group sometimes called "skilled" witnesses, such as bankers or landowners testifying to land values.

2000 Amendment Committee Note

Rule 702 has been amended in response to *Daubert v. Merrell Dow Pharmaceuticals, Inc.*, 509 U.S. 579 (1993), and to the many cases applying *Daubert*, including *Kumho Tire Co. v. Carmichael*, 119 S.Ct. 1167 (1999). In *Daubert* the Court charged trial judges with the responsibility of acting as gatekeepers to exclude unreliable expert testimony, and the Court in *Kumho* clarified that this gatekeeper function applies to all expert testimony, not just testimony based in science. *See also Kumho*, 119 S.Ct. at 1178 (citing the Committee Note to the proposed amendment to Rule 702, which had been released for public comment before the date of the *Kumho* decision). The amendment affirms the trial court's role as gatekeeper and provides some general standards that the trial court must use to assess the reliability and helpfulness of proffered expert testimony. Consistently with *Kumho*, the Rule as amended provides that all types of expert testimony present questions of admissibility for the trial court in deciding whether the evidence is reliable and helpful. Consequently, the admissibility of all expert testimony is governed by the principles of Rule 104(a). Under that Rule, the proponent has the burden of establishing that the pertinent admissibility requirements are met by a preponderance of the evidence. *See Bourjaily v. United States*, 483 U.S. 171 (1987).

Daubert set forth a non-exclusive checklist for trial courts to use in assessing the reliability of scientific expert testimony. The specific factors explicated by the *Daubert* Court are (1) whether the expert's technique or theory can be or has been tested—that is, whether the expert's theory can be challenged in some objective sense, or whether it is instead simply a subjective, conclusory approach that cannot reasonably be assessed for reliability; (2) whether the technique or theory has been subject to peer review and publication; (3) the known or potential rate of error of the technique or theory when applied; (4) the existence and maintenance of standards and controls; and (5) whether the technique or theory has been generally accepted in the scientific community. The Court in *Kumho* held that these factors might also be applicable in assessing the reliability of non-scientific expert testimony, depending upon "the particular circumstances of the particular case at issue." 119 S.Ct. at 1175.

No attempt has been made to "codify" these specific factors. *Daubert* itself emphasized that the factors were neither exclusive nor dispositive. Other cases have recognized that not all of the specific *Daubert* factors can apply to every type of expert testimony. In addition to *Kumho*, 119 S.Ct. at 1175, *see Tyus v. Urban Search Management*. 102 F.3d 256 (7th Cir. 1996) (noting that the factors mentioned by the Court in *Daubert* do not neatly apply to expert testimony from a sociologist). *See also Kannankeril v. Terminix Int'l. Inc.*, 128 F.3d 802, 809 (3d Cir. 1997) (holding that lack of peer review or publication was not dispositive where the expert's opinion was supported by "widely accepted scientific knowledge"). The standards set forth in the amendment are broad enough to require consideration of any or all of the specific *Daubert* factors where appropriate.

Courts both before and after *Daubert* have found other factors relevant in determining whether expert testimony is sufficiently reliable to be considered by the trier of fact. These factors include:

(1)   Whether experts are "proposing to testify about matters growing naturally and directly out of research they have conducted independent of the litigation, or whether they have developed their opinions expressly for purposes of testifying." *Daubert v. Merrell Dow Pharmaceuticals, Inc.*, 43 F.3d 1311, 1317 (9th Cir. 1995).

(2)   Whether the expert has unjustifiably extrapolated from an accepted premise to an unfounded conclusion. *See General Elec. Co. v. Joiner*, 522 U.S. 136, 146 (1997) (noting that in some cases a trial court "may conclude that there is simply too great an analytical gap between the data and the opinion proffered").

(3)   Whether the expert has adequately accounted for obvious alternative explanations. *See Claar v. Burlington N.R.R.*, 29 F.3d 499 (9th Cir. 1994) (testimony excluded where the expert failed to consider other obvious causes for the plaintiff's condition). *Compare Ambrosini v. Labarraque*, 101 F.3d 129 (D.C. Cir. 1996) (the possibility of some uneliminated causes presents a question of weight, so long as the most obvious causes have been considered and reasonably ruled out by the expert).

(4)   Whether the expert "is being as careful as he would be in his regular professional work outside his paid litigation consulting." *Sheehan v. Daily Racing Form, Inc.*, 104 F.3d 940, 942 (7th Cir. 1997). *See Kumho Tire Co. v. Carmichael*, 119 S.Ct. 1167, 1176 (1999) (*Daubert* requires the trial court to assure itself that the expert "employs in the courtroom the same level of intellectual rigor that characterizes the practice of an expert in the relevant field").

(5)   Whether the field of expertise claimed by the expert is known to reach reliable results for the type of opinion the expert would give. *See Kumho Tire Co. v. Carmichael*, 119 S.Ct. 1167, 1175 (1999) (*Daubert's* general acceptance factor does not "help show that an expert's testimony is reliable where the discipline itself lacks reliability, as for example, do theories grounded in any so-called generally accepted principles of astrology or necromancy."), *Moore v. Ashland Chemical, Inc.*, 151 F.3d 269 (5th Cir. 1998) (en banc) (clinical doctor was properly precluded from testifying to the toxicological cause of the plaintiff's respiratory problem, where the opinion was not sufficiently grounded in scientific methodology); *Sterling v. Velsicol Chem. Corp.*, 855 F.2d 1188 (6th Cir. 1988) (rejecting testimony based on "clinical ecology" as unfounded and unreliable).

All of these factors remain relevant to the determination of the reliability of expert testimony under the Rule as amended. Other factors may also be relevant. *See Kumho*, 119 S.Ct. 1167, 1176 ("[W]e conclude that the trial judge must have considerable leeway in deciding in a particular case how to go about determining whether particular expert testimony is reliable."). Yet no single factor is necessarily dispositive of the reliability of a particular expert's testimony. *See, e.g., Heller v. Shaw Industries, Inc.*, 167 F.3d 146, 155 (3d Cir. 1999) ("not only must each stage of the expert's testimony be reliable, but each stage must be evaluated practically and flexibly without bright-line exclusionary (or inclusionary) rules."); *Daubert v. Merrell Dow Pharmaceuticals, Inc.*, 43 F.3d 1311, 1317, n.5 (9th Cir. 1995) (noting that some expert disciplines "have the courtroom as a principal theatre of operations" and as to these disciplines "the fact that the expert has developed an expertise principally for purposes of litigation will obviously not be a substantial consideration.").

A review of the caselaw after *Daubert* shows that the rejection of expert testimony is the exception rather than the rule. *Daubert* did not work a "seachange over federal evidence law," and "the trial court's role as gatekeeper is not intended to serve as a replacement for the adversary system." *United States v. 14.38 Acres of Land Situated in Leflore County, Mississippi,* 80 F.3d 1074, 1078 (5th Cir. 1996). As the Court in *Daubert* stated: "Vigorous cross-examination, presentation of contrary evidence, and careful instruction on the burden of proof are the traditional and appropriate means of attacking shaky but admissible evidence." 509 U.S. at 595. Likewise, this amendment is not intended to provide an excuse for an automatic challenge to the testimony of every expert. *See Kumho Tire Co. v. Carmichael,* 119 S.Ct. 1167, 1176 (1999) (noting that the trial judge has the discretion "both to avoid unnecessary 'reliability' proceedings in ordinary cases where the reliability of an expert's methods is properly taken for granted, and to require appropriate proceedings in the less usual or more complex cases where cause for questioning the expert's reliability arises.").

When a trial court, applying this amendment, rules that an expert's testimony is reliable, this does not necessarily mean that contradictory expert testimony is unreliable. The amendment is broad enough to permit testimony that is the product of competing principles or methods in the same field of expertise. *See, e.g., Heller v. Shaw Industries, Inc.,* 167 F.3d 146, 160 (3d Cir. 1999) (expert testimony cannot be excluded simply because the expert uses one test rather than another, when both tests are accepted in the field and both reach reliable results). As the court stated in *In re Paoli R.R. Yard PCB Litigation,* 35 F.3d 717, 744 (3d Cir. 1994), proponents "do not have to demonstrate to the judge by a preponderance of the evidence that the assessments of their experts are correct, they only have to demonstrate by a preponderance of evidence that their opinions are reliable. . . . The evidentiary requirement of reliability is lower than the merits standard of correctness." *See also Daubert v. Merrell Dow Pharmaceuticals, Inc.,* 43 F.3d 1311, 1318 (9th Cir. 1995) (scientific experts might be permitted to testify if they could show that the methods they used were also employed by "a recognized minority of scientists in their field."); *Ruiz-Troche v. Pepsi Cola,* 161 F.3d 77, 85 (1st Cir. 1998) ("*Daubert* neither requires nor empowers trial courts to determine which of several competing scientific theories has the best provenance.").

The Court in *Daubert* declared that the "focus, of course, must be solely on principles and methodology, not on the conclusions they generate." 509 U.S. at 595. Yet as the Court later recognized, "conclusions and methodology are not entirely distinct from one another." *General Elec. Co. v. Joiner,* 522 U.S. 136, 146 (1997). Under the amendment, as under *Daubert,* when an expert purports to apply principles and methods in accordance with professional standards, and yet reaches a conclusion that other experts in the field would not reach, the trial court may fairly suspect that the principles and methods have not been faithfully applied. *See Lust v. Merrell Dow Pharmaceuticals, Inc.,* 89 F.3d 594, 598 (9th Cir. 1996). The amendment specifically provides that the trial court must scrutinize not only the principles and methods used by the expert, but also whether those principles and methods have been properly applied to the facts of the case. As the court noted in *In re Paoli R.R. Yard PCB Litig.,* 35 F.3d 717, 745 (3d Cir. 1994), "*any* step that renders the analysis unreliable . . . renders the expert's testimony inadmissible. *This is true whether the step completely changes a reliable methodology or merely misapplies that methodology.*"

If the expert purports to apply principles and methods to the facts of the case, it is important that this application be conducted reliably. Yet it might also be important in some cases for an expert to educate the factfinder about general principles, without ever attempting to apply these principles to the specific facts of the case. For example, experts might instruct the factfinder on the principles of thermodynamics, or bloodclotting, or on how financial markets respond to corporate reports, without ever knowing about or trying to tie their testimony into the facts of the case. The amendment does not alter the venerable practice of using expert testimony to educate the factfinder on general principles. For this kind of generalized testimony, Rule 702 simply requires that: (1) the expert be qualified; (2) the testimony address a subject matter on which the factfinder can be assisted by an expert; (3) the testimony be reliable; and (4) the testimony "fit" the facts of the case.

As stated earlier, the amendment does not distinguish between scientific and other forms of expert testimony. The trial court's gatekeeping function applies to testimony by any expert. *See Kumho Tire Co. v. Carmichael*, 119 S.Ct. 1167, 1171 (1999) ("We conclude that *Daubert's* general holding—setting forth the trial judge's general 'gatekeeping' obligation—applies not only to testimony based on 'scientific' knowledge, but also to testimony based on 'technical' and 'other specialized' knowledge."). While the relevant factors for determining reliability will vary from expertise to expertise, the amendment rejects the premise that an expert's testimony should be treated more permissively simply because it is outside the realm of science. An opinion from an expert who is not a scientist should receive the same degree of scrutiny for reliability as an opinion from an expert who purports to be a scientist. *See Watkins v. Telsmith, Inc.*, 121 F.3d 984, 991 (5th Cir. 1997) ("[I]t seems exactly backwards that experts who purport to rely on general engineering principles and practical experience might escape screening by the district court simply by stating that their conclusions were not reached by any particular method or technique."). Some types of expert testimony will be more objectively verifiable, and subject to the expectations of falsifiability, peer review, and publication, than others. Some types of expert testimony will not rely on anything like a scientific method, and so will have to be evaluated by reference to other standard principles attendant to the particular area of expertise. The trial judge in all cases of proffered expert testimony must find that it is properly grounded, well-reasoned, and not speculative before it can be admitted. The expert's testimony must be grounded in an accepted body of learning or experience in the expert's field, and the expert must explain how the conclusion is so grounded. *See, e.g.,* American College of Trial Lawyers, *Standards and Procedures for Determining the Admissibility of Expert Testimony after Daubert*, 157 F.R.D. 571, 579 (1994) ("[W]hether the testimony concerns economic principles, accounting standards, property valuation or other non-scientific subjects, it should be evaluated by reference to the 'knowledge and experience' of that particular field.").

The amendment requires that the testimony must be the product of reliable principles and methods that are reliably applied to the facts of the case. While the terms "principles" and "methods" may convey a certain impression when applied to scientific knowledge, they remain relevant when applied to testimony based on technical or other specialized knowledge. For example, when a law enforcement agent testifies regarding the use of code words in a drug transaction, the principle used by the agent is that participants in such transactions regularly use code words to conceal the nature of their activities. The method used by the agent is the application of extensive experience to analyze the meaning of the conversations. So long as the principles and methods are reliable and applied reliably to the facts of the case, this type of testimony should be admitted.

Nothing in this amendment is intended to suggest that experience alone— or experience in conjunction with other knowledge, skill, training or education— may not provide a sufficient foundation for expert testimony. To the contrary, the text of Rule 702 expressly contemplates that an expert may be qualified on the basis of experience. In certain fields, experience is the predominant, if not sole, basis for a great deal of reliable expert testimony. *See, e.g., United States v. Jones*, 107 F.3d 1147 (6th Cir. 1997) (no abuse of discretion in admitting the testimony of a handwriting examiner who had years of practical experience and extensive training, and who explained his methodology in detail); *Tassin v. Sears Roebuck*, 946 F.Supp. 1241, 1248 (M.D.La. 1996) (design engineer's testimony can be admissible when the expert's opinions "are based on facts, a reasonable investigation, and traditional technical/mechanical expertise, and he provides a reasonable link between the information and procedures he uses and the conclusions he reaches"). *See also Kumho Tire Co. v. Carmichael*, 119 S.Ct. 1167, 1178 (1999) (stating that "no one denies that an expert might draw a conclusion from a set of observations based on extensive and specialized experience.").

If the witness is relying solely or primarily on experience, then the witness must explain how that experience leads to the conclusion reached, why that experience is a sufficient basis for the opinion, and how that experience is reliably applied to the facts. The trial court's gatekeeping function requires more than simply "taking the expert's word for it." *See Daubert v. Merrell Dow Pharmaceuticals, Inc.*, 43 F.3d 1311, 1319 (9th Cir. 1995) ("We've been presented with only the experts' qualifications, their conclusions and their assurances of reliability. Under *Daubert*, that's not enough."). The more subjective and controversial the expert's inquiry, the more likely the testimony should be excluded as unreliable. *See O'Conner v. Commonwealth Edison Co.*, 13 F.3d 1090 (7th Cir. 1994) (expert testimony based on a completely subjective methodology held properly excluded). *See also Kumho Tire Co. v. Carmichael*, 119 S.Ct. 1167, 1176 (1999) ("[I]t will at times be useful to ask even of a witness whose expertise is based purely on experience, say, a perfume tester able to distinguish among 140 odors at a sniff, whether his preparation is of a kind that others in the field would recognize as acceptable.").

Subpart (1) of Rule 702 calls for a quantitative rather than qualitative analysis. The amendment requires that expert testimony be based on sufficient underlying "facts or data." The term "data" is intended to encompass the reliable opinions of other experts. See the original Advisory Committee Note to Rule 703. The language "facts or data" is broad enough to allow an expert to rely on hypothetical facts that are supported by the evidence. *Id.*

When facts are in dispute, experts sometimes reach different conclusions based on competing versions of the facts. The emphasis in the amendment on "sufficient facts or data" is not intended to authorize a trial court to exclude an expert's testimony on the ground that the court believes one version of the facts and not the other.

There has been some confusion over the relationship between Rules 702 and 703. The amendment makes clear that the sufficiency of the basis of an expert's testimony is to be decided under Rule 702. Rule 702 sets forth the overarching requirement of reliability, and an analysis of the sufficiency of the expert's basis cannot be divorced from the ultimate reliability of the expert's opinion. In contrast, the "reasonable reliance" requirement of Rule 703 is a relatively narrow inquiry. When an expert relies on inadmissible information, Rule 703 requires the trial court to determine whether that information is of a type reasonably relied on by other experts in the field. If so, the expert can rely on the information in reaching an opinion. However, the question whether the expert is relying on a *sufficient* basis of information—whether admissible information or not—is governed by the requirements of Rule 702.

The amendment makes no attempt to set forth procedural requirements for exercising the trial court's gatekeeping function over expert testimony. *See* Daniel J. Capra, *The Daubert Puzzle*, 32 Ga.L.Rev. 699, 766 (1998) ("Trial courts should be allowed substantial discretion in dealing with *Daubert* questions; any attempt to codify procedures will likely give rise to unnecessary changes in practice and create difficult questions for appellate review."). Courts have shown considerable ingenuity and flexibility in considering challenges to expert testimony under *Daubert*, and it is contemplated that this will continue under the amended Rule. *See, e.g., Cortes-Irizarry v. Corporacion Insular*, 111 F.3d 184 (1st Cir. 1997) (discussing the application of *Daubert* in ruling on a motion for summary judgment); *In re Paoli R.R. Yard PCB Litig.*, 35 F.3d 717, 736, 739 (3d Cir. 1994) (discussing the use of *in limine* hearings); *Claar v. Burlington N.R.R.*, 29 F.3d 499, 502–05 (9th Cir. 1994) (discussing the trial court's technique of ordering experts to submit serial affidavits explaining the reasoning and methods underlying their conclusions).

The amendment continues the practice of the original Rule in referring to a qualified witness as an "expert." This was done to provide continuity and to minimize change. The use of the term "expert" in the Rule does not, however, mean that a jury should actually be informed that a qualified witness is testifying as an "expert." Indeed, there is much to be said for a practice that prohibits the use of the term "expert" by both the parties and the court at trial. Such a practice "ensures that trial courts do not inadvertently put their stamp of authority" on a witness's opinion, and protects against the jury's being "overwhelmed by the so-called 'experts'." Hon. Charles Richey, *Proposals to Eliminate the Prejudicial Effect of the Use of the Word "Expert" Under the Federal Rules of Evidence in Criminal and Civil Jury Trials*, 154 F.R.D. 537, 559 (1994) (setting forth limiting instructions and a standing order employed to prohibit the use of the term "expert" injury trials).

Rule 703. Bases of an Expert's Opinion Testimony

An expert may base an opinion on facts or data in the case that the expert has been made aware of or personally observed. If experts in the particular field would reasonably rely on those kinds of facts or data in forming an opinion on the subject, they need not be admissible for the opinion to be admitted. But if the facts or data would otherwise be inadmissible, the proponent of the opinion may disclose them to the jury only if their probative value in helping the jury evaluate the opinion substantially outweighs their prejudicial effect.

(As amended Mar. 2, 1987, eff. Oct. 1, 1987; Apr. 17, 2000, eff. Dec. 1, 2000; Apr. 26, 2011, eff. Dec. 1, 2011.)

RESTYLED RULE 703 COMMITTEE NOTE

The language of Rule 703 has been amended as part of the general restyling of the Evidence Rules to make them more easily understood and to make style and terminology consistent throughout the rules. These changes are intended to be stylistic only. There is no intent to change any result in any ruling on evidence admissibility.

The Committee deleted all reference to an "inference" on the grounds that the deletion made the Rule flow better and easier to read, and because any "inference" is covered by the broader term "opinion." Courts have not made substantive decisions on the basis of any distinction between an opinion and an inference. No change in current practice is intended.

REPORTER'S COMMENT ON RESTYLED RULE 703

The references to "inference" throughout original Rule 703 were deleted as superfluous. See the explanation in the Reporter's Comment on Restyled Rule 701. The use of "inference" was especially problematic in original Rule 703 because it was inconsistent. The last sentence of the original rule referred to opinion without referring to inference.

Section references, McCormick 7th ed.

§ 10, §§ 13–16, § 324.3

Note by Federal Judicial Center

The rule enacted by the Congress is the rule prescribed by the Supreme Court without change.

Advisory Committee's Note

56 F.R.D. 183, 283

Facts or data upon which expert opinions are based may, under the rule, be derived from three possible sources. The first is the firsthand observation of the witness, with opinions based thereon traditionally allowed. A treating physician affords an example. Rheingold, The Basis of Medical Testimony, 15 Vand.L.Rev. 473, 489 (1962). Whether he must first relate his observations is treated in Rule 705. The second source, presentation at the trial, also reflects existing practice. The technique may be the familiar hypothetical question or having the expert attend the trial and hear the testimony establishing the facts. Problems of determining what testimony the expert relied upon, when the latter technique is employed and the testimony is in conflict, may be resolved by resort to Rule 705. The third source contemplated by the rule consists of presentation of data to the expert outside of court and other than by his own perception. In this respect the rule is designed to broaden the basis for expert opinions beyond that current in many jurisdictions and to bring the judicial practice into line with the practice of the experts themselves when not in court. Thus a physician in his own practice bases his diagnosis on information from numerous sources and of considerable variety, including statements by patients and relatives, reports and opinions from nurses, technicians and other doctors, hospital records, and X rays. Most of them are admissible in evidence, but only with the expenditure of substantial time in producing and examining various authenticating witnesses. The physician makes life-and-death decisions in reliance upon them. His validation, expertly performed and subject to cross-examination, ought to suffice for judicial purposes. Rheingold, *supra*, at 531; McCormick § 15. A similar provision is California Evidence Code § 801(b).

The rule also offers a more satisfactory basis for ruling upon the admissibility of public opinion poll evidence. Attention is directed to the validity of the techniques employed rather than to relatively fruitless inquiries whether hearsay is involved. See Judge Feinberg's careful analysis in Zippo Mfg. Co. v. Rogers Imports, Inc., 216 F.Supp. 670 (S.D.N.Y. 1963). *See also* Blum et al., The Art of Opinion Research: A Lawyer's Appraisal of an Emerging Service, 24 U.Chi.L.Rev. 1 (1956); Bonynge, Trademark Surveys and Techniques and Their Use in Litigation, 48 A.B.A.J. 329 (1962); Zeisel, The Uniqueness of Survey Evidence, 45 Cornell L.Q. 322 (1960); Annot., 76 A.L.R.2d 919.

If it be feared that enlargement of permissible data may tend to break down the rules of exclusion unduly, notice should be taken that the rule requires that the facts or data "be of a type reasonably relied upon by experts in the particular field." The language would not warrant admitting in evidence the opinion of an "accidentologist" as to the point of impact in an automobile collision based on statements of bystanders, since this requirement is not satisfied. See Comment, Cal.Law Rev.Comm'n, Recommendation Proposing an Evidence Code 148–150 (1965).

1987 Amendment Committee Note

The amendment is technical. No substantive change is intended.

2000 Amendment Committee Note

Rule 703 has been amended to emphasize that when an expert reasonably relies on inadmissible information to form an opinion or inference, the underlying information is not admissible simply because the opinion or inference is admitted. Courts have reached different results on how to treat inadmissible information when it is reasonably relied upon by an expert in forming an opinion or drawing an inference. *Compare United States v. Rollins*, 862 F.2d 1282 (7th Cir. 1988) (admitting, as part of the basis of an FBI agent's expert opinion on the meaning of code language, the hearsay statements of an informant), *with United States v. 0.59 Acres of Land*, 109 F.3d 1493 (9th Cir. 1997) (error to admit hearsay offered as the basis of an expert opinion, without a limiting instruction). Commentators have also taken differing views. *See, e.g.*, Ronald Carlson, *Policing the Bases of Modern Expert Testimony*, 39 Vand.L.Rev. 577 (1986) (advocating limits on the jury's consideration of otherwise inadmissible evidence used as the basis for an expert opinion); Paul Rice, *Inadmissible Evidence as a Basis for Expert Testimony: A Response to Professor Carlson*, 40 Vand.L.Rev. 583 (1987) (advocating unrestricted use of information reasonably relied upon by an expert).

When information is reasonably relied upon by an expert and yet is admissible only for the purpose of assisting the jury in evaluating an expert's opinion, a trial court applying this Rule must consider the information's probative value in assisting the jury to weigh the expert's opinion on the one hand, and the risk of prejudice resulting from the jury's potential misuse of the information for substantive purposes on the other. The information may be disclosed to the jury, upon objection, only if the trial court finds that the probative value of the information in assisting the jury to evaluate the expert's opinion substantially outweighs its prejudicial effect. If the otherwise inadmissible information is admitted under this balancing test, the trial judge must give a limiting instruction upon request, informing the jury that the underlying information must not be used for substantive purposes. *See* Rule 105. In determining the appropriate course, the trial court should consider the probable effectiveness or lack of effectiveness of a limiting instruction under the particular circumstances.

The amendment governs only the disclosure to the jury of information that is reasonably relied on by an expert, when that information is not admissible for substantive purposes. It is not intended to affect the admissibility of an expert's testimony. Nor does the amendment prevent an expert from relying on information that is inadmissible for substantive purposes.

Nothing in this Rule restricts the presentation of underlying expert facts or data when offered by an adverse party. *See* Rule 705. Of course, an adversary's attack on an expert's basis will often open the door to a proponent's rebuttal with information that was reasonably relied upon by the expert, even if that information would not have been discloseable initially under the balancing test provided by this amendment. Moreover, in some circumstances the proponent might wish to disclose information that is relied upon by the expert in order to "remove the sting" from the opponent's anticipated attack, and thereby prevent the jury from drawing an unfair negative inference. The trial court should take this consideration into account in applying the balancing test provided by this amendment.

This amendment covers facts or data that cannot be admitted for any purpose other than to assist the jury to evaluate the expert's opinion. The balancing test provided in this amendment is not applicable to facts or data that are admissible for any other purpose but have not yet been offered for such a purpose at the time the expert testifies.

The amendment provides a presumption against disclosure to the jury of information used as the basis of an expert's opinion and not admissible for any substantive purpose, when that information is offered by the proponent of the expert. In a multi-party case, where one party proffers an expert whose testimony is also beneficial to other parties, each such party should be deemed a "proponent" within the meaning of the amendment.

Rule 704. Opinion on an Ultimate Issue

(a) In General—Not Automatically Objectionable. An opinion is not objectionable just because it embraces an ultimate issue.

(b) Exception. In a criminal case, an expert witness must not state an opinion about whether the defendant did or did not have a mental state or condition that constitutes an element of the crime charged or of a defense. Those matters are for the trier of fact alone.

(As amended Pub.L. 98–473, Title II, § 406, Oct. 12, 1984, 98 Stat. 2067; Apr. 26, 2011, Dec. 1, 2011.)

RESTYLED RULE 704 COMMITTEE NOTE

The language of Rule 704 has been amended as part of the general restyling of the Evidence Rules to make them more easily understood and to make style and terminology consistent throughout the rules. These changes are intended to be stylistic only. There is no intent to change any result in any ruling on evidence admissibility.

The Committee deleted all reference to an "inference" on the grounds that the deletion made the Rule flow better and easier to read, and because any "inference" is covered by the broader term "opinion." Courts have not made substantive decisions on the basis of any distinction between an opinion and an inference. No change in current practice is intended.

REPORTER'S COMMENT ON RESTYLED RULE 704

The references in the original Rule 704(a) to an "inference" were deleted as superfluous. See the explanation in the Reporter's Comment to Restyled Rule 701.

The restylist sought to delete the last sentence of Rule 704(b) on the ground that it was a "redundant intensifier." But the Advisory Committee objected. The Committee was of the opinion that it was useful to emphasize the point that ultimate issues of the defendant's intent are for the jury. For one thing, the sentence has been relied on by trial courts to explain to litigants *why* experts are not permitted to testify to whether the defendant had the requisite mental state to commit the charged crime.

Section references, McCormick 7th ed.

§ 12, § 14, § 206

Editorial Note

Subdivision (a) is the entire rule prescribed by the Supreme Court and enacted without change by Congress when it enacted the Rules of Evidence in 1974 (though subsequently restyled).

Subdivision (b) was added by the Congress in 1984 as a part of the Insanity Defense Reform Act of 1984. P.L. 98–473, Title II, ch. IV, § 406. The legislative history of that provision is set forth below, after the Advisory Committee Note to the original rule.

Advisory Committee's Note

56 F.R.D. 183, 284

[Subdivision (a)—Ed.] The basic approach to opinions, lay and expert, in these rules is to admit them when helpful to the trier of fact. In order to render this approach fully effective and to allay any doubt on the subject, the so-called "ultimate issue" rule is specifically abolished by the instant rule.

The older cases often contained strictures against allowing witnesses to express opinions upon ultimate issues, as a particular aspect of the rule against opinions. The rule was unduly restrictive, difficult of application, and generally served only to deprive the trier of fact of useful information. 7 Wigmore §§ 1920, 1921; McCormick § 12. The basis usually assigned for the rule, to prevent the witness from "usurping the province of the jury," is aptly characterized as "empty rhetoric." 7 Wigmore § 1920, p. 17. Efforts to meet the felt needs of particular situations led to odd verbal circumlocutions which were said not to violate the rule. Thus a witness could express his estimate of the criminal responsibility of an accused in terms of sanity or insanity, but not in terms of ability to tell right from wrong or other more modern standard. And in cases of medical causation, witnesses were sometimes required to couch their opinions in cautious phrases of "might or could," rather than "did," though the result was to deprive many opinions of the positiveness to which they were entitled, accompanied by the hazard of a ruling of insufficiency to support a verdict. In other instances the rule was simply disregarded, and, as concessions to need, opinions were allowed upon such matters as intoxication, speed, handwriting, and value, although more precise coincidence with an ultimate issue would scarcely be possible.

Many modern decisions illustrate the trend to abandon the rule completely. People v. Wilson, 25 Cal.2d 341, 153 P.2d 720 (1944), whether abortion necessary to save life of patient; Clifford-Jacobs Forging Co. v. Industrial Comm., 19 Ill.2d 236, 166 N.E.2d 582 (1960), medical causation; Dowling v. L.H. Shattuck, Inc., 91 N.H. 234, 17 A.2d 529 (1941), proper method of shoring ditch; Schweiger v. Solbeck, 191 Or. 454, 230 P.2d 195 (1951), cause of landslide. In each instance the opinion was allowed.

The abolition of the ultimate issue rule does not lower the bars so as to admit all opinions. Under Rules 701 and 702, opinions must be helpful to the trier of fact, and Rule 403 provides for exclusion of evidence which wastes time. These provisions afford ample assurances against the admission of opinions which would merely tell the jury what result to reach, somewhat in the manner of the oath-helpers of an earlier day. They also stand ready to exclude opinions phrased in terms of inadequately explored legal criteria. Thus the question, "Did T have capacity to make a will?" would be excluded, while the question, "Did T have sufficient mental capacity to know the nature and extent of his property and the natural objects of his bounty and to formulate a rational scheme of distribution?" would be allowed. McCormick § 12.

For similar provisions see Uniform Rule 56(4); California Evidence Code § 805; Kansas Code of Civil Procedure § 60–456(d); New Jersey Evidence Rule 56(3).

Senate Report No. 98–225 (adding subdivision (b) in 1984)

S.Rep. No. 225, 98th Cong. 2d Sess. pp. 230–31(1984); 1984 U.S.Code Cong. & Ad.News, 3412–13

With respect to limitations on the scope of expert testimony by psychiatrists and other mental health experts, section 406 of title IV of the bill amends Rule 704 of the Federal Rules of Evidence to provide:

> No expert witness testifying with respect to the mental state or condition of a defendant in a criminal case may state an opinion or inference as to whether the defendant did or did not have the mental state or condition constituting an element of the crime or of a defense thereto. Such ultimate issues are matters for the trier of fact alone.

The purpose of this amendment is to eliminate the confusing spectacle of competing expert witnesses testifying to directly contradictory conclusions as to the ultimate legal issue to be found by the trier of fact. Under this proposal, expert psychiatric testimony would be limited to presenting and explaining their diagnoses, such as whether the defendant had a severe mental disease or defect and what the characteristics of such a disease or defect, if any, may have been.

The basis for this limitation on expert testimony in insanity cases is ably stated by the American Psychiatric Association:

> [I]t is clear that psychiatrists are experts in medicine, not the law. As such, it is clear that the psychiatrist's first obligation and expertise in the courtroom is to do psychiatry, *i.e.*, to present medical information and opinion about the defendant's mental state and motivation and to explain in detail the reason for his medical-psychiatric conclusions. When, however, ultimate issue questions are formulated by the law and put to the expert witness who must then say yea or nay, then the expert witness is required to make a leap in logic. He no longer addresses himself to medical concepts but instead must infer or intuit what is in fact unspeakable, namely, the probable relationship between medical concepts and legal or moral constructs such as free will. These impermissible leaps in logic made by expert witnesses confuse the jury. [Footnote omitted.] Juries thus find themselves listening to conclusory and seemingly contradictory psychiatric testimony that defendants are either sane or insane or that they do or do not meet the relevant legal test for insanity. This state of affairs does considerable injustice to psychiatry and, we believe, possibly to criminal defendants. In fact, in many criminal insanity trials both prosecution and defense psychiatrists do agree about the nature and even the extent of mental disorder exhibited by the defendant at the time of the act.

> Psychiatrists, of course, must be permitted to testify fully about the defendant's diagnosis, mental state and motivation (in clinical and commonsense terms) at the time of the alleged act so as to permit the jury or judge to reach the ultimate conclusion about which they and only they are expert. Determining whether a criminal defendant was legally insane is a matter for legal fact-finders, not for experts. [American Psychiatric Association Statement on the Insanity Defense at 18–19. *See also* Hearings, Limiting the Insanity Defense at 256–258 (statement of Dr. Loren Roth, University of Pittsburgh) and 272–273 (statement of Dr. Seymour L. Halleck, University of North Carolina.]

Moreover, the rationale for precluding ultimate opinion psychiatric testimony extends beyond the insanity defense to any ultimate mental state of the defendant that is relevant to the legal conclusion sought to be proven. The Committee has fashioned its Rule 704 provision to reach all such ultimate issues, *e.g.*, premeditation in a homicide case, or lack of predisposition in entrapment.

Rule 705. Disclosing the Facts or Data Underlying an Expert's Opinion

Unless the court orders otherwise, an expert may state an opinion—and give the reasons for it—without first testifying to the underlying facts or data. But the expert may be required to disclose those facts or data on cross-examination.

(As amended Mar. 2, 1987, eff. Oct. 1, 1987; Apr. 22, 1993, eff. Dec. 1, 1993; Apr. 26, 2011, eff. Dec. 1, 2011.)

RESTYLED RULE 705 COMMITTEE NOTE

The language of Rule 705 has been amended as part of the general restyling of the Evidence Rules to make them more easily understood and to make style and terminology consistent throughout the rules. These changes are intended to be stylistic only. There is no intent to change any result in any ruling on evidence admissibility.

The Committee deleted all reference to an "inference" on the grounds that the deletion made the Rule flow better and easier to read, and because any "inference" is covered by the broader term "opinion." Courts have not made substantive decisions on the basis of any distinction between an opinion and an inference. No change in current practice is intended.

REPORTER'S COMMENT ON RESTYLED RULE 705

The word "inference" in the original rule was deleted as superfluous, completely encompassed by the word "opinion." See the discussion in the Reporter's Comment on Restyled Rule 701.

Section references, McCormick 7th ed.

§ 15, § 32

Note by Federal Judicial Center

The rule enacted by the Congress is the rule prescribed by the Supreme Court, amended only by substituting "court" in place of "judge."

Advisory Committee's Note

56 F.R.D. 183, 285

The hypothetical question has been the target of a great deal of criticism as encouraging partisan bias, affording an opportunity for summing up in the middle of the case, and as complex and time consuming. Ladd, Expert Testimony, 5 Vand.L.Rev. 414, 426–427 (1952). While the rule allows counsel to make disclosure of the underlying facts or data as a preliminary to the giving of an expert opinion, if he chooses, the instances in which he is required to do so are reduced. This is true whether the expert bases his opinion on data furnished him at secondhand or observed by him at firsthand.

The elimination of the requirement of preliminary disclosure at the trial of underlying facts or data has a long background of support. In 1937 the Commissioners on Uniform State Laws incorporated a provision to this effect in their Model Expert Testimony Act, which furnished the basis for Uniform Rules 57 and 58. Rule 4515, N.Y.CPLR (McKinney 1963), provides:

> "Unless the court orders otherwise, questions calling for the opinion of an expert witness need not be hypothetical in form, and the witness may state his opinion and reasons without first specifying the data upon which it is based. Upon cross-examination, he may be required to specify the data. . . . "

See also California Evidence Code § 802; Kansas Code of Civil Procedure §§ 60–456, 60–457; New Jersey Evidence Rules 57, 58.

If the objection is made that leaving it to the cross-examiner to bring out the supporting data is essentially unfair, the answer is that he is under no compulsion to bring out any facts or data except those unfavorable to the opinion. The answer assumes that the cross-examiner has the advance knowledge which is essential for effective cross-examination. This advance knowledge has been afforded, though imperfectly, by the traditional foundation requirement. Rule 26(b)(4) of the Rules of Civil Procedure, as revised, provides for substantial discovery in this area, obviating in large measure the obstacles which have been raised in some instances to discovery of findings, underlying data, and even the identity of the experts. Friedenthal, Discovery and Use of an Adverse Party's Expert Information, 14 Stan.L.Rev. 455 (1962).

These safeguards are reinforced by the discretionary power of the judge to require preliminary disclosure in any event.

1987 Amendment Committee Note

The amendment is technical. No substantive change is intended.

1993 Amendment Committee Note

This rule, which relates to the manner of presenting testimony at trial, is revised to avoid an arguable conflict with revised Rules 26(a)(2)(B) and 26(e)(1) of the Federal Rules of Civil Procedure or with revised Rule 16 of the Federal Rules of Criminal Procedure, which require disclosure in advance of trial of the basis and reasons for an expert's opinions.

If a serious question is raised under Rule 702 or 703 as to the admissibility of expert testimony, disclosure of the underlying facts or data on which opinions are based may, of course, be needed by the court before deciding whether, and to what extent, the person should be allowed to testify. This rule does not preclude such an inquiry.

Rule 706. Court-Appointed Expert Witnesses

(a) Appointment Process. On a party's motion or on its own, the court may order the parties to show cause why expert witnesses should not be appointed and may ask the parties to submit nominations. The court may appoint any expert that the parties agree on and any of its own choosing. But the court may only appoint someone who consents to act.

(b) Expert's Role. The court must inform the expert of the expert's duties. The court may do so in writing and have a copy filed with the clerk or may do so orally at a conference in which the parties have an opportunity to participate. The expert:

> **(1)** must advise the parties of any findings the expert makes;

> **(2)** may be deposed by any party;

> **(3)** may be called to testify by the court or any party; and

> **(4)** may be cross-examined by any party, including the party that called the expert.

(c) Compensation. The expert is entitled to a reasonable compensation, as set by the court. The compensation is payable as follows:

> **(1)** in a criminal case or in a civil case involving just compensation under the Fifth Amendment, from any funds that are provided by law; and

> **(2)** in any other civil case, by the parties in the proportion and at the time that the court directs—and the compensation is then charged like other costs.

(d) Disclosing the Appointment to the Jury. The court may authorize disclosure to the jury that the court appointed the expert.

(e) Parties' Choice of Their Own Experts. This rule does not limit a party in calling its own experts.

(As amended Mar. 2, 1987, eff. Oct. 1, 1987; Apr. 26, 2011, eff. Dec. 1, 2011.)

RESTYLED RULE 706 COMMITTEE NOTE

The language of Rule 706 has been amended as part of the restyling of the Evidence Rules to make them more easily understood and to make style and terminology consistent throughout the rules. These changes are intended to be stylistic only. There is no intent to change any result in any ruling on evidence admissibility.

REPORTER'S COMMENT ON RESTYLED RULE 706

One look at original Rule 706(a) indicated that it cried out for restyling. It was a mass of jumbled sentences, which dealt with two separate subjects in one overlong subdivision: 1) how an expert is to be appointed; and 2) what the expert is supposed to do when appointed. The Restyled Rule separates out these concepts into two separate subdivisions. This restructuring will create some difficulties with electronic searches—typing "Rule 706(a)" into Westlaw for research on Restyled Rule 706(a) will not be a perfect fit for cases decided before the Restyling. But the Committee determined that the cost would be worth it, especially because there is not much case law to search for under Rule 706.

Section references, McCormick 7th ed.

§ 8, § 17

Note by Federal Judicial Center

The rule enacted by the Congress is the rule prescribed by the Supreme Court, amended by substituting "court" in place of "judge," with conforming pronominal changes, and, in subdivision (b), by substituting the phrase "and civil actions and proceedings" in place of "and cases" before "involving" in the second sentence.

Advisory Committee's Note

56 F.R.D. 183, 286

The practice of shopping for experts, the venality of some experts, and the reluctance of many reputable experts to involve themselves in litigation, have been matters of deep concern. Though the contention is made that court appointed experts acquire an aura of infallibility to which they are not entitled, Levy, Impartial Medical Testimony—Revisited, 34 Temple L.Q. 416 (1961), the trend is increasingly to provide for their use. While experience indicates that actual appointment is a relatively infrequent occurrence, the assumption may be made that the availability of the procedure in itself decreases the need for resorting to it. The ever-present possibility that the judge *may* appoint an expert in a given case must inevitably exert a sobering effect on the expert witness of a party and upon the person utilizing his services.

The inherent power of a trial judge to appoint an expert of his own choosing is virtually unquestioned. Scott v. Spanjer Bros., Inc., 298 F.2d 928 (2d Cir. 1962); Danville Tobacco Assn. v. Bryant-Buckner Associates, Inc., 333 F.2d 202 (4th Cir. 1964); Sink, The Unused Power of a Federal Judge to Call His Own Expert Witnesses, 29 S.Cal.L.Rev. 195 (1956); 2 Wigmore § 563, 9 *id.* § 2484; Annot., 95 A.L.R.2d 383. Hence the problem becomes largely one of detail.

The New York plan is well known and is described in Report by Special Committee of the Association of the Bar of the City of New York: Impartial Medical Testimony (1956). On recommendation of the Section of Judicial Administration, local adoption of an impartial medical plan was endorsed by the American Bar Association. 82 A.B.A.Rep. 184–185 (1957). Descriptions and analyses of plans in effect in various parts of the country are found in Van Dusen, A United States District Judge's View of the Impartial Medical Expert System, 32 F.R.D. 498 (1963); Wick and Kightlinger, Impartial Medical Testimony Under the Federal Civil Rules: A Tale of Three Doctors, 34 Ins. Counsel J. 115 (1967); and numerous articles collected in Klein, Judicial Administration and the Legal Profession 393 (1963). Statutes and rules include California Evidence Code §§ 730–733; Illinois Supreme Court Rule 215(d), Ill.Rev.Stat. 1969, c. 110A, § 215(d); Burns Indiana Stats. 1956, § 9–1702; Wisconsin Stats.Annot. 1958, § 957.27.

In the federal practice, a comprehensive scheme for court appointed experts was initiated with the adoption of Rule 28 of the Federal Rules of Criminal Procedure in 1946. The Judicial Conference of the United States in 1953 considered court appointed experts in civil cases, but only with respect to whether they should be compensated from public funds, a proposal which was rejected. Report of the Judicial Conference of the United States 23 (1953). The present rule expands the practice to include civil cases.

[Editor's Note: Rule 706 was restructured in the 2011 restyling; the references to subdivisions below do not accord with the restyled Rule.]

Subdivision (a) is based on Rule 28 of the Federal Rules of Criminal Procedure, with a few changes, mainly in the interest of clarity. Language has been added to provide specifically for the appointment either on motion of a party or on the judge's own motion. A provision subjecting the court appointed expert to deposition procedures has been incorporated. The rule has been revised to make definite the right of any party, including the party calling him, to cross-examine.

Subdivision (b) combines the present provision for compensation in criminal cases with what seems to be a fair and feasible handling of civil cases, originally found in the Model Act and carried from there into Uniform Rule 60. *See also* California Evidence Code §§ 730–731. The special provision for Fifth Amendment compensation cases is designed to guard against reducing constitutionally guaranteed just compensation by requiring the recipient to pay costs. See Rule 71A(*l*) of the Rules of Civil Procedure.

Subdivision (c) seems to be essential if the use of court appointed experts is to be fully effective. Uniform Rule 61 so provides.

Subdivision (d) is in essence the last sentence of Rule 28(a) of the Federal Rules of Criminal Procedure.

1987 Amendment Committee Note

The amendments are technical. No substantive change is intended.

ARTICLE VIII. HEARSAY

Rule 801. **Definitions That Apply to This Article; Exclusions from Hearsay**

(a) Statement. "Statement" means a person's oral assertion, written assertion, or nonverbal conduct, if the person intended it as an assertion.

(b) Declarant. "Declarant" means the person who made the statement.

(c) Hearsay. "Hearsay" means a statement that:

(1) the declarant does not make while testifying at the current trial or hearing; and

(2) a party offers in evidence to prove the truth of the matter asserted in the statement.

(d) Statements That Are Not Hearsay. A statement that meets the following conditions is not hearsay:

(1) *A Declarant-Witness's Prior Statement.* The declarant testifies and is subject to cross-examination about a prior statement, and the statement:

(A) is inconsistent with the declarant's testimony and was given under penalty of perjury at a trial, hearing, or other proceeding or in a deposition;

(B) is consistent with the declarant's testimony and is offered:

(i) to rebut an express or implied charge that the declarant recently fabricated it or acted from a recent improper influence or motive in so testifying; or

(ii) to rehabilitate the declarant's credibility as a witness when attacked on another ground; or

(C) identifies a person as someone the declarant perceived earlier.

(2) *An Opposing Party's Statement.* The statement is offered against an opposing party and:

(A) was made by the party in an individual or representative capacity;

(B) is one the party manifested that it adopted or believed to be true;

(C) was made by a person whom the party authorized to make a statement on the subject;

(D) was made by the party's agent or employee on a matter within the scope of that relationship and while it existed; or

(E) was made by the party's co-conspirator during and in furtherance of the conspiracy.

The statement must be considered but does not by itself establish the declarant's authority under (C); the existence or scope of the relationship under (D); or the existence of the conspiracy or participation in it under (E).

(As amended Pub.L. 94–113, § 1, Oct. 16, 1975, 89 Stat. 576; Mar. 2, 1987, eff. Oct. 1, 1987, Apr. 11, 1997, eff. Dec. 1, 1997; Apr. 26, 2011, eff. Dec. 1, 2011; Apr. 25, 2014, eff. Dec. 1, 2014.)

RESTYLED RULE 801 COMMITTEE NOTE

The language of Rule 801 has been amended as part of the general restyling of the Evidence Rules to make them more easily understood and to make style and terminology consistent throughout the rules. These changes are intended to be stylistic only. There is no intent to change any result in any ruling on evidence admissibility.

Statements falling under the hearsay exclusion provided by Rule 801(d)(2) are no longer referred to as "admissions" in the title to the subdivision. The term "admissions" is confusing because not all statements covered by the exclusion are admissions in the colloquial sense—a statement can be within the exclusion even if it "admitted" nothing and was not against the party's interest when made. The term "admissions" also raises confusion in comparison with the Rule 804(b)(3) exception for declarations against interest. No change in application of the exclusion is intended.

REPORTER'S COMMENT ON RESTYLED RULE 801

Restyling Rule 801 raised a number of difficult drafting and policy questions:

1.   *Rule 801(a)*—the original rule was vague on whether an oral or written assertion must be intended as an assertion in order to qualify as hearsay. The "it" in the rule was placed in a way that appeared to make the intent requirement applicable only to nonverbal conduct. The Committee considered whether to clarify whether the intent requirement applied to oral and written assertions. It determined that the case law was not uniform on whether there is an intent requirement for implied assertions to be considered hearsay. Clarifying the rule to reject an intent requirement would therefore result in a change of case law in the many courts which hold that an implied assertion is not hearsay unless there is an intent to communicate what is implied in the statement. And clarifying the rule to include an intent requirement for implied assertions would change the case law in courts that have come out the other way. Any change would thus be substantive under the protocol used by the Advisory Committee, and so was not a candidate for a change within the context of restyling. When the Restyled Rule 801(a) went before the Supreme Court, the Court suggested that the Rule be clarified—but it accepted the Advisory Committee's explanation that such clarification would be substantive. For more on implied assertions and Rule 801(a) see Saltzburg, Martin and Capra, *4 Federal Rules of Evidence Manual,* Par. 801.02 (11th ed. 2015).

2.   *Rule 801(c)*—the definition of hearsay has received a helpful clarification, which is consistent with the case law. The original rule provided that a statement is hearsay if offered for the "truth of the matter asserted." A novice might well ask, "asserted where?" The Restyled Rule answers that the focus is on the proffered out-of-court statement and what is asserted *in that statement*. Hopefully the "in the statement" clarification will help students in understanding the hearsay rule.

3.   *Rule 801(d)(2)*—"admissions." The term "admissions" is an inaccurate description of those statements that are admissible under Rule 801(d)(2). A party might make a statement that "admits" nothing—indeed it could be expressly made to deny something. Yet if such a statement can be used against the party at trial—for example an alibi by the defendant that turns out to be without support—it is admissible despite the fact that it is hearsay. So a statement admissible under Rule 801(d)(2) does not have to be an "admission" of anything. The term "admissions" also has given rise to courts and litigants talking about "admissions against interest." And that inaccurate term has raised confusion with

the separate exception in Rule 804(b)(3) for declarations against interest. Accordingly, the Advisory Committee thought it helpful to completely eliminate any reference to "admissions" in the Restyled Rules of Evidence. They are now called statements by an "opposing party." This change was properly within the confines of the Restyling Project as it alters no result in any case. It only changes the inaccurate language used to come to the correct result of admitting against a party the statements made by that party or its agents.

Section references, McCormick 7th ed.

§§ 246–251, §§ 254–262

Note by Federal Judicial Center

The rule enacted by the Congress is the rule prescribed by the Supreme Court, with an amendment to subdivision (d)(1). The amendment inserted in item (A), after "testimony," adds the phrase "and was given under oath subject to the penalty of perjury at a trial, hearing, or other proceeding, or in a deposition." The reasons for the amendment are stated in the Report of the House Committee on the Judiciary, the Report of the Senate Committee on the Judiciary, and the Conference Report.

Advisory Committee's Introductory Note to Article VIII

INTRODUCTORY NOTE: THE HEARSAY PROBLEM

The factors to be considered in evaluating the testimony of a witness are perception, memory, and narration. Morgan, Hearsay Dangers and the Application of the Hearsay Concept, 62 Harv.L.Rev. 177 (1948), Selected Writings on Evidence and Trial 764, 765 (Fryer ed. 1957); Shientag, Cross-Examination— A Judge's Viewpoint, 3 Record 12 (1948); Strahorn, A Reconsideration of the Hearsay Rule and Admissions, 85 U.Pa.L.Rev. 484, 485 (1937), Selected Writings, *supra*, 756, 757; Weinstein, Probative Force of Hearsay, 46 Iowa L.Rev. 331 (1961). Sometimes a fourth is added, sincerity, but in fact it seems merely to be an aspect of the three already mentioned.

In order to encourage the witness to do his best with respect to each of these factors, and to expose any inaccuracies which may enter in, the Anglo-American tradition has evolved three conditions under which witnesses will ideally be required to testify: (1) under oath, (2) in the personal presence of the trier of fact, (3) subject to cross-examination.

(1) Standard procedure calls for the swearing of witnesses. While the practice is perhaps less effective than in an earlier time, no disposition to relax the requirement is apparent, other than to allow affirmation by persons with scruples against taking oaths.

(2) The demeanor of the witness traditionally has been believed to furnish trier and opponent with valuable clues. Universal Camera Corp. v. N.L.R.B., 340 U.S. 474, 495–496, 71 S.Ct. 456, 95 L.Ed. 456 (1951); Sahm, Demeanor Evidence: Elusive and Intangible Imponderables, 47 A.B.A.J. 580 (1961), quoting numerous authorities. The witness himself will probably be impressed with the solemnity of the occasion and the possibility of public disgrace. Willingness to falsify may reasonably become more difficult in the presence of the person against whom directed. Rules 26 and 43(a) of the Federal Rules of Criminal and Civil Procedure, respectively, include the general requirement that testimony be taken orally in open court. The Sixth Amendment right of confrontation is a manifestation of these beliefs and attitudes.

(3) Emphasis on the basis of the hearsay rule today tends to center upon the condition of cross-examination. All may not agree with Wigmore that cross-

examination is "beyond doubt the greatest legal engine ever invented for the discovery of truth," but all will agree with his statement that it has become a "vital feature" of the Anglo-American system. 5 Wigmore, § 1367, p. 29. The belief, or perhaps hope, that cross-examination, is effective in exposing imperfections of perception, memory, and narration is fundamental. Morgan, Foreword to Model Code of Evidence 37 (1942).

The logic of the preceding discussion might suggest that no testimony be received unless in full compliance with the three ideal conditions. No one advocates this position. Common sense tells that much evidence which is not given under the three conditions may be inherently superior to much that is. Moreover, when the choice is between evidence which is less than best and no evidence at all, only clear folly would dictate an across-the-board policy of doing without. The problem thus resolves itself into effecting a sensible accommodation between these considerations and the desirability of giving testimony under the ideal conditions.

The solution evolved by the common law has been a general rule excluding hearsay but subject to numerous exceptions under circumstances supposed to furnish guarantees of trustworthiness. Criticisms of this scheme are that it is bulky and complex, fails to screen good from bad hearsay realistically, and inhibits the growth of the law of evidence.

Since no one advocates excluding all hearsay, three possible solutions may be considered: (1) abolish the rule against hearsay and admit all hearsay; (2) admit hearsay possessing sufficient probative force, but with procedural safeguards; (3) revise the present system of class exceptions.

(1)   Abolition of the hearsay rule would be the simplest solution. The effect would not be automatically to abolish the giving of testimony under ideal conditions. If the declarant were available, compliance with the ideal conditions would be optional with either party. Thus the proponent could call the declarant as a witness as a form of presentation more impressive than his hearsay statement. Or the opponent could call the declarant to be cross-examined upon his statement. This is the tenor of Uniform Rule 63(1), admitting the hearsay declaration of a person "who is present at the hearing and available for cross-examination." Compare the treatment of declarations of available declarants in Rule 801(d)(1) of the instant rules. If the declarant were unavailable, a rule of free admissibility would make no distinctions in terms of degrees of noncompliance with the ideal conditions and would exact no quid pro quo in the form of assurances of trustworthiness. Rule 503 of the Model Code did exactly that, providing for the admissibility of any hearsay declaration by an unavailable declarant, finding support in the Massachusetts act of 1898, enacted at the instance of Thayer, Mass.Gen.L. 1932, c. 233 § 65, and in the English act of 1938, St. 1938, c. 28, Evidence. Both are limited to civil cases. The draftsmen of the Uniform Rules chose a less advanced and more conventional position. Comment, Uniform Rule 63. The present Advisory Committee has been unconvinced of the wisdom of abandoning the traditional requirement of some particular assurance of credibility as a condition precedent to admitting the hearsay declaration of an unavailable declarant.

In criminal cases, the Sixth Amendment requirement of confrontation would no doubt move into a large part of the area presently occupied by the hearsay rule in the event of the abolition of the latter. The resultant split between civil and criminal evidence is regarded as an undesirable development.

(2)   Abandonment of the system of class exceptions in favor of individual treatment in the setting of the particular case, accompanied by procedural safeguards, has been impressively advocated. Weinstein, The Probative Force of Hearsay, 46 Iowa L.Rev. 331 (1961). Admissibility would be determined by weighing the probative force of the evidence against the possibility of prejudice,

waste of time, and the availability of more satisfactory evidence. The bases of the traditional hearsay exceptions would be helpful in assessing probative force. Ladd, The Relationship of the Principles of Exclusionary Rules of Evidence to the Problem of Proof, 18 Minn.L.Rev. 506 (1934). Procedural safeguards would consist of notice of intention to use hearsay, free comment by the judge on the weight of the evidence, and a greater measure of authority in both trial and appellate judges to deal with evidence on the basis of weight. The Advisory Committee has rejected this approach to hearsay as involving too great a measure of judicial discretion, minimizing the predictability of rulings, enhancing the difficulties of preparation for trial, adding a further element to the already over-complicated congeries of pretrial procedures, and requiring substantially different rules for civil and criminal cases. The only way in which the probative force of hearsay differs from the probative force of other testimony is in the absence of oath, demeanor, and cross-examination as aids in determining credibility. For a judge to exclude evidence because he does not believe it has been described as "altogether atypical, extraordinary. . . ." Chadbourn, Bentham and the Hearsay Rule—A Benthamic View of Rule 63(4)(c) of the Uniform Rules of Evidence, 75 Harv.L.Rev. 932, 947 (1962).

(3)   The approach to hearsay in these rules is that of the common law, *i.e.*, a general rule excluding hearsay, with exceptions under which evidence is not required to be excluded even though hearsay. The traditional hearsay exceptions are drawn upon for the exceptions, collected under two rules, one dealing with situations where availability of the declarant is regarded as immaterial and the other with those where unavailability is made a condition to the admission of the hearsay statement. Each of the two rules concludes with a provision for hearsay statements not within one of the specified exceptions "but having comparable [equivalent] circumstantial guarantees of trustworthiness." Rules 803(24) and 804(b)(6)[5]. **[Those two rules have been transferred to a single rule, Rule 807.—Ed.]**This plan is submitted as calculated to encourage growth and development in this area of the law, while conserving the values and experience of the past as a guide to the future.

CONFRONTATION AND DUE PROCESS

[Editor's Note: Most of the Advisory Committee's discussion on constitutional issues, set forth immediately below, has become outdated by the Supreme Court's subsequently decided cases on the Confrontation Clause.]

Until very recently, decisions invoking the confrontation clause of the Sixth Amendment were surprisingly few, a fact probably explainable by the former inapplicability of the clause to the states and by the hearsay rule's occupancy of much the same ground. The pattern which emerges from the earlier cases invoking the clause is substantially that of the hearsay rule, applied to criminal cases: an accused is entitled to have the witnesses against him testify under oath, in the presence of himself and trier, subject to cross-examination; yet considerations of public policy and necessity require the recognition of such exceptions as dying declarations and former testimony of unavailable witnesses. Mattox v. United States, 156 U.S. 237, 15 S.Ct. 337, 39 L.Ed. 409 (1895); Motes v. United States, 178 U.S. 458, 20 S.Ct. 993, 44 L.Ed. 1150 (1900); Delaney v. United States, 263 U.S. 586, 44 S.Ct. 206, 68 L.Ed. 462 (1924). Beginning with Snyder v. Massachusetts, 291 U.S. 97, 54 S.Ct. 330, 78 L.Ed. 674 (1934), the Court began to speak of confrontation as an aspect of procedural due process, thus extending its applicability to state cases and to federal cases other than criminal. The language of *Snyder* was that of an elastic concept of hearsay. The deportation case of Bridges v. Wixon, 326 U.S. 135, 65 S.Ct. 1443, 89 L.Ed. 2103 (1945), may be read broadly as imposing a strictly construed right of confrontation in all kinds of cases or narrowly as the product of a failure of the Immigration and Naturalization Service to follow its own rules. In re Oliver, 333 U.S. 257, 68 S.Ct.

499, 92 L.Ed. 682 (1948), ruled that cross-examination was essential to due process in a state contempt proceeding, but in United States v. Nugent, 346 U.S. 1, 73 S.Ct. 991, 97 L.Ed. 1417 (1953), the court held that it was not an essential aspect of a "hearing" for a conscientious objector under the Selective Service Act. Stein v. New York, 346 U.S. 156, 196, 73 S.Ct. 1077, 97 L.Ed. 1522 (1953), disclaimed any purpose to read the hearsay rule into the Fourteenth Amendment, but in Greene v. McElroy, 360 U.S. 474, 79 S.Ct. 1400, 3 L.Ed.2d 1377 (1959), revocation of security clearance without confrontation and cross-examination was held unauthorized, and a similar result was reached in Willner v. Committee on Character, 373 U.S. 96, 83 S.Ct. 1175, 10 L.Ed.2d 224 (1963). Ascertaining the constitutional dimensions of the confrontation-hearsay aggregate against the background of these cases is a matter of some difficulty, yet the general pattern is at least not inconsistent with that of the hearsay rule.

In 1965 the confrontation clause was held applicable to the states. Pointer v. Texas, 380 U.S. 400, 85 S.Ct. 1065, 13 L.Ed.2d 923 (1965). Prosecution use of former testimony given at a preliminary hearing where petitioner was not represented by counsel was a violation of the clause. The same result would have followed under conventional hearsay doctrine read in the light of a constitutional right to counsel, and nothing in the opinion suggests any difference in essential outline between the hearsay rule and the right of confrontation. In the companion case of Douglas v. Alabama, 380 U.S. 415, 85 S.Ct. 1074, 13 L.Ed.2d 934 (1965), however, the result reached by applying the confrontation clause is one reached less readily via the hearsay rule. A confession implicating petitioner was put before the jury by reading it to the witness in portions and asking if he made that statement. The witness refused to answer on grounds of self-incrimination. The result, said the Court, was to deny cross-examination, and hence confrontation. True, it could broadly be said that the confession was a hearsay statement which for all practical purposes was put in evidence. Yet a more easily accepted explanation of the opinion is that its real thrust was in the direction of curbing undesirable prosecutorial behavior, rather than merely applying rules of exclusion, and that the confrontation clause was the means selected to achieve this end. Comparable facts and a like result appeared in Brookhart v. Janis, 384 U.S. 1, 86 S.Ct. 1245, 16 L.Ed.2d 314 (1966).

The pattern suggested in *Douglas* was developed further and more distinctly in a pair of cases at the end of the 1966 term. United States v. Wade, 388 U.S. 218, 87 S.Ct. 1926, 18 L.Ed.2d 1149 (1967), and Gilbert v. California, 388 U.S. 263, 87 S.Ct. 1951, 18 L.Ed.2d 1178 (1967), hinged upon practices followed in identifying accused persons before trial. This pretrial identification was said to be so decisive an aspect of the case that accused was entitled to have counsel present; a pretrial identification made in the absence of counsel was not itself receivable in evidence and, in addition, might fatally infect a courtroom identification. The presence of counsel at the earlier identification was described as a necessary prerequisite for "a meaningful confrontation at trial." United States v. Wade, *supra*, 388 U.S. at p. 236, 87 S.Ct. at p. 1937. *Wade* involved no evidence of the fact of a prior identification and hence was not susceptible of being decided on hearsay grounds. In *Gilbert,* witnesses did testify to an earlier identification, readily classifiable as hearsay under a fairly strict view of what constitutes hearsay. The Court, however, carefully avoided basing the decision on the hearsay ground, choosing confrontation instead. 388 U.S. 263, 272, n. 3, 87 S.Ct. 1951. *See also* Parker v. Gladden, 385 U.S. 363, 87 S.Ct. 468, 17 L.Ed.2d 420 (1966), holding that the right of confrontation was violated when the bailiff made prejudicial statements to jurors, and Note, 75 Yale L.J. 1434 (1966).

Under the earlier cases, the confrontation clause may have been little more than a constitutional embodiment of the hearsay rule, even including traditional exceptions but with some room for expanding them along similar lines. But under the recent cases the impact of the clause clearly extends beyond the confines of the hearsay rule. These considerations have led the Advisory Committee to conclude that a hearsay rule can function usefully as an adjunct to the confrontation right in constitutional areas and independently in nonconstitutional areas. In recognition of the separateness of the confrontation clause and the hearsay rule, and to avoid inviting collisions between them or between the hearsay rule and other exclusionary principles, the exceptions set forth in Rules 803 and 804 are stated in terms of exemption from the general exclusionary mandate of the hearsay rule, rather than in positive terms of admissibility. See Uniform Rule 63(1) to (31) and California Evidence Code §§ 1200–1340.

Advisory Committee's Note to Rule 801

56 F.R.D. 183, 293

Subdivision (a). The definition of "statement" assumes importance because the term is used in the definition of hearsay in subdivision (c). The effect of the definition of "statement" is to exclude from the operation of the hearsay rule all evidence of conduct, verbal or nonverbal, not intended as an assertion. The key to the definition is that nothing is an assertion unless intended to be one.

It can scarcely be doubted that an assertion made in words is intended by the declarant to be an assertion. Hence verbal assertions readily fall into the category of "statement." Whether nonverbal conduct should be regarded as a statement for purposes of defining hearsay requires further consideration. Some nonverbal conduct, such as the act of pointing to identify a suspect in a lineup, is clearly the equivalent of words, assertive in nature, and to be regarded as a statement. Other nonverbal conduct, however, may be offered as evidence that the person acted as he did because of his belief in the existence of the condition sought to be proved, from which belief the existence of the condition may be inferred. This sequence is, arguably, in effect an assertion of the existence of the condition and hence properly includable within the hearsay concept. See Morgan, Hearsay Dangers and the Application of the Hearsay Concept, 62 Harv.L.Rev. 177, 214, 217 (1948), and the elaboration in Finman, Implied Assertions as Hearsay: Some Criticisms of the Uniform Rules of Evidence, 14 Stan.L.Rev. 682 (1962). Admittedly evidence of this character is untested with respect to the perception, memory, and narration (or their equivalents) of the actor, but the Advisory Committee is of the view that these dangers are minimal in the absence of an intent to assert and do not justify the loss of the evidence on hearsay grounds. No class of evidence is free of the possibility of fabrication, but the likelihood is less with nonverbal than with assertive verbal conduct. The situations giving rise to the nonverbal conduct are such as virtually to eliminate questions of sincerity. Motivation, the nature of the conduct, and the presence or absence of reliance will bear heavily upon the weight to be given the evidence. Falknor, The "Hear-Say" Rule as a "See-Do" Rule: Evidence of Conduct, 33 Rocky Mt.L.Rev. 133 (1961). Similar considerations govern nonassertive verbal conduct and verbal conduct which is assertive but offered as a basis for inferring something other than the matter asserted, also excluded from the definition of hearsay by the language of subdivision (c).

When evidence of conduct is offered on the theory that it is not a statement, and hence not hearsay, a preliminary determination will be required to determine whether an assertion is intended. The rule is so worded as to place the burden upon the party claiming that the intention existed; ambiguous and doubtful cases will be resolved against him and in favor of admissibility. The determination involves no greater difficulty than many other preliminary questions of fact. Maguire, The Hearsay System: Around and Through the Thicket, 14 Vand.L.Rev. 741, 765–767 (1961).

For similar approaches, see Uniform Rule 62(1); California Evidence Code §§ 225, 1200; Kansas Code of Civil Procedure § 60–459(a); New Jersey Evidence Rule 62(1).

[Editor's Note: There is no Committee Note for Subdivision (b).]

Subdivision (c). The definition follows along familiar lines in including only statements offered to prove the truth of the matter asserted. McCormick § 225; 5 Wigmore § 1361, 6 *id.* § 1766. If the significance of an offered statement lies solely in the fact that it was made, no issue is raised as to the truth of anything asserted, and the statement is not hearsay. Emich Motors Corp. v. General Motors Corp., 181 F.2d 70 (7th Cir. 1950), rev'd on other grounds 340 U.S. 558, 71 S.Ct. 408, 95 L.Ed. 534, letters of complaint from customers offered as a reason for cancellation of dealer's franchise, to rebut contention that franchise was revoked for refusal to finance sales through affiliated finance company. The effect is to exclude from hearsay the entire category of "verbal acts" and "verbal parts of an act," in which the statement itself affects the legal rights of the parties or is a circumstance bearing on conduct affecting their rights.

The definition of hearsay must, of course, be read with reference to the definition of statement set forth in subdivision (a).

Testimony given by a witness in the course of court proceedings is excluded since there is compliance with all the ideal conditions for testifying.

Subdivision (d). Several types of statements which would otherwise literally fall within the definition are expressly excluded from it:

(1) *Prior statement by witness.* Considerable controversy has attended the question whether a prior out-of-court statement by a person now available for cross-examination concerning it, under oath and in the presence of the trier of fact, should be classed as hearsay. If the witness admits on the stand that he made the statement and that it was true, he adopts the statement and there is no hearsay problem. The hearsay problem arises when the witness on the stand denies having made the statement or admits having made it but denies its truth. The argument in favor of treating these latter statements as hearsay is based upon the ground that the conditions of oath, cross-examination, and demeanor observation did not prevail at the time the statement was made and cannot adequately be supplied by the later examination. The logic of the situation is troublesome. So far as concerns the oath, its mere presence has never been regarded as sufficient to remove a statement from the hearsay category, and it receives much less emphasis than cross-examination as a truth-compelling device. While strong expressions are found to the effect that no conviction can be had or important right taken away on the basis of statements not made under fear of prosecution for perjury, Bridges v. Wixon, 326 U.S. 135, 65 S.Ct. 1443, 89 L.Ed. 2103 (1945), the fact is that, of the many common law exceptions to the hearsay rule, only that for reported testimony has required the statement to have been made under oath. **[It should be noted, however, that rule 801(d)(1)(A), as enacted by the Congress, requires that a prior inconsistent statement have been made under oath.—Ed.]** Nor is it satisfactorily explained why cross-examination cannot be conducted subsequently with success. The decisions contending most vigorously for its inadequacy in fact demonstrate quite thorough exploration of the weaknesses and doubts attending the earlier statement. State v. Saporen, 205 Minn. 358, 285 N.W. 898 (1939); Ruhala v. Roby, 379 Mich. 102, 150 N.W.2d 146 (1967); People v. Johnson, 68 Cal.2d 646, 68 Cal.Rptr. 599, 441 P.2d 111 (1968). In respect to demeanor, as Judge Learned Hand observed in Di Carlo v. United States, 6 F.2d 364 (2d Cir. 1925), when the jury decides that the truth is not what the witness says now, but what he said before, they are still deciding from what they see and hear in court. The bulk of the case law nevertheless has been against allowing prior statements of witnesses to be used

generally as substantive evidence. Most of the writers and Uniform Rule 63(1) have taken the opposite position.

The position taken by the Advisory Committee in formulating this part of the rule is founded upon an unwillingness to countenance the general use of prior prepared statements as substantive evidence, but with a recognition that particular circumstances call for a contrary result. The judgment is one more of experience than of logic. The rule requires in each instance, as a general safeguard, that the declarant actually testify as a witness, and it then enumerates three situations in which the statement is excepted from the category of hearsay. Compare Uniform Rule 63(1) which allows any out-of-court statement of a declarant who is present at the trial and available for cross-examination.

(A) Prior inconsistent statements traditionally have been admissible to impeach but not as substantive evidence. Under the rule they are substantive evidence. **[Editor's Note: The Advisory Committee proposal was narrowed by Congress to provide for substantive admissibility of prior inconsistent statements of testifying witnesses only if the prior statement was made under oath at a formal proceeding.]** As has been said by the California Law Revision Commission with respect to a similar provision:

"Section 1235 admits inconsistent statements of witnesses because the dangers against which the hearsay rule is designed to protect are largely nonexistent. The declarant is in court and may be examined and cross-examined in regard to his statements and their subject matter. In many cases, the inconsistent statement is more likely to be true than the testimony of the witness at the trial because it was made nearer in time to the matter to which it relates and is less likely to be influenced by the controversy that gave rise to the litigation. The trier of fact has the declarant before it and can observe his demeanor and the nature of his testimony as he denies or tries to explain away the inconsistency. Hence, it is in as good a position to determine the truth or falsity of the prior statement as it is to determine the truth or falsity of the inconsistent testimony given in court. Moreover, Section 1235 will provide a party with desirable protection against the 'turncoat' witness who changes his story on the stand and deprives the party calling him of evidence essential to his case." Comment, California Evidence Code § 1235. *See also* McCormick § 39. The Advisory Committee finds these views more convincing than those expressed in People v. Johnson, 68 Cal.2d 646, 68 Cal.Rptr. 599, 441 P.2d 111 (1968). The constitutionality of the Advisory Committee's view was upheld in California v. Green, 399 U.S. 149, 90 S.Ct. 1930, 26 L.Ed.2d 489 (1970). Moreover, the requirement that the statement be inconsistent with the testimony given assures a thorough exploration of both versions while the witness is on the stand and bars any general and indiscriminate use of previously prepared statements. [It should be noted that the rule as enacted by the Congress also requires that the prior inconsistent statement have been made under oath.][16]

Report of House Committee on the Judiciary on Rule 801(d)(1)(A)

House Comm. on Judiciary, Fed.Rules of Evidence, H.R.Rep. No. 650, 93d Cong., 1st Sess., p. 13 (1973); 1975 U.S. Code Cong. & Ad.News 7075, 7086

Present federal law, except in the Second Circuit, permits the use of prior inconsistent statements of a witness for impeachment only. Rule 801(d)(1) as proposed by the Court would have permitted all such statements to be admissible as substantive evidence, an approach followed by a small but growing number of State jurisdictions and recently held constitutional in California v. Green, 399 U.S. 149 (1970). Although there was some support expressed for the Court Rule, based largely on the need to counteract the effect of witness intimidation in

---

[16] The rest of the Advisory Committee Note on Rule 801(d) continues after the Congressional Reports on Rule 801(d)(1)(A).—Ed.

criminal cases, the Committee decided to adopt a compromise version of the Rule similar to the position of the Second Circuit. The Rule as amended draws a distinction between types of prior inconsistent statements (other than statements of identification of a person made after perceiving him which are currently admissible, see United States v. Anderson, 406 F.2d 719, 720 (4th Cir.), cert. denied, 395 U.S. 967 (1969)) and allows only those made while the declarant was subject to cross-examination at a trail [trial] or hearing or in a deposition, to be admissible for their truth. Compare United States v. DeSisto, 329 F.2d 929 (2nd Cir.), cert. denied, 377 U.S. 979 (1964); United States v. Cunningham, 446 F.2d 194 (2nd Cir. 1971) (restricting the admissibility of prior inconsistent statements as substantive evidence to those made under oath in a formal proceeding, but not requiring that there have been an opportunity for cross-examination). The rationale for the Committee's decision is that (1) unlike in most other situations involving unsworn or oral statements, there can be no dispute as to whether the prior statement was made; and (2) the context of a formal proceeding, an oath, and the opportunity for cross-examination provide firm additional assurances of the reliability of the prior statement.

Report of Senate Committee on the Judiciary on Rule 801(d)(1)(A)

Senate Comm. on Judiciary, Fed.Rules of Evidence, S.Rep. No. 1277, 93d Cong., 2d Sess., p. 15 (1974); 1974 U.S. Code Cong. & Ad.News 7051, 7062

Rule 801 defines what is and what is not hearsay for the purpose of admitting a prior statement as substantive evidence. A prior statement of a witness at a trial or hearing which is inconsistent with his testimony is, of course, always admissible for the purpose of impeaching the witness' credibility.

As submitted by the Supreme Court, subdivision (d)(1)(A) made admissible as substantive evidence the prior statement of a witness inconsistent with this present testimony.

The House severely limited the admissibility of prior inconsistent statements by adding a requirement that the prior statement must have been subject to cross-examination, thus precluding even the use of grand jury statements. The requirement that the prior statement must have been subject to cross-examination appears unnecessary since this rule comes into play only when the witness testifies in the present trial. At that time, he is on the stand and can explain an earlier position and be cross-examined as to both.

The requirement that the statement be under oath also appears unnecessary. Notwithstanding the absence of an oath contemporaneous with the statement, the witness, when on the stand, qualifying or denying the prior statement, is under oath. In any event, of all the many recognized exceptions to the hearsay rule, only one (former testimony) requires that the out-of-court statement have been made under oath. With respect to the lack of evidence of the demeanor of the witness at the time of the prior statement, it would be difficult to improve upon Judge Learned Hand's observation that when the jury decides that the truth is not what the witness says now but what he said before, they are still deciding from what they see and hear in court.[17]

The rule as submitted by the Court has positive advantages. The prior statement was made nearer in time to the events, when memory was fresher and intervening influences had not been brought into play. A realistic method is provided for dealing with the turncoat witness who changes his story on the stand.[18]

---

[17]   Di Carlo v. United States, 6 F.2d 364 (2d Cir. 1925).—Ed.

[18]   See Comment, California Evidence Code § 1235; McCormick, Evidence, § 38 (2nd ed. 1972).—Ed.

New Jersey, California, and Utah have adopted a rule similar to this one; and Nevada, New Mexico, and Wisconsin have adopted the identical Federal rule.

For all of these reasons, we think the House amendment should be rejected and the rule as submitted by the Supreme Court reinstated.[19]

Conference Report on Rule 801(d)(1)(A)

H.R., Fed.Rules of Evidence, Conf.Rep. No. 1597, 93d Cong., 2d Sess., p. 10 (1974); 1974 U.S. Code Cong. & Ad.News 7098, 7104

The House bill provides that a statement is not hearsay if the declarant testifies and is subject to cross-examination concerning the statement and if the statement is inconsistent with his testimony and was given under oath subject to cross-examination and subject to the penalty of perjury at a trial or hearing or in a deposition. The Senate amendment drops the requirement that the prior statement be given under oath subject to cross-examination and subject to the penalty of perjury at a trial or hearing or in a deposition.

The Conference adopts the Senate amendment with an amendment, so that the rule now requires that the prior inconsistent statement be given under oath subject to the penalty of perjury at a trial, hearing, or other proceeding, or in a deposition. The rule as adopted covers statements before a grand jury. Prior inconsistent statements may, of course, be used for impeaching the credibility of a witness. When the prior inconsistent statement is one made by a defendant in a criminal case, it is covered by Rule 801(d)(2).

Advisory Committee's Note on Rule 801(d)(1)(B)

56 F.R.D. 183, 296

(B)   Prior consistent statements traditionally have been admissible to rebut charges of recent fabrication or improper influence or motive but not as substantive evidence. Under the rule they are substantive evidence. The prior statement is consistent with the testimony given on the stand and, if the opposite party wishes to open the door for its admission in evidence, no sound reason is apparent why it should not be received generally.

Editorial Note on Rule 801(d)(1)(C)

Subdivision (d)(1)(C) was included in the rule as prescribed by the Supreme Court but was deleted by the Congress in enacting the rules. The Senate initially rejected the proposed Rule 801(d)(1)(C); the House acquiesced in order to ensure passage of the Rules of Evidence. Statement of Rep. Hungate, Cong. Rec. H. 9653 (Oct. 6, 1975). The Senate had deleted the provision because of strenuous objection by Senator Ervin. He was concerned that a conviction could be based solely on unsworn hearsay. Cong. Rec. H. 9654 (Oct. 6, 1975).

But Congress then amended Rule 801(d)(1) in 1975 to add back the Advisory Committee's proposal. P.L. 94–113 (1975). The report from the Senate Judiciary Committee on the 1975 amendment found that Senator Ervin's concerns were "misdirected." The report makes four points: 1) the rule is addressed to admissibility, not sufficiency; 2) most of the hearsay exceptions allow statements into evidence that were not made under oath; 3) the declarant who made the identification must under the rule be testifying subject to cross-examination, assuring that "if any

---

[19]   It would appear that some of the opposition to this Rule is based on a concern that a person could be convicted solely upon evidence admissible under this Rule. The Rule, however, is not addressed to the question of the sufficiency of evidence to send a case to the jury, but merely as to its admissibility. Factual circumstances could well arise where, if this were the sole evidence, dismissal would be appropriate.—Ed.

discrepancy occurs between the witness's in-court and out-of-court testimony, the opportunity is available to probe, with the witness under oath, the reasons for that discrepancy so that the trier of fact might determine which statement is to be believed"; and 4) the identification must pass constitutional muster under Supreme Court decisions excluding identification evidence if tainted by impermissible police suggestiveness. Report of the Committee on the Judiciary, Senate, 94th Cong., 1st Sess., No. 94–199 (1975).

Because the Advisory Committee's proposed Rule 801(d)(1)(C) was eventually enacted by Congress, the Committee Note to that provision is set forth below:

Advisory Committee's Note on Rule 801(d)(1)(C)

56 F.R.D. 183, 296

(C) The admission of evidence of identification finds substantial support, although it falls beyond a doubt in the category of prior out-of-court statements. Illustrative are People v. Gould, 54 Cal.2d 621, 7 Cal.Rptr. 273, 354 P.2d 865 (1960); Judy v. State, 218 Md. 168, 146 A.2d 29 (1958); State v. Simmons, 63 Wash.2d 17, 385 P.2d 389 (1963); California Evidence Code § 1238; New Jersey Evidence Rule 63(1)(c); N.Y.Code of Criminal Procedure § 393–b. Further cases are found in 4 Wigmore § 1130. The basis is the generally unsatisfactory and inconclusive nature of courtroom identifications as compared with those made at an earlier time under less suggestive conditions. The Supreme Court considered the admissibility of evidence of prior identification in Gilbert v. California, 388 U.S. 263, 87 S.Ct. 1951, 18 L.Ed.2d 1178 (1967). Exclusion of lineup identification was held to be required because the accused did not then have the assistance of counsel. Significantly, the Court carefully refrained from placing its decision on the ground that testimony as to the making of a prior out-of-court identification ("That's the man") violated either the hearsay rule or the right of confrontation because not made under oath, subject to immediate cross-examination, in the presence of the trier. Instead the Court observed:

> "There is a split among the States concerning the admissibility of prior extra-judicial identifications, as independent evidence of identity, both by the witness and third parties present at the prior identification. See 71 A.L.R.2d 449. It has been held that the prior identification is hearsay, and, when admitted through the testimony of the identifier, is merely a prior consistent statement. The recent trend, however, is to admit the prior identification under the exception that admits as substantive evidence a prior communication by a witness who is available for cross-examination at the trial. See 5 A.L.R.2d Later Case Service 1225–1228. . . . " 388 U.S. at 272, n. 3, 87 S.Ct. at 1956.

Advisory Committee Note to Rule 801(d)(2)

(2) *Admissions*. [The term "admissions" was deleted in the 2011 restyling in favor of the term "statements by an opposing party." See the Restyling Committee Note, supra.—Ed.] Admissions by a party-opponent are excluded from the category of hearsay on the theory that their admissibility in evidence is the result of the adversary system rather than satisfaction of the conditions of the hearsay rule. Strahorn, A Reconsideration of the Hearsay Rule and Admissions, 85 U.Pa.L.Rev. 484, 564 (1937); Morgan, Basic Problems of Evidence 265 (1962); 4 Wigmore § 1048. No guarantee of trustworthiness is required in the case of an admission. The freedom which admissions have enjoyed from technical demands of searching for an assurance of trustworthiness in some against-interest circumstance, and from the restrictive influences of the opinion rule and the rule requiring firsthand knowledge, when taken with the apparently

prevalent satisfaction with the results, calls for generous treatment of this avenue to admissibility.

The rule specifies five categories of statements for which the responsibility of a party is considered sufficient to justify reception in evidence against him:

(A)   A party's own statement is the classic example of an admission. If he has a representative capacity and the statement is offered against him in that capacity, no inquiry whether he was acting in the representative capacity in making the statement is required; the statement need only be relevant to representative affairs. To the same effect is California Evidence Code § 1220. Compare Uniform Rule 63(7), requiring a statement to be made in a representative capacity to be admissible against a party in a representative capacity.

(B)   Under established principles an admission may be made by adopting or acquiescing in the statement of another. While knowledge of contents would ordinarily be essential, this is not inevitably so: "X is a reliable person and knows what he is talking about." See McCormick § 246, p. 527, n. 15. Adoption or acquiescence may be manifested in any appropriate manner. When silence is relied upon, the theory is that the person would, under the circumstances, protest the statement made in his presence, if untrue. The decision in each case calls for an evaluation in terms of probable human behavior. In civil cases, the results have generally been satisfactory. In criminal cases, however, troublesome questions have been raised by decisions holding that failure to deny is an admission: the inference is a fairly weak one, to begin with; silence may be motivated by advice of counsel or realization that "anything you say may be used against you"; unusual opportunity is afforded to manufacture evidence; and encroachment upon the privilege against self-incrimination seems inescapably to be involved. However, recent decisions of the Supreme Court relating to custodial interrogation and the right to counsel appear to resolve these difficulties. Hence the rule contains no special provisions concerning failure to deny in criminal cases.

(C)   No authority is required for the general proposition that a statement authorized by a party to be made should have the status of an admission by the party. However, the question arises whether only statements to third persons should be so regarded, to the exclusion of statements by the agent to the principal. The rule is phrased broadly so as to encompass both. While it may be argued that the agent authorized to make statements to his principal does not speak for him, Morgan, Basic Problems of Evidence 273 (1962), communication to an outsider has not generally been thought to be an essential characteristic of an admission. Thus a party's books or records are usable against him, without regard to any intent to disclose to third persons. 5 Wigmore § 1557. *See also* McCormick § 78, pp. 159–161. In accord is New Jersey Evidence Rule 63(8)(a). Cf. Uniform Rule 63(8)(a) and California Evidence Code § 1222 which limit status as an admission in this regard to statements authorized by the party to be made "for" him, which is perhaps an ambiguous limitation to statements to third persons. Falknor, Vicarious Admissions and the Uniform Rules, 14 Vand.L.Rev. 855, 860–861 (1961).

(D)   The tradition has been to test the admissibility of statements by agents, as admissions, by applying the usual test of agency. Was the admission made by the agent acting in the scope of his employment? Since few principals employ agents for the purpose of making damaging statements, the usual result was exclusion of the statement. Dissatisfaction with this loss of valuable and helpful evidence has been increasing. A substantial trend favors admitting statements related to a matter within the scope of the agency or employment. Grayson v. Williams, 256 F.2d 61 (10th Cir. 1958); Koninklijke Luchtvaart Maatschappij N.V. KLM Royal Dutch Airlines v. Tuller, 110 U.S.App.D.C. 282, 292 F.2d 775, 784 (1961); Martin v. Savage Truck Lines, Inc., 121 F.Supp. 417

(D.D.C. 1954), and numerous state court decisions collected in 4 Wigmore, 1964 Supp., pp. 66–73, with comments by the editor that the statements should have been excluded as not within scope of agency. For the traditional view see Northern Oil Co. v. Socony Mobile [sic] Oil Co., 347 F.2d 81, 85 (2d Cir. 1965) and cases cited therein. Similar provisions are found in Uniform Rule 63(9)(a), Kansas Code of Civil Procedure § 60–460(i)(1), and New Jersey Evidence Rule 63(9)(a).

(E)   The limitation upon the admissibility of statements of co-conspirators to those made "during the course and in furtherance of the conspiracy" is in the accepted pattern. While the broadened view of agency taken in item (iv) might suggest wider admissibility of statements of co-conspirators, the agency theory of conspiracy is at best a fiction and ought not to serve as a basis for admissibility beyond that already established. See Levie, Hearsay and Conspiracy, 52 Mich.L.Rev. 1159 (1954); Comment, 25 U.Chi.L.Rev. 530 (1958). The rule is consistent with the position of the Supreme Court in denying admissibility to statements made after the objectives of the conspiracy have either failed or been achieved. Krulewitch v. United States, 336 U.S. 440, 69 S.Ct. 716, 93 L.Ed. 790 (1949); Wong Sun v. United States, 371 U.S. 471, 490, 83 S.Ct. 407, 9 L.Ed.2d 441 (1963). For similarly limited provisions see California Evidence Code § 1223 and New Jersey Rule 63(9)(b). Cf. Uniform Rule 63(9)(b).

Report of Senate Committee on the Judiciary on Rule 801(d)(2)(E)

Senate Comm. on Judiciary, Fed.Rules of Evidence, S.Rep. No. 1277, 93d Cong., 2d Sess., p. 26 (1974); 1974 U.S. Code Cong. & Ad.News 7051, 7073

The House approved the long-accepted rule that "a statement by a coconspirator of a party during the course and in furtherance of the conspiracy" is not hearsay as it was submitted by the Supreme Court. While the rule refers to a coconspirator, it is this committee's understanding that the rule is meant to carry forward the universally accepted doctrine that a joint venturer is considered as a coconspirator for the purposes of this rule even though no conspiracy has been charged. United States v. Rinaldi, 393 F.2d 97, 99 (2d Cir.), cert. denied 393 U.S. 913 (1968); United States v. Spencer, 415 F.2d 1301, 1304 (7th Cir. 1969).

1987 Amendment Committee Note

The amendments are technical. No substantive change is intended.

1997 Amendment Committee Note on Amendment to Rule 801(d)(2)

Rule 801(d)(2) has been amended in order to respond to three issues raised by *Bourjaily v. United States*, 483 U.S. 171 (1987). First, the amendment codifies the holding in *Bourjaily* by stating expressly that a court shall consider the contents of a coconspirator's statement in determining "the existence of the conspiracy and the participation therein of the declarant and the party against whom the statement is offered." According to *Bourjaily*, Rule 104(a) requires these preliminary questions to be established by a preponderance of the evidence.

Second, the amendment resolves an issue on which the Court had reserved decision. It provides that the contents of the declarant's statement do not alone suffice to establish a conspiracy in which the declarant and the defendant participated. The court must consider in addition the circumstances surrounding the statement, such as the identity of the speaker, the context in which the statement was made, or evidence corroborating the contents of the statement in making its determination as to each preliminary question. This amendment is in accordance with existing practice. Every court of appeals that has resolved this issue requires some evidence in addition to the contents of the statement. *See, e.g., United States v. Beckham*, 968 F.2d 47, 51 (D.C.Cir. 1992); *United States v. Sepulveda*, 15 F.3d 1161, 1181–82 (1st Cir. 1993), *cert. denied*, 114 S.Ct. 2714

(1994); *United States v. Daly*, 842 F.2d 1380, 1386 (2d Cir.), *cert. denied*, 488 U.S. 821 (1988); *United States v. Clark*, 18 F.3d 1337, 1341–42 (6th Cir.), *cert. denied*, 115 S.Ct. 152 (1994); *United States v. Zambrana*, 841 F.2d 1320, 1344–45 (7th Cir. 1988); *United States v. Silverman*, 861 F.2d 571, 577 (9th Cir. 1988); *United States v. Gordon*, 844 F.2d 1397, 1402 (9th Cir. 1988); *United States v. Hernandez*, 829 F.2d 988, 993 (10th Cir. 1987), *cert. denied*, 485 U.S. 1013 (1988); *United States v. Byrom*, 910 F.2d 725, 736 (11th Cir. 1990).

Third, the amendment extends the reasoning of *Bourjaily* to statements offered under subdivisions (C) and (D) of Rule 801 (d)(2). In *Bourjaily*, the Court rejected treating foundational facts pursuant to the law of agency in favor of an evidentiary approach governed by Rule 104(a). The Advisory Committee believes it appropriate to treat analogously preliminary questions relating to the declarant's authority under subdivision (C), and the agency or employment relationship and scope thereof under subdivision (D).

2014 Amendment Committee Note on Amendment to Rule 801(d)(1)(B)

Rule 801(d)(1)(B), as originally adopted, provided for substantive use of certain prior consistent statements of a witness subject to cross-examination. As the Advisory Committee noted, "[t]he prior statement is consistent with the testimony given on the stand, and, if the opposite party wishes to open the door for its admission in evidence, no sound reason is apparent why it should not be received generally."

Though the original Rule 801(d)(1)(B) provided for substantive use of certain prior consistent statements, the scope of that Rule was limited. The Rule covered only those consistent statements that were offered to rebut charges of recent fabrication or improper motive or influence. The Rule did not, for example, provide for substantive admissibility of consistent statements that are probative to explain what otherwise appears to be an inconsistency in the witness's testimony. Nor did it cover consistent statements that would be probative to rebut a charge of faulty memory. Thus, the Rule left many prior consistent statements potentially admissible only for the limited purpose of rehabilitating a witness's credibility. The original Rule also led to some conflict in the cases; some courts distinguished between substantive and rehabilitative use for prior consistent statements, while others appeared to hold that prior consistent statements must be admissible under Rule 801(d)(1)(B) or not at all.

The amendment retains the requirement set forth in *Tome v. United States*, 513 U.S. 150 (1995): that under Rule 801(d)(1)(B), a consistent statement offered to rebut a charge of recent fabrication or improper influence or motive must have been made before the alleged fabrication or improper influence or motive arose. The intent of the amendment is to extend substantive effect to consistent statements that rebut other attacks on a witness—such as the charges of inconsistency or faulty memory.

The amendment does not change the traditional and well-accepted limits on bringing prior consistent statements before the factfinder for credibility purposes. It does not allow impermissible bolstering of a witness. As before, prior consistent statements under the amendment may be brought before the factfinder only if they properly rehabilitate a witness whose credibility has been attacked. As before, to be admissible for rehabilitation, a prior consistent statement must satisfy the strictures of Rule 403. As before, the trial court has ample discretion to exclude prior consistent statements that are cumulative accounts of an event. The amendment does not make any consistent statement admissible that was not admissible previously—the only difference is that prior consistent statements otherwise admissible for rehabilitation are now admissible substantively as well.

———————————

Rule 802. The Rule Against Hearsay

Hearsay is not admissible unless any of the following provides otherwise:

- a federal statute;
- these rules; or
- other rules prescribed by the Supreme Court.

(As amended Apr. 26, 2011, eff. Dec. 1, 2011.)

RESTYLED RULE 802 COMMITTEE NOTE

The language of Rule 802 has been amended as part of the restyling of the Evidence Rules to make them more easily understood and to make style and terminology consistent throughout the rules. These changes are intended to be stylistic only. There is no intent to change any result in any ruling on evidence admissibility.

REPORTER'S COMMENT ON RESTYLED RULE 802

The Restyling changed "the hearsay rule" to "the rule against hearsay." That title is carried through to the exceptions, see Rules 803 and 804. The thought was that the new title is more descriptive—it says not only that it is a rule but something about what the rule does.

On the use of bullet points, see the Reporter's Comment on Restyled Rule 402.

The restyling deleted the language "pursuant to statutory authority" that Congress had added in describing rules prescribed by the Supreme Court that could override Rule 802. One of the goals of restyling is to delete superfluous language—and the phrase about statutory authority was found superfluous, given the fact that Supreme Court rulemaking for national rules of procedure is in fact pursuant to statutory authority.

Section references, McCormick 7th ed.

§ 246

Note by Federal Judicial Center

The rule enacted by the Congress is the rule prescribed by the Supreme Court, amended by substituting "prescribed" in place of "adopted" and by inserting the phrase "pursuant to statutory authority."

Advisory Committee's Note

56 F.R.D. 183, 299

The provision excepting from the operation of the rule hearsay which is made admissible by other rules adopted by the Supreme Court or by Act of Congress continues the admissibility thereunder of hearsay which would not qualify under these Evidence Rules. The following examples illustrate the working of the exception:

FEDERAL RULES OF CIVIL PROCEDURE

Rule 4(g): proof of service by affidavit.

Rule 32: admissibility of depositions.

Rule 43(e): affidavits when motion based on facts not appearing of record.

Rule 56: affidavits in summary judgment proceedings.

Rule 65(b): showing by affidavit for temporary restraining order.

FEDERAL RULES OF CRIMINAL PROCEDURE

Rule 4(a): affidavits to show grounds for issuing warrants.

Rule 12(b)(4): affidavits to determine issues of fact in connection with motions.

ACTS OF CONGRESS

10 U.S.C. § 7730: affidavits of unavailable witnesses in actions for damages caused by vessel in naval service, or towage or salvage of same, when taking of testimony or bringing of action delayed or stayed on security grounds.

29 U.S.C. § 161(4): affidavit as proof of service in NLRB proceedings.

38 U.S.C. § 5206: affidavit as proof of posting notice of sale of unclaimed property by Veterans Administration.

———————

Rule 803. Exceptions to the Rule Against Hearsay—Regardless of Whether the Declarant Is Available as a Witness

The following are not excluded by the rule against hearsay, regardless of whether the declarant is available as a witness:

(1) *Present Sense Impression.* A statement describing or explaining an event or condition, made while or immediately after the declarant perceived it.

(2) *Excited Utterance.* A statement relating to a startling event or condition, made while the declarant was under the stress of excitement that it caused.

(3) *Then-Existing   Mental,   Emotional,   or   Physical Condition.* A statement of the declarant's then-existing state of mind (such as motive, intent, or plan) or emotional, sensory, or physical condition (such as mental feeling, pain, or bodily health), but not including a statement of memory or belief to prove the fact remembered or believed unless it relates to the validity or terms of the declarant's will.

(4) *Statement Made for Medical Diagnosis or Treatment.* A statement that:

(A) is made for—and is reasonably pertinent to—medical diagnosis or treatment; and

(B) describes medical history; past or present symptoms or sensations; their inception; or their general cause.

(5) *Recorded Recollection.* A record that:

(A) is on a matter the witness once knew about but now cannot recall well enough to testify fully and accurately;

(B) was made or adopted by the witness when the matter was fresh in the witness's memory; and

(C) accurately reflects the witness's knowledge.

If admitted, the record may be read into evidence but may be received as an exhibit only if offered by an adverse party.

(6) *Records of a Regularly Conducted Activity.* A record of an act, event, condition, opinion, or diagnosis if:

(A) the record was made at or near the time by—or from information transmitted by—someone with knowledge;

(B) the record was kept in the course of a regularly conducted activity of a business, organization, occupation, or calling, whether or not for profit;

(C) making the record was a regular practice of that activity;

(D) all these conditions are shown by the testimony of the custodian or another qualified witness, or by a certification that complies with Rule 902(11) or (12) or with a statute permitting certification; and

(E) the opponent does not show that the source of information or the method or circumstances of preparation indicate a lack of trustworthiness.

(7) *Absence of a Record of a Regularly Conducted Activity.* Evidence that a matter is not included in a record described in paragraph (6) if:

(A) the evidence is admitted to prove that the matter did not occur or exist;

(B) a record was regularly kept for a matter of that kind; and

(C) the opponent does not show that the possible source of the information or other circumstances indicate a lack of trustworthiness.

(8) *Public Records.* A record or statement of a public office if:

(A) it sets out:

(i) the office's activities;

(ii) a matter observed while under a legal duty to report, but not including, in a criminal case, a matter observed by law-enforcement personnel; or

(iii) in a civil case or against the government in a criminal case, factual findings from a legally authorized investigation; and

(B) the opponent does not show that the source of information or other circumstances indicate a lack of trustworthiness.

(9) *Public Records of Vital Statistics.* A record of a birth, death, or marriage, if reported to a public office in accordance with a legal duty.

(10) *Absence of a Public Record.* Testimony—or a certification under Rule 902—that a diligent search failed to disclose a public record or statement if:

(A) the testimony or certification is admitted to prove that

(i) the record or statement does not exist; or

(ii) a matter did not occur or exist, if a public office regularly kept a record or statement for a matter of that kind; and

(B) in a criminal case, a prosecutor who intends to offer a certification provides written notice of that intent at least 14 days before trial, and the defendant does not object in writing within 7 days of receiving the notice—unless the court sets a different time for the notice or the objection.

(11) *Records of Religious Organizations Concerning Personal or Family History.* A statement of birth, legitimacy, ancestry, marriage, divorce, death, relationship by blood or marriage, or similar facts of personal or family history, contained in a regularly kept record of a religious organization.

(12) *Certificates of Marriage, Baptism, and Similar Ceremonies.* A statement of fact contained in a certificate:

(A) made by a person who is authorized by a religious organization or by law to perform the act certified;

    (B) attesting that the person performed a marriage or similar ceremony or administered a sacrament; and

    (C) purporting to have been issued at the time of the act or within a reasonable time after it.

(13) *Family Records.* A statement of fact about personal or family history contained in a family record, such as a Bible, genealogy, chart, engraving on a ring, inscription on a portrait, or engraving on an urn or burial marker.

(14) *Records of Documents That Affect an Interest in Property.* The record of a document that purports to establish or affect an interest in property if:

    (A) the record is admitted to prove the content of the original recorded document, along with its signing and its delivery by each person who purports to have signed it;

    (B) the record is kept in a public office; and

    (C) a statute authorizes recording documents of that kind in that office.

(15) *Statements in Documents That Affect an Interest in Property.* A statement contained in a document that purports to establish or affect an interest in property if the matter stated was relevant to the document's purpose—unless later dealings with the property are inconsistent with the truth of the statement or the purport of the document.

(16) *Statements in Ancient Documents.* A statement in a document that is at least 20 years old that was prepared before January 1, 1998, and whose authenticity is established.

(17) *Market Reports and Similar Commercial Publications.* Market quotations, lists, directories, or other compilations that are generally relied on by the public or by persons in particular occupations.

(18) *Statements in Learned Treatises, Periodicals, or Pamphlets.* A statement contained in a treatise, periodical, or pamphlet if:

    (A) the statement is called to the attention of an expert witness on cross-examination or relied on by the expert on direct examination; and

    (B) the publication is established as a reliable authority by the expert's admission or testimony, by another expert's testimony, or by judicial notice.

If admitted, the statement may be read into evidence but not received as an exhibit.

(19) *Reputation Concerning Personal or Family History.* A reputation among a person's family by blood, adoption, or marriage—or among a person's associates or in the community—concerning the person's birth, adoption, legitimacy, ancestry, marriage, divorce, death, relationship by blood, adoption, or marriage, or similar facts of personal or family history.

(20) *Reputation Concerning Boundaries or General History.* A reputation in a community—arising before the controversy—

concerning boundaries of land in the community or customs that affect the land, or concerning general historical events important to that community, state, or nation.

(21) *Reputation Concerning Character.* A reputation among a person's associates or in the community concerning the person's character.

(22) *Judgment of a Previous Conviction.* Evidence of a final judgment of conviction if:

> **(A)** the judgment was entered after a trial or guilty plea, but not a nolo contendere plea;

> **(B)** the conviction was for a crime punishable by death or by imprisonment for more than a year;

> **(C)** the evidence is admitted to prove any fact essential to the judgment; and

> **(D)** when offered by the prosecutor in a criminal case for a purpose other than impeachment, the judgment was against the defendant.

The pendency of an appeal may be shown but does not affect admissibility.

(23) *Judgments Involving Personal, Family, or General History, or a Boundary.* A judgment that is admitted to prove a matter of personal, family, or general history, or boundaries, if the matter:

> **(A)** was essential to the judgment; and

> **(B)** could be proved by evidence of reputation.

(24) *[Other Exceptions.]* [Transferred to Rule 807.]

(As amended P.L. 94–149, § 1(11), Dec. 12, 1975, 89 Stat. 805; Mar. 2, 1987, eff. Oct. 1, 1987, Apr.11, 1997, eff. Dec. 1, 1997, Apr. 17, 2000, eff. Dec. 1, 2000; Apr. 26, 2011, eff. Dec. 1, 2011; April 16, 2013, eff. Dec. 1, 2013; Apr. 25, 2014, eff. Dec. 1, 2014; Apr. 27, 2017, eff. Dec. 1, 2017.)

RESTYLED RULE 803 COMMITTEE NOTE

The language of Rule 803 has been amended as part of the restyling of the Evidence Rules to make them more easily understood and to make style and terminology consistent throughout the rules. These changes are intended to be stylistic only. There is no intent to change any result in any ruling on evidence admissibility.

REPORTER'S COMMENT ON RESTYLED RULE 803

Numbering

The hearsay exceptions in Rule 803 are numbered inconsistently with style conventions. A number follows a number, *e.g.,* "Rule 803(1)." Proper numbering of subdivisions would be 803(a), 803(b) and so forth. The restylist proposed this renumbering but it was emphatically rejected by the Advisory Committee. The Committee concluded that the benefits of proper numbering were far outweighed by the costs of upsetting electronic searches for cases decided under Rule 803, as well as the common understanding and lexicon used by courts and litigants for some of the most important rules in the Federal Rules of Evidence. The transaction costs of renumbering would be substantial.

Paper-Based Rules

Note that many of the Rule 803 exceptions cover documents, records, treatises, etc. The Restyled Rules make two innovations regarding these paper-based exceptions. First, the multiple references to "records, memoranda, documents," etc. are streamlined by defining "record" to include all similar terms. See Rule 101(b)(4). Second, these rules now explicitly cover electronic evidence—by way of a definition providing that any kind of written material to include information in electronic form. See Rule 101(b)(6).

Rule 803(8), Trustworthiness Clause

The Restyled Rule 803(8) places the trustworthiness clause in a separate paragraph, in order to clear up an ambiguity in the original rule—whether the trustworthiness clause applies only to investigative reports or to all reports. (The original rule was ambiguous because the trustworthiness clause was tacked on to the end of the rule, connected by a comma to the description of reports admissible under then subsection (C)). Commentators and case law indicate that the trustworthiness requirement should apply and was intended to apply to *all* public reports (and so would be parallel with business records, as the trustworthiness clause in that exception applies to all records proffered under it). So the Restyling clarifies the rule in accordance with its original intent and with the case law.

Section references, McCormick 7th ed.

§§ 268–300, §§ 321–323

Note by Federal Judicial Center

The rule enacted by the Congress retains the 24 exceptions set forth in the rule prescribed by the Supreme Court. [Now there are 23, as the residual exception set forth in Rule 803(24) has been moved to Rule 807.—Ed.] Three of the exceptions, numbered (6), (8), and (24) have been amended in respects that may fairly be described as substantial. Others, numbered (5), (7), (14), and (16), have been amended in lesser ways. The remaining 17 are unchanged. The amendments are, in numerical order, as follows.

Exception (5) as prescribed by the Supreme Court was amended by inserting after "made" the phrase "or adopted by the witness."

Exception (6) as prescribed by the Supreme Court was amended by substituting the phrase, "if kept in the course of a regularly conducted business activity, and if it was the regular practice of that business activity to make the memorandum, report, record, or data compilation, all," in place of "all in the course of a regularly conducted activity"; by substituting "source" in place of "sources"; by substituting the phrase, "the method or circumstances of preparation," in place of "other circumstances"; and by adding the second sentence.

Exception (7) as prescribed by the Supreme Court was amended by substituting the phrase, "kept in accordance with the provisions of paragraph (6)," in place of "of a regularly conducted activity." The exception prescribed by the Supreme Court included a comma after "memoranda," while the congressional enactment does not.

Exception (8) as prescribed by the Supreme Court was amended by inserting in item (B) after "law" the phrase, "as to which matters there was a duty to report, excluding, however, in criminal cases matters observed by police officers and other law enforcement personnel," and by substituting in item (C) the phrase "civil actions and proceedings," in place of "civil cases."

Exception (14) as prescribed by the Supreme Court was amended by substituting "authorizes" in place of "authorized."

Exception (16) as prescribed by the Supreme Court was amended by substituting the phrase, "the authenticity of which," in place of "whose authenticity."

Exception (24) as prescribed by the Supreme Court was amended by substituting "equivalent" in place of "comparable," and adding all that appears after "trustworthiness" in the exception as enacted by the Congress. [Subsequently moved to Rule 807.—Ed.]

Advisory Committee's Note[20]

56 F.R.D. 183, 303

The exceptions are phrased in terms of nonapplication of the hearsay rule, rather than in positive terms of admissibility, in order to repel any implication that other possible grounds for exclusion are eliminated from consideration.

The present rule proceeds upon the theory that under appropriate circumstances a hearsay statement may possess circumstantial guarantees of trustworthiness sufficient to justify nonproduction of the declarant in person at the trial even though he may be available. The theory finds vast support in the many exceptions to the hearsay rule developed by the common law in which unavailability of the declarant is not a relevant factor. The present rule is a synthesis of them, with revision where modern developments and conditions are believed to make that course appropriate.

In a hearsay situation, the declarant is, of course, a witness, and neither this rule nor Rule 804 dispenses with the requirement of firsthand knowledge. It may appear from his statement or be inferable from circumstances. See Rule 602.

Exceptions (1) and (2). In considerable measure these two [exceptions] overlap, though based on somewhat different theories. The most significant practical difference will lie in the time lapse allowable between event and statement.

The underlying theory of Exception (1) is that substantial contemporaneity of event and statement negative the likelihood of deliberate or conscious misrepresentation. Moreover, if the witness is the declarant, he may be examined on the statement. If the witness is not the declarant, he may be examined as to the circumstances as an aid in evaluating the statement. Morgan, Basic Problems of Evidence 340–341 (1962).

The theory of Exception (2) is simply that circumstances may produce a condition of excitement which temporarily stills the capacity of reflection and produces utterances free of conscious fabrication. 6 Wigmore § 1747, p. 135. Spontaneity is the key factor in each instance, though arrived at by somewhat different routes. Both are needed in order to avoid needless niggling.

While the theory of Exception (2) has been criticized on the ground that excitement impairs accuracy of observation as well as eliminating conscious fabrication, Hutchins and Slesinger, Some Observations on the Law of Evidence: Spontaneous Exclamations, 28 Colum.L.Rev. 432 (1928), it finds support in cases without number. See cases in 6 Wigmore § 1750; Annot., 53 A.L.R.2d 1245 (statements as to cause of or responsibility for motor vehicle accident); Annot., 4 A.L.R.3d 149 (accusatory statements by homicide victims). Since unexciting events are less likely to evoke comment, decisions involving Exception (1) are far less numerous. Illustrative are Tampa Elec. Co. v. Getrost, 151 Fla. 558, 10 So.2d

---

[20] The Congressional comment on individual subdivisions of Rule 803 are included immediately after the Advisory Committee Note on the particular subdivision.—Ed.

83 (1942); Houston Oxygen Co. v. Davis, 139 Tex. 1, 161 S.W.2d 474 (1942); and cases cited in McCormick § 273, p. 585, n. 4.

With respect to the *time element,* Exception (1) recognizes that in many, if not most, instances precise contemporaneity is not possible, and hence a slight lapse is allowable. Under Exception (2) the standard of measurement is the duration of the state of excitement. "How long can excitement prevail? Obviously there are no pat answers and the character of the transaction or event will largely determine the significance of the time factor." Slough, Spontaneous Statements and State of Mind, 46 Iowa L.Rev. 224, 243 (1961); McCormick § 272, p. 580.

Participation by the declarant is not required: a non-participant may be moved to describe what he perceives, and one may be startled by an event in which he is not an actor. Slough, *supra*; McCormick, *supra*; 6 Wigmore § 1755; Annot., 78 A.L.R.2d 300.

Whether *proof of the startling event* may be made by the statement itself is largely an academic question, since in most cases there is present at least circumstantial evidence that something of a startling nature must have occurred. For cases in which the evidence consists of the condition of the declarant (injuries, state of shock), see Insurance Co. v. Mosely, 75 U.S. (8 Wall.) 397, 19 L.Ed. 437 (1869); Wheeler v. United States, 93 U.S.App.D.C. 159, 211 F.2d 19 (1953), cert. denied 347 U.S. 1019, 74 S.Ct. 876, 98 L.Ed. 1140; Wetherbee v. Safety Casualty Co., 219 F.2d 274 (5th Cir. 1955); Lampe v. United States, 97 U.S.App.D.C. 160, 229 F.2d 43 (1956). Nevertheless, on occasion the only evidence may be the content of the statement itself, and rulings that it may be sufficient are described as "increasing," Slough, *supra* at 246, and as the "prevailing practice," McCormick § 272, p. 579. Illustrative are Armour & Co. v. Industrial Commission, 78 Colo. 569, 243 P. 546 (1926); Young v. Stewart, 191 N.C. 297, 131 S.E. 735 (1926). Moreover, under Rule 104(a) the judge is not limited by the hearsay rule in passing upon preliminary questions of fact.

Proof of declarant's perception by his statement presents similar considerations when declarant is identified. People v. Poland, 22 Ill.2d 175, 174 N.E.2d 804 (1961). However, when declarant is an unidentified bystander, the cases indicate hesitancy in upholding the statement alone as sufficient, Garrett v. Howden, 73 N.M. 307, 387 P.2d 874 (1963); Beck v. Dye, 200 Wash. 1, 92 P.2d 1113 (1939), a result which would under appropriate circumstances be consistent with the rule.

Permissible *subject matter* of the statement is limited under Exception (1) to description or explanation of the event or condition, the assumption being that spontaneity, in the absence of a startling event, may extend no farther. In Exception (2), however, the statement need only "relate" to the startling event or condition, thus affording a broader scope of subject matter coverage. 6 Wigmore §§ 1750, 1754. See Sanitary Grocery Co. v. Snead, 67 App.D.C. 129, 90 F.2d 374 (1937), slip-and-fall case sustaining admissibility of clerk's statement, "That has been on the floor for a couple of hours," and Murphy Auto Parts Co., Inc. v. Ball, 101 U.S.App.D.C. 416, 249 F.2d 508 (1957), upholding admission, on issue of driver's agency, of his statement that he had to call on a customer and was in a hurry to get home. Quick, Hearsay, Excitement, Necessity and the Uniform Rules: A Reappraisal of Rule 63(4), 6 Wayne L.Rev. 204, 206–209 (1960).

Similar provisions are found in Uniform Rule 63(4)(a) and (b); California Evidence Code § 1240 (as to Exception (2) only); Kansas Code of Civil Procedure § 60–460(d)(1) and (2); New Jersey Evidence Rule 63(4).

Exception (3) is essentially a specialized application of Exception (1), presented separately to enhance its usefulness and accessibility. See McCormick §§ 265, 268.

The exclusion of "statements of memory or belief to prove the fact remembered or believed" is necessary to avoid the virtual destruction of the hearsay rule which would otherwise result from allowing state of mind, provable by a hearsay statement, to serve as the basis for an inference of the happening of the event which produced the state of mind. Shepard v. United States, 290 U.S. 96, 54 S.Ct. 22, 78 L.Ed. 196 (1933); Maguire, The Hillmon Case—Thirty-three Years After, 38 Harv.L.Rev. 709, 719–731 (1925); Hinton, States of Mind and the Hearsay Rule, 1 U.Chi.L.Rev. 394, 421–423 (1934). The rule of Mutual Life Ins. Co. v. Hillmon, 145 U.S. 285, 12 S.Ct. 909, 36 L.Ed. 706 (1892), allowing evidence of intention as tending to prove the doing of the act intended, is, of course, left undisturbed.

The carving out, from the exclusion mentioned in the preceding paragraph, of declarations relating to the execution, revocation, identification, or terms of declarant's will represents an *ad hoc* judgment which finds ample reinforcement in the decisions, resting on practical grounds of necessity and expediency rather than logic. McCormick § 271, pp. 577–578; Annot., 34 A.L.R.2d 588, 62 A.L.R.2d 855. A similar recognition of the need for and practical value of this kind of evidence is found in California Evidence Code § 1260.

Report of House Committee on the Judiciary on Rule 803(3)

House Comm. on Judiciary, Fed.Rules of Evidence, H.R.Rep. No. 650, 93d Cong., 1st Sess., p. 13 (1973); 1974 U.S.Code Cong. & Ad.News 7075, 7087

Rule 803(3) was approved in the form submitted by the Court to Congress. However, the Committee intends that the Rule be construed to limit the doctrine of Mutual Life Insurance Co. v. Hillmon, 145 U.S. 285, 295–300 (1892), so as to render statements of intent by a declarant admissible only to prove his future conduct, not the future conduct of another person.

Advisory Committee's Note on Rule 803(4)

56 F.R.D. 183, 306

Exception (4). Even those few jurisdictions which have shied away from generally admitting statements of present condition have allowed them if made to a physician for purposes of diagnosis and treatment in view of the patient's strong motivation to be truthful. McCormick § 266, p. 563. The same guarantee of trustworthiness extends to statements of past conditions and medical history, made for purposes of diagnosis or treatment. It also extends to statements as to causation, reasonably pertinent to the same purposes, in accord with the current trend, Shell Oil Co. v. Industrial Commission, 2 Ill.2d 590, 119 N.E.2d 224 (1954); McCormick § 266, p. 564; New Jersey Evidence Rule 63(12)(c). Statements as to fault would not ordinarily qualify under this latter language. Thus a patient's statement that he was struck by an automobile would qualify but not his statement that the car was driven through a red light. Under the exception the statement need not have been made to a physician. Statements to hospital attendants, ambulance drivers, or even members of the family might be included.

Conventional doctrine has excluded from the hearsay exception, as not within its guarantee of truthfulness, statements to a physician consulted only for the purpose of enabling him to testify. While these statements were not admissible as substantive evidence, the expert was allowed to state the basis of his opinion, including statements of this kind. The distinction thus called for was one most unlikely to be made by juries. The rule accordingly rejects the limitation. This position is consistent with the provision of Rule 703 that the facts on which expert testimony is based need not be admissible in evidence if of a kind ordinarily relied upon by experts in the field.

Report of House Committee on the Judiciary on Rule 803(4)

House Comm. on Judiciary, Fed.Rules of Evidence, H.R.Rep. No. 650, 93d Cong., 1st Sess., p. 14 (1973); 1974 U.S.Code Cong. & Ad.News 7075, 7087

After giving particular attention to the question of physical examination made solely to enable a physician to testify, the Committee approved Rule 803(4) as submitted to Congress, with the understanding that it is not intended in any way to adversely affect present privilege rules or those subsequently adopted.

Report of Senate Committee on the Judiciary on Rule 803(4)

Senate Comm. on Judiciary, Fed.Rules of Evidence, S.Rep. No. 1277, 93d Cong., 2d Sess., p. 27 (1974); 1974 U.S.Code Cong. & Ad.News 7051, 7073

The House approved this rule as it was submitted by the Supreme Court "with the understanding that it is not intended in any way to adversely affect present privilege rules." We also approve this rule, and we would point out with respect to the question of its relation to privileges, it must be read in conjunction with rule 35 of the Federal Rules of Civil Procedure which provides that whenever the physical or mental condition of a party (plaintiff or defendant) is in controversy, the court may require him to submit to an examination by a physician. It is these examinations which will normally be admitted under this exception.

Advisory Committee's Note on Rule 803(5)

56 F.R.D. 183, 306

Exception (5). A hearsay exception for recorded recollection is generally recognized and has been described as having "long been favored by the federal and practically all the state courts that have had occasion to decide the question." United States v. Kelly, 349 F.2d 720, 770 (2d Cir. 1965), citing numerous cases and sustaining the exception against a claimed denial of the right of confrontation. Many additional cases are cited in Annot., 82 A.L.R.2d 473, 520. The guarantee of trustworthiness is found in the reliability inherent in a record made while events were still fresh in mind and accurately reflecting them. Owens v. State, 67 Md. 307, 316, 10 A. 210, 212 (1887).

The principal controversy attending the exception has centered, not upon the propriety of the exception itself, but upon the question whether a preliminary requirement of impaired memory on the part of the witness should be imposed. The authorities are divided. If regard be had only to the accuracy of the evidence, admittedly impairment of the memory of the witness adds nothing to it and should not be required. McCormick § 277, p. 593; 3 Wigmore § 738, p. 76; Jordan v. People, 151 Colo. 133, 376 P.2d 699 (1962), cert. denied 373 U.S. 944, 83 S.Ct. 1553, 10 L.Ed.2d 699; Hall v. State, 223 Md. 158, 162 A.2d 751 (1960); State v. Bindhammer, 44 N.J. 372, 209 A.2d 124 (1965). Nevertheless, the absence of the requirement, it is believed, would encourage the use of statements carefully prepared for purposes of litigation under the supervision of attorneys, investigators, or claim adjusters. Hence the example includes a requirement that the witness not have "sufficient recollection to enable him to testify fully and accurately." To the same effect are California Evidence Code § 1237 and New Jersey Rule 63(1)(b), and this has been the position of the federal courts. Vicksburg & Meridian R.R. v. O'Brien, 119 U.S. 99, 7 S.Ct. 118, 30 L.Ed. 299 (1886); Ahern v. Webb, 268 F.2d 45 (10th Cir. 1959); and see N.L.R.B. v. Hudson Pulp and Paper Corp., 273 F.2d 660, 665 (5th Cir. 1960); N.L.R.B. v. Federal Dairy Co., 297 F.2d 487 (1st Cir. 1962). But cf. United States v. Adams, 385 F.2d 548 (2d Cir. 1967).

No attempt is made in the exception to spell out the method of establishing the initial knowledge or the contemporaneity and accuracy of the record, leaving them to be dealt with as the circumstances of the particular case might indicate. Multiple person involvement in the process of observing and recording, as in Rathbun v. Brancatella, 93 N.J.L. 222, 107 A. 279 (1919), is entirely consistent with the exception.

Locating the exception at this place in the scheme of the rules is a matter of choice. There were two other possibilities. The first was to regard the statement as one of the group of prior statements of a testifying witness which are excluded entirely from the category of hearsay by Rule 801(d)(1). That category, however, requires that declarant be "subject to cross-examination," as to which the impaired memory aspect of the exception raises doubts. The other possibility was to include the exception among those covered by Rule 804. Since unavailability is required by that rule and lack of memory is listed as a species of unavailability by the definition of the term in Rule 804(a)(3), that treatment at first impression would seem appropriate. The fact is, however, that the unavailability requirement of the exception is of a limited and peculiar nature. Accordingly, the exception is located at this point rather than in the context of a rule where unavailability is conceived of more broadly.

Report of House Committee on the Judiciary on Rule 803(5)

House Comm. on Judiciary, Fed.Rules of Evidence, H.R.Rep. No. 650, 93d Cong., 1st Sess., p. 14 (1973); 1974 U.S.Code Cong. & Ad.News 7075, 7087

Rule 803(5) as submitted by the Court permitted the reading into evidence of a memorandum or record concerning a matter about which a witness once had knowledge but now has insufficient recollection to enable him to testify accurately and fully, "shown to have been made when the matter was fresh in his memory and to reflect that knowledge correctly." The Committee amended this Rule to add the words "or adopted by the witness" after the phrase "shown to have been made", a treatment consistent with the definition of "statement" in the Jencks Act, 18 U.S.C. 3500. Moreover, it is the Committee's understanding that a memorandum or report, although barred under this Rule, would nonetheless be admissible if it came within another hearsay exception. This last stated principle is deemed applicable to all the hearsay rules.

Report of Senate Committee on the Judiciary on Rule 803(5)

Senate Comm. on Judiciary, Fed.Rules of Evidence, S.Rep. No. 1277, 93d Cong., 2d Sess., p. 27 (1974); 1974 U.S.Code Cong. & Ad.News 7051, 7073

Rule 803(5) as submitted by the Court permitted the reading into evidence of a memorandum or record concerning a matter about which a witness once had knowledge but now has insufficient recollection to enable him to testify accurately and fully, "shown to have been made when the matter was fresh in his memory and to reflect that knowledge correctly." The House amended the rule to add the words "or adopted by the witness" after the phrase "shown to have been made," language parallel to the Jencks Act.[21]

The committee accepts the House amendment with the understanding and belief that it was not intended to narrow the scope of applicability of the rule. In fact, we understand it to clarify the rule's applicability to a memorandum adopted by the witness as well as one made by him. While the rule as submitted by the Court was silent on the question of who made the memorandum, we view the House amendment as a helpful clarification, noting, however, that the Advisory Committee's note to this rule suggests that the important thing is the accuracy of the memorandum rather than who made it.

The committee does not view the House amendment as precluding admissibility in situations in which multiple participants were involved.

---

[21] 18 U.S.C. § 3500.—Ed.

When the verifying witness has not prepared the report, but merely examined it and found it accurate, he has adopted the report, and it is therefore admissible. The rule should also be interpreted to cover other situations involving multiple participants, *e.g.*, employer dictating to secretary, secretary making memorandum at direction of employer, or information being passed along a chain of persons, as in Curtis v. Bradley.[22]

The committee also accepts the understanding of the House that a memorandum or report, although barred under this rule, would nonetheless be admissible if it came within another hearsay exception. We consider this principle to be applicable to all the hearsay rules.

Advisory Committee's Note on Rule 803(6)

56 F.R.D. 183, 307

Exception (6) represents an area which has received much attention from those seeking to improve the law of evidence. The Commonwealth Fund Act was the result of a study completed in 1927 by a distinguished committee under the chairmanship of Professor Morgan. Morgan et al., The Law of Evidence: Some Proposals for its Reform 63 (1927). With changes too minor to mention, it was adopted by Congress in 1936 as the rule for federal courts. 28 U.S.C. § 1732. A number of states took similar action. The Commissioners on Uniform State Laws in 1936 promulgated the Uniform Business Records as Evidence Act, 9A U.L.A. 506, which has acquired a substantial following in the states. Model Code Rule 514 and Uniform Rule 63(13) also deal with the subject. Difference of varying degrees of importance exist among these various treatments.

These reform efforts were largely within the context of business and commercial records, as the kind usually encountered, and concentrated considerable attention upon relaxing the requirement of producing as witnesses, or accounting for the nonproduction of, all participants in the process of gathering, transmitting, and recording information which the common law had evolved as a burdensome and crippling aspect of using records of this type. In their areas of primary emphasis on witnesses to be called and the general admissibility of ordinary business and commercial records, the Commonwealth Fund Act and the Uniform Act appear to have worked well. The exception seeks to preserve their advantages.

On the subject of what witnesses must be called, the Commonwealth Fund Act eliminated the common law requirement of calling or accounting for all participants by failing to mention it. United States v. Mortimer, 118 F.2d 266 (2d Cir. 1941); La Porte v. United States, 300 F.2d 878 (9th Cir. 1962); McCormick § 290, p. 608. Model Code Rule 514 and Uniform Rule 63(13) did likewise. The Uniform Act, however, abolished the common law requirement in express terms, providing that the requisite foundation testimony might be furnished by "the custodian or other qualified witness." Uniform Business Records as Evidence Act, § 2; 9A U.L.A. 506. The exception follows the Uniform Act in this respect.

The element of unusual reliability of business records is said variously to be supplied by systematic checking, by regularity and continuity which produce habits of precision, by actual experience of business in relying upon them, or by a duty to make an accurate record as part of a continuing job or occupation. McCormick §§ 281, 286, 287; Laughlin, Business Entries and the Like, 46 Iowa L.Rev. 276 (1961). The model statutes and rules have sought to capture these factors and to extend their impact by employing the phrase "regular course of business," in conjunction with a definition of "business" far broader than its ordinarily accepted meaning. The result is a tendency unduly to emphasize a

---

[22] 65 Conn. 99, 31 Atl. 591 (1894). *See also* Rathbun v. Brancatella, 93 N.J.L. 222, 107 Atl. 279 (1919); *see also* McCormick on Evidence, § 303 (2d ed. 1972).—Ed.

requirement of routineness and repetitiveness and an insistence that other types of records be squeezed into the fact patterns which give rise to traditional business records. The rule therefore adopts the phrase "the course of a regularly conducted activity" as capturing the essential basis of the hearsay exception as it has evolved and the essential element which can be abstracted from the various specifications of what is a "business." **[Editor's note: This terminology was rejected by Congress.]**

Amplification of the kinds of activities producing admissible records has given rise to problems which conventional business records by their nature avoid. They are problems of the source of the recorded information, of entries in opinion form, of motivation, and of involvement as participant in the matters recorded.

Sources of information presented no substantial problem with ordinary business records. All participants, including the observer or participant furnishing the information to be recorded, were acting routinely, under a duty of accuracy, with employer reliance on the result, or in short "in the regular course of business." If, however, the supplier of the information does not act in the regular course, an essential link is broken; the assurance of accuracy does not extend to the information itself, and the fact that it may be recorded with scrupulous accuracy is of no avail. An illustration is the police report incorporating information obtained from a bystander: the officer qualifies as acting in the regular course but the informant does not. The leading case, Johnson v. Lutz, 253 N.Y. 124, 170 N.E. 517 (1930), held that a report thus prepared was inadmissible. Most of the authorities have agreed with the decision. Gencarella v. Fyfe, 171 F.2d 419 (1st Cir. 1948); Gordon v. Robinson, 210 F.2d 192 (3d Cir. 1954); Standard Oil Co. of California v. Moore, 251 F.2d 188, 214 (9th Cir. 1957), cert. denied 356 U.S. 975, 78 S.Ct. 1139, 2 L.Ed.2d 1148; Yates v. Bair Transport, Inc., 249 F.Supp. 681 (S.D.N.Y. 1965); Annot., 69 A.L.R.2d 1148. Cf. Hawkins v. Gorea Motor Express, Inc., 360 F.2d 933 (2d Cir. 1966). Contra, 5 Wigmore § 1530a, n. 1, pp. 391–392. The point is not dealt with specifically in the Commonwealth Fund Act, the Uniform Act, or Uniform Rule 63(13). However, Model Code Rule 514 contains the requirement "that it was the regular course of that business for one with personal knowledge . . . to make such a memorandum or record or to transmit information thereof to be included in such a memorandum or record. . . ." The rule follows this lead in requiring an informant with knowledge acting in the course of the regularly conducted activity.

Entries in the form of opinions were not encountered in traditional business records in view of the purely factual nature of the items recorded, but they are now commonly encountered with respect to medical diagnoses, prognoses, and test results, as well as occasionally in other areas. The Commonwealth Fund Act provided only for records of an "act, transaction, occurrence, or event," while the Uniform Act, Model Code Rule 514, and Uniform Rule 63(13) merely added the ambiguous term "condition." The limited phrasing of the Commonwealth Fund Act, 28 U.S.C. § 1732, may account for the reluctance of some federal decisions to admit diagnostic entries. New York Life Ins. Co. v. Taylor, 79 U.S.App.D.C. 66, 147 F.2d 297 (1945); Lyles v. United States, 103 U.S.App.D.C. 22, 254 F.2d 725 (1957), cert. denied 356 U.S. 961, 78 S.Ct. 997, 2 L.Ed.2d 1067; England v. United States, 174 F.2d 466 (5th Cir. 1949); Skogen v. Dow Chemical Co., 375 F.2d 692 (8th Cir. 1967). Other federal decisions, however, experienced no difficulty in freely admitting diagnostic entries. Reed v. Order of United Commercial Travelers, 123 F.2d 252 (2d Cir. 1941); Buckminster's Estate v. Commissioner of Internal Revenue, 147 F.2d 331 (2d Cir. 1944); Medina v. Erickson, 226 F.2d 475 (9th Cir. 1955); Thomas v. Hogan, 308 F.2d 355 (4th Cir. 1962); Glawe v. Rulon, 284 F.2d 495 (8th Cir. 1960). In the state courts, the trend favors admissibility. Borucki v. MacKenzie Bros. Co., 125 Conn. 92, 3 A.2d 224 (1938); Allen v. St. Louis Public Service Co., 365 Mo. 677, 285 S.W.2d 663, 55 A.L.R.2d 1022 (1956); People v. Kohlmeyer, 284 N.Y. 366, 31 N.E.2d 490 (1940); Weis v. Weis, 147 Ohio St. 416, 72 N.E.2d 245 (1947). In order to make clear its adherence to the latter position, the rule specifically includes both diagnoses and opinions, in addition to acts, events, and conditions, as proper subjects of admissible entries.

Problems of the motivation of the informant have been a source of difficulty and disagreement. In Palmer v. Hoffman, 318 U.S. 109, 63 S.Ct. 477, 87 L.Ed. 645 (1943), exclusion of an accident report made by the since deceased engineer, offered by defendant railroad trustees in a grade crossing collision case, was upheld. The report was not "in the regular course of business," not a record of the systematic conduct of the business as a business, said the Court. The report was prepared for use in litigating, not railroading. While the opinion mentions the motivation of the engineer only obliquely, the emphasis on records of routine operations is significant only by virtue of impact on motivation to be accurate. Absence of routineness raises lack of motivation to be accurate. The opinion of the Court of Appeals had gone beyond mere lack of motive to be accurate: the engineer's statement was "dripping with motivations to misrepresent." Hoffman v. Palmer, 129 F.2d 976, 991 (2d Cir. 1942). The direct introduction of motivation is a disturbing factor, since absence of motive to misrepresent has not traditionally been a requirement of the rule; that records might be self-serving has not been a ground for exclusion. Laughlin, Business Records and the Like, 46 Iowa L.Rev. 276, 285 (1961). As Judge Clark said in his dissent, "I submit that there is hardly a grocer's account book which could not be excluded on that basis." 129 F.2d at 1002. A physician's evaluation report of a personal injury litigant would appear to be in the routine of his business. If the report is offered by the party at whose instance it was made, however, it has been held inadmissible, Yates v. Bair Transport, Inc., 249 F.Supp. 681 (S.D.N.Y. 1965), otherwise if offered by the opposite party, Korte v. New York, N.H. & H.R. Co., 191 F.2d 86 (2d Cir. 1951), cert. denied 342 U.S. 868, 72 S.Ct. 108, 96 L.Ed. 652.

The decisions hinge on motivation and which party is entitled to be concerned about it. Professor McCormick believed that the doctor's report or the accident report were sufficiently routine to justify admissibility. McCormick § 287, p. 604. Yet hesitation must be experienced in admitting everything which is observed and recorded in the course of a regularly conducted activity. Efforts to set a limit are illustrated by Hartzog v. United States, 217 F.2d 706 (4th Cir. 1954), error to admit worksheets made by since deceased deputy collector in preparation for the instant income tax evasion prosecution, and United States v. Ware, 247 F.2d 698 (7th Cir. 1957), error to admit narcotics agents' records of purchases. *See also* Exception (8), *infra*, as to the public record aspects of records of this nature. Some decisions have been satisfied as to motivation of an accident report if made pursuant to statutory duty, United States v. New York Foreign Trade Zone Operators, 304 F.2d 792 (2d Cir. 1962); Taylor v. Baltimore & O.R. Co., 344 F.2d 281 (2d Cir. 1965), since the report was oriented in a direction other than the litigation which ensued. Cf. Matthews v. United States, 217 F.2d 409 (5th Cir. 1954). The formulation of specific terms which would assure satisfactory results in all cases is not possible. Consequently the rule proceeds from the base that records made in the course of a regularly conducted activity will be taken as admissible but subject to authority to exclude if "the sources of information or other circumstances indicate lack of trustworthiness."

Occasional decisions have reached for enhanced accuracy by requiring involvement as a participant in matters reported. Clainos v. United States, 82 U.S.App.D.C. 278, 163 F.2d 593 (1947), error to admit police records of convictions; Standard Oil Co. of California v. Moore, 251 F.2d 188 (9th Cir. 1957), cert. denied 356 U.S. 975, 78 S.Ct. 1139, 2 L.Ed.2d 1148, error to admit employees' records of observed business practices of others. The rule includes no requirement of this nature. Wholly acceptable records may involve matters merely observed, *e.g.* the weather.

The form which the "record" may assume under the rule is described broadly as a "memorandum, report, record, or data compilation, in any form." The expression "data compilation" is used as broadly descriptive of any means of storing information other than the conventional words and figures in written or documentary form. It includes, but is by no means limited to, electronic computer storage. The term is borrowed from revised Rule 34(a) of the Rules of Civil Procedure.

Report of House Committee on the Judiciary on Rule 803(6)

House Comm. on Judiciary, Fed.Rules of Evidence, H.R.Rep. No. 650, 93d Cong., 1st Sess., p. 14 (1973); 1974 U.S.Code Cong. & Ad.News 7075, 7087

Rule 803(6) as submitted by the Court permitted a record made "in the course of a regularly conducted activity" to be admissible in certain circumstances. The Committee believed there were insufficient guarantees of reliability in records made in the course of activities falling outside the scope of "business" activities as that term is broadly defined in 28 U.S.C. 1732. Moreover, the Committee concluded that the additional requirement of Section 1732 that it must have been the regular practice of a business to make the record is a necessary further assurance of its trustworthiness. The Committee accordingly amended the Rule to incorporate these limitations.

Report of Senate Committee on the Judiciary on Rule 803(6)

Senate Comm. on Judiciary, Fed.Rules of Evidence, S.Rep. No. 1277, 93d Cong., 2d Sess., p. 16 (1974); 1974 U.S.Code Cong. & Ad.News 7051, 7063

Rule 803(6) as submitted by the Supreme Court permitted a record made in the course of a regularly conducted activity to be admissible in certain circumstances. This rule constituted a broadening of the traditional business records hearsay exception which has been long advocated by scholars and judges active in the law of evidence.

The House felt there were insufficient guarantees of reliability of records not within a broadly defined business records exception. We disagree. Even under the House definition of "business" including profession, occupation, and "calling of every kind," the records of many regularly conducted activities will, or may be, excluded from evidence. Under the principle of ejusdem generis, the intent of "calling of every kind" would seem to be related to work-related endeavors—*e.g.*, butcher, baker, artist, etc.

Thus, it appears that the records of many institutions or groups might not be admissible under the House amendments. For example, schools, churches, and hospitals will not normally be considered businesses within the definition. Yet, these are groups which keep financial and other records on a regular basis in a manner similar to business enterprises. We believe these records are of equivalent trustworthiness and should be admitted into evidence.

Three states, which have recently codified their evidence rules, have adopted the Supreme Court version of rule 803(6), providing for admission of memoranda of a "regularly conducted activity." None adopted the words "business activity" used in the House amendment.[23]

Therefore, the committee deleted the word "business" as it appears before the word "activity". The last sentence then is unnecessary and was also deleted.

It is the understanding of the committee that the use of the phrase "person with knowledge" is not intended to imply that the party seeking to introduce the memorandum, report, record, or data compilation must be able to produce, or even identify, the specific individual upon whose first-hand knowledge the memorandum, report, record or data compilation was based. A sufficient foundation for the introduction of such evidence will be laid if the party seeking

---

[23] See Nev.Rev.Stats. § 15.135; N.Mex.Stats. (1973 Supp.) § 20–4–803(6); West's Wis.Stats.Anno. (1973 Supp.) § 908.03(6).—Ed.

to introduce the evidence is able to show that it was the regular practice of the activity to base such memorandums, reports, records, or data compilations upon a transmission from a person with knowledge, *e.g.*, in the case of the content of a shipment of goods, upon a report from the company's receiving agent or in the case of a computer printout, upon a report from the company's computer programmer or one who has knowledge of the particular record system. In short, the scope of the phrase "person with knowledge" is meant to be coterminous with the custodian of the evidence or other qualified witness. The committee believes this represents the desired rule in light of the complex nature of modern business organizations.

Conference Report on Rule 803(6)

H.R., Fed.Rules of Evidence, Conf.Rep. No. 1597, 93d Cong., 2d Sess., p. 11 (1974); 1974 U.S.Code Cong. & Ad.News 7098, 7104

The House bill provides in subsection (6) that records of a regularly conducted "business" activity qualify for admission into evidence as an exception to the hearsay rule. "Business" is defined as including "business, profession, occupation and calling of every kind." The Senate amendment drops the requirement that the records be those of a "business" activity and eliminates the definition of "business." The Senate amendment provides that records are admissible if they are records of a regularly conducted "activity."

The Conference adopts the House provision that the records must be those of a regularly conducted "business" activity. The Conferees changed the definition of "business" contained in the House provision in order to make it clear that the records of institutions and associations like schools, churches and hospitals are admissible under this provision. The records of public schools and hospitals are also covered by Rule 803(8), which deals with public records and reports.

Advisory Committee's Note on Rule 803(7)

56 F.R.D. 183, 311

Exception (7). Failure of a record to mention a matter which would ordinarily be mentioned is satisfactory evidence of its nonexistence. Uniform Rule 63(14), Comment. While probably not hearsay as defined in Rule 801, *supra,* decisions may be found which class the evidence not only as hearsay but also as not within any exception. In order to set the question at rest in favor of admissibility, it is specifically treated here. McCormick § 289, p. 609; Morgan, Basic Problems of Evidence 314 (1962); 5 Wigmore § 1531; Uniform Rule 63(14); California Evidence Code § 1272; Kansas Code of Civil Procedure § 60–460(n); New Jersey Evidence Rule 63(14).

Report of House Committee on the Judiciary on Rule 803(7)

House Comm. on Judiciary, Fed.Rules of Evidence, H.R.Rep. No. 650, 93d Cong., 1st Sess., p. 14 (1973); 1974 U.S.Code Cong. & Ad.News 7075, 7088

Rule 803(7) as submitted by the Court concerned the *absence* of entry in the records of a "regularly conducted activity." The Committee amended this Rule to conform with its action with respect to Rule 803(6).

Advisory Committee's Note on Rule 803(8)

56 F.R.D. 183, 311

Exception (8). Public records are a recognized hearsay exception at common law and have been the subject of statutes without number. McCormick § 291. See, for example, 28 U.S.C. § 1733, the relative narrowness of which is illustrated by its nonapplicability to non-federal public agencies, thus necessitating resort to the less appropriate business record exception to the hearsay rule. Kay v. United States, 255 F.2d 476 (4th Cir. 1958). The rule makes no distinction between federal and nonfederal offices and agencies.

Justification for the exception is the assumption that a public official will perform his duty properly and the unlikelihood that he will remember details independently of the record. Wong Wing Foo v. McGrath, 196 F.2d 120 (9th Cir. 1952), and see Chesapeake & Delaware Canal Co. v. United States, 250 U.S. 123, 39 S.Ct. 407, 63 L.Ed. 889 (1919). As to items (A) and (B), further support is found in the reliability factors underlying records of regularly conducted activities generally. See Exception (6), *supra.*

(A) **[Restyled as (A)(i).—Ed.]** Cases illustrating the admissibility of records of the office's or agency's own activities are numerous. Chesapeake & Delaware Canal Co. v. United States, 250 U.S. 123, 39 S.Ct. 407, 63 L.Ed. 889 (1919), Treasury records of miscellaneous receipts and disbursements; Howard v. Perrin, 200 U.S. 71, 26 S.Ct. 195, 50 L.Ed. 374 (1906), General Land Office records; Ballew v. United States, 160 U.S. 187, 16 S.Ct. 263, 40 L.Ed. 388 (1895), Pension Office records.

(B) **[Restyled as (A)(ii).—Ed.]** Cases sustaining admissibility of records of matters observed are also numerous. United States v. Van Hook, 284 F.2d 489 (7th Cir. 1960), remanded for resentencing 365 U.S. 609, 81 S.Ct. 823, 5 L.Ed.2d 821, letter from induction officer to District Attorney, pursuant to army regulations, stating fact and circumstances of refusal to be inducted; T'Kach v. United States, 242 F.2d 937 (5th Cir. 1957), affidavit of White House personnel officer that search of records showed no employment of accused, charged with fraudulently representing himself as an envoy of the President; Minnehaha County v. Kelley, 150 F.2d 356 (8th Cir. 1945); Weather Bureau records of rainfall; United States v. Meyer, 113 F.2d 387 (7th Cir. 1940), cert. denied 311 U.S. 706, 61 S.Ct. 174, 85 L.Ed. 459, map prepared by government engineer from information furnished by men working under his supervision.

(C) **[Restyled as (A)(iii).—Ed.]** The more controversial area of public records is that of the so-called "evaluative" report. The disagreement among the decisions has been due in part, no doubt, to the variety of situations encountered, as well as to differences in principle. Sustaining admissibility are such cases as United States v. Dumas, 149 U.S. 278, 13 S.Ct. 872, 37 L.Ed. 734 (1893), statement of account certified by Postmaster General in action against postmaster; McCarty v. United States, 185 F.2d 520 (5th Cir. 1950), reh. denied 187 F.2d 234, Certificate of Settlement of General Accounting Office showing indebtedness and letter from Army official stating Government had performed, in action on contract to purchase and remove waste food from Army camp; Moran v. Pittsburgh-Des Moines Steel Co., 183 F.2d 467 (3d Cir. 1950), report of Bureau of Mines as to cause of gas tank explosion; Petition of W___, 164 F.Supp. 659 (E.D.Pa. 1958), report by Immigration and Naturalization Service investigator that petitioner was known in community as wife of man to whom she was not married. To the opposite effect and denying admissibility are Franklin v. Skelly Oil Co., 141 F.2d 568 (10th Cir. 1944), State Fire Marshal's report of cause of gas explosion; Lomax Transp. Co. v. United States, 183 F.2d 331 (9th Cir. 1950), Certificate of Settlement from General Accounting Office in action for naval supplies lost in warehouse fire; Yung Jin Teung v. Dulles, 229 F.2d 244 (2d Cir. 1956), "Status Reports" offered to justify delay in processing passport applications. Police reports have generally been excluded except to the extent to which they incorporate firsthand observations of the officer. Annot., 69 A.L.R.2d 1148. Various kinds of evaluative reports are admissible under federal statutes: 7 U.S.C. § 78, findings of Secretary of Agriculture prima facie evidence of true grade of grain; 7 U.S.C. § 210(f), findings of Secretary of Agriculture prima facie evidence in action for damages against stockyard owner; 7 U.S.C. § 292, order by Secretary of Agriculture prima facie evidence in judicial enforcement proceedings against producers association monopoly; 7 U.S.C. § 1622(h), Department of

Agriculture inspection certificates of products shipped in interstate commerce prima facie evidence; 8 U.S.C. § 1440(c), separation of alien from military service on conditions other than honorable provable by certificate from department in proceedings to revoke citizenship; 18 U.S.C. § 4245, certificate of Director of Prisons that convicted person has been examined and found probably incompetent at time of trial prima facie evidence in court hearing on competency; 42 U.S.C. § 269(b), bill of health by appropriate official prima facie evidence of vessel's sanitary history and condition and compliance with regulations; 46 U.S.C. § 679, certificate of consul presumptive evidence of refusal of master to transport destitute seamen to United States. While these statutory exceptions to the hearsay rule are left undisturbed, Rule 802, the willingness of Congress to recognize a substantial measure of admissibility for evaluative reports is a helpful guide.

Factors which may be of assistance in passing upon the admissibility of evaluative reports include: (1) the timeliness of the investigation, McCormick, Can the Courts Make Wider Use of Reports of Official Investigations? 42 Iowa L.Rev. 363 (1957); (2) the special skill or experience of the official, *id.,* (3) whether a hearing was held and the level at which conducted, Franklin v. Skelly Oil Co., 141 F.2d 568 (10th Cir. 1944); (4) possible motivation problems suggested by Palmer v. Hoffman, 318 U.S. 109, 63 S.Ct. 477, 87 L.Ed. 645 (1943). Others no doubt could be added.

The formulation of an approach which would give appropriate weight to all possible factors in every situation is an obvious impossibility. Hence the rule, as in Exception (6), assumes admissibility in the first instance but with ample provision for escape if sufficient negative factors are present. In one respect, however, the rule with respect to evaluative reports under item (c) [now (A)(iii)— Ed.] is very specific: they are admissible only in civil cases and against the government in criminal cases in view of the almost certain collision with confrontation rights which would result from their use against the accused in a criminal case.

Report of House Committee on the Judiciary on Rule 803(8)

House Comm. on Judiciary, Fed.Rules of Evidence, H.R.Rep. No. 650, 93d Cong., 1st Sess., p. 14 (1973); 1974 U.S.Code Cong. & Ad.News 7075, 7088

The Committee approved Rule 803(8) without substantive change from the form in which it was submitted by the Court. The Committee intends that the phrase "factual findings" be strictly construed and that evaluations or opinions contained in public reports shall not be admissible under this Rule.

Report of Senate Committee on the Judiciary on Rule 803(8)

Senate Comm. on Judiciary, Fed.Rules of Evidence, S.Rep. No. 1277, 93d Cong., 2d Sess., p. 17 (1974); 1974 U.S.Code Cong. & Ad.News 7051, 7064

The House approved rule 803(8), as submitted by the Supreme Court, with one substantive change. It excluded from the hearsay exception reports containing matters observed by police officers and other law enforcement personnel in criminal cases. Ostensibly, the reason for this exclusion is that observations by police officers at the scene of the crime or the apprehension of the defendant are not as reliable as observations by public officials in other cases because of the adversarial nature of the confrontation between the police and the defendant in criminal cases.

The committee accepts the House's decision to exclude such recorded observations where the police officer is available to testify in court about his observation. However, where he is unavailable as unavailability is defined in rule 804(a)(4) and (a)(5), the report should be admitted as the best available evidence. Accordingly, the Committee has amended rule 803(8) to refer to the provision of rule 804(b)(5), which allows the admission of such reports, records, or other statements where the police officer or other law enforcement officer is unavailable because of death, then existing physical or mental illness or infirmity, or not being successfully subject to legal process. **[This amendment did not get enacted into law.—Ed.]**

The House Judiciary Committee report contained a statement of intent that "the phrase 'factual findings' in subdivision (c) [now (A)(iii)—Ed.] be strictly construed and that evaluations or opinions contained in public reports shall not be admissible under this rule." The committee takes strong exception to this limiting understanding of the application of the rule. We do not think it reflects an understanding of the intended operation of the rule as explained in the Advisory Committee notes to this subsection. The Advisory Committee notes on subsection (c) [now (A)(iii)—Ed.] of this subdivision point out that various kinds of evaluative reports are now admissible under Federal statutes. 7 U.S.C. § 78, findings of Secretary of Agriculture prima facie evidence of true grade of grain; 42 U.S.C. § 269(b), bill of health by appropriate official prima facie evidence of vessel's sanitary history and condition and compliance with regulations. These statutory exceptions to the hearsay rule are preserved. Rule 802. The willingness of Congress to recognize these and other such evaluative reports provides a helpful guide in determining the kind of reports which are intended to be admissible under this rule. We think the restrictive interpretation of the House overlooks the fact that while the Advisory Committee assumes admissibility in the first instance of evaluative reports, they are not admissible if, as the rule states, "the sources of information or other circumstances indicate lack of trustworthiness."

The Advisory Committee explains the factors to be considered:

> Factors which may be assistance in passing upon the admissibility of evaluative reports include: (1) the timeliness of the investigation, McCormick, Can the Courts Make Wider Use of Reports of Official Investigations? 42 Iowa L.Rev. 363 (1957); (2) the special skill or experience of the official, *id.*; (3) whether a hearing was held and the level at which conducted, Franklin v. Skelly Oil Co., 141 F.2d 568 (19th Cir. 1944): (4) possible motivation problems suggested by Palmer v. Hoffman, 318 U.S. 109, 63 S.Ct. 477, 87 L.Ed. 645 (1943). Others no doubt could be added.[24]

The committee concludes that the language of the rule together with the explanation provided by the Advisory Committee furnish sufficient guidance on the admissibility of evaluative reports.

Conference Report on Rule 803(8)

H.R., Fed.Rules of Evidence, Conf.Rep. No. 1597, 93d Cong., 2d Sess., p. 11 (1974); 1974 U.S.Code Cong. & Ad.News 7098, 7104

The Senate amendment adds language, not contained in the House bill, that refers to another rule that was added by the Senate in another amendment. (Rule 804(b)(5)—Criminal law enforcement records and reports).

In view of its action on Rule 804(b)(5) (Criminal law enforcement records and reports), the Conference does not adopt the Senate amendment and restores the bill to the House version.

Advisory Committee's Note on Rule 803(9)–(13)

56 F.R.D. 183, 313

Exception (9). Records of vital statistics are commonly the subject of particular statutes making them admissible in evidence, Uniform Vital Statistics Act, 9C U.L.A. 350 (1957). The rule is in principle narrower than Uniform Rule

---

[24] Advisory Committee's notes, to Rule 803(8)(c) [now (A)(iii)].—Ed.

63(16) which includes reports required of persons performing functions authorized by statute, yet in practical effect the two are substantially the same. Comment Uniform Rule 63(16). The exception as drafted is in the pattern of California Evidence Code § 1281.

Exception (10). The principle of proving nonoccurrence of an event by evidence of the absence of a record which would regularly be made of its occurrence, developed in Exception (7) with respect to regularly conducted [business] activities, is here extended to public records of the kind mentioned in Exceptions (8) and (9). 5 Wigmore § 1633(6), p. 519. Some harmless duplication no doubt exists with Exception (7). For instances of federal statutes recognizing this method of proof, see 8 U.S.C. § 1284(b), proof of absence of alien crewman's name from outgoing manifest prima facie evidence of failure to detain or deport, and 42 U.S.C. § 405(c)(3), (4)(B), (4)(C), absence of HEW record prima facie evidence of no wages or self-employment income.

The rule includes situations in which absence of a record may itself be the ultimate focal point of inquiry, *e.g.* People v. Love, 310 Ill. 558, 142 N.E. 204 (1923), certificate of Secretary of State admitted to show failure to file documents required by Securities Law, as well as cases where the absence of a record is offered as proof of the non-occurrence of an event ordinarily recorded.

The refusal of the common law to allow proof by certificate of the lack of a record or entry has no apparent justification, 5 Wigmore § 1678(7), p. 752. The rule takes the opposite position, as do Uniform Rule 63(17); California Evidence Code § 1284; Kansas Code of Civil Procedure § 60–460(c); New Jersey Evidence Rule 63(17). Congress has recognized certification as evidence of the lack of a record. 8 U.S.C. § 1360(d), certificate of Attorney General or other designated officer that no record of Immigration and Naturalization Service of specified nature or entry therein is found, admissible in alien cases.

Exception (11). Records of activities of religious organizations are currently recognized as admissible at least to the extent of the business records exception to the hearsay rule, 5 Wigmore § 1523, p. 371, and Exception (6) would be applicable. However, both the business record doctrine and Exception (6) require that the person furnishing the information be one in the business or activity. The result is such decisions as Daily v. Grand Lodge, 311 Ill. 184, 142 N.E. 478 (1924), holding a church record admissible to prove fact, date, and place of baptism, but not age of child except that he had at least been born at the time. In view of the unlikelihood that false information would be furnished on occasions of this kind, the rule contains no requirement that the informant be in the course of the activity. See California Evidence Code § 1315 and Comment.

Exception (12). The principle of proof by certification is recognized as to public officials in Exceptions (8) and (10), and with respect to authentication in Rule 902. The present exception is a duplication to the extent that it deals with a certificate by a public official, as in the case of a judge who performs a marriage ceremony. The area covered by the rule is, however, substantially larger and extends the certification procedure to clergymen and the like who perform marriages and other ceremonies or administer sacraments. Thus certificates of such matters as baptism or confirmation, as well as marriage, are included. In principle they are as acceptable evidence as certificates of public officers. See 5 Wigmore § 1645, as to marriage certificates. When the person executing the certificate is not a public official, the self-authenticating character of documents purporting to emanate from public officials, see Rule 902, is lacking and proof is required that the person was authorized and did make the certificate. The time element, however, may safely be taken as supplied by the certificate, once authority and authenticity are established, particularly in view of the presumption that a document was executed on the date it bears.

For similar rules, some limited to certificates of marriage, with variations in foundation requirements, see Uniform Rule 63(18); California Evidence Code § 1316; Kansas Code of Civil Procedure § 60–460(p); New Jersey Evidence Rule 63(18).

Exception (13). Records of family history kept in family Bibles have by long tradition been received in evidence. 5 Wigmore §§ 1495, 1496, citing numerous statutes and decisions. *See also* Regulations, Social Security Administration, 20 C.F.R. § 404.703(c), recognizing family Bible entries as proof of age in the absence of public or church records. Opinions in the area also include inscriptions on tombstones, publicly displayed pedigrees, and engravings on rings. Wigmore, *supra*. The rule is substantially identical in coverage with California Evidence Code § 1312.

Report of House Committee on the Judiciary on Rule 803(13)

House Comm. on Judiciary, Fed.Rules of Evidence, H.R.Rep. No. 650, 93d Cong., 1st Sess., p. 15 (1973); 1974 U.S.Code Cong. & Ad.News 7075, 7088

The Committee approved this Rule in the form submitted by the Court, intending that the phrase "Statements of fact concerning personal or family history" be read to include the specific types of such statements enumerated in Rule 803(11).

Advisory Committee's Notes on Rule 803(14)–(23)

56 F.R.D. 183, 315

Exception (14). The recording of title documents is a purely statutory development. Under any theory of the admissibility of public records, the records would be receivable as evidence of the contents of the recorded document, else the recording process would be reduced to a nullity. When, however, the record is offered for the further purpose of proving execution and delivery, a problem of lack of first-hand knowledge by the recorder, not present as to contents, is presented. This problem is solved, seemingly in all jurisdictions, by qualifying for recording only those documents shown by a specified procedure, either acknowledgement or a form of probate, to have been executed and delivered. 5 Wigmore §§ 1647–1651. Thus what may appear in the rule, at first glance, as endowing the record with an effect independently of local law and inviting difficulties of an *Erie* nature under Cities Service Oil Co. v. Dunlap, 308 U.S. 208, 60 S.Ct. 201, 84 L.Ed. 196 (1939), is not present, since the local law in fact governs under the example [exception].

Exception (15). Dispositive documents often contain recitals of fact. Thus a deed purporting to have been executed by an attorney in fact may recite the existence of the power of attorney, or a deed may recite that the grantors are all the heirs of the last record owner. Under the rule, these recitals are exempted from the hearsay rule. The circumstances under which dispositive documents are executed and the requirement that the recital be germane to the purpose of the document are believed to be adequate guarantees of trustworthiness, particularly in view of the nonapplicability of the rule if dealings with the property have been inconsistent with the document. The age of the document is of no significance, though in practical application the document will most often be an ancient one. See Uniform Rule 63(29), Comment.

Similar provisions are contained in Uniform Rule 63(29); California Evidence Code § 1330; Kansas Code of Civil Procedure § 60–460(aa); New Jersey Evidence Rule 63(29).

Exception (16). Authenticating a document as ancient, essentially in the pattern of the common law, as provided in Rule 901(b)(8), leaves open as a separate question the admissibility of assertive statements contained therein as against a hearsay objection. 7 Wigmore § 2145a. Wigmore further states that the ancient document technique of authentication is universally conceded to apply to all sorts of documents, including letters, records, contracts, maps, and certificates, in addition to title documents, citing numerous decisions. *Id.* § 2145. Since most of these items are significant evidentially only insofar as they are assertive, their admission in evidence must be as a hearsay exception. But see 5 *id.* § 1573, p. 429, referring to recitals in ancient deeds as a "limited" hearsay exception. The former position is believed to be the correct one in reason and authority. As pointed out in McCormick § 298, danger of mistake is minimized by authentication requirements, and age affords assurance that the writing antedates the present controversy. See Dallas County v. Commercial Union Assurance Co., 286 F.2d 388 (5th Cir. 1961), upholding admissibility of 58-year-old newspaper story. Cf. Morgan, Basic Problems of Evidence 364 (1962), but see *id.* 254.

For a similar provision, but with the added requirement that "the statement has since generally been acted upon as true by persons having an interest in the matter," see California Evidence Code § 1331.

Exception (17). Ample authority at common law supported the admission in evidence of items falling in this category. While Wigmore's text is narrowly oriented to lists, etc., prepared for the use of a trade or profession, 6 Wigmore § 1702, authorities are cited which include other kinds of publications, for example, newspaper market reports, telephone directories, and city directories. *Id.* §§ 1702–1706. The basis of trustworthiness is general reliance by the public or by a particular segment of it, and the motivation of the compiler to foster reliance by being accurate.

For similar provisions, see Uniform Rule 63(30); California Evidence Code § 1340; Kansas Code of Civil Procedure § 60–460(bb); New Jersey Evidence Rule 63(30). Uniform Commercial Code § 2–724 provides for admissibility in evidence of "reports in official publications or trade journals or in newspapers or periodicals of general circulation published as the reports of such [established commodity] market."

Exception (18). The writers have generally favored the admissibility of learned treatises, McCormick § 296, p. 621; Morgan, Basic Problems of Evidence 366 (1962); 6 Wigmore § 1692, with the support of occasional decisions and rules, City of Dothan v. Hardy, 237 Ala. 603, 188 So. 264 (1939); Lewandowski v. Preferred Risk Mut. Ins. Co., 33 Wis.2d 69, 146 N.W.2d 505 (1966), 66 Mich.L.Rev. 183 (1967); Uniform Rule 63(31); Kansas Code of Civil Procedure § 60–460(cc), but the great weight of authority has been that learned treatises are not admissible as substantive evidence though usable in the cross-examination of experts. The foundation of the minority view is that the hearsay objection must be regarded as unimpressive when directed against treatises since a high standard of accuracy is engendered by various factors: the treatise is written primarily and impartially for professionals, subject to scrutiny and exposure for inaccuracy, with the reputation of the writer at stake. 6 Wigmore § 1692. Sound as this position may be with respect to trustworthiness, there is, nevertheless, an additional difficulty in the likelihood that the treatise will be misunderstood and misapplied without expert assistance and supervision. This difficulty is recognized in the cases demonstrating unwillingness to sustain findings relative to disability on the basis of judicially noticed medical texts. Ross v. Gardner, 365 F.2d 554 (6th Cir. 1966); Sayers v. Gardner, 380 F.2d 940 (6th Cir. 1967); Colwell v. Gardner, 386 F.2d 56 (6th Cir. 1967); Glendenning v. Ribicoff, 213 F.Supp. 301 (W.D.Mo. 1962); Cook v. Celebrezze, 217 F.Supp. 366 (W.D.Mo. 1963); Sosna v. Celebrezze, 234 F.Supp. 289 (E.D.Pa. 1964); and see McDaniel v. Celebrezze, 331 F.2d 426 (4th Cir. 1964). The rule avoids the danger of misunderstanding and misapplication by limiting the use of treatises as substantive evidence to situations in which an expert is on the stand and available to explain and assist in the application of the treatise if desired. The limitation upon receiving the publication itself physically in evidence, contained in the last sentence, is designed to further this policy.

The relevance of the use of treatises on cross-examination is evident. This use of treatises has been the subject of varied views. The most restrictive position is that the witness must have stated expressly on direct his reliance upon the treatise. A slightly more liberal approach still insists upon reliance but allows it to be developed on cross-examination. Further relaxation dispenses with reliance but requires recognition as an authority by the witness, developable on cross-examination. The greatest liberality is found in decisions allowing use of the treatise on cross-examination when its status as an authority is established by any means. Annot., 60 A.L.R.2d 77. The exception is hinged upon this last position, which is that of the Supreme Court, Reilly v. Pinkus, 338 U.S. 269, 70 S.Ct. 110, 94 L.Ed. 63 (1949), and of recent well considered state court decisions, City of St. Petersburg v. Ferguson, 193 So.2d 648 (Fla.App. 1967), cert. denied Fla., 201 So.2d 556; Darling v. Charleston Memorial Community Hospital, 33 Ill.2d 326, 211 N.E.2d 253 (1965); Dabroe v. Rhodes Co., 64 Wash.2d 431, 392 P.2d 317 (1964).

In Reilly v. Pinkus, *supra*, the Court pointed out that testing of professional knowledge was incomplete without exploration of the witness' knowledge of and attitude toward established treatises in the field. The process works equally well in reverse and furnishes the basis of the rule.

The rule does not require that the witness rely upon or recognize the treatise as authoritative, thus avoiding the possibility that the expert may at the outset block cross-examination by refusing to concede reliance or authoritativeness. Dabroe v. Rhodes Co., *supra*. Moreover, the rule avoids the unreality of admitting evidence for the purpose of impeachment only, with an instruction to the jury not to consider it otherwise. The parallel to the treatment of prior inconsistent statements will be apparent. See Rules 613(b) and 801(d)(1).

Exceptions (19), (20), and (21). Trustworthiness in reputation evidence is found "when the topic is such that the facts are likely to have been inquired about and that persons having personal knowledge have disclosed facts which have thus been discussed in the community; and thus the community's conclusion, if any has been formed, is likely to be a trustworthy one." 5 Wigmore § 1580, p. 444, and *see also* § 1583. On this common foundation, reputation as to land boundaries, customs, general history, character, and marriage have come to be regarded as admissible. The breadth of the underlying principle suggests the formulation of an equally broad exception, but tradition has in fact been much narrower and more particularized, and this is the pattern of these exceptions in the rule.

Exception (19) is concerned with matters of personal and family history. Marriage is universally conceded to be a proper subject of proof by evidence of reputation in the community. 5 Wigmore § 1602. As to such items as legitimacy, relationship, adoption, birth, and death, the decisions are divided. *Id.* § 1605. All seem to be susceptible to being the subject of well founded repute. The "world" in which the reputation may exist may be family, associates, or community. This world has proved capable of expanding with changing times from the single uncomplicated neighborhood, in which all activities take place, to the multiple and unrelated worlds of work, religious affiliation, and social activity, in each of which a reputation may be generated. People v. Reeves, 360 Ill. 55, 195 N.E. 443 (1935); State v. Axilrod, 248 Minn. 204, 79 N.W.2d 677 (1956); Mass.Stat. 1947, c. 410, M.G.L.A. c. 233 § 21A; 5 Wigmore § 1616. The family has often served as the point of beginning for allowing community reputation. 5 Wigmore § 1488. For comparable provisions see Uniform Rule 63(26), (27)(c); California Evidence Code §§ 1313, 1314; Kansas Code of Civil Procedure § 60–460(x), (y)(3); New Jersey Evidence Rule 63(26), (27)(c).

The first portion of Exception (20) is based upon the general admissibility of evidence of reputation as to land boundaries and land customs, expanded in this country to include private as well as public boundaries. McCormick § 299, p. 625. The reputation is required to antedate the controversy, though not to be ancient. The second portion is likewise supported by authority, *id.*, and is designed to facilitate proof of events when judicial notice is not available. The historical character of the subject matter dispenses with any need that the reputation antedate the controversy with respect to which it is offered. For similar provisions see Uniform Rule 63(27)(a), (b); California Evidence Code §§ 1320–1322; Kansas Code of Civil Procedure § 60–460(y), (1), (2); New Jersey Evidence Rule 63(27)(a), (b).

Exception (21) recognizes the traditional acceptance of reputation evidence as a means of proving human character. McCormick §§ 44, 158. The exception deals only with the hearsay aspect of this kind of evidence. Limitations upon admissibility based on other grounds will be found in Rules 404, relevancy of character evidence generally, and 608, character of witness. The exception is in effect a reiteration, in the context of hearsay, of Rule 405(a). Similar provisions are contained in Uniform Rule 63(28); California Evidence Code § 1324; Kansas Code of Civil Procedure § 60–460(z); New Jersey Evidence Rule 63(28).

Exception (22). When the status of a former judgment is under consideration in subsequent litigation, three possibilities must be noted: (1) the former judgment is conclusive under the doctrine of res judicata, either as a bar or a collateral estoppel; or (2) it is admissible in evidence for what it is worth; or (3) it may be of no effect at all. The first situation does not involve any problem of evidence except in the way that principles of substantive law generally bear upon the relevancy and materiality of evidence. The rule does not deal with the substantive effect of the judgment as a bar or collateral estoppel. When, however, the doctrine of res judicata does not apply to make the judgment either a bar or a collateral estoppel, a choice is presented between the second and third alternatives. The rule adopts the second for judgments of criminal conviction of felony grade. This is the direction of the decisions, Annot., 18 A.L.R.2d 1287, 1299, which manifest an increasing reluctance to reject *in toto* the validity of the law's factfinding processes outside the confines of res judicata and collateral estoppel. While this may leave a jury with the evidence of conviction but without means to evaluate it, as suggested by Judge Hinton, Note 27 Ill.L.Rev. 195 (1932), it seems safe to assume that the jury will give it substantial effect unless defendant offers a satisfactory explanation, a possibility not foreclosed by the provision. But see North River Ins. Co. v. Militello, 104 Colo. 28, 88 P.2d 567 (1939), in which the jury found for plaintiff on a fire policy despite the introduction of his conviction for arson. For supporting federal decisions see Clark, J., in New York & Cuba Mail S.S. Co. v. Continental Cas. Co., 117 F.2d 404, 411 (2d Cir. 1941); Connecticut Fire Ins. Co. v. Farrara, 277 F.2d 388 (8th Cir. 1960).

Practical considerations require exclusion of convictions of minor offenses, not because the administration of justice in its lower echelons must be inferior, but because motivation to defend at this level is often minimal or nonexistent. Cope v. Goble, 39 Cal.App.2d 448, 103 P.2d 598 (1940); Jones v. Talbot, 87 Idaho 498, 394 P.2d 316 (1964); Warren v. Marsh, 215 Minn. 615, 11 N.W.2d 528 (1943); Annot., 18 A.L.R.2d 1287, 1295–1297; 16 Brooklyn L.Rev. 286 (1950); 50 Colum.L.Rev. 529 (1950); 35 Cornell L.Q. 872 (1950). Hence the rule includes only convictions of felony grade, measured by federal standards.

Judgments of conviction based upon pleas of *nolo contendere* are not included. This position is consistent with the treatment of *nolo* pleas in Rule 410 and the authorities cited in the Advisory Committee's Note in support thereof.

While these rules do not in general purport to resolve constitutional issues, they have in general been drafted with a view to avoiding collision with constitutional principles. Consequently the exception does not include evidence of the conviction of a third person, offered against the accused in a criminal prosecution to prove any fact essential to sustain the judgment of conviction. A contrary position would seem clearly to violate the right of confrontation. Kirby v. United States, 174 U.S. 47, 19 S.Ct. 574, 43 L.Ed. 890 (1899), error to convict of possessing stolen postage stamps with the only evidence of theft being the record of conviction of the thieves. The situation is to be distinguished from cases in which conviction of another person is an element of the crime, *e.g.* 15 U.S.C. § 902(d), interstate shipment of firearms to a known convicted felon, and, as specifically provided, from impeachment.

For comparable provisions see Uniform Rule 63(20); California Evidence Code § 1300; Kansas Code of Civil Procedure § 60–460(r); New Jersey Evidence Rule 63(20).

Exception (23). A hearsay exception in this area was originally justified on the ground that verdicts were evidence of reputation. As trial by jury graduated from the category of neighborhood inquests, this theory lost its validity. It was never valid as to chancery decrees. Nevertheless the rule persisted, though the judges and writers shifted ground and began saying that the judgment or decree was as good evidence as reputation. See City of London v. Clerke, Carth. 181, 90 Eng.Rep. 710 (K.B. 1691); Neill v. Duke of Devonshire, 8 App.Cas. 135 (1882). The shift appears to be correct, since the process of inquiry, sifting, and scrutiny which is relied upon to render reputation reliable is present in perhaps greater measure in the process of litigation. While this might suggest a broader area of application, the affinity to reputation is strong, and paragraph (23) goes no further, not even including character.

The leading case in the United States, Patterson v. Gaines, 47 U.S. (6 How.) 550, 599, 12 L.Ed. 553 (1847), follows in the pattern of the English decisions, mentioning as illustrative matters thus provable: manorial rights, public rights of way, immemorial custom, disputed boundary, and pedigree. More recent recognition of the principle is found in Grant Bros. Construction Co. v. United States, 232 U.S. 647, 34 S.Ct. 452, 58 L.Ed. 776 (1914), in action for penalties under Alien Contract Labor Law, decision of board of inquiry of Immigration Service admissible to prove alienage of laborers, as a matter of pedigree; United States v. Mid-Continent Petroleum Corp., 67 F.2d 37 (10th Cir. 1933), records of commission enrolling Indians admissible on pedigree; Jung Yen Loy v. Cahill, 81 F.2d 809 (9th Cir. 1936), board decisions as to citizenship of plaintiff's father admissible in proceeding for declaration of citizenship. Contra, In re Estate of Cunha, 49 Haw. 273, 414 P.2d 925 (1966).

Exception (24). [Editor's Note: This rule was moved to Rule 807. See the Committee Note and the relevant legislative history under that rule, *infra*.]

1987 Amendment Committee Note

The amendments are technical. No substantive change is intended.

1997 Amendment Committee Note

The contents of Rule 803(24) and Rule 804(b)(5) have been combined and transferred to a new Rule 807. This was done to facilitate additions to Rules 803 and 804. No change in meaning is intended.

Committee Note to the 2000 Amendment to Rule 803(6)

The amendment provides that the foundation requirements of Rule 803(6) can be satisfied under certain circumstances without the expense and inconvenience of producing time-consuming foundation witnesses. Under current law, courts have generally required foundation witnesses to testify. *See, e.g., Tongil Co., Ltd. v. Hyundai Merchant Marine Corp.*, 968 F.2d 999 (9th Cir. 1992) (reversing a judgment based on business records where a qualified person filed an affidavit but did not testify). Protections are provided by the authentication requirements of Rule 902(11) for domestic records, Rule 902(12) for foreign records in civil cases, and 18 U.S.C. § 3505 for foreign records in criminal cases.

Committee Note to the 2013 Amendment to Rule 803(10)

Rule 803(10) has been amended in response to *Melendez-Diaz v. Massachusetts*, 557 U.S. 305 (2009). The *Melendez-Diaz* Court declared that a testimonial certificate could be admitted if the accused is given advance notice and does not timely demand the presence of the official who prepared the certificate. The amendment incorporates, with minor variations, a "notice-and-demand" procedure that was approved by the *Melendez-Diaz* Court. See Tex. Code Crim. P. Ann., art. 38.41.

Committee Notes to the 2014 Amendments to Rules 803(6)–(8)

Rule 803(6):

The Rule has been amended to clarify that if the proponent has established the stated requirements of the exception—regular business with regularly kept record, source with personal knowledge, record made timely, and foundation testimony or certification—then the burden is on the opponent to show that the source of information or the method or circumstances of preparation indicate a lack of trustworthiness. While most courts have imposed that burden on the opponent, some have not. It is appropriate to impose this burden on the opponent, as the basic admissibility requirements are sufficient to establish a presumption that the record is reliable.

The opponent, in meeting its burden, is not necessarily required to introduce affirmative evidence of untrustworthiness. For example, the opponent might argue that a record was prepared in anticipation of litigation and is favorable to the preparing party without needing to introduce evidence on the point. A determination of untrustworthiness necessarily depends on the circumstances.

Rule 803(7):

The Rule has been amended to clarify that if the proponent has established the stated requirements of the exception—set forth in Rule 803(6)—then the burden is on the opponent to show that the possible source of the information or other circumstances indicate a lack of trustworthiness. The amendment maintains consistency with the proposed amendment to the trustworthiness clause of Rule 803(6).

Rule 803(8):

The Rule has been amended to clarify that if the proponent has established that the record meets the stated requirements of the exception—prepared by a public office and setting out information as specified in the Rule—then the burden is on the opponent to show that the source of information or other circumstances indicate a lack of trustworthiness. While most courts have imposed that burden on the opponent, some have not. Public records have justifiably carried a presumption of reliability, and it should be up to the opponent to "demonstrate why a time-tested and carefully considered presumption is not appropriate." *Ellis v. International Playtex, Inc.*, 745 F.2d 292, 301 (4th Cir. 1984). The amendment maintains consistency with the proposed amendment to the trustworthiness clause of Rule 803(6).

The opponent, in meeting its burden, is not necessarily required to introduce affirmative evidence of untrustworthiness. For example, the opponent might argue that a record was prepared in anticipation of litigation and is favorable to the preparing party without needing to introduce evidence on the point. A determination of untrustworthiness necessarily depends on the circumstances.

Committee Note to the 2017 Amendment to Rule 803(16)

The ancient documents exception to the rule against hearsay has been limited to statements in documents prepared before January 1, 1998. The Committee has determined that the ancient documents exception should be limited due to the risk that it will be used as a vehicle to admit vast amounts of unreliable electronically stored information (ESI). Given the exponential development and growth of electronic information since 1998, the hearsay exception for ancient documents has now become a possible open door for large amounts of unreliable ESI, as no showing of reliability needs to be made to qualify under the exception.

The Committee is aware that in certain cases—such as cases involving latent diseases and environmental damage—parties must rely on hardcopy documents from the past. The ancient documents exception remains available for such cases for documents prepared before 1998. Going forward, it is anticipated that any need to admit old hardcopy documents produced after January 1, 1998 will decrease, because reliable ESI is likely to be available and can be offered under a reliability-based hearsay exception. Rule 803(6) may be used for many of these ESI documents, especially given its flexible standards on which witnesses might be qualified to provide an adequate foundation. And Rule 807 can be used to admit old documents upon a showing of reliability—which will often (though not always) be found by circumstances such as that the document was prepared with no litigation motive in mind, close in time to the relevant events. The limitation of the ancient documents exception is not intended to raise an inference that 20 year-old documents are, as a class, unreliable, or that they should somehow not qualify for admissibility under Rule 807. Finally, many old documents can be admitted for the non-hearsay purpose of proving notice, or as party-opponent statements.

The limitation of the ancient documents hearsay exception is not intended to have any effect on authentication of ancient documents. The possibility of authenticating an old document under Rule 901(b)(8)—or under any ground available for any other document—remains unchanged.

The Committee carefully considered, but ultimately rejected, an amendment that would preserve the ancient documents exception for hardcopy evidence only. A party will often offer hardcopy that is derived from ESI. Moreover, a good deal of old information in hardcopy has been digitized or will be so in the future. Thus, the line between ESI and hardcopy was determined to be one that could not be drawn usefully.

The Committee understands that the choice of a cut-off date has a degree of arbitrariness. But January 1, 1998 is a rational date for treating concerns about old and unreliable ESI. And the date is no more arbitrary than the 20-year cutoff date in the original rule. See Committee Note to Rule 901(b)(8) ("Any time period selected is bound to be arbitrary.").

Under the amendment, a document is "prepared" when the statement proffered was recorded in that document. For example, if a hardcopy document is prepared in 1995, and a party seeks to admit a scanned copy of that document, the date of preparation is 1995 even though the scan was made long after that—the subsequent scan does not alter the document. The relevant point is the date on which the information is recorded, not when the information is prepared for trial. However, if the content of the document is *itself* altered after the cut-off date, then the hearsay exception will not apply to statements that were added in the alteration.

———————————

Rule 804. Exceptions to the Rule Against Hearsay—When the Declarant Is Unavailable as a Witness

(a) Criteria for Being Unavailable. A declarant is considered to be unavailable as a witness if the declarant:

(1) is exempted from testifying about the subject matter of the declarant's statement because the court rules that a privilege applies;

(2) refuses to testify about the subject matter despite a court order to do so;

(3) testifies to not remembering the subject matter;

(4) cannot be present or testify at the trial or hearing because of death or a then-existing infirmity, physical illness, or mental illness; or

(5) is absent from the trial or hearing and the statement's proponent has not been able, by process or other reasonable means, to procure:

(A) the declarant's attendance, in the case of a hearsay exception under Rule 804(b)(1) or (6); or

(B) the declarant's attendance or testimony, in the case of a hearsay exception under Rule 804(b) (2), (3), or (4).

But this subdivision (a) does not apply if the statement's proponent procured or wrongfully caused the declarant's unavailability as a witness in order to prevent the declarant from attending or testifying.

(b) The Exceptions. The following are not excluded by the rule against hearsay if the declarant is unavailable as a witness:

(1) *Former Testimony.* Testimony that:

(A) was given as a witness at a trial, hearing, or lawful deposition, whether given during the current proceeding or a different one; and

(B) is now offered against a party who had—or, in a civil case, whose predecessor in interest had—an opportunity and similar motive to develop it by direct, cross-, or redirect examination.

(2) *Statement Under the Belief of Imminent Death.* In a prosecution for homicide or in a civil case, a statement that the declarant, while believing the declarant's death to be imminent, made about its cause or circumstances.

(3) *Statement Against Interest.* A statement that:

(A) a reasonable person in the declarant's position would have made only if the person believed it to be true because, when made, it was so contrary to the declarant's proprietary or pecuniary interest or had so great a tendency to invalidate the declarant's claim against someone else or to expose the declarant to civil or criminal liability; and

(B) is supported by corroborating circumstances that clearly indicate its trustworthiness, if it is offered in a criminal case as one that tends to expose the declarant to criminal liability.

(4) *Statement of Personal or Family History.* A statement about:

(A) the declarant's own birth, adoption, legitimacy, ancestry marriage, divorce, relationship by blood, adoption, or marriage, or similar facts of personal or family history, even though the declarant had no way of acquiring personal knowledge about that fact; or

(B) another person concerning any of these facts, as well as death, if the declarant was related to the person by blood, adoption or marriage or was so intimately associated with the person's family that the declarant's information is likely to be accurate.

(5) *[Other Exceptions.]* [Transferred to Rule 807.]

(6) *Statement Offered Against a Party That Wrongfully Caused the Declarant's Unavailability.* A statement offered against a party that wrongfully caused—or acquiesced in wrongfully causing— the declarant's unavailability as a witness, and did so intending that result.

(As amended P.L. 94–149, § 1(12), (13), Dec. 12, 1975, 89 Stat. 806; Mar. 2, 1987, eff. Oct. 1, 1987; Nov. 18, 1988, P.L. 100–690, Title II, § 7075(b), 102 Stat. 4405, Apr. 11, 1997, eff. Dec. 1, 1997; Apr. 28, 2010, eff. Dec. 1, 2010; Apr. 26, 2011, eff. Dec. 1, 2011.)

RESTYLED RULE 804 COMMITTEE NOTE

The language of Rule 804 has been amended as part of the general restyling of the Evidence Rules to make them more easily understood and to make style and terminology consistent throughout the rules. These changes are intended to be stylistic only. There is no intent to change any result in any ruling on evidence admissibility.

No style changes were made to Rule 804(b)(3), because it was already restyled in conjunction with a substantive amendment, effective December 1, 2010.

Section references, McCormick 7th ed.

§ 253, §§ 301–320

Note by Federal Judicial Center

The rule prescribed by the Supreme Court was amended by the Congress in a number of respects as follows:

Subdivision (a). Paragraphs (1) and (2) were amended by substituting "court" in place of "judge," and paragraph (5) was amended by inserting "(or in the case of a hearsay exception under subdivision (b)(2), (3), or (4), his attendance or testimony)".

Subdivision (b). Exception (1) was amended by inserting "the same or" after "course of," and by substituting the phrase "if the party against whom the testimony is now offered, or, in a civil action or proceeding, a predecessor in interest, had an opportunity and similar motive to develop the testimony by direct, cross, or redirect examination" in place of "at the instance of or against a party with an opportunity to develop the testimony by direct, cross, or redirect examination, with motive and interest similar to those of the party against whom now offered."

Exception (2) as prescribed by the Supreme Court, dealing with statements of recent perception, was deleted by the Congress. [This rejected rule, for statements of recent perception, can be found in the section on "Deleted and Superseded Materials" *infra* in this Book.]

Exception (2) as enacted by the Congress is Exception (3) prescribed by the Supreme Court, amended by inserting at the beginning, "In a prosecution for homicide or in a civil action or proceeding".

Exception (3) as enacted by the Congress is Exception (4) prescribed by the Supreme Court, amended in the first sentence by deleting, after "another," the phrase "or to make him an object of hatred, ridicule, or disgrace," and amended in the second sentence by substituting, after "unless," the phrase, "corroborating circumstances clearly indicate the trustworthiness of the statement," in place of "corroborated."

Exception (4) as enacted by the Congress is Exception (5) prescribed by the Supreme Court without change.

Exception (5) as enacted by the Congress is Exception (6) prescribed by the Supreme Court, amended by substituting "equivalent" in place of "comparable" and by adding additional admissibility requirements after "trustworthiness." **[This rule has been transferred to Rule 807 and the Congressional changes are discussed there.—Ed.]**

Advisory Committee's Note[25]

56 F.R.D. 183, 322

As to firsthand knowledge on the part of hearsay declarants, see the introductory portion of the Advisory Committee's Note to Rule 803.

Subdivision (a). The definition of unavailability implements the division of hearsay exceptions into two categories by Rules 803 and 804(b).

At common law the unavailability requirement was evolved in connection with particular hearsay exceptions rather than along general lines. For example, see the separate explications of unavailability in relation to former testimony, declarations against interest, and statements of pedigree, separately developed in McCormick §§ 234, 257, and 297. However, no reason is apparent for making distinctions as to what satisfies unavailability for the different exceptions. The treatment in the rule is therefore uniform although differences in the range of process for witnesses between civil and criminal cases will lead to a less exacting requirement under item (5). See Rule 45(e) of the Federal Rules of Civil Procedure and Rule 17(e) of the Federal Rules of Criminal Procedure.

Five instances of unavailability are specified:

(1)   Substantial authority supports the position that exercise of a claim of privilege by the declarant satisfies the requirement of unavailability (usually in connection with former testimony). Wyatt v. State, 35 Ala.App. 147, 46 So.2d 837 (1950); State v. Stewart, 85 Kan. 404, 116 P. 489 (1911); Annot., 45 A.L.R.2d 1354; Uniform Rule 62(7)(a); California Evidence Code § 240(a)(1); Kansas Code of Civil Procedure § 60–459(g)(1). A ruling by the judge is required, which clearly implies that an actual claim of privilege must be made.

(2)   A witness is rendered unavailable if he simply refuses to testify concerning the subject matter of his statement despite judicial pressures to do so, a position supported by similar considerations of practicality. Johnson v. People, 152 Colo. 586, 384 P.2d 454 (1963); People v. Pickett, 339 Mich. 294, 63 N.W.2d 681, 45 A.L.R.2d 1341 (1954). Contra, Pleau v. State, 255 Wis. 362, 38 N.W.2d 496 (1949).

---

[25] Congressional comment on particular subdivisions is included immediately after the Advisory Committee Note on the affected subdivision.—Ed.

(3) The position that a claimed lack of memory by the witness of the subject matter of his statement constitutes unavailability likewise finds support in the cases, though not without dissent. McCormick § 234, p. 494. If the claim is successful, the practical effect is to put the testimony beyond reach, as in the other instances. In this instance, however, it will be noted that the lack of memory must be established by the testimony of the witness himself, which clearly contemplates his production and subjection to cross-examination.

Report of House Committee on the Judiciary on Rule 804(a)(3)

House Comm. on Judiciary, Fed.Rules of Evidence, H.R.Rep. No. 650, 93d Cong., 1st Sess., p. 15 (1973); 1974 U.S.Code Cong. & Ad.News 7075, 7088

Rule 804(a)(3) was approved in the form submitted by the Court. However, the Committee intends no change in existing federal law under which the court may choose to disbelieve the declarant's testimony as to his lack of memory. See United States v. Insana, 423 F.2d 1165, 1169–1170 (2nd Cir.), cert. denied, 400 U.S. 841 (1970).

Advisory Committee's Note to Rule 804(a)(4)–(5)

56 F.R.D. 183, 322

[(a)](4) Death and infirmity find general recognition as grounds. McCormick §§ 234, 257, 297; Uniform Rule 62(7)(c); California Evidence Code § 240(a)(3); Kansas Code of Civil Procedure § 60–459(g)(3); New Jersey Evidence Rule 62(6)(c). *See also* the provisions on use of depositions in Rule 32(a)(3) of the Federal Rules of Civil Procedure and Rule 15(e) of the Federal Rules of Criminal Procedure.

[(a)](5) Absence from the hearing coupled with inability to compel attendance by process or other reasonable means also satisfies the requirement. McCormick § 234; Uniform Rule 62(7)(d) and (e); California Evidence Code § 240(a)(4) and (5); Kansas Code of Civil Procedure § 60–459(g)(4) and (5); New Jersey Rule 62(6)(b) and (d). See the discussion of procuring attendance of witnesses who are nonresidents or in custody in Barber v. Page, 390 U.S. 719, 88 S.Ct. 1318, 20 L.Ed.2d 255 (1968).

If the conditions otherwise constituting unavailability result from the procurement or wrongdoing of the proponent of the statement, the requirement is not satisfied. The rule contains no requirement that an attempt be made to take the deposition of the declarant. **[Editor's Note: Congress subsequently added the requirement that the proponent attempt to take a deposition when unavailability is asserted on the grounds of absence. See the text of Rule 804(a)(5) and the explanation in the Congressional Reports immediately below.]**

Report of House Committee on the Judiciary on Rule 804(a)(5)

House Comm. on Judiciary, Fed.Rules of Evidence, H.R.Rep. No. 650, 93d Cong., 1st Sess., p. 15 (1973); 1974 U.S.Code Cong. & Ad.News 7075, 7088

Rule 804(a)(5) as submitted to the Congress provided, as one type of situation in which a declarant would be deemed "unavailable", that he be "absent from the hearing and the proponent of his statement has been unable to procure his attendance by process or other reasonable means." The Committee amended the Rule to insert after the word "attendance" the parenthetical expression "(or, in the case of a hearsay exception under subdivision (b)(2), (3), or (4), his attendance or testimony)". The amendment is designed primarily to require that an attempt be made to depose a witness (as well as to seek his attendance) as a precondition to the witness being deemed unavailable. The Committee, however, recognized the propriety of an exception to this additional requirement when it is the declarant's former testimony that is sought to be admitted under subdivision (b)(1).

Report of Senate Committee on the Judiciary on Rule 804(a)(5)

Senate Comm. on Judiciary, Fed.Rules of Evidence, S.Rep. No. 1277, 93d Cong., 2d Sess., p. 20 (1974); 1974 U.S.Code Cong. & Ad.News 7051, 7066

Subdivision (a) of rule 804 as submitted by the Supreme Court defined the conditions under which a witness was considered to be unavailable. It was amended in the House.

The purpose of the amendment, according to the report of the House Committee on the Judiciary, is "primarily to require that an attempt be made to depose a witness (as well as to seek his attendance) as a precondition to the witness being unavailable."[1]

Under the House amendment, before a witness is declared unavailable, a party must try to depose a witness (declarant) with respect to dying declarations, declarations against interest, and declarations of pedigree. None of these situations would seem to warrant this needless, impractical and highly restrictive complication. A good case can be made for eliminating the unavailability requirement entirely for declarations against interest cases.[2]

In dying declaration cases, the declarant will usually, though not necessarily, be deceased at the time of trial. Pedigree statements which are admittedly and necessarily based largely on word of mouth are not greatly fortified by a deposition requirement.

Depositions are expensive and time-consuming. In any event, deposition procedures are available to those who wish to resort to them. Moreover, the deposition procedures of the Civil Rules and Criminal Rules are only imperfectly adapted to implementing the amendment. No purpose is served unless the deposition, if taken, may be used in evidence. Under Civil Rule (a)(3) and Criminal Rule 15(e), a deposition, though taken, may not be admissible, and under Criminal Rule 15(a) substantial obstacles exist in the way of even taking a deposition.

For these reasons, the committee deleted the House amendment.

The committee understands that the rule as to unavailability, as explained by the Advisory Committee "contains no requirement that an attempt be made to take the deposition of a declarant." In reflecting the committee's judgment, the statement is accurate insofar as it goes. Where, however, the proponent of the statement, with knowledge of the existence of the statement, fails to confront the declarant with the statement at the taking of the deposition, then the proponent should not, in fairness, be permitted to treat the declarant as "unavailable" simply because the declarant was not amenable to process compelling his attendance at trial. The committee does not consider it necessary to amend the rule to this effect because such a situation abuses, not conforms to, the rule. Fairness would preclude a person from introducing a hearsay statement on a particular issue if the person taking the deposition was aware of the issue at the time of the deposition but failed to depose the unavailable witness on that issue.

Conference Report on Rule 804(a)(5)

H.R., Fed.Rules of Evidence, Conf.Rep. No. 1597, 93d Cong., 2d Sess., p. 12 (1974); 1974 U.S.Code Cong. & Ad. News 7098, 7105

Subsection (a) defines the term "unavailability as a witness". The House bill provides in subsection (a)(5) that the party who desires to use the statement must

---

[1] H.Rept. 93–650, at p. 15.

[2] Uniform Rule 63(10); Kan.Stat.Anno. 60–460(j); 2A N.J.Stats.Anno. 84–63(10).

be unable to procure the declarant's attendance by process or other reasonable means. In the case of dying declarations, statements against interest and statements of personal or family history, the House bill requires that the proponent must also be unable to procure the declarant's *testimony* (such as by deposition or interrogatories) by process or other reasonable means. The Senate amendment eliminates this latter provision.

The Conference adopts the provision contained in the House bill.

Advisory Committee's Note to Rule 804(b)

56 F.R.D. 183, 323

Subdivision (b). Rule 803, *supra*, is based upon the assumption that a hearsay statement falling within one of its exceptions possesses qualities which justify the conclusion that whether the declarant is available or unavailable is not a relevant factor in determining admissibility. The instant rule proceeds upon a different theory: hearsay which admittedly is not equal in quality to testimony of the declarant on the stand may nevertheless be admitted if the declarant is unavailable and if his statement meets a specified standard. The rule expresses preferences: testimony given on the stand in person is preferred over hearsay, and hearsay, if of the specified quality, is preferred over complete loss of the evidence of the declarant. The exceptions evolved at common law with respect to declarations of unavailable declarants furnish the basis for the exceptions enumerated in the proposal. The term "unavailable" is defined in subdivision (a).

Exception [1]. Former testimony does not rely upon some set of circumstances to substitute for oath and cross-examination, since both oath and opportunity to cross-examine were present in fact. The only missing one of the ideal conditions for the giving of testimony is the presence of trier and opponent ("demeanor evidence"). This is lacking with all hearsay exceptions. Hence it may be argued that former testimony is the strongest hearsay and should be included under Rule 803, *supra*. However, opportunity to observe demeanor is what in a large measure confers depth and meaning upon oath and cross-examination. Thus in cases under Rule 803 demeanor lacks the significance which it possesses with respect to testimony. In any event, the tradition, founded in experience, uniformly favors production of the witness if he is available. The exception indicates continuation of the policy. This preference for the presence of the witness is apparent also in rules and statutes on the use of depositions, which deal with substantially the same problem.

Under the exception, the testimony may be offered (1) against the party *against* whom it was previously offered or (2) against the party *by* whom it was previously offered. In each instance the question resolves itself into whether fairness allows imposing, upon the party against whom now offered, the handling of the witness on the earlier occasion. (1) If the party against whom now offered is the one against whom the testimony was offered previously, no unfairness is apparent in requiring him to accept his own prior conduct of cross-examination or decision not to cross-examine. Only demeanor has been lost, and that is inherent in the situation. (2) If the party against whom now offered is the one *by* whom the testimony was offered previously, a satisfactory answer becomes somewhat more difficult. One possibility is to proceed somewhat along the line of an adoptive admission, *i.e.* by offering the testimony proponent in effect adopts it. However, this theory savors of discarded concepts of witnesses' belonging to a party, of litigants' ability to pick and choose witnesses, and of vouching for one's own witnesses. Cf. McCormick § 246, pp. 526–527; 4 Wigmore § 1075. A more direct and acceptable approach is simply to recognize direct and redirect examination of one's own witness as the equivalent of cross-examining an opponent's witness. Falknor, Former Testimony and the Uniform Rules: A Comment, 38 N.Y.U.L.Rev. 651, n. 1 (1963); McCormick § 231, p. 483. *See also* 5

Wigmore § 1389. Allowable techniques for dealing with hostile, double-crossing, forgetful, and mentally deficient witnesses leave no substance to a claim that one could not adequately develop his own witness at the former hearing. An even less appealing argument is presented when failure to develop fully was the result of a deliberate choice.

The common law did not limit the admissibility of former testimony to that given in an earlier trial of the same case, although it did require identity of issues as a means of insuring that the former handling of the witness was the equivalent of what would now be done if the opportunity were presented. Modern decisions reduce the requirement to "substantial" identity. McCormick § 233. Since identity of issues is significant only in that it bears on motive and interest in developing fully the testimony of the witness, expressing the matter in the latter terms is preferable. *Id.* Testimony given at a preliminary hearing was held in California v. Green, 399 U.S. 149, 90 S.Ct. 1930, 26 L.Ed.2d 489 (1970), to satisfy confrontation requirements in this respect.

As a further assurance of fairness in thrusting upon a party the prior handling of the witness, the common law also insisted upon identity of parties, deviating only to the extent of allowing substitution of successors in a narrowly construed privity. Mutuality as an aspect of identity is now generally discredited, and the requirement of identity of the offering party disappears except as it might affect motive to develop the testimony. Falknor, *supra*, at 652; McCormick § 232, pp. 487–488. The question remains whether strict identity, or privity, should continue as a requirement with respect to the party against whom offered. The rule departs to the extent of allowing substitution of one with the right and opportunity to develop the testimony with similar motive and interest. The position is supported by modern decisions. McCormick § 232. pp. 487–88; 5 Wigmore § 1388. **[Editor's Note: Congress modified the Advisory Committee proposal, so that the rule enacted provides that prior testimony cannot be used against a party unless that party—or a predecessor in interest—had a similar motive and opportunity to develop the testimony. See the Congressional reports immediately below.]**

Provisions of the same tenor will be found in Uniform Rule 63(3)(b); California Evidence Code §§ 1290–1292; Kansas Code of Civil Procedure § 60460(c)(2); New Jersey Evidence Rule 63(3). Unlike the rule, the latter three provide either that former testimony is not admissible if the right of confrontation is denied or that it is not admissible if the accused was not a party to the prior hearing. The genesis of these limitations is a caveat in Uniform Rule 63(3) Comment that use of former testimony against an accused may violate his right of confrontation. Mattox v. United States, 156 U.S. 237, 15 S.Ct. 337, 39 L.Ed. 409 (1895), held that the right was not violated by the government's use, on a retrial of the same case, of testimony given at the first trial by two witnesses since deceased. The decision leaves open the question (1) whether direct and redirect are equivalent to cross-examination for purposes of confrontation, (2) whether testimony given in a different proceeding is acceptable, and (3) whether the accused must himself have been a party to the earlier proceeding or whether a similarly situated person will serve the purpose. Professor Falknor concluded that, if a dying declaration untested by cross-examination is constitutionally admissible, former testimony tested by the cross-examination of one similarly situated does not offend against confrontation. Falknor, *supra*, at 659–60. The constitutional acceptability of dying declarations has often been conceded. Mattox v. United States, 156 U.S. 237, 243, 15 S.Ct. 337, 39 L.Ed. 409 (1895); Kirby v. United States, 174 U.S. 47, 61, 19 S.Ct. 574, 43 L.Ed. 890 (1899); Pointer v. Texas, 380 U.S. 400, 407, 85 S.Ct. 1065, 13 L.Ed. 2d 923 (1965).

Report of House Committee on the Judiciary on Rule 804(b)(1)

House Comm. on Judiciary, Fed.Rules of Evidence, H.R.Rep. No. 650, 93d Cong., 1st Sess., p. 15 (1973); 1974 U.S.Code Cong. & Ad.News 7075, 7088

Rule 804(b)(1) as submitted by the Court allowed prior testimony of an unavailable witness to be admissible if the party against whom it is offered or a person "with motive and interest similar" to his had an opportunity to examine the witness. The Committee considered that it is generally unfair to impose upon the party against whom the hearsay evidence is being offered responsibility for the manner in which the witness was previously handled by another party. The sole exception to this, in the Committee's view, is when a party's predecessor in interest in a civil action or proceeding had an opportunity and similar motive to examine the witness. The Committee amended the Rule to reflect these policy determinations.

Report of Senate Committee on the Judiciary on Rule 804(b)(1)

Senate Comm. on Judiciary, Fed.Rules of Evidence, S.Rep. No. 1277, 93d Cong., 2d Sess., p. 21 (1974); 1974 U.S.Code Cong. & Ad.News 7051, 7067

Former testimony.—Rule 804(b)(1) as submitted by the Court allowed prior testimony of an unavailable witness to be admissible if the party against whom it is offered or a person "with motive and interest similar" to his had an opportunity to examine the witness.

The House amended the rule to apply only to a party's predecessor in interest. Although the committee recognizes considerable merit to the rule submitted by the Supreme Court, a position which has been advocated by many scholars and judges, we have concluded that the difference between the two versions is not great and we accept the House amendment.

Advisory Committee's Note to Rule 804(b)(2)

56 F.R.D. 183, 326

Exception [2]. The exception is the familiar dying declaration of the common law, expanded somewhat beyond its traditionally narrow limits. While the original religious justification for the exception may have lost its conviction for some persons over the years, it can scarcely be doubted that powerful psychological pressures are present. See 5 Wigmore § 1443 and the classic statement of Chief Baron Eyre in Rex v. Woodcock, 1 Leach 500, 502, 168 Eng.Rep. 352, 353 (K.B. 1789).

The common law required that the statement be that of the victim, offered in a prosecution for criminal homicide. Thus declarations by victims in prosecutions for other crimes, *e.g.* a declaration by a rape victim who dies in childbirth, and all declarations in civil cases were outside the scope of the exception. An occasional statute has removed these restrictions, as in Colo.R.S. § 52–1–20, or has expanded the area of offenses to include abortions, 5 Wigmore § 1432, p. 224, n. 4. Kansas by decision extended the exception to civil cases. Thurston v. Fritz, 91 Kan. 468, 138 P. 625 (1914). While the common law exception no doubt originated as a result of the exceptional need for the evidence in homicide cases, the theory of admissibility applies equally in civil cases and in prosecutions for crimes other than homicide. **[Editor's Note: Congress refused to extend the dying declaration exception to crimes other than homicide.]** The same considerations suggest abandonment of the limitation to circumstances attending the event in question, yet when the statement deals with matters other than the supposed death, its influence is believed to be sufficiently attenuated to justify the limitation. Unavailability is not limited to death. See subdivision (a) of this rule. Any problem as to declarations phrased in terms of opinion is laid at rest by Rule 701, and continuation of a requirement of first-hand knowledge is assured by Rule 602.

Comparable provisions are found in Uniform Rule 63(5); California Evidence Code § 1242; Kansas Code of Civil Procedure § 60–460(e); New Jersey Evidence Rule 63(5).

Report of House Committee on the Judiciary on Rule 804(b)(2)

House Comm. on Judiciary, Fed.Rules of Evidence, H.R.Rep. No. 650, 93d Cong., 1st Sess., p. 15 (1973); 1974 U.S.Code Cong. & Ad.News 7075, 7089

Rule 804(b)(3) as submitted by the Court (now Rule 804(b)(2) in the bill) proposed to expand the traditional scope of the dying declaration exception (*i.e.* a statement of the victim in a homicide case as to the cause or circumstances of his believed imminent death) to allow such statements in all criminal and civil cases. The Committee did not consider dying declarations as among the most reliable forms of hearsay. Consequently, it amended the provision to limit their admissibility in criminal cases to homicide prosecutions, where exceptional need for the evidence is present. This is existing law. At the same time, the Committee approved the expansion to civil actions and proceedings where the stakes do not involve possible imprisonment, although noting that this could lead to forum shopping in some instances.

Advisory Committee's Note to Rule 804(b)(3)

56 F.R.D. 183, 327

Exception [3]. The circumstantial guaranty of reliability for declarations against interest is the assumption that persons do not make statements which are damaging to themselves unless satisfied for good reason that they are true. Hileman v. Northwest Engineering Co., 346 F.2d 668 (6th Cir. 1965). If the statement is that of a party, offered by his opponent, it comes in as an admission, Rule 803(d)(2) **[Now Rule 801(d)(2)—Ed.]**, and there is no occasion to inquire whether it is against interest, this not being a condition precedent to admissibility of admissions by opponents.

The common law required that the interest declared against be pecuniary or proprietary but within this limitation demonstrated striking ingenuity in discovering an against-interest aspect. Higham v. Ridgway, 10 East 109, 103 Eng.Rep. 717 (K.B. 1808); Reg. v. Overseers of Birmingham, 1 B. & S. 763, 121 Eng.Rep. 897 (Q.B. 1861); McCormick, § 256, p. 551, nn. 2 and 3.

The exception discards the common law limitation and expands to the full logical limit. One result is to remove doubt as to the admissibility of declarations tending to establish a tort liability against the declarant or to extinguish one which might be asserted by him, in accordance with the trend of the decisions in this country. McCormick, § 254, pp. 548–549. Another is to allow statements tending to expose declarant to hatred, ridicule, or disgrace, the motivation here being considered to be as strong as when financial interests are at stake. McCormick § 255, p. 551. **[Editor's Note: The exception as adopted by Congress does not include statements tending to expose declarants to hatred, ridicule or disgrace.]** And finally, exposure to criminal liability satisfies the against-interest requirement. The refusal of the common law to concede the adequacy of a penal interest was no doubt indefensible in logic, see the dissent of Mr. Justice Holmes in Donnelly v. United States, 228 U.S. 243, 33 S.Ct. 449, 57 L.Ed. 820 (1913), but one senses in the decisions a distrust of evidence of confessions by third persons offered to exculpate the accused arising from suspicions of fabrication either of the fact of the making of the confession or in its contents, enhanced in either instance by the required unavailability of the declarant. Nevertheless, an increasing amount of decisional law recognizes exposure to punishment for crime as a sufficient stake. People v. Spriggs, 60

Cal.2d 868, 36 Cal.Rptr. 841, 389 P.2d 377 (1964); Sutter v. Easterly, 354 Mo. 282, 189 S.W.2d 284 (1945); Band's Refuse Removal, Inc. v. Fairlawn Borough, 62 N.J.Super. 522, 163 A.2d 465 (1960); Newberry v. Commonwealth, 191 Va. 445, 61 S.E.2d 318 (1950); Annot., 162 A.L.R. 446. The requirement of corroboration is included in the rule in order to effect an accommodation between these competing considerations. When the statement is offered by the accused by way of exculpation, the resulting situation is not adapted to control by rulings as to the weight of the evidence, and hence the provision is cast in terms of a requirement preliminary to admissibility. Cf. Rule 406(a). The requirement of corroboration should be construed in such a manner as to effectuate its purpose of circumventing fabrication.

Ordinarily the third-party confession is thought of in terms of exculpating the accused, but this is by no means always or necessarily the case: it may include statements implicating him, and under the general theory of declarations against interest they would be admissible as related statements. Douglas v. Alabama, 380 U.S. 415, 85 S.Ct. 1074, 13 L.Ed.2d 934 (1965), and Bruton v. United States, 389 U.S. 818, 88 S.Ct. 126, 19 L.Ed.2d 70 (1968), both involved confessions by codefendants which implicated the accused. While the confession was not actually offered in evidence in *Douglas,* the procedure followed effectively put it before the jury, which the Court ruled to be error. Whether the confession might have been admissible as a declaration against penal interest was not considered or discussed. *Bruton* assumed the inadmissibility, as against the accused, of the implicating confession of his codefendant, and centered upon the question of the effectiveness of a limiting instruction. These decisions, however, by no means require that all statements implicating another person be excluded from the category of declarations against interest. Whether a statement is in fact against interest must be determined from the circumstances of each case. Thus a statement admitting guilt and implicating another person, made while in custody, may well be motivated by a desire to curry favor with the authorities and hence fail to qualify as against interest. See the dissenting opinion of Mr. Justice White in *Bruton.* On the other hand, the same words spoken under different circumstances, *e.g.,* to an acquaintance, would have no difficulty in qualifying. The rule does not purport to deal with questions of the right of confrontation.

The balancing of self-serving against disserving aspects of a declaration is discussed in McCormick § 256.

For comparable provisions, see Uniform Rule 63(10); California Evidence Code § 1230; Kansas Code of Civil Procedure § 60–460(j); New Jersey Evidence Rule 63(10).

Report of House Committee on the Judiciary on Rule 804(b)(3)

House Comm. on Judiciary, Fed.Rules of Evidence, H.R.Rep. No. 650, 93d Cong., 1st Sess., p. 16 (1973); 1974 U.S.Code Cong. & Ad.News 7075, 7089

Rule 804(b)(4) as submitted by the Court (now Rule 804(b)(3) in the bill) provided as follows:

> *Statement against interest.*—A statement which was at the time of its making so far contrary to the declarant's pecuniary or proprietary interest or so far tended to subject him to civil or criminal liability or to render invalid a claim by him against another or to make him an object of hatred, ridicule, or disgrace, that a reasonable man in his position would not have made the statement unless he believed it to be true. A statement tending to exculpate the accused is not admissible unless corroborated.

The Committee determined to retain the traditional hearsay exception for statements against pecuniary or proprietary interest. However, it deemed the Court's additional references to statements tending to subject a declarant to civil liability or to render invalid a claim by him against another to be redundant as included within the scope of the reference to statements against pecuniary or proprietary interest. See Gichner v. Antonio Triano Tile and Marble Co., 410 F.2d 238 (D.C.Cir. 1968). Those additional references were accordingly deleted.

The Court's Rule also proposed to expand the hearsay limitation from its present federal limitation to include statements subjecting the declarant to criminal liability and statements tending to make him an object of hatred, ridicule, or disgrace. The Committee eliminated the latter category from the subdivision as lacking sufficient guarantees of reliability. See United States v. Dovico, 380 F.2d 325, 327 nn. 2, 4 (2nd Cir.), cert. denied, 389 U.S. 944 (1967). As for statements against penal interest, the Committee shared the view of the Court that some such statements do possess adequate assurances of reliability and should be admissible. It believed, however, as did the Court, that statements of this type tending to exculpate the accused are more suspect and so should have their admissibility conditioned upon some further provision insuring trustworthiness. The proposal in the Court Rule to add a requirement of simple corroboration was, however, deemed ineffective to accomplish this purpose since the accused's own testimony might suffice while not necessarily increasing the reliability of the hearsay statement. The Committee settled upon the language "unless corroborating circumstances clearly indicate the trustworthiness of the statement" as affording a proper standard and degree of discretion. It was contemplated that the result in such cases as Donnelly v. United States, 228 U.S. 243 (1912), where the circumstances plainly indicated reliability, would be changed. The Committee also added to the Rule the final sentence from the 1971 Advisory Committee draft, designed to codify the doctrine of Bruton v. United States, 391 U.S. 123 (1968). The Committee does not intend to affect the existing exception to the *Bruton* principle where the codefendant takes the stand and is subject to cross-examination, but believed there was no need to make specific provision for this situation in the Rule, since in that event the declarant would not be "unavailable".

Report of Senate Committee on the Judiciary on Rule 804(b)(3)

Senate Comm. on Judiciary, Fed.Rules of Evidence, S.Rep. No. 1277, 93d Cong., 2d Sess., p. 21 (1974); 1974 U.S.Code Cong. & Ad.News 7051, 7067

The rule defines those statements which are considered to be against interest and thus of sufficient trustworthiness to be admissible even though hearsay. With regard to the type of interest declared against, the version submitted by the Supreme Court included inter alia, statements tending to subject a declarant to civil liability or to invalidate a claim by him against another. The House struck these provisions as redundant. In view of the conflicting case law construing pecuniary or proprietary interests narrowly so as to exclude, *e.g.*, tort cases, this deletion could be misconstrued.

Three States which have recently codified their rules of evidence have followed the Supreme Court's version of this rule, *i.e.*, that a statement is against interest if it tends to subject a declarant to civil liability.[3]

The committee believes that the reference to statements tending to subject a person to civil liability constitutes a desirable clarification of the scope of the rule. Therefore, we have reinstated the Supreme Court language on this matter.

The Court rule also proposed to expand the hearsay limitation from its present federal limitation to include statements subjecting the declarant to statements tending to make him an object of hatred, ridicule, or disgrace. The House eliminated the latter category from the subdivision as lacking sufficient guarantees of reliability. Although there is considerable support for the

---

[3] Nev.Rev.Stats. § 51.345; N.Mex.Stats. (1973 Supp.) § 20–4–804(4); West's Wis.Stats.Anno. (1973 Supp.) § 908.045(4).

admissibility of such statements (all three of the State rules referred to *supra*, would admit such statements), we accept the deletion by the House.

The House amended this exception to add a sentence making inadmissible a statement or confession offered against the accused in a criminal case, made by a codefendant or other person implicating both himself and the accused. The sentence was added to codify the constitutional principle announced in Bruton v. United States, 391 U.S. 123 (1968). *Bruton* held that the admission of the extrajudicial hearsay statement of one codefendant inculpating a second codefendant violated the confrontation clause of the sixth amendment.

The committee decided to delete this provision because the basic approach of the rules is to avoid codifying, or attempting to codify, constitutional evidentiary principles, such as the fifth amendment's right against self-incrimination and, here, the sixth amendment's right of confrontation. Codification of a constitutional principle is unnecessary and, where the principle is under development, often unwise. Furthermore, the House provision does not appear to recognize the exceptions to the *Bruton* rule, *e.g.* where the codefendant takes the stand and is subject to cross examination; where the accused confessed, see United States v. Mancusi, 404 F.2d 296 (2d Cir. 1968), cert. denied 397 U.S. 942 (1907); where the accused was placed at the scene of the crime, see United States v. Zelker, 452 F.2d 1009 (2d Cir. 1971). For these reasons, the committee decided to delete this provision.

Conference Report on Rule 804(b)(3)

H.R., Fed.Rules of Evidence, Conf.Rep. No. 1597, 93d Cong., 2d Sess., p. 12 (1974); 1974 U.S.Code Cong. & Ad.News 7098, 7105

The Senate amendment to subsection (b)(3) provides that a statement is against interest and not excluded by the hearsay rule when the declarant is unavailable as a witness, if the statement tends to subject a person to civil or criminal liability or renders invalid a claim by him against another. The House bill did not refer specifically to civil liability and to rendering invalid a claim against another. The Senate amendment also deletes from the House bill the provision that subsection (b)(3) does not apply to a statement or confession, made by a codefendant or another, which implicates the accused and the person who made the statement, when that statement or confession is offered against the accused in a criminal case.

The Conference adopts the Senate amendment. The Conferees intend to include within the purview of this rule, statements subjecting a person to civil liability and statements rendering claims invalid. The Conferees agree to delete the provision regarding statements by a codefendant, thereby reflecting the general approach in the Rules of Evidence to avoid attempting to codify constitutional evidentiary principles.

Advisory Committee's Note to Rule 804(b)(4)

56 F.R.D. 183, 328

Exception [4]. The general common law requirement that a declaration in this area must have been made *ante litem motam* has been dropped, as bearing more appropriately on weight than admissibility. See 5 Wigmore § 1483. Item (i) specifically disclaims any need of firsthand knowledge respecting declarant's own personal history. In some instances it is self-evident (marriage) and in others impossible and traditionally not required (date of birth). Item (ii) deals with declarations concerning the history of another person. As at common law, declarant is qualified if related by blood or marriage. 5 Wigmore, § 1489. In addition, and contrary to the common law, declarant qualifies by virtue of intimate association with the family. *Id.*, § 1487. The requirement sometimes encountered that when the subject of the statement is the relationship between two other persons the declarant must qualify as to both is omitted. Relationship is reciprocal. *Id.*, § 1491.

For comparable provisions, see Uniform Rule 63(23), (24), (25); California Evidence Code §§ 1310, 1311; Kansas Code of Civil Procedure § 60–460(u), (v), (w); New Jersey Evidence Rules 63(23), 63(24), 63(25).

[Editor's Note: Rule 804(b)(5) was transferred with Rule 803(24) to make a combined residual exception. See the Committee Note and relevant legislative history under Rule 807.]

1987 Amendment Committee Note

The amendments are technical. No substantive change is intended.

1997 Amendment Committee Note, to Transfer of Rule 804(b)(5) and to addition of Rule 804(b)(6)

Subdivision (b)(5). The contents of Rule 803(24) and Rule 804(b)(5) have been combined and transferred to a new Rule 807. This was done to facilitate additions to Rules 803 and 804. No change in meaning is intended.

Subdivision (b)(6). Rule 804(b)(6) has been added to provide that a party forfeits the right to object on hearsay grounds to the admission of a declarant's prior statement when the party's deliberate wrongdoing or acquiescence therein procured the unavailability of the declarant as a witness. This recognizes the need for a prophylactic rule to deal with abhorrent behavior "which strikes at the heart of the system of justice itself." *United States v. Mastrangelo*, 693 F.2d 269, 273 (2d Cir. 1982), *cert. denied*, 467 U.S. 1204 (1984). The wrongdoing need not consist of a criminal act. The rule applies to all parties, including the government. It applies to actions taken after the event to prevent a witness from testifying.

Every circuit that has resolved the question has recognized the principle of forfeiture by misconduct, although the tests for determining whether there is a forfeiture have varied. *See, e.g., United States v. Aguiar*, 975 F.2d 45, 47 (2d Cir. 1992); *United States v. Potamitis*, 739 F.2d 784, 789 (2d Cir.), *cert. denied*, 469 U.S. 918 (1984); *Steele v. Taylor*, 684 F.2d 1193, 1199 (6th Cir. 1982), *cert. denied*, 460 U.S. 1053 (1983); United *States v. Balano*, 618 F.2d 624, 629 (10th Cir. 1979), *cert. denied*, 449 U.S. 840 (1980); *United States v. Carlson*, 547 F.2d 1346, 1358–59 (8th Cir.), *cert. denied*, 431 U.S. 914 (1977). The foregoing cases apply a preponderance of the evidence standard. *Contra United States v. Thevis*, 665 F.2d 616, 631 (5th Cir.) (clear and convincing standard), *cert. denied*, 459 U.S. 825 (1982). The usual Rule 104(a) preponderance of the evidence standard has been adopted in light of the behavior the new Rule 804(b)(6) seeks to discourage.

2010 Committee Note to an Amendment to Rule 804(b)(3)

Rule 804(b)(3) has been amended to provide that the corroborating circumstances requirement applies to all declarations against penal interest offered in criminal cases. A number of courts have applied the corroborating circumstances requirement to declarations against penal interest offered by the prosecution, even though the text of the Rule did not so provide. *See, e.g., United States v. Alvarez*, 584 F.2d 694, 701 (5th Cir. 1978) ("by transplanting the language governing exculpatory statements onto the analysis for admitting inculpatory hearsay, a unitary standard is derived which offers the most workable basis for applying Rule 804(b)(3)"); *United States v. Shukri*, 207 F.3d 412 (7th Cir. 2000) (requiring corroborating circumstances for against-penal-interest statements offered by the government). A unitary approach to declarations against penal interest assures both the prosecution and the accused that the Rule will not be abused and that only reliable hearsay statements will be admitted under the exception.

All other changes to the structure and wording of the rule are intended to be stylistic only. There is no intent to change any other result in any ruling on evidence admissibility.

The amendment does not address the use of the corroborating circumstances for declarations against penal interest offered in civil cases.

In assessing whether corroborating circumstances exist, some courts have focused on the credibility of the witness who relates the hearsay statement in court. But the credibility of the witness who relates the statement is not a proper factor for the court to consider in assessing corroborating circumstances. To base admission or exclusion of a hearsay statement on the witness's credibility would usurp the jury's role of determining the credibility of testifying witnesses.

Rule 805. Hearsay Within Hearsay

Hearsay within hearsay is not excluded by the rule against hearsay if each part of the combined statements conforms with an exception to the rule.

(As amended Apr. 26, 2011, eff. Dec. 1, 2011.)

RESTYLED RULE 805 COMMITTEE NOTE

The language of Rule 805 has been amended as part of the restyling of the Evidence Rules to make them more easily understood and to make style and terminology consistent throughout the rules. These changes are intended to be stylistic only. There is no intent to change any result in any ruling on evidence admissibility.

Section references, McCormick 7th ed.

§ 324.1

Note by Federal Judicial Center

The rule enacted by the Congress is the rule prescribed by the Supreme Court without change.

Advisory Committee's Note

56 F.R.D. 183, 329

On principle it scarcely seems open to doubt that the hearsay rule should not call for exclusion of a hearsay statement which includes a further hearsay statement when both conform to the requirements of a hearsay exception. Thus a hospital record might contain an entry of the patient's age based on information furnished by his wife. The hospital record would qualify as a regular entry except that the person who furnished the information was not acting in the routine of the business. However, her statement independently qualifies as a statement of pedigree (if she is unavailable) or as a statement made for purposes of diagnosis or treatment, and hence each link in the chain falls under sufficient assurances. Or, further to illustrate, a dying declaration may incorporate a declaration against interest by another declarant. See McCormick § 290, p. 611.

Rule 806. Attacking and Supporting the Declarant's Credibility

When a hearsay statement—or a statement described in Rule 801(d)(2)(C), (D), or (E)—has been admitted in evidence, the declarant's credibility may be attacked, and then supported, by any evidence that would be admissible for those purposes if the declarant had testified as a witness. The court may admit evidence of the declarant's inconsistent statement or conduct, regardless of when it occurred or whether the declarant had an opportunity to explain or deny it. If the party against whom the statement was admitted calls the declarant as a witness, the party may examine the declarant on the statement as if on cross-examination.

(As amended Mar. 2, 1987, eff. Oct. 1, 1987; Apr. 11, 1997, eff. Dec. 1, 1997; Apr. 26, 2011, eff. Dec. 1, 2011.)

RESTYLED RULE 806 COMMITTEE NOTE

The language of Rule 806 has been amended as part of the restyling of the Evidence Rules to make them more easily understood and to make style and terminology consistent throughout the rules. These changes are intended to be stylistic only. There is no intent to change any result in any ruling on evidence admissibility.

REPORTER'S COMMENT ON RESTYLED RULE 806

The Restyling fixed a glitch in the original rule. The rule is intended to allow an adversary to impeach a hearsay declarant to the same extent as if the declarant were testifying—because in effect the declarant *is* testifying when their out-of-court statement is offered for its truth. The first sentence of the rule indicates that statements of party-opponents' agents—while denominated "not hearsay"—are covered by the rule to the same extent as statements admitted under the hearsay exceptions. This makes sense because those statements are offered for their truth and the opponent should be allowed to attack the declarant's credibility to the same extent as if the agent testified at trial. Calling them "not hearsay" is simply a device used in the Federal Rules designed to differentiate such statements from those that are admitted because they are reliable, but functionally a statement admitted under Rule 801(d) has the same effect as a statement admitted under a hearsay "exception."

The problem with the original rule was that the reference to agency-statements set forth in the first sentence was not carried through to the second and third sentences, which provide details on how to attack the credibility of a hearsay declarant. That is, those latter sentences referred to "hearsay" without also referring to statements admitted under Rule 801(d)(2)(C), (D) or (E). The Restyling fixes the anomaly by simply deleting the references to hearsay in the second and third sentences. There is no need to keep referring to hearsay, as the first sentence adequately states the problem being treated and any further reference is superfluous—and in this case incomplete.

Section references, McCormick 7th ed.

§ 324.2

Note by Federal Judicial Center

The rule enacted by the Congress is the rule prescribed by the Supreme Court, amended by inserting the phrase "or a statement defined in Rule 801(d)(2), (C), (D), or (E)."

Advisory Committee's Note

56 F.R.D. 183, 329

The declarant of a hearsay statement which is admitted in evidence is in effect a witness. His credibility should in fairness be subject to impeachment and support as though he had in fact testified. See Rules 608 and 609. There are however, some special aspects of the impeaching of a hearsay declarant which require consideration. These special aspects center upon impeachment by inconsistent statement, arise from factual differences which exist between the use of hearsay and an actual witness and also between various kinds of hearsay, and involve the question of applying to declarants the general rule disallowing evidence of an inconsistent statement to impeach a witness unless he is afforded an opportunity to deny or explain. See Rule 613(b).

The principle [sic] difference between using hearsay and an actual witness is that the inconsistent statement will in the case of the witness almost inevitably of necessity in the nature of things be a *prior* statement, which it is entirely possible and feasible to call to his attention, while in the case of hearsay the inconsistent statement may well be a *subsequent* one, which practically precludes calling it to the attention of the declarant. The result of insisting upon observation of this impossible requirement in the hearsay situation is to deny the opponent, already barred from cross-examination, any benefit of this important technique of impeachment. The writers favor allowing the subsequent statement. McCormick, § 37, p. 69; 3 Wigmore § 1033. The cases, however, are divided. Cases allowing the impeachment include People v. Collup, 27 Cal.2d 829, 167 P.2d 714 (1946); People v. Rosoto, 58 Cal.2d 304, 23 Cal.Rptr. 779, 373 P.2d 867 (1962); Carver v. United States, 164 U.S. 694, 17 S.Ct. 228, 41 L.Ed. 602 (1897). Contra, Mattox v. United States, 156 U.S. 237, 15 S.Ct. 337, 39 L.Ed. 409 (1895); People v. Hines, 284 N.Y. 93, 29 N.E.2d 483 (1940). The force of *Mattox,* where the hearsay was the former testimony of a deceased witness and the denial of use of a subsequent inconsistent statement was upheld, is much diminished by *Carver,* where the hearsay was a dying declaration and denial of use of a subsequent inconsistent statement resulted in reversal. The difference in the particular brand of hearsay seems unimportant when the inconsistent statement is a *subsequent* one. True, the opponent is not totally deprived of cross-examination when the hearsay is former testimony or a deposition but he is deprived of cross-examining on the statement or along lines suggested by it. Mr. Justice Shiras, with two justices joining him, dissented vigorously in *Mattox.*

When the impeaching statement was made *prior* to the hearsay statement, differences in the kinds of hearsay appear which arguably may justify differences in treatment. If the hearsay consisted of a simple statement by the witness, *e.g.* a dying declaration or a declaration against interest, the feasibility of affording him an opportunity to deny or explain encounters the same practical impossibility as where the statement is a subsequent one, just discussed, although here the impossibility arises from the total absence of anything resembling a hearing at which the matter could be put to him. The courts by a large majority have ruled in favor of allowing the statement to be used under these circumstances. McCormick § 37, p. 69; 3 Wigmore § 1033. If, however, the hearsay consists of former testimony or a deposition, the possibility of calling the prior statement to the attention of the witness or deponent is not ruled out, since the opportunity to cross-examine was available. It might thus be concluded that with former testimony or depositions the conventional foundation should be insisted upon. Most of the cases involve depositions, and Wigmore describes them as divided. 3 Wigmore § 1031. Deposition procedures at best are cumbersome and expensive, and to require the laying of the foundation may impose an undue burden. Under the federal practice, there is no way of knowing with certainty at the time of taking a deposition whether it is merely for discovery or will ultimately end up in evidence. With respect to both former testimony and depositions the possibility exists that knowledge of the statement might not be acquired until after the time of the cross-examination. Moreover, the expanded admissibility of former testimony and depositions under Rule 804(b)(1) calls for a correspondingly expanded approach to impeachment. The rule dispenses with the requirement in all hearsay situations, which is readily administered and best calculated to lead to fair results.

Notice should be taken that Rule 26(f) of the Federal Rules of Civil Procedure, as originally submitted by the Advisory Committee, ended with the following:

> " . . . and, without having first called them to the deponent's attention, may show statements contradictory thereto made at any time by the deponent."

This language did not appear in the rule as promulgated in December, 1937. See 4 Moore's Federal Practice 26.01[9], 26.35 (2d ed. 1967). In 1951, Nebraska adopted a provision strongly resembling the one stricken from the federal rule:

> "Any party may impeach any adverse deponent by self-contradiction without having laid foundation for such impeachment at the time such deposition was taken." R.S.Neb. § 25–1267.07.

For similar provisions, see Uniform Rule 65; California Evidence Code § 1202; Kansas Code of Civil Procedure § 60–462; New Jersey Evidence Rule 65.

The provision for cross-examination of a declarant upon his hearsay statement is a corollary of general principles of cross-examination. A similar provision is found in California Evidence Code § 1203.

Report of Senate Committee on the Judiciary

Senate Comm. on Judiciary, Fed.Rules of Evidence, S.Rep. No. 1277, 93d Cong., 2d Sess., p. 22 (1974); 1974 U.S.Code Cong. & Ad.News 7051, 7068

Rule 906 [now 806], as passed by the House and as proposed by the Supreme Court provides that whenever a hearsay statement is admitted, the credibility of the declarant of the statement may be attacked, and if attacked may be supported, by any evidence which would be admissible for those purposes if the declarant had testified as a witness. Rule 801 defines what is a hearsay statement. While statements by a person authorized by a party-opponent to make a statement concerning the subject, by the party-opponent's agent or by a coconspirator of a party—see rule 801(d)(2)(c), (d) and (e)—are traditionally defined as exceptions to the hearsay rule, rule 801 defines such admission by a party-opponent as statements which are not hearsay. Consequently, rule 806 by referring exclusively to the admission of hearsay statements, does not appear to allow the credibility of the declarant to be attacked when the declarant is a coconspirator, agent or authorized spokesman. The committee is of the view that such statements should open the declarant to attacks on his credibility. Indeed, the reason such statements are excluded from the operation of rule 806 is likely attributable to the drafting technique used to codify the hearsay rule, viz. some statements, instead of being referred to as exceptions to the hearsay rule, are defined as statements which are not hearsay. The phrase "or a statement defined in rule 801(d)(2)(c), (d) and (e)" is added to the rule in order to subject the declarant of such statements, like the declarant of hearsay statements, to attacks on his credibility.[1]

---

[1]   The committee considered it unnecessary to include statements contained in rule 801(d)(2)(A) and (B)—the statement by the party-opponent himself or the statement of which he has manifested his adoption—because the credibility of the party-opponent is always subject to an attack on his credibility.

Conference Report

H.R., Fed.Rules of Evidence, Conf.Rep. No. 1597, 93d Cong., 2d Sess., p. 13 (1974); 1974 U.S.Code Cong. & Ad.News 7098, 7106

The Senate amendment permits an attack upon the credibility of the declarant of a statement if the statement is one by a person authorized by a party-opponent to make a statement concerning the subject, only by an agent of a party-opponent, or one by a coconspirator of the party-opponent, as these statements are defined in Rules 801(d)(2)(C), (D) and (E). The House bill has no such provision.

The Conference adopts the Senate amendment. The Senate amendment conforms the rule to present practice.

1987 Amendment Committee Note

The amendments are technical. No substantive change is intended.

1997 Amendment Committee Note

The amendment is technical. No substantive change is intended.

Rule 807. Residual Exception

(a) In General. Under the following circumstances, a hearsay statement is not excluded by the rule against hearsay even if the statement is not specifically covered by a hearsay exception in Rule 803 or 804:

    (1) the statement has equivalent circumstantial guarantees of trustworthiness;

    (2) it is offered as evidence of a material fact;

    (3) it is more probative on the point for which it is offered than any other evidence that the proponent can obtain through reasonable efforts; and

    (4) admitting it will best serve the purposes of these rules and the interests of justice.

(b) Notice. The statement is admissible only if, before the trial or hearing, the proponent gives an adverse party reasonable notice of the intent to offer the statement and its particulars, including the declarant's name and address, so that the party has a fair opportunity to meet it.

(As amended Apr. 26, 2011, eff. Dec. 1, 2011.)

RESTYLED RULE 807 COMMITTEE NOTE

The language of Rule 807 has been amended as part of the restyling of the Evidence Rules to make them more easily understood and to make style and terminology consistent throughout the rules. These changes are intended to be stylistic only. There is no intent to change any result in any ruling on evidence admissibility.

Amendments to Rule 807, scheduled to take effect on December 1, 2019

Rule 807. Residual Exception

(a) In General. Under the following ~~circumstances~~ conditions, a hearsay statement is not excluded by the rule against hearsay even if the statement is not ~~specifically covered by~~ admissible under a hearsay exception in Rule 803 or 804:

    (1) the statement ~~has equivalent circumstantial~~ is supported by sufficient guarantees of trustworthiness—after considering the totality of circumstances under which it was made and   evidence, if any, corroborating the statement; and

    ~~(2)~~   ~~it is offered as evidence of a material fact;~~

    (~~3~~ 2)   it is more probative on the point for which it is offered than any other evidence that the proponent can obtain through reasonable efforts~~; and~~

    ~~(4)~~   ~~admitting it will best serve the purposes of these rules and the interests of justice~~.

(b) Notice. The statement is admissible only if~~, before the trial or hearing,~~ the proponent gives an adverse party reasonable notice of the intent to offer the statement~~ and its particulars, including the declarant's name and address,~~ including its substance and the declarant's name—so that the party has a fair opportunity to meet it. The notice must be provided in writing before the trial or hearing—or in any form during the trial or hearing if the court, for good cause, excuses a lack of earlier notice.

Committee Note to Amendments to Rule 807, scheduled to take effect on December 1, 2019

Rule 807 has been amended to fix a number of problems that the courts have encountered in applying it.

Courts have had difficulty with the requirement that the proffered hearsay carry "equivalent" circumstantial guarantees of trustworthiness. The "equivalence" standard is difficult to apply, given the different types of guarantees of reliability, of varying strength, found among the categorical exceptions (as well as the fact that some hearsay exceptions, e.g., Rule 804(b)(6), are not based on reliability at all). The "equivalence" standard" has not served to guide a court's discretion to admit hearsay, because the court is free to choose among a spectrum of exceptions for comparison. Moreover, experience has shown that some statements offered as residual hearsay cannot be compared usefully to any of the categorical exceptions and yet might well be trustworthy. Thus the requirement of an equivalence analysis has been eliminated. Under the amendment, the court should proceed directly to a determination of whether the hearsay is supported by guarantees of trustworthiness. See Rule 104(a). As with any hearsay statement offered under an exception, the court's threshold finding that admissibility requirements are met merely means that the jury may consider the statement and not that it must assume the statement to be true.

The amendment specifically requires the court to consider corroborating evidence in the trustworthiness enquiry. Most courts have required the consideration of corroborating evidence, though some courts have disagreed. The rule now provides for a uniform approach, and recognizes that the existence or absence of corroboration is relevant to, but not dispositive of, whether a statement should be admissible under this exception. Of course, the court must consider not only the existence of corroborating evidence but also the strength and quality of that evidence.

The amendment does not alter the case law prohibiting parties from proceeding directly to the residual exception, without considering admissibility of the hearsay under Rules 803 and 804. A court is not required to make a finding that no other hearsay exception is applicable. But the opponent cannot seek admission under Rule 807 if it is apparent that the hearsay could be admitted under another exception.

The rule in its current form applies to hearsay "not specifically covered" by a Rule 803 or 804 exception. The amendment makes the rule applicable to hearsay "not admissible under" those exceptions. This clarifies that a court assessing guarantees of trustworthiness may consider whether the statement is a "near-miss" of one of the Rule 803 or 804 exceptions. If the court employs a "near-miss" analysis it should—in addition to evaluating all relevant guarantees of trustworthiness—take into account the reasons that the hearsay misses the admissibility requirements of the standard exception.

In deciding whether the statement is supported by sufficient guarantees of trustworthiness, the court should not consider the credibility of any witness who relates the declarant's hearsay statement in court. The credibility of an in-court witness does not present a hearsay question. To base admission or exclusion of a hearsay statement on the witness's credibility would usurp the jury's role of determining the credibility of testifying witnesses. The rule provides that the focus for trustworthiness is on circumstantial guarantees surrounding the making of the statement itself, as well as any independent evidence corroborating the statement. The credibility of the witness relating the statement is not a part of either enquiry.

Of course, even if the court finds sufficient guarantees of trustworthiness, the independent requirements of the Confrontation Clause must be satisfied if the hearsay statement is offered against a defendant in a criminal case.

The Committee decided to retain the requirement that the proponent must show that the hearsay statement is more probative than any other evidence that the proponent can reasonably obtain. This necessity requirement will continue to serve to prevent the residual exception from being used as a device to erode the categorical exceptions.

The requirements that residual hearsay must be evidence of a material fact and that its admission will best serve the purposes of these rules and the interests of justice have been deleted. These requirements have proved to be superfluous in that they are already found in other rules. See Rules 102, 401.

The notice provision has been amended to make four changes in the operation of the rule:

- First, the amendment requires the proponent to disclose the "substance" of the statement. This term is intended to require a description that is sufficiently specific under the circumstances to allow the opponent a fair opportunity to meet the evidence. See Rule 103(a)(2) (requiring the party making an offer of proof to inform the court of the "substance" of the evidence).

- Second, the prior requirement that the declarant's address must be disclosed has been deleted. That requirement was nonsensical when the declarant was unavailable, and unnecessary in the many cases in which the declarant's address was known or easily obtainable. If prior disclosure of the declarant's address is critical and cannot be obtained by the opponent through other means, then the opponent can seek relief from the court.

- Third, the amendment requires that the pretrial notice be in writing— which is satisfied by notice in electronic form. See Rule 101(b)(6). Requiring the notice to be in writing provides certainty and reduces arguments about whether notice was actually provided.

- Finally, the pretrial notice provision has been amended to provide for a good cause exception. Most courts have applied a good cause exception under Rule 807 even though the rule in its current form does not provide for it, while some courts have read the rule as it was written. Experience under the residual exception has shown that a good cause exception is necessary in certain limited situations. For example, the proponent may not become aware of the existence of the hearsay statement until after the trial begins; or the proponent may plan to call a witness who without warning becomes unavailable during trial, and the proponent might then need to resort to residual hearsay.

The rule retains the requirement that the opponent receive notice in a way that provides a fair opportunity to meet the evidence. When notice is provided during trial after a finding of good cause, the court may need to consider protective measures, such as a continuance, to assure that the opponent is not prejudiced.

[Editor's Note: In 1997, original Rules 803(24) and 804(b)(5) were combined into a single residual exception, Rule 807. What follows are the Advisory Committee Notes to Rules 803(24) and 804(b)(5) and the relevant legislative history regarding those rules.]

Advisory Committee's Note to Rule 803(24)

The preceding 23 exceptions of Rule 803 and the first five [four] exceptions of Rule 804(b), *infra*, are designed to take full advantage of the accumulated wisdom and experience of the past in dealing with hearsay. It would, however, be presumptuous to assume that all possible desirable exceptions to the hearsay rule have been catalogued and to pass the hearsay rule to oncoming generations as a closed system. Exception (24) and its companion provision in Rule 804(b)(6)[5] are accordingly included. They do not contemplate an unfettered exercise of judicial discretion, but they do provide for treating new and presently unanticipated situations which demonstrate a trustworthiness within the spirit of the specifically stated exceptions. Within this framework, room is left for growth and development of the law of evidence in the hearsay area, consistently with the broad purposes expressed in Rule 102. See Dallas County v. Commercial Union Assur. Co., 286 F.2d 388 (5th Cir. 1961).

Advisory Committee's Note to Rule 804(b)(5)

In language and purpose, this exception is identical with Rule 803(24). See the Advisory Committee's Note to that provision.

Report of House Committee on the Judiciary
on Rules 803(24) and 804(b)(5)

House Comm. on Judiciary, Fed.Rules of Evidence, H.R.Rep. No. 650, 93d Cong., 1st Sess., p. 5 (1973); 1974 U.S.Code Cong. & Ad.News 7075, 7079

The proposed Rules of Evidence submitted to Congress contained identical provisions in Rules 803 and 804 (which set forth the various hearsay exceptions), to the effect that the federal courts could admit any hearsay statement not specifically covered by any of the stated exceptions, if the hearsay statement was found to have "comparable circumstantial guarantees of trustworthiness."

The Committee deleted these provisions (proposed Rules 803(24) and 804(b)(6)) as injecting too much uncertainty into the law of evidence and impairing the ability of practitioners to prepare for trial. It was noted that Rule 102 directs the courts to construe the Rules of Evidence so as to promote "growth and development." The Committee believed that if additional hearsay exceptions are to be created, they should be by amendments to the Rules, not on a case-by-case basis.

Report of Senate Committee on the Judiciary
on Rules 803(24) and 804(b)(5)

Senate Comm. on Judiciary, Fed.Rules of Evidence, S.Rep. No. 1277, 93d Cong., 2d Sess., p. 18 (1974); 1974 U.S.Code Cong. & Ad.News 7051, 7065

The proposed Rules of Evidence submitted to Congress contained identical provisions in rules 803 and 804 (which set forth the various hearsay exceptions), admitting any hearsay statement not specifically covered by any of the stated exceptions, if the hearsay statement was found to have "comparable circumstantial guarantees of trustworthiness." The House deleted these provisions (proposed rules 803(24) and 804(b)(6)) as injecting "too much uncertainty" into the law of evidence and impairing the ability of practitioners to prepare for trial. The House felt that rule 102, which directs the courts to construe the Rules of Evidence so as to promote growth and development, would permit sufficient flexibility to admit hearsay evidence in appropriate cases under various factual situations that might arise.

We disagree with the total rejection of a residual hearsay exception. While we view rule 102 as being intended to provide for a broader construction and interpretation of these rules, we feel that, without a separate residual provision, the specifically enumerated exceptions could become tortured beyond any reasonable circumstances which they were intended to include (even if broadly construed). Moreover, these exceptions, while they reflect the most typical and well recognized exceptions to the hearsay rule, may not encompass every situation in which the reliability and appropriateness of a particular piece of hearsay evidence make clear that it should be heard and considered by the trier of fact.

The committee believes that there are certain exceptional circumstances where evidence which is found by a court to have guarantees of trustworthiness equivalent to or exceeding the guarantees reflected by the presently listed exceptions, and to have a high degree of probativeness and necessity could properly be admissible.

The case of Dallas County v. Commercial Union Assoc. Co., Ltd., 286 F.2d 388 (5th Cir. 1961) illustrates the point. The issue in that case was whether the tower of the county courthouse collapsed because it was struck by lightning (covered by insurance) or because of structural weakness and deterioration of the structure (not covered). Investigation of the structure revealed the presence of charcoal and charred timbers. In order to show that lightning may not have been the cause of the charring, the insurer offered a copy of a local newspaper published over 50 years earlier containing an unsigned article describing a fire in the courthouse while it was under construction. The Court found that the newspaper did not qualify for admission as a business record or an ancient document and did not fit within any other recognized hearsay exception. The court concluded, however, that the article was trustworthy because it was inconceivable that a newspaper reporter in a small town would report a fire in the courthouse if none had occurred. *See also* United States v. Barbati, 284 F.Supp. 409 (E.D.N.Y. 1968).

Because exceptional cases like the *Dallas County* case may arise in the future, the committee has decided to reinstate a residual exception for rules 803 and 804(b).

The committee, however, also agrees with those supporters of the House version who felt that an overly broad residual hearsay exception could emasculate the hearsay rule and the recognized exceptions or vitiate the rationale behind codification of the rules.

Therefore, the committee has adopted a residual exception for rules 803 and 804(b) of much narrower scope and applicability than the Supreme Court version. In order to qualify for admission, a hearsay statement not falling within one of the recognized exceptions would have to satisfy at least four conditions. First, it must have "equivalent circumstantial guarantees of trustworthiness." Second, it must be offered as evidence of a material fact. Third, the court must determine that the statement "is more probative on the point for which it is offered than any other evidence which the proponent can procure through reasonable efforts." This requirement is intended to insure that only statements which have high probative value and necessity may qualify for admission under the residual exceptions. Fourth, the court must determine that "the general purposes of these rules and the interests of justice will best be served by admission of the statement into evidence."

It is intended that the residual hearsay exceptions will be used very rarely, and only in exceptional circumstances. The committee does not intend to establish a broad license for trial judges to admit hearsay statements that do not fall within one of the other exceptions contained in rules 803 and 804(b). The residual exceptions are not meant to authorize major judicial revisions of the hearsay rule, including its present exceptions. Such major revisions are best accomplished by legislative action. It is intended that in any case in which evidence is sought to be admitted under these subsections, the trial judge will exercise no less care, reflection and caution than the courts did under the common law in establishing the now-recognized exceptions to the hearsay rule.

In order to establish a well-defined jurisprudence, the special facts and circumstances which, in the court's judgment, indicates that the statement has a sufficiently high degree of trustworthiness and necessity to justify its admission should be stated on the record. It is expected that the court will give the opposing party a full and adequate opportunity to contest the admission of any statement sought to be introduced under these subsections.

Conference Report on Rule 803(24)

H.R., Fed.Rules of Evidence, Conf.Rep. No. 1597, 93d Cong., 2d Sess., p. 11 (1974); 1974 U.S.Code Cong. & Ad.News 7098, 7105

The Senate amendment adds a new subsection, (24), which makes admissible a hearsay statement not specifically covered by any of the previous twenty-three subsections, if the statement has equivalent circumstantial guarantees of trustworthiness and if the court determines that (A) the statement is offered as evidence of a material fact; (B) the statement is more probative on the point for which it is offered than any other evidence the proponent can procure through reasonable efforts; and (C) the general purposes of these rules and the interests of justice will best be served by admission of the statement into evidence.

The House bill eliminated a similar, but broader, provision because of the conviction that such a provision injected too much uncertainty into the law of evidence regarding hearsay and impaired the ability of a litigant to prepare adequately for trial.

The Conference adopts the Senate amendment with an amendment that provides that a party intending to request the court to use a statement under this provision must notify any adverse party of this intention as well as of the particulars of the statement, including the name and address of the declarant. This notice must be given sufficiently in advance of the trial or hearing to provide any adverse party with a fair opportunity to prepare to contest the use of the statement.

Conference Report on Rule 804(b)(5)

The Senate amendment adds a new subsection, (b)(6) [renumbered (5)], which makes admissible a hearsay statement not specifically covered by any of the five [four] previous subsections, if the statement has equivalent circumstantial guarantees of trustworthiness and if the court determines that (A) the statement is offered as evidence of a material fact; (B) the statement is more probative on the point for which it is offered than any other evidence the proponent can procure through reasonable efforts; and (C) the general purposes of these rules and the interests of justice will best be served by admission of the statement into evidence.

The House bill eliminated a similar, but broader, provision because of the conviction that such a provision injected too much uncertainty into the law of evidence regarding hearsay and impaired the ability of a litigant to prepare adequately for trial.

The Conference adopts the Senate amendment with an amendment that renumbers this subsection and provides that a party intending to request the court to use a statement under this provision must notify any adverse party of this intention as well as of the particulars of the statement, including the name and address of the declarant. This notice must be given sufficiently in advance of the trial or hearing to provide any adverse party with a fair opportunity to prepare to contest the use of the statement.

1997 Amendment Committee Note (adding Rule 807)

The contents of Rule 803(24) and Rule 804(b)(5) have been combined and transferred to a new Rule 807. This was done to facilitate additions to Rules 803 and 804. No change in meaning is intended.

ARTICLE IX. AUTHENTICATION AND IDENTIFICATION

Rule 901. Authenticating or Identifying Evidence

(a) **In General.** To satisfy the requirement of authenticating or identifying an item of evidence, the proponent must produce evidence sufficient to support a finding that the item is what the proponent claims it is.

(b) **Examples.** The following are examples only—not a complete list— of evidence that satisfies the requirement:

(1) *Testimony of a Witness with Knowledge.* Testimony that an item is what it is claimed to be.

(2) *Nonexpert Opinion About Handwriting.* A nonexpert's opinion that handwriting is genuine, based on a familiarity with it that was not acquired for the current litigation.

(3) *Comparison by an Expert Witness or the Trier of Fact.* A comparison with an authenticated specimen by an expert witness or the trier of fact.

(4) *Distinctive Characteristics and the Like.* The appearance, contents, substance, internal patterns, or other distinctive characteristics of the item, taken together with all the circumstances.

(5) *Opinion About a Voice.* An opinion identifying a person's voice—whether heard firsthand or through mechanical or electronic transmission or recording—based on hearing the voice at any time under circumstances that connect it with the alleged speaker.

(6) *Evidence About a Telephone Conversation.* For a telephone conversation, evidence that a call was made to the number assigned at the time to:

(A) a particular person, if circumstances, including self-identification, show that the person answering was the one called; or

(B) a particular business, if the call was made to a business and the call related to business reasonably transacted over the telephone.

(7) *Evidence About Public Records.* Evidence that:

(A) a document was recorded or filed in a public office as authorized by law; or

(B) a purported public record or statement is from the office where items of this kind are kept.

(8) *Evidence About Ancient Documents or Data Compilations.* For a document or data compilation, evidence that it:

(A) is in a condition that creates no suspicion about its authenticity;

(B) was in a place where, if authentic, it would likely be; and

(C) is at least 20 years old when offered.

(9) *Evidence About a Process or System.* Evidence describing a process or system and showing that it produces an accurate result.

(10) *Methods Provided by a Statute or Rule.* Any method of authentication or identification allowed by a federal statute or a rule prescribed by the Supreme Court.

(As amended Apr. 26, 2011, eff. Dec. 1, 2011.)

RESTYLED RULE 901 COMMITTEE NOTE

The language of Rule 901 has been amended as part of the restyling of the Evidence Rules to make them more easily understood and to make style and terminology consistent throughout the rules. These changes are intended to be stylistic only. There is no intent to change any result in any ruling on evidence admissibility.

REPORTER'S COMMENT ON RESTYLED RULE 901

The Reporter objected to the use of the term "item of evidence"—seen in the first sentence of the Restyled Rule and throughout—as an inaccurate way to describe all the evidence subject to the authentication requirement. Many forms of evidence that aren't "items" may nonetheless require authentication. For example, a purported phone conversation with a party cannot be admitted unless it is shown that the party was the one talking. But a conversation is not an "item" in any user-friendly sense. The Reporter argued that limiting authenticity questions to "items" is likely to be found a substantive change. The Reporter suggested that it would be more accurate and clear to simply refer to proffered evidence, *i.e.,* "to satisfy the requirement of authenticating proffered evidence, the proponent must produce evidence sufficient to support a finding . . ." But the restylist argued that the use of the same term "evidence" twice would be confusing, *i.e.,* evidence must be authenticated by evidence. Eventually the Advisory Committee determined that the use of the term "item of evidence" would not constitute a substantive change. And under the protocol used for restyling, the restylists had the final word on questions of style.

Section references, McCormick 7th ed.

§§ 221–228

Note by Federal Judicial Center

The rule enacted by the Congress is the rule prescribed by the Supreme Court, amended in subdivision (b)(10) by substituting "prescribed" in place of "adopted," and by adding "pursuant to statutory authority." [That phrase was deleted in the Restyling on the ground that it was superfluous.—Ed.]

Advisory Committee's Note

56 F.R.D. 183, 332

Subdivision (a). Authentication and identification represent a special aspect of relevancy. Michael and Adler, Real Proof, 5 Vand.L.Rev. 344, 362 (1952); McCormick §§ 179, 185; Morgan, Basic Problems of Evidence 378 (1962). Thus a telephone conversation may be irrelevant because on an unrelated topic or because the speaker is not identified. The latter aspect is the one here involved. Wigmore describes the need for authentication as "an inherent logical necessity." 7 Wigmore § 2129, p. 564.

This requirement of showing authenticity or identity falls in the category of relevancy dependent upon fulfillment of a condition of fact and is governed by the procedure set forth in Rule 104(b).

The common law approach to authentication of documents has been criticized as an "attitude of agnosticism," McCormick, Cases on Evidence 388, n. 4 (3rd ed. 1956), as one which "departs sharply from men's customs in ordinary affairs," and as presenting only a slight obstacle to the introduction of forgeries in comparison to the time and expense devoted to proving genuine writings which correctly show their origin on their face, McCormick § 185, pp. 395, 396. Today, such available procedures as requests to admit and pretrial conference afford the means of eliminating much of the need for authentication or identification. Also, significant inroads upon the traditional insistence on authentication and identification have been made by accepting as at least prima facie genuine items of the kind treated in Rule 902, *infra*. However, the need for suitable methods of proof still remains, since criminal cases pose their own obstacles to the use of preliminary procedures, unforeseen contingencies may arise, and cases of genuine controversy will still occur.

Subdivision (b). The treatment of authentication and identification draws largely upon the experience embodied in the common law and in statutes to furnish illustrative applications of the general principle set forth in subdivision (a). The examples are not intended as an exclusive enumeration of allowable methods but are meant to guide and suggest, leaving room for growth and development in this area of the law.

The examples relate for the most part to documents, with some attention given to voice communications and computer print-outs. As Wigmore noted, no special rules have been developed for authenticating chattels. Wigmore, Code of Evidence § 2086 (3rd ed. 1942).

It should be observed that compliance with requirements of authentication or identification by no means assures admission of an item into evidence, as other bars, hearsay for example, may remain.

Example (1) contemplates a broad spectrum ranging from testimony of a witness who was present at the signing of a document to testimony establishing narcotics as taken from an accused and accounting for custody through the period until trial, including laboratory analysis. See California Evidence Code § 1413, eyewitness to signing.

Example (2) states conventional doctrine as to lay identification of handwriting, which recognizes that a sufficient familiarity with the handwriting of another person may be acquired by seeing him write, by exchanging correspondence, or by other means, to afford a basis for identifying it on subsequent occasions. McCormick § 189. *See also* California Evidence Code § 1416. Testimony based upon familiarity acquired for purposes of the litigation is reserved to the expert under the example which follows.

Example (3). The history of common law restrictions upon the technique of proving or disproving the genuineness of a disputed specimen of handwriting through comparison with a genuine specimen, by either the testimony of expert witnesses or direct viewing by the triers themselves, is detailed in 7 Wigmore §§ 1991–1994. In breaking away, the English Common Law Procedure Act of 1854, 17 and 18 Vict., c. 125, § 27, cautiously allowed expert or trier to use exemplars "proved to the satisfaction of the judge to be genuine" for purposes of comparison. The language found its way into numerous statutes in this country, *e.g.*, California Evidence Code §§ 1417, 1418. While explainable as a measure of prudence in the process of breaking with precedent in the handwriting situation, the reservation to the judge of the question of the genuineness of exemplars and the imposition of an unusually high standard of persuasion are at variance with the general treatment of relevancy which depends upon fulfillment of a condition of fact. Rule 104(b). No similar attitude is found in other comparison situations, *e.g.*, ballistics comparison by jury, as in Evans v. Commonwealth, 230 Ky. 411, 19 S.W.2d 1091 (1929), or by experts, Annot., 26 A.L.R.2d 892, and no reason appears for its continued existence in handwriting cases. Consequently Example (3) sets no higher standard for handwriting specimens and treats all comparison situations alike, to be governed by Rule 104(b). This approach is consistent with 28 U.S.C. § 1731: "The admitted or proved handwriting of any person shall be admissible, for purposes of comparison, to determine genuineness of other handwriting attributed to such person."

Precedent supports the acceptance of visual comparison as sufficiently satisfying preliminary authentication requirements for admission in evidence. Brandon v. Collins, 267 F.2d 731 (2d Cir. 1959); Wausau Sulphate Fibre Co. v. Commissioner of Internal Revenue, 61 F.2d 879 (7th Cir. 1932); Desimone v. United States, 227 F.2d 864 (9th Cir. 1955).

Example (4). The characteristics of the offered item itself, considered in the light of circumstances, afford authentication techniques in great variety. Thus a document or telephone conversation may be shown to have emanated from a particular person by virtue of its disclosing knowledge of facts known peculiarly to him; Globe Automatic Sprinkler Co. v. Braniff, 89 Okl. 105, 214 P. 127 (1923); California Evidence Code § 1421; similarly, a letter may be authenticated by content and circumstances indicating it was in reply to a duly authenticated one. McCormick § 192; California Evidence Code § 1420. Language patterns may indicate authenticity or its opposite. Magnuson v. State, 187 Wis. 122, 203 N.W. 749 (1925); Arens and Meadow, Psycholinguistics and the Confession Dilemma, 56 Colum.L.Rev. 19 (1956).

Example (5). Since aural voice identification is not a subject of expert testimony, the requisite familiarity may be acquired either before or after the particular speaking which is the subject of the identification, in this respect resembling visual identification of a person rather than identification of handwriting. Cf. Example (2), *supra,* People v. Nichols, 378 Ill. 487, 38 N.E.2d 766 (1942); McGuire v. State, 200 Md. 601, 92 A.2d 582 (1952); State v. McGee, 336 Mo. 1082, 83 S.W.2d 98 (1935).

Example (6). The cases are in agreement that a mere assertion of his identity by a person talking on the telephone is not sufficient evidence of the authenticity of the conversation and that additional evidence of his identity is required. The additional evidence need not fall in any set pattern. Thus the content of his statements or the reply technique, under Example (4), *supra,* or voice identification under Example (5), may furnish the necessary foundation. Outgoing calls made by the witness involve additional factors bearing upon authenticity. The calling of a number assigned by the telephone company reasonably supports the assumption that the listing is correct and that the number is the one reached. If the number is that of a place of business, the mass of authority allows an ensuing conversation if it relates to business reasonably transacted over the telephone, on the theory that the maintenance of the telephone connection is an invitation to do business without further identification. Matton v. Hoover Co., 350 Mo. 506, 166 S.W.2d 557 (1942); City of Pawhuska v. Crutchfield, 147 Okl. 4, 293 P. 1095 (1930); Zurich General Acc. & Liability Ins. Co. v. Baum, 159 Va. 404, 165 S.E. 518 (1932). Otherwise, some additional circumstance of identification of the speaker is required. The authorities divide on the question whether the self-identifying statement of the person answering suffices. Example (6) answers in the affirmative on the assumption that usual conduct respecting telephone calls furnish adequate assurances of regularity, bearing in mind that the entire matter is open to exploration before the trier of fact. In general, see McCormick § 193; 7 Wigmore § 2155; Annot., 71 A.L.R. 5, 105 *id.* 326.

Example (7). Public records are regularly authenticated by proof of custody, without more. McCormick § 191; 7 Wigmore §§ 2158, 2159. The example extends the principle to include data stored in computers and similar methods, of which increasing use in the public records area may be expected. See California Evidence Code §§ 1532, 1600.

Example (8). The familiar ancient document rule of the common law is extended to include data stored electronically or by other similar means. Since the importance of appearance diminishes in this situation, the importance of custody or place where found increases correspondingly. This expansion is necessary in view of the widespread use of methods of storing data in forms other than conventional written records.

Any time period selected is bound to be arbitrary. The common law period of 30 years is here reduced to 20 years, with some shift of emphasis from the probable unavailability of witnesses to the unlikeliness of a still viable fraud after the lapse of time. The shorter period is specified in the English Evidence Act of 1938, 1 & 2 Geo. 6, c. 28, and in Oregon R.S. 1963, § 41.360(34). *See also* the numerous statutes prescribing periods of less than 30 years in the case of recorded documents. 7 Wigmore § 2143.

The application of Example (8) is not subject to any limitation to title documents or to any requirement that possession, in the case of a title document, has been consistent with the document. See McCormick § 190.

Example (9) is designed for situations in which the accuracy of a result is dependent upon a process or system which produces it. X rays afford a familiar instance. Among more recent developments is the computer, as to which see Transport Indemnity Co. v. Seib, 178 Neb. 253, 132 N.W.2d 871 (1965); State v. Veres, 7 Ariz.App. 117, 436 P.2d 629 (1968); Merrick v. United States Rubber Co., 7 Ariz.App. 433, 440 P.2d 314 (1968); Freed, Computer Print-Outs as Evidence, 16 Am.Jur.Proof of Facts 273; Symposium, Law and Computers in the Mid-Sixties, ALI-ABA (1966); 37 Albany L.Rev. 61 (1967). Example (9) does not, of course, foreclose taking judicial notice of the accuracy of the process or system.

Example (10). The example makes clear that methods of authentication provided by Act of Congress and by the Rules of Civil and Criminal Procedure or by Bankruptcy Rules are not intended to be superseded. Illustrative are the provisions for authentication of official records in Civil Procedure Rule 44 and Criminal Procedure Rule 27, for authentication of records of proceedings by court reporters in 28 U.S.C. § 753(b) and Civil Procedure Rule 80(c), and for authentication of depositions in Civil Procedure Rule 30(f).

Rule 902.   Evidence That Is Self-Authenticating

The following items of evidence are self-authenticating; they require no extrinsic evidence of authenticity in order to be admitted:

(1) ***Domestic Public Documents That Are Sealed and Signed.*** A document that bears:

> **(A)** a seal purporting to be that of the United States; any state, district, commonwealth, territory, or insular possession of the United States; the former Panama Canal Zone; the Trust Territory of the Pacific Islands; a political subdivision of any of these entities; or a department, agency, or officer of any entity named above; and

> **(B)** a signature purporting to be an execution or attestation.

(2) ***Domestic Public Documents That Are Not Sealed but Are Signed and Certified.*** A document that bears no seal if:

> **(A)** it bears the signature of an officer or employee of an entity named in Rule 902(1)(A); and

> **(B)** another public officer who has a seal and official duties within that same entity certifies under seal—or its equivalent—that the signer has the official capacity and that the signature is genuine.

(3) ***Foreign Public Documents.*** A document that purports to be signed or attested by a person who is authorized by a foreign country's law to do so. The document must be accompanied by a final certification that certifies the genuineness of the signature and official position of the signer or attester—or of any foreign official whose certificate of genuineness relates to the signature or attestation or is in a chain of certificates of genuineness relating to the signature or attestation. The certification may be made by a secretary of a United States embassy or legation; by a consul general, vice consul, or consular agent of the United States; or by a diplomatic or consular official of the foreign country assigned or accredited to the United States. If all parties have been given a reasonable opportunity to investigate the document's authenticity and accuracy, the court may, for good cause, either:

> **(A)** order that it be treated as presumptively authentic without final certification; or

> **(B)** allow it to be evidenced by an attested summary with or without final certification.

(4) ***Certified Copies of Public Records.*** A copy of an official record— or a copy of a document that was recorded or filed in a public office as authorized by law—if the copy is certified as correct by:

> **(A)** the custodian or another person authorized to make the certification; or

> **(B)** a certificate that complies with Rule 902(1), (2), or (3), a federal statute, or a rule prescribed by the Supreme Court.

(5) ***Official Publications.*** A book, pamphlet, or other publication purporting to be issued by a public authority.

(6) ***Newspapers and Periodicals.*** Printed material purporting to be a newspaper or periodical.

(7) ***Trade Inscriptions and the Like.*** An inscription, sign, tag, or label purporting to have been affixed in the course of business and indicating origin, ownership, or control.

(8) *Acknowledged Documents.* A document accompanied by a certificate of acknowledgment that is lawfully executed by a notary public or another officer who is authorized to take acknowledgments.

(9) *Commercial Paper and Related Documents.* Commercial paper, a signature on it, and related documents, to the extent allowed by general commercial law.

(10) *Presumptions Under a Federal Statute.* A signature, document, or anything else that a federal statute declares to be presumptively or prima facie genuine or authentic.

(11) *Certified Domestic Records of a Regularly Conducted Activity.* The original or a copy of a domestic record that meets the requirements of Rule 803(6)(A)–(C), as shown by a certification of the custodian or another qualified person that complies with a federal statute or a rule prescribed by the Supreme Court. Before the trial or hearing, the proponent must give an adverse party reasonable written notice of the intent to offer the record—and must make the record and certification available for inspection—so that the party has a fair opportunity to challenge them.

(12) *Certified Foreign Records of a Regularly Conducted Activity.* In a civil case, the original or a copy of a foreign record that meets the requirements of Rule 902(11), modified as follows: the certification, rather than complying with a federal statute or Supreme Court rule, must be signed in a manner that, if falsely made, would subject the maker to a criminal penalty in the country where the certification is signed. The proponent must also meet the notice requirements of Rule 902(11).

(13) *Certified Records Generated by an Electronic Process or System.* A record generated by an electronic process or system that produces an accurate result, as shown by a certification of a qualified person that complies with the certification requirements of Rule 902(11) or (12). The proponent must also meet the notice requirements of Rule 902(11).

(14) *Certified Data Copied from an Electronic Device, Storage Medium, or File.* Data copied from an electronic device, storage medium, or file, if authenticated by a process of digital identification, as shown by a certification of a qualified person that complies with the certification requirements of Rule 902(11) or (12). The proponent also must meet the notice requirements of Rule 902(11).

(As amended Mar. 2, 1987, eff. Oct. 1, 1987; Apr. 25, 1988, eff. Nov. 1, 1988; Apr. 17, 2000, eff. Dec. 1, 2000; Apr. 26, 2011, eff. Dec. 1, 2011; Apr. 27, 2017, eff. Dec. 1, 2017.)

RESTYLED RULE 902 COMMITTEE NOTE

The language of Rule 902 has been amended as part of the restyling of the Evidence Rules to make them more easily understood and to make style and terminology consistent throughout the rules. These changes are intended to be stylistic only. There is no intent to change any result in any ruling on evidence admissibility.

REPORTER'S COMMENT ON RESTYLED RULE 902

The title of the rule is changed from "Self-authentication" to "Evidence That Is Self-Authenticating." The Advisory Committee thought that the use of the bare term "self-authentication" would be odd to novices—it sounds like a party has to be authenticating himself. The restylist proposed the title "Items That Need Not Be Authenticated" but accepted the Reporter's suggestion for the change ultimately made. The Reporter was uncomfortable with the use of the term "item"—see the Reporter's Comment to Rule 901—and the use of "evidence" rather than "item" works well in the title.

§ 229, § 229.1

Note by Federal Judicial Center

The rule enacted by the Congress is the rule prescribed by the Supreme Court, amended as follows:

Paragraph (4) was amended by substituting "prescribed" in place of "adopted," and by adding "pursuant to statutory authority." [The phrase was deleted by the Restyling on the ground that it was superfluous.—Ed.]

Paragraph (8) was amended by substituting "in the manner provided by law by" in place of "under the hand and seal of."

Advisory Committee's Note

56 F.R.D. 183, 337

Case law and statutes have, over the years, developed a substantial body of instances in which authenticity is taken as sufficiently established for purposes of admissibility without extrinsic evidence to that effect, sometimes for reasons of policy but perhaps more often because practical considerations reduce the possibility of unauthenticity to a very small dimension. The present rule collects and incorporates these situations, in some instances expanding them to occupy a larger area which their underlying considerations justify. In no instance is the opposite party foreclosed from disputing authenticity.

Paragraph (1). The acceptance of documents bearing a public seal and signature, most often encountered in practice in the form of acknowledgments or certificates authenticating copies of public records, is actually of broad application. Whether theoretically based in whole or in part upon judicial notice, the practical underlying considerations are that forgery is a crime and detection is fairly easy and certain. 7 Wigmore § 2161, p. 638; California Evidence Code § 1452. More than 50 provisions for judicial notice of official seals are contained in the United States Code.

Paragraph (2). While statutes are found which raise a presumption of genuineness of purported official signatures in the absence of an official seal, 7 Wigmore § 2167; California Evidence Code § 1453, the greater ease of effecting a forgery under these circumstances is apparent. Hence this paragraph of the rule calls for authentication by an officer who has a seal. Notarial acts by members of the armed forces and other special situations are covered in paragraph (10).

Paragraph (3) provides a method for extending the presumption of authenticity to foreign official documents by a procedure of certification. It is derived from Rule 44(a)(2) of the Rules of Civil Procedure but is broader in applying to public documents rather than being limited to public records.

Paragraph (4). The common law and innumerable statutes have recognized the procedure of authenticating copies of public records by certificate. The certificate qualifies as a public document, receivable as authentic when in conformity with paragraph (1), (2), or (3). Rule 44(a) of the Rules of Civil Procedure and Rule 27 of the Rules of Criminal Procedure have provided authentication procedures of this nature for both domestic and foreign public records. It will be observed that the certification procedure here provided extends only to public records, reports, and recorded documents, all including data compilations, and does not apply to public documents generally. Hence documents provable when presented in original form under paragraphs (1), (2), or (3) may not be provable by certified copy under paragraph (4).

Paragraph (5). Dispensing with preliminary proof of the genuineness of purportedly official publications, most commonly encountered in connection with statutes, court reports, rules, and regulations, has been greatly enlarged by statutes and decisions. 5 Wigmore § 1684. Paragraph (5), it will be noted, does not confer admissibility upon all official publications; it merely provides a means whereby their authenticity may be taken as established for purposes of admissibility. Rule 44(a) of the Rules of Civil Procedure has been to the same effect.

Paragraph (6). The likelihood of forgery of newspapers or periodicals is slight indeed. Hence no danger is apparent in receiving them. Establishing the authenticity of the publication may, of course, leave still open questions of authority and responsibility for items therein contained. See 7 Wigmore § 2150. Cf. 39 U.S.C. § 4005(b), public advertisement prima facie evidence of agency of person named, in postal fraud order proceeding; Canadian Uniform Evidence Act, Draft of 1936, printed copy of newspaper prima facie evidence that notices or advertisements were authorized.

Paragraph (7). Several factors justify dispensing with preliminary proof of genuineness of commercial and mercantile labels and the like. The risk of forgery is minimal. Trademark infringement involves serious penalties. Great efforts are devoted to inducing the public to buy in reliance on brand names, and substantial protection is given them. Hence the fairness of this treatment finds recognition in the cases. Curtiss Candy Co. v. Johnson, 163 Miss. 426, 141 So. 762 (1932), Baby Ruth candy bar; Doyle v. Continental Baking Co., 262 Mass. 516, 160 N.E. 325 (1928), loaf of bread; Weiner v. Mager & Throne, Inc., 167 Misc. 338, 3 N.Y.S.2d 918 (1938), same. And see W.Va.Code 1966, § 47–3–5, trade-mark on bottle prima facie evidence of ownership. Contra, Keegan v. Green Giant Co., 150 Me. 283, 110 A.2d 599 (1954); Murphy v. Campbell Soup Co., 62 F.2d 564 (1st Cir. 1933). Cattle brands have received similar acceptance in the western states. Rev.Code Mont. 1947, § 46–606; State v. Wolfley, 75 Kan. 406, 89 P. 1046 (1907); Annot., 11 L.R.A.(N.S.) 87. Inscriptions on trains and vehicles are held to be prima facie evidence of ownership or control. Pittsburgh, Ft. W. & C. Ry. v. Callaghan, 157 Ill. 406, 41 N.E. 909 (1895); 9 Wigmore § 2510a. *See also* the provision of 19 U.S.C. § 1615(2) that marks, labels, brands, or stamps indicating foreign origin are prima facie evidence of foreign origin of merchandise.

Paragraph (8). In virtually every state, acknowledged title documents are receivable in evidence without further proof. Statutes are collected in 5 Wigmore § 1676. If this authentication suffices for documents of the importance of those affecting titles, logic scarcely permits denying this method when other kinds of documents are involved. Instances of broadly inclusive statutes are California Evidence Code § 1451 and N.Y.CPLR 4538, McKinney's Consol.Laws 1963.

Report of House Committee on the Judiciary on Rule 902(8)

House Comm. on Judiciary, Fed.Rules of Evidence, H.R.Rep. No. 650, 93d Cong., 1st Sess., p. 17 (1973); 1974 U.S.Code Cong. & Ad.News 7075, 7090

Rule 902(8) as submitted by the Court referred to certificates of acknowledgment "under the hand and seal of" a notary public or other officer authorized by law to take acknowledgments. The Committee amended the Rule to eliminate the requirement, believed to be inconsistent with the law in some States, that a notary public must affix a seal to a document acknowledged before him. As amended the Rule merely requires that the document be executed in the manner prescribed by State law.

Advisory Committee's Note to Rule 902(9)

56 F.R.D. 183, 339

Paragraph (9). Issues of the authenticity of commercial paper in federal courts will usually arise in diversity cases, will involve an element of a cause of action or defense, and with respect to presumptions and burden of proof will be controlled by Erie Railroad Co. v. Tompkins, 304 U.S. 64, 58 S.Ct. 817, 82 L.Ed 1188 (1938). Rule 302, *supra.* There may, however, be questions of authenticity involving lesser segments of a case or the case may be one governed by federal common law. Clearfield Trust Co. v. United States, 318 U.S. 363, 63 S.Ct. 573, 87 L.Ed. 838 (1943). Cf. United States v. Yazell, 382 U.S. 341, 86 S.Ct. 500, 15 L.Ed.2d 404 (1966). In these situations, resort to the useful authentication provisions of the Uniform Commercial Code is provided for. While the phrasing is in terms of "general commercial law," in order to avoid the potential complications inherent in borrowing local statutes, today one would have difficulty in determining the general commercial law without referring to the Code. See Williams v. Walker-Thomas Furniture Co., 121 U.S.App.D.C. 315, 350 F.2d 445 (1965). Pertinent Code provisions are sections 1–202, 3–307, and 3–510, dealing with third-party documents, signatures on negotiable instruments, protests, and statements of dishonor.

Report of House Committee on the Judiciary on Rule 902(9)

House Comm. on Judiciary, Fed.Rules of Evidence, H.R.Rep. No. 650, 93d Cong., 1st Sess., p. 17 (1973); 1974 U.S.Code Cong. & Ad.News 7075, 7090

The Committee approved Rule 902(9) as submitted by the Court. With respect to the meaning of the phrase "general commercial law", the Committee intends that the Uniform Commercial Code, which has been adopted in virtually every State, will be followed generally, but that federal commercial law will apply where federal commercial paper is involved. See Clearfield Trust Co. v. United States, 318 U.S. 363 (1943). Further, in those instances in which the issues are governed by Erie R. Co. v. Tompkins, 304 U.S. 64 (1938), State law will apply irrespective of whether it is the Uniform Commercial Code.

Advisory Committee's Note to Rule 902(10)

56 F.R.D. 183, 340

Paragraph (10). The paragraph continues in effect dispensations with preliminary proof of genuineness provided in various Acts of Congress. See, for example, 10 U.S.C. § 936, signature, without seal, together with title, prima facie evidence of authenticity of acts of certain military personnel who are given notarial powers; 15 U.S.C. § 77f(a), signature on SEC registration presumed genuine; 26 U.S.C. § 6064, signature to tax return prima facie genuine.

1987 Amendment Committee Note

The amendments are technical. No substantive change is intended.

1988 Amendment Committee Note

Two sentences were inadvertently eliminated from the 1987 amendment. The amendment is technical. No substantive change is intended.

2000 Committee Note to an Amendment Adding Rules 902(11) and (12)

The amendment adds two new paragraphs to the rule on self-authentication. It sets forth a procedure by which parties can authenticate certain records of regularly conducted activity, other than through the testimony of a foundation witness. See the amendment to Rule 803(6). 18 U.S.C. § 3505 currently provides a means for certifying foreign records of regularly conducted activity in criminal cases, and this amendment is intended to establish a similar procedure for domestic records, and for foreign records offered in civil cases.

A declaration that satisfies 28 U.S.C. § 1746 would satisfy the declaration requirement of Rule 902(11), as would any comparable certification under oath.

The notice requirement in Rules 902(11) and (12) is intended to give the opponent of the evidence a full opportunity to test the adequacy of the foundation set forth in the declaration.

2017 Committee Note to an Amendment Adding Rule 902(13)

The amendment sets forth a procedure by which parties can authenticate certain electronic evidence other than through the testimony of a foundation witness. As with the provisions on business records in Rules 902(11) and (12), the Committee has found that the expense and inconvenience of producing a witness to authenticate an item of electronic evidence is often unnecessary. It is often the case that a party goes to the expense of producing an authentication witness and then the adversary either stipulates authenticity before the witness is called or fails to challenge the authentication testimony once it is presented. The amendment provides a procedure under which the parties can determine in advance of trial whether a real challenge to authenticity will be made, and can then plan accordingly.

Nothing in the amendment is intended to limit a party from establishing authenticity of electronic evidence on any ground provided in these Rules, including through judicial notice where appropriate.

A proponent establishing authenticity under this Rule must present a certification containing information that would be sufficient to establish authenticity were that information provided by a witness at trial. If the certification provides information that would be insufficient to authenticate the record if the certifying person testified, then authenticity is not established under this Rule. The Rule specifically allows the authenticity foundation that satisfies Rule 901(b)(9) to be established by a certification rather than the testimony of a live witness.

The reference to the "certification requirements of Rule 902(11) or (12)" is only to the procedural requirements for a valid certification. There is no intent to require, or permit, a certification under this rule to prove the requirements of Rule 803(6). Rule 902(13) is solely limited to authentication and any attempt to satisfy a hearsay exception must be made independently.

A certification under this Rule can establish only that the proffered item has satisfied the admissibility requirements for authenticity. The opponent remains free to object to admissibility of the proffered item on other grounds—including hearsay, relevance, or in criminal cases the right to confrontation. For example, assume that a plaintiff in a defamation case offers what purports to be a printout of a webpage on which a defamatory statement was made. Plaintiff offers a certification under this Rule in which a qualified person describes the process by which the webpage was retrieved. Even if that certification sufficiently establishes that the webpage is authentic, defendant remains free to object that the statement on the webpage was not placed there by defendant. Similarly, a certification authenticating a computer output, such as a spreadsheet, does not preclude an objection that the information produced is unreliable—the authentication establishes only that the output came from the computer.

A challenge to the authenticity of electronic evidence may require technical information about the system or process at issue, including possibly retaining a forensic technical expert; such factors will effect whether the opponent has a fair opportunity to challenge the evidence given the notice provided.

The reference to Rule 902(12) is intended to cover certifications that are made in a foreign country.

2017 Committee Note to an Amendment Adding Rule 902(14)

The amendment sets forth a procedure by which parties can authenticate data copied from an electronic device, storage medium, or an electronic file, other than through the testimony of a foundation witness. As with the provisions on business records in Rules 902(11) and (12), the Committee has found that the expense and inconvenience of producing an authenticating witness for this evidence is often unnecessary. It is often the case that a party goes to the expense of producing an authentication witness, and then the adversary either stipulates authenticity before the witness is called or fails to challenge the authentication testimony once it is presented. The amendment provides a procedure in which the parties can determine in advance of trial whether a real challenge to authenticity will be made, and can then plan accordingly.

Today, data copied from electronic devices, storage media, and electronic files are ordinarily authenticated by "hash value." A hash value is a number that is often represented as a sequence of characters and is produced by an algorithm based upon the digital contents of a drive, medium, or file. If the hash values for the original and copy are different, then the copy is not identical to the original. If the hash values for the original and copy are the same, it is highly improbable that the original and copy are not identical. Thus, identical hash values for the original and copy reliably attest to the fact that they are exact duplicates. This amendment allows self-authentication by a certification of a qualified person that she checked the hash value of the proffered item and that it was identical to the original. The rule is flexible enough to allow certifications through processes other than comparison of hash value, including by other reliable means of identification provided by future technology.

Nothing in the amendment is intended to limit a party from establishing authenticity of electronic evidence on any ground provided in these Rules, including through judicial notice where appropriate.

A proponent establishing authenticity under this Rule must present a certification containing information that would be sufficient to establish authenticity were that information provided by a witness at trial. If the certification provides information that would be insufficient to authenticate the record if the certifying person testified, then authenticity is not established under this Rule.

The reference to the "certification requirements of Rule 902(11) or (12)" is only to the procedural requirements for a valid certification. There is no intent to require, or permit, a certification under this rule to prove the requirements of Rule 803(6). Rule 902(14) is solely limited to authentication and any attempt to satisfy a hearsay exception must be made independently.

A certification under this Rule can only establish that the proffered item is authentic. The opponent remains free to object to admissibility of the proffered item on other grounds—including hearsay, relevance, or in criminal cases the right to confrontation. For example, in a criminal case in which data copied from a hard drive is proffered, the defendant can still challenge hearsay found in the hard drive, and can still challenge whether the information on the hard drive was placed there by the defendant.

A challenge to the authenticity of electronic evidence may require technical information about the system or process at issue, including possibly retaining a forensic technical expert; such factors will effect whether the opponent has a fair opportunity to challenge the evidence given the notice provided.

The reference to Rule 902(12) is intended to cover certifications that are made in a foreign country.

———————————

Rule 903. Subscribing Witness's Testimony

A subscribing witness's testimony is necessary to authenticate a writing only if required by the law of the jurisdiction that governs its validity.

(As amended Apr. 26, 2011, eff. Dec. 1, 2011.)

RESTYLED RULE 903 COMMITTEE NOTE

The language of Rule 903 has been amended as part of the restyling of the Evidence Rules to make them more easily understood and to make style and terminology consistent throughout the rules. These changes are intended to be stylistic only. There is no intent to change any result in any ruling on evidence admissibility.

Section references, McCormick 7th ed.

None

Note by Federal Judicial Center

The rule enacted by the Congress is the rule prescribed by the Supreme Court without change.

Advisory Committee's Note

56 F.R.D. 183, 340

The common law required that attesting witnesses be produced or accounted for. Today the requirement has generally been abolished except with respect to documents which must be attested to be valid, *e.g.* wills in some states. McCormick § 188. Uniform Rule 71; California Evidence Code § 1411; Kansas Code of Civil Procedure § 60–468; New Jersey Evidence Rule 71; New York CPLR Rule 4537.

ARTICLE X. CONTENTS OF WRITINGS, RECORDINGS, AND PHOTOGRAPHS

Rule 1001. Definitions That Apply to This Article

In this article:

(a) A "writing" consists of letters, words, numbers, or their equivalent set down in any form.

(b) A "recording" consists of letters, words, numbers, or their equivalent recorded in any manner.

(c) A "photograph" means a photographic image or its equivalent stored in any form.

(d) An "original" of a writing or recording means the writing or recording itself or any counterpart intended to have the same effect by the person who executed or issued it. For electronically stored information, "original" means any printout—or other output readable by sight—if it accurately reflects the information. An "original" of a photograph includes the negative or a print from it.

(e) A "duplicate" means a counterpart produced by a mechanical, photographic, chemical, electronic, or other equivalent process or technique that accurately reproduces the original.

(As amended Apr. 26, 2011, eff. Dec. 1, 2011.)

RESTYLED RULE 1001 COMMITTEE NOTE

The language of Rule 1001 has been amended as part of the restyling of the Evidence Rules to make them more easily understood and to make style and terminology consistent throughout the rules. These changes are intended to be stylistic only. There is no intent to change any result in any ruling on evidence admissibility.

REPORTER'S COMMENT ON RESTYLED RULE 1001

The Restyling changes the subdivisions of Rule 1001 to accord with standard rulemaking numbering, *i.e.*, a letter follows a number. The Advisory Committee recognized that the change could disrupt electronic searches—for example, using "1001(a)" to search for cases on a writing would not uncover the pertinent cases decided before the restyling under then-Rule 1001(1). But the Committee thought that the disruption would be minimal as this definitions section is not often cited or applied in the cases—unlike the Rule 803 exceptions, where the numbering was not changed, in recognition of the substantial Rule 803 case law.

Restyled Rule 1001 also breaks out the definitions of "writing" and "recording" into separate subdivisions.

Section references, McCormick 7th ed.

§§ 230–236

Note by Federal Judicial Center

The rule enacted by the Congress is the rule prescribed by the Supreme Court, amended in paragraph (2) by inserting "video tapes."

Advisory Committee's Note

[Editor's Note: The restyling changed the numbered paragraphs of Rule 1001 to letters, in accordance with standard conventions of rule drafting. The restyling also provides separate subdivisions for definitions of "writing" and "recording" so the Advisory Committee's Note on Paragraph (1) applies to both.]

56 F.R.D. 183, 341

In an earlier day, when discovery and other related procedures were strictly limited, the misleading named "best evidence rule" afforded substantial guarantees against inaccuracies and fraud by its insistence upon production of original documents. The great enlargement of the scope of discovery and related procedures in recent times has measurably reduced the need for the rule. Nevertheless important areas of usefulness persist: discovery of documents outside the jurisdiction may require substantial outlay of time and money; the unanticipated document may not practically be discoverable; criminal cases have built-in limitations on discovery. Cleary and Strong, The Best Evidence Rule: An Evaluation in Context, 51 Iowa L.Rev. 825 (1966).

Paragraph (1) [now (a) and (b)]. Traditionally the rule requiring the original centered upon accumulations of data and expressions affecting legal relations set forth in words and figures. This meant that the rule was one essentially related to writings. Present day techniques have expanded methods of storing data, yet the essential form which the information ultimately assumes for usable purposes is words and figures. Hence the considerations underlying the rule dictate its expansion to include computers, photographic systems, and other modern developments.

Report of House Committee on the Judiciary

House Comm. on Judiciary, Fed.Rules of Evidence, H.R.Rep. No. 650, 93d Cong., 1st Sess., p. 17 (1973); 1974 U.S.Code Cong. & Ad.News 7075, 7090

The Committee amended this Rule expressly to include "video tapes" in the definition of "photographs."

Advisory Committee's Note
to Rule 1001(3) and (4)

56 F.R.D. 183, 341

Paragraph (3) [now (d)]. In most instances, what is an original will be self-evident and further refinement will be unnecessary. However, in some instances particularized definition is required. A carbon copy of a contract executed in duplicate becomes an original, as does a sales ticket carbon copy given to a customer. While strictly speaking the original of a photograph might be thought to be only the negative, practicality and common usage require that any print from the negative be regarded as an original. Similarly, practicality and usage confer the status of original upon any computer printout. Transport Indemnity Co. v. Seib, 178 Neb. 253, 132 N.W.2d 871 (1965).

Paragraph (4) [now (e)]. The definition describes "copies" produced by methods possessing an accuracy which virtually eliminates the possibility of error. Copies thus produced are given the status of originals in large measure by Rule 1003, *infra*. Copies subsequently produced manually, whether handwritten or typed, are not within the definition. It should be noted that what is an original for some purposes may be a duplicate for others. Thus a bank's microfilm record of checks cleared is the original as a record. However, a print offered as a copy of a check whose contents are in controversy is a duplicate. This result is substantially consistent with 28 U.S.C. § 1732(b). Compare 26 U.S.C. § 7513(c), giving full status as originals to photographic reproductions of tax returns and other documents, made by authority of the Secretary of the Treasury, and 44 U.S.C. § 399(a), giving original status to photographic copies in the National Archives.

Rule 1002. Requirement of the Original

An original writing, recording, or photograph is required in order to prove its content unless these rules or a federal statute provides otherwise.

(As amended Apr. 26, 2011, eff. Dec. 1, 2011.)

RESTYLED RULE 1002 COMMITTEE NOTE

The language of Rule 1002 has been amended as part of the restyling of the Evidence Rules to make them more easily understood and to make style and terminology consistent throughout the rules. These changes are intended to be stylistic only. There is no intent to change any result in any ruling on evidence admissibility.

Note by Federal Judicial Center

The rule enacted by the Congress is the rule prescribed by the Supreme Court without change.

Section references, McCormick 7th ed.

§ 235

Advisory Committee's Note

56 F.R.D. 183, 342

The rule is the familiar one requiring production of the original of a document to prove its contents, expanded to include writings, recordings, and photographs, as defined in Rule 1001(1) and (2), *supra*.

Application of the rule requires a resolution of the question whether contents are sought to be proved. Thus an event may be proved by nondocumentary evidence, even though a written record of it was made. If, however, the event is sought to be proved by the written record, the rule applies. For example, payment may be proved without producing the written receipt which was given. Earnings may be proved without producing books of account in which they are entered. McCormick § 198; 4 Wigmore § 1245. Nor does the rule apply to testimony that books or records have been examined and found not to contain any reference to a designated matter.

The assumption should not be made that the rule will come into operation on every occasion when use is made of a photograph in evidence. On the contrary, the rule will seldom apply to ordinary photographs. In most instances a party *wishes* to introduce the item and the question raised is the propriety of receiving it in evidence. Cases in which an offer is made of the testimony of a witness as to what he saw in a photograph or motion picture, without producing the same, are most unusual. The usual course is for a witness on the stand to identify the photograph or motion picture as a correct representation of events which he saw or of a scene with which he is familiar. In fact he adopts the picture as his testimony, or, in common parlance, uses the picture to illustrate his testimony. Under these circumstances, no effort is made to prove the contents of the picture, and the rule is inapplicable. Paradis, The Celluloid Witness, 37 U.Colo.L.Rev. 235, 249–251 (1965).

On occasion, however, situations arise in which contents are sought to be proved. Copyright, defamation, and invasion of privacy by photograph or motion picture falls in this category. Similarly as to situations in which the picture is offered as having independent probative value, *e.g.* automatic photograph of bank robber. See People v. Doggett, 83 Cal.App.2d 405, 188 P.2d 792 (1948), photograph of defendants engaged in indecent act; Mouser and Philbin, Photographic Evidence—Is There a Recognized Basis for Admissibility? 8 Hastings L.J. 310 (1957). The most commonly encountered of this latter group is of course, the X-ray, with substantial authority calling for production of the original. Daniels v. Iowa City, 191 Iowa 811, 183 N.W. 415 (1921); Cellamare v. Third Ave. Transit Corp., 273 App.Div. 260, 77 N.Y.S.2d 91 (1948); Patrick & Tilman v. Matkin, 154 Okl. 232, 7 P.2d 414 (1932); Mendoza v. Rivera, 78 P.R.R. 569 (1955).

It should be noted, however, that Rule 703, *supra*, allows an expert to give an opinion based on matters not in evidence, and the present rule must be read as being limited accordingly in its application. Hospital records which may be admitted as business records under Rule 803(6) commonly contain reports interpreting X rays by the staff radiologist, who qualifies as an expert, and these reports need not be excluded from the records by the instant rule.

The references to Acts of Congress is made in view of such statutory provisions as 26 U.S.C. § 7513, photographic reproductions of tax returns and documents, made by authority of the Secretary of the Treasury, treated as originals, and 44 U.S.C. § 399(a), photographic copies in National Archives treated as originals.

Rule 1003. Admissibility of Duplicates

A duplicate is admissible to the same extent as the original unless a genuine question is raised about the original's authenticity or the circumstances make it unfair to admit the duplicate.

(As amended Apr. 26, 2011, eff. Dec. 1, 2011.)

RESTYLED RULE 1003 COMMITTEE NOTE

The language of Rule 1003 has been amended as part of the restyling of the Evidence Rules to make them more easily understood and to make style and terminology consistent throughout the rules. These changes are intended to be stylistic only. There is no intent to change any result in any ruling on evidence admissibility.

Section references, McCormick 7th ed.

§ 236

Note by Federal Judicial Center

The rule enacted by the Congress is the rule prescribed by the Supreme Court without change.

Advisory Committee's Note

56 F.R.D. 183, 343

When the only concern is with getting the words or other contents before the court with accuracy and precision, then a counterpart serves equally as well as the original, if the counterpart is the product of a method which insures accuracy and genuineness. By definition in Rule 1001(4), *supra*, a "duplicate" possesses this character.

Therefore, if no genuine issue exists as to authenticity and no other reason exists for requiring the original, a duplicate is admissible under the rule. This position finds support in the decisions, Myrick v. United States, 332 F.2d 279 (5th Cir. 1964), no error in admitting photostatic copies of checks instead of original microfilm in absence of suggestion to trial judge that photostats were incorrect; Johns v. United States, 323 F.2d 421 (5th Cir. 1963), not error to admit concededly accurate tape recording made from original wire recording; Sauget v. Johnston, 315 F.2d 816 (9th Cir. 1963), not error to admit copy of agreement when opponent had original and did not on appeal claim any discrepancy. Other reasons for requiring the original may be present when only a part of the original is reproduced and the remainder is needed for cross-examination or may disclose matters qualifying the part offered or otherwise useful to the opposing party. United States v. Alexander, 326 F.2d 736 (4th Cir. 1964). And see Toho Bussan Kaisha, Ltd. v. American President Lines, Ltd., 265 F.2d 418, 76 A.L.R.2d 1344 (2d Cir. 1959).

Report of House Committee on the Judiciary

House Comm. on Judiciary, Fed.Rules of Evidence, 93d Cong., 1st Sess., p. 17 (1973); 1974 U.S.Code Cong. & Ad.News 7075, 7090

The Committee approved this Rule in the form submitted by the Court, with the expectation that the courts would be liberal in deciding that a "genuine question is raised as to the authenticity of the original."

Rule 1004. Admissibility of Other Evidence of Content

An original is not required and other evidence of the content of a writing, recording, or photograph is admissible if:

(a) all the originals are lost or destroyed, and not by the proponent acting in bad faith;

(b) an original cannot be obtained by any available judicial process;

(c) the party against whom the original would be offered had control of the original; was at that time put on notice, by pleadings or otherwise, that the original would be a subject of proof at the trial or hearing; and fails to produce it at the trial or hearing; or

(d) the writing, recording, or photograph is not closely related to a controlling issue.

(As amended Mar. 2, 1987, eff. Oct. 1, 1987; Apr. 26, 2011, eff. Dec. 1, 2011.)

RESTYLED RULE 1004 COMMITTEE NOTE

The language of Rule 1004 has been amended as part of the restyling of the Evidence Rules to make them more easily understood and to make style and terminology consistent throughout the rules. These changes are intended to be stylistic only. There is no intent to change any result in any ruling on evidence admissibility.

REPORTER'S COMMENT ON RESTYLED RULE 1004

The subdivisions are now lettered rather than numbered in accordance with standard conventions of rulemaking and statutory drafting—a numbered rule is followed by a lettered subdivision. Redesignation creates a risk of disruption to electronic searches, but Rule 1004 is so infrequently cited that the Advisory Committee deemed the risk to be minimal.

Section references, McCormick 7th ed.

§§ 237–239

Note by Federal Judicial Center

The rule enacted by the Congress is the rule prescribed by the Supreme Court without change.

Advisory Committee's Note

56 F.R.D. 183, 344

Basically the rule requiring the production of the original as proof of contents has developed as a rule of preference: if failure to produce the original is satisfactorily explained, secondary evidence is admissible. The instant rule specifies the circumstances under which production of the original is excused.

The rule recognizes no "degrees" of secondary evidence. While strict logic might call for extending the principle of preference beyond simply preferring the original, the formulation of a hierarchy of preferences and a procedure for making it effective is believed to involve unwarranted complexities. Most, if not all, that would be accomplished by an extended scheme of preferences will, in any event, be achieved through the normal motivation of a party to present the most convincing evidence possible and the arguments and procedures available to his opponent if he does not. Compare McCormick § 207.

Paragraph (1) [now Restyled as (a)—Ed.]. Loss or destruction of the original, unless due to bad faith of the proponent, is a satisfactory explanation of nonproduction. McCormick § 201.

Report of House Committee on the Judiciary

House Comm. on Judiciary, Fed.Rules of Evidence, H.R.Rep. No. 650, 93d Cong., 1st Sess., p. 17 (1973); 1974 U.S.Code Cong. & Ad.News 7075, 7090

The Committee approved Rule 1004(1) **[now (a)—Ed.]** in the form submitted to Congress. However, the Committee intends that loss or destruction of an original by another person at the instigation of the proponent should be considered as tantamount to loss or destruction in bad faith by the proponent himself.

Advisory Committee's Note to Rule 1004(2)–(4)

56 F.R.D. 183, 344

Paragraph (2) [now restyled as (b)—Ed.]. When the original is in the possession of a third person, inability to procure it from him by resort to process or other judicial procedure is a sufficient explanation of nonproduction. Judicial procedure includes subpoena duces tecum as an incident to the taking of a deposition in another jurisdiction. No further showing is required. See McCormick § 202.

Paragraph (3) [now restyled as (c)—Ed.]. A party who has an original in his control has no need for the protection of the rule if put on notice that proof of contents will be made. He can ward off secondary evidence by offering the original. The notice procedure here provided is not to be confused with orders to produce or other discovery procedures, as the purpose of the procedure under this rule is to afford the opposite party an opportunity to produce the original, not to compel him to do so. McCormick § 203.

Paragraph (4) [now restyled as (d)—Ed.]. While difficult to define with precision, situations arise in which no good purpose is served by production of the original. Examples are the newspaper in an action for the price of publishing defendant's advertisement, Foster-Holcomb Investment Co. v. Little Rock Publishing Co., 151 Ark. 449, 236 S.W. 597 (1922), and the streetcar transfer of plaintiff claiming status as a passenger, Chicago City Ry. Co. v. Carroll, 206 Ill. 318, 68 N.E. 1087 (1903). Numerous cases are collected in McCormick § 200, p. 412, n. 1.

1987 Amendment Committee Note

The amendments are technical. No substantive change is intended.

Rule 1005. Copies of Public Records to Prove Content

The proponent may use a copy to prove the content of an official record—or of a document that was recorded or filed in a public office as authorized by law—if these conditions are met: the record or document is otherwise admissible; and the copy is certified as correct in accordance with Rule 902(4) or is testified to be correct by a witness who has compared it with the original. If no such copy can be obtained by reasonable diligence, then the proponent may use other evidence to prove the content.

(As amended Apr. 26, 2011, eff. Dec. 1, 2011.)

RESTYLED RULE 1005 COMMITTEE NOTE

The language of Rule 1005 has been amended as part of the restyling of the Evidence Rules to make them more easily understood and to make style and terminology consistent throughout the rules. These changes are intended to be stylistic only. There is no intent to change any result in any ruling on evidence admissibility.

REPORTER'S COMMENT ON RESTYLED RULE 1005

Rule 1005 illustrates an example of the Restyling's attempt to make the Evidence Rules more user-friendly. The original Rule referred to certification "in accordance with Rule 902." The Restyled version adds a more specific reference to the subdivision of Rule 902 that is applicable—Rule 902(4). Hopefully this will aid courts and litigants in applying Rule 1005.

Section references, McCormick 7th ed.

§ 240

Note by Federal Judicial Center

The rule enacted by the Congress is the rule prescribed by the Supreme Court without change.

Advisory Committee's Note

56 F.R.D. 183, 345

Public records call for somewhat different treatment. Removing them from their usual place of keeping would be attended by serious inconvenience to the public and to the custodian. As a consequence judicial decisions and statutes commonly hold that no explanation need be given for failure to produce the original of a public record. McCormick § 204; 4 Wigmore §§ 1215–1228. This blanket dispensation from producing or accounting for the original would open the door to the introduction of every kind of secondary evidence of contents of public records were it not for the preference given certified or compared copies. Recognition of degrees of secondary evidence in this situation is an appropriate *quid pro quo* for not applying the requirement of producing the original.

The provisions of 28 U.S.C. § 1733(b) apply only to departments or agencies of the United States. The rule, however, applies to public records generally and is comparable in scope in this respect to Rule 44(a) of the Rules of Civil Procedure.

Rule 1006. Summaries to Prove Content

The proponent may use a summary, chart, or calculation to prove the content of voluminous writings, recordings, or photographs that cannot be conveniently examined in court. The proponent must make the originals or duplicates available for examination or copying, or both, by other parties at a reasonable time and place. And the court may order the proponent to produce them in court.

(As amended Apr. 26, 2011; eff. Dec. 1, 2011.)

RESTYLED RULE 1006 COMMITTEE NOTE

The language of Rule 1006 has been amended as part of the restyling of the Evidence Rules to make them more easily understood and to make style and terminology consistent throughout the rules. These changes are intended to be stylistic only. There is no intent to change any result in any ruling on evidence admissibility.

Section references, McCormick 7th ed.

§ 241

Note by Federal Judicial Center

The rule enacted by the Congress is the rule prescribed by the Supreme Court without change.

Advisory Committee's Note

56 F.R.D. 183, 346

The admission of summaries of voluminous books, records, or documents offers the only practicable means of making their contents available to judge and jury. The rule recognizes this practice, with appropriate safeguards. 4 Wigmore § 1230.

Rule 1007. Testimony or Statement of a Party to Prove Content

The proponent may prove the content of a writing, recording, or photograph by the testimony, deposition, or written statement of the party against whom the evidence is offered. The proponent need not account for the original.

(As amended Mar. 2, 1987, eff. Oct. 1, 1987; Apr. 26, 2011, eff. Dec. 1, 2011.)

RESTYLED RULE 1007 COMMITTEE NOTE

The language of Rule 1007 has been amended as part of the restyling of the Evidence Rules to make them more easily understood and to make style and terminology consistent throughout the rules. These changes are intended to be stylistic only. There is no intent to change any result in any ruling on evidence admissibility.

REPORTER'S COMMENT ON RESTYLED RULE 1007

The Rule carries over the Advisory Committee's decision to eliminate any reference to party "admissions." See the Reporter's Comment to Restyled Rule 801. The original reference to a party's "written admission" has been changed to "written statement"—consistent with the language used in Rule 801.

Section references, McCormick 7th ed.

§ 242

Note by Federal Judicial Center

The rule enacted by the Congress is the rule prescribed by the Supreme Court without change.

Advisory Committee's Note

56 F.R.D. 183, 356

While the parent case, Slatterie v. Pooley, 6 M. & W. 664, 151 Eng.Rep. 579 (Exch. 1840), allows proof of contents by evidence of an oral admission by the party against whom offered, without accounting for nonproduction of the original, the risk of inaccuracy is substantial and the decision is at odds with the purpose of the rule giving preference to the original. See 4 Wigmore § 1255. The instant rule follows Professor McCormick's suggestion of limiting this use of admissions to those made in the course of giving testimony or in writing. McCormick § 208, p. 424. The limitation, of course, does not call for excluding evidence of an oral admission when nonproduction of the original has been accounted for and secondary evidence generally has become admissible. Rule 1004, *supra*.

A similar provision is contained in New Jersey Evidence Rule 70(1)(h).

1987 Amendment Committee Note

The amendment is technical. No substantive change is intended.

Rule 1008. Functions of Court and Jury

Ordinarily, the court determines whether the proponent has fulfilled the factual conditions for admitting other evidence of the content of a writing, recording, or photograph under Rule 1004 or 1005. But in a jury trial, the jury determines—in accordance with Rule 104(b)—any issue about whether:

(a) an asserted writing, recording, or photograph ever existed;

(b) another one produced at the trial or hearing is the original; or

(c) other evidence of content accurately reflects the content.

(As amended Apr. 26, 2011; eff. Dec. 1, 2011.)

RESTYLED RULE 1008 COMMITTEE NOTE

The language of Rule 1008 has been amended as part of the restyling of the Evidence Rules to make them more easily understood and to make style and terminology consistent throughout the rules. These changes are intended to be stylistic only. There is no intent to change any result in any ruling on evidence admissibility.

REPORTER'S COMMENT ON RESTYLED RULE 1008

Restyled Rule 1008 showcases two aspects of the Restyling that were designed to make the Evidence Rules more user-friendly. First, it unpacks the existing rule to make it easier to approach visually—the subdivisions are broken out of the mass of the rule and laid out in vertical form. Second, the Restyled Rule provides more specific references to the rules referred to in the text, so that they can be more easily accessed by courts and litigants.

Section references, McCormick 7th ed.

§ 243

Note by Federal Judicial Center

The rule enacted by the Congress is the rule prescribed by the Supreme Court, amended by substituting "court" in place of "judge," and by adding at the end of the first sentence the phrase "in accordance with the provisions of rule 104."

Advisory Committee's Note

56 F.R.D. 183, 347

Most preliminary questions of fact in connection with applying the rule preferring the original as evidence of contents are for the judge, under the general principles announced in Rule 104, *supra.* Thus, the question whether the loss of the originals has been established, or of the fulfillment of other conditions specified in Rule 1004, *supra,* is for the judge. However, questions may arise which go beyond the mere administration of the rule preferring the original and into the merits of the controversy. For example, plaintiff offers secondary evidence of the contents of an alleged contract, after first introducing evidence of loss of the original, and defendant counters with evidence that no such contract was ever executed. If the judge decides that the contract was never executed and excludes the secondary evidence, the case is at an end without ever going to the jury on a central issue. Levin, Authentication and Content of Writings, 10 Rutgers L.Rev. 632, 644 (1956). The latter portion of the instant rule is designed to insure treatment of these situations as raising jury questions. The decision is not one for uncontrolled discretion of the jury but is subject to the control exercised generally by the judge over jury determinations. See Rule 104(b), *supra.*

For similar provisions, see Uniform Rule 70(2); Kansas Code of Civil Procedure § 60–467(b); New Jersey Evidence Rule 70(2), (3).

ARTICLE XI. MISCELLANEOUS RULES

Rule 1101. Applicability of the Rules

(a) To Courts and Judges. These rules apply to proceedings before:

- United States district courts;
- United States bankruptcy and magistrate judges;
- United States courts of appeals;
- the United States Court of Federal Claims; and
- the district courts of Guam, the Virgin Islands, and the Northern Mariana Islands.

(b) To Cases and Proceedings. These rules apply in:

- civil cases and proceedings, including bankruptcy, admiralty, and maritime cases;
- criminal cases and proceedings; and
- contempt proceedings, except those in which the court may act summarily.

(c) Rules on Privilege. The rules on privilege apply to all stages of a case or proceeding.

(d) Exceptions. These rules—except for those on privilege—do not apply to the following:

(1) the court's determination, under Rule 104(a), on a preliminary question of fact governing admissibility;

(2) grand-jury proceedings; and

(3) miscellaneous proceedings such as:

- extradition or rendition;
- issuing an arrest warrant, criminal summons, or search warrant;
- a preliminary examination in a criminal case;
- sentencing;
- granting or revoking probation or supervised release; and
- considering whether to release on bail or otherwise.

(e) Other Statutes and Rules. A federal statute or a rule prescribed by the Supreme Court may provide for admitting or excluding evidence independently from these rules.

(As amended P.L. 94–149, § 1(14), Dec. 12, 1975, 89 Stat. 806; P.L. 95–598, Title II, § 251, Nov. 6, 1978, 92 Stat. 2673; P.L. 97–164, Title I, § 142, Apr. 2, 1982, 96 Stat. 45; Mar. 2, 1987, eff. Oct. 1, 1987; Apr. 25, 1988, eff. Nov. 1, 1988; Nov. 18, 1988, Pub.L. 100–690, Title VII, § 7075(c), 102 Stat. 4405; Apr. 22, 1993, eff. Dec. 1, 1993; Apr. 26, 2011, eff. Dec. 1, 2011.)

RESTYLED RULE 1101 COMMITTEE NOTE

The language of Rule 1101 has been amended as part of the restyling of the Evidence Rules to make them more easily understood and to make style and terminology consistent throughout the rules. These changes are intended to be stylistic only. There is no intent to change any result in any ruling on evidence admissibility.

REPORTER'S COMMENT ON RESTYLED RULE 1101

Rule 1101(d)(3) lists certain "miscellaneous proceedings" in which the Evidence Rules are inapplicable. Case law indicates that the list is not exclusive. *See, e.g., United States v. Palesky,* 855 F.2d 34 (1st Cir. 1988) (Evidence Rules are not applicable in hearings held to determine whether a person will be committed to or released from a psychiatric facility—Rule 1101(d)(3) not read to provide an exclusive list). The Advisory Committee believed that it was important to provide notification to courts and especially to litigants that the list is not exclusive—*i.e.,* there are a number of other proceedings in which the Evidence Rules have been found inapplicable. Accordingly, the words "such as" were added before the list in Rule 1101(d)(3). The list was also modified to recognize that supervised release has replaced probation in the Federal system.

The original Evidence Rule 1101(e) set forth a laundry list of proceedings in which the Evidence Rules are applicable only to the extent that matters of evidence are not governed by other specified rules or statutes. After substantial research, the Advisory Committee determined that this provision was devoid of substantive effect. All of the proceedings specified were civil actions or proceedings tried in the federal courts. The Evidence Rules are already applicable to these proceedings under the provisions of Rule 1101(a) and (c). So the only apparent purpose for subdivision (e) was to highlight the fact that other rules and statutes might trump the Evidence Rules in particular circumstances. Yet this merely states the obvious. There are a large number of statutes that trump the Evidence Rules in specific circumstances. Rule 1101(e) was not comprehensive; and moreover some of the statutes that were referred to in the rule have been abrogated or repealed.

The Advisory Committee considered whether Rule 1101(e) should be retained in order to prevent the enumerated statutes from being superseded by the (later-enacted) amendment to Rule 1101. But the Committee determined that these statutes would not be superseded by amending Rule 1101(e). This is because the Evidence Rules are written so as not to supersede any statutory rule of evidence. The statutory rules of evidence generally govern one of five topics: 1) presumptions; 2) relevance and prejudice; 3) privilege; 4) hearsay; and 5) authentication. On none of these topics do the Evidence Rules preclude statutory authority from determining whether evidence is admissible. For example, Rule 301 provides a rule on presumptions to the extent not otherwise provided for by federal statute. Rule 402 says that relevant evidence is admissible, unless otherwise provided by federal statute, etc. Rule 501 provides for a federal common law of privilege except as otherwise provided by statute, etc. Rule 802 provides that hearsay is not admissible except as otherwise provided by statute, etc. And Rule 901 governs authenticity, but does not purport to supersede statutes that provide for authentication; the examples in 901 are illustrative only.

Accordingly, the Advisory Committee deleted the laundry list of proceedings in Rule 1101(e) and substituted general language cautioning the user that other statutes and rules may trump the Evidence Rules in determining admissibility in certain proceedings.

Section references, McCormick 7th ed.

None

Note by Federal Judicial Center

The rule enacted by the Congress is the rule prescribed by the Supreme Court, amended as follows:

Subdivision (a) was amended in the first sentence by inserting "the Court of Claims" and by inserting "actions, cases, and." It was amended in the second sentence by substituting "terms" in place of "word," by inserting the phrase "and 'court'," and by adding "commissioners of the Court of Claims."

Subdivision (b) was amended by substituting "civil actions and proceedings" in place of "civil actions," and by substituting "criminal cases and proceedings" in place of "criminal proceedings."

Subdivision (c) was amended by substituting "rule" in place of "rules" and by changing the verb to the singular.

Subdivision (d) was amended by deleting "those" after "other than" and by substituting "Rule 104" in place of "Rule 104(a)."

Subdivision (e) was amended by substituting "prescribed" in place of "adopted" and by adding "pursuant to statutory authority." The form of the statutory citations was also changed.

Advisory Committee's Note

56 F.R.D. 183, 348

Subdivision (a). [Editor's Note: This portion of the Advisory Committee's Note discussed the courts for which the various enabling acts granted the Supreme Court power to prescribe rules. Congressional enactment of the Evidence Rules has rendered the discussion moot. The enabling acts did not include the Court of Claims which the Congress added to Rule 1101(a)].

Report of House Committee on the Judiciary

House Comm. on Judiciary, Fed.Rules of Evidence, H.R.Rep. No. 650, 93d Cong., 1st Sess., p. 17 (1973); 1974 U.S.Code Cong. & Ad.News 7075, 7090

Subdivision (a) as submitted to the Congress, in stating the courts and judges to which the Rules of Evidence apply, omitted the Court of Claims and commissioners of that Court. At the request of the Court of Claims, the Committee amended the Rule to include the Court and its commissioners within the purview of the Rules.

Advisory Committee's Note to Rule 1101(b)–(e)

56 F.R.D. 183, 351

Subdivision (b) is a combination of the language of the enabling acts, *supra*, with respect to the kinds of proceedings in which the making of rules is authorized. It is subject to the qualifications expressed in the subdivisions which follow.

Subdivision (c), singling out the rules of privilege for special treatment, is made necessary by the limited applicability of the remaining rules.

Subdivision (d). The rule is not intended as an expression as to when due process or other constitutional provisions may require an evidentiary hearing. Paragraph (1) restates, for convenience, the provisions of the second sentence of Rule 104(a), *supra*. See Advisory Committee's Note to that rule.

(2)   While some states have statutory requirements that indictments be based on "legal evidence," and there is some case law to the effect that the rules of evidence apply to grand jury proceedings, 1 Wigmore § 4(5), the Supreme Court has not accepted this view. In Costello v. United States, 350 U.S. 359, 76 S.Ct. 406, 100 L.Ed. 397 (1965), the Court refused to allow an indictment to be attacked,

for either constitutional or policy reasons, on the ground that only hearsay evidence was presented.

"It would run counter to the whole history of the grand jury institution, in which laymen conduct their inquiries unfettered by technical rules. Neither justice nor the concept of a fair trial requires such a change." *Id.* at 364. The rule as drafted does not deal with the evidence required to support an indictment.

(3)   The rule exempts preliminary examinations in criminal cases. Authority as to the applicability of the rules of evidence to preliminary examinations has been meagre and conflicting. Goldstein, The State and the Accused: Balance of Advantage in Criminal Procedure, 69 Yale L.J. 1149, 1168, n. 53 (1960); Comment, Preliminary Hearings on Indictable Offenses in Philadelphia, 106 U. of Pa.L.Rev. 589, 592–593 (1958). Hearsay testimony is, however, customarily received in such examinations. Thus in a Dyer Act case, for example, an affidavit may properly be used in a preliminary examination to prove ownership of the stolen vehicle, thus saving the victim of the crime the hardship of having to travel twice to a distant district for the sole purpose of testifying as to ownership. It is believed that the extent of the applicability of the Rules of Evidence to preliminary examinations should be appropriately dealt with by the Federal Rules of Criminal Procedure which regulate those proceedings.

Extradition and rendition proceedings are governed in detail by statute. 18 U.S.C. §§ 3181–3195. They are essentially administrative in character. Traditionally the rules of evidence have not applied. 1 Wigmore § 4(6). Extradition proceedings are accepted from the operation of the Rules of Criminal Procedure. Rule 54(b)(5) of Federal Rules of Criminal Procedure.

The rules of evidence have not been regarded as applicable to sentencing or probation proceedings, where great reliance is placed upon the presentence investigation and report. Rule 32(c) of the Federal Rules of Criminal Procedure requires a presentence investigation and report in every case unless the court otherwise directs. In Williams v. New York, 337 U.S. 241, 69 S.Ct. 1079, 93 L.Ed. 1337 (1949), in which the judge overruled a jury recommendation of life imprisonment and imposed a death sentence, the Court said that due process does not require confrontation or cross-examination in sentencing or passing on probation, and that the judge has broad discretion as to the sources and types of information relied upon. Compare the recommendation that the substance of all derogatory information be disclosed to the defendant, in A.B.A. Project on Minimum Standards for Criminal Justice, Sentencing Alternatives and Procedures § 4.4, Tentative Draft (1967, Sobeloff, Chm.). Williams was adhered to in Specht v. Patterson, 386 U.S. 605, 87 S.Ct. 1209, 18 L.Ed.2d 326 (1967), but not extended to a proceeding under the Colorado Sex Offenders Act, which was said to be a new charge leading in effect to punishment, more like the recidivist statutes where opportunity must be given to be heard on the habitual criminal issue.

Warrants for arrest, criminal summonses, and search warrants are issued upon complaint or affidavit showing probable cause. Rules 4(a) and 41(c) of the Federal Rules of Criminal Procedure. The nature of the proceedings makes application of the formal rules of evidence inappropriate and impracticable.

Criminal contempts are punishable summarily if the judge certifies that he saw or heard the contempt and that it was committed in the presence of the court. Rule 42(a) of the Federal Rules of Criminal Procedure. The circumstances which preclude application of the rules of evidence in this situation are not present, however, in other cases of criminal contempt.

Proceedings with respect to release on bail or otherwise do not call for application of the rules of evidence. The governing statute specifically provides:

"Information stated in, or offered in connection with, any order entered pursuant to this section need not conform to the rules pertaining to the admissibility of evidence in a court of law." 18 U.S.C.A. § 3146(f).

This provision is consistent with the type of inquiry contemplated in A.B.A. Project on Minimum Standards for Criminal Justice, Standards Relating to Pretrial Release, § 4.5(b), (c), p. 16 (1968). The references to the weight of the evidence against the accused, in Rule 46(a)(1), (c) of the Federal Rules of Criminal Procedure and in 18 U.S.C.A. § 3146(b), as a factor to be considered, clearly do not have in view evidence introduced at a hearing under the rules of evidence.

The rule does not exempt habeas corpus proceedings. The Supreme Court held in Walker v. Johnston, 312 U.S. 275, 61 S.Ct. 574, 85 L.Ed. 830 (1941), that the practice of disposing of matters of fact on affidavit, which prevailed in some circuits, did not "satisfy the command of the statute that the judge shall proceed 'to determine the facts of the case, by hearing the testimony and arguments.'" This view accords with the emphasis in Townsend v. Sain, 372 U.S. 293, 83 S.Ct. 745, 9 L.Ed.2d 770 (1963), upon trial-type proceedings, *id.* 311, 83 S.Ct. 745, with demeanor evidence as a significant factor, *id.* 322, 83 S.Ct. 745, in applications by state prisoners aggrieved by unconstitutional detentions. Hence subdivision (e) applies the rules to habeas corpus proceedings to the extent not inconsistent with the statute.

Subdivision (e). [Deleted in the 2011 Restyling.—Ed.] In a substantial number of special proceedings, *ad hoc* evaluation has resulted in the promulgation of particularized evidentiary provisions, by Act of Congress or by rule adopted by the Supreme Court. Well adapted to the particular proceedings, though not apt candidates for inclusion in a set of general rules, they are left undisturbed. Otherwise, however, the rules of evidence are applicable to the proceedings enumerated in the subdivision.

Report of House Committee on the Judiciary

House Comm. on Judiciary, Fed.Rules of Evidence, H.R.Rep. No. 650, 93d Cong., 1st Sess., p. 17 (1973); 1974 U.S.Code Cong. & Ad.News 7075, 7090

Subdivision (e) was amended merely to substitute positive law citations for those which were not.

1987 Amendment Committee Note

Subdivision (a) is amended to delete the reference to the District Court for the District of the Canal Zone, which no longer exists, and to add the District Court for the Northern Mariana Islands. The United States bankruptcy judges are added to conform the subdivision with Rule 1101(b) and Bankruptcy Rule 9017.

1988 Amendment Committee Note

The amendment is technical. No substantive change is intended.

1993 Amendment Committee Note

This revision is made to conform the rule to changes in terminology made by Rule 58 of the Federal Rules of Criminal Procedure and to the changes in the title of United States magistrates made by the Judicial Improvements Act of 1990.

Rule 1102. Amendments

These rules may be amended as provided in 28 U.S.C. § 2072.

(As amended Apr. 30, 1991, eff. Dec. 1, 1991; Apr. 26, 2011, eff. Dec. 1, 2011.)

RESTYLED RULE 1102 COMMITTEE NOTE

The language of Rule 1102 has been amended as part of the restyling of the Evidence Rules to make them more easily understood and to make style and terminology consistent throughout the rules. These changes are intended to be stylistic only. There is no intent to change any result in any ruling on evidence admissibility.

Note by Federal Judicial Center

This rule was not included among those prescribed by the Supreme Court. The rule prescribed by the Court as 1102 now appears as 1103.

Advisory Committee's Note

1991 Amendment

The amendment is technical. No substantive change is intended.

Rule 1103. Title

These rules may be cited as the Federal Rules of Evidence.

(As amended Apr. 26, 2011, eff. Dec. 1, 2011.)

RESTYLED RULE 1103 COMMITTEE NOTE

The language of Rule 1103 has been amended as part of the restyling of the Evidence Rules to make them more easily understood and to make style and terminology consistent throughout the rules. These changes are intended to be stylistic only. There is no intent to change any result in any ruling on evidence admissibility.

Note by Federal Judicial Center

The rule enacted by the Congress is the rule prescribed by the Supreme Court as Rule 1102 without change.

DELETED AND SUPERSEDED MATERIALS

*[**Editor's Note:** The following provisions, prescribed by the Supreme Court, were excised by the Congress from the finally-enacted version of the Rules. However, they are useful in understanding the policies of the drafters, the federal law on the matters involved, and the thinking underlying similar provisions in some state rules or codes.]*

ARTICLE I. GENERAL PROVISIONS

Rule 105. Summing Up and Comment by Judge [Not enacted.]

After the close of the evidence and arguments of counsel, the judge may fairly and impartially sum up the evidence and comment to the jury upon the weight of the evidence and the credibility of the witnesses, if he also instructs the jury that they are to determine for themselves the weight of the evidence and the credit to be given to the witnesses and that they are not bound by the judge's summation or comment.

Note by Federal Judicial Center

The foregoing rule prescribed by the Supreme Court was deleted from the rules enacted by the Congress.

Advisory Committee's Note

The rule states the present rule in the federal courts. Capital Traction Co. v. Hof, 174 U.S. 1, 13–14, 19 S.Ct. 580, 43 L.Ed. 873 (1899). The judge must, of course, confine his remarks to what is disclosed by the evidence. He cannot convey to the jury his purely personal reaction to credibility or to the merits of the case; he can be neither argumentative nor an advocate. Quercia v. United States, 289 U.S. 466, 469, 53 S.Ct. 698, 77 L.Ed. 1321 (1933); Billeci v. United States, 87 U.S.App.D.C. 274, 184 F.2d 394, 402, 24 A.L.R.2d 881 (1950). For further discussion see the series of articles by Wright, The Invasion of Jury: Temperature of the War, 27 Temp.L.Q. 137 (1953), Instructions to the Jury: Summary Without Comment, 1954 Wash.U.L.Q. 177, Adequacy of Instructions to the Jury, 53 Mich.L.Rev. 505, 813 (1955); A.L.I. Model Code of Evidence, Comment to Rule 8; Maguire, Weinstein, et al., Cases and Materials on Evidence 737–740 (5th ed. 1965); Vanderbilt, Minimum Standards of Judicial Administration 224–229 (1949).

Report of the House Committee on the Judiciary

Rule 105 as submitted by the Supreme Court concerned the issue of summing up and comment by the judge. It provided that after the close of the evidence and the arguments of counsel, the presiding judge could fairly and impartially sum up the evidence and comment to the jury upon its weight and the credibility of the witnesses, if he also instructed the jury that it was not bound thereby and must make its own determination of those matters. The Committee recognized that the Rule as submitted is consistent with long standing and current federal practice. However, the aspect of the Rule dealing with the authority of a judge to comment on the weight of the evidence and the credibility of witnesses—an authority not granted to judges in most State courts—was highly controversial. After much debate the Committee determined to delete the entire Rule, intending that its action be understood as reflecting no conclusion as to the merits of the proposed Rule and that the subject should be left for separate consideration at another time.

Report of Senate Committee on the Judiciary

This rule as submitted by the Supreme Court permitted the judge to sum up and comment on the evidence. The House struck the rule.

The committee accepts the House action with the understanding that the present Federal practice, taken from the common law, of the trial judge's discretionary authority to comment on and summarize the evidence is left undisturbed.

ARTICLE III. PRESUMPTIONS IN CIVIL CASES

Rule 301. Presumptions in General [As prescribed by Supreme Court]

In all cases not otherwise provided for by Act of Congress or by these rules a presumption imposes on the party against whom it is directed the burden of proving that the nonexistence of the presumed fact is more probable than its existence.

Rule 301. Presumptions in General in Civil Actions and Proceedings [As passed by House of Representatives]

In all civil actions and proceedings not otherwise provided for by Act of Congress or by these rules, a presumption imposes on the party against whom it is directed the burden of going forward with the evidence, and, even though met with contradicting evidence, a presumption is sufficient evidence of the fact presumed, to be considered by the trier of the facts.

Note by Federal Judicial Center

Neither of the above versions of Rule 301 was enacted.

Advisory Committee's Note

This rule governs presumptions generally. See Rule 302 for presumptions controlled by state law and Rule 303 for those against an accused in a criminal case.

Presumptions governed by this rule are given the effect of placing upon the opposing party the burden of establishing the nonexistence of the presumed fact, once the party invoking the presumption establishes the basic facts giving rise to it. The same considerations of fairness, policy, and probability which dictate the allocation of the burden of the various elements of a case as between the prima facie case of a plaintiff and affirmative defenses also underlie the creation of presumptions. These considerations are not satisfied by giving a lesser effect to presumptions. Morgan and Maguire, Looking Backward and Forward at Evidence, 50 Harv.L.Rev. 909, 913 (1937); Morgan, Instructing the Jury upon Presumptions and Burden of Proof, 47 Harv.L.Rev. 59, 82 (1933); Cleary, Presuming and Pleading: An Essay on Juristic Immaturity, 12 Stan.L.Rev. 5 (1959).

The so-called "bursting bubble" theory, under which a presumption vanishes upon the introduction of evidence which would support a finding of the nonexistence of the presumed fact, even though not believed, is rejected as according presumptions too "slight and evanescent" an effect. Morgan and Maguire, *supra,* at p. 913.

In the opinion of the Advisory Committee, no constitutional infirmity attends this view of presumptions. In Mobile, J. & K.C.R. Co. v. Turnipseed, 219 U.S. 35, 31 S.Ct. 136, 55 L.Ed. 78 (1910), the Court upheld a Mississippi statute which provided that in actions against railroads proof of injury inflicted by the running of trains should be prima facie evidence of negligence by the railroad. The injury in the case had resulted from a derailment. The opinion made the points (1) that the only effect of the statute was to impose on the railroad the duty of producing some evidence to the contrary, (2) that an inference may be supplied by law if there is a rational connection between the fact proved and the fact presumed, as long as the opposite party is not precluded from presenting his evidence to the contrary, and (3) that considerations of public policy arising from the character of the business justified the application in question. Nineteen years later, in Western & Atlantic R. Co. v. Henderson, 279 U.S. 639, 49 S.Ct. 445, 73

L.Ed. 884 (1929), the Court overturned a Georgia statute making railroads liable for damages done by trains, unless the railroad made it appear that reasonable care had been used, the presumption being against the railroad. The declaration alleged the death of plaintiff's husband from a grade crossing collision, due to specified acts of negligence by defendant. The jury were instructed that proof of the injury raised a presumption of negligence; the burden shifted to the railroad to prove ordinary care; and unless it did so, they should find for plaintiff. The instruction was held erroneous in an opinion stating (1) that there was no rational connection between the mere fact of collision and negligence on the part of anyone, and (2) that the statute was different from that in *Turnipseed* in imposing a burden upon the railroad. The reader is left in a state of some confusion. Is the difference between a derailment and a grade crossing collision of no significance? Would the *Turnipseed* presumption have been bad if it had imposed a burden of persuasion on defendant, although that would in nowise have impaired its "rational connection"? If *Henderson* forbids imposing a burden of persuasion on defendants, what happens to affirmative defenses?

Two factors serve to explain *Henderson*. The first was that it was common ground that negligence was indispensable to liability. Plaintiff thought so, drafted her complaint accordingly, and relied upon the presumption. But how in logic could the same presumption establish her alternative grounds of negligence that the engineer was so blind he could not see decedent's truck and that he failed to stop after he saw it? Second, take away the basic assumption of no liability without fault, as *Turnipseed* intimated might be done ("considerations of public policy arising out of the character of the business"), and the structure of the decision in *Henderson* fails. No question of logic would have arisen if the statute had simply said: a prima facie case of liability is made by proof of injury by a train; lack of negligence is an affirmative defense, to be pleaded and proved as other affirmative defenses. The problem would be one of economic due process only. While it seems likely that the Supreme Court of 1929 would have voted that due process was denied, that result today would be unlikely. See, for example, the shift in the direction of absolute liability in the consumer cases. Prosser, The Assault upon the Citadel (Strict Liability to the Consumer), 69 Yale L.J. 1099 (1960).

Any doubt as to the constitutional permissibility of a presumption imposing a burden of persuasion of the nonexistence of the presumed fact in civil cases is laid at rest by Dick v. New York Life Ins. Co., 359 U.S. 437, 79 S.Ct. 921, 3 L.Ed.2d 935 (1959). The Court unhesitatingly applied the North Dakota rule that the presumption against suicide imposed on defendant the burden of proving that the death of insured, under an accidental death clause, was due to suicide.

"Proof of coverage and of death by gunshot wound shifts the burden to the insurer to establish that the death of the insured was due to his suicide." 359 U.S. at 443, 79 S.Ct. at 925.

"In a case like this one, North Dakota presumes that death was accidental and places on the insurer the burden of proving that death resulted from suicide." *Id.* at 446, 79 S.Ct. at 927.

The rational connection requirement survives in criminal cases, Tot v. United States, 319 U.S. 463, 63 S.Ct. 1241, 87 L.Ed. 1519 (1943), because the Court has been unwilling to extend into that area the greater-includes-the-lesser theory of Ferry v. Ramsey, 277 U.S. 88, 48 S.Ct. 443, 72 L.Ed. 796 (1928). In that case the Court sustained a Kansas statute under which bank directors were personally liable for deposits made with their assent and with knowledge of insolvency, and the fact of insolvency was prima facie evidence of assent and knowledge of insolvency. Mr. Justice Holmes pointed out that the state legislature could have made the directors personally liable to depositors in every case. Since the statute imposed a less stringent liability, "the thing to be considered is the result reached, not the possibly inartificial or clumsy way of reaching it." *Id.* at

94, 48 S.Ct. at 444. Mr. Justice Sutherland dissented: though the state could have created an absolute liability, it did not purport to do so; a rational connection was necessary, but lacking, between the liability created and the prima facie evidence of it; the result might be different if the basis of the presumption were being open for business.

The Sutherland view has prevailed in criminal cases by virtue of the higher standard of notice there required. The fiction that everyone is presumed to know the law is applied to the substantive law of crimes as an alternative to complete unenforceability. But the need does not extend to criminal evidence and procedure, and the fiction does not encompass them. "Rational connection" is not fictional or artificial, and so it is reasonable to suppose that Gainey should have known that his presence at the site of an illicit still could convict him of being connected with (carrying on) the business, United States v. Gainey, 380 U.S. 63, 85 S.Ct. 754, 13 L.Ed.2d 658 (1965), but not that Romano should have known that his presence at a still could convict him of possessing it, United States v. Romano, 382 U.S. 136, 86 S.Ct. 279, 15 L.Ed.2d 210 (1965).

In his dissent in Gainey, Mr. Justice Black put it more artistically:

> "It might be argued, although the Court does not so argue or hold, that Congress if it wished could make presence at a still a crime in itself, and so Congress should be free to create crimes which are called 'possession' and 'carrying on an illegal distillery business' but which are defined in such a way that unexplained presence is sufficient and indisputable evidence in all cases to support conviction for those offenses. See Ferry v. Ramsey, 277 U.S. 88, 48 S.Ct. 443, 72 L.Ed. 796. Assuming for the sake of argument that Congress could make unexplained presence a criminal act, and ignoring also the refusal of this Court in other cases to uphold a statutory presumption on such a theory, see Heiner v. Donnan, 285 U.S. 312, 52 S.Ct. 358, 76 L.Ed. 772, there is no indication here that Congress intended to adopt such a misleading method of draftsmanship, nor in my judgment could the statutory provisions if so construed escape condemnation for vagueness, under the principles applied in Lanzetta v. New Jersey, 306 U.S. 451, 59 S.Ct. 618, 83 L.Ed. 888, and many other cases." 380 U.S. at 84, n. 12, 85 S.Ct. at 766.

And the majority opinion in *Romano* agreed with him:

> "It may be, of course, that Congress has the power to make presence at an illegal still a punishable crime, but we find no clear indication that it intended to so exercise this power. The crime remains possession, not presence, and with all due deference to the judgment of Congress, the former may not constitutionally be inferred from the latter." 382 U.S. at 144, 86 S.Ct. at 284.

The rule does not spell out the procedural aspects of its application. Questions as to when the evidence warrants submission of a presumption and what instructions are proper under varying states of fact are believed to present no particular difficulties.

Report of House Committee on the Judiciary

Rule 301 as submitted by the Supreme Court provided that in all cases a presumption imposes on the party against whom it is directed the burden of proving that the nonexistence of the presumed fact is more probable than its existence. The Committee limited the scope of Rule 301 to "civil actions and proceedings" to effectuate its decision not to deal with the question of presumptions in criminal cases. (See note on Rule 303 in discussion of Rules deleted). With respect to the weight to be given a presumption in a civil case, the Committee agreed with the judgment implicit in the Court's version that the so-called "bursting bubble" theory of presumptions, whereby a presumption vanishes upon the appearance of any contradicting evidence by the other party, gives to presumptions too slight an effect. On the other hand, the Committee believed that the Rule proposed by the Court, whereby a presumption permanently alters the burden of persuasion, no matter how much contradicting evidence is introduced— a view shared by only a few courts—lends too great a force to presumptions. Accordingly, the Committee amended the Rule to adopt an intermediate position under which a presumption does not vanish upon the introduction of contradicting evidence, and does not change the burden of persuasion; instead it is merely deemed sufficient evidence of the fact presumed, to be considered by the jury or other finder of fact.

Rule 303.   Presumptions in Criminal Cases [Not enacted.]

(a) Scope. Except as otherwise provided by Act of Congress, in criminal cases, presumptions against an accused, recognized at common law or created by statute, including statutory provisions that certain facts are prima facie evidence of other facts or of guilt, are governed by this rule.

(b) Submission to jury. The judge is not authorized to direct the jury to find a presumed fact against the accused. When the presumed fact establishes guilt or is an element of the offense or negatives a defense, the judge may submit the question of guilt or of the existence of the presumed fact to the jury, if, but only if, a reasonable juror on the evidence as a whole, including the evidence of the basic facts, could find guilt or the presumed fact beyond a reasonable doubt. When the presumed fact has a lesser effect, its existence may be submitted to the jury if the basic facts are supported by substantial evidence, or are otherwise established, unless the evidence as a whole negatives the existence of the presumed fact.

(c) Instructing the jury. Whenever the existence of a presumed fact against the accused is submitted to the jury, the judge shall give an instruction that the law declares that the jury may regard the basic facts as sufficient evidence of the presumed fact but does not require it to do so. In addition, if the presumed fact establishes guilt or is an element of the offense or negatives a defense, the judge shall instruct the jury that its existence must, on all the evidence, be proved beyond a reasonable doubt.

Note by Federal Judicial Center

The foregoing rule prescribed by the Supreme Court was deleted from the rules enacted by the Congress.

Advisory Committee's Note

Subdivision (a). This rule is based largely upon A.L.I. Model Penal Code § 1.12(5) P.O.D. (1962) and United States v. Gainey, 380 U.S. 63, 85 S.Ct. 754, 13 L.Ed.2d 658 (1965). While the rule, unlike the Model Penal Code provision, spells out the effect of common law presumptions as well as those created by statute, cases involving the latter are no doubt of more frequent occurrence. Congress has enacted numerous provisions to lessen the burden of the prosecution, principally though not exclusively in the fields of narcotics control and taxation of liquor. Occasionally, in the pattern of the usual common law treatment of such matters as insanity, they take the form of assigning to the defense the responsibility of raising specified matters as affirmative defenses, which are not within the scope of these rules. See Comment, A.L.I. Model Penal Code § 1.13, T.D. No. 4 (1955). In other instances they assume a variety of forms which are the concern of this rule. The provision may be that proof of a specified fact (possession or presence) is sufficient to authorize conviction. 26 U.S.C. § 4704(a), unlawful to buy or sell opium except from original stamped package—absence of stamps from package prima facie evidence of violation by person in possession; 26 U.S.C. § 4724(c), unlawful for person who has not registered and paid special tax to possess narcotics—possession presumptive evidence of violation. Sometimes the qualification is added, "unless the defendant explains the possession [presence] to the satisfaction of the jury." 18 U.S.C. § 545, possession of unlawfully imported goods sufficient for conviction of smuggling, unless explained; 21 U.S.C. § 174, possession sufficient for conviction of buying or selling narcotics known to have been imported unlawfully, unless explained. *See also* 26 U.S.C. § 5601(a)(1), (a)(4), (a)(8), (b)(1), (b)(2), (b)(4), relating to distilling operations. Another somewhat different pattern makes possession evidence of a particular element of the crime. 21 U.S.C. § 176b, crime to furnish unlawfully imported heroin to juveniles—possession sufficient proof of unlawful importation, unless explained;

50 U.S.C.A.App. § 462(b), unlawful to possess draft card not lawfully issued to holder, with intent to use for purposes of false identification—possession sufficient evidence of intent, unless explained. *See also* 15 U.S.C. § 902(f), (i).

Differences between the permissible operation of presumptions against the accused in criminal cases and in other situations prevent the formulation of a comprehensive definition of the term "presumption," and none is attempted. Nor do these rules purport to deal with problems of the validity of presumptions except insofar as they may be found reflected in the formulation of permissible procedures.

The presumption of innocence is outside the scope of the rule and unaffected by it.

Subdivisions (b) and (c). It is axiomatic that a verdict cannot be directed against the accused in a criminal case, 9 Wigmore § 2495, p. 312, with the corollary that the judge is without authority to direct the jury to find against the accused as to any element of the crime, A.L.I. Model Penal Code § 1.12(1) P.O.D. (1962). Although arguably the judge could direct the jury to find against the accused as to a lesser fact, the tradition is against it, and this rule makes no use of presumptions to remove any matters from final determination by the jury.

The only distinction made among presumptions under this rule is with respect to the measure of proof required in order to justify submission to the jury. If the effect of the presumption is to establish guilt or an element of the crime or to negative a defense, the measure of proof is the one widely accepted by the Courts of Appeals as the standard for measuring the sufficiency of the evidence in passing on motions for directed verdict (now judgment of acquittal): an acquittal should be directed when reasonable jurymen must have a reasonable doubt. Curley v. United States, 81 U.S.App.D.C. 389, 160 F.2d 229 (1947), cert. denied 331 U.S. 837, 67 S.Ct. 1511, 91 L.Ed. 1850; United States v. Honeycutt, 311 F.2d 660 (4th Cir. 1962); Stephens v. United States, 354 F.2d 999 (5th Cir. 1965); Lambert v. United States, 261 F.2d 799 (5th Cir. 1958); United States v. Leggett, 292 F.2d 423 (6th Cir. 1961); Cape v. United States, 283 F.2d 430 (9th Cir. 1960); Cartwright v. United States, 335 F.2d 919 (10th Cir. 1964). Cf. United States v. Gonzales Castro, 228 F.2d 807 (2d Cir. 1956); United States v. Masiello, 235 F.2d 279 (2d Cir. 1956), cert. denied Stickel v. United States, 352 U.S. 882, 77 S.Ct. 100, 1 L.Ed.2d 79; United States v. Feinberg, 140 F.2d 592 (2d Cir. 1944). But cf. United States v. Arcuri, 282 F.Supp. 347 (E.D.N.Y. 1968), aff'd. 405 F.2d 691, cert. denied 395 U.S. 913; United States v. Melillo, 275 F.Supp. 314 (E.D.N.Y. 1968). If the presumption operates upon a lesser aspect of the case than the issue of guilt itself or an element of the crime or negativing a defense, the required measure of proof is the less stringent one of substantial evidence, consistently with the attitude usually taken with respect to particular items of evidence. 9 Wigmore § 2497, p. 324.

The treatment of presumptions in the rule is consistent with United States v. Gainey, 380 U.S. 63, 85 S.Ct. 754, 13 L.Ed.2d 658 (1965), where the matter was considered in depth. After sustaining the validity of the provision of 26 U.S.C. § 5601(b)(2) that presence at the site is sufficient to convict of the offense of carrying on the business of distiller without giving bond, unless the presence is explained to the satisfaction of the jury, the Court turned to procedural considerations and reached several conclusions. The power of the judge to withdraw a case from the jury for insufficiency of evidence is left unimpaired; he may submit the case on the basis of presence alone, but he is not required to do so. Nor is he precluded from rendering judgment notwithstanding the verdict. It is proper to tell the jury about the "statutory inference," if they are told it is not conclusive. The jury may still acquit, even if it finds defendant present and his presence is unexplained. [Compare the mandatory character of the instruction condemned in Bollenbach v. United States, 326 U.S. 607, 66 S.Ct. 402, 90 L.Ed. 350 (1945).] To avoid any implication that the statutory language relative to explanation be taken as directing attention to failure of the accused to testify, the better practice, said the Court, would be to instruct the jury that they may draw the inference unless the evidence provides a satisfactory explanation of defendant's presence, omitting any explicit reference to the statute.

The Final Report of the National Commission on Reform of Federal Criminal Laws § 103(4) and (5) (1971) contains a careful formulation of the consequences of a statutory presumption with an alternative formulation set forth in the Comment thereto, and also of the effect of a prima facie case. In the criminal code there proposed, the terms "presumption" and "prima facie case" are used with precision and with reference to these meanings. In the federal criminal law as it stands today, these terms are not used with precision. Moreover, common law presumptions continue. Hence it is believed that the rule here proposed is better adapted to the present situation until such time as the Congress enacts legislation covering the subject, which the rule takes into account. If the subject of common law presumptions is not covered by legislation, the need for the rule in that regard will continue.

Report of House Committee on the Judiciary

Rule 303, as submitted by the Supreme Court was directed to the issues of when, in criminal cases, a court may submit a presumption to a jury and the type of instruction it should give. The Committee deleted this Rule since the subject of presumptions in criminal cases is addressed in detail in bills now pending before the Committee to revise the federal criminal code. The Committee determined to consider this question in the course of its study of these proposals.

ARTICLE IV. RELEVANCE AND ITS LIMITS

Rule 406. Habit; Routine Practice [Subdivision (b) not enacted.]

(b) Method of proof. Habit or routine practice may be proved by testimony in the form of an opinion or by specific instances of conduct sufficient in number to warrant a finding that the habit existed or that the practice was routine.

Advisory Committee's Note

* * *

Subdivision (b). Permissible methods of proving habit or routine conduct include opinion and specific instances sufficient in number to warrant a finding that the habit or routine practice in fact existed. Opinion evidence must be "rationally based on the perception of the witness" and helpful, under the provisions of Rule 701. Proof by specific instances may be controlled by the overriding provisions of Rule 403 for exclusion on grounds of prejudice, confusion, misleading the jury, or waste of time. Thus the illustrations following A.L.I. Model Code of Evidence Rule 307 suggests the possibility of admitting testimony by W that on numerous occasions he had been with X when X crossed a railroad track and that on each occasion X had first stopped and looked in both directions, but discretion to exclude offers of 10 witnesses, each testifying to a different occasion.

Similar provisions for proof by opinion or specific instances are found in Uniform Rule 50 and Kansas Code of Civil Procedure § 60–450. New Jersey Rule 50 provides for proof by specific instances but is silent as to opinion. The California Evidence Code is silent as to methods of proving habit, presumably proceeding on the theory that any method is relevant and all relevant evidence is admissible unless otherwise provided. Tentative Recommendation and a Study Relating to the Uniform Rules of Evidence (Art. VI. Extrinsic Policies Affecting Admissibility), Rep., Rec. & Study, Cal.Law Rev.Comm'n, 620 (1964).

Report of House Committee on the Judiciary

[Reasons for deleting subdivision (b) are stated in the report, which is set forth in the main text under rule 406, *supra*.]

ARTICLE V. PRIVILEGES

Note by Federal Judicial Center

The 13 rules numbered 501–513 prescribed by the Supreme Court as Article V were replaced by a single rule 501 in the rules enacted by the Congress. The rules are included here for informational purposes only.

Rule 501. Privileges Recognized Only as Provided [Not enacted.]

Except as otherwise required by the Constitution of the United States or provided by Act of Congress, and except as provided in these rules or in other rules adopted by the Supreme Court, no person has a privilege to:

(1)   Refuse to be a witness; or

(2)   Refuse to disclose any matter; or

(3)   Refuse to produce any object or writing; or

(4)   Prevent another from being a witness or disclosing any matter of producing any object or writing.

Advisory Committee's Note

No attempt is made in these rules to incorporate the constitutional provisions which relate to the admission and exclusion of evidence, whether denominated as privileges or not. The grand design of these provisions does not readily lend itself to codification. The final reference must be the provisions themselves and the decisions construing them. Nor is formulating a rule an appropriate means of settling unresolved constitutional questions.

Similarly, privileges created by act of Congress are not within the scope of these rules. These privileges do not assume the form of broad principles; they are the product of resolving particular problems in particular terms. Among them are included such provisions as 13 U.S.C. § 9, generally prohibiting official disclosure of census information and conferring a privileged status on retained copies of census reports; 42 U.S.C. § 2000e–5(a), making inadmissible in evidence anything said or done during Equal Employment Opportunity conciliation proceeding; 42 U.S.C. § 2240, making required reports of incidents by nuclear facility licensees inadmissible in actions for damages; 45 U.S.C. §§ 33, 41, similarly as to reports of accidents by railroads; 49 U.S.C. § 1441(e), declaring C.A.B. accident investigation reports inadmissible in actions for damages. The rule leaves them undisturbed.

The reference to other rules adopted by the Supreme Court makes clear that provisions relating to privilege in those rules will continue in operation. See, for example, the "work product" immunity against discovery spelled out under the Rules of Civil Procedure in Hickman v. Taylor, 329 U.S. 495, 67 S.Ct. 385, 91 L.Ed. 451 (1947), now formalized in revised Rule 26(b)(3) of the Rules of Civil Procedure, and the secrecy of grand jury proceedings provided by Criminal Rule 6.

With respect to privileges created by state law, these rules in some instances grant them greater status than has heretofore been the case by according them recognition in federal criminal proceedings, bankruptcy, and federal question litigation. See Rules 502 and 510. There is, however, no provision generally adopting state-created privileges.

In federal criminal prosecutions the primacy of federal law as to both substance and procedure has been undoubted. See, for example, United States v. Krol, 374 F.2d 776 (7th Cir. 1967), sustaining the admission in a federal prosecution of evidence obtained by electronic eavesdropping, despite a state statute declaring the use of these devices unlawful and evidence obtained therefrom inadmissible. This primacy includes matters of privilege. As stated in 4 Barron, Federal Practice and Procedure § 2151, p. 175 (1951):

"The determination of the question whether a matter is privileged is governed by federal decisions and the state statutes or rules of evidence have no application."

In Funk v. United States, 290 U.S. 371, 54 S.Ct. 212, 78 L.Ed. 369 (1933), the Court had considered the competency of a wife to testify for her husband and concluded that, absent congressional action or direction, the federal courts were to follow the common law as they saw it "in accordance with present day standards of wisdom and justice." And in Wolfle v. United States, 291 U.S. 7, 54 S.Ct. 279, 78 L.Ed. 617 (1934), the Court said with respect to the standard appropriate in determining a claim of privilege for an alleged confidential communication between spouses in a federal criminal prosecution:

"So our decision here, in the absence of Congressional legislation on the subject, is to be controlled by common law principles, not by local statute." *Id.*, 13, 54 S.Ct. at 280.

On the basis of *Funk* and *Wolfle,* the Advisory Committee on Rules of Criminal Procedure formulated Rule 26, which was adopted by the Court. The pertinent part of the rule provided:

"The . . . privileges of witnesses shall be governed, except when an act of Congress or these rules otherwise provide, by the principles of the common law as they may be interpreted . . . in the light of reason and experience."

As regards bankruptcy, section 21(a) of the Bankruptcy Act provides for examination of the bankrupt and his spouse concerning the acts, conduct, or property of the bankrupt. The Act limits examination of the spouse to business transacted by her or to which she is a party but provides "That the spouse may be so examined, any law of the United States or of any State to the contrary notwithstanding." 11 U.S.C. § 44(a). The effect of the quoted language is clearly to override any conflicting state rule of incompetency or privilege against spousal testimony. A fair reading would also indicate an overriding of any contrary state rule of privileged confidential spousal communications. Its validity has never been questioned and seems most unlikely to be. As to other privileges, the suggestion has been made that state law applies, though with little citation of authority, 2 Moore's Collier on Bankruptcy ¶ 21.13, p. 297 (14th ed. 1961). This position seems to be contrary to the expression of the Court in McCarthy v. Arndstein, 266 U.S. 34, 39, 45 S.Ct. 16, 69 L.Ed. 158 (1924), which speaks in the pattern of Rule 26 of the Federal Rules of Criminal Procedure:

"There is no provision [in the Bankruptcy Act] prescribing the rules by which the examination is to be governed. These are, impliedly, the general rules governing the admissibility of evidence and the competency and compellability of witnesses."

With respect to federal question litigation, the supremacy of federal law may be less clear, yet indications that state privileges are inapplicable preponderate in the circuits. In re Albert Lindley Lee Memorial Hospital, 209 F.2d 122 (2d Cir. 1953), cert. denied Cincotta v. United States, 347 U.S. 960, 74 S.Ct. 709, 98 L.Ed. 1104; Colton v. United States, 306 F.2d 633 (2d Cir. 1962); Falsone v. United States, 205 F.2d 734 (5th Cir. 1953); Fraser v. United States, 145 F.2d 139 (6th Cir. 1944), cert. denied 324 U.S. 849, 65 S.Ct. 684, 89 L.Ed. 1409; United States v. Brunner, 200 F.2d 276 (6th Cir. 1952). *Contra,* Baird v. Koerner, 279 F.2d 623 (9th Cir. 1960). Additional decisions of district courts are collected in Annot., 95 A.L.R.2d 320, 336. While a number of the cases arise from administrative income tax investigations, they nevertheless support the broad proposition of the inapplicability of state privileges in federal proceedings.

In view of these considerations, it is apparent that, to the extent that they accord state privileges standing in federal criminal cases, bankruptcy, and federal question cases, the rules go beyond what previously has been thought necessary or proper.

On the other hand, in diversity cases, or perhaps more accurately cases in which state law furnishes the rule of decision, the rules avoid giving state privileges the effect which substantial authority has thought necessary and proper. Regardless of what might once have been thought to be the command of Erie R. Co. v. Tompkins, 304 U.S. 64, 58 S.Ct. 817, 82 L.Ed. 1188 (1938), as to observance of state created privileges in diversity cases, Hanna v. Plumer, 380 U.S. 460, 85 S.Ct. 1136, 14 L.Ed.2d 8 (1965), is believed to locate the problem in the area of choice rather than necessity. Wright, Procedural Reform: Its Limitations and Its Future, 1 Ga.L.Rev. 563, 572–573 (1967). Contra, Republic Gear Co. v. Borg-Warner Corp., 381 F.2d 551, 555, n. 2 (2d Cir. 1967), and see authorities there cited. Hence all significant policy factors need to be considered in order that the choice may be a wise one.

The arguments advanced in favor of recognizing state privileges are: a state privilege is an essential characteristic of a relationship or status created by state law and thus is substantive in the *Erie* sense; state policy ought not to be frustrated by the accident of diversity; the allowance or denial of a privilege is so likely to affect the outcome of litigation as to encourage forum selection on that basis, not a proper function of diversity jurisdiction. There are persuasive answers to these arguments.

(1)   As to the question of "substance," it is true that a privilege commonly represents an aspect of a relationship created and defined by a State. For example, a confidential communications privilege is often an incident of marriage. However, in litigation involving the relationship itself, the privilege is not ordinarily one of the issues. In fact, statutes frequently make the communication privilege inapplicable in cases of divorce. McCormick § 88, p. 177. The same is true with respect to the attorney-client privilege when the parties to the relationship have a falling out. The reality of the matter is that privilege is called into operation, not when the relation giving rise to the privilege is being litigated, but when the litigation involves something substantively devoid of relation to the privilege. The appearance of privilege in the case is quite by accident, and its effect is to block off the tribunal from a source of information. Thus its real impact is on the method of proof in the case, and in comparison any substantive aspect appears tenuous.

(2)   By most standards, criminal prosecutions are attended by more serious consequences than civil litigation, and it must be evident that the criminal area has the greatest sensitivity where privilege is concerned. Nevertheless, as previously noted, state privileges traditionally have given way in federal criminal prosecutions. If a privilege is denied in the area of greatest sensitivity, it tends to become illusory as a significant aspect of the relationship out of which it arises. For example, in a state having by statute an accountant's privilege, only the most imperceptible added force would be given the privilege by putting the accountant in a position to assure his client that, while he could not block disclosure in a federal criminal prosecution, he could do so in diversity cases as well as in state court proceedings. Thus viewed, state interest in privilege appears less substantial than at first glance might seem to be the case.

Moreover, federal interest is not lacking. It can scarcely be contended that once diversity is invoked the federal government no longer has a legitimate concern in the quality of judicial administration conducted under its aegis. The demise of conformity and the adoption of the Federal Rules of Civil Procedure stand as witness to the contrary.

(3)   A large measure of forum shopping is recognized as legitimate in the American judicial system. Subject to the limitations of jurisdiction and the relatively modest controls imposed by venue provisions and the doctrine of forum non conveniens, plaintiffs are allowed in general a free choice of forum. Diversity jurisdiction has as its basic purpose the giving of a choice, not only to plaintiffs but, in removal situations, also to defendants. In principle, the basis of the choice is the supposed need to escape from local prejudice. If the choice were tightly confined to that basis, then complete conformity to local procedure as well as substantive law would be required. This, of course, is not the case, and the choice may in fact be influenced by a wide range of factors. As Dean Ladd has pointed out, a litigant may select the federal court "because of the federal procedural rules, the liberal discovery provisions, the quality of jurors expected in the federal court, the respect held for federal judges, the control of federal judges over a trial, the summation and comment upon the weight of evidence by the judge, or the authority to grant a new trial if the judge regards the verdict against the weight of the evidence." Ladd, Privileges, 1969 Ariz.St.L.J. 555, 564. Present Rule 43(a) of the Civil Rules specifies a broader range of admissibility in federal than in state courts and makes no exception for diversity cases. Note should also be taken that Rule 26(b)(2) of the Rules of Civil Procedure, as revised, allows discovery to be had of liability insurance, without regard to local state law upon the subject.

When attention is directed to the practical dimensions of the problem, they are found not to be great. The privileges affected are few in number. Most states provide a physician-patient privilege; the proposed rules limit the privilege to a psychotherapist-patient relationship. See Advisory Committee's Note to Rule 504. The area of marital privilege under the proposed rules is narrower than in most states. See Rule 505. Some states recognize privileges for journalists and accountants; the proposed rules do not.

Physician-patient is the most widely recognized privilege not found in the proposed rules. As a practical matter it was largely eliminated in diversity cases when Rule 35 of the Rules of Civil Procedure became effective in 1938. Under that rule, a party physically examined pursuant to court order, by requesting and obtaining a copy of the report or by taking the deposition of the examiner, waives any privilege regarding the testimony of every other person who has examined him in respect of the same condition. While waiver may be avoided by neither requesting the report nor taking the examiner's deposition, the price is one which most litigant-patients are probably not prepared to pay.

Rule 502. Required Reports Privileged by Statute [Not enacted.]

A person, corporation, association, or other organization or entity, either public or private, making a return or report required by law to be made has a privilege to refuse to disclose and to prevent any other person from disclosing the return or report, if the law requiring it to be made so provides. A public officer or agency to whom a return or report is required by law to be made has a privilege to refuse to disclose the return or report if the law requiring it to be made so provides. No privilege exists under this rule in actions involving perjury, false statements, fraud in the return or report, or other failure to comply with the law in question.

Advisory Committee's Note

Statutes which require the making of returns or reports sometimes confer on the reporting party a privilege against disclosure, commonly coupled with a prohibition against disclosure by the officer to whom the report is made. Some of the federal statutes of this kind are mentioned in the Advisory Committee's Note to Rule 501, *supra. See also* the Note to Rule 402, *supra.* A provision against disclosure may be included in a statute for a variety of reasons, the chief of which are probably assuring the validity of the statute against claims of self-incrimination, honoring the privilege against self-incrimination, and encouraging the furnishing of the required information by assuring privacy.

These statutes, both state and federal, may generally be assumed to embody policies of significant dimension. Rule 501 insulates the federal provisions against disturbance by these rules; the present rule reiterates a result commonly specified in federal statutes and extends its application to state statutes of similar character. Illustrations of the kinds of returns and reports contemplated by the rule appear in the cases, in which a reluctance to compel disclosure is manifested. In re Reid, 155 F. 933 (E.D.Mich. 1906), assessor not compelled to produce bankrupt's property tax return in view of statute forbidding disclosure; In re Valecia Condensed Milk Co., 240 F. 310 (7th Cir. 1917), secretary of state tax commission not compelled to produce bankrupt's income tax returns in violation of statute; Herman Bros. Pet Supply, Inc. v. N.L.R.B., 360 F.2d 176 (6th Cir. 1966), subpoena denied for production of reports to state employment security commission prohibited by statute, in proceeding for back wages. And see the discussion of motor vehicle accident reports in Krizak v. W.C. Brooks & Sons, Inc., 320 F.2d 37, 42–43 (4th Cir. 1963). Cf. In re Hines, 69 F.2d 52 (2d Cir. 1934).

Rule 503. Lawyer-Client Privilege [Not enacted.]

(a) Definitions. As used in this rule:

(1) A "client" is a person, public officer, or corporation, association, or other organization or entity, either public or private, who is rendered professional legal services by a lawyer, or who consults a lawyer with a view to obtaining professional legal services from him.

(2) A "lawyer" is a person authorized, or reasonably believed by the client to be authorized, to practice law in any state or nation.

(3) A "representative of the lawyer" is one employed to assist the lawyer in the rendition of professional legal services.

(4) A communication is "confidential" if not intended to be disclosed to third persons other than those to whom disclosure is in furtherance of the rendition of professional legal services to the client or those reasonably necessary for the transmission of the communication.

(b) General rule of privilege. A client has a privilege to refuse to disclose and to prevent any other person from disclosing confidential communications made for the purpose of facilitating the rendition of professional legal services to the client, (1) between himself or his representative and his lawyer or his lawyer's representative, or (2) between his lawyer and the lawyer's representative, or (3) by him or his lawyer to a lawyer representing another in a matter of common interest, or (4) between representatives of the client or between the client and a representative of the client, or (5) between lawyers representing the client.

(c) Who may claim the privilege. The privilege may be claimed by the client, his guardian or conservator, the personal representative of a deceased client, or the successor, trustee, or similar representative of a corporation, association, or other organization, whether or not in existence. The person who was the lawyer at the time of the communication may claim the privilege but only on behalf of the client. His authority to do so is presumed in the absence of evidence to the contrary.

(d) Exceptions. There is no privilege under this rule:

(1) *Furtherance of crime or fraud.* If the services of the lawyer were sought or obtained to enable or aid anyone to commit or plan to commit what the client knew or reasonably should have known to be a crime or fraud; or

(2) *Claimants through same deceased client.* As to a communication relevant to an issue between parties who claim through the same deceased client, regardless of whether the claims are by testate or intestate succession or by *inter vivos* transaction; or

(3) *Breach of duty by lawyer or client.* As to a communication relevant to an issue of breach of duty by the lawyer to his client or by the client to his lawyer; or

(4) *Document attested by lawyer.* As to a communication relevant to an issue concerning an attested document to which the lawyer is an attesting witness; or

(5) *Joint clients.* As to a communication relevant to a matter of common interest between two or more clients if the communication was made by any of them to a lawyer retained or consulted in common, when offered in an action between any of the clients.

Advisory Committee's Note

Subdivision (a). (1) The definition of "client" includes governmental bodies, Connecticut Mutual Life Ins. Co. v. Shields, 18 F.R.D. 448 (S.D.N.Y. 1955); People ex rel. Department of Public Works v. Glen Arms Estate, Inc., 230 Cal.App.2d 841, 41 Cal.Rptr. 303 (1965); Rowley v. Ferguson, 48 N.E.2d 243 (Ohio App. 1942); and corporations, Radiant Burners, Inc. v. American Gas Assn., 320 F.2d 314 (7th Cir. 1963). *Contra,* Gardner, A Personal Privilege for Communications of Corporate Clients—Paradox or Public Policy, 40 U.Det.L.J. 299, 323, 376 (1963). The definition also extends the status of client to one consulting a lawyer preliminarily with a view to retaining him, even though actual employment does not result. McCormick, § 92, p. 184. The client need not be involved in litigation; the rendition of legal service or advice under any circumstances suffices. 8 Wigmore § 2294 (McNaughton Rev. 1961). The services must be professional legal services; purely business or personal matters do not qualify. McCormick § 92, p. 184.

The rule contains no definition of "representative of the client." In the opinion of the Advisory Committee, the matter is better left to resolution by decision on a case-by-case basis. The most restricted position is the "control group" test, limiting the category to persons with authority to seek and act upon legal advice for the client. *See, e.g.,* City of Philadelphia v. Westinghouse Electric Corp., 210 F.Supp. 483 (E.D.Pa. 1962), mandamus and prohibition denied *sub nom.* General Electric Co. v. Kirkpatrick, 312 F.2d 742 (3d Cir.), cert. denied 372 U.S. 943; Garrison v. General Motors Corp., 213 F.Supp. 515 (S.D.Cal. 1963); Hogan v. Zletz, 43 F.R.D. 308 (N.D.Okla. 1967), aff'd *sub nom.* Natta v. Hogan, 392 F.2d 686 (10th Cir. 1968); Day v. Illinois Power Co., 50 Ill.App.2d 52, 199 N.E.2d 802 (1964). Broader formulations are found in other decisions. *See, e.g.,* United States v. United Shoe Machinery Corp., 89 F.Supp. 357 (D.Mass. 1950); Zenith Radio Corp. v. Radio Corp. of America, 121 F.Supp. 792 (D.Del. 1954); Harper & Row Publishers, Inc. v. Decker, 423 F.2d 487 (7th Cir. 1970), aff'd without opinion by equally divided court 400 U.S. 955 (1971), reh. denied 401 U.S. 950; D.I. Chadbourne, Inc. v. Superior Court, 60 Cal.2d 723, 36 Cal.Rptr. 468, 388 P.2d 700 (1964). Cf. Rucker v. Wabash R. Co., 418 F.2d 146 (7th Cir. 1969). *See generally,* Simon, The Attorney-Client Privilege as Applied to Corporations, 65 Yale L.J. 953, 956–966 (1956); Note, Attorney-Client Privilege for Corporate Clients: The Control Group Test, 84 Harv.L.Rev. 424 (1970).

The status of employees who are used in the process of communicating, as distinguished from those who are parties to the communication, is treated in paragraph (4) of subdivision (a) of the rule.

(2) A "lawyer" is a person licensed to practice law in any state or nation. There is no requirement that the licensing state or nation recognize the attorney-client privilege, thus avoiding excursions into conflict of laws questions. "Lawyer" also includes a person reasonably believed to be a lawyer. For similar provisions, see California Evidence Code § 950.

(3) The definition of "representative of the lawyer" recognizes that the lawyer may, in rendering legal services, utilize the services of assistants in addition to those employed in the process of communicating. Thus the definition includes an expert employed to assist in rendering legal advice. United States v. Kovel, 296 F.2d 918 (2d Cir. 1961) (accountant). Cf. Himmelfarb v. United States, 175 F.2d 924 (9th Cir. 1949). It also includes an expert employed to assist in the planning and conduct of litigation, though not one employed to testify as a witness. Lalance & Grosjean Mfg. Co. v. Haberman Mfg. Co., 87 F. 563 (S.D.N.Y. 1898), and see revised Civil Rule 26(b)(4). The definition does not, however, limit "representative of the lawyer" to experts. Whether his compensation is derived immediately from the lawyer or the client is not material.

(4)   The requisite confidentiality of communication is defined in terms of intent. A communication made in public or meant to be relayed to outsiders or which is divulged by the client to third persons can scarcely be considered confidential. McCormick § 95. The intent is inferable from the circumstances. Unless intent to disclose is apparent, the attorney-client communication is confidential. Taking or failing to take precautions may be considered as bearing on intent.

Practicality requires that some disclosure be allowed beyond the immediate circle of lawyer-client and their representatives without impairing confidentiality. Hence the definition allows disclosure to persons "to whom disclosure is in furtherance of the rendition of professional legal services to the client," contemplating those in such relation to the client as "spouse, parent, business associate, or joint client." Comment, California Evidence Code § 952.

Disclosure may also be made to persons "reasonably necessary for the transmission of the communication," without loss of confidentiality.

Subdivision (b) sets forth the privilege, using the previously defined terms: client, lawyer, representative of the lawyer, and confidential communication.

Substantial authority has in the past allowed the eavesdropper to testify to overheard privileged conversations and has admitted intercepted privileged letters. Today, the evolution of more sophisticated techniques of eavesdropping and interception calls for abandonment of this position. The rule accordingly adopts a policy of protection against these kinds of invasion of the privilege.

The privilege extends to communications (1) between client or his representative and lawyer or his representative, (2) between lawyer and lawyer's representative, (3) by client or his lawyer to a lawyer representing another in a matter of common interest, (4) between representatives of the client or the client and a representative of the client, and (5) between lawyers representing the client. All these communications must be specifically for the purpose of obtaining legal services for the client; otherwise the privilege does not attach.

The third type of communication occurs in the "joint defense" or "pooled information" situation, where different lawyers represent clients who have some interests in common. In Chahoon v. Commonwealth, 62 Va. 822 (1871), the court said that the various clients might have retained one attorney to represent all; hence everything said at a joint conference was privileged, and one of the clients could prevent another from disclosing what the other had himself said. The result seems to be incorrect in overlooking a frequent reason for retaining different attorneys by the various clients, namely actually or potentially conflicting interests in addition to the common interest which brings them together. The needs of these cases seem better to be met by allowing each client a privilege as to his own statements. Thus if all resist disclosure, none will occur. Continental Oil Co. v. United States, 330 F.2d 347 (9th Cir. 1964). But, if for reasons of his own, a client wishes to disclose his own statements made at the joint conference, he should be permitted to do so, and the rule is to that effect. The rule does not apply to situations where there is no common interest to be promoted by a joint consultation, and the parties meet on a purely adversary basis. Vance v. State, 190 Tenn. 521, 230 S.W.2d 987 (1950), cert. denied 339 U.S. 988, 70 S.Ct. 1010, 94 L.Ed. 1389. Cf. Hunydee v. United States, 355 F.2d 183 (9th Cir. 1965).

Subdivision (c). The privilege is, of course, that of the client, to be claimed by him or by his personal representative. The successor of a dissolved corporate client may claim the privilege. California Evidence Code § 953; New Jersey Evidence Rule 26(1). *Contra,* Uniform Rule 26(1).

The lawyer may not claim the privilege on his own behalf. However, he may claim it on behalf of the client. It is assumed that the ethics of the profession will require him to do so except under most unusual circumstances. American Bar

Association, Canons of Professional Ethics, Canon 37. His authority to make the claim is presumed unless there is evidence to the contrary, as would be the case if the client were now a party to litigation in which the question arose and were represented by other counsel. Ex parte Lipscomb, 111 Tex. 409, 239 S.W. 1101 (1922).

Subdivision (d) in general incorporates well established exceptions.

(1) The privilege does not extend to advice in aid of future wrongdoing. 8 Wigmore § 2298 (McNaughton Rev. 1961). The wrongdoing need not be that of the client. The provision that the client knew or reasonably should have known of the criminal or fraudulent nature of the act is designed to protect the client who is erroneously advised that a proposed action is within the law. No preliminary finding that sufficient evidence aside from the communication has been introduced to warrant a finding that the services were sought to enable the commission of a wrong is required. Cf. Clark v. United States, 289 U.S. 1, 15–16, 53 S.Ct. 465, 77 L.Ed. 993 (1933); Uniform Rule 26(2)(a). While any general exploration of what transpired between attorney and client would, of course, be inappropriate, it is wholly feasible, either at the discovery stage or during trial, so to focus the inquiry by specific questions as to avoid any broad inquiry into attorney-client communications. Numerous cases reflect this approach.

(2) Normally the privilege survives the death of the client and may be asserted by his representative. Subdivision (c), *supra*. When, however, the identity of the person who steps into the client's shoes is in issue, as in a will contest, the identity of the person entitled to claim the privilege remains undetermined until the conclusion of the litigation. The choice is thus between allowing both sides or neither to assert the privilege, with authority and reason favoring the latter view. McCormick § 98; Uniform Rule 26(2)(b); California Evidence Code § 957; Kansas Code of Civil Procedure § 60–426(b)(2); New Jersey Evidence Rule 26(2)(b).

(3) The exception is required by considerations of fairness and policy when questions arise out of dealings between attorney and client, as in cases of controversy over attorney's fees, claims of inadequacy of representation, or charges of professional misconduct. McCormick § 95; Uniform Rule 26(2)(c); California Evidence Code § 958; Kansas Code of Civil Procedure § 60–426(b)(3); New Jersey Evidence Rule 26(2)(c).

(4) When the lawyer acts as attesting witness, the approval of the client to his so doing may safely be assumed, and waiver of the privilege as to any relevant lawyer-client communications is a proper result. McCormick § 92, p. 184; Uniform Rule 26(2)(d); California Evidence Code § 959; Kansas Code of Civil Procedure § 60–426(b)(d) [*sic*].

(5) The subdivision states existing law. McCormick § 95, pp. 192–193. For similar provisions, see Uniform Rule 26(2)(e); California Evidence Code § 962; Kansas Code of Civil Procedure § 60–426(b)(4); New Jersey Evidence Rule 26(2). The situation with which this provision deals is to be distinguished from the case of clients with a common interest who retain different lawyers. See subdivision (b)(3) of this rule, *supra*.

Rule 504. Psychotherapist-Patient Privilege [Not enacted.]

(a) Definitions.

(1)   A "patient" is a person who consults or is examined or interviewed by a psychotherapist.

(2)   A "psychotherapist" is (A) a person authorized to practice medicine in any state or nation, or reasonably believed by the patient so to be, while engaged in the diagnosis or treatment of a mental or emotional condition, including drug addiction, or (B) a person licensed or certified as a psychologist under the laws of any state or nation, while similarly engaged.

(3)   A communication is "confidential" if not intended to be disclosed to third persons other than those present to further the interest of the patient in the consultation, examination, or interview, or persons reasonably necessary for the transmission of the communication, or persons who are participating in the diagnosis and treatment under the direction of the psychotherapist, including members of the patient's family.

(b) General rule of privilege.
A patient has a privilege to refuse to disclose and to prevent any other person from disclosing confidential communications, made for the purposes of diagnosis or treatment of his mental or emotional condition, including drug addiction, among himself, his psychotherapist, or persons who are participating in the diagnosis or treatment under the direction of the psychotherapist, including members of the patient's family.

(c) Who may claim the privilege.
The privilege may be claimed by the patient, by his guardian or conservator, or by the personal representative of a deceased patient. The person who was the psychotherapist may claim the privilege but only on behalf of the patient. His authority so to do is presumed in the absence of evidence to the contrary.

(d) Exceptions.

(1)   *Proceedings for hospitalization.* There is no privilege under this rule for communications relevant to an issue in proceedings to hospitalize the patient for mental illness, if the psychotherapist in the course of diagnosis or treatment has determined that the patient is in need of hospitalization.

(2)   *Examination by order of judge.* If the judge orders an examination of the mental or emotional condition of the patient, communications made in the course thereof are not privileged under this rule with respect to the particular purpose for which the examination is ordered unless the judge orders otherwise.

(3)   *Condition an element of claim or defense.* There is no privilege under this rule as to communications relevant to an issue of the mental or emotional condition of the patient in any proceeding in which he relies upon the condition as an element of his claim or defense, or, after the patient's death, in any proceeding in which any party relies upon the condition as an element of his claim or defense.

Advisory Committee's Note

The rules contain no provision for a general physician-patient privilege. While many states have by statute created the privilege, the exceptions which have been found necessary in order to obtain information required by the public interest or to avoid fraud are so numerous as to leave little if any basis for the privilege. Among the exclusions from the statutory privilege, the following may be enumerated; communications not made for purposes of diagnosis and treatment; commitment and restoration proceedings; issues as to wills or otherwise between parties claiming by succession from the patient; actions on insurance policies; required reports (venereal diseases, gunshot wounds, child abuse); communications in furtherance of crime or fraud; mental or physical condition put in issue by patient (personal injury cases); malpractice actions; and some or all criminal prosecutions. California, for example, excepts cases in which the patient puts his condition in issue, all criminal proceedings, will and similar contests, malpractice cases, and disciplinary proceedings, as well as certain other situations, thus leaving virtually nothing covered by the privilege. California Evidence Code §§ 990–1007. For other illustrative statutes see Ill.Rev.Stat. 1967, c. 51, § 5.1; N.Y.C.P.L.R. § 4504; N.C.Gen.Stat. 1953, § 8–53. Moreover, the possibility of compelling gratuitous disclosure by the physician is foreclosed by his standing to raise the question of relevancy. See Note on "Official Information" Privilege following Rule 509, *infra*.

The doubts attendant upon the general physician-patient privilege are not present when the relationship is that of psychotherapist and patient. While the common law recognized no general physician-patient privilege, it had indicated a disposition to recognize a psychotherapist-patient privilege, Note, Confidential Communications to a Psychotherapist: A New Testimonial Privilege, 47 Nw.U.L.Rev. 384 (1952), when legislatures began moving into the field.

The case for the privilege is convincingly stated in Report No. 45, Group for the Advancement of Psychiatry 92 (1960):

"Among physicians, the psychiatrist has a special need to maintain confidentiality. His capacity to help his patients is completely dependent upon their willingness and ability to talk freely. This makes it difficult if not impossible for him to function without being able to assure his patients of confidentiality and, indeed, privileged communication. Where there may be exceptions to this general rule * * *, there is wide agreement that confidentiality is a *sine qua non* for successful psychiatric treatment. The relationship may well be likened to that of the priest-penitent or the lawyer-client. Psychiatrists not only explore the very depths of their patients' conscious, but their unconscious feelings and attitudes as well. Therapeutic effectiveness necessitates going beyond a patient's awareness and, in order to do this, it must be possible to communicate freely. A threat to secrecy blocks successful treatment."

A much more extended exposition of the case for the privilege is made in Slovenko, Psychiatry and a Second Look at the Medical Privilege, 6 Wayne L.Rev. 175, 184 (1960), quoted extensively in the careful Tentative Recommendation and Study Relating to the Uniform Rules of Evidence (Article V. Privileges), Cal.Law Rev.Comm'n, 417 (1964). The conclusion is reached that Wigmore's four conditions needed to justify the existence of a privilege are amply satisfied.

Illustrative statutes are Cal.Evidence Code §§ 1010–1026; Ga.Code § 38–418 (1961 Supp.); Conn.Gen.Stat., § 52–146a (1966 Supp.); Ill.Rev.Stat. 1967, c. 51, § 5.2.

While many of the statutes simply place the communications on the same basis as those between attorney and client, 8 Wigmore § 2286, n. 23 (McNaughton Rev. 1961), basic differences between the two relationships forbid resorting to attorney-client save as a helpful point of departure. Goldstein and Katz, Psychiatrist-Patient Privilege: The GAP Proposal and the Connecticut Statute, 36 Conn.B.J. 175, 182 (1962).

Subdivision (a). (1) The definition of patient does not include a person submitting to examination for scientific purposes. Cf. Cal.Evidence Code § 1101. Attention is directed to 42 U.S.C. 242a(2), as amended by the Drug Abuse and Control Act of 1970, P.L. 91–513, authorizing the Secretary of Health, Education, and Welfare to withhold the identity of persons who are the subjects of research on the use and effect of drugs. The rule would leave this provision in full force. See Rule 501.

(2)   The definition of psychotherapist embraces a medical doctor while engaged in the diagnosis or treatment of mental or emotional conditions, including drug addiction, in order not to exclude the general practitioner and to avoid the making of needless refined distinctions concerning what is and what is not the practice of psychiatry. The requirement that the psychologist be in fact licensed, and not merely be believed to be so, is believed to be justified by the number of persons, other than psychiatrists, purporting to render psychotherapeutic aid and the variety of their theories. Cal.Law Rev.Comm'n, *supra,* at pp. 434–437.

The clarification of mental or emotional condition as including drug addiction is consistent with current approaches to drug abuse problems. *See, e.g.,* the definition of "drug dependent person" in 42 U.S.C. 201(q), added by the Drug Abuse Prevention and Control Act of 1970, P.L. 91–513.

(3)   Confidential communication is defined in terms conformable with those of the lawyer-client privilege. Rule 503(a)(4), *supra,* with changes appropriate to the difference in circumstance.

Subdivisions (b) and (c). The lawyer-client rule is drawn upon for the phrasing of the general rule of privilege and the determination of those who may claim it. See Rule 503(b) and (c).

The specific inclusion of communications made for the diagnosis and treatment of drug addiction recognizes the continuing contemporary concern with rehabilitation of drug dependent persons and is designed to implement that policy by encouraging persons in need thereof to seek assistance. The provision is in harmony with Congressional actions in this area. See 42 U.S.C. § 260, providing for voluntary hospitalization of addicts or persons with drug dependence problems and prohibiting use of evidence of admission or treatment in any proceeding against him, and 42 U.S.C. § 3419 providing that in voluntary or involuntary commitment of addicts the results of any hearing, examination, test, or procedure used to determine addiction shall not be used against the patient in any criminal proceeding.

Subdivision (d). The exceptions differ substantially from those of the attorney-client privilege, as a result of the basic differences in the relationships. While it has been argued convincingly that the nature of the psychotherapist-patient relationship demands complete security against legally coerced disclosure in all circumstances, Louisell, The Psychologist in Today's Legal World: Part II, 41 Minn.L.Rev. 731, 746 (1957), the committee of psychiatrists and lawyers who drafted the Connecticut statute concluded that in three instances the need for disclosure was sufficiently great to justify the risk of possible impairment of the relationship. Goldstein and Katz, Psychiatrist-Patient Privilege: The GAP Proposal and the Connecticut Statute, 36 Conn.B.J. 175 (1962). These three exceptions are incorporated in the present rule.

(1)   The interests of both patient and public call for a departure from confidentiality in commitment proceedings. Since disclosure is authorized only when the psychotherapist determines that hospitalization is needed, control over disclosure is placed largely in the hands of a person in whom the patient has already manifested confidence. Hence damage to the relationship is unlikely.

(2)   In a court ordered examination, the relationship is likely to be an arm's length one, though not necessarily so. In any event, an exception is necessary for the effective utilization of this important and growing procedure. The exception, it will be observed, deals with a court ordered examination rather than with a court appointed psychotherapist. Also, the exception is effective only with respect to the particular purpose for which the examination is ordered. The rule thus

conforms with the provisions of 18 U.S.C. § 4244 that no statement made by the accused in the course of an examination into competency to stand trial is admissible on the issue of guilt and of 42 U.S.C. § 3420 that a physician conducting an examination in a drug addiction commitment proceeding is a competent and compellable witness.

(3)   By injecting his condition into litigation, the patient must be said to waive the privilege, in fairness and to avoid abuses. Similar considerations prevail after the patient's death.

––––––––––––

Rule 505. Husband-Wife Privilege [Not enacted.]

(a) **General rule of privilege.** An accused in a criminal proceeding has a privilege to prevent his spouse from testifying against him.

(b) **Who may claim the privilege.** The privilege may be claimed by the accused or by the spouse on his behalf. The authority of the spouse to do so is presumed in the absence of evidence to the contrary.

(c) **Exceptions.** There is no privilege under this rule (1) in proceedings in which one spouse is charged with a crime against the person or property of the other or of a child of either, or with a crime against the person or property of a third person committed in the course of committing a crime against the other, or (2) as to matters occurring prior to the marriage, or (3) in proceedings in which a spouse is charged with importing an alien for prostitution or other immoral purpose in violation of 8 U.S.C. § 1328, with transporting a female in interstate commerce for immoral purposes or other offense in violation of 18 U.S.C. §§ 2421–2424, or with violation of other similar statutes.

Advisory Committee's Note

Subdivision (a). Rules of evidence have evolved around the marriage relationship in four respects: (1) incompetency of one spouse to testify for the other; (2) privilege of one spouse not to testify against the other; (3) privilege of one spouse not to have the other testify against him; and (4) privilege against disclosure of confidential communications between spouses, sometimes extended to information learned by virtue of the existence of the relationship. Today these matters are largely governed by statutes.

With the disappearance of the disqualification of parties and interested persons, the basis for spousal incompetency no longer existed, and it, too, virtually disappeared in both civil and criminal actions. Usually reached by statute, this result was reached for federal courts by the process of decision. Funk v. United States, 290 U.S. 371, 54 S.Ct. 212, 78 L.Ed. 369 (1933). These rules contain no recognition of incompetency of one spouse to testify for the other.

While some 10 jurisdictions recognize a privilege not to testify against one's spouse in a criminal case, and a much smaller number do so in civil cases, the great majority recognizes no privilege on the part of the testifying spouse, and this is the position taken by the rule. Compare Wyatt v. United States, 362 U.S. 525, 80 S.Ct. 901, 4 L.Ed.2d 931 (1960), a Mann Act prosecution in which the wife was the victim. The majority opinion held that she could not claim privilege and was compellable to testify. The holding was narrowly based: The Mann Act presupposed that the women with whom it dealt had no independent wills of their own, and this legislative judgment precluded allowing a victim-wife an option whether to testify, lest the policy of the statute be defeated. A vigorous dissent took the view that nothing in the Mann Act required departure from usual doctrine, which was conceived to be one of allowing the injured party to claim or waive privilege.

About 30 jurisdictions recognize a privilege of an accused in a criminal case to prevent his or her spouse from testifying. It is believed to represent the one aspect of marital privilege the continuation of which is warranted. In Hawkins v. United States, 358 U.S. 74, 79 S.Ct. 136, 3 L.Ed.2d 125 (1958) it was sustained. Cf. McCormick § 66; 8 Wigmore § 2228 (McNaughton Rev. 1961): Comment, Uniform Rule 23(2).

The rule recognizes no privilege for confidential communications. The traditional justifications for privileges not to testify against a spouse and not to be testified against by one's spouse have been the prevention of marital dissension and the repugnancy of requiring a person to condemn or be condemned by his spouse. 8 Wigmore §§ 2228, 2241 (McNaughton Rev. 1961). These considerations bear no relevancy to marital communications. Nor can it be assumed that marital conduct will be affected by a privilege for confidential communications of whose existence the parties in all likelihood are unaware. The other communication privileges, by way of contrast, have as one party a professional person who can be expected to inform the other of the existence of the privilege. Moreover, the relationships from which those privileges arise are essentially and almost exclusively verbal in nature, quite unlike marriage. See Hutchins and Slesinger, Some Observations on the Law of Evidence: Family Relations, 13 Minn.L.Rev. 675 (1929). Cf. McCormick § 90; 8 Wigmore § 2337 (McNaughton Rev. 1961).

The parties are not spouses if the marriage was a sham, Lutwak v. United States, 344 U.S. 604 (1953), or they have been divorced, Barsky v. United States, 339 F.2d 180 (9th Cir. 1964), and therefore the privilege is not applicable.

Subdivision (b). This provision is a counterpart of Rules 503(c), 504(c), and 506(c). Its purpose is to provide a procedure for preventing the taking of the spouse's testimony notably in grand jury proceedings, when the accused is absent and does not know that a situation appropriate for a claim of privilege is presented. If the privilege is not claimed by the spouse, the protection of Rule 512 is available.

Subdivision (c) contains three exceptions to the privilege against spousal testimony in criminal cases.

(1)   The need of limitation upon the privilege in order to avoid grave injustice in cases of offenses against the other spouse or a child of either can scarcely be denied. 8 Wigmore § 2239 (McNaughton Rev. 1961). The rule therefore disallows any privilege against spousal testimony in these cases and in this respect is in accord with the result reached in Wyatt v. United States, 362 U.S. 525, 80 S.Ct. 901, 4 L.Ed.2d 931 (1960), a Mann Act prosecution, denying the accused the privilege of excluding his wife's testimony, since she was the woman who was transported for immoral purposes.

(2)   The second exception renders the privilege inapplicable as to matters occurring prior to the marriage. This provision eliminates the possibility of suppressing testimony by marrying the witness.

(3)   The third exception continues and expands established Congressional policy. In prosecutions for importing aliens for immoral purposes, Congress has specifically denied the accused any privilege not to have his spouse testify against him. 8 U.S.C. § 1328. No provision of this nature is included in the Mann Act, and in Hawkins v. United States, 358 U.S. 74, 79 S.Ct. 136, 3 L.Ed.2d 125 (1958), the conclusion was reached that the common law privilege continued. Consistency requires similar results in the two situations. The rule adopts the Congressional approach, as based upon a more realistic appraisal of the marriage relationship in cases of this kind, in preference to the specific result in *Hawkins*. Note the common law treatment of pimping and sexual offenses with third persons as exceptions to marital privilege. 8 Wigmore § 2239 (McNaughton Rev. 1961).

With respect to bankruptcy proceedings, the smallness of the area of spousal privilege under the rule and the general inapplicability of privileges created by state law render unnecessary any special provision for examination of the spouse of the bankrupt, such as that now contained in section 21(a) of the Bankruptcy Act. 11 U.S.C. § 44(a).

For recent statutes and rules dealing with husband-wife privileges, see California Evidence Code §§ 970–973, 980–987; Kansas Code of Civil Procedure §§ 60–423(b), 60–428; New Jersey Evidence Rules 23(2), 28.

Rule 506. Communications to Clergymen [Not enacted.]

(a) Definitions. As used in this rule:

(1) A "clergyman" is a minister, priest, rabbi, or other similar functionary of a religious organization, or an individual reasonably believed so to be by the person consulting him.

(2) A communication is "confidential" if made privately and not intended for further disclosure except to other persons present in furtherance of the purpose of the communication.

(b) General rule of privilege. A person has a privilege to refuse to disclose and to prevent another from disclosing a confidential communication by the person to a clergyman in his professional character as spiritual adviser.

(c) Who may claim the privilege. The privilege may be claimed by the person, by his guardian or conservator, or by his personal representative if he is deceased. The clergyman may claim the privilege on behalf of the person. His authority so to do is presumed in the absence of evidence to the contrary.

Advisory Committee's Note

The considerations which dictate the recognition of privileges generally seem strongly to favor a privilege for confidential communications to clergymen. During the period when most of the common law privileges were taking shape, no clear-cut privilege for communications between priest and penitent emerged. 8 Wigmore § 2394 (McNaughton Rev. 1961). The English political climate of the time may well furnish the explanation. In this country, however, the privilege has been recognized by statute in about two-thirds of the states and occasionally by the common law process of decision. *Id.,* § 2395; Mullen v. United States, 105 U.S.App.D.C. 25, 263 F.2d 275 (1959).

Subdivision (a). Paragraph (1) defines a clergyman as a "minister, priest, rabbi, or other similar functionary of a religious organization." The concept is necessarily broader than that inherent in the ministerial exemption for purposes of Selective Service. See United States v. Jackson, 369 F.2d 936 (4th Cir. 1966). However, it is not so broad as to include all self-denominated "ministers." A fair construction of the language requires that the person to whom the status is sought to be attached be regularly engaged in activities conforming at least in a general way with those of a Catholic priest, Jewish rabbi, or minister of an established Protestant denomination, though not necessarily on a full-time basis. No further specification seems possible in view of the lack of licensing and certification procedures for clergymen. However, this lack seems to have occasioned no particular difficulties in connection with the solemnization of marriages, which suggests that none may be anticipated here. For similar definitions of "clergyman" see California Evidence Code § 1030; New Jersey Evidence Rule 29.

The "reasonable belief" provision finds support in similar provisions for lawyer-client in Rule 503 and for psychotherapist-patient in Rule 504. A parallel is also found in the recognition of the validity of marriages performed by unauthorized persons if the parties reasonably believed them legally qualified. Harper and Skolnick, Problems of the Family 153 (Rev.Ed. 1962).

(2) The definition of "confidential" communication is consistent with the use of the term in Rule 503(a)(5) for lawyer-client and in Rule 504(a)(3) for psychotherapist-patient, suitably adapted to communications to clergymen.

Subdivision (b). The choice between a privilege narrowly restricted to doctrinally required confessions and a privilege broadly applicable to all confidential communications with a clergyman in his professional character as spiritual adviser has been exercised in favor of the latter. Many clergymen now receive training in marriage counseling and the handling of personality problems. Matters of this kind fall readily into the realm of the spirit. The same considerations which underlie the psychotherapist-patient privilege of Rule 504 suggest a broad application of the privilege for communications to clergymen.

State statutes and rules fall in both the narrow and the broad categories. A typical narrow statute proscribes disclosure of "a confession * * * made * * * in the course of discipline enjoined by the church to which he belongs." Ariz.Rev.Stats.Ann. 1956, § 12–2233. *See also* California Evidence Code § 1032; Uniform Rule 29. Illustrative of the broader privilege are statutes applying to "information communicated to him in a confidential manner, properly entrusted to him in his professional capacity, and necessary to enable him to discharge the functions of his office according to the usual course of his practice or discipline, wherein such person so communicating * * * is seeking spiritual counsel and advice," Fla.Stats.Ann. 1960, § 90.241, or to any "confidential communication properly entrusted to him in his professional capacity, and necessary and proper to enable him to discharge the functions of his office according to the usual course of practice or discipline," Iowa Code Ann. 1950, § 622.10. *See also* Ill.Rev.Stats. 1967, c. 51, § 48.1; Minn.Stats.Ann. 1945, § 595.02(3); New Jersey Evidence Rule 29.

Under the privilege as phrased, the communicating person is entitled to prevent disclosure not only by himself but also by the clergyman and by eavesdroppers. For discussion see Advisory Committee's Note under lawyer-client privilege, Rule 503(b).

The nature of what may reasonably be considered spiritual advice makes it unnecessary to include in the rule a specific exception for communications in furtherance of crime or fraud, as in Rule 503(d)(1).

Subdivision (c) makes clear that the privilege belongs to the communicating person. However, a prima facie authority on the part of the clergyman to claim the privilege on behalf of the person is recognized. The discipline of the particular church and the discreetness of the clergyman are believed to constitute sufficient safeguards for the absent communicating person. See Advisory Committee's Note to the similar provision with respect to attorney-client in Rule 503(c).

Rule 507. Political Vote [Not enacted.]

Every person has a privilege to refuse to disclose the tenor of his vote at a political election conducted by secret ballot unless the vote was cast illegally.

Advisory Committee's Note

Secrecy in voting is an essential aspect of effective democratic government, insuring free exercise of the franchise and fairness in elections. Secrecy after the ballot has been cast is as essential as secrecy in the act of voting. Nutting, Freedom of Silence: Constitutional Protection Against Governmental Intrusion in Political Affairs, 47 Mich.L.Rev. 181, 191 (1948). Consequently a privilege has long been recognized on the part of a voter to decline to disclose how he voted. Required disclosure would be the exercise of "a kind of inquisitorial power unknown to the principles of our government and constitution, and might be highly injurious to the suffrages of a free people, as well as tending to create cabals and disturbances between contending parties in popular elections." Johnston v. Charleston, 1 Bay 441, 442 (S.C. 1795).

The exception for illegally cast votes is a common one under both statutes and case law, Nutting, *supra,* at p. 192; 8 Wigmore § 2214, p. 163 (McNaughton Rev. 1961). The policy considerations which underlie the privilege are not applicable to the illegal voter. However, nothing in the exception purports to foreclose an illegal voter from invoking the privilege against self-incrimination under appropriate circumstances.

For similar provisions, see Uniform Rule 31; California Evidence Code § 1050; Kansas Code of Civil Procedure § 60–431; New Jersey Evidence Rule 31.

Rule 508. Trade Secrets [Not enacted.]

A person has a privilege, which may be claimed by him or his agent or employee, to refuse to disclose and to prevent other persons from disclosing a trade secret owned by him, if the allowance of the privilege will not tend to conceal fraud or otherwise work injustice. When disclosure is directed, the judge shall take such protective measure as the interests of the holder of the privilege and of the parties and the furtherance of justice may require.

Advisory Committee's Note

While sometimes said not to be a true privilege, a qualified right to protection against disclosure of trade secrets has found ample recognition, and, indeed, a denial of it would be difficult to defend. 8 Wigmore § 2212(3) (McNaughton Rev. 1961). And see 4 Moore's Federal Practice ¶¶ 30.12 and 34.15 (2nd ed. 1963 and Supp. 1965) and 2A Barron and Holtzoff, Federal Practice and Procedure § 715.1 (Wright ed. 1961). Congressional policy is reflected in the Securities Exchange Act of 1934, 15 U.S.C. § 78x, and the Public Utility Holding Company Act of 1933, *id.* § 79v, which deny the Securities and Exchange Commission authority to require disclosure of trade secrets or processes in applications and reports. *See also* Rule 26(c)(7) of the Rules of Civil Procedure, as revised, mentioned further hereinafter.

Illustrative cases raising trade-secret problems are: E.I. Du Pont de Nemours Powder Co. v. Masland, 244 U.S. 100, 37 S.Ct. 575, 61 L.Ed. 1016 (1917), suit to enjoin former employee from using plaintiff's secret processes, countered by defense that many of the processes were well known to the trade: Segal Lock & Hardware Co. v. FTC, 143 F.2d 935 (2d Cir. 1944), question whether expert locksmiths employed by FTC should be required to disclose methods used by them in picking petitioner's "pick-proof" locks; Dobson v. Graham, 49 F. 17 (E.D.Pa. 1889), patent infringement suit in which plaintiff sought to elicit from former employees now in the hire of defendant the respects in which defendant's machinery differed from plaintiff's patented machinery: Putney v. Du Bois Co., 240 Mo.App. 1075, 226 S.W.2d 737 (1950), action for injuries allegedly sustained from using defendant's secret formula dishwashing compound. See 8 Wigmore § 2212(3) (McNaughton Rev. 1961); Annot., 17 A.L.R.2d 383; 49 Mich.L.Rev. 133 (1950). The need for accommodation between protecting trade secrets, on the one hand, and eliciting facts required for full and fair presentation of a case, on the other hand, is apparent. Whether disclosure should be required depends upon a weighing of the competing interests involved against the background of the total situation, including consideration of such factors as the dangers of abuse, good faith, adequacy of protective measures, and the availability of other means of proof.

The cases furnish examples of the bringing of judicial ingenuity to bear upon the problem of evolving protective measures which achieve a degree of control over disclosure. Perhaps the most common is simply to take testimony *in camera.* Annot., 62 A.L.R.2d 509. Other possibilities include making disclosure to opposing counsel but not to his client, E.I. Du Pont de Nemours Powder Co. v. Masland, 244 U.S. 100, 37 S.Ct. 575, 61 L.Ed. 1016 (1917); making disclosure only to the judge (hearing examiner), Segal Lock & Hardware Co. v. FTC, 143 F.2d 935 (2d Cir. 1944); and placing those present under oath not to make disclosure, Paul v. Sinnott, 217 F.Supp. 84 (W.D.Pa. 1963).

Rule 26(c) of the Rules of Civil Procedure, as revised, provides that the judge may make "any order which justice requires to protect a party or person from annoyance, embarrassment, oppression, or undue burden or expense, including one or more of the following: * * * (7) that a trade secret or other confidential research, development, or commercial information not be disclosed or be disclosed only in a designated way * * *." While the instant evidence rule extends this underlying policy into the trial, the difference in circumstances between discovery stage and trial may well be such as to require a different ruling at the trial.

For other rules recognizing privilege for trade secrets, see Uniform Rule 32; California Evidence Code § 1060; Kansas Code of Civil Procedure § 60–432; New Jersey Evidence Rule 32.

———————————

Rule 509.   Secrets of State and Other Official Information [Not enacted.]

(a) Definitions.

(1)   Secret of state. A "secret of state" is a governmental secret relating to the national defense or the international relations of the United States.

(2)   Official information. "Official information" is information within the custody or control of a department or agency of the government the disclosure of which is shown to be contrary to the public interest and which consists of: (A) intragovernmental opinions or recommendations submitted for consideration in the performance of decisional or policymaking functions, or (B) subject to the provisions of 18 U.S.C. § 3500, investigatory files compiled for law enforcement purposes and not otherwise available, or (C) information within the custody or control of a governmental department or agency whether initiated within the department or agency or acquired by it in its exercise of its official responsibilities and not otherwise available to the public pursuant to 5 U.S.C. § 552.

(b)   General rule of privilege. The government has a privilege to refuse to give evidence and to prevent any person from giving evidence upon a showing of reasonable likelihood of danger that the evidence will disclose a secret of state or official information, as defined in this rule.

(c)   Procedures. The privilege for secrets of state may be claimed only by the chief officer of the government agency or department administering the subject matter which the secret information sought concerns, but the privilege for official information may be asserted by any attorney representing the government. The required showing may be made in whole or in part in the form of a written statement. The judge may hear the matter in chambers, but all counsel are entitled to inspect the claim and showing and to be heard thereon, except that, in the case of secrets of state, the judge upon motion of the government, may permit the government to make the required showing in the above form *in camera.* If the judge sustains the privilege upon a showing *in camera,* the entire text of the government's statements shall be sealed and preserved in the court's records in the event of appeal. In the case of privilege claimed for official information the court may require examination *in camera* of the information itself. The judge may take any protective measure which the interests of the government and the furtherance of justice may require.

(d)   Notice to government. If the circumstances of the case indicate a substantial possibility that a claim of privilege would be appropriate but has not been made because of oversight or lack of knowledge, the judge shall give or cause notice to be given to the officer entitled to claim the privilege and shall stay further proceedings a reasonable time to afford opportunity to assert a claim of privilege.

(e)   Effect of sustaining claim. If a claim of privilege is sustained in a proceeding to which the government is a party and it appears that another party is thereby deprived of material evidence, the judge shall make any further orders which the interests of justice require, including striking the testimony of a witness, declaring a mistrial, finding against the government upon an issue as to which the evidence is relevant, or dismissing the action.

Advisory Committee's Note

Subdivision (a). (1) The rule embodies the privilege protecting military and state secrets described as "well established in the law of evidence," United States

v. Reynolds, 345 U.S. 1, 6, 73 S.Ct. 528, 97 L.Ed. 727 (1953), and as one "the existence of which has never been doubted," 8 Wigmore § 2378, p. 794 (McNaughton Rev. 1961).

The use of the term "national defense," without attempt at further elucidation, finds support in the similar usage in statutory provisions relating to the crimes of gathering, transmitting, or losing defense information, and gathering or delivering defense information to aid a foreign government. 18 U.S.C. §§ 793, 794. *See also* 5 U.S.C. § 1002; 50 U.S.C.App. § 2152(d). In determining whether military or state secrets are involved, due regard will, of course, be given to classification pursuant to executive order.

(2)   The rule also recognizes a privilege for specified types of official information and in this respect is designed primarily to resolve questions of the availability to litigants of data in the files of governmental departments and agencies. In view of the lesser danger to the public interest than in cases of military and state secrets, the official information privilege is subject to a generally overriding requirement that disclosure would be contrary to the public interest. It is applicable to three categories of information.

(A)   Intergovernmental opinions or recommendations submitted for consideration in the performance of decisional or policy making functions. The policy basis of this aspect of the privilege is found in the desirability of encouraging candor in the exchange of views within the government. Kaiser Aluminum & Chemical Corp. v. United States, 141 Ct.Cl. 38, 157 F.Supp. 939 (1958); Davis v. Braswell Motor Freight Lines, Inc., 363 F.2d 600 (5th Cir. 1966); Ackerly v. Ley, 420 F.2d 1336 (D.C.Cir. 1969). A privilege of this character is consistent with the Freedom of Information Act, 5 U.S.C. § 552(b)(5), and with the standing of the agency to raise questions of relevancy, though not a party, recognized in such decisions as Boeing Airplane Co. v. Coggeshall, 108 U.S.App.D.C. 106, 280 F.2d 654, 659 (1960) (Renegotiation Board) and Freeman v. Seligson, 132 U.S.App.D.C. 56, 405 F.2d 1326, 1334 (1968) (Secretary of Agriculture).

(B)   Investigatory files compiled for law enforcement purposes. This category is expressly made subject to the provisions of the Jencks Act, 18 U.S.C. § 3500, which insulates prior statements or reports of government witnesses in criminal cases against subpoena, discovery, or inspection until the witness has testified on direct examination at the trial but then entitles the defense to its production. Rarely will documents of this nature be relevant until the author has testified and thus placed his credibility in issue. Further protection against discovery of government files in criminal cases is found in Criminal Procedure Rule 16(a) and (b). The breadth of discovery in civil cases, however, goes beyond ordinary bounds of relevancy and raises problems calling for the exercise of judicial control, and in making provision for it the rule implements the Freedom of Information Act, 18 U.S.C. § 552(b)(7).

(C)   Information exempted from disclosure under the Freedom of Information Act, 5 U.S.C. § 552. In 1958 the old "housekeeping" statute which had been relied upon as a foundation for departmental regulations curtailing disclosure was amended by adding a provision that it did not authorize withholding information from the public. In 1966 the Congress enacted the Freedom of Information Act for the purpose of making information in the files of departments and agencies, subject to certain specified exceptions, available to the mass media and to the public generally. 5 U.S.C. § 552. These enactments are significant expressions of Congressional policy. The exceptions in the Act are not framed in terms of evidentiary privilege, thus recognizing by clear implication that the needs of litigants may stand on somewhat different footing from those of the public generally. Nevertheless, the exceptions are based on values obviously entitled to weighty consideration in formulating rules of evidentiary privilege. In some instances in these rules, exceptions in the Act have been made the subject of specific privileges, *e.g.,* military and state secrets in the present rule and trade secrets in Rule 508. The purpose of the present provision is to incorporate the remaining exceptions of the Act into the qualified privilege here created, thus subjecting disclosure of the information to judicial determination with respect to the effect of disclosure on the public interest. This approach appears to afford a satisfactory resolution of the problems which may arise.

Subdivision (b). The rule vests the privileges in the government where they properly belong rather than a party or witness. See United States v. Reynolds, *supra,* p. 7, 73 S.Ct. 528. The showing required as a condition precedent to claiming the privilege represents a compromise between complete judicial control and accepting as final the decision of a departmental officer. See Machin v. Zuckert, 114 U.S.App.D.C. 335, 316 F.2d 336 (1963), rejecting in part a claim of privilege by the Secretary of the Air Force and ordering the furnishing of information for use in private litigation. This approach is consistent with *Reynolds.*

Subdivision (c). In requiring the claim of privilege for state secrets to be made by the chief departmental officer, the rule again follows *Reynolds,* insuring consideration by a high-level officer. This provision is justified by the lesser participation by the judge in cases of state secrets. The full participation by the judge in official information cases, on the contrary, warrants allowing the claim of privilege to be made by a government attorney.

Subdivision (d). spells out and emphasizes a power and responsibility on the part of the trial judge. An analogous provision is found in the requirement that the court certify to the Attorney General when the constitutionality of an act of Congress is in question in an action to which the government is not a party. 28 U.S.C. § 2403.

Subdivision (e). If privilege is successfully claimed by the government in litigation to which it is not a party, the effect is simply to make the evidence unavailable, as though a witness had died or claimed the privilege against self-incrimination, and no specification of the consequences is necessary. The rule therefore deals only with the effect of a successful claim of privilege by the government in proceedings to which it is a party. Reference to other types of cases serves to illustrate the variety of situations which may arise and the impossibility of evolving a single formula to be applied automatically to all of them. The privileged materials may be the statement of a government witness, as under the *Jencks* statute, which provides that, if the government elects not to produce the statement, the judge is to strike the testimony of the witness, or that he may declare a mistrial if the interests of justice so require. 18 U.S.C. § 3500(d). Or the privileged materials may disclose a possible basis for applying pressure upon witnesses. United States v. Beekman, 155 F.2d 580 (2d Cir. 1946). Or they may bear directly upon a substantive element of a criminal case, requiring dismissal in the event of a successful claim of privilege. United States v. Andolschek, 142 F.2d 503 (2d Cir. 1944); and see United States v. Reynolds, 345 U.S. 1, 73 S.Ct. 528, 97 L.Ed. 727 (1953). Or they may relate to an element of a plaintiff's claim against the government, with the decisions indicating unwillingness to allow the government's claim of privilege for secrets of state to be used as an offensive weapon against it. United States v. Reynolds, *supra;* Republic of China v. National Union Fire Ins. Co., 142 F.Supp. 551 (D.Md. 1956).

Rule 510. Identity of Informer [Not enacted.]

(a) **Rule of privilege.** The government or a state or subdivision thereof has a privilege to refuse to disclose the identity of a person who has furnished information relating to or assisting in an investigation of a possible violation of law to a law enforcement officer or member of a legislative committee or its staff conducting an investigation.

(b) **Who may claim.** The privilege may be claimed by an appropriate representative of the government, regardless of whether the information was furnished to an officer of the government or of a state or subdivision thereof. The privilege may be claimed by an appropriate representative of a state or subdivision if the information was furnished to an officer thereof, except that in criminal cases the privilege shall not be allowed if the government objects.

(c) **Exceptions.**

(1) *Voluntary disclosure; informer a witness.* No privilege exists under this rule if the identity of the informer or his interest in the subject matter of his communication has been disclosed to those who would have cause to resent the communication by a holder of the privilege or by the informer's own action, or if the informer appears as a witness for the government.

(2) *Testimony on merits.* If it appears from the evidence in the case or from other showing by a party that an informer may be able to give testimony necessary to a fair determination of the issue of guilt or innocence in a criminal case or of a material issue on the merits in a civil case to which the government is a party, and the government invokes the privilege, the judge shall give the government an opportunity to show *in camera* facts relevant to determining whether the informer can, in fact, supply that testimony. The showing will ordinarily be in the form of affidavits, but the judge may direct that testimony be taken if he finds that the matter cannot be resolved satisfactorily upon affidavit. If the judge finds that there is a reasonable probability that the informer can give the testimony, and the government elects not to disclose his identity, the judge on motion of the defendant in a criminal case shall dismiss the charges to which the testimony would relate, and the judge may do so on his own motion. In civil cases, he may make any order that justice requires. Evidence submitted to the judge shall be sealed and preserved to be made available to the appellate court in the event of an appeal, and the contents shall not otherwise be revealed without consent of the government. All counsel and parties shall be permitted to be present at every stage of proceedings under this subdivision except a showing *in camera,* at which no counsel or party shall be permitted to be present.

(3) *Legality of obtaining evidence.* If information from an informer is relied upon to establish the legality of the means by which evidence was obtained and the judge is not satisfied that the information was received from an informer reasonably believed to be reliable or credible, he may require the identity of the informer to be disclosed. The judge shall, on request of the government, direct that the disclosure be made *in camera.* All counsel and parties concerned with the issue of legality shall be permitted to be present at every stage of proceedings under this subdivision except a disclosure *in camera,* at which no counsel or party shall be permitted to be present. If disclosure of the identity of the informer is made *in camera,* the record thereof shall be sealed and preserved to be made available to the appellate court in the event of an appeal, and the contents shall not otherwise be revealed without consent of the government.

Advisory Committee's Note

The rule recognizes the use of informers as an important aspect of law enforcement, whether the informer is a citizen who steps forward with information or a paid undercover agent. In either event, the basic importance of anonymity in the effective use of informers is apparent, Bocchicchio v. Curtis Publishing Co., 203 F.Supp. 403 (E.D.Pa. 1962), and the privilege of withholding their identity was well established at common law. Roviaro v. United States, 353 U.S. 53, 59, 77 S.Ct. 623, 1 L.Ed.2d 639 (1957); McCormick § 148; 8 Wigmore § 2374 (McNaughton Rev. 1961).

Subdivision (a). The public interest in law enforcement requires that the privilege be that of the government, state, or political subdivision, rather than that of the witness. The rule blankets in as an informer anyone who tells a law enforcement officer about a violation of law without regard to whether the officer is one charged with enforcing the particular law. The rule also applies to disclosures to legislative investigating committees and their staffs, and is sufficiently broad to include continuing investigations.

Although the tradition of protecting the identity of informers has evolved in an essentially criminal setting, noncriminal law enforcement situations involving possibilities of reprisal against informers fall within the purview of the considerations out of which the privilege originated. In Mitchell v. Roma, 265 F.2d 633 (3d Cir. 1959), the privilege was given effect with respect to persons informing as to violations of the Fair Labor Standards Act, and in Wirtz v. Continental Finance & Loan Co., 326 F.2d 561 (5th Cir. 1964), a similar case, the privilege was recognized, although the basis of decision was lack of relevancy to the issues in the case.

Only identity is privileged; communications are not included except to the extent that disclosure would operate also to disclose the informer's identity. The common law was to the same effect. 8 Wigmore § 2374, at p. 765 (McNaughton Rev. 1961). *See also* Roviaro v. United States, *supra*, 353 U.S. at p. 60, 77 S.Ct. 623; Bowman Dairy Co. v. United States, 341 U.S. 214, 221, 71 S.Ct. 675, 95 L.Ed. 879 (1951).

The rule does not deal with the question whether presentence reports made under Criminal Procedure Rule 32(c) should be made available to an accused.

Subdivision (b). Normally the "appropriate representative" to make the claim will be counsel. However, it is possible that disclosure of the informer's identity will be sought in proceedings to which the government, state, or subdivision, as the case may be, is not a party. Under these circumstances effective implementation of the privilege requires that other representatives be considered "appropriate." See, for example, Bocchicchio v. Curtis Publishing Co., 203 F.Supp. 403 (E.D.Pa. 1962), a civil action for libel, in which a local police officer not represented by counsel successfully claimed the informer privilege.

The privilege may be claimed by a state or subdivision of a state if the information was given to its officer, except that in criminal cases it may not be allowed if the government objects.

Subdivision (c) deals with situations in which the informer privilege either does not apply or is curtailed.

(1)   If the identity of the informer is disclosed, nothing further is to be gained from efforts to suppress it. Disclosure may be direct, or the same practical effect may result from action revealing the informer's interest in the subject matter. See, for example, Westinghouse Electric Corp. v. City of Burlington, 122 U.S.App.D.C. 65, 351 F.2d 762 (1965), on remand City of Burlington v. Westinghouse Electric Corp., 246 F.Supp. 839 (D.D.C. 1965), which held that the filing of civil antitrust actions destroyed as to plaintiffs the informer privilege claimed by the Attorney General with respect to complaints of criminal antitrust

violations. While allowing the privilege in effect to be waived by one not its holder, *i.e.* the informer himself, is something of a novelty in the law of privilege, if the informer chooses to reveal his identity, further efforts to suppress it are scarcely feasible.

The exception is limited to disclosure to "those who would have cause to resent the communication," in the language of Roviaro v. United States, 353 U.S. 53, 60, 77 S.Ct. 623, 1 L.Ed.2d 639 (1957), since disclosure otherwise, *e.g.* to another law enforcing agency, is not calculated to undercut the objects of the privilege.

If the informer becomes a witness for the government, the interests of justice in disclosing his status as a source of bias or possible support are believed to outweigh any remnant of interest in nondisclosure which then remains. See Harris v. United States, 371 F.2d 365 (9th Cir. 1967), in which the trial judge permitted detailed inquiry into the relationship between the witness and the government. Cf. Attorney General v. Briant, 15 M. & W. 169, 153 Eng.Rep. 808 (Exch. 1846). The purpose of the limitation to witnesses for the government is to avoid the possibility of calling persons as witnesses as a means of discovery whether they are informers.

(2)   The informer privilege, it was held by the leading case, may not be used in a criminal prosecution to suppress the identity of a witness when the public interest in protecting the flow of information is outweighed by the individual's right to prepare his defense. Roviaro v. United States, *supra.* The rule extends this balancing to include civil as well as criminal cases and phrases it in terms of "a reasonable probability that the informer may be able to give testimony necessary to a fair determination of the issue of guilt or innocence in a criminal case or of a material issue on the merits in a civil case." Once the privilege is invoked a procedure is provided for determining whether the informer can in fact supply testimony of such nature as to require disclosure of his identity, thus avoiding a "judicial guessing game" on the question. United States v. Day, 384 F.2d 464, 470 (3d Cir. 1967). An investigation *in camera* is calculated to accommodate the conflicting interests involved. The rule also spells out specifically the consequences of a successful claim of the privilege in a criminal case; the wider range of possibilities in civil cases demands more flexibility in treatment. See Advisory Committee's Note to Rule 509(e), *supra.*

(3)   One of the acute conflicts between the interest of the public in nondisclosure and the avoidance of unfairness to the accused as a result of nondisclosure arises when information from an informer is relied upon to legitimate a search and seizure by furnishing probable cause for an arrest without a warrant or for the issuance of a warrant for arrest or search. McCray v. Illinois, 386 U.S. 300, 87 S.Ct. 1056, 18 L.Ed.2d 62 (1967), rehearing denied 386 U.S. 1042. A hearing *in camera* provides an accommodation of these conflicting interests. United States v. Jackson, 384 F.2d 825 (3d Cir. 1967). The limited disclosure to the judge avoids any significant impairment of secrecy, while affording the accused a substantial measure of protection against arbitrary police action. The procedure is consistent with McCray and the decisions there discussed.

Rule 511. Waiver of Privilege by Voluntary Disclosure [Not enacted.]

A person upon whom these rules confer a privilege against disclosure of the confidential matter or communication waives the privilege if he or his predecessor while holder of the privilege voluntarily discloses or consents to disclosure of any significant part of the matter or communication. This rule does not apply if the disclosure is itself a privileged communication.

Advisory Committee's Note

The central purpose of most privileges is the promotion of some interest or relationship by endowing it with a supporting secrecy or confidentiality. It is evident that the privilege should terminate when the holder by his own act destroys this confidentiality. McCormick §§ 87, 97, 106; 8 Wigmore §§ 2242, 2327–2329, 2374, 2389–2390 (McNaughton Rev. 1961).

The rule is designed to be read with a view to what it is that the particular privilege protects. For example, the lawyer-client privilege covers only communications, and the fact that a client has discussed a matter with his lawyer does not insulate the client against disclosure of the subject matter discussed, although he is privileged not to disclose the discussion itself. See McCormick § 93. The waiver here provided for is similarly restricted. Therefore a client, merely by disclosing a subject which he had discussed with his attorney, would not waive the applicable privilege; he would have to make disclosure of the communication itself in order to effect a waiver.

By traditional doctrine, waiver is the intentional relinquishment of a known right. Johnson v. Zerbst, 304 U.S. 458, 464, 58 S.Ct. 1019, 82 L.Ed. 1461 (1938). However, in the confidential privilege situations, once confidentiality is destroyed through voluntary disclosure, no subsequent claim of privilege can restore it, and knowledge or lack of knowledge of the existence of the privilege appears to be irrelevant. California Evidence Code § 912; 8 Wigmore § 2327 (McNaughton Rev. 1961).

Rule 512. Privileged Matter Disclosed Under Compulsion or Without Opportunity to Claim Privilege [Not enacted.]

Evidence of a statement or other disclosure of privileged matter is not admissible against the holder of the privilege if the disclosure was (a) compelled erroneously or (b) made without opportunity to claim the privilege.

Advisory Committee's Note

Ordinarily a privilege is invoked in order to forestall disclosure. However, under some circumstances consideration must be given to the status and effect of a disclosure already made. Rule 511, immediately preceding, gives voluntary disclosure the effect of a waiver, while the present rule covers the effect of disclosure made under compulsion or without opportunity to claim the privilege.

Confidentiality, once destroyed, is not susceptible of restoration, yet some measure of repair may be accomplished by preventing use of the evidence against the holder of the privilege. The remedy of exclusion is therefore made available when the earlier disclosure was compelled erroneously or without opportunity to claim the privilege.

With respect to erroneously compelled disclosure, the argument may be made that the holder should be required in the first instance to assert the privilege, stand his ground, refuse to answer, perhaps incur a judgment of contempt, and exhaust all legal recourse, in order to sustain his privilege. See Fraser v. United States, 145 F.2d 139 (6th Cir. 1944), cert. denied 324 U.S. 849, 65 S.Ct. 684, 89 L.Ed. 1409; United States v. Johnson, 76 F.Supp. 538 (M.D.Pa. 1947), aff'd 165 F.2d 42 (3d Cir. 1947), cert. denied 332 U.S. 852, 68 S.Ct. 355, 92 L.Ed. 422, reh. denied 333 U.S. 834, 68 S.Ct. 457, 92 L.Ed. 1118. However, this exacts of the holder greater fortitude in the face of authority than ordinary individuals are likely to possess, and assumes unrealistically that a judicial remedy is always available. In self-incrimination cases, the writers agree that erroneously compelled disclosures are inadmissible in a subsequent criminal prosecution of the holder, Maguire, Evidence of Guilt 66 (1959); McCormick § 127; 8 Wigmore § 2270 (McNaughton Rev. 1961), and the principle is equally sound when applied to other privileges. The modest departure from usual principles of res judicata which occurs when the compulsion is judicial is justified by the advantage of having one simple rule, assuring at least one opportunity for judicial supervision in every case.

The second circumstance stated as a basis for exclusion is disclosure made without opportunity to the holder to assert his privilege. Illustrative possibilities are disclosure by an eavesdropper, by a person used in the transmission of a privileged communication, by a family member participating in psychotherapy, or privileged data improperly made available from a computer bank.

Rule 513. Comment upon or Inference from Claim of Privilege; Instruction [Not enacted.]

(a) Comment or inference not permitted. The claim of a privilege, whether in the present proceeding or upon a prior occasion, is not a proper subject of comment by judge or counsel. No inference may be drawn therefrom.

(b) Claiming privilege without knowledge of jury. In jury cases, proceedings shall be conducted, to the extent practicable, so as to facilitate the making of claims of privilege without the knowledge of the jury.

(c) Jury instruction. Upon request, any party against whom the jury might draw an adverse inference from a claim of privilege is entitled to an instruction that no inference may be drawn therefrom.

Advisory Committee's Note

Subdivision (a). In Griffin v. California, 380 U.S. 609, 614, 85 S.Ct. 1229, 14 L.Ed.2d 106 (1965), the Court pointed out that allowing comment upon the claim of a privilege "cuts down on the privilege by making its assertion costly." Consequently it was held that comment upon the election of the accused not to take the stand infringed upon his privilege against self-incrimination so substantially as to constitute a constitutional violation. While the privileges governed by these rules are not constitutionally based, they are nevertheless founded upon important policies and are entitled to maximum effect. Hence the present subdivision forbids comment upon the exercise of a privilege, in accord with the weight of authority. Courtney v. United States, 390 F.2d 521 (9th Cir. 1968); 8 Wigmore §§ 2243, 2322, 2386; Barnhart, Privilege in the Uniform Rules of Evidence, 24 Ohio St.L.J. 131, 137–138 (1963). Cf. McCormick § 80.

Subdivision (b). The value of a privilege may be greatly depreciated by means other than expressly commenting to a jury upon the fact that it was exercised. Thus, the calling of a witness in the presence of the jury and subsequently excusing him after a sidebar conference may effectively convey to the jury the fact that a privilege has been claimed, even though the actual claim has not been made in their hearing. Whether a privilege will be claimed is usually ascertainable in advance and the handling of the entire matter outside the presence of the jury is feasible. Destruction of the privilege by innuendo can and should be avoided. Tallo v. United States, 344 F.2d 467 (1st Cir. 1965); United States v. Tomaiolo, 249 F.2d 683 (2d Cir. 1957); San Fratello v. United States, 343 F.2d 711 (5th Cir. 1965); Courtney v. United States, 390 F.2d 521 (9th Cir. 1968); 6 Wigmore § 1808, pp. 275–276; 6 U.C.L.A.Rev. 455 (1959). This position is in accord with the general agreement of the authorities that an accused cannot be forced to make his election not to testify in the presence of the jury. 8 Wigmore § 2268, p. 407 (McNaughton Rev. 1961).

Unanticipated situations are, of course, bound to arise, and much must be left to the discretion of the judge and the professional responsibility of counsel.

Subdivision (c). Opinions will differ as to the effectiveness of a jury instruction not to draw an adverse inference from the making of a claim of privilege. See Bruton v. United States, 389 U.S. 818, 88 S.Ct. 126, 19 L.Ed.2d 70 (1968). Whether an instruction shall be given is left to the sound judgment of counsel for the party against whom the adverse inference may be drawn. The instruction is a matter of right, if requested. This is the result reached in Bruno v. United States, 308 U.S. 287, 60 S.Ct. 198, 84 L.Ed. 257 (1939), holding that an accused is entitled to an instruction under the statute (now 18 U.S.C. § 3481) providing that his failure to testify creates no presumption against him.

The right to the instruction is not impaired by the fact that the claim of privilege is by a witness, rather than by a party, provided an adverse inference against the party may result.

———————————

ARTICLE VIII. HEARSAY

Rule 804. Hearsay   Exceptions: Declarant   Unavailable
[Subdivision (b)(2) not enacted.]

* * *

(b) Hearsay exceptions. The following are not excluded by the hearsay rule if the declarant is unavailable as a witness:

* * *

(2) *Statement of recent perception.* A statement, not in response to the instigation of a person engaged in investigating, litigating, or settling a claim, which narrates, describes, or explains an event or condition recently perceived by the declarant, made in good faith, not in contemplation of pending or anticipated litigation in which he was interested, and while his recollection was clear.

Note by Federal Judicial Center

Hearsay exception (b)(2) is set forth above as prescribed by the Supreme Court. It was not included in the rules enacted by the Congress but is reproduced here for such value as it may have for purposes of interpretation.

Advisory Committee's Note

Exception (2). The rule finds support in several directions. The well known Massachusetts Act of 1898 allows in evidence the declaration of any deceased person made in good faith before the commencement of the action and upon personal knowledge. Mass.G.L., c. 233, § 65. To the same effect is R.I.G.L. § 9–19–11. Under other statutes, a decedent's statement is admissible on behalf of his estate in actions against it, to offset the presumed inequality resulting from allowing a surviving opponent to testify. California Evidence Code § 1261; Conn.G.S., § 52–172; and statutes collected in 5 Wigmore § 1576. *See also* Va.Code § 8–286, allowing statements made when capable by a party now incapable of testifying.

In 1938 the Committee on Improvements in the Law of Evidence of the American Bar Association recommended adoption of a statute similar to that of Massachusetts but with the concept of unavailability expanded to include, in addition to death, cases of insanity or inability to produce a witness or take his deposition. 63 A.B.A. Reports 570, 584, 600 (1938). The same year saw enactment of the English Evidence Act of 1938, allowing written statements made on personal knowledge, if declarant is deceased or otherwise unavailable or if the court is satisfied that undue delay or expense would otherwise be caused, unless declarant was an interested person in pending or anticipated relevant proceedings. Evidence Act of 1938, 1 & 2 Geo. 6, c. 28; Cross on Evidence 482 (3rd ed. 1967).

Model Code Rule 503(a) provided broadly for admission of any hearsay declaration of an unavailable declarant. No circumstantial guarantees of trustworthiness were required. Debate upon the floor of the American Law Institute did not seriously question the propriety of the rule but centered upon what should constitute unavailability. 18 A.L.I. Proceedings 90–134 (1941).

The Uniform Rules draftsman took a less advanced position, more in the pattern of the Massachusetts statute, and invoked several assurances of accuracy: recency of perception, clarity of recollection, good faith, and antecedence to the commencement of the action. Uniform Rule 63(4)(c).

Opposition developed to the Uniform Rule because of its countenancing of the use of statements carefully prepared under the tutelage of lawyers, claim adjusters, or investigators with a view to pending or prospective litigation. Tentative Recommendation and a Study Relating to the Uniform Rules of Evidence (Art. VIII. Hearsay Evidence), Cal.Law Rev.Comm'n, 318 (1962); Quick, Excitement, Necessity and the Uniform Rules: A Reappraisal of Rule 63(4), 6 Wayne L.Rev. 204, 219–224 (1960). To meet this objection, the rule excludes statements made at the instigation of a person engaged in investigating, litigating, or setting a claim. It also incorporates as safeguards the good faith and clarity of recollection required by the Uniform Rule and the exclusion of a statement by a person interested in the litigation provided by the English act.

With respect to the question whether the introduction of a statement under this exception against the accused in a criminal case would violate his right of confrontation, reference is made to the last paragraph of the Advisory Committee's Note under Exception (1), *supra*.

Report of House Committee on the Judiciary

Rule 804(b)(2), a hearsay exception submitted by the Court, titled "Statement of recent perception," read as follows:

A statement, not in response to the instigation of a person engaged in investigating, litigating, or settling a claim, which narrates, describes, or explains an event or condition recently perceived by the declarant, made in good faith, not in contemplation of pending or anticipated litigation in which he was interested, and while his recollection was clear.

The Committee eliminated this Rule as creating a new and unwarranted hearsay exception of great potential breadth. The Committee did not believe that statements of the type referred to bore sufficient guarantees of trustworthiness to justify admissibility.

INDEX TO FEDERAL RULES OF EVIDENCE

A

ABSENCE OF ENTRY
Business record, Rule 803(6), (7)
Public record, Rule 803(8)–(10)

ABSENCE OF MISTAKE OR ACCIDENT, Rule 404(b)

ACADEMIC PEER REVIEW PRIVILEGE, Rule 501

ACCIDENTS
Other or similar, Rule 403

ACKNOWLEDGED DOCUMENTS
Authentication, Rules 901 and 902

ADJUDICATIVE FACTS
Judicial notice, Rule 201

ADMISSIBILITY
See also Relevancy
Generally, Rules 401–403
Limited, Rule 105, Rule 703
Preliminary questions of fact, Rules 104, 1008

ADOPTIVE STATEMENTS, Rule 801(d)(2)(B)

ADVERSE WITNESS, Rule 611

AFFIRMATION, Rule 603

AGENT STATEMENTS, Rule 801(d)(2)

ALCOHOL USE
Competency as witness, Rule 601
Habit, Rule 406
Impeachment, Rule 607

AMBIGUOUS QUESTION, Rule 611

ANCIENT DOCUMENTS
Authentication, Rule 901(b)(8)
Hearsay exception, Rule 803(16)

ANNULMENT OF CONVICTION, Rule 609

APPLICABILITY OF RULES
Generally, Rules 101, 1101
Judicial notice, Rule 201
Preliminary questions, Rule 104
Privilege, Rule 1101

ARGUMENTATIVE QUESTION, Rule 611

ASKED AND ANSWERED, Rule 611

ASSERTIONS, Rule 801(a)–(c)

ASSUMING FACTS IN QUESTION, Rule 611

ATTACKING AND SUPPORTING CREDIBILITY OF HEARSAY DECLARANT, Rule 806

ATTACKING VALIDITY OF VERDICT OR INDICTMENT, Rule 606

INDEX

ATTORNEY-CLIENT PRIVILEGE
See Lawyer-Client Privilege

AUTHENTICATION
   See also Self-Authentication
  Generally, Rule 901
Ancient documents, Rule 901
Certifications, Rule 902 (11)–(14)
Chain of custody, Rule 901
Comparison by expert witness, Rule 901
Comparison by trier of fact, Rule 901
Conditional relevancy, Rule 104, Rule 901
Distinctive characteristics, Rule 901
Exemplars, Rule 901
Handwriting,
  Expert opinion, Rule 901
  Non-expert opinion, Rule 901
Judge and jury, Rule 901
Methods provided by statute or rule, Rule 901
Process or system, Rule 901
Public records or reports, Rules 901, 902
Reply letter doctrine, Rule 901
Subscribing witnesses, Rule 903
Substantially same condition, Rule 401, Rule 901
Telephone conversations, Rule 901
Voice identification, Rule 901
Wills, Rule 903
Witness with knowledge, Rule 901

B

BACKGROUND INFORMATION, Rule 401, Rule 608

BAIL
Applicability of rules, Rule 1101

BAPTISMAL CERTIFICATES, Rule 803(12)

BEST EVIDENCE RULE
  Generally, Rule 1002
Admissibility of other evidence of contents, Rule 1004
Certified copy of public record, Rule 1005
Chattels, inscribed, Rule 1001
Collateral matters, Rule 1004
Compared copy, public records, Rule 1005
Counterparts, Rule 1001
Destroyed original, Rule 1004
Duplicates,
  Admissibility, Rule 1003
  Definition, Rule 1001
Inscribed chattels, Rule 1001
Judge and jury, Rule 1008
Lost or destroyed original, Rule 1004
Notice to produce, Rule 1004
Original,
  Definition, Rule 1001
  Requirement of, Rule 1002
Original in possession of opponent, Rule 1004
Original lost or destroyed, Rule 1004
Original not obtainable, Rule 1004
Photographs, Rule 1001, Rule 1002
Possession of opponent, Rule 1004
Preliminary questions of fact, Rule 1008
Public records, Rule 1005
Reasonable reliance by expert, Rule 703
Recordings, Rule 1001
Secondary evidence, Rule 1004
Statement of party-opponent, Rule 1007
Summaries, Rule 1006

INDEX

Testimony of party, Rule 1007
Writing, definition of, Rule 1001

BIAS, Rule 607

BODILY CONDITION
Statement of, Rule 803(3)

BODILY DEMONSTRATIONS, Rule 401

BOLSTERING WITNESS, Rule 607; Rule 608

BOUNDARIES
Judgment as to, Rule 803(23)
Reputation concerning, Rule 803(20)

BRAND NAMES
Authentication, Rule 902

BUSINESS RECORDS, Rule 803(6), (7); Rule 805; Rule 902(11), (12)

BUSINESS ROUTINE, Rule 406

C

CERTIFIED BUSINESS RECORDS, Rule 902(11), (12)

CERTIFIED COPIES OF PUBLIC RECORDS
Best Evidence Rule, Rule 1005
Self-authentication, Rule 902

CHAIN OF CUSTODY, Rule 901

CHARACTER EVIDENCE
See also Character for Truthfulness; Reputation
Generally, Rules 404, 405, 413–415
Accused, Rule 404(a); Rule 404(b), Rule 405, Rules 413, 414
Character "in issue," Rule 404(a); Rule 405
Civil cases, Rules 404, 405, 415
Criminal cases, Rules 404, 405, 413, 414
Cross-examination of character witnesses, Rule 404(a), Rule 405, Rule 608
Decedent, Rule 404(a)
Element of charge, claim, or defense, Rule 404(a); Rule 405
Expert opinion testimony, Rule 405
Good character instruction, Rule 404(a)
Method of proof, Rule 404(a), Rule 405, Rule 413; Rule 414; Rule 415; Rule 608
Opinion testimony, Rule 404(a), Rule 405, Rule 608
Other crimes, wrongs, or acts, Rules 404(b), 413, 414, 415
Party, Rule 404(a); Rule 404(b), Rules 405, 413, 414, 415
Qualifications of character witness, Rule 405; Rule 608
Reputation, hearsay exception, Rule 803(21)
Reputation testimony, Rule 404(a), Rule 405, Rule 608
Specific instances of conduct, Rule 404(a), Rule 404(b), Rules 405, 413, 414, 415, Rule 608
Victim, Rule 404(a), Rule 405, Rule 412
Witness, Rule 404(a); Rules 608–609

CHARACTER FOR TRUTHFULNESS
Generally, Rule 608, Rule 609
Convictions, Rule 609
Cross-examination, Rule 608, Rule 609
Form of questions, Rule 608
Opinion testimony, Rule 608
Rehabilitation, Rule 608
Reputation, hearsay exception, Rule 803(21)
Reputation testimony, Rule 608
Specific acts of fact witness, Rule 608

CHARACTER IN ISSUE, Rule 404(a); Rule 405

CHARACTER OF ACCUSED, Rule 404(a), Rule 404(b); Rule 405, Rules 413, 414

CHARACTER OF CIVIL PARTY, Rule 404(a); Rules 405, 415

INDEX

INDEX

INDEX

Disclosure of hearsay, Rule 703; Rule 705
Exclusion of, Rule 615, Rule 702
General acceptance of scientific principle, Rule 702
Handwriting, Rule 901
Hearsay, Rule 703, Rule 705
Helpfulness of testimony, Rule 702, Rule 704
Hypothetical question, Rule 703; Rule 705
Impeachment, Rule 705
Learned treatises, Rule 803(18)
Novel scientific evidence, Rule 702
Opinion on ultimate issue, Rule 702, Rule 704
Personal knowledge, Rule 602, Rule 703
Procedure for determining reliability, Rule 702
Qualifications, Rule 702
Reasonable reliance, Rule 703
Scientific evidence, Rule 702
Subject matter, Rule 702
Sufficient basis, Rule 702
Technical knowledge, Rule 702
Ultimate issue, Rule 702, Rule 704
Unexplored legal criteria, Rule 702, Rule 704

EXTRADITION
Or rendition, applicability of rules, Rule 1101

EXTRANEOUS OFFENSES, Rule 404(b), 413, 414, 415

EXTRINSIC EVIDENCE
Bad acts, Rule 608(b)
Bias or interest, Rule 607
Capacity, Rule 607
Contradiction, Rule 607
Convictions, Rule 609
Prior inconsistent statement, Rule 613

F

FACT OF CONSEQUENCE, Rule 401

FACTS NOT IN DISPUTE, Rule 401, Rule 404(b)

FACTUAL FINDINGS
Public records and reports, Rule 803(8)

FAMILY HISTORY, Rules 803(19), 804(b)(4)

FAMILY RECORDS, Rule 803(13)

FINANCIAL INTEREST, Rule 408, Rule 607

FOREIGN DOCUMENTS, Rule 902

FORFEITURE BY WRONGDOING, Rule 804(b)(6)

FORM OF QUESTION
Generally, Rule 611
Specific objections, Rule 611

FORMER TESTIMONY, Rule 804(b)(1)

FOUNDATION
Authentication, Rule 401, Rule 901
Bias, Rule 607
Interest, Rule 607
Opinion of expert witness, Rules 702, 705
Opinion of lay witness, Rule 701
Opinion testimony as to character, generally, Rule 405
Opinion testimony as to truthful character, Rule 608
Personal knowledge, Rule 602
Prior inconsistent statement, Rule 613
Reputation testimony as to character, generally, Rule 405
Reputation testimony as to truthful character, Rule 608

INDEX

FUNCTIONS OF JUDGE AND JURY
Generally, Rule 104
Authentication, Rule 901
Original Writing Rule, Rule 1008

G

GENERAL ACCEPTANCE OF SCIENTIFIC PRINCIPLE, Rule 702

GENERAL OBJECTIONS, Rule 103

GRAND JURY
Applicability of rules, Rule 1101

GRAND JURY TESTIMONY, Rule 801(d)(1)(A)

GUILTY PLEAS
See also Pleas
Generally, Rule 410

H

HABIT
Generally, Rule 406,
Business routine, Rule 406
Compared to character, Rule 406
Defined, Rule 406
Industry standards, Rule 406
Proof, Rule 406
Trade custom, Rule 406

HANDWRITING
Expert opinion, Rule 702, Rule 901
Non-expert opinion, Rule 701, Rule 901

HARASSING WITNESS, Rule 611

HARMLESS ERROR, Rule 103

HEARING IN PRESENCE OF JURY
Generally, Rules 103, 104

HEARSAY
Admissibility, Rule 802
Assertions, Rule 801(a)–(c)
Basis for expert testimony, Rule 703
Confrontation Clause, Rule 703, Rule 802
Definition, Rule 801
Exceptions,
Declarant unavailability immaterial, Rule 803
Declarant unavailability required, Rule 804
Grand jury testimony, Rule 801(d)(1)(A)
Impeaching declarant, Rule 806
Multiple, Rule 805
Nonhearsay statements, Rule 801(a)–(c)
Nonverbal conduct intended as an assertion, Rule 801(a)–(c)
Nonverbal nonassertive conduct, Rule 801(a)–(c)
Operative fact, Rule 801(a)–(c)
Prior consistent statements, Rule 607, Rule 801(d)(1)(B)
Prior identification, Rule 801(d)(1)(C)
Prior inconsistent statements, Rule 607, Rule 613, Rule 801(d)(1)(A)
Statements by party-opponent, Rule 801(d)(2)
Verbal acts, Rule 801(a)–(c)
Verbal assertions, Rule 801(a)–(c)

HEARSAY EXCEPTIONS, AVAILABILITY OF DECLARANT IMMATERIAL
Generally, Rule 803
Absence of entry,
Business record, Rule 803(6), (7)
Public record, Rule 803(8), (10)
Ancient documents, Rule 803(16)

324

INDEX

INDEX

INDEX

INDEX

LAWYER-CLIENT PRIVILEGE
Attorney-Client Privilege, Rule 501, Rule 502
Limitations on Waiver, Rule 502

LAY WITNESS
See Opinion of Lay Witness

LEADING QUESTIONS, Rule 611

LEARNED TREATISES, Rule 803(18)

LEGISLATIVE FACTS, Rule 201

LIMITED ADMISSIBILITY, Rule 105, Rule 404(b), Rule 703

LIMITING INSTRUCTIONS, Rule 105, Rule 403, Rule 404(b)

M

MAGISTRATES
Applicability of rules, Rule 1101

MARKET REPORTS, Rule 803(17)

MARRIAGE CERTIFICATES, Rule 803(12)

MATTER ASSERTED, Rule 801(a)–(c)

MEDICAL DIAGNOSIS OR TREATMENT
Statements, Rule 803(4)

MEDICAL RECORDS
Hearsay, Rule 803(6), (7)

MENTAL COMPETENCY
Competency of witness, Rule 601
Impeachment, Rule 607

MISCONDUCT
Other, Rule 404(b), 413, 414, 415

MISTAKE
Absence of, Rule 404(b)

MODE OF INTERROGATION AND PRESENTATION, Rule 611

"MODUS OPERANDI", Rule 404(b)

MOTION TO STRIKE, Rule 103

MOTIONS IN LIMINE, Rule 103

MOTIVE, Rule 404(b)

MULTIPLE HEARSAY, Rule 805

N

NARRATIVE ANSWER, Rule 611

NEGOTIABLE INSTRUMENTS
Authentication, Rule 902

NEWSPAPERS AND PERIODICALS
Authentication, Rule 902(6)

NOLO CONTENDERE
See also Pleas
Generally, Rule 410
Judgment of Conviction, Rule 803(22)

NONASSERTIVE CONDUCT, Rule 801(a)–(c)

NONHEARSAY STATEMENTS, Rule 801(a)–(c)

INDEX

NONRESPONSIVE ANSWER, Rule 611

NONVERBAL CONDUCT
Intended as an assertion, Rule 801(a)–(c)
Nonassertive, Rule 801(a)–(c)

NOTARIZED DOCUMENTS, Rule 902(8)

NOTICE
Other crimes, wrongs, or acts, Rules 404(b), 413, 414, 415
Notice and Demand, Rule 803(10)
Rape shield rule, Rule 412
Residual exception, Rule 807
To produce, Best Evidence Rule, Rule 1004

O

OATH, Rule 603

OBJECTIONS
Competency of judge as witness, Rule 605
Continuing, Rule 103
Depositions, Rule 103
"Door opening," Rule 106
General, Rule 103
Grounds for, Rule 103
Hearing of jury, Rule 103
Interrogation of witness by court, Rule 614
Motion in limine, Rule 103
Motion to strike, Rule 103
Necessity for, Rule 103
Oath, Rule 603
Offer of proof, Rule 103
Relevancy, Rules 401, 403
Specificity required, Rule 103
Time of objecting, Rule 103
Waiver, Rule 103

OFFER OF PROOF, Rule 103

OFFERS TO COMPROMISE
See Compromise

OFFICIAL PUBLICATIONS
Authentication, Rule 902(5)

"OPENING THE DOOR", Rule 106, Rule 403

OPERATIVE FACT, Rule 801(a)–(c)

OPINION OF LAY WITNESS
Conclusory, Rule 701
Fact versus opinion, Rule 701
Helpfulness, Rule 701
Illustrations, Rule 701
Personal knowledge, Rule 701
Testifying as expert, Rule 701, Rule 702
Ultimate issue, Rule 701, Rule 704

OPINIONS
 See also Character Evidence; Expert Witness; Opinion of Lay Witness
Business records, Rule 803(6)
Hearsay, Rule 801(d)(2), Rule 803(6)
Public records, Rule 803(8)
Ultimate issue, Rule 701, Rule 702, Rule 704

INDEX

INDEX

INDEX

Q

QUALIFICATIONS OF EXPERT WITNESS, Rule 702

R

RAPE
    See also Sexual Conduct of Victim, Sexual Offenses
Child molestation, Rules 414, 415
Rape shield provision, Rule 412
Similar acts in sexual assault cases, Rules 413, 415

REAL EVIDENCE
Authentication, Rule 401, Rule 901
Definition, Rule 401
Relevancy, Rule 401

REASONABLE RELIANCE BY EXPERT, Rule 703

RECENT FABRICATION, Rule 607, Rule 801(d)(1)(B)

RECORDED RECOLLECTION, Rule 612, Rule 803(5)

RECORDS OF REGULARLY CONDUCTED ACTIVITY, Rules 803(6), (7); Rules 902(11), (12)

RECROSS EXAMINATION, Rule 611

REDIRECT EXAMINATION, Rule 611

REFRESHING RECOLLECTION
Before testifying, Rule 612
Documents, Rule 612
During deposition, Rule 612
Jencks Act, Rule 612
Leading questions, Rule 611
Past recollection recorded distinguished, Rule 612, Rule 803(5)
While testifying, Rule 612

REHABILITATION OF WITNESS
    See also Cross-Examination; Impeachment
Bolstering distinguished, Rule 607, Rule 608
Character for truthfulness, Rule 607, Rule 608
Explaining prior convictions, Rule 609
Hearsay exception, Rule 801(d)(1)(B)
Prior consistent statement, Rule 801(d)(1)(B)

RELATED WRITINGS OR RECORDED STATEMENTS, Rule 106

RELEVANCY
    Generally, Rules 401–403
Background information, Rule 401
Circumstantial evidence, Rule 401, Rule 404(a)
Conditional, Rule 104(b)
Confusion of issues, Rule 403
Connecting up, Rule 104
Cumulative evidence, Rule 403
Definition and nature, Rule 401, Rule 403
Demonstrative evidence, Rule 401
Exclusion of relevant evidence, Rules 402, 403
Fact of consequence, Rule 401
Irrelevant evidence, Rule 402
Logical relevancy, Rule 401
Misleading, Rule 403
Other,
    Accidents, Rule 401
    Contracts, Rule 401
    Crimes, wrongs, or acts, Rules 404(b), 413, 414, 415
    Frauds or misconduct, Rule 404(b)
Preliminary questions of fact, Rule 104
Probative value, Rule 401; Rule 403

INDEX

Real evidence, Rule 401
Relevancy conditioned on fact, Rule 104(b); Rules 404(b), 413, 414, 415; Rule 901(a)
Similar events and transactions, Rule 401
Surprise, Rule 403
Trial court discretion, Rule 403
Undisputed facts, Rule 401, Rule 404(b)
Undue delay, Rule 403
Unfair prejudice, Rule 403; Rule 404(b), Rule 413; Rule 414; Rule 415
Waste of time, Rule 403

RELIGIOUS BELIEFS OR OPINIONS, Rule 601, Rule 603, Rule 610

RELIGIOUS ORGANIZATIONS
Records of, Rule 803(11)

REMAINDER OF WRITINGS OR RECORDED STATEMENTS, Rule 106

REMEDIAL MEASURES
See Subsequent Remedial Measures

REMOVING THE STING, Rule 607

RENDITION
Applicability of rules, Rule 1101

REPUTATION
Boundaries, Rule 803(20)
Character, Rule 404(a), Rule 405, Rule 803(21)
General history, Rule 803(20)
Personal and family history, Rule 803(23)
Truthfulness, Rule 608

RESIDUAL HEARSAY EXCEPTION, Rule 807

REVERSIBLE ERROR, Rule 103

ROUTINE PRACTICE, Rule 406

RULE OF COMPLETENESS, Rule 106

RULINGS ON EVIDENCE, Rule 103

S

SCOPE OF CROSS-EXAMINATION, Rule 611

SEARCH WARRANTS
Applicability of rules, Rule 1101

SECONDARY EVIDENCE
Best Evidence Rule, Rules 1002, 1004

SELF-AUTHENTICATION
    Generally, Rule 902
Acknowledged documents, Rule 902(8)
Certification to prove authenticity, Rules 902(11)–(14)
Certified business records, Rule 902(11), (12)
Certified copies of public records, Rule 902
Commercial paper, Rule 902
Domestic public documents not under seal, Rule 902(2)
Domestic public documents under seal, Rule 902(1)
Foreign public documents, Rule 902(3)
Newspapers and periodicals, Rule 902(6)
Official publications, Rule 902(5)
Statutes or other rules, Rule 902
Trade inscriptions, Rule 902(7)

SELF-DEFENSE, Rule 404(a)

SEQUESTRATION OF WITNESSES, Rule 615

SETTLEMENT
See Compromise

INDEX

INDEX

INDEX

WITHDRAWN PLEAS, Rule 410

WITNESSES
> See also Character Evidence; Cross-Examination; Expert Witness; Impeachment; Marital Privileges; Rehabilitation of Witness

Bolstering, Rule 608
Competency, Rule 405, Rule 601
Exclusion, Rule 615
Interrogation by court, Rule 614
Leading questions, Rule 611
Occupation, Rule 608
Power of court to call, Rule 614
Residence, Rule 608
Sequestration, Rule 615

X

X-RAYS, Rule 1002

Appendix I

UNIFORM RULES OF EVIDENCE (AS AMENDED IN 2005)

Table of Contents

APPENDIX I

UNIFORM RULES OF EVIDENCE

UNIFORM RULES OF EVIDENCE

PREFATORY NOTE

Codification of rules of evidence has proven to be more of a "work in progress" enterprise than was originally anticipated by the various drafting bodies at work in the 1970's. Societal changes, advances in both the hard and soft science and improvements in information technology have exposed many problematic evidentiary situations routinely faced by lawyers and judges. With increasing frequency, the rules fail to fit into a new environment, or alternatively, if they fit, they produce measurable inequity. It is within this context that the Drafting Committee to revise the Uniform Rules of Evidence of 1974, as amended, presented its final work product to the National Conference of Commissioners on Uniform State Laws at its 1999 Annual Meeting in Denver, Colorado.

The assignment from the Conference's Scope and Program and Executive Committees authorized a comprehensive analysis of significant problems, with directions to keep in mind that the law of evidence, being applicable to an almost unlimited range of subject matter, does not reasonably respond to micro-management by the rule maker.

It may be prudent to anticipate one area of inquiry arising from an earlier mandate directed to the Drafting Committee that concluded its work with the 1986 amendments adopted at the Boston Conference. Responding to the expanding interstate and intercourt nature of the practice of law, the Drafting Committee was charged with bringing the language of the Uniform Rules of Evidence into line with comparable provisions in the Federal Rules of Evidence, where reasonably possible. The underlying theory was, apparently, that a trial practitioner need master only one set of rules to comfortably practice in both

APPENDIX I

federal and state forums located in various States, Districts, and Circuits. However, in practice, this theory does not seem to work as well as expected. In operation, the same words are often construed differently by different courts, even by sister federal circuits and state jurisdictions. Thus, the careful lawyer must continue to research certain rules of evidence on a case-by-case basis.

As a result, the current Drafting Committee has endeavored to draft the amended rules in clear and reasonably understandable terms without slavish regard for other existing work product. In this context, you will note, for the first time, that we have created a definitions rule, as amended Rule 101, containing terms that are used in several different Uniform Rules. The Drafting Committee is also proposing a unique approach to accommodate the admissibility of electronic evidence through the use of the term "record" throughout the rules in lieu of the terminology "writings," "recordings," and "photographs" and appropriately defining "record" in Rule 101(3). Numerous stylistic changes have also been made throughout the Uniform Rules as recommended by the Committee on Style.

The Drafting Committee also met on October 30–November 1, 1998 and February 26–28, 1999 to consider the comments, criticisms and suggestions of the Committee of the Whole of the Conference at the First Reading in 1988 of proposed amendments to the Uniform Rules. Hopefully, the Committee gave due consideration to all of the views expressed by Commissioners at the First Reading even though for various reasons all of them were not recommended or adopted. Among the Uniform Rules in which substantive revisions have been made based upon recommendations of the Committee of the Whole are: Rule 404(c) narrowing the scope of the procedural rules to apply in criminal cases when evidence of other crimes, wrongs or acts is offered against an accused; Rule 407 clarifying the meaning of an event in determining the applicability of the rule excluding evidence of subsequent remedial measures; Rules 803(6) and 803(8) to provide that public records inadmissible under Rule 803(8) are inadmissible as business records under Rule 803(6); and Rule 807 which tightens up the criteria for determining the admissibility of statements of children relating to neglect, or physical or sexual abuse.

It should also again be noted that Congress added Rules 413 through 415 of the Federal Rules of Evidence on September 13, 1994, Pub. L. 103–222, § 320935(a), 108 Stat. 2135, effective July 9, 1995. Rules 413 through 415 permit respectively, (1) the admissibility of evidence of prior offenses of sexual assault when, in a criminal proceeding, a person is accused of such an offense; (2) the admissibility of evidence of prior offenses of child molestation when, in a criminal proceeding, a person is accused of child molestation, and (3) the admissibility of evidence of prior offenses of sexual assault, or of child molestation when, in a civil proceeding, a claim for damages or other relief is sought against a party who is alleged to have committed an act of sexual assault or child molestation.

The overwhelming majority of judges, lawyers, law professors and legal organizations who responded to the Federal Advisory Committee's call for public response opposed the enactment of Rules 413 through 415 without equivocation. The principal objections expressed were twofold. First, the rules would permit the admission of unfairly prejudicial evidence by focusing on convicting a criminal defendant for what the defendant *is* rather than what the defendant *has done*.

Second, the rules contained numerous drafting problems apparently not intended by their authors. For example, mandating the admissibility of the evidence without regard to the other rules of evidence such as the Rule 403 balancing test and the hearsay rule. In turn, it was believed that serious constitutional questions would arise in criminal proceedings in which the rules were invoked. For these and related reasons, the Advisory Committee on the Federal Rules of Evidence, the Standing Committee on Rules of Practice and

UNIFORM RULES OF EVIDENCE

Procedure and the Judicial Conference of the United States opposed the enactment of Rules 413 through 415.

Alternatively, the Standing Committee and the Judicial Conference recommended the adoption of an amendment to Rules 404 and 405 of the Federal Rules of Evidence proposed by the Advisory Committee which would provide for the admission of such evidence under limited conditions. However, Congress elected not to accept the recommendation.

In spite of the expressed concerns for the constitutionality of Rules 413 through 415, they are being given surprising vitality among the federal circuit courts that have considered the issue. These courts have held that the rules do not violate the Due Process Clause subject to the balancing of relevancy against unfair prejudice as provided in Rule 403 of the Federal Rules of Evidence. *See United States v. Mound*, 149 F.3d 799 (8th Cir. 1998); *United States v. Summer*, 119 F.3d 658 (8th Cir. 1997); *United States v. Castillo*, 140 F.3d 874 (10th Cir. 1998); *United States v. Guardia*, 135 F.3d 1326 (10th Cir. 1998); *United States v. Enjady*, 134 F.3d 1427 (10th Cir. 1998); and *United States v. Larson*, 112 F.3d 600 (2d Cir. 1997).

However, there is still some lingering for the constitutionality of these rules. *See* the dissenting opinion from an order denying a petition for rehearing *en banc* in *United States v. Mound*, 157 F.3d 1153 (8th Cir. 1998), in which it is argued that an *en banc* court ought to consider the constitutionality of Rule 413 because the rule "presents [so] great a risk that the jury will convict a defendant for his past conduct or unsavory character" that it violates due process. *Id.* at 157 F.3d 1153. *See further*, M.A. Sheft, *Federal Rules of Evidence 413: A Dangerous New Frontier*, 33 Am. Crim. L. Rev. 57, 77–82 (1995).

In any event, the propriety of including Rules 413 through 415 in the Uniform Rules of Evidence was considered questionable at best. There is no state which has adopted these rules to date. In Arizona, their adoption was considered by the Supreme Court of Arizona, but was rejected largely for the same reasons they were rejected by the Judicial Conference of the United States. *See* Robert L. Gottsfield, *We Just Don't Get It: Improper Admission of Other Acts Under Evidence Rule 404(B) as Needless Cause of Reversal in Civil and Criminal Cases*, Ariz. Att'y, Apr. 1997 at 24. Connecticut has reprinted Federal Rules 413 through 415 in its Trial Lawyers Guide to Evidence, but they are inapplicable in state court proceedings. Indiana has a rule similar to Federal Rule 414, but it is more carefully drawn with procedural safeguards. *See* Ind. Code Ann. § 35–37–4–15 (West 1997). California also has statutes authorizing the introduction of prior sexual offenses or acts of domestic violence subject to balancing relevancy against unfair prejudice. *See* Cal. Evid. Code §§ 1108, 1109 (West 1997). Section 1108 has been held constitutional by the California Court of Appeal in *People v. Fitch* (App. 3 Dist. 1997), 63 Cal. Rptr. 753, 55 Cal. App. 4th 172. Missouri also had a blanket statutory rule, since held unconstitutional, admitting evidence of prior acts of child molestation similar to Federal Rule 414. *See* Mo. Ann. Stat. § 566.025 (West 1978).

For the foregoing reasons and apparent lack of support to date among the several states for the enactment of rules similar to Rules 413 through 415, the Drafting Committee, at its meeting in Cleveland, Ohio, on October 46, 1996, voted unanimously not to include or recommend the adoption of Rules 413 through 415 by the Conference.

Similarly, the Drafting Committee did not recommend the adoption of the Advisory Committee's earlier carefully drawn proposed amendment to Rule 404 of the Federal Rules of Evidence to deal with the issue.

These decisions of the Drafting Committee have now been reinforced by the decision of the Supreme Court of Missouri in *State v. Burns*, 978 S.W.2d 759 (Mo. 1998), holding that Section 566.025, *supra*, contravened the Missouri

APPENDIX I

Constitution. In Burns, a prosecution for statutory sodomy, the trial court admitted the testimony of two witnesses relating to prior uncharged acts of sexual abuse committed by the defendant pursuant to Section 566.025, RSMo 1994, providing that evidence of other charged and uncharged crimes "shall be admissible for the purpose of showing the propensity of the defendant to commit the crime or crimes with which he is charged."

The Missouri Supreme Court reasoned that Section 566.025 violated Article I, Section 17 providing "[t]hat no person shall be prosecuted criminally for felony or misdemeanor otherwise than by indictment or information" and Article I, Section 18(a) providing "[t]hat in criminal prosecutions the accused shall have the right . . . to demand the nature and cause of the accusation; . . . ." In doing so it rejected the state's argument that Section 566.062 did not violate Sections 17 and 18(a) of Article I since the defendant was not "on trial" for the uncharged conduct because he could be convicted only for the formally charged crime. This interpretation, the Court reasoned, would enable the jury to "improperly convict the defendant because of his propensity to commit such crimes without regard to whether he is actually guilty of the charged crime. * * * As a result, the defendant is forced to defend against the uncharged conduct in addition to the charged crime."

The Court also rejected the State's argument that in determining the admissibility of propensity evidence under Section 566.025 the trial court can balance the value and effect of evidence of other crimes. This interpretation, the Court also reasoned, would require ignoring the Legislature's use of the mandatory term "shall," an approach which has largely been ignored by the federal circuit courts in dealing with this issue. Finally, the defendant also contended that Section 566.025 violated the Fifth, Sixth, and Fourteenth Amendments to the United States Constitution. However, the Court did not reach these issues by concluding that the challenge under the Missouri Constitution was dispositive.

Within the foregoing approach the proposed amendments of the Uniform Rules of Evidence (1999) were approved and recommended for enactment in all states at the Conference's Annual Meeting, meeting in its One-Hundred-and-Eighth Year in Denver, Colorado, July 23–30, 1999.

ARTICLE I

GENERAL PROVISIONS

Rule 101.   Definitions.

In these rules:

(1)   "Person" means an individual, corporation, business trust, estate, trust, partnership, limited liability company, association, joint venture, government; governmental subdivision, agency, or instrumentality; public corporation; or any other legal or commercial entity.

(2)   "Public record" means a record of a public office or agency in which the record is prepared, filed, or recorded pursuant to law.

(3)   "Record" means information that is inscribed on a tangible medium or that is stored in an electronic or other medium and is retrievable in perceivable form.

(4)   "State" means a State of the United States, the District of Columbia, Puerto Rico, the United States Virgin Islands, or any territory or insular possession subject to the jurisdiction of the United States.

Rule 102.   Scope, Purpose, and Construction.

(a)   Rules applicable. Except as otherwise provided in subdivision (b), these rules apply to all actions and proceedings in the courts of this State.

(b)   Rules inapplicable. These rules, other than those applicable to privileges, do not apply in:

(1)   the determination of questions of fact preliminary to admissibility of evidence if the issue is to be determined by the court under Rule 104(a);

(2)   proceedings before grand juries;

(3)   proceedings for contempt in which the court may act summarily; and

(4)   miscellaneous proceedings, such as proceedings involving extradition or rendition; [preliminary] [probable cause] hearings in criminal cases; [sentencing]; granting or revoking probation; issuance of warrants for arrest, criminal summonses, and search warrants; and release on bail or otherwise.

(c)   Purpose and construction. These rules must be construed to secure fairness, eliminate unjustifiable expense and delay, and promote the growth and development of the law of evidence, to the end that truth may be ascertained and issues justly determined.

Rule 103.   Rulings on Evidence.

(a)   Effect of erroneous ruling. Error may not be predicated upon a ruling that admits or excludes evidence unless a substantial right of the party is affected, and:

(1)   if the ruling is one admitting evidence, a timely objection or motion to strike appears of record, stating the specific ground of objection, if the specific ground was not apparent from the context; or

343

(2)   if the ruling is one excluding evidence, the substance of the evidence was made known to the court by offer or was apparent from the context within which questions were asked.

(b)   Record of offer and ruling. The court may add any other or further statement that shows the character of the evidence, the form in which it was offered, the objection made, and the ruling thereon. It may direct the making of an offer in question and answer form.

(c)   Effect of pretrial ruling. If the court makes a definitive pretrial ruling on the record admitting or excluding evidence, a party need not renew an objection or offer of proof at trial to preserve a claim of error for appeal.

(d)   Hearing of jury. In jury cases, proceedings must be conducted, to the extent practicable, so as to prevent inadmissible evidence from being suggested to the jury by any means, such as making statements or offers of proof or asking questions within the hearing of the jury.

(e)   Errors affecting substantial rights. This rule does not preclude a court from taking notice of an error affecting a substantial right even if it was not brought to the attention of the trial court.

Rule 104.   Preliminary Questions.

(a)   Questions of admissibility generally. Preliminary questions concerning the qualification of an individual to be a witness, the existence of a privilege, or the admissibility of evidence must be determined by the court, subject to subdivision (b). In making its determination, the court is not bound by the rules of evidence except the rules with respect to privileges.

(b)   Determination of privilege. A person claiming a privilege must prove that the conditions prerequisite to the existence of the privilege are more probably true than not. A person claiming an exception to a privilege must prove that the conditions prerequisite to the applicability of the exception are more probably true than not. If there is a factual basis to support a good faith belief that a review of the allegedly privileged material is necessary, the court, in making its determination, may review the material outside the presence of any other person.

(c)   Relevancy conditioned on fact. If the relevancy of evidence depends upon the fulfillment of a condition of fact, the court shall admit it upon, in the court's discretion, subject to the introduction of evidence sufficient to support a finding of the fulfillment of the condition.

(d)   Hearing of jury. A hearing on the admissibility of a confession in a criminal case must be conducted out of the hearing of the jury. A hearing on any other preliminary matter must be so conducted if the interests of justice require or, in a criminal case, an accused is a witness and so requests.

(e)   Testimony by accused. An accused, by testifying upon a preliminary matter, does not become subject to cross-examination as to other issues in the case.

(f)   Weight and credibility. This rule does not limit the right of a party to introduce before the jury evidence relevant to weight or credibility.

Rule 105.   Limited Admissibility.

If evidence that is admissible as to one party or for one purpose but not admissible as to another party or for another purpose is admitted, the court, upon request, shall restrict the evidence to its proper scope and instruct the jury accordingly.

Comment

This rule is not intended to affect a power of a court to order a severance or separate trial of issues in a multi-party case.

Rule 106.   Remainder of, or Related, Record.

If a record or part thereof is introduced by a party, an adverse party may require the introduction at that time of any other part or any other record that in fairness ought to be considered contemporaneously with it.

APPENDIX I

ARTICLE II

JUDICIAL NOTICE

Rule 201.   Judicial Notice of Adjudicative Facts.

(a)   Scope of rule. This rule governs only judicial notice of adjudicative facts.

(b)   Kinds of facts. A judicially noticed fact must be one that is not subject to reasonable dispute because it is:

(1)   generally known within the territorial jurisdiction of the trial court; or

(2)   capable of accurate and ready determination by resort to sources whose accuracy cannot reasonably be questioned.

(c)   When discretionary. A court may take judicial notice, whether requested or not.

(d)   When mandatory. A court shall take judicial notice if requested by a party and supplied with the necessary information.

(e)   Opportunity to be heard. A party is entitled upon timely request to an opportunity to be heard as to the propriety of taking judicial notice and the tenor of the matter noticed. In the absence of earlier notification, the request may be made after judicial notice has been taken.

(f)   Time of taking notice. Judicial notice may be taken at any stage of the proceeding.

(g)   Instructing jury. The court shall instruct the jury to accept as conclusive a fact judicially noticed.

ARTICLE III

PRESUMPTIONS

Rule 301.   Definitions.

In this article:

(1) "Basic fact" means a fact or group of facts that give rise to a presumption.

(2) "Inconsistent presumption" means that the presumed fact of one presumption is inconsistent with the presumed fact of another presumption.

(3) "Presumed fact" means a fact that is assumed upon the finding of a basic fact.

(4) "Presumption" means that when a basic fact is found to exist, the presumed fact is assumed to exist until the nonexistence of the presumed fact is determined as provided in Rules 302 and 303.

Rule 302.   Effect of Presumptions in Civil Cases.

(a) General rule. In a civil action or proceeding, unless otherwise provided by statute, judicial decision, or these rules, a presumption imposes on the party against whom it is directed the burden of proving that the nonexistence of the presumed fact is more probable than its existence.

(b) Inconsistent presumptions. If presumptions are inconsistent, the presumption applies that is founded upon weightier considerations of policy. If considerations of policy are of equal weight, neither presumption applies.

(c) Effect if federal law provides the rule of decision. The effect of presumption respecting a fact that is an element of a claim or defense as to which federal law provides the rule of decision is determined in accordance with federal law.

Rule 303.   Scope and Effect of Presumptions in Criminal Cases.

(a) Scope. Except as otherwise provided by statute or judicial decision, this rule governs presumptions against an accused in criminal cases, recognized at common law or created by statute, including statutory provisions that certain facts are prima facie evidence of other facts or of guilt.

(b) Submission to jury. The court may not direct the jury to find a presumed fact against an accused. If a presumed fact establishes guilt, is an element of the offense, or negates a defense, the court may submit the question of guilt or of the existence of the presumed fact to the jury, but only if a reasonable juror on the evidence as a whole, including the evidence of the basic fact, could find guilt or the presumed fact beyond a reasonable doubt. If the presumed fact has a lesser effect, the question of its existence may be submitted to the jury if the basic fact is supported by substantial evidence or is otherwise established, unless the court determines that a reasonable juror could not find on the evidence as a whole the existence of the presumed fact.

(c) Instructing the jury. At the time the existence of a presumed fact against the accused is submitted to the jury, the court shall instruct the jury that it may regard the basic fact as sufficient evidence of the presumed fact but is not required to do so. In addition, if a presumed fact establishes guilt, is an element of the offense, or negates a defense, the court shall instruct the jury that its existence, on all the evidence, must be proved beyond a reasonable doubt.

ARTICLE IV

RELEVANCY AND ITS LIMITS

Rule 401.   Definition of "Relevant Evidence."

In this article, relevant evidence means evidence having any tendency to make the existence of any fact that is of consequence to the determination of the action more probable or less probable than it would be without the evidence.

Rule 402.   Relevant Evidence Generally Admissible; Irrelevant Evidence Inadmissible.

All relevant evidence is admissible, except as otherwise provided by statute, these rules, or other rules applicable in the courts of this State. Evidence that is not relevant is not admissible.

Rule 403.   Exclusion of Relevant Evidence on Grounds of Prejudice, Confusion, or Waste of Time.

Although relevant, evidence may be excluded if its probative value is substantially outweighed by the danger of unfair prejudice, confusion of the issues, or misleading the jury, or by considerations of undue delay, waste of time, or needless presentation of cumulative evidence.

Rule 404.   Character Evidence Not Admissible to Prove Conduct, Exceptions; Other Crimes.

(a)   Character evidence generally. Evidence of a person's character or a trait of character is not admissible for the purpose of proving the person acted in conformity therewith on a particular occasion, except:

(1)   evidence of a pertinent trait of the accused's character offered by an accused, or by the prosecution to rebut that evidence;

(2)   evidence of a pertinent trait of character of the alleged victim of the crime offered by an accused, or by the prosecution to rebut that evidence, or evidence of a character trait of peacefulness of the alleged victim offered by the prosecution in a homicide case to rebut evidence that the alleged victim was the first aggressor; and

(3)   evidence of the character of a witness, as provided in Rules 607, 608, and 609.

(b)   Other crimes, wrongs, or acts. Evidence of other crimes, wrongs, or acts is not admissible to prove the character of a person in order to show the person acted in conformity therewith. However, it may be admissible for another purpose, such as proof of motive, opportunity, intent, preparation, plan, knowledge, identity, or absence of mistake or accident.

(c)   Determination of admissibility. Evidence is not admissible under subdivision (b) unless:

(1)   the proponent gives to all adverse parties reasonable notice in advance of trial, or during trial if the court excuses pretrial notice for good cause shown, of the nature of the evidence the proponent intends to introduce at trial;

(2) if offered against an accused in a criminal case, the court conducts a hearing to determine the admissibility of the evidence and finds:

> (A) by clear and convincing evidence, that the other crime, wrong, or act was committed;

> (B) that the evidence is relevant to a purpose for which the evidence is admissible under subdivision (b); and

> (C) that the probative value of the evidence outweighs the danger of unfair prejudice; and

(3) upon the request of a party, the court gives an instruction on the limited admissibility of the evidence pursuant to Rule 105.

Rule 405.   Methods of Proving Character.

(a) Reputation or opinion. If evidence of character or a trait of character of a person is admissible, proof may be by testimony as to reputation or in the form of opinion. On cross-examination, inquiry is allowable into relevant specific instances of conduct.

(b) Specific instances of conduct. If character or a trait of character of a person is an essential element of a charge, claim, or defense, proof may also be made of specific instances of the person's conduct.

Rule 406.   Habit; Routine Practice.

(a) Admissibility. Evidence of the habit of an individual or of the routine practice of a person other than an individual, whether corroborated or not and regardless of the presence of eyewitnesses, is relevant to prove that the conduct of the individual or other person on a particular occasion was in conformity with the habit or routine practice.

(b) Method of proof. Habit or routine practice may be proved by testimony in the form of an opinion or by specific instances of conduct sufficient in number to warrant a finding that the habit existed or that the practice was routine.

Rule 407.   Subsequent Remedial Measures.

If, after an event, measures are taken that, if taken previously, would have made injury or harm less likely to occur, evidence of the subsequent measures is not admissible to prove negligence, culpable conduct, a defect in a product, a defect in a product's design, or a need for a warning or instruction. Evidence of subsequent measures may be admissible if offered for another purpose, such as impeachment or, if controverted, proof of ownership, control, or feasibility of precautionary measures. An event includes the sale of a product to a user or consumer.

Rule 408.   Compromise and Offers to Compromise.

Evidence of furnishing, offering, promising to furnish, or accepting, offering, or promising to accept, a valuable consideration in compromising or attempting to compromise a claim that was disputed as to either validity or amount is not admissible to prove liability for, invalidity of, or amount of the claim, or any other claim. Evidence of conduct or statements made in compromise negotiations is likewise not admissible. This rule does not require the exclusion of evidence otherwise discoverable merely because it is presented in the course of compromise negotiations. This rule also does not require exclusion if the evidence is offered for another purpose, such as proving bias or prejudice of a witness, negating a contention of undue delay, or proving an effort to obstruct a criminal investigation or prosecution.

Rule 409.   Payment of Medical and Similar Expenses.

Evidence of furnishing, offering, or promising to pay medical, hospital, or similar expenses occasioned by an injury is not admissible to prove liability for the injury.

Rule 410.   Inadmissibility of Pleas, Plea Discussions, and Related Statements.

(a)   General. Except as otherwise provided in subdivision (b), evidence of the following is not admissible in a civil or criminal proceeding against the defendant who made the plea or was a participant in the plea discussions:

(1)   a plea of guilty that was later withdrawn;

(2)   a plea of nolo contendere;

(3)   a statement made in the course of any proceedings under Rule 11 of the Federal Rules of Criminal Procedure, [Rules 443 and 444 of the Uniform Rules of Criminal Procedure, or comparable state procedure of this or any other State] regarding either of the foregoing pleas; and

(4)   a statement made in the course of plea discussions with an attorney for the prosecuting authority which do not result in a plea of guilty or which result in a plea of guilty later withdrawn.

(b)   Exceptions. A statement described in subdivision (a) is admissible:

(1)   in a proceeding in which another statement made in the course of the same plea or plea discussions has been introduced and, in fairness, the statement should be considered contemporaneously with the other statement; and

(2)   in a criminal proceeding for perjury or false statement if the statement was made by the defendant under oath, on the record, and in the presence of counsel.

Rule 411.   Liability Insurance.

Evidence that a person was or was not insured against liability is not admissible upon the issue as to whether the person acted negligently or otherwise wrongfully. This rule does not require the exclusion of evidence of insurance against liability when offered for another purpose, such as proof of agency, ownership, or control, or bias or prejudice of a witness.

Rule 412.   Sexual Behavior.

(a)   Definition. In this rule, "sexual behavior" means behavior relating to the sexual activities of an individual, including the individual's experience or observation of sexual intercourse or sexual contact, use of contraceptives, history of marriage or divorce, sexual predisposition, expressions of sexual ideas or emotions, and activities of the mind such as fantasies or dreams.

(b)   Evidence of sexual behavior generally inadmissible. Except as otherwise provided in subdivisions (c) and (d), in a criminal proceeding involving the alleged sexual misconduct of an accused, evidence may not be admitted to prove that the alleged victim engaged in other sexual behavior.

(c)   Exceptions. Evidence of specific instances of an alleged victim's sexual behavior, if otherwise admissible under these rules, is admissible to prove:

(1)   that a person other than the accused was the source of the semen, injury, disease, other physical evidence, or pregnancy;

(2)   that a person other than the accused was the source of the alleged victim's knowledge of sexual behavior;

(3)   consent, if the alleged victim's sexual behavior involved the accused or constituted conduct so distinctive and which so closely resembles the accused's version of the sexual behavior of the alleged victim at the time of the alleged sexual misconduct that it corroborates the accused's claim of reasonable belief that the alleged victim consented to the alleged misconduct; or

(4)   a fact of consequence whose exclusion would violate the constitutional rights of the accused.

(d)   Procedure to determine admissibility. Evidence is not admissible under subdivision (c) unless:

(1)   the proponent gives to all parties and to the alleged victim, or the alleged victim's guardian or representative, reasonable notice in advance of trial, or during trial if the court excuses pretrial notice for good cause shown, of the nature of such evidence the proponent intends to introduce at trial;

(2)   the court conducts a hearing in chambers, affords the alleged victim and the parties a right to attend the hearing and be heard, and finds:

(A)   that the evidence is relevant to a fact of consequence for which the evidence is admissible under subdivision (c); and

(B)   that the probative value of the evidence is not substantially outweighed by the danger of harm to the alleged victim or of unfair prejudice to any party; and

(3)   upon request, the court gives an instruction on the limited admissibility of the evidence, pursuant to Rule 105.

ARTICLE V

PRIVILEGES

Rule 501.   Privileges Recognized Only as Provided.

Except as otherwise provided by constitution or statute or by these or other rules promulgated by [the Supreme Court of this State], no person has a privilege to:

(1)   refuse to be a witness;

(2)   refuse to disclose any matter;

(3)   refuse to produce any object or record; or

(4)   prevent another from being a witness or disclosing any matter or producing any object or record.

Comment

The word "record" has been substituted for the word "writing." See the Comment to Rule 101.

Rule 502.   Lawyer-Client Privilege.

(a)   Definitions. In this rule:

(1)   "Client" means a person for whom a lawyer renders professional legal services or who consults a lawyer with a view to obtaining professional legal services from the lawyer.

(2)   A communication is "confidential" if it is not intended to be disclosed to third persons other than those to whom disclosure is made in furtherance of the rendition of professional legal services to the client or those reasonably necessary for the transmission of the communication.

(3)   "Lawyer" means a person authorized, or reasonably believed by the client to be authorized, to engage in the practice of law in any State or country.

(4)   "Representative of the client" means a person having authority to obtain professional legal services, or to act on legal advice rendered, on behalf of the client or a person who, for the purpose of effectuating legal representation for the client, makes or receives a confidential communication while acting in the scope of employment for the client.

(5)   "Representative of the lawyer" means a person employed, or reasonably believed by the client to be employed, by the lawyer to assist the lawyer in rendering professional legal services.

(b)   General rule of privilege. A client has a privilege to refuse to disclose and to prevent any other person from disclosing a confidential communication made for the purpose of facilitating the rendition of professional legal services to the client:

(1)   between the client or a representative of the client and the client's lawyer or a representative of the lawyer;

(2)   between the lawyer and a representative of the lawyer;

(3)   by the client or a representative of the client or the client's lawyer or a representative of the lawyer to a lawyer or a representative of a lawyer representing another party in a pending action and concerning a matter of common interest therein;

(4)   between representatives of the client or between the client and a representative of the client; or

(5)   among lawyers and their representatives representing the same client.

(c)   Who may claim privilege. The privilege under this rule may be claimed by the client, the client's guardian or conservator, the personal representative of a deceased client, or the successor, trustee, or similar representative of a corporation, association, or other organization, whether or not in existence. A person who was the lawyer or the lawyer's representative at the time of the communication is presumed to have authority to claim the privilege, but only on behalf of the client.

(d)   Exceptions. There is no privilege under this rule:

(1)   if the services of the lawyer were sought or obtained to enable or aid anyone to commit or plan to commit what the client knew or reasonably should have known was a crime or fraud;

(2)   as to a communication relevant to an issue between parties who claim through the same deceased client, regardless of whether the claims are by testate or intestate succession or by transaction inter vivos;

(3)   as to a communication relevant to an issue of breach of duty by a lawyer to the client or by a client to the lawyer;

(4)   as to a communication necessary for a lawyer to defend in a legal proceeding an accusation that the lawyer assisted the client in criminal or fraudulent conduct;

(5)   as to a communication relevant to an issue concerning an attested document to which the lawyer is an attesting witness;

(6)   as to a communication relevant to a matter of common interest between or among two or more clients if the communication was made by any of them to a lawyer retained or consulted in common, when offered in an action between or among any of the clients; or

(7)   as to a communication between a public officer or agency and its lawyers unless the communication concerns a pending investigation, claim, or action and the court determines that disclosure will seriously impair the ability of the public officer or agency to act upon the claim or conduct a pending investigation, litigation, or proceeding in the public interest.

Rule 503.   [Psychotherapist] [Physician and Psychotherapist] [Physician and Mental-Health Provider] [Mental-Health Provider]-Patient Privilege.

(a)   Definitions. In this rule:

(1)   A communication is "confidential" if it is not intended to be disclosed to third persons, except those present to further the interest of the patient in the consultation, examination, or interview, those reasonably necessary for the transmission of the communication, and

persons who are participating in the diagnosis and treatment of the patient under the direction of a [psychotherapist] [physician or psychotherapist] [physician or mental-health provider] [mental-health provider], including members of the patient's family.

[(2) "Mental-health provider" means a person authorized, in any State or country, or reasonably believed by the patient to be authorized, to engage in the diagnosis or treatment of a mental or emotional condition, including addiction to alcohol or drugs.]

[(3) "Patient" means an individual who consults or is examined or interviewed by a[psychotherapist] [physician or psychotherapist] [physician or mental-health provider] [mental-health provider].]

[(4) "Physician" means a person authorized in any State or country, or reasonably believed by the patient to be authorized to practice medicine.]

[(5) "Psychotherapist" means a person authorized in any State or country, or reasonably believed by the patient to be authorized, to practice medicine, while engaged in the diagnosis or treatment of a mental or emotional condition, including addiction to alcohol or drugs, or a person licensed or certified under the laws of any State or country, or reasonably believed by the patient to be licensed or certified, as a psychologist, while similarly engaged.]

(b)   General rule of privilege. A patient has a privilege to refuse to disclose and to prevent any other person from disclosing confidential communications made for the purpose of diagnosis or treatment of the patient's [physical,] mental[,] or emotional condition, including addiction to alcohol or drugs, among the patient, the patient's [psychotherapist] [physician or psychotherapist] [physician or mental-health provider] [mental-health provider] and persons, including members of the patient's family, who are participating in the diagnosis or treatment under the direction of the [psychotherapist] [physician or psychotherapist] [physician or mental-health provider] [mental-health provider].

(c)   Who may claim the privilege. The privilege under this rule may be claimed by the patient, the patient's guardian or conservator, or the personal representative of a deceased patient. The person who was the [psychotherapist] [physician or psychotherapist] [physician or mental-health provider] [mental-health provider] at the time of the communication is presumed to have authority to claim the privilege, but only on behalf of the patient.

(d)   Exceptions. There is no privilege under this rule for a communication:

(1)   relevant to an issue in proceedings to hospitalize the patient for mental illness, if the [psychotherapist] [physician or psychotherapist] [physician or mental-health provider] [mental-health provider], in the course of diagnosis or treatment, has determined that the patient is in need of hospitalization;

(2)   made in the course of a court-ordered investigation or examination of the [physical,] mental[,] or emotional condition of the patient, whether a party or a witness, with respect to the particular purpose for which the examination is ordered, unless the court orders otherwise;

(3) relevant to an issue of the [physical,] mental[,] or emotional condition of the patient in any proceeding in which the patient relies upon the condition as an element of the patient's claim or defense or, after the patient's death, in any proceeding in which any party relies upon the condition as an element of the party's claim or defense;

(4) if the services of the [psychotherapist] [physician or psychotherapist] [physician or mental-health provider] [mental-health provider] were sought or obtained to enable or aid anyone to commit or plan to commit what the patient knew, or reasonably should have known, was a crime or fraud or mental or physical injury to the patient or another individual;

(5) in which the patient has expressed an intent to engage in conduct likely to result in imminent death or serious bodily injury to the patient or another individual;

(6) relevant to an issue in a proceeding challenging the competency of the [psychotherapist] [physician or psychotherapist] [physician or mental-health provider] [mental-health provider];

(7) relevant to a breach of duty by the [psychotherapist] [physician or psychotherapist] [physician or mental-health provider] [mental-health provider]; or

(8) that is subject to a duty to disclose under [statutory law].

Rule 504.   Spousal Privilege.

(a) Confidential communication. A communication is confidential if it is made privately by an individual to the individual's spouse and is not intended for disclosure to any other person.

(b) Marital communications. An individual has a privilege to refuse to testify and to prevent the individual's spouse or former spouse from testifying as to any confidential communication made by the individual to the spouse during their marriage. The privilege may be waived only by the individual holding the privilege or by the holder's guardian or conservator, or the individual's personal representative if the individual is deceased.

(c) Spousal testimony in criminal proceeding. The spouse of an accused in a criminal proceeding has a privilege to refuse to testify against the accused spouse.

(d) Exceptions. There is no privilege under this rule:

(1) in any civil proceeding in which the spouses are adverse parties;

(2) in any criminal proceeding in which an unrefuted showing is made that the spouses acted jointly in the commission of the crime charged,;

(3) in any proceeding in which one spouse is charged with a crime or tort against the person or property of the other, a minor child of either, an individual residing in the household of either, or a third person if the crime or tort is committed in the course of committing a crime or tort against the other spouse, a minor child of either spouse, or an individual residing in the household of either spouse; or

(4)   in any other proceeding, in the discretion of the court, if the interests of a minor child of either spouse may be adversely affected by invocation of the privilege.

Rule 505.   Religious Privilege.

(a)   Definitions. In this rule:

(1)   "Cleric" means a minister, priest, rabbi, accredited Christian Science Practitioner, or other similar functionary of a religious organization, or an individual reasonably believed so to be by the individual consulting the cleric.

(2)   A communication is "confidential" if it is made privately and not intended for further disclosure except to other persons present in furtherance of the purpose of the communication.

(b)   General rule of privilege. An individual has a privilege to refuse to disclose and to prevent another from disclosing a confidential communication by the individual to a cleric in the cleric's professional capacity as spiritual adviser.

(c)   Who may claim the privilege. The privilege under this rule may be claimed by an individual or the individual's guardian or conservator, or the individual's personal representative if the individual is deceased. The individual who was the cleric at the time of the communication is presumed to have authority to claim the privilege but only on behalf of the communicant.

Rule 506.   Political Vote.

(a)   General rule of privilege. An individual has a privilege to refuse to disclose the tenor of the individual's vote at a political election conducted by secret ballot.

(b)   Exceptions. The privilege under subdivision (a) does not apply if the court finds that the vote was cast illegally or determines that disclosure should be compelled pursuant to [the election laws of the State].

Rule 507.   Trade Secrets.

A person has a privilege, which may be claimed by the person or the person's agent or employee, to refuse to disclose and to prevent other persons from disclosing a trade secret owned by the person, if the allowance of the privilege will not tend to conceal fraud or otherwise work injustice. If disclosure is directed, the court shall take such protective measures as the interest of the holder of the privilege and of the parties and the interests of justice require.

Rule 508.   Secrets of State and Other Official Information; Governmental Privileges.

(a)   Claim of privilege under law of United States. If the law of the United States creates a governmental privilege that the courts of this State must recognize under the Constitution of the United States, the privilege may be claimed as provided by the law of the United States.

(b)   Privileges created by laws of State. No governmental privilege is recognized except as provided in subdivision (a) or created by the constitution, statutes, or rules of this State.

(c)   Effect of sustaining claim. If a claim of governmental privilege is sustained and it appears that a party is thereby deprived of material evidence, the court shall make any further orders the interests of justice require, including striking the testimony of a witness, declaring a mistrial, finding upon an issue as to which the evidence is relevant, or dismissing the action.

Rule 509.   Identity of Informer.

(a)   Rule of privilege. The United States or a State has a privilege to refuse to disclose the identity of an individual who has furnished information relating to or assisted in an investigation of a possible violation of a law to a law enforcement officer or member of a legislative committee or its staff conducting an investigation.

(b)   Who may claim. The privilege under this rule may be claimed by an appropriate representative of the government to which the information was furnished.

(c)   Exceptions. There is no privilege under this rule if the identity of the informer or the informer's interest in the subject matter of the informer's communication has been disclosed by a holder of the privilege or by the informer's own action to persons who would have cause to resent the communication or if the informer appears as a witness for the government.

(d)   Procedures. If it appears that an informer may be able to give testimony relevant to an issue in a criminal case, or to a fair determination of a material issue on the merits in a civil case to which the government is a party, and the informed government invokes the privilege, the court shall give the government an opportunity to show in chambers facts relevant to whether the informer can, in fact, supply the testimony. The showing ordinarily will be by affidavit, but the court may direct that testimony be taken if it finds that the matter cannot be resolved satisfactorily upon affidavit. If the court finds there is a reasonable probability that the informer can give the testimony, and the government elects not to disclose the informer's identity, in criminal cases the court on motion of the defendant or on its own motion shall grant appropriate relief, which may include one or more of the following: requiring the prosecuting attorney to comply, granting the defendant additional time or a continuance, relieving the defendant from making disclosures otherwise required of the defendant, prohibiting the prosecuting attorney from introducing specified evidence, and dismissing charges. In civil cases, the court may issue any order the interests of justice require. Evidence submitted to the court must be sealed and preserved to be made available to the appellate court in the event of an appeal, and the contents may not otherwise be revealed without consent of the informed government. All counsel and parties may be present at every stage of a proceeding under this subdivision except a showing in chambers, if the court has determined that no counsel or party may be present.

Rule 510.   Waiver of Privilege.

(a)   Voluntary disclosure. A person upon whom these rules confer a privilege against disclosure waives the privilege if the person or the person's predecessor, while holder of the privilege, voluntarily discloses or consents to disclosure of any significant part of the privileged matter. This rule does not apply if the disclosure itself is privileged.

(b)   Involuntary disclosure. A claim of privilege is not waived by a disclosure that was compelled erroneously or made without an opportunity to claim the privilege.

Rule 511.   Comment Upon or Inference From Claim of Privilege; Instruction.

(a)   Comment or inference not permitted. A claim of privilege, whether in the present proceeding or upon a previous occasion, is not a proper subject of comment by judge or counsel. No inference may be drawn from the claim.

(b)   Claiming privilege without knowledge of jury. In jury cases, proceedings must be conducted, to the extent practicable, so as to facilitate the making of claims of privilege without the knowledge of the jury.

(c)   Jury instruction. Upon request, any party against whom the jury might draw an adverse inference from a claim of privilege is entitled to an instruction that no inference may be drawn therefrom.

APPENDIX I

ARTICLE VI

WITNESSES

Rule 601.   General Rule of Competency.

Every individual is competent to be a witness except as otherwise provided in these rules.

Rule 602.   Lack of Personal Knowledge.

A witness may not testify to a matter unless evidence is introduced sufficient to support a finding that the witness has personal knowledge of the matter. Evidence to prove personal knowledge may, but need not, consist of the witness's own testimony. This rule is subject to Rule 703, relating to opinion testimony by expert witnesses.

Rule 603.   Oath or Affirmation.

Before testifying, each witness must declare under oath or affirmation that the witness will testify truthfully. The oath or affirmation must be administered in a form calculated to awaken the witness's conscience and impress the witness's mind with the duty to testify truthfully.

Rule 604.   Interpreters.

An interpreter is subject to the provisions of these rules relating to qualification as an expert and the administration of an oath or affirmation to make a true and complete rendition of all communications made during the interpretive process to the best of the interpreter's knowledge and belief.

Rule 605.   Competency of Judge as Witness.

The judge presiding at a trial may not testify in that trial as a witness. An objection need not be made to preserve the point.

Rule 606.   Competency of Juror as Witness.

(a)   At the trial. A member of a jury may not testify as a witness before the jury in the trial of the case in which the juror is sitting. If the juror is called so to testify, the parties must be afforded an opportunity to object out of the presence of the jury.

(b)   Inquiry into validity of verdict or indictment. Upon an inquiry into the validity of a verdict or indictment the following rules apply:

(1)   A juror may not testify to a matter or statement occurring during the course of the jury's deliberations or to the effect of anything upon that or any other juror's mind or emotions as influencing the juror to assent to or dissent from the verdict or indictment or concerning the juror's mental processes in connection therewith.

(2)   A juror's affidavit or evidence of any statement by the juror concerning a matter about which the juror would be precluded from testifying may not be received.

(3)   A juror may testify as to whether extraneous prejudicial information was improperly brought to the jury's attention or whether any outside influence was improperly brought to bear upon a juror.

Rule 607.   Who May Impeach.

The credibility of a witness may be attacked by any party, including the party calling the witness.

Rule 608.   Evidence of Character and Conduct of Witness.

(a)   Opinion and reputation evidence of character. The credibility of a witness may be attacked or supported by evidence in the form of opinion or reputation, subject to the following:

(1)   The evidence may refer only to character for truthfulness or untruthfulness, and

(2)   Evidence of truthful character is admissible only after the character of the witness for truthfulness has been attacked by opinion or reputation evidence or otherwise.

(b)   Specific instances of conduct. Specific instances of the conduct of a witness, for the purpose of attacking or supporting the witness's credibility, other than conviction of crime as provided in Rule 609, may not be proved by extrinsic evidence. However, in the discretion of the court, if probative of truthfulness or untruthfulness, they may be inquired into on cross-examination of the witness (i) concerning the witness's character for truthfulness or untruthfulness, or (ii) concerning the character for truthfulness or untruthfulness of another witness as to which character the witness being cross-examined has testified.

(c)   Privilege against self-incrimination. The giving of testimony, whether by an accused or by any other witness, does not operate as a waiver of the accused's or the witness's privilege against self-incrimination when examined with respect to matters that relate only to credibility.

Rule 609.   Impeachment by Evidence of Conviction of Crime.

(a)   General rule. For the purpose of attacking the credibility of a witness:

(1)   Evidence that a witness other than an accused has been convicted of a crime is admissible, subject to Rule 403, if the crime was punishable by death or imprisonment in excess of one year under the law under which the witness was convicted, and evidence that an accused has been convicted of such a crime is admissible if the court determines that the probative value of the evidence substantially outweighs the danger of unfair prejudice the accused.

(2)   Evidence that a witness has been convicted of a crime of untruthfulness or falsification is admissible, regardless of punishment, if the statutory elements of the crime necessarily involve untruthfulness or falsification.

(b)   Time limit. Evidence of a conviction is not admissible under this rule if a period of more than 10 years has elapsed since the date of the conviction or of the release of the witness from the confinement imposed for the conviction, whichever is the later date, unless the court determines, in the interests of justice, that the probative value of evidence of the conviction supported by specific facts and circumstances substantially outweighs its unfair prejudicial effect.

(c) Effect of pardon, annulment, or certificate of rehabilitation. Evidence of a conviction is not admissible under this rule if the conviction has been:

(1) the subject of a pardon, annulment, certificate of rehabilitation, or other equivalent procedure based on a finding of the rehabilitation of the individual convicted, and that individual has not been convicted of a subsequent crime punishable by death or imprisonment in excess of one year; or

(2) the subject of a pardon, annulment, or other equivalent procedure based on a finding of innocence.

(d) Juvenile adjudications. Evidence of a juvenile adjudication is generally not admissible under this rule. Except as otherwise provided by statute, however, in a criminal case the court may allow evidence of a juvenile adjudication of a witness other than the accused if conviction of the offense would be admissible to attack the credibility of an adult and the court is satisfied that admission of the evidence is necessary for a fair determination of the issue of guilt or innocence.

(e) Pendency of appeal. The pendency of an appeal from a conviction does not render evidence of the conviction inadmissible. Evidence of the pendency of an appeal is admissible.

(f) Notice. Evidence is not admissible under this rule unless the proponent of the evidence gives to all adverse parties reasonable notice in advance of trial, or during trial if the court excuses pretrial notice for good cause shown, of the nature of the conviction.

(g) Record. If objection is made to evidence offered pursuant to subdivision (a)(1) or (2), the court shall state on the record the factors it considered in determining admissibility.

(h) Evidence. If admissible, evidence of a conviction may be by testimony of the witness during direct or cross-examination, by the introduction of a public record, or by other extrinsic evidence if the public record is not available and good cause is shown.

Rule 610.   Religious Beliefs and Opinions.

Evidence of the beliefs or opinions of a witness on matters of religion is not admissible for the purpose of showing that by reason of their nature the witness's credibility is impaired or enhanced.

Rule 611.   Mode and Order of Interrogation and Presentation.

(a) Control by court. The court shall exercise reasonable control over the mode and order of interrogating witnesses and presenting evidence so as to make the interrogation and presentation effective for the ascertainment of the truth, avoid needless consumption of time, and protect witnesses from harassment or undue embarrassment.

(b) Scope of cross-examination. Cross-examination should be limited to the subject matter of the direct examination and matters affecting the credibility of the witness. The court, in the exercise of discretion, may permit inquiry into additional matters as if on direct examination.

(c) Leading questions. Leading questions should not be used on the direct examination of a witness except as is necessary to develop the witness's testimony. Ordinarily leading questions should be permitted on cross-examination. A party may interrogate a hostile witness, an adverse party, or a witness identified with an adverse party, by leading questions.

Rule 612.   Record or Object Used to Refresh Memory.

(a)   While testifying. If, while testifying, a witness uses a record or object to refresh the witness's memory, an adverse party is entitled to have the record or object produced at the trial, hearing, or deposition in which the witness is testifying.

(b)   Before testifying. If, before testifying, a witness uses a record or object to refresh memory for the purpose of testifying and the court in its discretion determines that the interests of justice so require, an adverse party is entitled to have the record or object produced, if practicable, at the trial, hearing, or deposition in which the witness is testifying.

(c)   Terms and conditions of production and use. A party entitled to have a record or object produced under this rule is entitled to inspect it, cross-examine the witness thereon, and introduce in evidence portions of the record which relate to the testimony of the witness. If production of the record or object at the trial, hearing, or deposition is impracticable, the court may order it made available for inspection. If it is claimed that the record or object contains matter not related to the subject matter of the testimony, the court shall examine the record or object in chambers, excise any portions not so related, and order delivery of the remainder to the party entitled thereto. Any portion withheld over objections must be preserved and made available to the appellate court in the event of an appeal. If a record or object is not produced, made available for inspection, or delivered pursuant to order under this rule, the court shall make any order justice requires, but in criminal cases if the prosecution elects not to comply, the order must be one striking the testimony or, if the court in its discretion determines that the interests of justice so require, declaring a mistrial.

Rule 613.   Prior Statement of Witness.

(a)   Examining witness concerning prior statement. In examining a witness concerning a prior statement made by the witness, whether in a record or not, the statement need not be shown nor its contents disclosed to the witness at that time, but on request it must be shown or disclosed to opposing counsel.

(b)   Extrinsic evidence of prior inconsistent statement of witness. Extrinsic evidence of a prior inconsistent statement by a witness is not admissible unless the witness is afforded an opportunity to explain or deny the statement and the opposing party is afforded an opportunity to interrogate the witness thereon, or the interests of justice otherwise require. This subdivision does not apply to admissions of a party-opponent as defined in Rule 801(d)(2).

Rule 614.   Calling and Interrogation of Witness by Court.

(a)   Calling by court. The court, at the suggestion of a party or on its own motion, may call a witness, and all parties may cross-examine the witness thus called.

(b)   Interrogation by court. The court may interrogate a witness, whether called by the court or a party.

(c) Objection. An objection to the calling or interrogation of a witness by the court may be made at the time or at the next available opportunity when the jury is not present.

Rule 615.   Exclusion of Witnesses.

At the request of a party the court shall order witnesses excluded so that they cannot hear the testimony of other witnesses, and it may make the order on its own motion. This Rule does not authorize exclusion of a party who is an individual, an officer or employee of a party that is not an individual designated as its representative by its attorney, or an individual whose presence is shown by a party to be essential to the presentation of the party's cause or is otherwise authorized by statute, judicial decision, or court rule.

Rule 616.   Bias of Witness.

For the purpose of attacking the credibility of a witness, evidence of bias, prejudice, or interest of the witness for or against a party to the case is admissible.

ARTICLE VII

OPINIONS AND EXPERT TESTIMONY

Rule 701.   Opinion Testimony by Lay Witnesses.

If a witness's testimony is not based on scientific, technical, or other specialized knowledge within the scope of Rule 702, the witness's testimony in the form of opinions or inferences is limited to those opinions or inferences that are rationally based on the perception of the witness, and helpful to a clear understanding of the witness's testimony or the determination of a fact in issue.

Rule 702.   Testimony by Experts.

(a)   General rule. If a witness's testimony is based on scientific, technical, or other specialized knowledge, the witness may testify in the form of opinion or otherwise if the court determines the following are satisfied:

(1)   the testimony will assist the trier of fact to understand evidence or determine a fact in issue;

(2)   the witness is qualified by knowledge, skill, experience, training, or education as an expert in the scientific, technical, or other specialized field;

(3)   the testimony is based upon principles or methods that are reasonably reliable, as established under subdivision (b), (c), (d), or (e);

(4)   the testimony is based upon sufficient and reliable facts or data; and

(5)   the witness has applied the principles or methods reliably to the facts of the case.

(b)   Reliability deemed to exist. A principle or method is reasonably reliable if its reliability has been established by controlling legislation or judicial decision.

(c)   Presumption of reliability. A principle or method is presumed to be reasonably reliable if it has substantial acceptance within the relevant scientific, technical, or specialized community. A party may rebut the presumption by proving that it is more probable than not that the principle or method is not reasonably reliable.

(d)   Presumption of unreliability. A principle or method is presumed not to be reasonably reliable if it does not have substantial acceptance within the relevant scientific, technical, or specialized community. A party may rebut the presumption by proving that it is more probable than not that the principle or method is reasonably reliable.

(e)   Other reliability factors. In determining the reliability of a principle or method, the court shall consider all relevant additional factors, which may include:

(1)   the extent to which the principle or method has been tested;

(2)   the adequacy of research methods employed in testing the principle or method;

(3)   the extent to which the principle or method has been published and subjected to peer review;

(4)   the rate of error in the application of the principle or method;

(5)   the experience of the witness in the application of the principle or method;

(6)   the extent to which the principle or method has gained acceptance within the relevant scientific, technical, or specialized community; and

(7)   the extent to which the witness's specialized field of knowledge has gained acceptance within the general scientific, technical, or specialized community.

Rule 703.   Basis of Opinion Testimony by Expert.

The facts or data in a particular case upon which an expert bases an opinion or inference may be those perceived by or made known to the expert at or before the hearing. If of a type reasonably relied upon by experts in the particular field in forming opinions or inferences upon the subject, the facts or data need not be admissible in evidence for the opinion or inference to be admissible.

Rule 704.   Opinion on Ultimate Issue.

Testimony in the form of an opinion or inference otherwise admissible is not objectionable because it embraces an ultimate issue to be decided by the trier of fact.

Rule 705.   Disclosure of Facts or Data Underlying Expert Opinion.

An expert may testify in terms of opinion or inference and give reasons therefore without previous disclosure of the underlying facts or data, unless the court requires otherwise. The expert may be required to disclose the underlying facts or data on cross-examination.

Rule 706.   Court Appointed Expert Witness.

(a)   Appointment. The court, on motion of any party or its own motion, may issue an order to show cause why an expert witness should not be appointed, and may request the parties to submit nominations. The court may appoint an expert witness agreed upon by the parties, and may appoint an expert witness of its own selection. An expert witness may not be appointed by the court unless the witness consents to act. A witness so appointed must be informed of the witness's duties by the court in writing, a copy of which must be filed with the clerk, or at a conference in which the parties have an opportunity to participate. A witness so appointed shall advise the parties of the witness's findings, if any. The witness's deposition may be taken by any party. The witness may be called to testify by the court or any party. The witness is subject to cross-examination by each party, including a party calling the witness.

(b)   Compensation. An expert witness appointed by the court is entitled to reasonable compensation as determined by the court. The compensation is payable from funds that are provided by law in criminal cases and in civil actions and proceedings involving just compensation for the taking of property. In other civil actions and proceedings the parties shall pay the compensation in such proportion and at such time as the court directs, and the compensation is to be charged as costs.

(c)   Disclosure of appointment. The court may authorize disclosure to the jury of the fact that the court appointed the expert witness.

(d)   Parties' experts of own selection. This rule does not limit the parties in calling expert witnesses of their own selection.

APPENDIX I

ARTICLE VIII

HEARSAY

Rule 801.   Definitions; Exclusions.

(a)   General. In this article:

(1)   "Declarant" means a person who makes a statement.

(2)   "Hearsay" means a statement, other than one made by the declarant while testifying at the trial or hearing, offered in evidence to prove the truth of the matter asserted.

(3)   "Statement" means an oral assertion, an assertion in a record, or nonverbal conduct of a person who intends it as an assertion.

(b)   A statement is not hearsay if:

(1)   the declarant testifies at the trial or hearing, is subject to cross-examination concerning the statement, and the statement is:

(A)   inconsistent with the declarant's testimony and was given under oath and subject to the penalty of perjury at a trial, hearing, or other proceeding, or in a deposition;

(B)   consistent with the declarant's testimony, is offered to rebut an express or implied charge against the declarant of recent fabrication or improper influence or motive and was made before the supposed fabrication, influence, or motive arose; or

(C)   one of identification made shortly after perceiving the individual identified.

(2)   the statement is offered against a party and is:

(A)   the party's own statement, in either an individual or a representative capacity;

(B)   a statement of which the party has manifested adoption or belief in its truth;

(C)   a statement by an individual authorized by the party to make a statement concerning the subject;

(D)   a statement by the party's agent or servant concerning a matter within the scope of the agency or employment, made during the existence of the relationship; or

(E)   a statement by a coconspirator of a party during the course and in furtherance of the conspiracy.

Rule 802.   Hearsay Rule.

Hearsay Is Not Admissible Except as Provided by Law or by These rules.

Rule 803.   Hearsay   Exceptions: Availability   of   Declarant Immaterial.

The following are not excluded by the hearsay rule, even if the declarant is available as a witness:

(1)   Present sense impression. A statement describing or explaining an event or condition made while the declarant was perceiving the event or condition, or immediately thereafter.

(2)   Excited utterance. A statement relating to a startling event or condition made while the declarant was under the stress of excitement caused by the event or condition.

(3)   Then existing mental, emotional, or physical condition. A statement of the declarant's then existing state of mind, emotion, sensation, or physical condition, such as intent, plan, motive, design, mental feeling, pain, and bodily health, but not a statement of memory or belief to prove the fact remembered or believed unless it relates to the execution, revocation, identification, or terms of declarant's will.

(4)   Statements for purposes of medical diagnosis or treatment. Statements made for purposes of medical diagnosis or treatment and describing medical history, or past or present symptoms, pain, or sensation, or the inception or general character of the cause or external source thereof insofar as reasonably pertinent to diagnosis or treatment.

(5)   Recorded recollection. A record concerning a matter about which a witness once had knowledge but now has insufficient recollection to testify fully and accurately, shown to have been made or adopted by the witness when the matter was fresh in the witness's memory and to reflect that knowledge correctly, which record may be read into evidence but may not be received as an exhibit unless offered by an adverse party.

(6)   Record of regularly conducted business activity. A record of acts, events, conditions, opinions, or diagnoses, made at or near the time by, or from information transmitted by, a person having knowledge, if kept in the course of a regularly conducted business activity, and if it was the regular practice of that business activity to make the record, all as shown by the testimony of the custodian or other qualified witness, or by certification that complies with Rule 902(11) or (12), or with a statute providing for certification, unless the sources of information or the method or circumstances of preparation indicate lack of trustworthiness. In this paragraph, business includes business, institution, association, profession, occupation, and calling of every kind, whether or not conducted for profit. A public record inadmissible under paragraph (8) is inadmissible under this exception.

(7)   Absence of entry in records kept in accordance with paragraph (6). Evidence that a matter is not included in the records kept in accordance with paragraph (6), to prove the nonoccurrence or nonexistence of the matter, if the matter was of a kind of which a record was regularly made and preserved, all as shown by the testimony of the custodian or other qualified witness, or by certification that complies with Rule 902(11) or (12), or with a statute providing for certification, unless the sources of information or other circumstances indicate lack of trustworthiness.

(8)   Record or report of public office. Unless the sources of information or other circumstances indicate lack of trustworthiness, a record of a public office or agency setting forth its regularly conducted and regularly recorded activities, or matters observed pursuant to duty imposed by law and as to which there was a duty to report, or factual findings resulting from an investigation made pursuant to authority granted by law. The following are not within this exception to the hearsay rule:

(A) an investigative report by police and other law enforcement personnel, except when offered by an accused in a criminal case;

(B) an investigative report prepared by or for a government, public office, or agency when offered by it in a case in which it is a party;

(C) factual findings offered by the government in criminal cases; and

(D) factual findings resulting from special investigation of a particular complaint, case, or incident, unless offered by an accused in a criminal case.

(9) Record of vital statistics. A record of birth, fetal death, death, or marriage, if the report thereof was made to a public office.

(10) Absence of record or entry. To prove the absence of a record, or the nonoccurrence or nonexistence of a matter of which a record was regularly made and preserved by a public office or agency, evidence in the form of a certification in accordance with Rule 902, or testimony, that diligent search failed to disclose the record, or entry.

(11) Record of religious organization. A statement of birth, marriage, divorce, death, legitimacy, ancestry, relationship by blood or marriage, or other similar fact of personal or family history, contained in a regularly kept record of a religious organization.

(12) Marriage, baptismal, and similar certified record. A statement of fact contained in a certified record that the maker performed a marriage or other ceremony or administered a sacrament, made by a cleric, public official, or other person authorized by the rules or practices of a religious organization or by law to perform the act certified, and purporting to have been issued at the time of the act or within a reasonable time thereafter.

(13) Family record. A statement of fact concerning personal or family history contained in a family Bible, genealogy, chart, engraving on a ring, an inscription on a family portrait, an engraving on an urn, crypt, or tombstone, or the like.

(14) Record of document affecting an interest in property. A public record purporting to establish or affect an interest in property, as proof of the content of the original recorded document and its execution and delivery by each person by whom it purports to have been executed and delivered.

(15) Statement in record affecting an interest in property. A statement contained in a record purporting to establish or affect an interest in property if the matter stated was relevant to the purpose of the record, unless dealings with the property since the record was made have been inconsistent with the truth of the statement or the purport of the record.

(16) Statement in ancient record. A statement in a record in existence 20 years or more, the authenticity of which is established.

(17) Market report, commercial publication. Market quotation, tabulation, list, directory, or other published or publicly recorded compilations, generally used and relied upon by the public or by persons in particular occupations.

(18) Learned treatise. To the extent called to the attention of an expert witness upon cross-examination or relied upon by the witness in direct examination, a statement contained in a published treatise, periodical, or pamphlet on a subject of history, medicine, or other science or art, established

as a reliable authority by testimony or admission of the witness, by other expert testimony, or by judicial notice. If admitted, the statement may be read into evidence but may not be received as an exhibit.

(19) *Reputation concerning personal or family history.* Reputation among members of an individual's family by blood, adoption, or marriage, or among the individual's associates, or in the community, concerning the individual's birth, adoption, marriage, divorce, death, legitimacy, relationship by blood, adoption, or marriage, ancestry, or other similar fact of the individual's personal or family history.

(20) *Reputation concerning boundaries or general history.* Reputation in a community, arising before the controversy, as to boundaries of or customs affecting land in the community, and reputation as to an event of general history important to the community, State, or country in which located.

(21) *Reputation as to character.* Reputation of a person's character among the person's associates or in the community.

(22) *Judgment of previous conviction.* Evidence of a final judgment adjudging a person guilty of a crime punishable by death or imprisonment in excess of one year, to prove any fact essential to sustain the judgment, but not including, when offered by the State in a criminal prosecution for purposes other than impeachment, a judgment against a person other than the accused. The pendency of an appeal may be shown but does not affect admissibility.

(23) *Judgment as to personal, family, or general history, or boundaries.* A judgment as proof of a matter of personal, family or general history, or boundaries, essential to the judgment, if the matter is provable by evidence of reputation.

Rule 804.   Hearsay Exceptions: Declarant Unavailable.

(a)   Unavailability as a witness. In this rule:

(1)   Unavailability as a witness includes situations in which the declarant:

(A) is exempted by ruling of the court on the ground of privilege from testifying concerning the subject matter of the declarant's statement;

(B) persists in refusing to testify concerning the subject matter of the declarant's statement despite an order of the court to do so;

(C) testifies to a lack of memory of the subject matter of the declarant's statement;

(D) is unable to be present or to testify at the hearing because of death or then existing physical or mental illness or infirmity; or

(E) is absent from the hearing and the proponent of the declarant's statement has been unable to procure the declarant's attendance, or in the case of a hearsay exception under subdivision (b)(2), (3), or (4), the declarant's attendance or testimony, by process or other reasonable means.

(2)   A declarant is not unavailable as a witness if the declarant's exemption, refusal, claim of lack of memory, inability, or absence is due to the procurement or wrongdoing of the proponent of the declarant's

statement for the purpose of preventing the declarant from attending or testifying.

(b) Hearsay exceptions. The following are not excluded by the hearsay rule if the declarant is unavailable as a witness:

(1) Former testimony. Testimony given as a witness at another hearing of the same or a different proceeding, or in a deposition taken in compliance with law in the course of the same or another proceeding, if the party against whom the testimony is now offered, or, in a civil action or proceeding a predecessor in interest, had an opportunity and similar motive to develop the testimony by direct, cross, or redirect examination.

(2) Statement under belief of impending death. A statement made by a declarant while believing that the declarant's death was imminent, concerning the cause or circumstances of what the declarant believed to be the declarant's impending death.

(3) Statement against interest. A statement that at the time of its making was so far contrary to the declarant's pecuniary or proprietary interest, or so far tended to subject the declarant to civil or criminal liability or to render invalid a claim by the declarant against another or to make the declarant an object of hatred, ridicule, or disgrace, that a reasonable individual in the declarant's position would not have made the statement unless the individual believed it to be true. A statement tending to expose the declarant to criminal liability and offered to exculpate an accused is not admissible unless corroborating circumstances clearly indicate the trustworthiness of the statement. A statement or confession offered against the accused in a criminal case, made by a codefendant or other individual implicating both the codefendant or other individual and the accused, is not within this exception.

(4) Statement of personal or family history. A statement concerning:

(A) the declarant's own birth, adoption, marriage, divorce, legitimacy, relationship by blood, adoption, marriage, ancestry, or other similar fact of personal or family history, even though declarant had no means of acquiring personal knowledge of the matter stated or

(B) the matters listed in subparagraph (A) or the death of another individual if the declarant was related to the other individual by blood, adoption, or marriage or was so intimately associated with the other individual's family as to be likely to have accurate information concerning the matter declared.

(5) Forfeiture by wrongdoing. A statement offered against a party that has engaged or acquiesced in wrongdoing that was intended to and did cause the unavailability of the declarant as a witness.

Rule 805.   Hearsay Within Hearsay.

Hearsay included within hearsay is not excluded under the hearsay rule if each part of the combined statements conforms with an exception to the hearsay rule provided in these rules.

Rule 806.   Attacking and Supporting Credibility of Declarant.

If a hearsay statement, or a statement described in Rule 801(b)(2)(C), (D), or (E), has been admitted in evidence, the credibility of the declarant may be attacked, and if attacked may be supported, by any evidence that would be admissible for those purposes if the declarant had testified as a witness. Evidence of a statement or conduct by the declarant inconsistent with the declarant's hearsay statement is not subject to a requirement that the declarant has been afforded an opportunity to deny or explain. If the party against whom a hearsay statement has been admitted calls the declarant as a witness, the party may examine the declarant on the statement as if under cross-examination.

Rule 807.   Statement of Child Victim.

(a) Statement of child not excluded. A statement made by a child under [seven] years of age describing an alleged act of neglect, physical or sexual abuse, or sexual contact performed against, with, or on the child by another individual is not excluded by the hearsay rule if:

(1) subject to subdivision (b), the court conducts a hearing outside the presence of the jury and finds that the statement concerns an event within the child's personal knowledge and is inherently trustworthy; and

(2) the child testifies at the proceeding [or pursuant to an applicable state procedure for the giving of testimony by a child], or the child is unavailable to testify at the proceeding, as defined in Rule 804(a), and, in the latter case, there is evidence corroborative of the alleged act of neglect, physical or sexual abuse, or sexual contact.

(b) Determining trustworthiness. In determining the trustworthiness of a child's statement, the court shall consider the circumstances surrounding the making of the statement, including:

(1) the child's ability to observe, remember, and relate the details of the event;

(2) the child's age and mental and physical maturity;

(3) whether the child used terminology not reasonably expected of a child of similar age, mental and physical maturity, and socioeconomic circumstances;

(4) the child's relationship to the alleged offender;

(5) the nature and duration of the alleged neglect, physical or sexual abuse, or sexual contact;

(6) whether any other descriptions of the event by the child have been consistent with the statement;

(7) whether the child had a motive to fabricate the statement;

(8) the identity, knowledge and experience of the person taking the statement;

(9) whether there is a video or audio recording of the statement and, if so, the circumstances surrounding the taking of the statement; and

(10) whether the child made the statement spontaneously or in response to suggestive or leading questions.

(c) Making a record. The court shall state on the record the circumstances that support its determination of the admissibility of the statement offered pursuant to subdivision (a).

(d) Notice. Evidence is not admissible under this rule unless the proponent gives to all adverse parties reasonable notice in advance of trial, or during trial if the court excuses pretrial notice for good cause shown, of the nature of any such evidence the proponent intends to introduce at trial.

Rule 808.   Residual Exception.

(a) Exception. In exceptional circumstances a statement not covered by Rules 803, 804, or 807 but possessing equivalent, though not identical, circumstantial guarantees of trustworthiness, is not excluded by the hearsay rule if the court determines that

(1) the statement is offered as evidence of a fact of consequence;

(2) the statement is more probative on the point for which it is offered than any other evidence that the proponent can procure through reasonable efforts; and

(3) the general purposes of these rules and the interests of justice will best be served by admission of the statement into evidence.

(b) Making a record. The court shall state on the record the circumstances that support its determination of the admissibility of the statement offered pursuant to subdivision (a).

(c) Notice. A statement is not admissible under this exception unless the proponent gives to all parties reasonable notice in advance of trial, or during trial if the court excuses pretrial notice for good cause shown, of the substance of the statement and the identity of the declarant.

ARTICLE IX

AUTHENTICATION AND IDENTIFICATION

Rule 901.   Requirement of Authentication or Identification.

(a)   General   provision.   The   requirement   of   authentication   or identification as a condition precedent to admissibility is satisfied by evidence sufficient to support a finding that the matter in question is what its proponent claims.

(b)   Illustrations. By way of illustration only, and not by way of limitation, the following are examples of authentication or identification conforming with the requirements of this rule:

(1)   Testimony of witness having knowledge. Testimony of a witness with knowledge that a matter is what it is claimed to be.

(2)   Nonexpert opinion on handwriting. Nonexpert opinion as to the genuineness of handwriting, based upon familiarity not acquired for purposes of the litigation.

(3)   Comparison by trier or expert witness. Comparison by the trier of fact or by an expert witness with a specimen that has been authenticated.

(4)   Distinctive characteristics and the like. Appearance, contents, substance, internal patterns, or other distinctive characteristics, taken in conjunction with circumstances.

(5)   Voice identification. Identification of a voice, whether heard firsthand or through mechanical or electronic transmission or recording, by opinion based upon hearing the voice under circumstances connecting it with the alleged speaker.

(6)   Telephone   conversations.   Telephone   conversations,   by evidence that a call was made to the number assigned at the time by the telephone company to a particular person, if:

(A)   in the case of an individual, circumstances, including self-identification, which show that the individual who answered was the one called; or

(B)   in the case of a person other than an individual, the call was made to a place of business and the conversation related to business reasonably transacted over the telephone.

(7)   Public records or reports. Evidence that a public record or a purported public record is from the public office where items of this nature are kept.

(8)   Ancient records. Evidence that a record is in such condition as to create no suspicion concerning its authenticity, was in a place where it, if authentic, would likely be, and has been in existence 20 years or more at the time it is offered.

(9)   Process or system. Evidence describing a process or system used to produce a result and showing that the process or system produces an accurate result.

(10) Method   provided   by   statute   or   rule.   Any   method   of authentication or identification provided by [the Supreme Court of this State or by] a statute or as provided in the constitution of this State.

Rule 902.   Self-Authentication.

Extrinsic evidence of authenticity as a condition precedent to admissibility is not required with respect to the following:

(1)   Domestic public document under seal. A document bearing a seal purporting to be that of the United States, or of any State, or of a political subdivision, department, officer, or agency of one of them, and a signature purporting to be an attestation or execution.

(2)   Domestic public document not under seal. A document purporting to bear a signature in the official capacity of an officer or employee of any entity designated in paragraph (1), having no seal, if a public officer having a seal and having official duties in the district or political subdivision of the officer or employee certifies under seal that the signer has the official capacity and that the signature is genuine.

(3)   Foreign public document. A document purporting to be executed or attested in the official capacity of an individual authorized by the laws of a foreign country to make the execution or attestation, and accompanied by a final certification as to the genuineness of the signature and official position (i) of the executing or attesting individual, or (ii) of any foreign official whose certificate of genuineness of signature and official position relates to the execution or attestation or is in a chain of certificates of genuineness of signature and official position relating to the execution or attestation. A final certification may be made by a secretary of embassy or legation, consul general, consul, vice consul, or consular agent of the United States, or a diplomatic or consular official of the foreign country assigned or accredited to the United States. If all parties have been given a reasonable opportunity to investigate the authenticity and accuracy of an official document, the court may for good cause shown order that it be treated as presumptively authentic without final certification or permit it to be evidenced by an attested summary with or without final certification.

(4)   Certified copy of public record. A copy of a public record or report or entry therein, or of a document authorized by law to be recorded or filed and actually recorded or filed in a public office, certified as correct by the custodian or other authorized person by certificate complying with paragraph (1), (2), or (3) or complying with any law of the United States or of this State.

(5)   Official publication. A book, pamphlet, publication, or other publicly issued record issued by public authority, if in a form indicative of the genuineness of such a record.

(6)   Newspaper or periodical. Publicly distributed material purporting to be a newspaper or periodical.

(7)   Trade inscriptions and the like. Inscriptions, signs, tags, or labels purporting to have been affixed in the course of business and indicating ownership, control, or origin.

(8)   Acknowledged record. A record accompanied by a certificate of acknowledgment executed in the manner provided by law by a notary public or other officer authorized by law to take acknowledgments.

(9)   Commercial paper and related record. Commercial paper, a signature thereon, and a record relating thereto or having the same legal effect as commercial paper, to the extent provided by general commercial law.

(10) *Presumption created by law.* A signature, document, or other matter declared by any law of the United States or of this State to be presumptively or prima facie genuine or authentic.

(11) *Certified domestic record of regularly conducted business activity.* The original or a duplicate of a domestic record of regularly conducted activity, within the scope of Rule 803(6), which the custodian thereof acts, events, conditions, opinions, or diagnoses if:

(A) the document is accompanied by a written declaration under oath of the custodian of the record or other qualified individual that the record was made, at or near the time of the occurrence of the matters set forth, by, or from information transmitted by, a person having knowledge of those matters; was kept in the course of the regularly conducted business activity; and was made pursuant to the regularly conducted activity;

(B) the party intending to offer the record in evidence gives notice of that intention to all adverse parties and makes the record available for inspection sufficiently in advance of its offer to provide the adverse parties with a fair opportunity to challenge the record; and

'(C) notice is not given to the proponent, sufficiently in advance of the offer to provide the proponent with a fair opportunity to meet the objection or obtain the testimony of a foundation witness, raising a genuine question as to the trustworthiness or authenticity of the record.

(12) *Certified foreign record of regularly conducted business activity.* The original or a duplicate of a record from a foreign country of acts, events, conditions, opinions, or diagnoses if:

(A) the document is accompanied by a written declaration under oath of the custodian of the record or other qualified individual that the record was made, at or near the time of the occurrence of the matters set forth, by or from information transmitted by a person having knowledge of those matters, was kept in the course of a regularly conducted business activity, and was made pursuant to the regularly conducted activity;

(B) the party intending to offer the record in evidence gives notice of that intention to all adverse parties and makes the record available for inspection sufficiently in advance of its offer to provide the adverse parties with a fair opportunity to challenge the record; and

(C) notice is not given to the proponent, sufficiently in advance of the offer to provide the proponent with a fair opportunity to meet the objection or obtain the testimony of a foundation witness, raising a genuine question as to the trustworthiness or authenticity of the record.

Rule 903. Subscribing Witness' Testimony Unnecessary.

The testimony of a subscribing witness is not necessary to authenticate a record unless required by the laws of the jurisdiction whose laws govern the validity of the record.

APPENDIX I

ARTICLE X

CONTENT OF RECORD, WRITING, RECORDING,
PHOTOGRAPH, IMAGE, AND OTHER RECORD

Rule 1001. Definitions.

In this article:

(1) "Duplicate" means a counterpart in the form of a record produced by the same impression as the original, from the same matrix, by means of photography, including enlargements and miniatures, by mechanical or electronic re-recording, by chemical reproduction, or by another equivalent technique that accurately reproduces the original.

(2) "Image" means a form of a record which consists of a digitized copy or image of information.

(3) An "original" of a writing, recording, or other record means the writing, recording, or other record itself or any counterpart intended to have the same effect by a person executing or issuing it. The term, when applied to a photograph, includes the negative or any print therefrom. The term includes a printout or other perceivable output of a record of data or images stored in a computer or similar device, if shown to reflect the data or images accurately.

(4) "Photograph" means a form of a record which consists of a still photograph, stored image, X-ray film, video tape, or motion picture.

(5) "Writing" and "recording" mean letters, words, sounds, or numbers, or their equivalent, inscribed on a tangible medium or stored in an electronic or other machine and retrievable in perceivable form by handwriting, typewriting, printing, photostating, photographing, mechanical or electronic recording, or other technique.

Rule 1002. Requirement of Original.

To prove the content of a writing, recording, photograph, or other record, the original record, writing, recording, photograph, or other record is required, except as otherwise provided in these rules or by [rules adopted by the Supreme Court of this State or by] statute.

Rule 1003. Admissibility of Duplicates.

A duplicate is admissible to the same extent as an original unless a genuine question is raised as to the authenticity or continuing effectiveness of the original or in the circumstances it would be unfair to admit the duplicate in lieu of the original.

Rule 1004. Admissibility of Other Evidence of Contents.

The original is not required, and other evidence of the contents of a record is admissible if:

(1) all originals are lost or have been destroyed, unless the proponent lost or destroyed them in bad faith;

(2) an original cannot be obtained by any available judicial process or procedure;

(3)   at a time when an original was under the control of the party against whom offered, the party was put on notice, by the pleadings or otherwise, that the contents would be a subject of proof at the hearing, and the party does not produce the original at the hearing; or

(4)   the record is not closely related to a controlling issue.

Rule 1005.   Public Records.

The contents of an official record, or of a private record authorized to be recorded or filed in the public records and actually recorded or filed, if otherwise admissible, may be proved by a copy in perceivable form, certified as correct in accordance with Rule 902 or testified to be correct by a witness who has compared it with the original. If a copy complying with the foregoing cannot be obtained by the exercise of reasonable diligence, other evidence of the contents may be admitted.

Rule 1006.   Summaries.

The contents of voluminous records which cannot conveniently be examined in court may be presented in the form of a chart, summary, calculation, or other perceivable presentation. The original, or a duplicate, must be made available for examination or copying, or both, by other parties at a reasonable time and place. The court may order that they be produced in court.

Rule 1007.   Testimony, or Admission in Record of Party.

The contents of a record may be proved by the testimony or deposition of the party against whom offered or by that party's written admission without accounting for the nonproduction of the original.

Rule 1008.   Functions of Court and Jury.

If the admissibility under these rules of other evidence of the contents of a record depends upon the fulfillment of a condition of fact, the question whether the condition has been fulfilled is ordinarily for the court to determine in accordance with Rule 104. However, if an issue is raised as to whether the asserted record ever existed, another record produced at the trial is the original, or other evidence of contents correctly reflects the contents, the issue is for the trier of fact to determine.

RULE 1101   APPENDIX I

                          ARTICLE XI

                  MISCELLANEOUS RULES

Rule 1101.   Title.

   These rules shall be known and may be cited as Uniform Rules of
Evidence.

Appendix II

CALIFORNIA EVIDENCE CODE

DIVISION 1. PRELIMINARY PROVISIONS AND CONSTRUCTION

DIVISION 2. WORDS AND PHRASES DEFINED

APPENDIX II

CALIFORNIA EVIDENCE CODE

APPENDIX II

CALIFORNIA EVIDENCE CODE

APPENDIX II

CALIFORNIA EVIDENCE CODE

CALIFORNIA EVIDENCE CODE

CALIFORNIA EVIDENCE CODE

CALIFORNIA EVIDENCE CODE

CHAPTER 2. MEDIATION

CHAPTER 3. OTHER EVIDENCE AFFECTED OR EXCLUDED BY EXTRINSIC POLICIES

APPENDIX II

DIVISION 10. HEARSAY EVIDENCE

CHAPTER 1. GENERAL PROVISIONS

CHAPTER 2. EXCEPTIONS TO THE HEARSAY RULE

ARTICLE 1. CONFESSIONS AND ADMISSIONS

CALIFORNIA EVIDENCE CODE

APPENDIX II

CALIFORNIA EVIDENCE CODE

APPENDIX II

DIVISION 1. PRELIMINARY PROVISIONS AND CONSTRUCTION

§ 1. Short title

This code shall be known as the Evidence Code.

§ 2. Abrogation of common law rule of strict construction; liberal construction

The rule of the common law, that statutes in derogation thereof are to be strictly construed, has no application to this code. This code establishes the law of this state respecting the subject to which it relates, and its provisions are to be liberally construed with a view to effecting its objects and promoting justice.

§ 3. Severability

If any provision or clause of this code or application thereof to any person or circumstances is held invalid, such invalidity shall not affect other provisions or applications of the code which can be given effect without the invalid provision or application, and to this end the provisions of this code are declared to be severable.

§ 4. Construction of code

Unless the provision or context otherwise requires, these preliminary provisions and rules of construction shall govern the construction of this code.

§ 5. Construction of headings

Division, chapter, article, and section headings do not in any manner affect the scope, meaning, or intent of the provisions of this code.

§ 6. References to statutes; application

Whenever any reference is made to any portion of this code or of any other statute, such reference shall apply to all amendments and additions heretofore or hereafter made.

§ 7. Definitions

Unless otherwise expressly stated:

(a) "Division" means a division of this code.

(b) "Chapter" means a chapter of the division in which that term occurs.

(c) "Article" means an article of the chapter in which that term occurs.

(d) "Section" means a section of this code.

(e) "Subdivision" means a subdivision of the section in which that term occurs.

(f) "Paragraph" means a paragraph of the subdivision in which that term occurs.

§ 8. Construction of tenses

The present tense includes the past and future tenses; and the future, the present.

§ 9. Construction of gender references

The masculine gender includes the feminine and neuter.

§ 10. Construction of singular and plural

The singular number includes the plural; and the plural, the singular.

§ 11. "Shall" and "may"

"Shall" is mandatory and "may" is permissive.

§ 12. Operative date of code; effect on pending proceedings

(a) This code shall become operative on January 1, 1967, and shall govern proceedings in actions brought on or after that date and, except as provided in subdivision (b), further proceedings in actions pending on that date.

(b) Subject to subdivision (c), a trial commenced before January 1, 1967, shall not be governed by this code. For the purpose of this subdivision:

(1) A trial is commenced when the first witness is sworn or the first exhibit is admitted into evidence and is terminated when the issue upon which such evidence is received is submitted to the trier of fact. A new trial, or a separate trial of a different issue, commenced on or after January 1, 1967, shall be governed by this code.

(2) If an appeal is taken from a ruling made at a trial commenced before January 1, 1967, the appellate court shall apply the law applicable at the time of the commencement of the trial.

(c) The provisions of Division 8 (commencing with Section 900) relating to privileges shall govern any claim of privilege made after December 31, 1966.

DIVISION 2. WORDS AND PHRASES DEFINED

§ 100. Application of definitions

Unless the provision or context otherwise requires, these definitions govern the construction of this code.

§ 105. "Action"

"Action" includes a civil action and a criminal action.

LAW REVISION COMMISSION COMMENT

Defining the word "action" to include both a civil action or proceeding and a criminal action or proceeding eliminates the necessity of repeating "civil action and criminal action" in numerous code sections. [7 Cal.L.Rev.Comm. Reports 1 (1965)]

§ 110. "Burden of producing evidence"

"Burden of producing evidence" means the obligation of a party to introduce evidence sufficient to avoid a ruling against him on the issue.

§ 115. "Burden of proof"

"Burden of proof" means the obligation of a party to establish by evidence a requisite degree of belief concerning a fact in the mind of the trier of fact or the court. The burden of proof may require a party to raise a reasonable doubt concerning the existence or nonexistence of a fact or that he establish the existence or nonexistence of a fact by a preponderance of the evidence, by clear and convincing proof, or by proof beyond a reasonable doubt.

Except as otherwise provided by law, the burden of proof requires proof by a preponderance of the evidence.

§ 120. "Civil action"

"Civil action" includes civil proceedings.

§ 125. "Conduct"

"Conduct" includes all active and passive behavior, both verbal and nonverbal.

§ 130. "Criminal action"

"Criminal action" includes criminal proceedings.

§ 135. "Declarant"

"Declarant" is a person who makes a statement.

§ 140. "Evidence"

"Evidence" means testimony, writings, material objects, or other things presented to the senses that are offered to prove the existence or nonexistence of a fact.

§ 145. "The hearing"

"The hearing" means the hearing at which a question under this code arises, and not some earlier or later hearing.

§ 150. "Hearsay evidence"

"Hearsay evidence" is defined in Section 1200.

§ 160. "Law"

"Law" includes constitutional, statutory, and decisional law.

§ 165. "Oath"

"Oath" includes affirmation or declaration under penalty of perjury.

§ 170. "Perceive"

"Perceive" means to acquire knowledge through one's senses.

§ 175. "Person"

"Person" includes a natural person, firm, association, organization, partnership, business trust, corporation, limited liability company, or public entity.

§ 177. "Dependent person"

"Dependent person" means a person, regardless of whether the person lives independently, who has a physical or mental impairment that substantially restricts his or her ability to carry out normal activities or to protect his or her rights, including, but not limited to, persons who have physical or developmental disabilities or whose physical or mental abilities have significantly diminished because of age. "Dependent person" includes any person who is admitted as an inpatient to a 24-hour health facility, as defined in Sections 1250, 1250.2, and 1250.3 of the Health and Safety Code.

§ 180. "Personal property"

"Personal property" includes money, goods, chattels, things in action, and evidences of debt.

§ 185. "Property"

"Property" includes both real and personal property.

§ 190. "Proof"

"Proof" is the establishment by evidence of a requisite degree of belief concerning a fact in the mind of the trier of fact or the court.

§ 195. "Public employee"

"Public employee" means an officer, agent, or employee of a public entity.

§ 200. "Public entity"

"Public entity" includes a nation, state, county, city and county, city, district, public authority, public agency, or any other political subdivision or public corporation, whether foreign or domestic.

§ 205. "Real property"

"Real property" includes lands, tenements, and hereditaments.

§ 210. "Relevant evidence"

"Relevant evidence" means evidence, including evidence relevant to the credibility of a witness or hearsay declarant, having any tendency in reason to prove or disprove any disputed fact that is of consequence to the determination of the action.

§ 215. "Spouse"

"Spouse" includes "registered domestic partner," as required by Secion 297.5 of the Family Code.

§ 220. "State"

"State" means the State of California, unless applied to the different parts of the United States. In the latter case, it includes any state, district, commonwealth, territory, or insular possession of the United States.

§ 225. "Statement"

"Statement" means (a) oral or written verbal expression or (b) nonverbal conduct of a person intended by him as a substitute for oral or written verbal expression.

§ 230. "Statute"

"Statute" includes a treaty and a constitutional provision.

§ 235. "Trier of fact"

"Trier of fact" includes (a) the jury and (b) the court when the court is trying an issue of fact other than one relating to the admissibility of evidence.

§ 240. "Unavailable as a witness"

(a) Except as otherwise provided in subdivision (b), "unavailable as a witness" means that the declarant is any of the following:

(1) Exempted or precluded on the ground of privilege from testifying concerning the matter to which his or her statement is relevant.

(2) Disqualified from testifying to the matter.

(3) Dead or unable to attend or to testify at the hearing because of then-existing physical or mental illness or infirmity.

(4) Absent from the hearing and the court is unable to compel his or her attendance by its process.

(5) Absent from the hearing and the proponent of his or her statement has exercised reasonable diligence but has been unable to procure his or her attendance by the court's process.

(6) Persistent in refusing to testify concerning the subject matter of the declarant's statement despite having been found in contempt for refusal to testify.

(b) A declarant is not unavailable as a witness if the exemption, preclusion, disqualification, death, inability, or absence of the declarant was brought about by the procurement or wrongdoing of the proponent of his or her statement for the purpose of preventing the declarant from attending or testifying.

(c) Expert testimony that establishes that physical or mental trauma resulting from an alleged crime has caused harm to a witness of sufficient severity that the witness is physically unable to testify or is unable to testify without suffering substantial trauma may constitute a sufficient showing of unavailability pursuant to paragraph (3) of subdivision (a). As used in this section, the term "expert" means a physician and surgeon, including a psychiatrist, or any person described by subdivision (b), (c), or (e) of Section 1010.

The introduction of evidence to establish the unavailability of a witness under this subdivision shall not be deemed procurement of unavailability, in absence of proof to the contrary.

§ 250. "Writing"

"Writing" means handwriting, typewriting, printing, photostating, photographing, photocopying, transmitting by electronic mail or facsimile, and every other means of recording upon any tangible thing, any form of communication or representation, including letters, words, pictures, sounds, or symbols, or combinations thereof, and any record thereby created, regardless of the manner in which the record has been stored.

§ 255. "Original"

"Original" means the writing itself or any counterpart intended to have the same effect by a person executing or issuing it. An "original" of a photograph includes the negative or any print therefrom. If data are stored in a computer or similar device, any printout or other output readable by sight, shown to reflect the data accurately, is an "original."

§ 260. "Duplicate"

A "duplicate" is a counterpart produced by the same impression as the original, or from the same matrix, or by means of photography, including enlargements and miniatures, or by mechanical or electronic rerecording, or by chemical reproduction, or by other equivalent technique which accurately reproduces the original.

DIVISION 3. GENERAL PROVISIONS

CHAPTER 1. APPLICABILITY OF CODE

§ 300. Applicability of code

Except as otherwise provided by statute, this code applies in every action before the Supreme Court or a court of appeal or superior court, including proceedings in such actions conducted by a referee, court commissioner, or similar officer, but does not apply in grand jury proceedings.

2002 Amendment Section 300 is amended to reflect unification of the municipal superior courts pursuant to Article VI, Section 5(e) of the California Constitution. [32 Cal.L.Rev.Comm. Reports 157 (2002)]

CHAPTER 2. PROVINCE OF COURT AND JURY

§ 310. Questions of law for court

(a) All questions of law (including but not limited to questions concerning the construction of statutes and other writings, the admissibility of evidence, and other rules of evidence) are to be decided by the court. Determination of issues of fact preliminary to the admission of evidence are to be decided by the court as provided in Article 2 (commencing with Section 400) of Chapter 4.

(b) Determination of the law of an organization of nations or of the law of a foreign nation or a public entity in a foreign nation is a question of law to be determined in the manner provided in Division 4 (commencing with Section 450).

§ 311. Foreign law applicable; law undetermined; procedures

If the law of an organization of nations, a foreign nation or a state other than this state, or a public entity in a foreign nation or a state other than this state, is applicable and such law cannot be determined, the court may, as the ends of justice require, either:

(a) Apply the law of this state if the court can do so consistently with the Constitution of the United States and the Constitution of this state; or

(b) Dismiss the action without prejudice or, in the case of a reviewing court, remand the case to the trial court with directions to dismiss the action without prejudice.

§ 312. Jury as trier of fact

Except as otherwise provided by law, where the trial is by jury:

(a) All questions of fact are to be decided by the jury.

(b) Subject to the control of the court, the jury is to determine the effect and value of the evidence addressed to it, including the credibility of witnesses and hearsay declarants.

APPENDIX II

CHAPTER 3. ORDER OF PROOF

§ 320. Power of court to regulate order of proof

Except as otherwise provided by law, the court in its discretion shall regulate the order of proof.

CHAPTER 4. ADMITTING AND EXCLUDING EVIDENCE

ARTICLE 1. GENERAL PROVISIONS

§ 350. Only relevant evidence admissible

No evidence is admissible except relevant evidence.

§ 351. Admissibility of relevant evidence

Except as otherwise provided by statute, all relevant evidence is admissible.

§ 351.1. Polygraph examinations; results, opinion of examiner or reference; exclusion

(a) Notwithstanding any other provision of law, the results of a polygraph examination, the opinion of a polygraph examiner, or any reference to an offer to take, failure to take, or taking of a polygraph examination, shall not be admitted into evidence in any criminal proceeding, including pretrial and post conviction motions and hearings, or in any trial or hearing of a juvenile for a criminal offense, whether heard in juvenile or adult court, unless all parties stipulate to the admission of such results.

(b) Nothing in this section is intended to exclude from evidence statements made during a polygraph examination which are otherwise admissible.

§ 351.2. Evidence of immigration status; exclusion from certain civil actions

(a) In a civil action for personal injury or wrongful death, evidence of a person's immigration status shall not be admitted into evidence, nor shall discovery into a person's immigration status be permitted.

(b) This section does not affect the standards of relevance, admissibility, or discovery prescribed by Section 3339 of the Civil Code, Section 7285 of the Government Code, Section 24000 of the Health and Safety Code, and Section 1171.5 of the Labor Code.

§ 351.3. Evidence of immigration status; civil actions not governed by § 351.2

(a) In a civil action not governed by Section 351.2, evidence of a person's immigration status shall not be disclosed in open court by a party or his or her attorney unless the judge presiding over the matter first determines that the evidence is admissible in an in camera hearing requested by the party seeking disclosure of the person's immigration status.

(b) This section does not do any of the following:

(1) Apply to cases in which a person's immigration status is necessary to prove an element of a claim or an affirmative defense.

(2) Impact otherwise applicable laws governing the relevance of immigration status to liability or the standards applicable to inquiries regarding immigration status in discovery or proceedings in a civil action, including Section 3339 of the Civil Code, Section 7285 of the Government Code, Section 24000 of the Health and Safety Code, and Section 1171.5 of the Labor Code.

(3) Prohibit a person or his or her attorney from voluntarily revealing his or her immigration status to the court.

(c) This section shall remain in effect only until January 1, 2022, and as of that date is repealed.

§ 351.4. Evidence of immigration status; criminal actions

(a) In a criminal action, evidence of a person's immigration status shall not be disclosed in open court by a party or his or her attorney unless the judge presiding over the matter first determines that the evidence is admissible in an in camera hearing requested by the party seeking disclosure of the person's immigration status.

(b) This section does not do any of the following:

(1) Apply to cases in which a person's immigration status is necessary to prove an element of an offense or an affirmative defense.

(2) Limit discovery in a criminal action.

(3) Prohibit a person or his or her attorney from voluntarily revealing his or her immigration status to the court.

(c) This section shall remain in effect only until January 1, 2022, and as of that date is repealed.

§ 352. Discretion of court to exclude evidence

The court in its discretion may exclude evidence if its probative value is substantially outweighed by the probability that its admission will (a) necessitate undue consumption of time or (b) create substantial danger of undue prejudice, of confusing the issues, or of misleading the jury.

§ 352.1. Criminal sex acts; victim's address and telephone number

In any criminal proceeding under Section 261, 262, or 264.1, subdivision (d) of Section 286, or subdivision (d) of Section 287 of, or former Section 288a of, the Penal Code, or in any criminal proceeding under subdivision (c) of Section 286 or subdivision (c) of Section 287 of, or former Section 288a of, the Penal Code in which the defendant is alleged to have compelled the participation of the victim by force, violence, duress, menace, or threat of great bodily harm, the district attorney may, upon written motion with notice to the defendant or the defendant's attorney, if he or she is represented by an attorney, within a reasonable time prior to any hearing, move to exclude from evidence the current address and telephone number of any victim at the hearing.

The court may order that evidence of the victim's current address and telephone number be excluded from any hearings conducted pursuant to the criminal proceeding if the court finds that the probative value of the evidence is outweighed by the creation of substantial danger to the victim.

Nothing in this section shall abridge or limit the defendant's right to discover or investigate the information.

§ 353. Erroneous admission of evidence; effect

A verdict or finding shall not be set aside, nor shall the judgment or decision based thereon be reversed, by reason of the erroneous admission of evidence unless:

(a)   There appears of record an objection to or a motion to exclude or to strike the evidence that was timely made and so stated as to make clear the specific ground of the objection or motion; and

(b)   The court which passes upon the effect of the error or errors is of the opinion that the admitted evidence should have been excluded on the ground stated and that the error or errors complained of resulted in a miscarriage of justice.

§ 354. Erroneous exclusion of evidence; effect

A verdict or finding shall not be set aside, nor shall the judgment or decision based thereon be reversed, by reason of the erroneous exclusion of evidence unless the court which passes upon the effect of the error or errors is of the opinion that the error or errors complained of resulted in a miscarriage of justice and it appears of record that:

(a)   The substance, purpose, and relevance of the excluded evidence was made known to the court by the questions asked, an offer of proof, or by any other means;

(b)   The rulings of the court made compliance with subdivision (a) futile; or

(c)   The evidence was sought by questions asked during cross-examination or recross-examination.

§ 355. Limited admissibility

When evidence is admissible as to one party or for one purpose and is inadmissible as to another party or for another purpose, the court upon request shall restrict the evidence to its proper scope and instruct the jury accordingly.

§ 356. Entire act, declaration, conversation, or writing, to elucidate part offered

Where part of an act, declaration, conversation, or writing is given in evidence by one party, the whole on the same subject may be inquired into by an adverse party; when a letter is read, the answer may be given; and when a detached act, declaration, conversation, or writing is given in evidence, any other act, declaration, conversation, or writing which is necessary to make it understood may also be given in evidence.

ARTICLE 2. PRELIMINARY DETERMINATIONS ON ADMISSIBILITY OF EVIDENCE

§ 400. "Preliminary fact" defined

As used in this article, "preliminary fact" means a fact upon the existence or nonexistence of which depends the admissibility or inadmissibility of evidence. The phrase "the admissibility or inadmissibility of evidence" includes the qualification or disqualification of a person to be a witness and the existence or nonexistence of a privilege.

§ 401. "Proffered evidence" defined

As used in this article, "proffered evidence" means evidence, the admissibility or inadmissibility of which is dependent upon the existence or nonexistence of a preliminary fact.

§ 402. Procedure for determining foundational and other preliminary facts

(a) When the existence of a preliminary fact is disputed, its existence or nonexistence shall be determined as provided in this article.

(b) The court may hear and determine the question of the admissibility of evidence out of the presence or hearing of the jury; but in a criminal action, the court shall hear and determine the question of the admissibility of a confession or admission of the defendant out of the presence and hearing of the jury if any party so requests.

(c) A ruling on the admissibility of evidence implies whatever finding of fact is prerequisite thereto; a separate or formal finding is unnecessary unless required by statute.

§ 403. Determination of foundational and other preliminary facts where relevancy, personal knowledge, or authenticity is disputed

(a) The proponent of the proffered evidence has the burden of producing evidence as to the existence of the preliminary fact, and the proffered evidence is inadmissible unless the court finds that there is evidence sufficient to sustain a finding of the existence of the preliminary fact, when:

(1) The relevance of the proffered evidence depends on the existence of the preliminary fact;

(2) The preliminary fact is the personal knowledge of a witness concerning the subject matter of his testimony;

(3) The preliminary fact is the authenticity of a writing; or

(4) The proffered evidence is of a statement or other conduct of a particular person and the preliminary fact is whether that person made the statement or so conducted himself.

(b) Subject to Section 702, the court may admit conditionally the proffered evidence under this section, subject to evidence of the preliminary fact being supplied later in the course of the trial.

(c) If the court admits the proffered evidence under this section, the court:

(1) May, and on request shall, instruct the jury to determine whether the preliminary fact exists and to disregard the proffered evidence unless the jury finds that the preliminary fact does exist.

(2) Shall instruct the jury to disregard the proffered evidence if the court subsequently determines that a jury could not reasonably find that the preliminary fact exists.

§ 404. Determination of whether proffered evidence is incriminatory

Whenever the proffered evidence is claimed to be privileged under Section 940, the person claiming the privilege has the burden of showing that the proffered evidence might tend to incriminate him; and the proffered evidence is inadmissible unless it clearly appears to the court that the proffered evidence cannot possibly have a tendency to incriminate the person claiming the privilege.

§ 405. Determination of foundational and other preliminary facts in other cases

With respect to preliminary fact determinations not governed by Section 403 or 404:

(a) When the existence of a preliminary fact is disputed, the court shall indicate which party has the burden of producing evidence and the burden of proof on the issue as implied by the rule of law under which the question arises. The court shall determine the existence or nonexistence of the preliminary fact and shall admit or exclude the proffered evidence as required by the rule of law under which the question arises.

(b) If a preliminary fact is also a fact in issue in the action:

(1) The jury shall not be informed of the court's determination as to the existence or nonexistence of the preliminary fact.

(2) If the proffered evidence is admitted, the jury shall not be instructed to disregard the evidence if its determination of the fact differs from the court's determination of the preliminary fact.

§ 406. Evidence affecting weight or credibility

This article does not limit the right of a party to introduce before the trier of fact evidence relevant to weight or credibility.

CHAPTER 5. WEIGHT OF EVIDENCE GENERALLY

§ 410. "Direct evidence" defined

As used in this chapter, "direct evidence" means evidence that directly proves a fact, without an inference or presumption, and which in itself, if true, conclusively establishes that fact.

§ 411. Direct evidence of one witness sufficient

Except where additional evidence is required by statute, the direct evidence of one witness who is entitled to full credit is sufficient for proof of any fact.

§ 412. Party having power to produce better evidence

If weaker and less satisfactory evidence is offered when it was within the power of the party to produce stronger and more satisfactory evidence, the evidence offered should be viewed with distrust.

§ 413. Party's failure to explain or deny evidence

In determining what inferences to draw from the evidence or facts in the case against a party, the trier of fact may consider, among other things, the party's failure to explain or to deny by his testimony such evidence or facts in the case against him, or his willful suppression of evidence relating thereto, if such be the case.

APPENDIX II

DIVISION 4. JUDICIAL NOTICE

§ 450. Judicial notice may be taken only as authorized by law

Judicial notice may not be taken of any matter unless authorized or required by law.

§ 451. Matters which must be judicially noticed

Judicial notice shall be taken of the following:

(a) The decisional, constitutional, and public statutory law of this state and of the United States and the provisions of any charter described in Section 3, 4, or 5 of Article XI of the California Constitution.

(b) Any matter made a subject of judicial notice by Section 11343.6, 11344.6, or 18576 of the Government Code or by Section 1507 of Title 44 of the United States Code.

(c) Rules of professional conduct for members of the bar adopted pursuant to Section 6076 of the Business and Professions Code and rules of practice and procedure for the courts of this state adopted by the Judicial Council.

(d) Rules of pleading, practice, and procedure prescribed by the United States Supreme Court, such as the Rules of the United States Supreme Court, the Federal Rules of Civil Procedure, the Federal Rules of Criminal Procedure, the Admiralty Rules, the Rules of the Court of Claims, the Rules of the Customs Court, and the General Orders and Forms in Bankruptcy.

(e) The true signification of all English words and phrases and of all legal expressions.

(f) Facts and propositions of generalized knowledge that are so universally known that they cannot reasonably be the subject of dispute.

§ 452. Matters which may be judicially noticed

Judicial notice may be taken of the following matters to the extent that they are not embraced within Section 451:

(a) The decisional, constitutional, and statutory law of any state of the United States and the resolutions and private acts of the Congress of the United States and of the Legislature of this state.

(b) Regulations and legislative enactments issued by or under the authority of the United States or any public entity in the United States.

(c) Official acts of the legislative, executive, and judicial departments of the United States and of any state of the United States.

(d) Records of (1) any court of this state or (2) any court of record of the United States or of any state of the United States.

(e) Rules of court of (1) any court of this state or (2) any court of record of the United States or of any state of the United States.

(f) The law of an organization of nations and of foreign nations and public entities in foreign nations.

(g) Facts and propositions that are of such common knowledge within the territorial jurisdiction of the court that they cannot reasonably be the subject of dispute.

(h)   Facts and propositions that are not reasonably subject to dispute and are capable of immediate and accurate determination by resort to sources of reasonably indisputable accuracy.

§ 452.5.   Criminal conviction records; computer-generated records and electronically digitalized copies; admissibility

(a)   The official acts and records specified in subdivisions (c) and (d) of Section 452 include any computer-generated official court records, as specified by the Judicial Council, that relate to criminal convictions, when the record is certified by a clerk of the superior court pursuant to Section 69844.5 of the Government Code at the time of computer entry.

(b)(1)   An official record of conviction certified in accordance with subdivision (a) of Section 1530, or an electronically digitized copy thereof, is admissible under Section 1280 to prove the commission, attempted commission, or solicitation of a criminal offense, prior conviction, service of a prison term, or other act, condition, or event recorded by the record.

(2)   For purposes of this subdivision, "electronically digitized copy" means a copy that is made by scanning, photographing, or otherwise exactly reproducing a document, is stored or maintained in a digitized format, and meets either of the following requirements:

(A)   The copy bears an electronic signature or watermark unique to the entity responsible for certifying the document.

(B)   The copied document is an official record of conviction, certified in accordance with subdivision (a) of Section 1530, that is transmitted by the clerk of the superior court in a manner showing that the copy was prepared and transmitted by that clerk of the superior court. A seal, signature, or other indicia of the court shall constitute adequate showing.

§ 453.   Compulsory judicial notice upon request

The trial court shall take judicial notice of any matter specified in Section 452 if a party requests it and:

(a)   Gives each adverse party sufficient notice of the request, through the pleadings or otherwise, to enable such adverse party to prepare to meet the request; and

(b)   Furnishes the court with sufficient information to enable it to take judicial notice of the matter.

§ 454.   Information that may be used in taking judicial notice

(a)   In determining the propriety of taking judicial notice of a matter, or the tenor thereof:

(1)   Any source of pertinent information, including the advice of persons learned in the subject matter, may be consulted or used, whether or not furnished by a party.

(2)   Exclusionary rules of evidence do not apply except for Section 352 and the rules of privilege.

(b)   Where the subject of judicial notice is the law of an organization of nations, a foreign nation, or a public entity in a foreign nation and the court resorts to the advice of persons learned in the subject matter, such advice, if not received in open court, shall be in writing.

§ 455.　Opportunity to present information to court

With respect to any matter specified in Section 452 or in subdivision (f) of Section 451 that is of substantial consequence to the determination of the action:

(a)　If the trial court has been requested to take or has taken or proposes to take judicial notice of such matter, the court shall afford each party reasonable opportunity, before the jury is instructed or before the cause is submitted for decision by the court, to present to the court information relevant to (1) the propriety of taking judicial notice of the matter and (2) the tenor of the matter to be noticed.

(b)　If the trial court resorts to any source of information not received in open court, including the advice of persons learned in the subject matter, such information and its source shall be made a part of the record in the action and the court shall afford each party reasonable opportunity to meet such information before judicial notice of the matter may be taken.

§ 456.　Noting denial of request to take judicial notice

If the trial court denies a request to take judicial notice of any matter, the court shall at the earliest practicable time so advise the parties and indicate for the record that it has denied the request.

§ 457.　Instructing jury on matter judicially noticed

If a matter judicially noticed is a matter which would otherwise have been for determination by the jury, the trial court may, and upon request shall, instruct the jury to accept as a fact the matter so noticed.

§ 458.　Judicial notice by trial court in subsequent proceedings

The failure or refusal of the trial court to take judicial notice of a matter, or to instruct the jury with respect to the matter, does not preclude the trial court in subsequent proceedings in the action from taking judicial notice of the matter in accordance with the procedure specified in this division.

§ 459.　Judicial notice by reviewing court

(a)　The reviewing court shall take judicial notice of (1) each matter properly noticed by the trial court and (2) each matter that the trial court was required to notice under Section 451 or 453. The reviewing court may take judicial notice of any matter specified in Section 452. The reviewing court may take judicial notice of a matter in a tenor different from that noticed by the trial court.

(b)　In determining the propriety of taking judicial notice of a matter, or the tenor thereof, the reviewing court has the same power as the trial court under Section 454.

(c)　When taking judicial notice under this section of a matter specified in Section 452 or in subdivision (f) of Section 451 that is of substantial consequence to the determination of the action, the reviewing court shall comply with the provisions of subdivision (a) of Section 455 if the matter was not theretofore judicially noticed in the action.

(d) In determining the propriety of taking judicial notice of a matter specified in Section 452 or in subdivision (f) of Section 451 that is of substantial consequence to the determination of the action, or the tenor thereof, if the reviewing court resorts to any source of information not received in open court or not included in the record of the action, including the advice of persons learned in the subject matter, the reviewing court shall afford each party reasonable opportunity to meet such information before judicial notice of the matter may be taken.

§ 460. Appointment of expert by court

Where the advice of persons learned in the subject matter is required in order to enable the court to take judicial notice of a matter, the court on its own motion or on motion of any party may appoint one or more such persons to provide such advice. If the court determines to appoint such a person, he shall be appointed and compensated in the manner provided in Article 2 (commencing with Section 730) of Chapter 3 of Division 6.

DIVISION 5. BURDEN OF PROOF; BURDEN OF PRODUCING EVIDENCE; PRESUMPTIONS AND INFERENCES

CHAPTER 1. BURDEN OF PROOF

ARTICLE 1. GENERAL

§ 500. Party who has the burden of proof

Except as otherwise provided by law, a party has the burden of proof as to each fact the existence or nonexistence of which is essential to the claim for relief or defense that he is asserting.

§ 501. Criminal actions; statutory assignment of burden of proof; controlling section

Insofar as any statute, except Section 522, assigns the burden of proof in a criminal action, such statute is subject to Penal Code Section 1096.

§ 502. Instructions on burden of proof

The court on all proper occasions shall instruct the jury as to which party bears the burden of proof on each issue and as to whether that burden requires that a party raise a reasonable doubt concerning the existence or nonexistence of a fact or that he establish the existence or nonexistence of a fact by a preponderance of the evidence, by clear and convincing proof, or by proof beyond a reasonable doubt.

ARTICLE 2. BURDEN OF PROOF ON SPECIFIC ISSUES

§ 520. Claim that person guilty of crime or wrongdoing

The party claiming that a person is guilty of crime or wrongdoing has the burden of proof on that issue.

§ 521. Claim that person did not exercise care

The party claiming that a person did not exercise a requisite degree of care has the burden of proof on that issue.

§ 522. Claim that person is or was insane

The party claiming that any person, including himself, is or was insane has the burden of proof on that issue.

§ 523. Historic locations of water; claims involving state land patents or grants

In any action where the state is a party, regardless of who is the moving party, where (a) the boundary of land patented or otherwise granted by the state is in dispute, or (b) the validity of any state patent or grant dated prior to 1950 is in dispute, the state shall have the burden of proof on all issues relating to the historic locations of rivers, streams, and other water bodies and the authority of the state in issuing the patent or grant.

This section is not intended to nor shall it be construed to supersede existing statutes governing disputes where the state is a party and regarding title to real property.

§ 524. Burden of proof in cases involving State Board of Equalization; unreasonable search or access to records prohibited; taxpayer defined

(a) Notwithstanding any other provision of law, in a civil proceeding to which the State Board of Equalization is a party, that board shall have the burden of proof by clear and convincing evidence in sustaining its assertion of a penalty for intent to evade or fraud against a taxpayer, with respect to any factual issue relevant to ascertaining the liability of a taxpayer.

(b) Nothing in this section shall be construed to override any requirement for a taxpayer to substantiate any item on a return or claim filed with the State Board of Equalization.

(c) Nothing in this section shall subject a taxpayer to unreasonable search or access to records in violation of the United States Constitution, the California Constitution, or any other law.

(d) For purposes of this section, "taxpayer" includes a person on whom fees administered by the State Board of Equalization are imposed.

CHAPTER 2. BURDEN OF PRODUCING EVIDENCE

§ 550. Party who has the burden of producing evidence

(a) The burden of producing evidence as to a particular fact is on the party against whom a finding on that fact would be required in the absence of further evidence.

(b) The burden of producing evidence as to a particular fact is initially on the party with the burden of proof as to that fact.

CHAPTER 3. PRESUMPTIONS AND INFERENCES

ARTICLE 1. GENERAL

§ 600. "Presumption" and "inference" defined

(a) A presumption is an assumption of fact that the law requires to be made from another fact or group of facts found or otherwise established in the action. A presumption is not evidence.

(b) An inference is a deduction of fact that may logically and reasonably be drawn from another fact or group of facts found or otherwise established in the action.

§ 601. Classification of presumptions

A presumption is either conclusive or rebuttable. Every rebuttable presumption is either (a) a presumption affecting the burden of producing evidence or (b) a presumption affecting the burden of proof.

§ 602. Statute making one fact prima facie evidence of another fact

A statute providing that a fact or group of facts is prima facie evidence of another fact establishes a rebuttable presumption.

§ 603. Presumption affecting the burden of producing evidence defined

A presumption affecting the burden of producing evidence is a presumption established to implement no public policy other than to facilitate the determination of the particular action in which the presumption is applied.

§ 604. Effect of presumption affecting burden of producing evidence

The effect of a presumption affecting the burden of producing evidence is to require the trier of fact to assume the existence of the presumed fact unless and until evidence is introduced which would support a finding of its nonexistence, in which case the trier of fact shall determine the existence or nonexistence of the presumed fact from the evidence and without regard to the presumption. Nothing in this section shall be construed to prevent the drawing of any inference that may be appropriate.

§ 605. "Presumption affecting the burden of proof" defined

A presumption affecting the burden of proof is a presumption established to implement some public policy other than to facilitate the determination of the particular action in which the presumption is applied, such as the policy in favor of establishment of a parent and child relationship, the validity of marriage, the stability of titles to property, or the security of those who entrust themselves or their property to the administration of others.

§ 606. Effect of presumption affecting burden of proof

The effect of a presumption affecting the burden of proof is to impose upon the party against whom it operates the burden of proof as to the nonexistence of the presumed fact.

§ 607. Effect of certain presumptions in a criminal action

When a presumption affecting the burden of proof operates in a criminal action to establish presumptively any fact that is essential to the defendant's guilt, the presumption operates only if the facts that give rise to the presumption have been found or otherwise established beyond a reasonable doubt and, in such case, the defendant need only raise a reasonable doubt as to the existence of the presumed fact.

ARTICLE 2. CONCLUSIVE PRESUMPTIONS

§ 620. Conclusive presumptions

The presumptions established by this article, and all other presumptions declared by law to be conclusive, are conclusive presumptions.

§ 621. Repealed by Stats.1992, c. 162 (A.B.2650), § 8, operative Jan. 1, 1994

§ 621.1. Repealed by Stats.1993, c. 219 (A.B.1500), § 76

§ 622. Facts recited in written instrument

The facts recited in a written instrument are conclusively presumed to be true as between the parties thereto, or their successors in interest; but this rule does not apply to the recital of a consideration.

§ 623. Estoppel by own statement or conduct

Whenever a party has, by his own statement or conduct, intentionally and deliberately led another to believe a particular thing true and to act upon such belief, he is not, in any litigation arising out of such statement or conduct, permitted to contradict it.

§ 624. Estoppel of tenant to deny title of landlord

A tenant is not permitted to deny the title of his landlord at the time of the commencement of the relation.

ARTICLE 3. PRESUMPTIONS AFFECTING THE BURDEN OF PRODUCING EVIDENCE

§ 630. Presumptions affecting the burden of producing evidence

The presumptions established by this article, and all other rebuttable presumptions established by law that fall within the criteria of Section 603, are presumptions affecting the burden of producing evidence.

§ 631. Money delivered by one to another

Money delivered by one to another is presumed to have been due to the latter.

§ 632. Thing delivered by one to another

A thing delivered by one to another is presumed to have belonged to the latter.

§ 633. Obligation delivered up to the debtor

An obligation delivered up to the debtor is presumed to have been paid.

§ 634. Person in possession of order on self

A person in possession of an order on himself for the payment of money, or delivery of a thing, is presumed to have paid the money or delivered the thing accordingly.

§ 635. Obligation possessed by creditor

An obligation possessed by the creditor is presumed not to have been paid.

§ 636. Payment of earlier rent or installments

The payment of earlier rent or installments is presumed from a receipt for later rent or installments.

§ 637. Ownership of things possessed

The things which a person possesses are presumed to be owned by him.

§ 638. Property ownership acts

A person who exercises acts of ownership over property is presumed to be the owner of it.

§ 639. Judgment correctly determines rights of parties

A judgment, when not conclusive, is presumed to correctly determine or set forth the rights of the parties, but there is no presumption that the facts essential to the judgment have been correctly determined.

§ 640. Writing truly dated

A writing is presumed to have been truly dated.

§ 641. Letter received in ordinary course of mail

A letter correctly addressed and properly mailed is presumed to have been received in the ordinary course of mail.

§ 642. Conveyance by person having duty to convey real property

A trustee or other person, whose duty it was to convey real property to a particular person, is presumed to have actually conveyed to him when such presumption is necessary to perfect title of such person or his successor in interest.

§ 643. Authenticity of ancient document

A deed or will or other writing purporting to create, terminate, or affect an interest in real or personal property is presumed to be authentic if it:

(a)   Is at least 30 years old;

(b)   Is in such condition as to create no suspicion concerning its authenticity;

(c)   Was kept, or if found was found, in a place where such writing, if authentic, would be likely to be kept or found; and

(d)   Has been generally acted upon as authentic by persons having an interest in the matter.

§ 644. Book purporting to be published by public authority

A book, purporting to be printed or published by public authority, is presumed to have been so printed or published.

§ 645. Book purporting to contain reports of cases

A book, purporting to contain reports of cases adjudged in the tribunals of the state or nation where the book is published, is presumed to contain correct reports of such cases.

§ 645.1. Printed materials purporting to be particular newspaper or periodical

Printed materials, purporting to be a particular newspaper or periodical, are presumed to be that newspaper or periodical if regularly issued at average intervals not exceeding three months.

§ 646. Res ipsa loquitur; instruction

(a) As used in this section, "defendant" includes any party against whom the res ipsa loquitur presumption operates.

(b) The judicial doctrine of res ipsa loquitur is a presumption affecting the burden of producing evidence.

(c) If the evidence, or facts otherwise established, would support a res ipsa loquitur presumption and the defendant has introduced evidence which would support a finding that he was not negligent or that any negligence on his part was not a proximate cause of the occurrence, the court may, and upon request shall, instruct the jury to the effect that:

(1) If the facts which would give rise to a res ipsa loquitur presumption are found or otherwise established, the jury may draw the inference from such facts that a proximate cause of the occurrence was some negligent conduct on the part of the defendant; and

(2) The jury shall not find that a proximate cause of the occurrence was some negligent conduct on the part of the defendant unless the jury believes, after weighing all the evidence in the case and drawing such inferences therefrom as the jury believes are warranted, that it is more probable than not that the occurrence was caused by some negligent conduct on the part of the defendant.

§ 647. Return of process served by registered process server

The return of a process server registered pursuant to Chapter 16 (commencing with Section 22350) of Division 8 of the Business and Professions Code upon process or notice establishes a presumption, affecting the burden of producing evidence, of the facts stated in the return.

ARTICLE 4. PRESUMPTIONS AFFECTING THE BURDEN OF PROOF

§ 660. Presumptions affecting the burden of proof

The presumptions established by this article, and all other rebuttable presumptions established by law that fall within the criteria of Section 605, are presumptions affecting the burden of proof.

§ 661. Repealed by Stats. 1975, c. 1244, p. 3202, § 14

§ 662. Owner of legal title to property is owner of beneficial title

The owner of the legal title to property is presumed to be the owner of the full beneficial title. This presumption may be rebutted only by clear and convincing proof.

§ 663. Ceremonial marriage

A ceremonial marriage is presumed to be valid.

§ 664. Official duty regularly performed

It is presumed that official duty has been regularly performed. This presumption does not apply on an issue as to the lawfulness of an arrest if it is found or otherwise established that the arrest was made without a warrant.

§ 665. Ordinary consequences of voluntary act

A person is presumed to intend the ordinary consequences of his voluntary act. This presumption is inapplicable in a criminal action to establish the specific intent of the defendant where specific intent is an element of the crime charged.

§ 666. Judicial action lawful exercise of jurisdiction

Any court of this state or the United States, or any court of general jurisdiction in any other state or nation, or any judge of such a court, acting as such, is presumed to have acted in the lawful exercise of its jurisdiction. This presumption applies only when the act of the court or judge is under collateral attack.

§ 667. Death of person not heard from in five years

A person not heard from in five years is presumed to be dead.

§ 668. Unlawful intent

An unlawful intent is presumed from the doing of an unlawful act. This presumption is inapplicable in a criminal action to establish the specific intent of the defendant where specific intent is an element of the crime charged.

§ 669. Due care; failure to exercise

(a)   The failure of a person to exercise due care is presumed if:

(1)   He violated a statute, ordinance, or regulation of a public entity;

(2)   The violation proximately caused death or injury to person or property;

(3)   The death or injury resulted from an occurrence of the nature which the statute, ordinance, or regulation was designed to prevent; and

(4)   The person suffering the death or the injury to his person or property was one of the class of persons for whose protection the statute, ordinance, or regulation was adopted.

(b)   This presumption may be rebutted by proof that:

(1)   The person violating the statute, ordinance, or regulation did what might reasonably be expected of a person of ordinary prudence, acting under similar circumstances, who desired to comply with the law; or

(2)   The person violating the statute, ordinance, or regulation was a child and exercised the degree of care ordinarily exercised by persons of his maturity, intelligence, and capacity under similar circumstances, but the presumption may not be rebutted by such proof if the violation occurred in the course of an activity normally engaged in only by adults and requiring adult qualifications.

§ 669.1.   Standards of conduct for public employees; presumption of failure to exercise due care

A rule, policy, manual, or guideline of state or local government setting forth standards of conduct or guidelines for its employees in the conduct of their public employment shall not be considered a statute, ordinance, or regulation of that public entity within the meaning of Section 669, unless the rule, manual, policy, or guideline has been formally adopted as a statute, as an ordinance of a local governmental entity in this state empowered to adopt ordinances, or as a regulation by an agency of the state pursuant to the Administrative Procedure Act (Chapter 3.5 (commencing with Section 11340) of Division 3 of Title 2 of the Government Code), or by an agency of the United States government pursuant to the federal Administrative Procedure Act (Chapter 5 (commencing with Section 5001) of Title 5 of the United States Code). This section affects only the presumption set forth in Section 669, and is not otherwise intended to affect the admissibility or inadmissibility of the rule, policy, manual, or guideline under other provisions of law.

§ 669.5.   Ordinances limiting building permits or development of buildable lots for residential purposes; impact on supply of residential units; actions challenging validity

(a)   Any ordinance enacted by the governing body of a city, county, or city and county which (1) directly limits, by number, the building permits that may be issued for residential construction or the buildable lots which may be developed for residential purposes, or (2) changes the standards of residential development on vacant land so that the governing body's zoning is rendered in violation of Section 65913.1 of the Government Code is presumed to have an impact on the supply of residential units available in an area which includes territory outside the jurisdiction of the city, county, or city and county.

(b)   With respect to any action which challenges the validity of an ordinance specified in subdivision (a) the city, county, or city and county enacting the ordinance shall bear the burden of proof that the ordinance is necessary for the protection of the public health, safety, or welfare of the population of the city, county, or city and county.

(c)   This section does not apply to state and federal building code requirements or local ordinances which (1) impose a moratorium, to protect the public health and safety, on residential construction for a specified period of time, if, under the terms of the ordinance, the moratorium will cease when the public health or safety is no longer jeopardized by the construction, (2) create agricultural preserves under Chapter 7 (commencing with Section 51200) of Part 1 of Division 1 of Title 5 of the Government Code, or (3) restrict the number of buildable parcels or designate lands within a zone for nonresidential uses in order to protect agricultural uses as defined in subdivision (b) of Section 51201 of the Government Code or open-space land as defined in subdivision (h) of Section 65560 of the Government Code.

(d)   This section shall not apply to a voter approved ordinance adopted by referendum or initiative prior to the effective date of this section which (1) requires the city, county, or city and county to establish a population growth limit which represents its fair share of each year's statewide population growth, or (2) which sets a growth rate of no more than the average population growth rate experienced by the state as a whole. Paragraph (2) of subdivision (a) does not apply to a voter-approved ordinance adopted by referendum or initiative which exempts housing affordable to persons and families of low or moderate income, as defined in Section 50093 of the Health and Safety Code, or which otherwise provides low-and moderate-income housing sites equivalent to such an exemption.

§ 670.   Payments by check

(a)   In any dispute concerning payment by means of a check, a copy of the check produced in accordance with Section 1550 of the Evidence Code, together with the original bank statement that reflects payment of the check by the bank on which it was drawn or a copy thereof produced in the same manner, creates a presumption that the check has been paid.

(b)   As used in this section:

(1)   "Bank" means any person engaged in the business of banking and includes, in addition to a commercial bank, a savings and loan association, savings bank, or credit union.

(2)   "Check" means a draft, other than a documentary draft, payable on demand and drawn on a bank, even though it is described by another term, such as "share draft" or "negotiable order of withdrawal."

DIVISION 6. WITNESSES

CHAPTER 1. COMPETENCY

§ 700. General rule as to competency

Except as otherwise provided by statute, every person, irrespective of age, is qualified to be a witness and no person is disqualified to testify to any matter.

§ 701. Disqualification of witness

(a) A person is disqualified to be a witness if he or she is:

(1) Incapable of expressing himself or herself concerning the matter so as to be understood, either directly or through interpretation by one who can understand him; or

(2) Incapable of understanding the duty of a witness to tell the truth.

(b) In any proceeding held outside the presence of a jury, the court may reserve challenges to the competency of a witness until the conclusion of the direct examination of that witness.

§ 702. Personal knowledge of witness

(a) Subject to Section 801, the testimony of a witness concerning a particular matter is inadmissible unless he has personal knowledge of the matter. Against the objection of a party, such personal knowledge must be shown before the witness may testify concerning the matter.

(b) A witness' personal knowledge of a matter may be shown by any otherwise admissible evidence, including his own testimony.

§ 703. Judge as witness

(a) Before the judge presiding at the trial of an action may be called to testify in that trial as a witness, he shall, in proceedings held out of the presence and hearing of the jury, inform the parties of the information he has concerning any fact or matter about which he will be called to testify.

(b) Against the objection of a party, the judge presiding at the trial of an action may not testify in that trial as a witness. Upon such objection, the judge shall declare a mistrial and order the action assigned for trial before another judge.

(c) The calling of the judge presiding at a trial to testify in that trial as a witness shall be deemed a consent to the granting of a motion for mistrial, and an objection to such calling of a judge shall be deemed a motion for mistrial.

(d) In the absence of objection by a party, the judge presiding at the trial of an action may testify in that trial as a witness.

§ 703.5. Judges, arbitrators or mediators as witnesses; subsequent civil proceeding

No person presiding at any judicial or quasi-judicial proceeding, and no arbitrator or mediator, shall be competent to testify, in any subsequent civil proceeding, as to any statement, conduct, decision, or ruling, occurring at or in conjunction with the prior proceeding, except as to a statement or conduct that could (a) give rise to civil or criminal contempt, (b) constitute a crime, (c) be the subject of investigation by the State Bar or Commission on Judicial Performance, or (d) give rise to disqualification proceedings under paragraph (1) or (6) of subdivision (a) of Section 170.1 of the Code of Civil Procedure. However, this section does not apply to a mediator with regard to any mediation under Chapter 11 (commencing with Section 3160) of Part 2 of Division 8 of the Family Code.

§ 704.   Juror as witness

(a)   Before a juror sworn and impaneled in the trial of an action may be called to testify before the jury in that trial as a witness, he shall, in proceedings conducted by the court out of the presence and hearing of the remaining jurors, inform the parties of the information he has concerning any fact or matter about which he will be called to testify.

(b)   Against the objection of a party, a juror sworn and impaneled in the trial of an action may not testify before the jury in that trial as a witness. Upon such objection, the court shall declare a mistrial and order the action assigned for trial before another jury.

(c)   The calling of a juror to testify before the jury as a witness shall be deemed a consent to the granting of a motion for mistrial, and an objection to such calling of a juror shall be deemed a motion for mistrial.

(d)   In the absence of objection by a party, a juror sworn and impaneled in the trial of an action may be compelled to testify in that trial as a witness.

CHAPTER 2. OATH AND CONFRONTATION

§ 710.   Oath required

Every witness before testifying shall take an oath or make an affirmation or declaration in the form provided by law, except that a child under the age of 10 or a dependent person with a substantial cognitive impairment, in the court's discretion, may be required only to promise to tell the truth.

§ 711.   Confrontation

At the trial of an action, a witness can be heard only in the presence and subject to the examination of all the parties to the action, if they choose to attend and examine.

§ 712.   Blood samples; technique in taking; affidavits in criminal actions; service; objections

Notwithstanding Sections 711 and 1200, at the trial of a criminal action, evidence of the technique used in taking blood samples may be given by a registered nurse, licensed vocational nurse, or licensed clinical laboratory technologist or clinical laboratory bioanalyst, by means of an affidavit. The affidavit shall be admissible, provided the party offering the affidavit as evidence has served all other parties to the action, or their counsel, with a copy of the affidavit no less than 10 days prior to trial. Nothing in this section shall preclude any party or his counsel from objecting to the introduction of the affidavit at any time, and requiring the attendance of the affiant, or compelling attendance by subpoena.

CHAPTER 3. EXPERT WITNESSES

ARTICLE 1. EXPERT WITNESSES GENERALLY

§ 720. Qualification as an expert witness

(a) A person is qualified to testify as an expert if he has special knowledge, skill, experience, training, or education sufficient to qualify him as an expert on the subject to which his testimony relates. Against the objection of a party, such special knowledge, skill, experience, training, or education must be shown before the witness may testify as an expert.

(b) A witness' special knowledge, skill, experience, training, or education may be shown by any otherwise admissible evidence, including his own testimony.

§ 721. Cross-examination of expert witness

(a) Subject to subdivision (b), a witness testifying as an expert may be cross-examined to the same extent as any other witness and, in addition, may be fully cross-examined as to (1) his or her qualifications, (2) the subject to which his or her expert testimony relates, and (3) the matter upon which his or her opinion is based and the reasons for his or her opinion.

(b) If a witness testifying as an expert testifies in the form of an opinion, he or she may not be cross-examined in regard to the content or tenor of any scientific, technical, or professional text, treatise, journal, or similar publication unless any of the following occurs:

(1) The witness referred to, considered, or relied upon such publication in arriving at or forming his or her opinion.

(2) The publication has been admitted in evidence.

(3) The publication has been established as a reliable authority by the testimony or admission of the witness or by other expert testimony or by judicial notice.

If admitted, relevant portions of the publication may be read into evidence but may not be received as exhibits.

§ 722. Credibility of expert witness

(a) The fact of the appointment of an expert witness by the court may be revealed to the trier of fact.

(b) The compensation and expenses paid or to be paid to an expert witness by the party calling him is a proper subject of inquiry by any adverse party as relevant to the credibility of the witness and the weight of his testimony.

§ 723. Limit on number of expert witnesses

The court may, at any time before or during the trial of an action, limit the number of expert witnesses to be called by any party.

ARTICLE 2. APPOINTMENT OF EXPERT WITNESS BY COURT

§ 730. Appointment of expert by court

When it appears to the court, at any time before or during the trial of an action, that expert evidence is or may be required by the court or by any party to the action, the court on its own motion or on motion of any party may appoint one or more experts to investigate, to render a report as may be ordered by the court, and to testify as an expert at the trial of the action relative to the fact or matter as to which the expert evidence is or may be required. The court may fix the compensation for these services, if any, rendered by any person appointed under this section, in addition to any service as a witness, at the amount as seems reasonable to the court.

Nothing in this section shall be construed to permit a person to perform any act for which a license is required unless the person holds the appropriate license to lawfully perform that act.

§ 731. Payment of court-appointed expert

(a)(1) In all criminal actions and juvenile court proceedings, the compensation fixed under Section 730 shall be a charge against the county in which the action or proceeding is pending and shall be paid out of the treasury of that county on order of the court.

(2) Notwithstanding paragraph (1), if the expert is appointed for the court's needs, the compensation shall be a charge against the court.

(b) In any county in which the superior court so provides, the compensation fixed under Section 730 for medical experts appointed for the court's needs in civil actions shall be a charge against the court. In any county in which the board of supervisors so provides, the compensation fixed under Section 730 for medical experts appointed in civil actions, for purposes other than the court's needs, shall be a charge against and paid out of the treasury of that county on order of the court.

(c) Except as otherwise provided in this section, in all civil actions, the compensation fixed under Section 730 shall, in the first instance, be apportioned and charged to the several parties in a proportion as the court may determine and may thereafter be taxed and allowed in like manner as other costs.

§ 732. Calling and examining court-appointed expert

Any expert appointed by the court under Section 730 may be called and examined by the court or by any party to the action. When such witness is called and examined by the court, the parties have the same right as is expressed in Section 775 to cross-examine the witness and to object to the questions asked and the evidence adduced.

§ 733. Right to produce other expert evidence

Nothing contained in this article shall be deemed or construed to prevent any party to any action from producing other expert evidence on the same fact or matter mentioned in Section 730; but, where other expert witnesses are called by a party to the action, their fees shall be paid by the party calling them and only ordinary witness fees shall be taxed as costs in the action.

CHAPTER 4. INTERPRETERS AND TRANSLATORS

§ 750. Rules relating to witnesses apply to interpreters and translators

A person who serves as an interpreter or translator in any action is subject to all the rules of law relating to witnesses.

§ 751. Oath required of interpreters and translators

(a) An interpreter shall take an oath that he or she will make a true interpretation to the witness in a language that the witness understands and that he or she will make a true interpretation of the witness' answers to questions to counsel, court, or jury, in the English language, with his or her best skill and judgment.

(b) In any proceeding in which a deaf or hard-of-hearing person is testifying under oath, the interpreter certified pursuant to subdivision (f) of Section 754 shall advise the court whenever he or she is unable to comply with his or her oath taken pursuant to subdivision (a).

(c) A translator shall take an oath that he or she will make a true translation in the English language of any writing he or she is to decipher or translate.

(d) An interpreter or translator regularly employed by the court and certified or registered in accordance with Article 4 (commencing with Section 68560) of Chapter 2 of Title 8 of the Government Code, or a translator regularly employed by the court, may file an oath as prescribed by this section with the clerk of the court. The filed oath shall serve for all subsequent court proceedings until the appointment is revoked by the court.

§ 752. Interpreters for witnesses; compensation

(a) When a witness is incapable of understanding the English language or is incapable of expressing himself or herself in the English language so as to be understood directly by counsel, court, and jury, an interpreter whom the witness can understand and who can understand the witness shall be sworn to interpret for the witness.

(b) The record shall identify the interpreter, who may be appointed and compensated as provided in Article 2 (commencing with Section 730) of Chapter 3, with that compensation charged as follows:

(1) In all criminal actions and juvenile court proceedings, the compensation for an interpreter under this section shall be a charge against the court.

(2) In all civil actions, the compensation for an interpreter under this section shall, in the first instance, be apportioned and charged to the several parties in a proportion as the court may determine and may thereafter be taxed and allowed in a like manner as other costs.

§ 753. Translators of writings; compensation

(a) When the written characters in a writing offered in evidence are incapable of being deciphered or understood directly, a translator who can decipher the characters or understand the language shall be sworn to decipher or translate the writing.

(b)　The record shall identify the translator, who may be appointed and compensated as provided in Article 2 (commencing with Section 730) of Chapter 3, with that compensation charged as follows:

(1)　In all criminal actions and juvenile court proceedings, the compensation for a translator under this section shall be a charge against the court.

(2)　In all civil actions, the compensation for a translator under this section shall, in the first instance, be apportioned and charged to the several parties in a proportion as the court may determine and may thereafter be taxed and allowed in like manner as other costs.

§ 754.　Deaf or hard of hearing persons; interpreters; qualifications; guidelines; compensation; questioning; use of statements

(a)　As used in this section, "individual who is deaf or hard of hearing" means an individual with a hearing loss so great as to prevent his or her understanding language spoken in a normal tone, but does not include an individual who is hard of hearing provided with, and able to fully participate in the proceedings through the use of, an assistive listening system or computer-aided transcription equipment provided pursuant to Section 54.8 of the Civil Code.

(b)　In a civil or criminal action, including an action involving a traffic or other infraction, a small claims court proceeding, a juvenile court proceeding, a family court proceeding or service, or a proceeding to determine the mental competency of a person, in a court-ordered or court-provided alternative dispute resolution, including mediation and arbitration, or in an administrative hearing, where a party or witness is an individual who is deaf or hard of hearing is present and participating, the proceeding shall be interpreted in a language that the individual who is deaf or hard of hearing understands by a qualified interpreter appointed by the court or other appointing authority, or as agreed upon.

(c)　For purposes of this section, "appointing authority" means a court, department, board, commission, agency, licensing or legislative body, or other body for proceedings requiring a qualified interpreter.

(d)　For purposes of this section, "interpreter" includes an oral interpreter, a sign language interpreter, or a deaf-blind interpreter, depending upon the needs of the individual who is deaf or hard of hearing.

(e)　For purposes of this section, "intermediary interpreter" means an individual who is deaf or hard of hearing, or a hearing individual who is able to assist in providing an accurate interpretation between spoken English and sign language or between variants of sign language or between American Sign Language and other foreign languages by acting as an intermediary between the individual who is deaf or hard of hearing and the qualified interpreter.

(f)　For purposes of this section, "qualified interpreter" means an interpreter who has been certified as competent to interpret court proceedings by a testing organization, agency, or educational institution approved by the Judicial Council as qualified to administer tests to court interpreters for individuals who are deaf or hard of hearing.

(g)　If the appointed interpreter is not familiar with the use of particular signs by the individual who is deaf or hard of hearing or his or her particular variant of sign language, the court or other appointing authority shall, in consultation with the individual who is deaf or hard of hearing or his or her representative, appoint an intermediary interpreter.

(h)(1) Before July 1, 1992, the Judicial Council shall conduct a study to establish the guidelines pursuant to which it shall determine which testing organizations, agencies, or educational institutions will be approved to administer tests for certification of court interpreters for individuals who are deaf or hard of hearing. It is the intent of the Legislature that the study obtain the widest possible input from the public, including, but not limited to, educational institutions, the judiciary, linguists, members of the State Bar of California, court interpreters, members of professional interpreting organizations, and members of the deaf and hard of hearing communities. After obtaining public comment and completing its study, the Judicial Council shall publish these guidelines. By January 1, 1997, the Judicial Council shall approve one or more entities to administer testing for court interpreters for individuals who are deaf or hard of hearing. Testing entities may include educational institutions, testing organizations, joint powers agencies or public agencies.

(2) Commencing July 1, 1997, court interpreters for individuals who are deaf or hard of hearing shall meet the qualifications specified in subdivision (f).

(i) Persons appointed to serve as interpreters under this section shall be paid, in addition to actual travel costs, the prevailing rate paid to persons employed by the court to provide other interpreter services unless such service is considered to be a part of the person's regular duties as an employee of the state, county, or other political subdivision of the state. Except as provided in subdivision (j), payment of the interpreter's fee in administrative proceedings shall be a charge against the appointing board or authority.

(j) Whenever a peace officer or any other person having a law enforcement or prosecutorial function in a criminal or quasi-criminal investigation or proceeding questions or otherwise interviews an alleged victim or witness who demonstrates or alleges deafness or hearing loss, a good faith effort to secure the services of an interpreter shall be made, without any unnecessary delay unless either the individual who is deaf or hard of hearing affirmatively indicates that he or she does not need or cannot use an interpreter, or an interpreter is not otherwise required by Title II of the federal Americans with Disabilities Act of 1990 (Public Law 101–336) and federal regulations adopted thereunder. Payment of the interpreter's fee shall be a charge against the county, or other political subdivision of the state, in which the action is pending.

(k) A statement, written or oral, made by an individual who the court finds is deaf or hard of hearing in reply to a question of a peace officer, or any other person having a law enforcement or prosecutorial function in a criminal or quasi-criminal investigation or proceeding, shall not be used against that individual who is deaf or hard of hearing unless the question was accurately interpreted and the statement was made knowingly, voluntarily, and intelligently and was accurately interpreted, or the court finds that either the individual could not have used an interpreter or an interpreter was not otherwise required by Title II of the federal Americans with Disabilities Act of 1990 (Public Law 101–336) and federal regulations adopted thereunder and that the statement was made knowingly, voluntarily, and intelligently.

(*l*) In obtaining services of an interpreter for purposes of subdivision (j) or (k), priority shall be given to first obtaining a qualified interpreter.

(m) Subdivisions (j) and (k) shall not be deemed to supersede the requirement of subdivision (b) for use of a qualified interpreter for an individual who is deaf or hard of hearing participating as a party or witness in a trial or hearing.

(n) In an action or proceeding in which an individual who is deaf or hard of hearing is a participant, the appointing authority shall not commence the action or proceeding until the appointed interpreter is in full view of and spatially situated to assure proper communication with the participating individual who is deaf or hard of hearing.

(o) Each superior court shall maintain a current roster of qualified interpreters certified pursuant to subdivision (f).

§ 754.5.   Privileged statements; deaf or hard of hearing persons; use of interpreter

Whenever an otherwise valid privilege exists between an individual who is deaf or hard of hearing and another person, that privilege is not waived merely because an interpreter was used to facilitate their communication.

§ 755.   Hearings or proceedings related to domestic violence; party not proficient in English; interpreters; fees

(a) In any action or proceeding under Division 10 (commencing with Section 6200) of the Family Code, and in any action or proceeding under the Uniform Parentage Act (Part 3 (commencing with Section 7600) of Division 12 of the Family Code) or for dissolution or nullity of marriage or legal separation of the parties in which a protective order has been granted or is being sought pursuant to Section 6221 of the Family Code, in which a party does not proficiently speak or understand the English language, and that party is present, an interpreter, as provided in this section, shall be present to interpret the proceedings in a language that the party understands, and to assist communication between the party and his or her attorney. Notwithstanding this requirement, a court may issue an ex parte order pursuant to Sections 2045 and 7710 of, and Article 1 (commencing with Section 6320) of Chapter 2 of Part 4 of Division 10 of the Family Code, without the presence of an interpreter. The interpreter selected shall be certified pursuant to Article 4 (commencing with Section 68560) of Chapter 2 of Title 8 of the Government Code, unless the court in its discretion appoints an interpreter who is not certified.

(b) The fees of interpreters utilized under this section shall be paid as provided in subdivision (b) of Section 68092 of the Government Code. However, the fees of an interpreter shall be waived for a party who needs an interpreter and appears in forma pauperis pursuant to Section 68511.3 of the Government Code. The Judicial Council shall amend subdivision (i) of California Rule of Court 985 and revise its forms accordingly by July 1, 1996.

(c) In any civil action in which an interpreter is required under this section, the court shall not commence proceedings until the appointed interpreter is present and situated near the party and his or her attorney. However, this section shall not prohibit the court from doing any of the following:

(1) Issuing an order when the necessity for the order outweighs the necessity for an interpreter.

(2) Extending the duration of a previously issued temporary order if an interpreter is not readily available.

(3) Issuing a permanent order where a party who requires an interpreter fails to make appropriate arrangements for an interpreter after receiving proper notice of the hearing with information about obtaining an interpreter.

(d) This section does not prohibit the presence of any other person to assist a party.

(e) A local public entity may, and the Judicial Council shall, apply to the appropriate state agency that receives federal funds authorized pursuant to the federal Violence Against Women Act (P.L. 103–322) for these federal funds or for funds from sources other than the state to implement this section. A local public entity and the Judicial Council shall comply with the requirements of this section only to the extent that any of these funds are made available.

(f) The Judicial Council shall draft rules and modify forms necessary to implement this section, including those for the petition for a temporary restraining order and related forms, to inform both parties of their right to an interpreter pursuant to this section.

§ 755.5. Medical examinations; parties not proficient in English language; interpreters; fees; admissibility of record

(a) During any medical examination, requested by an insurer or by the defendant, of a person who is a party to a civil action and who does not proficiently speak or understand the English language, conducted for the purpose of determining damages in a civil action, an interpreter shall be present to interpret the examination in a language that the person understands. The interpreter shall be certified pursuant to Article 8 (commencing with Section 11435.05) of Chapter 4.5 of Part 1 of Division 3 of Title 2 of the Government Code.

(b) The fees of interpreters used under subdivision (a) shall be paid by the insurer or defendant requesting the medical examination.

(c) The record of, or testimony concerning, any medical examination conducted in violation of subdivision (a) shall be inadmissible in the civil action for which it was conducted or any other civil action.

(d) This section does not prohibit the presence of any other person to assist a party.

(e) In the event that interpreters certified pursuant to Article 8 (commencing with Section 11435.05) of Chapter 4.5 of Part 1 of Division 3 of Title 2 of the Government Code cannot be present at the medical examination, upon stipulation of the parties the requester specified in subdivision (a) shall have the discretionary authority to provisionally qualify and use other interpreters.

§ 756. Court interpreter services provided in civil actions; reimbursement by Judicial Council; prioritization where funding is insufficient

(a) To the extent required by other state or federal laws, the Judicial Council shall reimburse courts for court interpreter services provided in civil actions and proceedings to any party who is present in court and who does not proficiently speak or understand the English language for the purpose of interpreting the proceedings in a language the party understands, and assisting communications between the party, his or her attorney, and the court.

(b)   If sufficient funds are not appropriated to provide an interpreter to every party that meets the standard of eligibility, court interpreter services in civil cases reimbursed by the Judicial Council, pursuant to subdivision (a), shall be prioritized by case type by each court in the following order:

(1)   Actions and proceedings under Division 10 (commencing with Section 6200) of the Family Code, actions or proceedings under the Uniform Parentage Act (Part 3 (commencing with Section 7600) of Division 12 of the Family Code) in which a protective order has been granted or is being sought pursuant to Section 6221 of the Family Code, and actions and proceedings for dissolution or nullity of marriage or legal separation of the parties in which a protective order has been granted or is being sought pursuant to Section 6221 of the Family Code; actions and proceedings under subdivision (w) of Section 527.6 of the Code of Civil Procedure; and actions and proceedings for physical abuse or neglect under the Elder Abuse and Dependent Adult Civil Protection Act (Chapter 11 (commencing with Section 15600) of Part 3 of Division 9 of the Welfare and Institutions Code).

(2)   Actions and proceedings relating to unlawful detainer.

(3)   Actions and proceedings to terminate parental rights.

(4)   Actions and proceedings relating to conservatorship or guardianship, including the appointment or termination of a probate guardian or conservator.

(5)   Actions and proceedings by a parent to obtain sole legal or physical custody of a child or rights to visitation.

(6)   All other actions and proceedings under Section 527.6 of the Code of Civil Procedure or the Elder Abuse and Dependent Adult Civil Protection Act (Chapter 11 (commencing with Section 15600) of Part 3 of Division 9 of the Welfare and Institutions Code).

(7)   All other actions and proceedings related to family law.

(8)   All other civil actions or proceedings.

(c)(1)   If funds are not available to provide an interpreter to every party that meets the standard of eligibility, preference shall be given for parties proceeding in forma pauperis pursuant to Section 68631 of the Government Code in any civil action or proceeding described in paragraph (3), (4), (5), (6), (7), or (8) of subdivision (b).

(2)   Courts may provide an interpreter to a party outside the priority order listed in subdivision (b) when a qualified interpreter is present and available at the court location and no higher priority action that meets the standard of eligibility described in subdivision (a) is taking place at that location during the period of time for which the interpreter has already been compensated.

(d)   A party shall not be charged a fee for the provision of a court interpreter.

(e)   In seeking reimbursement for court interpreter services, the court shall identify to the Judicial Council the case types for which the interpretation to be reimbursed was provided. Courts shall regularly certify that in providing the interpreter services, they have complied with the priorities and preferences set forth in subdivisions (b) and (c), which shall be subject to review by the Judicial Council.

(f) This section shall not be construed to alter, limit, or negate any right to an interpreter in a civil action or proceeding otherwise provided by state or federal law, or the right to an interpreter in criminal, traffic, or other infraction, juvenile, or mental competency actions or proceedings.

(g) This section shall not result in a reduction in staffing or compromise the quality of interpreting services in criminal, juvenile, or other types of matters in which interpreters are provided.

§ 757. Proceedings regarding special immigrant juvenile status; authority to provide interpreter

Pursuant to this chapter, other applicable law, and existing Judicial Council policy, including the policy adopted on January 23, 2014, existing authority to provide interpreters in civil court includes the authority to provide an interpreter in a proceeding in which a petitioner requests an order from the superior court to make the findings regarding special immigrant juvenile status pursuant to Section 1101(a)(27)(J) of Title 8 of the United States Code.

CHAPTER 5. METHOD AND SCOPE OF EXAMINATION

ARTICLE 1. DEFINITIONS

§ 760. Direct examination

"Direct examination" is the first examination of a witness upon a matter that is not within the scope of a previous examination of the witness.

§ 761. Cross-examination

"Cross-examination" is the examination of a witness by a party other than the direct examiner upon a matter that is within the scope of the direct examination of the witness.

§ 762. Redirect examination

"Redirect examination" is an examination of a witness by the direct examiner subsequent to the cross-examination of the witness.

§ 763. Recross-examination

"Recross-examination" is an examination of a witness by a cross-examiner subsequent to a redirect examination of the witness.

§ 764. Leading question

A "leading question" is a question that suggests to the witness the answer that the examining party desires.

ARTICLE 2. EXAMINATION OF WITNESSES

§ 765. Court to control mode of interrogation

(a)   The court shall exercise reasonable control over the mode of interrogation of a witness so as to make such interrogation as rapid, as distinct, and as effective for the ascertainment of the truth, as may be, and to protect the witness from undue harassment or embarrassment.

(b)   With a witness under the age of 14 or a dependant person with a substantial cognitive impairment, the court shall take special care to protect him or her from undue harassment or embarrassment, and to restrict the unnecessary repetition of questions. The court shall also take special care to ensure that questions are stated in a form which is appropriate to the age or cognitive level of the witness. The court may in the interests of justice, on objection by a party, forbid the asking of a question which is in a form that is not reasonably likely to be understood by a person of the age or cognitive level of the witness.

§ 766. Responsive answers

A witness must give responsive answers to questions, and answers that are not responsive shall be stricken on motion of any party.

§ 767. Leading questions

(a)   Except under special circumstances where the interests of justice otherwise require:

(1)   A leading question may not be asked of a witness on direct or redirect examination.

(2)   A leading question may be asked of a witness on cross-examination or recross-examination.

(b)   The court may in the interests of justice permit a leading question to be asked of a child under 10 years of age or a dependent person with a substantial cognitive impairment in a case involving a prosecution under Section 273a, 273d, 288.5, 368, or any of the acts described in Section 11165.1 or 11165.2 of the Penal Code.

§ 768. Writings

(a)   In examining a witness concerning a writing, it is not necessary to show, read, or disclose to him any part of the writing.

(b)   If a writing is shown to a witness, all parties to the action must be given an opportunity to inspect it before any question concerning it may be asked of the witness.

§ 769. Inconsistent statement or conduct

In examining a witness concerning a statement or other conduct by him that is inconsistent with any part of his testimony at the hearing, it is not necessary to disclose to him any information concerning the statement or other conduct.

§ 770. Evidence of inconsistent statement of witness; exclusion; exceptions

Unless the interests of justice otherwise require, extrinsic evidence of a statement made by a witness that is inconsistent with any part of his testimony at the hearing shall be excluded unless:

(a) The witness was so examined while testifying as to give him an opportunity to explain or to deny the statement; or

(b) The witness has not been excused from giving further testimony in the action.

§ 771. Production of writing used to refresh memory

(a) Subject to subdivision (c), if a witness, either while testifying or prior thereto, uses a writing to refresh his memory with respect to any matter about which he testifies, such writing must be produced at the hearing at the request of an adverse party and, unless the writing is so produced, the testimony of the witness concerning such matter shall be stricken.

(b) If the writing is produced at the hearing, the adverse party may, if he chooses, inspect the writing, cross-examine the witness concerning it, and introduce in evidence such portion of it as may be pertinent to the testimony of the witness.

(c) Production of the writing is excused, and the testimony of the witness shall not be stricken, if the writing:

(1) Is not in the possession or control of the witness or the party who produced his testimony concerning the matter; and

(2) Was not reasonably procurable by such party through the use of the court's process or other available means.

§ 772. Order of examination

(a) The examination of a witness shall proceed in the following phases: direct examination, cross-examination, redirect examination, recross-examination, and continuing thereafter by redirect and recross-examination.

(b) Unless for good cause the court otherwise directs, each phase of the examination of a witness must be concluded before the succeeding phase begins.

(c) Subject to subdivision (d), a party may, in the discretion of the court, interrupt his cross-examination, redirect examination, or recross-examination of a witness, in order to examine the witness upon a matter not within the scope of a previous examination of the witness.

(d) If the witness is the defendant in a criminal action, the witness may not, without his consent, be examined under direct examination by another party.

§ 773. Cross-examination

(a) A witness examined by one party may be cross-examined upon any matter within the scope of the direct examination by each other party to the action in such order as the court directs.

(b)   The cross-examination of a witness by any party whose interest is not adverse to the party calling him is subject to the same rules that are applicable to the direct examination.

§ 774.   Re-examination

A witness once examined cannot be reexamined as to the same matter without leave of the court, but he may be reexamined as to any new matter upon which he has been examined by another party to the action. Leave may be granted or withheld in the court's discretion.

§ 775.   Court may call witnesses

The court, on its own motion or on the motion of any party, may call witnesses and interrogate them the same as if they had been produced by a party to the action, and the parties may object to the questions asked and the evidence adduced the same as if such witnesses were called and examined by an adverse party. Such witnesses may be cross-examined by all parties to the action in such order as the court directs.

§ 776.   Examination of adverse party or person identified with adverse party

(a)   A party to the record of any civil action, or a person identified with such a party, may be called and examined as if under cross-examination by any adverse party at any time during the presentation of evidence by the party calling the witness.

(b)   A witness examined by a party under this section may be cross-examined by all other parties to the action in such order as the court directs; but, subject to subdivision (e), the witness may be examined only as if under redirect examination by:

(1)   In the case of a witness who is a party, his own counsel and counsel for a party who is not adverse to the witness.

(2)   In the case of a witness who is not a party, counsel for the party with whom the witness is identified and counsel for a party who is not adverse to the party with whom the witness is identified.

(c)   For the purpose of this section, parties represented by the same counsel are deemed to be a single party.

(d)   For the purpose of this section, a person is identified with a party if he is:

(1)   A person for whose immediate benefit the action is prosecuted or defended by the party.

(2)   A director, officer, superintendent, member, agent, employee, or managing agent of the party or of a person specified in paragraph (1), or any public employee of a public entity when such public entity is the party.

(3)   A person who was in any of the relationships specified in paragraph (2) at the time of the act or omission giving rise to the cause of action.

(4)   A person who was in any of the relationships specified in paragraph (2) at the time he obtained knowledge of the matter concerning which he is sought to be examined under this section.

(e)   Paragraph (2) of subdivision (b) does not require counsel for the party with whom the witness is identified and counsel for a party who is not adverse to the party with whom the witness is identified to examine the witness as if under redirect examination if the party who called the witness for examination under this section:

(1)   Is also a person identified with the same party with whom the witness is identified.

(2)   Is the personal representative, heir, successor, or assignee of a person identified with the same party with whom the witness is identified.

§ 777. Exclusion of witness

(a)   Subject to subdivisions (b) and (c), the court may exclude from the courtroom any witness not at the time under examination so that such witness cannot hear the testimony of other witnesses.

(b)   A party to the action cannot be excluded under this section.

(c)   If a person other than a natural person is a party to the action, an officer or employee designated by its attorney is entitled to be present.

§ 778. Recall of witness

After a witness has been excused from giving further testimony in the action, he cannot be recalled without leave of the court. Leave may be granted or withheld in the court's discretion.

CHAPTER 6. CREDIBILITY OF WITNESSES

ARTICLE 1. CREDIBILITY GENERALLY

§ 780. Testimony; proof of truthfulness; considerations

Except as otherwise provided by statute, the court or jury may consider in determining the credibility of a witness any matter that has any tendency in reason to prove or disprove the truthfulness of his testimony at the hearing, including but not limited to any of the following:

(a)   His demeanor while testifying and the manner in which he testifies.

(b)   The character of his testimony.

(c)   The extent of his capacity to perceive, to recollect, or to communicate any matter about which he testifies.

(d)   The extent of his opportunity to perceive any matter about which he testifies.

(e)   His character for honesty or veracity or their opposites.

(f)   The existence or nonexistence of a bias, interest, or other motive.

(g)   A statement previously made by him that is consistent with his testimony at the hearing.

(h)   A statement made by him that is inconsistent with any part of his testimony at the hearing.

(i)   The existence or nonexistence of any fact testified to by him.

(j)   His attitude toward the action in which he testifies or toward the giving of testimony.

(k)   His admission of untruthfulness.

§ 782. Sexual offenses; evidence of sexual conduct of complaining witness; procedure for admissibility; treatment of resealed affidavits

(a)   In any of the circumstances described in subdivision (c), if evidence of sexual conduct of the complaining witness is offered to attack the credibility of the complaining witness under Section 780, the following procedure shall be followed:

(1)   A written motion shall be made by the defendant to the court and prosecutor stating that the defense has an offer of proof of the relevancy of evidence of the sexual conduct of the complaining witness proposed to be presented and its relevancy in attacking the credibility of the complaining witness.

(2)   The written motion shall be accompanied by an affidavit in which the offer of proof shall be stated. The affidavit shall be filed under seal and only unsealed by the court to determine if the offer of proof is sufficient to order a hearing pursuant to paragraph (3). After that determination, the affidavit shall be resealed by the court.

(3)   If the court finds that the offer of proof is sufficient, the court shall order a hearing out of the presence of the jury, if any, and at the hearing allow the questioning of the complaining witness regarding the offer of proof made by the defendant.

(4)   At the conclusion of the hearing, if the court finds that evidence proposed to be offered by the defendant regarding the sexual conduct of the complaining witness is relevant pursuant to Section 780, and is not inadmissible pursuant to Section 352 of this code, the court may make an order stating what evidence may be introduced by the defendant, and the nature of the questions to be permitted. The defendant may then offer evidence pursuant to the order of the court.

(5)   An affidavit resealed by the court pursuant to paragraph (2) shall remain sealed, unless the defendant raises an issue on appeal or collateral review relating to the offer of proof contained in the sealed document. If the defendant raises that issue on appeal, the court shall allow the Attorney General and appellate counsel for the defendant access to the sealed affidavit. If the issue is raised on collateral review, the court shall allow the district attorney and defendant's counsel access to the sealed affidavit. The use of the information contained in the affidavit shall be limited solely to the pending proceeding.

(b)   As used in this section, "complaining witness" means:

(1)   The alleged victim of the crime charged, the prosecution of which is subject to this section, pursuant to paragraph (1) of subdivision (c).

(2)   An alleged victim offering testimony pursuant to paragraph (2) or paragraph (3) of subdivision (c).

(c)   The procedure provided by subdivision (a) shall apply in any of the following circumstances:

(1)   In a prosecution under Section 261, 262, 264.1, 286, 287, 288, 288.5, or 289 of, or former Section 288a of, the Penal Code, or for assault with intent to commit, attempt to commit, or conspiracy to commit any crime defined in any of those sections, except if the crime is alleged to have occurred in a local detention facility, as defined in Section 6031.4 of the Penal Code, or in the state prison, as defined in Section 4504.

(2)   When an alleged victim testifies pursuant to subdivision (b) of Section 1101 as a victim of a crime listed in Section 243.4, 261, 261.5, 269, 285, 286, 287, 288, 288.5, 289, 314, or 647.6 of, or former Section 288a of, the Penal Code, except if the crime is alleged to have occurred in a local detention facility, as defined in Section 6031.4 of the Penal Code, or in the state prison, as defined in Section 4504 of the Penal Code.

(3)   When an alleged victim of a sexual offense testifies pursuant to Section 1108, except if the crime is alleged to have occurred in a local detention facility, as defined in Section 6031.4 of the Penal Code, or in the state prison, as defined in Section 4504 of the Penal Code.

§ 782.1.   Possession of condoms; procedure for admissibility

In any prosecution under Sections 647 and 653.22 of the Penal Code, if the possession of one or more condoms is to be introduced as evidence in support of the commission of the crime, the following procedure shall be followed:

(a)   A written motion shall be made by the prosecutor to the court and to the defendant stating that the prosecution has an offer of proof of the relevancy of the possession by the defendant of one or more condoms.

(b)   The written motion shall be accompanied by an affidavit in which the offer of proof shall be stated. The affidavit shall be filed under seal and only unsealed by the court to determine if the offer of proof is sufficient to order a hearing pursuant to subdivision (c). After that determination, the affidavit shall be resealed by the court.

(c)   If the court finds that the offer of proof is sufficient, the court shall order a hearing out of the presence of the jury, if any, and at the hearing allow questioning regarding the offer of proof made by the prosecution.

(d)   At the conclusion of the hearing, if the court finds that evidence proposed to be offered by the prosecutor regarding the possession of condoms is relevant pursuant to Section 210, and is not inadmissible pursuant to Section 352, the court may make an order stating what evidence may be introduced by the prosecutor. The prosecutor may then offer evidence pursuant to the order of the court.

(e)   An affidavit resealed by the court pursuant to subdivision (b) shall remain sealed, unless the defendant raises an issue on appeal or collateral review relating to the offer of proof contained in the sealed document. If the defendant raises that issue on appeal, the court shall allow the Attorney General and appellate counsel for the defendant access to the sealed affidavit. If the issue is raised on collateral review, the court shall allow the district attorney and defendant's counsel access to the sealed affidavit. The use of the information contained in the affidavit shall be limited solely to the pending proceeding.

§ 783. Sexual harassment, sexual assault, or sexual battery cases; admissibility of evidence of plaintiff's sexual conduct; procedure

In any civil action alleging conduct which constitutes sexual harassment, sexual assault, or sexual battery, if evidence of sexual conduct of the plaintiff is offered to attack credibility of the plaintiff under Section 780, the following procedures shall be followed:

(a) A written motion shall be made by the defendant to the court and the plaintiff's attorney stating that the defense has an offer of proof of the relevancy of evidence of the sexual conduct of the plaintiff proposed to be presented.

(b) The written motion shall be accompanied by an affidavit in which the offer of proof shall be stated.

(c) If the court finds that the offer of proof is sufficient, the court shall order a hearing out of the presence of the jury, if any, and at the hearing allow the questioning of the plaintiff regarding the offer of proof made by the defendant.

(d) At the conclusion of the hearing, if the court finds that evidence proposed to be offered by the defendant regarding the sexual conduct of the plaintiff is relevant pursuant to Section 780, and is not inadmissible pursuant to Section 352, the court may make an order stating what evidence may be introduced by the defendant, and the nature of the questions to be permitted. The defendant may then offer evidence pursuant to the order of the court.

ARTICLE 2. ATTACKING OR SUPPORTING CREDIBILITY

§ 785. Parties may attack or support credibility

The credibility of a witness may be attacked or supported by any party, including the party calling him.

§ 786. Character evidence generally

Evidence of traits of his character other than honesty or veracity, or their opposites, is inadmissible to attack or support the credibility of a witness.

§ 787. Specific instances of conduct

Subject to Section 788, evidence of specific instances of his conduct relevant only as tending to prove a trait of his character is inadmissible to attack or support the credibility of a witness.

§ 788. Prior felony conviction

For the purpose of attacking the credibility of a witness, it may be shown by the examination of the witness or by the record of the judgment that he has been convicted of a felony unless:

(a) A pardon based on his innocence has been granted to the witness by the jurisdiction in which he was convicted.

(b) A certificate of rehabilitation and pardon has been granted to the witness under the provisions of Chapter 3.5 (commencing with Section 4852.01) of Title 6 of Part 3 of the Penal Code.

(c)   The accusatory pleading against the witness has been dismissed under the provisions of Penal Code Section 1203.4, but this exception does not apply to any criminal trial where the witness is being prosecuted for a subsequent offense.

(d)   The conviction was under the laws of another jurisdiction and the witness has been relieved of the penalties and disabilities arising from the conviction pursuant to a procedure substantially equivalent to that referred to in subdivision (b) or (c).

§ 789.   Religious belief

Evidence of his religious belief or lack thereof is inadmissible to attack or support the credibility of a witness.

§ 790.   Good character of witness

Evidence of the good character of a witness is inadmissible to support his credibility unless evidence of his bad character has been admitted for the purpose of attacking his credibility.

§ 791.   Prior consistent statement of witness

Evidence of a statement previously made by a witness that is consistent with his testimony at the hearing is inadmissible to support his credibility unless it is offered after:

(a)   Evidence of a statement made by him that is inconsistent with any part of his testimony at the hearing has been admitted for the purpose of attacking his credibility, and the statement was made before the alleged inconsistent statement; or

(b)   An express or implied charge has been made that his testimony at the hearing is recently fabricated or is influenced by bias or other improper motive, and the statement was made before the bias, motive for fabrication, or other improper motive is alleged to have arisen.

CHAPTER 7. HYPNOSIS OF WITNESSES

§ 795.   Testimony of hypnosis subject; admissibility; conditions

(a)   The testimony of a witness is not inadmissible in a criminal proceeding by reason of the fact that the witness has previously undergone hypnosis for the purpose of recalling events that are the subject of the witness's testimony, if all of the following conditions are met:

(1)   The testimony is limited to those matters that the witness recalled and related prior to the hypnosis.

(2)   The substance of the prehypnotic memory was preserved in a writing, audio recording, or video recording prior to the hypnosis.

(3)   The hypnosis was conducted in accordance with all of the following procedures:

(A) A written record was made prior to hypnosis documenting the subject's description of the event, and information that was provided to the hypnotist concerning the subject matter of the hypnosis.

(B)   The subject gave informed consent to the hypnosis.

(C) The hypnosis session, including the pre-and post-hypnosis interviews, was video recorded for subsequent review.

(D) The hypnosis was performed by a licensed physician and surgeon, psychologist, licensed clinical social worker, licensed marriage and family therapist, or licensed professional clinical counselor experienced in the use of hypnosis and independent of and not in the presence of law enforcement, the prosecution, or the defense.

(4) Prior to admission of the testimony, the court holds a hearing pursuant to Section 402 at which the proponent of the evidence proves by clear and convincing evidence that the hypnosis did not so affect the witness as to render the witness's prehypnosis recollection unreliable or to substantially impair the ability to cross-examine the witness concerning the witness's prehypnosis recollection. At the hearing, each side shall have the right to present expert testimony and to cross-examine witnesses.

(b) Nothing in this section shall be construed to limit the ability of a party to attack the credibility of a witness who has undergone hypnosis, or to limit other legal grounds to admit or exclude the testimony of that witness.

DIVISION 7. OPINION TESTIMONY AND SCIENTIFIC EVIDENCE

CHAPTER 1. EXPERT AND OTHER OPINION TESTIMONY

ARTICLE 1. EXPERT AND OTHER OPINION TESTIMONY GENERALLY

§ 800. Lay witnesses; opinion testimony

If a witness is not testifying as an expert, his testimony in the form of an opinion is limited to such an opinion as is permitted by law, including but not limited to an opinion that is:

(a) Rationally based on the perception of the witness; and

(b) Helpful to a clear understanding of his testimony.

§ 801. Expert witness; opinion testimony

If a witness is testifying as an expert, his testimony in the form of an opinion is limited to such an opinion as is:

(a) Related to a subject that is sufficiently beyond common experience that the opinion of an expert would assist the trier of fact; and

(b) Based on matter (including his special knowledge, skill, experience, training, and education) perceived by or personally known to the witness or made known to him at or before the hearing, whether or not admissible, that is of a type that reasonably may be relied upon by an expert in forming an opinion upon the subject to which his testimony relates, unless an expert is precluded by law from using such matter as a basis for his opinion.

§ 802. Statement of basis of opinion

A witness testifying in the form of an opinion may state on direct examination the reasons for his opinion and the matter (including, in the case of an expert, his special knowledge, skill, experience, training, and education) upon which it is based, unless he is precluded by law from using such reasons or matter as a basis for his opinion. The court in its discretion may require that a witness before testifying in the form of an opinion be first examined concerning the matter upon which his opinion is based.

§ 803. Opinion based on improper matter

The court may, and upon objection shall, exclude testimony in the form of an opinion that is based in whole or in significant part on matter that is not a proper basis for such an opinion. In such case, the witness may, if there remains a proper basis for his opinion, then state his opinion after excluding from consideration the matter determined to be improper.

§ 804. Opinion based on opinion or statement of another

(a) If a witness testifying as an expert testifies that his opinion is based in whole or in part upon the opinion or statement of another person, such other person may be called and examined by any adverse party as if under cross-examination concerning the opinion or statement.

(b) This section is not applicable if the person upon whose opinion or statement the expert witness has relied is (1) a party, (2) a person identified with a party within the meaning of subdivision (d) of Section 776, or (3) a witness who has testified in the action concerning the subject matter of the opinion or statement upon which the expert witness has relied.

(c)   Nothing in this section makes admissible an expert opinion that is inadmissible because it is based in whole or in part on the opinion or statement of another person.

(d)   An expert opinion otherwise admissible is not made inadmissible by this section because it is based on the opinion or statement of a person who is unavailable for examination pursuant to this section.

§ 805.   Opinion on ultimate issue

Testimony in the form of an opinion that is otherwise admissible is not objectionable because it embraces the ultimate issue to be decided by the trier of fact.

ARTICLE 2. EVIDENCE OF MARKET VALUE OF PROPERTY

§ 810.   Application of article

(a)   Except where another rule is provided by statute, this article provides special rules of evidence applicable to any action in which the value of property is to be ascertained.

(b)   This article does not govern ad valorem property tax assessment or equalization proceedings.

§ 811.   Value of property

As used in this article, "value of property" means market value of any of the following:

(a)   Real property or any interest therein.

(b)   Real property or any interest therein and tangible personal property valued as a unit.

§ 812.   Market value; interpretation of meaning

This article is not intended to alter or change the existing substantive law, whether statutory or decisional, interpreting the meaning of "market value," whether denominated "fair market value" or otherwise.

§ 813.   Value of property; authorized opinions; view of property; admissible evidence

(a)   The value of property may be shown only by the opinions of any of the following:

(1)   Witnesses qualified to express such opinions.

(2)   The owner or the spouse of the owner of the property or property interest being valued.

(3)   An officer, regular employee, or partner designated by a corporation, partnership, or unincorporated association that is the owner of the property or property interest being valued, if the designee is knowledgeable as to the value of the property or property interest.

(b)   Nothing in this section prohibits a view of the property being valued or the admission of any other admissible evidence (including but not limited to evidence as to the nature and condition of the property and, in an eminent domain proceeding, the character of the improvement proposed to be constructed by the plaintiff) for the limited purpose of enabling the court, jury, or referee to understand and weigh the testimony given under subdivision (a); and such evidence, except evidence of the character of the improvement proposed to be constructed by the plaintiff in an eminent domain proceeding, is subject to impeachment and rebuttal.

(c)   For the purposes of subdivision (a), "owner of the property or property interest being valued" includes, but is not limited to, the following persons:

(1)   A person entitled to possession of the property.

(2)   Either party in an action or proceeding to determine the ownership of the property between the parties if the court determines that it would not be in the interest of efficient administration of justice to determine the issue of ownership prior to the admission of the opinion of the party.

§ 814.   Matter upon which opinion must be based

The opinion of a witness as to the value of property is limited to such an opinion as is based on matter perceived by or personally known to the witness or made known to the witness at or before the hearing, whether or not admissible, that is of a type that reasonably may be relied upon by an expert in forming an opinion as to the value of property, including but not limited to the matters listed in Sections 815 to 821, inclusive, unless a witness is precluded by law from using such matter as a basis for an opinion.

§ 814.5.   Repealed by Stats. 1971, c. 1574, p. 3154, § 1.4, operative July 1, 1972

§ 815.   Sales of subject property

When relevant to the determination of the value of property, a witness may take into account as a basis for an opinion the price and other terms and circumstances of any sale or contract to sell and purchase which included the property or property interest being valued or any part thereof if the sale or contract was freely made in good faith within a reasonable time before or after the date of valuation, except that in an eminent domain proceeding where the sale or contract to sell and purchase includes only the property or property interest being taken or a part thereof, such sale or contract to sell and purchase may not be taken into account if it occurs after the filing of the lis pendens.

§ 816.   Comparable sales

When relevant to the determination of the value of property, a witness may take into account as a basis for his opinion the price and other terms and circumstances of any sale or contract to sell and purchase comparable property if the sale or contract was freely made in good faith within a reasonable time before or after the date of valuation. In order to be considered comparable, the sale or contract must have been made sufficiently near in time to the date of valuation, and the property sold must be located sufficiently near the property being valued, and must be sufficiently alike in respect to character, size, situation, usability, and improvements, to make it clear that the property sold and the property being valued are comparable in value and that the price realized for the property sold may fairly be considered as shedding light on the value of the property being valued.

§ 817. Leases of subject property

(a)   Subject to subdivision (b), when relevant to the determination of the value of property, a witness may take into account as a basis for an opinion the rent reserved and other terms and circumstances of any lease which included the property or property interest being valued or any part thereof which was in effect within a reasonable time before or after the date of valuation, except that in an eminent domain proceeding where the lease includes only the property or property interest being taken or a part thereof, such lease may not be taken into account in the determination of the value of property if it is entered into after the filing of the lis pendens.

(b)   A witness may take into account a lease providing for a rental fixed by a percentage or other measurable portion of gross sales or gross income from a business conducted on the leased property only for the purpose of arriving at an opinion as to the reasonable net rental value attributable to the property or property interest being valued as provided in Section 819 or determining the value of a leasehold interest.

§ 818. Comparable leases

For the purpose of determining the capitalized value of the reasonable net rental value attributable to the property or property interest being valued as provided in Section 819 or determining the value of a leasehold interest, a witness may take into account as a basis for his opinion the rent reserved and other terms and circumstances of any lease of comparable property if the lease was freely made in good faith within a reasonable time before or after the date of valuation.

§ 819. Capitalization of income

When relevant to the determination of the value of property, a witness may take into account as a basis for his opinion the capitalized value of the reasonable net rental value attributable to the land and existing improvements thereon (as distinguished from the capitalized value of the income or profits attributable to the business conducted thereon).

§ 820. Reproduction cost

When relevant to the determination of the value of property, a witness may take into account as a basis for his opinion the value of the property or property interest being valued as indicated by the value of the land together with the cost of replacing or reproducing the existing improvements thereon, if the improvements enhance the value of the property or property interest for its highest and best use, less whatever depreciation or obsolescence the improvements have suffered.

§ 821. Conditions in general vicinity of subject property

When relevant to the determination of the value of property, a witness may take into account as a basis for his opinion the nature of the improvements on properties in the general vicinity of the property or property interest being valued and the character of the existing uses being made of such properties.

§ 822. Matter upon which opinion may not be based

(a) In an eminent domain or inverse condemnation proceeding, notwithstanding the provisions of Sections 814 to 821, inclusive, the following matter is inadmissible as evidence and shall not be taken into account as a basis for an opinion as to the value of property:

(1) The price or other terms and circumstances of an acquisition of property or a property interest if the acquisition was for a public use for which the property could have been taken by eminent domain.

The price or other terms and circumstances shall not be excluded pursuant to this paragraph if the proceeding relates to the valuation of all or part of a water system as defined in section 240 of the Public Utilities Code.

(2) The price at which an offer or option to purchase or lease the property or property interest being valued or any other property was made, or the price at which such property or interest was optioned, offered, or listed for sale or lease, except that an option, offer, or listing may be introduced by a party as an admission of another party to the proceeding; but nothing in this subdivision permits an admission to be used as direct evidence upon any matter that may be shown only by opinion evidence under Section 813.

(3) The value of any property or property interest as assessed for taxation purposes or the amount of taxes which may be due on the property, but nothing in this subdivision prohibits the consideration of actual or estimated taxes for the purpose of determining the reasonable net rental value attributable to the property or property interest being valued.

(4) An opinion as to the value of any property or property interest other than that being valued.

(5) The influence upon the value of the property or property interest being valued of any noncompensable items of value, damage, or injury.

(6) The capitalized value of the income or rental from any property or property interest other than that being valued.

(b) In an action other than an eminent domain or inverse condemnation proceeding, the matters listed in subdivision (a) are not admissible as evidence, and may not be taken into account as a basis for an opinion as to the value of property, except to the extent permitted under the rules of law otherwise applicable.

§ 823. Property with no relevant, comparable market

Notwithstanding any other provision of this article, the value of property for which there is no relevant, comparable market may be determined by any method of valuation that is just and equitable.

§ 824. Nonprofit, special use property

(a) Notwithstanding any other provision of this article, a just and equitable method of determining the value of nonprofit, special use property, as defined by Section 1235.155 of the Code of Civil Procedure, for which there is no relevant, comparable market, is the cost of purchasing land and the reasonable cost of making it suitable for the conduct of the same nonprofit, special use, together with the cost of constructing similar improvements. The method for determining compensation for improvements shall be as set forth in subdivision (b).

(b)   Notwithstanding any other provision of this article, a witness providing opinion testimony on the value of nonprofit, special use property, as defined by Section 1235.155 of the Code of Civil Procedure, for which there is no relevant, comparable market, shall base his or her opinion on the value of reproducing the improvements without taking into consideration any depreciation or obsolescence of the improvements.

(c)   This section does not apply to actions or proceedings commenced by a public entity or public utility to acquire real property or any interest in real property for the use of water, sewer, electricity, telephone, natural gas, or flood control facilities or rights-of-way where those acquisitions neither require removal or destruction of existing improvements, nor render the property unfit for the owner's present or proposed use.

ARTICLE 3. OPINION TESTIMONY ON PARTICULAR SUBJECTS

§ 870.   Opinion as to sanity

A witness may state his opinion as to the sanity of a person when:

(a)   The witness is an intimate acquaintance of the person whose sanity is in question;

(b)   The witness was a subscribing witness to a writing, the validity of which is in dispute, signed by the person whose sanity is in question and the opinion relates to the sanity of such person at the time the writing was signed; or

(c)   The witness is qualified under Section 800 or 801 to testify in the form of an opinion.

CHAPTER 2. BLOOD TESTS TO DETERMINE PATERNITY [REPEALED]

§§ 890 to 895. Repealed by Stats.1992, c. 162 (A.B.2650), § 9, operative Jan. 1, 1994

§ 895.5.   Repealed by Stats.1993, c. 219 (A.B.1500), § 77

§§ 896, 897.   Repealed by Stats.1992, c. 162 (A.B.2650), § 9, operative Jan. 1, 1994

DIVISION 8. PRIVILEGES

CHAPTER 1. DEFINITIONS

§ 900. Application of definitions

Unless the provision or context otherwise requires, the definitions in this chapter govern the construction of this division. They do not govern the construction of any other division.

§ 901. Proceeding

"Proceeding" means any action, hearing, investigation, inquest, or inquiry (whether conducted by a court, administrative agency, hearing officer, arbitrator, legislative body, or any other person authorized by law) in which, pursuant to law, testimony can be compelled to be given.

§ 902. Civil proceeding

"Civil proceeding" means any proceeding except a criminal proceeding.

§ 903. Criminal proceeding

"Criminal proceeding" means:

(a) A criminal action; and

(b) A proceeding pursuant to Article 3 (commencing with Section 3060) of Chapter 7 of Division 4 of Title 1 of the Government Code to determine whether a public officer should be removed from office for willful or corrupt misconduct in office.

§ 904. Blank

§ 905. Presiding officer

"Presiding officer" means the person authorized to rule on a claim of privilege in the proceeding in which the claim is made.

CHAPTER 2. APPLICABILITY OF DIVISION

§ 910. Applicability of division

Except as otherwise provided by statute, the provisions of this division apply in all proceedings. The provisions of any statute making rules of evidence inapplicable in particular proceedings, or limiting the applicability of rules of evidence in particular proceedings, do not make this division inapplicable to such proceedings.

CHAPTER 3. GENERAL PROVISIONS RELATING TO PRIVILEGES

§ 911. Refusal to be or have another as witness, or disclose or produce any matter

Except as otherwise provided by statute:

(a) No person has a privilege to refuse to be a witness.

(b) No person has a privilege to refuse to disclose any matter or to refuse to produce any writing, object, or other thing.

(c) No person has a privilege that another shall not be a witness or shall not disclose any matter or shall not produce any writing, object, or other thing.

§ 912. Waiver of privilege

(a) Except as otherwise provided in this section, the right of any person to claim a privilege provided by Section 954 (lawyer-client privilege), 966 (lawyer referral service-client privilege), 980 (privilege for confidential marital communications), 994 (physician-patient privilege), 1014 (psychotherapist-patient privilege), 1033 (privilege of penitent), 1034 (privilege of clergy member), 1035.8 (sexual assault counselor-victim privilege), 1037.5 (domestic violence counselor-victim privilege), or 1038 (human trafficking caseworker-victim privilege) is waived with respect to a communication protected by the privilege if any holder of the privilege, without coercion, has disclosed a significant part of the communication or has consented to disclosure made by anyone. Consent to disclosure is manifested by any statement or other conduct of the holder of the privilege indicating consent to the disclosure, including failure to claim the privilege in any proceeding in which the holder has legal standing and the opportunity to claim the privilege.

(b) Where two or more persons are joint holders of a privilege provided by Section 954 (lawyer-client privilege), 966 (lawyer referral service-client privilege), 994 (physician-patient privilege), 1014 (psychotherapist-patient privilege), 1035.8 (sexual assault counselor-victim privilege), 1037.5 (domestic violence counselor-victim privilege), or 1038 (human trafficking caseworker-victim privilege), a waiver of the right of a particular joint holder of the privilege to claim the privilege does not affect the right of another joint holder to claim the privilege. In the case of the privilege provided by Section 980 (privilege for confidential marital communications), a waiver of the right of one spouse to claim the privilege does not affect the right of the other spouse to claim the privilege.

(c) A disclosure that is itself privileged is not a waiver of any privilege.

(d) A disclosure in confidence of a communication that is protected by a privilege provided by Section 954 (lawyer-client privilege), 966 (lawyer referral service-client privilege), 994 (physician-patient privilege), 1014 (psychotherapist-patient privilege), 1035.8 (sexual assault counselor-victim privilege), 1037.5 (domestic violence counselor-victim privilege), or 1038 (human trafficking caseworker-victim privilege), when disclosure is reasonably necessary for the accomplishment of the purpose for which the lawyer, lawyer referral service, physician, psychotherapist, sexual assault counselor, domestic violence counselor, or human trafficking caseworker was consulted, is not a waiver of the privilege.

§ 913. Comment on, and inferences from, exercise of privilege

(a) If in the instant proceeding or on a prior occasion a privilege is or was exercised not to testify with respect to any matter, or to refuse to disclose or to prevent another from disclosing any matter, neither the presiding officer nor counsel may comment thereon, no presumption shall arise because of the exercise of the privilege, and the trier of fact may not draw any inference therefrom as to the credibility of the witness or as to any matter at issue in the proceeding.

(b)   The court, at the request of a party who may be adversely affected because an unfavorable inference may be drawn by the jury because a privilege has been exercised, shall instruct the jury that no presumption arises because of the exercise of the privilege and that the jury may not draw any inference therefrom as to the credibility of the witness or as to any matter at issue in the proceeding.

§ 914.   Determination of claim of privilege; limitation on punishment for contempt

(a)   The presiding officer shall determine a claim of privilege in any proceeding in the same manner as a court determines such a claim under Article 2 (commencing with Section 400) of Chapter 4 of Division 3.

(b)   No person may be held in contempt for failure to disclose information claimed to be privileged unless he has failed to comply with an order of a court that he disclose such information. This subdivision does not apply to any governmental agency that has constitutional contempt power, nor does it apply to hearings and investigations of the Industrial Accident Commission, nor does it impliedly repeal Chapter 4 (commencing with Section 9400) of Part 1 of Division 2 of Title 2 of the Government Code. If no other statutory procedure is applicable, the procedure prescribed by Section 1991 of the Code of Civil Procedure shall be followed in seeking an order of a court that the person disclose the information claimed to be privileged.

§ 915.   Disclosure of privileged information or attorney work product in ruling on claim of privilege

(a)   Subject to subdivision (b), the presiding officer may not require disclosure of information claimed to be privileged under this division or attorney work product under subdivision (a) of Section 2018.030 of the Code of Civil Procedure in order to rule on the claim of privilege; provided, however, that in any hearing conducted pursuant to subdivision (c) of Section 1524 of the Penal Code in which a claim of privilege is made and the court determines that there is no other feasible means to rule on the validity of the claim other than to require disclosure, the court shall proceed in accordance with subdivision (b).

(b)   When a court is ruling on a claim of privilege under Article 9 (commencing with Section 1040) of Chapter 4 (official information and identity of informer) or under Section 1060 (trade secret) or under subdivision (b) of Section 2018.030 of the Code of Civil Procedure (attorney work product) and is unable to do so without requiring disclosure of the information claimed to be privileged, the court may require the person from whom disclosure is sought or the person authorized to claim the privilege, or both, to disclose the information in chambers out of the presence and hearing of all persons except the person authorized to claim the privilege and any other persons as the person authorized to claim the privilege is willing to have present. If the judge determines that the information is privileged, neither the judge nor any other person may ever disclose, without the consent of a person authorized to permit disclosure, what was disclosed in the course of the proceedings in chambers.

§ 916. Exclusion of privileged information where persons authorized to claim privilege are not present

(a)   The presiding officer, on his own motion or on the motion of any party, shall exclude information that is subject to a claim of privilege under this division if:

(1)   The person from whom the information is sought is not a person authorized to claim the privilege; and

(2)   There is no party to the proceeding who is a person authorized to claim the privilege.

(b)   The presiding officer may not exclude information under this section if:

(1)   He is otherwise instructed by a person authorized to permit disclosure; or

(2)   The proponent of the evidence establishes that there is no person authorized to claim the privilege in existence.

§ 917. Presumption that certain communications are confidential; privileged character of electronic communications

(a)   If a privilege is claimed on the ground that the matter sought to be disclosed is a communication made in confidence in the course of the lawyer-client, physician-patient, psychotherapist-patient, clergy-penitent, marital or domestic partnership, sexual assault counselor-victim, domestic violence counselor-victim relationship, or human-trafficking caseworker-victim relationship, the communication is presumed to have been made in confidence and the opponent of the claim of privilege has the burden of proof to establish that the communication was not confidential.

(b)   A communication between persons in a relationship listed in subdivision (a) does not lose its privileged character for the sole reason that it is communicated by electronic means or because persons involved in the delivery, facilitation, or storage of electronic communication may have access to the content of the communication.

(c)   For purposes of this section, "electronic" has the same meaning provided in Section 1633.2 of the Civil Code.

§ 918.   Error in overruling claim of privilege

A party may predicate error on a ruling disallowing a claim of privilege only if he is the holder of the privilege, except that a party may predicate error on a ruling disallowing a claim of privilege by his spouse under Section 970 or 971.

§ 919.   Admissibility where disclosure erroneously compelled; claim of privilege; coercion

(a)   Evidence of a statement or other disclosure of privileged information is inadmissible against a holder of the privilege if:

(1)   A person authorized to claim the privilege claimed it but nevertheless disclosure erroneously was required to be made; or

(2) The presiding officer did not exclude the privileged information as required by Section 916.

(b) If a person authorized to claim the privilege claimed it, whether in the same or a prior proceeding, but nevertheless disclosure erroneously was required by the presiding officer to be made, neither the failure to refuse to disclose nor the failure to seek review of the order of the presiding officer requiring disclosure indicates consent to the disclosure or constitutes a waiver and, under these circumstances, the disclosure is one made under coercion.

§ 920. Implied repeal of other statutes related to privileges

Nothing in this division shall be construed to repeal by implication any other statute relating to privileges.

CHAPTER 4. PARTICULAR PRIVILEGES

ARTICLE 1. PRIVILEGE OF DEFENDANT IN CRIMINAL CASE

§ 930. Privilege not to be called as a witness and not to testify

To the extent that such privilege exists under the Constitution of the United States or the State of California, a defendant in a criminal case has a privilege not to be called as a witness and not to testify.

ARTICLE 2. PRIVILEGE AGAINST SELF-INCRIMINATION

§ 940. Privilege against self-incrimination

To the extent that such privilege exists under the Constitution of the United States or the State of California, a person has a privilege to refuse to disclose any matter that may tend to incriminate him.

ARTICLE 3. LAWYER-CLIENT PRIVILEGE

§ 950. Lawyer

As used in this article, "lawyer" means a person authorized, or reasonably believed by the client to be authorized, to practice law in any state or nation.

§ 951. Client

As used in this article, "client" means a person who, directly or through an authorized representative, consults a lawyer for the purpose of retaining the lawyer or securing legal service or advice from him in his professional capacity, and includes an incompetent (a) who himself so consults the lawyer or (b) whose guardian or conservator so consults the lawyer in behalf of the incompetent.

§ 952. Confidential communication between client and lawyer

As used in this article, "confidential communication between client and lawyer" means information transmitted between a client and his or her lawyer in the course of that relationship and in confidence by a means which, so far as the client is aware, discloses the information to no third persons other than those who are present to further the interest of the client in the consultation or those to whom disclosure is reasonably necessary for the transmission of the information or the accomplishment of the purpose for which the lawyer is consulted, and includes a legal opinion formed and the advice given by the lawyer in the course of that relationship.

§ 953. Holder of the privilege

As used in this article, "holder of the privilege" means:

(a) The client, if the client has no guardian or conservator.

(b)(1) A guardian or conservator of the client, if the client has a guardian or conservator, except as provided in paragraph (2).

(2) If the guardian or conservator has an actual or apparent conflict of interest with the client, then the guardian or conservator does not hold the privilege.

(c) The personal representative of the client if the client is dead, including a personal representative appointed pursuant to Section 12252 of the Probate Code.

(d) A successor, assign, trustee in dissolution, or any similar representative of a firm, association, organization, partnership, business trust, corporation, or public entity that is no longer in existence.

§ 954. Lawyer-client privilege

Subject to Section 912 and except as otherwise provided in this article, the client, whether or not a party, has a privilege to refuse to disclose, and to prevent another from disclosing, a confidential communication between client and lawyer if the privilege is claimed by:

(a) The holder of the privilege;

(b) A person who is authorized to claim the privilege by the holder of the privilege; or

(c) The person who was the lawyer at the time of the confidential communication, but such person may not claim the privilege if there is no holder of the privilege in existence or if he is otherwise instructed by a person authorized to permit disclosure.

The relationship of attorney and client shall exist between a law corporation as defined in Article 10 (commencing with Section 6160) of Chapter 4 of Division 3 of the Business and Professions Code and the persons to whom it renders professional services, as well as between such persons and members of the State Bar employed by such corporation to render services to such persons. The word "persons" as used in this subdivision includes partnerships, corporations, limited liability companies, associations and other groups and entities.

§ 955. When lawyer required to claim privilege

The lawyer who received or made a communication subject to the privilege under this article shall claim the privilege whenever he is present when the communication is sought to be disclosed and is authorized to claim the privilege under subdivision (c) of Section 954.

§ 956. Exception: Crime or fraud

(a) There is no privilege under this article if the services of the lawyer were sought or obtained to enable or aid anyone to commit or plan to commit a crime or a fraud.

(b) This exception to the privilege granted by this article shall not apply to legal services rendered in compliance with state and local laws on medicinal cannabis or adult-use cannabis, and confidential communications provided for the purpose of rendering those services are confidential communications between client and lawyer, as defined in Section 952, provided the lawyer also advises the client on conflicts with respect to federal law.

§ 956.5. Exception; Prevention of criminal act likely to result in death or substantial bodily harm

There is no privilege under this article if the lawyer reasonably believes that disclosure of any confidential communication relating to representation of a client is necessary to prevent a criminal act that the lawyer reasonably believes is likely to result in the death of, or substantial bodily harm to, an individual.

§ 957. Exception: Parties claiming through deceased client

There is no privilege under this article as to a communication relevant to an issue between parties all of whom claim through a deceased client, regardless of whether the claims are by testate or intestate succession, nonprobate transfer, or inter vivos transaction.

§ 958. Exception: Breach of duty arising out of lawyer-client relationship

There is no privilege under this article as to a communication relevant to an issue of breach, by the lawyer or by the client, of a duty arising out of the lawyer-client relationship.

§ 959. Exception: Lawyer as attesting witness

There is no privilege under this article as to a communication relevant to an issue concerning the intention or competence of a client executing an attested document of which the lawyer is an attesting witness, or concerning the execution or attestation of such a document.

§ 960. Exception: Intention of deceased client concerning writing affecting property interest

There is no privilege under this article as to a communication relevant to an issue concerning the intention of a client, now deceased, with respect to a deed of conveyance, will, or other writing, executed by the client, purporting to affect an interest in property.

§ 961. Exception: Validity of writing affecting property interest

There is no privilege under this article as to a communication relevant to an issue concerning the validity of a deed of conveyance, will, or other writing, executed by a client, now deceased, purporting to affect an interest in property.

§ 962.   Exception: Joint clients

Where two or more clients have retained or consulted a lawyer upon a matter of common interest, none of them, nor the successor in interest of any of them, may claim a privilege under this article as to a communication made in the course of that relationship when such communication is offered in a civil proceeding between one of such clients (or his successor in interest) and another of such clients (or his successor in interest).

ARTICLE 3.5. LAWYER-CLIENT REFERRAL SERVICE—CLIENT PRIVILEGE

§ 965.   Definitions

For purposes of this article, the following terms have the following meanings:

(a)   "Client" means a person who, directly or through an authorized representative, consults a lawyer referral service for the purpose of retaining, or securing legal services or advice from, a lawyer in his or her professional capacity, and includes an incompetent who consults the lawyer referral service himself or herself or whose guardian or conservator consults the lawyer referral service on his or her behalf.

(b)   "Confidential communication between client and lawyer referral service" means information transmitted between a client and a lawyer referral service in the course of that relationship and in confidence by a means that, so far as the client is aware, does not disclose the information to third persons other than those who are present to further the interests of the client in the consultation or those to whom disclosure is reasonably necessary for the transmission of the information or the accomplishment of the purpose for which the lawyer referral service is consulted.

(c)   "Holder of the privilege" means any of the following:

(1)   The client, if the client has no guardian or conservator.

(2)   A guardian or conservator of the client, if the client has a guardian or conservator.

(3)   The personal representative of the client if the client is dead, including a personal representative appointed pursuant to Section 12252 of the Probate Code.

(4)   A successor, assign, trustee in dissolution, or any similar representative of a firm, association, organization, partnership, business trust, corporation, or public entity that is no longer in existence.

(d)   "Lawyer referral service" means a lawyer referral service certified under, and operating in compliance with, Section 6155 of the Business and Professions Code or an enterprise reasonably believed by the client to be a lawyer referral service certified under, and operating in compliance with, Section 6155 of the Business and Professions Code.

§ 966.   Lawyer referral service-client privilege

(a)   Subject to Section 912 and except as otherwise provided in this article, the client, whether or not a party, has a privilege to refuse to disclose, and to prevent another from disclosing, a confidential communication between client and lawyer referral service if the privilege is claimed by any of the following:

(1) The holder of the privilege.

(2) A person who is authorized to claim the privilege by the holder of the privilege.

(3) The lawyer referral service or a staff person thereof, but the lawyer referral service or a staff person thereof may not claim the privilege if there is no holder of the privilege in existence or if the lawyer referral service or a staff person thereof is otherwise instructed by a person authorized to permit disclosure.

(b) The relationship of lawyer referral service and client shall exist between a lawyer referral service, as defined in Section 965, and the persons to whom it renders services, as well as between such persons and anyone employed by the lawyer referral service to render services to such persons. The word "persons" as used in this subdivision includes partnerships, corporations, limited liability companies, associations, and other groups and entities.

§ 967. Claiming of privilege

A lawyer referral service that has received or made a communication subject to the privilege under this article shall claim the privilege if the communication is sought to be disclosed and the client has not consented to the disclosure.

§ 968. Exceptions to privilege

There is no privilege under this article if either of the following applies:

(a) The services of the lawyer referral service were sought or obtained to enable or aid anyone to commit or plan to commit a crime or a fraud.

(b) A staff person of the lawyer referral service who receives a confidential communication in processing a request for legal assistance reasonably believes that disclosure of the confidential communication is necessary to prevent a criminal act that the staff person of the lawyer referral service reasonably believes is likely to result in the death of, or substantial bodily harm to, an individual.

ARTICLE 4. PRIVILEGE NOT TO TESTIFY AGAINST SPOUSE

§ 970. Spouse's privilege not to testify against spouse; exception

Except as otherwise provided by statute, a married person has a privilege not to testify against his spouse in any proceeding.

§ 971. Privilege not to be called as a witness against spouse

Except as otherwise provided by statute, a married person whose spouse is a party to a proceeding has a privilege not to be called as a witness by an adverse party to that proceeding without the prior express consent of the spouse having the privilege under this section unless the party calling the spouse does so in good faith without knowledge of the marital relationship.

§ 972. Exceptions to privilege

A married person does not have a privilege under this article in:

(a) A proceeding brought by or on behalf of one spouse against the other spouse.

(b) A proceeding to commit or otherwise place his or her spouse or his or her spouse's property, or both, under the control of another because of the spouse's alleged mental or physical condition.

(c) A proceeding brought by or on behalf of a spouse to establish his or her competence.

(d) A proceeding under the Juvenile Court Law, Chapter 2 (commencing with Section 200) of Part 1 of Division 2 of the Welfare and Institutions Code.

(e) A criminal proceeding in which one spouse is charged with:

(1) A crime against the person or property of the other spouse or of a child, parent, relative, or cohabitant of either, whether committed before or during marriage.

(2) A crime against the person or property of a third person committed in the course of committing a crime against the person or property of the other spouse, whether committed before or during marriage.

(3) Bigamy.

(4) A crime defined by Section 270 or 270a of the Penal Code.

(f) A proceeding resulting from a criminal act which occurred prior to legal marriage of the spouses to each other regarding knowledge acquired prior to that marriage if prior to the legal marriage the witness spouse was aware that his or her spouse had been arrested for or had been formally charged with the crime or crimes about which the spouse is called to testify.

(g) A proceeding brought against the spouse by a former spouse so long as the property and debts of the marriage have not been adjudicated, or in order to establish, modify, or enforce a child, family or spousal support obligation arising from the marriage to the former spouse; in a proceeding brought against a spouse by the other parent in order to establish, modify, or enforce a child support obligation for a child of a nonmarital relationship of the spouse; or in a proceeding brought against a spouse by the guardian of a child of that spouse in order to establish, modify, or enforce a child support obligation of the spouse. The married person does not have a privilege under this subdivision to refuse to provide information relating to the issues of income, expenses, assets, debts, and employment of either spouse, but may assert the privilege as otherwise provided in this article if other information is requested by the former spouse, guardian, or other parent of the child.

Any person demanding the otherwise privileged information made available by this subdivision, who also has an obligation to support the child for whom an order to establish, modify, or enforce child support is sought, waives his or her marital privilege to the same extent as the spouse as provided in this subdivision.

§ 973. Waiver of privilege

(a) Unless erroneously compelled to do so, a married person who testifies in a proceeding to which his spouse is a party, or who testifies against his spouse in any proceeding, does not have a privilege under this article in the proceeding in which such testimony is given.

(b) There is no privilege under this article in a civil proceeding brought or defended by a married person for the immediate benefit of his spouse or of himself and his spouse.

ARTICLE 5. PRIVILEGE FOR CONFIDENTIAL MARITAL COMMUNICATIONS

§ 980. Confidential spousal communication privilege

Subject to Section 912 and except as otherwise provided in this article, a spouse (or his or guardian or conservator when he or she has a guardian or conservator), whether or not a party, has a privilege during the marital or domestic partnership relationship and afterwards to refuse to disclose, and to prevent another from disclosing, a communication if he or she claims the privilege and the communication was made in confidence between him or her and the other spouse while they were spouses.

§ 981. Exception: Crime or fraud

There is no privilege under this article if the communication was made, in whole or in part, to enable or aid anyone to commit or plan to commit a crime or a fraud.

§ 982. Commitment or similar proceeding

There is no privilege under this article in a proceeding to commit either spouse or otherwise place him or his property, or both, under the control of another because of his alleged mental or physical condition.

§ 983. Competency proceedings

There is no privilege under this article in a proceeding brought by or on behalf of either spouse to establish his competence.

§ 984. Proceeding between spouses

There is no privilege under this article in:

(a) A proceeding brought by or on behalf of one spouse against the other spouse.

(b) A proceeding between a surviving spouse and a person who claims through the deceased spouse, regardless of whether such claim is by testate or intestate succession or by inter vivos transaction.

§ 985. Criminal proceedings

There is no privilege under this article in a criminal proceeding in which one spouse is charged with:

(a) A crime committed at any time against the person or property of the other spouse or of a child of either.

(b)   A crime committed at any time against the person or property of a third person committed in the course of committing a crime against the person or property of the other spouse.

(c)   Bigamy.

(d)   A crime defined by Section 270 or 270a of the Penal Code.

§ 986.   Juvenile court proceedings

There is no privilege under this article in a proceeding under the Juvenile Court Law, Chapter 2 (commencing with Section 200) of Part 1 of Division 2 of the Welfare and Institutions Code.

§ 987.   Communication offered by spouse who is criminal defendant

There is no privilege under this article in a criminal proceeding in which the communication is offered in evidence by a defendant who is one of the spouses between whom the communication was made.

ARTICLE 6. PHYSICIAN-PATIENT PRIVILEGE

§ 990.   Physician

As used in this article, "physician" means a person authorized, or reasonably believed by the patient to be authorized, to practice medicine in any state or nation.

§ 991.   Patient

As used in this article, "patient" means a person who consults a physician or submits to an examination by a physician for the purpose of securing a diagnosis or preventive, palliative, or curative treatment of his physical or mental or emotional condition.

§ 992.   Confidential communication between patient and physician

As used in this article, "confidential communication between patient and physician" means information, including information obtained by an examination of the patient, transmitted between a patient and his physician in the course of that relationship and in confidence by a means which, so far as the patient is aware, discloses the information to no third persons other than those who are present to further the interest of the patient in the consultation or those to whom disclosure is reasonably necessary for the transmission of the information or the accomplishment of the purpose for which the physician is consulted, and includes a diagnosis made and the advice given by the physician in the course of that relationship.

§ 993.   Holder of the privilege

As used in this article, "holder of the privilege" means:

(a)   The patient when he has no guardian or conservator.

(b)   A guardian or conservator of the patient when the patient has a guardian or conservator.

(c)   The personal representative of the patient if the patient is dead.

§ 994. Physician-patient privilege

Subject to Section 912 and except as otherwise provided in this article, the patient, whether or not a party, has a privilege to refuse to disclose, and to prevent another from disclosing, a confidential communication between patient and physician if the privilege is claimed by:

(a) The holder of the privilege;

(b) A person who is authorized to claim the privilege by the holder of the privilege; or

(c) The person who was the physician at the time of the confidential communication, but such person may not claim the privilege if there is no holder of the privilege in existence or if he or she is otherwise instructed by a person authorized to permit disclosure.

The relationship of a physician and patient shall exist between a medical or podiatry corporation as defined in the Medical Practice Act and the patient to whom it renders professional services, as well as between such patients and licensed physicians and surgeons employed by such corporation to render services to such patients. The word "persons" as used in this subdivision includes partnerships, corporations, limited liability companies, associations, and other groups and entities.

§ 995. When physician required to claim privilege

The physician who received or made a communication subject to the privilege under this article shall claim the privilege whenever he is present when the communication is sought to be disclosed and is authorized to claim the privilege under subdivision (c) of Section 994.

§ 996. Patient-litigant exception

There is no privilege under this article as to a communication relevant to an issue concerning the condition of the patient if such issue has been tendered by:

(a) The patient;

(b) Any party claiming through or under the patient;

(c) Any party claiming as a beneficiary of the patient through a contract to which the patient is or was a party; or

(d) The plaintiff in an action brought under Section 376 or 377 of the Code of Civil Procedure for damages for the injury or death of the patient.

§ 997. Exception: Crime or tort

There is no privilege under this article if the services of the physician were sought or obtained to enable or aid anyone to commit or plan to commit a crime or a tort or to escape detection or apprehension after the commission of a crime or a tort.

§ 998. Exception: Criminal proceeding

There is no privilege under this article in a criminal proceeding.

§ 999. Communication relating to patient condition in proceeding to recover damages; good cause

There is no privilege under this article as to a communication relevant to an issue concerning the condition of the patient in a proceeding to recover damages on account of the conduct of the patient if good cause for disclosure of the communication is shown.

§ 1000. Parties claiming through deceased patient

There is no privilege under this article as to a communication relevant to an issue between parties all of whom claim through a deceased patient, regardless of whether the claims are by testate or intestate succession or by inter vivos transaction.

§ 1001. Breach of duty arising out of physician-patient relationship

There is no privilege under this article as to a communication relevant to an issue of breach, by the physician or by the patient, of a duty arising out of the physician-patient relationship.

§ 1002. Intention of deceased patient concerning writing affecting property interest

There is no privilege under this article as to a communication relevant to an issue concerning the intention of a patient, now deceased, with respect to a deed of conveyance, will, or other writing, executed by the patient, purporting to affect an interest in property.

§ 1003. Validity of writing affecting property interest

There is no privilege under this article as to a communication relevant to an issue concerning the validity of a deed of conveyance, will, or other writing, executed by a patient, now deceased, purporting to affect an interest in property.

§ 1004. Commitment or similar proceeding

There is no privilege under this article in a proceeding to commit the patient or otherwise place him or his property, or both, under the control of another because of his alleged mental or physical condition.

§ 1005. Proceeding to establish competence

There is no privilege under this article in a proceeding brought by or on behalf of the patient to establish his competence.

§ 1006. Required report

There is no privilege under this article as to information that the physician or the patient is required to report to a public employee, or as to information required to be recorded in a public office, if such report or record is open to public inspection.

§ 1007. Proceeding to terminate right, license or privilege

There is no privilege under this article in a proceeding brought by a public entity to determine whether a right, authority, license, or privilege (including the right or privilege to be employed by the public entity or to hold a public office) should be revoked, suspended, terminated, limited, or conditioned.

ARTICLE 7. PSYCHOTHERAPIST-PATIENT PRIVILEGE

§ 1010. Psychotherapist

As used in this article, "psychotherapist" means a person who is, or is reasonably believed by the patient to be:

(a)   A person authorized to practice medicine in any state or nation who devotes, or is reasonably believed by the patient to devote, a substantial portion of his or her time to the practice of psychiatry.

(b)   A person licensed as a psychologist under Chapter 6.6 (commencing with Section 2900) of Division 2 of the Business and Professions Code.

(c)   A person licensed as a clinical social worker under Chapter 14 (commencing with Section 4991) of Division 2 of the Business and Professions Code, when he or she is engaged in applied psychotherapy of a nonmedical nature.

(d)   A person who is serving as a school psychologist and holds a credential authorizing that service issued by the state.

(e)   A person licensed as a marriage and family therapist under Chapter 13 (commencing with Section 4980) of Division 2 of the Business and Professions Code.

(f)   A person registered as a psychological assistant who is under the supervision of a licensed psychologist or board certified psychiatrist as required by Section 2913 of the Business and Professions Code, or a person registered as an associate marriage and family therapist intern who is under the supervision of a licensed marriage and family therapist, a licensed clinical social worker, a licensed professional clinical counselor, a licensed psychologist, or a licensed physician and surgeon certified in psychiatry, as specified in Section 4980.44 of the Business and Professions Code.

(g)   A person registered as an associate clinical social worker who is under supervision as specified in Section 4996.23 of the Business and Professions Code.

(h)   A person registered with the Board of Psychology as a registered psychologist who is under the supervision of a licensed psychologist or board certified psychiatrist.

(i)   A psychological intern as defined in Section 2911 of the Business and Professions Code who is under the supervision of a licensed psychologist or board certified psychiatrist.

(j)   A trainee, as defined in subdivision (c) of Section 4980.03 of the Business and Professions Code, who is fulfilling his or her supervised practicum required by subparagraph (B) of paragraph (1) of subdivision (d) of Section 4980.36 of, or subdivision (c) of Section 4980.37 of, the Business and Professions Code and is supervised by a licensed psychologist, a board certified psychiatrist, a licensed clinical social worker, a licensed marriage and family therapist, or a licensed professional clinical counselor.

(k) A person licensed as a registered nurse pursuant to Chapter 6 (commencing with Section 2700) of Division 2 of the Business and Professions Code, who possesses a master's degree in psychiatric-mental health nursing and is listed as a psychiatric-mental health nurse by the Board of Registered Nursing.

(*l*) An advanced practice registered nurse who is certified as a clinical nurse specialist pursuant to Article 9 (commencing with Section 2838) of Chapter 6 of Division 2 of the Business and Professions Code and who participates in expert clinical practice in the specialty of psychiatric-mental health nursing.

(m) A person rendering mental health treatment or counseling services as authorized pursuant to Section 6924 of the Family Code.

(n) A person licensed as a professional clinical counselor under Chapter 16 (commencing with Section 4999.10) of Division 2 of the Business and Professions Code.

(o) A person registered as an associate professional clinical counselor who is under the supervision of a licensed professional clinical counselor, a licensed marriage and family therapist, a licensed clinical social worker, a licensed psychologist, or a licensed physician and surgeon certified in psychiatry, as specified in Sections 4999.42 to 4999.48, inclusive, of the Business and Professions Code.

(p) A clinical counselor trainee, as defined in subdivision (g) of Section 4999.12 of the Business and Professions Code, who is fulfilling his or her supervised practicum required by paragraph (3) of subdivision (c) of Section 4999.32 of, or paragraph (3) of subdivision (c) of Section 4999.33 of, the Business and Professions Code, and is supervised by a licensed psychologist, a board-certified psychiatrist, a licensed clinical social worker, a licensed marriage and family therapist, or a licensed professional clinical counselor.

§ 1010.5. Privileged communication between patient and educational psychologist

A communication between a patient and an educational psychologist, licensed under Article 5 (commencing with Section 4986) of Chapter 13 of Division 2 of the Business and Professions Code, shall be privileged to the same extent, and subject to the same limitations, as a communication between a patient and a psychotherapist described in subdivisions (c), (d), and (e) of Section 1010.

§ 1011. Patient

As used in this article, "patient" means a person who consults a psychotherapist or submits to an examination by a psychotherapist for the purpose of securing a diagnosis or preventive, palliative, or curative treatment of his mental or emotional condition or who submits to an examination of his mental or emotional condition for the purpose of scientific research on mental or emotional problems.

§ 1012. Confidential communication between patient and psychotherapist

As used in this article, "confidential communication between patient and psychotherapist" means information, including information obtained by an examination of the patient, transmitted between a patient and his psychotherapist in the course of that relationship and in confidence by a means which, so far as the patient is aware, discloses the information to no third persons other than those who are present to further the interest of the patient in the consultation, or those to whom disclosure is reasonably necessary for the transmission of the information or the accomplishment of the purpose for which the psychotherapist is consulted, and includes a diagnosis made and the advice given by the psychotherapist in the course of that relationship.

§ 1013. Holder of the privilege

As used in this article, "holder of the privilege" means:

(a)   The patient when he has no guardian or conservator.

(b)   A guardian or conservator of the patient when the patient has a guardian or conservator.

(c)   The personal representative of the patient if the patient is dead.

§ 1014. Psychotherapist-patient privilege; application to individuals and entities

Subject to Section 912 and except as otherwise provided in this article, the patient, whether or not a party, has a privilege to refuse to disclose, and to prevent another from disclosing, a confidential communication between patient and psychotherapist if the privilege is claimed by:

(a)   The holder of the privilege.

(b)   A person who is authorized to claim the privilege by the holder of the privilege.

(c)   The person who was the psychotherapist at the time of the confidential communication, but such person may not claim the privilege if there is no holder of the privilege in existence or if he or she is otherwise instructed by a person authorized to permit disclosure.

The relationship of a psychotherapist and patient shall exist between a psychological corporation as defined in Article 9 (commencing with Section 2995) of Chapter 6.6 of Division 2 of the Business and Professions Code, a marriage, family, and child counseling corporation as defined in Article 6 (commencing with Section 4987.5) of Chapter 13 of Division 2 of the Business and Professions Code, a licensed clinical social workers corporation as defined in Article 5 (commencing with Section 4998) of Chapter 14 of Division 2 of the Business and Professions Code, or a professional clinical counselor corporation as defined in Article 7 (commencing with Section 4999.123) of Chapter 16 of Division 2 of the Business and Professions Code, and the patient to whom it renders professional services, as well as between those patients and psychotherapists employed by those corporations to render services to those patients. The word "persons" as used in this subdivision includes partnerships, corporations, limited liability companies, associations and other groups and entities.

§ 1014.5. Repealed by Stats.1994, c. 1270 (A.B.2659), § 2

§ 1015. When psychotherapist required to claim privilege

The psychotherapist who received or made a communication subject to the privilege under this article shall claim the privilege whenever he is present when the communication is sought to be disclosed and is authorized to claim the privilege under subdivision (c) of Section 1014.

§ 1016. Exception: Patient-litigant exception

There is no privilege under this article as to a communication relevant to an issue concerning the mental or emotional condition of the patient if such issue has been tendered by:

(a) The patient;

(b) Any party claiming through or under the patient;

(c) Any party claiming as a beneficiary of the patient through a contract to which the patient is or was a party; or

(d) The plaintiff in an action brought under Sections 376 or 377 of the Code of Civil Procedure for damages for the injury or death of the patient.

§ 1017. Exception: Psychotherapist appointed by court or board of prison terms

(a) There is no privilege under this article if the psychotherapist is appointed by order of a court to examine the patient, but this exception does not apply where the psychotherapist is appointed by order of the court upon the request of the lawyer for the defendant in a criminal proceeding in order to provide the lawyer with information needed so that he or she may advise the defendant whether to enter or withdraw a plea based on insanity or to present a defense based on his or her mental or emotional condition.

(b) There is no privilege under this article if the psychotherapist is appointed by the Board of Prison Terms to examine a patient pursuant to the provisions of Article 4 (commencing with Section 2960) of Chapter 7 of Title 1 of Part 3 of the Penal Code.

§ 1018. Exception: Crime or tort

There is no privilege under this article if the services of the psychotherapist were sought or obtained to enable or aid anyone to commit or plan to commit a crime or a tort or to escape detection or apprehension after the commission of a crime or a tort.

§ 1019. Exception: Parties claiming through deceased patient

There is no privilege under this article as to a communication relevant to an issue between parties all of whom claim through a deceased patient, regardless of whether the claims are by testate or intestate succession or by inter vivos transaction.

§ 1020. Exception: Breach of duty arising out of psychotherapist-patient relationship

There is no privilege under this article as to a communication relevant to an issue of breach, by the psychotherapist or by the patient, of a duty arising out of the psychotherapist-patient relationship.

§ 1021. Exception: Intention of deceased patient concerning writing affecting property interest

There is no privilege under this article as to a communication relevant to an issue concerning the intention of a patient, now deceased, with respect to a deed of conveyance, will, or other writing, executed by the patient, purporting to affect an interest in property.

§ 1022. Exception: Validity of writing affecting property interest

There is no privilege under this article as to a communication relevant to an issue concerning the validity of a deed of conveyance, will, or other writing, executed by a patient, now deceased, purporting to affect an interest in property.

§ 1023. Exception: Proceeding to determine sanity of criminal defendant

There is no privilege under this article in a proceeding under Chapter 6 (commencing with Section 1367) of Title 10 of Part 2 of the Penal Code initiated at the request of the defendant in a criminal action to determine his sanity.

§ 1024. Exception: Patient dangerous to himself or others

There is no privilege under this article if the psychotherapist has reasonable cause to believe that the patient is in such mental or emotional condition as to be dangerous to himself or to the person or property of another and that disclosure of the communication is necessary to prevent the threatened danger.

§ 1025. Exception: Proceeding to establish competence

There is no privilege under this article in a proceeding brought by or on behalf of the patient to establish his competence.

§ 1026. Exception: Required report

There is no privilege under this article as to information that the psychotherapist or the patient is required to report to a public employee or as to information required to be recorded in a public office, if such report or record is open to public inspection.

§ 1027. Exception: Child under 16 victim of crime

There is no privilege under this article if all of the following circumstances exist:

(a) The patient is a child under the age of 16.

(b) The psychotherapist has reasonable cause to believe that the patient has been the victim of a crime and that disclosure of the communication is in the best interest of the child.

§ 1028. Repealed by Stats. 1985, c. 1077, §§ 1, 2

ARTICLE 8. CLERGY-PENITENT PRIVILEGES

§ 1030. Member of the clergy

As used in this article, "member of the clergy" means a priest, minister, religious practitioner, or similar functionary of a church or of a religious denomination or religious organization.

§ 1031. Penitent

As used in this article, "penitent" means a person who has made a penitential communication to a member of the clergy.

§ 1032. Penitential communication

As used in this article, "penitential communication" means a communication made in confidence, in the presence of no third person so far as the penitent is aware, to a member of the clergy who, in the course of the discipline or practice of the clergy member's church, denomination, or organization, is authorized or accustomed to hear such communications and, under the discipline or tenets of his or her church, denomination, or organization, has a duty to keep those communications secret.

§ 1033. Privilege of penitent

Subject to Section 912, a penitent, whether or not a party, has a privilege to refuse to disclose, and to prevent another from disclosing, a penitential communication if he or she claims the privilege.

§ 1034. Privilege of clergy

Subject to Section 912, a member of the clergy, whether or not a party, has a privilege to refuse to disclose a penitential communication if he or she claims the privilege.

ARTICLE 8.5. SEXUAL ASSAULT
COUNSELOR-VICTIM PRIVILEGE

§ 1035. Victim

As used in this article, "victim" means a person who consults a sexual assault counselor for the purpose of securing advice or assistance concerning a mental, physical, or emotional condition caused by a sexual assault.

§ 1035.2. Sexual assault counselor

As used in this article, "sexual assault counselor" means any of the following:

(a) A person who is engaged in any office, hospital, institution, or center commonly known as a rape crisis center, whose primary purpose is the rendering of advice or assistance to victims of sexual assault and who has received a certificate evidencing completion of a training program in the counseling of sexual assault victims issued by a counseling center that meets the criteria for the award of a grant established pursuant to Section 13837 of the Penal Code and who meets one of the following requirements:

    (1) Is a psychotherapist as defined in Section 1010; has a master's degree in counseling or a related field; or has one year of counseling experience, at least six months of which is in rape crisis counseling.

    (2) Has 40 hours of training as described below and is supervised by an individual who qualifies as a counselor under paragraph (1). The training, supervised by a person qualified under paragraph (1), shall include, but not be limited to, the following areas:

    (A) Law.

    (B) Medicine.

    (C) Societal attitudes.

    (D) Crisis intervention and counseling techniques.

    (E) Role playing.

    (F) Referral services.

    (G) Sexuality.

    (b) A person who is engaged in a program on the campus of a public or private institution of higher education, whose primary purpose is the rendering of advice or assistance to victims of sexual assault and who has received a certificate evidencing completion of a training program in the counseling of sexual assault victims issued by a counseling center that meets the criteria for the award of a grant established pursuant to Section 13837 of the Penal Code and who meets one of the following requirements:

    (1) Is a psychotherapist as defined in Section 1010; has a master's degree in counseling or a related field; or has one year of counseling experience, at least six months of which is in rape crisis counseling.

    (2) Has 40 hours of training as described below and is supervised by an individual who qualifies as a counselor under paragraph (1). The training, supervised by a person qualified under paragraph (1), shall include, but not be limited to, the following areas:

    (A) Law.

    (B) Medicine.

    (C) Societal attitudes.

    (D) Crisis intervention and counseling techniques.

    (E) Role playing.

    (F) Referral services.

    (G) Sexuality.

    (c) A person who is employed by any organization providing the programs specified in Section 13835.2 of the Penal Code, whether financially compensated or not, for the purpose of counseling and assisting sexual assault victims, and who meets one of the following requirements:

    (1) Is a psychotherapist as defined in Section 1010; has a master's degree in counseling or a related field; or has one year of counseling experience, at least six months of which is in rape assault counseling.

(2) Has the minimum training for sexual assault counseling required by guidelines established by the employing agency pursuant to subdivision (c) of Section 13835.10 of the Penal Code, and is supervised by an individual who qualifies as a counselor under paragraph (1). The training, supervised by a person qualified under paragraph (1), shall include, but not be limited to, the following areas:

    (A) Law.

    (B) Victimology.

    (C) Counseling.

    (D) Client and system advocacy.

    (E) Referral services.

§ 1035.4. Confidential communication between the sexual assault counselor and the victim; disclosure

As used in this article, "confidential communication between the sexual assault counselor and the victim" means information transmitted between the victim and the sexual assault counselor in the course of their relationship and in confidence by a means which, so far as the victim is aware, discloses the information to no third persons other than those who are present to further the interests of the victim in the consultation or those to whom disclosures are reasonably necessary for the transmission of the information or an accomplishment of the purposes for which the sexual assault counselor is consulted. The term includes all information regarding the facts and circumstances involving the alleged sexual assault and also includes all information regarding the victim's prior or subsequent sexual conduct, and opinions regarding the victim's sexual conduct or reputation in sexual matters.

The court may compel disclosure of information received by the sexual assault counselor which constitutes relevant evidence of the facts and circumstances involving an alleged sexual assault about which the victim is complaining and which is the subject of a criminal proceeding if the court determines that the probative value outweighs the effect on the victim, the treatment relationship, and the treatment services if disclosure is compelled. The court may also compel disclosure in proceedings related to child abuse if the court determines the probative value outweighs the effect on the victim, the treatment relationship, and the treatment services if disclosure is compelled.

When a court is ruling on a claim of privilege under this article, the court may require the person from whom disclosure is sought or the person authorized to claim the privilege, or both, to disclose the information in chambers out of the presence and hearing of all persons except the person authorized to claim the privilege and such other persons as the person authorized to claim the privilege is willing to have present. If the judge determines that the information is privileged and must not be disclosed, neither he or she nor any other person may ever disclose, without the consent of a person authorized to permit disclosure, what was disclosed in the course of the proceedings in chambers.

If the court determines certain information shall be disclosed, the court shall so order and inform the defendant. If the court finds there is a reasonable likelihood that particular information is subject to disclosure pursuant to the balancing test provided in this section, the following procedure shall be followed:

(1)   The court shall inform the defendant of the nature of the information which may be subject to disclosure.

(2)   The court shall order a hearing out of the presence of the jury, if any, and at the hearing allow the questioning of the sexual assault counselor regarding the information which the court has determined may be subject to disclosure.

(3)   At the conclusion of the hearing, the court shall rule which items of information, if any, shall be disclosed. The court may make an order stating what evidence may be introduced by the defendant and the nature of questions to be permitted. The defendant may then offer evidence pursuant to the order of the court. Admission of evidence concerning the sexual conduct of the complaining witness is subject to Sections 352, 782, and 1103.

§ 1035.6. Holder of the privilege

As used in this article, "holder of the privilege" means:

(a)   The victim when such person has no guardian or conservator.

(b)   A guardian or conservator of the victim when the victim has a guardian or conservator.

(c)   The personal representative of the victim if the victim is dead.

§ 1035.8. Sexual assault counselor privilege

A victim of a sexual assault, whether or not a party, has a privilege to refuse to disclose, and to prevent another from disclosing, a confidential communication between the victim and a sexual assault counselor if the privilege is claimed by any of the following:

(a)   The holder of the privilege;

(b)   A person who is authorized to claim the privilege by the holder of the privilege; or

(c)   The person who was the sexual assault counselor at the time of the confidential communication, but that person may not claim the privilege if there is no holder of the privilege in existence or if he or she is otherwise instructed by a person authorized to permit disclosure.

§ 1036. Claim of privilege by sexual assault counselor

The sexual assault counselor who received or made a communication subject to the privilege under this article shall claim the privilege if he or she is present when the communication is sought to be disclosed and is authorized to claim the privilege under subdivision (c) of Section 1035.8.

§ 1036.2. Sexual assault

As used in this article, "sexual assault" includes all of the following:

(a)   Rape, as defined in Section 261 of the Penal Code.

(b)   Unlawful sexual intercourse, as defined in Section 261.5 of the Penal Code.

(c)   Rape in concert with force and violence, as defined in Section 264.1 of the Penal Code.

(d)   Rape of a spouse, as defined in Section 262 of the Penal Code.

(e)   Sodomy, as defined in Section 286 of the Penal Code, except a violation of subdivision (e) of that section.

(f)   A violation of Section 288 of the Penal Code.

(g)   Oral copulation, as defined in Section 287 of, or former Section 288a of, the Penal Code, except a violation of subdivision (e) of those sections.

(h)   Penetration of the genital or anal openings of another person with a foreign object, substance, instrument, or device, as specified in Section 289 of the Penal Code.

(i)   Annoying or molesting a child under 18, as defined in Section 647a of the Penal Code.

(j)   Any attempt to commit any of the above acts.

ARTICLE 8.7. DOMESTIC VIOLENCE COUNSELOR-VICTIM PRIVILEGE

§ 1037. Victim

As used in this article, "victim" means any person who suffers domestic violence, as defined in Section 1037.7.

§ 1037.1. Domestic violence counselor; qualifications; domestic violence victim service organization

(a)(1)   As used in this article, "domestic violence counselor" means a person who is employed by a domestic violence victim service organization, as defined in this article, whether financially compensated or not, for the purpose or rendering advice or assistance to victims of domestic violence and who has at least 40 hours of training as specified in paragraph (2).

(2)   The 40 hours of training shall be supervised by an individual who qualifies as a counselor under paragraph (1), and who has at least one year of experience counseling domestic violence victims for the domestic violence victim service organization. The training shall include, but need not be limited to, the following areas: history of domestic violence, civil and criminal law as it relates to domestic violence, the domestic violence victim-counselor privilege and other laws that protect the confidentiality of victim records and information, societal attitudes towards domestic violence, peer counseling techniques, housing, public assistance and other financial resources available to meet the financial needs of domestic violence victims, and referral services available to domestic violence victims.

(3)   A domestic violence counselor who has been employed by the domestic violence victim service organization for a period of less than six months shall be supervised by a domestic violence counselor who has at least one year of experience counseling domestic violence victims for the domestic violence victim service organization.

(b)   As used in this article, "domestic violence victim service organization" means either of the following:

(1) A nongovernmental organization or entity that provides shelter, programs, or services to victims of domestic violence and their children, including, but not limited to, either of the following:

(A) Domestic violence shelter-based programs, as described in Section 18294 of the Welfare and Institutions Code.

(B) Other programs with the primary mission to provide services to victims of domestic violence whether or not that program exists in an agency that provides additional services.

(2) Programs on the campus of a public or private institution of higher education with the primary mission to provide support or advocacy services to victims of domestic violence.

§ 1037.2. Confidential communication; compulsion of disclosure by court; claim of privilege

(a) As used in this article, "confidential communication" means any information, including, but not limited to, written or oral communication, transmitted between the victim and the counselor in the course of their relationship and in confidence by a means which, so far as the victim is aware, discloses the information to no third persons other than those who are present to further the interests of the victim in the consultation or those to whom disclosures are reasonably necessary for the transmission of the information or an accomplishment of the purposes for which the domestic violence counselor is consulted. The term includes all information regarding the facts and circumstances involving all incidences of domestic violence, as well as all information about the children of the victim or abuser and the relationship of the victim with the abuser.

(b) The court may compel disclosure of information received by a domestic violence counselor which constitutes relevant evidence of the facts and circumstances involving a crime allegedly perpetrated against the victim or another household member and which is the subject of a criminal proceeding, if the court determines that the probative value of the information outweighs the effect of disclosure of the information on the victim, the counseling relationship, and the counseling services. The court may compel disclosure if the victim is either dead or not the complaining witness in a criminal action against the perpetrator. The court may also compel disclosure in proceedings related to child abuse if the court determines that the probative value of the evidence outweighs the effect of the disclosure on the victim, the counseling relationship, and the counseling services.

(c) When a court rules on a claim of privilege under this article, it may require the person from whom disclosure is sought or the person authorized to claim the privilege, or both, to disclose the information in chambers out of the presence and hearing of all persons except the person authorized to claim the privilege and such other persons as the person authorized to claim the privilege consents to have present. If the judge determines that the information is privileged and shall not be disclosed, neither he nor she nor any other person may disclose, without the consent of a person authorized to permit disclosure, any information disclosed in the course of the proceedings in chambers.

(d) If the court determines that information shall be disclosed, the court shall so order and inform the defendant in the criminal action. If the court finds there is a reasonable likelihood that any information is subject to disclosure pursuant to the balancing test provided in this section, the procedure specified in subdivisions (1), (2), and (3) of Section 1035.4 shall be followed.

§ 1037.3. Child abuse; reporting

Nothing in this article shall be construed to limit any obligation to report instances of child abuse as required by Section 11166 of the Penal Code.

§ 1037.4. Holder of the privilege

As used in this article, "holder of the privilege" means:

(a)   The victim when he or she has no guardian or conservator.

(b)   A guardian or conservator of the victim when the victim has a guardian or conservator, unless the guardian or conservator is accused of perpetrating domestic violence against the victim.

§ 1037.5. Privilege of refusal to disclose communication; claimants

A victim of domestic violence, whether or not a party to the action, has a privilege to refuse to disclose, and to prevent another from disclosing, a confidential communication between the victim and a domestic violence counselor in any proceeding specified in Section 901 if the privilege is claimed by any of the following persons:

(a)   The holder of the privilege.

(b)   A person who is authorized to claim the privilege by the holder of the privilege.

(c)   The person who was the domestic violence counselor at the time of the confidential communication. However, that person may not claim the privilege if there is no holder of the privilege in existence or if he or she is otherwise instructed by a person authorized to permit disclosure.

§ 1037.6. Claim of privilege by counselor

The domestic violence counselor who received or made a communication subject to the privilege granted by this article shall claim the privilege whenever he or she is present when the communication is sought to be disclosed and he or she is authorized to claim the privilege under subdivision (c) of Section 1037.5.

§ 1037.7. Domestic violence

As used in this article, "domestic violence" means "domestic violence" as defined in Section 6211 of the Family Code.

§ 1037.8. Notice; limitations on confidential communications

A domestic violence counselor shall inform a domestic violence victim of any applicable limitations on confidentiality of communications between the victim and the domestic violence counselor. This information may be given orally.

ARTICLE 8.8. HUMAN TRAFFICKING CASEWORKER-VICTIM PRIVILEGE

§ 1038. Privilege

(a) A trafficking victim, whether or not a party to the action, has a privilege to refuse to disclose, and to prevent another from disclosing, a confidential communication between the victim and a human trafficking caseworker if the privilege is claimed by any of the following persons:

(1) The holder of the privilege.

(2) A person who is authorized to claim the privilege by the holder of the privilege.

(3) The person who was the human trafficking caseworker at the time of the confidential communication. However, that person may not claim the privilege if there is no holder of the privilege in existence or if he or she is otherwise instructed by a person authorized to permit disclosure. The human trafficking caseworker who received or made a communication subject to the privilege granted by this article shall claim the privilege whenever he or she is present when the communication is sought to be disclosed and he or she is authorized to claim the privilege under this section.

(b) A human trafficking caseworker shall inform a trafficking victim of any applicable limitations on confidentiality of communications between the victim and the caseworker. This information may be given orally.

§ 1038.1. Compulsion of disclosure by court

(a) The court may compel disclosure of information received by a human trafficking caseworker that constitutes relevant evidence of the facts and circumstances involving a crime allegedly perpetrated against the victim and that is the subject of a criminal proceeding, if the court determines that the probative value of the information outweighs the effect of disclosure of the information on the victim, the counseling relationship, and the counseling services. The court may compel disclosure if the victim is either dead or not the complaining witness in a criminal action against the perpetrator.

(b) When a court rules on a claim of privilege under this article, it may require the person from whom disclosure is sought or the person authorized to claim the privilege, or both, to disclose the information in chambers out of the presence and hearing of all persons except the person authorized to claim the privilege and those other persons that the person authorized to claim the privilege consents to have present.

(c) If the judge determines that the information is privileged and shall not be disclosed, neither he nor she nor any other person may disclose, without the consent of a person authorized to permit disclosure, any information disclosed in the course of the proceedings in chambers. If the court determines that information shall be disclosed, the court shall so order and inform the defendant in the criminal action. If the court finds there is a reasonable likelihood that any information is subject to disclosure pursuant to the balancing test provided in this section, the procedure specified in paragraphs (1), (2), and (3) of Section 1035.4 shall be followed.

§ 1038.2. Definitions

(a) As used in this article, "victim" means any person who is a "trafficking victim" as defined in Section 236.1 of the Penal Code.

(b) As used in this article, "human trafficking caseworker" means any of the following:

(1) A person who is employed by any organization providing the programs specified in Section 18294 of the Welfare and Institutions Code, whether financially compensated or not, for the purpose of rendering advice or assistance to victims of human trafficking, who has received specialized training in the counseling of human trafficking victims, and who meets one of the following requirements:

(A) Has a master's degree in counseling or a related field; or has one year of counseling experience, at least six months of which is in the counseling of human trafficking victims.

(B) Has at least 40 hours of training as specified in this paragraph and is supervised by an individual who qualifies as a counselor under subparagraph (A), or is a psychotherapist, as defined in Section 1010. The training, supervised by a person qualified under subparagraph (A), shall include, but need not be limited to, the following areas: history of human trafficking, civil and criminal law as it relates to human trafficking, societal attitudes towards human trafficking, peer counseling techniques, housing, public assistance and other financial resources available to meet the financial needs of human trafficking victims, and referral services available to human trafficking victims. A portion of this training must include an explanation of privileged communication.

(2) A person who is employed by any organization providing the programs specified in Section 13835.2 of the Penal Code, whether financially compensated or not, for the purpose of counseling and assisting human trafficking victims, and who meets one of the following requirements:

(A) Is a psychotherapist as defined in Section 1010, has a master's degree in counseling or a related field, or has one year of counseling experience, at least six months of which is in rape assault counseling.

(B) Has the minimum training for human trafficking counseling required by guidelines established by the employing agency pursuant to subdivision (c) of Section 13835.10 of the Penal Code, and is supervised by an individual who qualifies as a counselor under subparagraph (A). The training, supervised by a person qualified under subparagraph (A), shall include, but not be limited to, law, victimology, counseling techniques, client and system advocacy, and referral services. A portion of this training must include an explanation of privileged communication.

(c) As used in this article, "confidential communication" means information transmitted between the victim and the caseworker in the course of their relationship and in confidence by a means which, so far as the victim is aware, discloses the information to no third persons other than those who are present to further the interests of the victim in the consultation or those to whom disclosures are reasonably necessary for the transmission of the information or an accomplishment of the purposes for which the human trafficking counselor is consulted. It includes all information regarding the facts and circumstances involving all incidences of human trafficking.

(d)   As used in this article, "holder of the privilege" means the victim when he or she has no guardian or conservator, or a guardian or conservator of the victim when the victim has a guardian or conservator.

ARTICLE 9. OFFICIAL INFORMATION AND IDENTITY OF INFORMER

§ 1040. Privilege for official information

(a)   As used in this section, "official information" means information acquired in confidence by a public employee in the course of his or her duty and not open, or officially disclosed, to the public prior to the time the claim of privilege is made.

(b)   A public entity has a privilege to refuse to disclose official information, and to prevent another from disclosing official information, if the privilege is claimed by a person authorized by the public entity to do so and either of the following apply:

(1)   Disclosure is forbidden by an act of the Congress of the United States or a statute of this state.

(2)   Disclosure of the information is against the public interest because there is a necessity for preserving the confidentiality of the information that outweighs the necessity for disclosure in the interest of justice; but no privilege may be claimed under this paragraph if any person authorized to do so has consented that the information be disclosed in the proceeding. In determining whether disclosure of the information is against the public interest, the interest of the public entity as a party in the outcome of the proceeding may not be considered.

(c)   Notwithstanding any other law, the Employment Development Department shall disclose to law enforcement agencies, in accordance with subdivision (i) of Section 1095 of the Unemployment Insurance Code, information in its possession relating to any person if an arrest warrant has been issued for the person for commission of a felony.

§ 1041. Privilege for identity of informer

(a)   Except as provided in this section, a public entity has a privilege to refuse to disclose the identity of a person who has furnished information as provided in subdivision (b) purporting to disclose a violation of a law of the United States or of this state or of a public entity in this state, and to prevent another from disclosing such identity, if the privilege is claimed by a person authorized by the public entity to do so and either of the following apply:

(1)   Disclosure is forbidden by an act of the Congress of the United States or a statute of this state.

(2)   Disclosure of the identity of the informer is against the public interest because there is a necessity for preserving the confidentiality of his or her identity outweighs the necessity for disclosure in the interest of justice. The privilege shall not be claimed under this paragraph if any person authorized to do so has consented that the identity of the informer be disclosed in the proceeding. In determining whether disclosure of the identity of the informer is against the public interest,

the interest of the public entity as a party in the outcome of the proceeding shall not be considered.

(b)   The privilege described in this section applies only if the information is furnished in confidence by the informer to any of the following:

(1)   A law enforcement officer.

(2)   A representative of an administrative agency charged with the administration or enforcement of the law alleged to be violated.

(3)   Any person for the purpose of transmittal to a person listed in paragraph (1) or (2). As used in this paragraph, "person" includes a volunteer or employee of a crime stopper organization.

(c)   The privilege described under this section shall not be construed to prevent the informer from disclosing his or her identity.

(d) As used in this section, "crime stopper organization" means a private, nonprofit organization that accepts and expends donations used to reward persons who report to the organization information concerning alleged criminal activity, and forwards the information to the appropriate law enforcement agency.

§ 1042. Adverse order or finding in certain cases

(a)   Except where disclosure is forbidden by an act of the Congress of the United States, if a claim of privilege under this article by the state or a public entity in this state is sustained in a criminal proceeding, the presiding officer shall make such order or finding of fact adverse to the public entity bringing the proceeding as is required by law upon any issue in the proceeding to which the privileged information is material.

(b)   Notwithstanding subdivision (a), where a search is made pursuant to a warrant valid on its face, the public entity bringing a criminal proceeding is not required to reveal to the defendant official information or the identity of an informer in order to establish the legality of the search or the admissibility of any evidence obtained as a result of it.

(c)   Notwithstanding subdivision (a), in any preliminary hearing, criminal trial, or other criminal proceeding, any otherwise admissible evidence of information communicated to a peace officer by a confidential informant, who is not a material witness to the guilt or innocence of the accused of the offense charged, is admissible on the issue of reasonable cause to make an arrest or search without requiring that the name or identity of the informant be disclosed if the judge or magistrate is satisfied, based upon evidence produced in open court, out of the presence of the jury, that such information was received from a reliable informant and in his discretion does not require such disclosure.

(d)   When, in any such criminal proceeding, a party demands disclosure of the identity of the informant on the ground the informant is a material witness on the issue of guilt, the court shall conduct a hearing at which all parties may present evidence on the issue of disclosure. Such hearing shall be conducted outside the presence of the jury, if any. During the hearing, if the privilege provided for in Section 1041 is claimed by a person authorized to do so or if a person who is authorized to claim such privilege refuses to answer any question on the ground that the answer would tend to disclose the identity of the informant, the prosecuting attorney may request that the court hold an in camera hearing. If such a request is made, the court shall hold such a hearing outside the presence of the defendant and his counsel. At the in camera hearing, the prosecution may offer evidence which would tend to disclose or which discloses the identity of the informant to aid the court in its determination whether there is a reasonable possibility that nondisclosure might deprive the defendant of a fair trial. A reporter shall be present at the in camera hearing. Any transcription of the proceedings at the in camera hearing, as well as any physical evidence presented at the hearing, shall be ordered sealed by the court, and only a court may have access to its contents. The court shall not order disclosure, nor strike the testimony of the witness who invokes the privilege, nor dismiss the criminal proceeding, if the party offering the witness refuses to disclose the identity of the informant, unless, based upon the evidence presented at the hearing held in the presence of the defendant and his counsel and the evidence presented at the in camera hearing, the court concludes that there is a reasonable possibility that nondisclosure might deprive the defendant of a fair trial.

§ 1043. Peace or custodial officer personnel records; discovery or disclosure; procedure

(a) In any case in which discovery or disclosure is sought of peace officer personnel records or records maintained pursuant to Section 832.5 of the Penal Code or information from those records, the party seeking the discovery or disclosure shall file a written motion with the appropriate court or administrative body upon written notice to the governmental agency which has custody and control of the records. The written notice shall be given at the times prescribed by subdivision (b) of Section 1005 of the Code of Civil Procedure. Upon receipt of the notice the governmental agency served shall immediately notify the individual whose records are sought.

(b) The motion shall include all of the following:

(1) Identification of the proceeding in which discovery or disclosure is sought, the party seeking discovery or disclosure, the peace officer whose records are sought, the governmental agency which has custody and control of the records, and the time and place at which the motion for discovery or disclosure shall be heard.

(2) A description of the type of records or information sought.

(3) Affidavits showing good cause for the discovery or disclosure sought, setting forth the materiality thereof to the subject matter involved in the pending litigation and stating upon reasonable belief that the governmental agency identified has the records or information from the records.

(c) No hearing upon a motion for discovery or disclosure shall be held without full compliance with the notice provisions of this section except upon a showing by the moving party of good cause for noncompliance, or upon a waiver of the hearing by the governmental agency identified as having the records.

§ 1044. Medical or psychological history records; right of access

Nothing in this article shall be construed to affect the right of access to records of medical or psychological history where such access would otherwise be available under Section 996 or 1016.

§ 1045. Peace or custodial officers; access to records of complaints, investigation of complaints, or discipline imposed; relevancy; protective orders

(a)   Nothing in this article shall be construed to affect the right of access to records of complaints, or investigations of complaints, or discipline imposed as a result of such investigations, concerning an event or transaction in which the peace officer participated, or which he perceived, and pertaining to the manner in which he performed his duties, provided that such information is relevant to the subject matter involved in the pending litigation.

(b)   In determining relevance the court shall examine the information in chambers in conformity with Section 915, and shall exclude from disclosure:

(1)   Information consisting of complaints concerning conduct occurring more than five years before the event or transaction which is the subject of the litigation in aid of which discovery or disclosure is sought.

(2)   In any criminal proceeding the conclusions of any officer investigating a complaint filed pursuant to Section 832.5 of the Penal Code.

(3)   Facts sought to be disclosed which are so remote as to make disclosure of little or no practical benefit.

(c)   In determining relevance where the issue in litigation concerns the policies or pattern of conduct of the employing agency, the court shall consider whether the information sought may be obtained from order records maintained by the employing agency in the regular course of agency business which would not necessitate the disclosure of individual personnel records.

(d)   Upon motion seasonably made by the governmental agency which has custody or control of the records to be examined or by the officer whose records are sought, and upon good cause showing the necessity thereof, the court may make any order which justice requires to protect the officer or agency from unnecessary annoyance, embarrassment or oppression.

(e)   The court shall, in any case or proceeding permitting the disclosure or discovery of any peace officer records requested pursuant to Section 1043, order that the records disclosed or discovered may not be used for any purpose other than a court proceeding pursuant to applicable law.

§ 1046. Allegation of excessive force by peace or custodial officer; copy of police or crime report

In any case, otherwise authorized by law, in which the party seeking disclosure is alleging excessive force by a peace officer or custodial officer, as defined in Section 831.5 of the Penal Code, in connection with the arrest of that party, or for conduct alleged to have occurred within a jail facility, the motion shall include a copy of the police report setting forth the circumstances under which the party was stopped and arrested, or a copy of the crime report setting forth the circumstances under which the conduct is alleged to have occurred within a jail facility.

§ 1047. Records of peace or custodial officers; exemption from disclosure

Records of peace officers or custodial officers, as defined in Section 831.5 of the Penal Code, including supervisorial officers, who either were not present during the arrest or had no contact with the party seeking disclosure from the time of the arrest until the time of booking, or who were not present at the time the conduct is alleged to have occurred within a jail facility, shall not be subject to disclosure.

ARTICLE 10. POLITICAL VOTE

§ 1050. Privilege to protect secrecy of vote

If he claims the privilege, a person has a privilege to refuse to disclose the tenor of his vote at a public election where the voting is by secret ballot unless he voted illegally or he previously made an unprivileged disclosure of the tenor of his vote.

ARTICLE 11. TRADE SECRET

§ 1060. Privilege to protect trade secret

If he or his agent or employee claims the privilege, the owner of a trade secret has a privilege to refuse to disclose the secret, and to prevent another from disclosing it, if the allowance of the privilege will not tend to conceal fraud or otherwise work injustice.

§ 1061. Procedure for assertion of trade secret privilege

(a) For purposes of this section, and Sections 1062 and 1063:

(1) "Trade secret" means "trade secret," as defined in subdivision (d) of Section 3426.1 of the Civil Code, or paragraph (9) of subdivision (a) of Section 499c of the Penal Code.

(2) "Article" means "article," as defined in paragraph (2) of subdivision (a) of Section 499c of the Penal Code.

(b) In addition to Section 1062, the following procedure shall apply whenever the owner of a trade secret wishes to assert his or her trade secret privilege, as provided in Section 1060, during a criminal proceeding:

(1) The owner of the trade secret shall file a motion for a protective order, or the People may file the motion on the owner's behalf and with the owner's permission. The motion shall include an affidavit based upon personal knowledge listing the affiant's qualifications to give an opinion concerning the trade secret at issue, identifying, without revealing, the alleged trade secret and articles which disclose the secret, and presenting evidence that the secret qualifies as a trade secret under either subdivision (d) of Section 3426.1 of the Civil Code or paragraph (9) of subdivision (a) of Section 499c of the Penal Code. The motion and affidavit shall be served on all parties in the proceeding.

(2) Any party in the proceeding may oppose the request for the protective order by submitting affidavits based upon the affiant's personal knowledge. The affidavits shall be filed under seal, but shall be provided to the owner of the trade secret and to all parties in the proceeding. Neither the owner of the trade secret nor any party in the

proceeding may disclose the affidavit to persons other than to counsel of record without prior court approval.

(3)   The movant shall, by a preponderance of the evidence, show that the issuance of a protective order is proper. The court may rule on the request without holding an evidentiary hearing. However, in its discretion, the court may choose to hold an in camera evidentiary hearing concerning disputed articles with only the owner of the trade secret, the People's representative, the defendant, and defendant's counsel present. If the court holds such a hearing, the parties' right to examine witnesses shall not be used to obtain discovery, but shall be directed solely toward the question of whether the alleged trade secret qualifies for protection.

(4)   If the court finds that a trade secret may be disclosed during any criminal proceeding unless a protective order is issued and that the issuance of a protective order would not conceal a fraud or work an injustice, the court shall issue a protective order limiting the use and dissemination of the trade secret, including, but not limited to, articles disclosing that secret. The protective order may, in the court's discretion, include the following provisions:

(A)   That the trade secret may be disseminated only to counsel for the parties, including their associate attorneys, paralegals, and investigators, and to law enforcement officials or clerical officials.

(B)   That the defendant may view the secret only in the presence of his or her counsel, or if not in the presence of his or her counsel, at counsel's offices.

(C)   That any party seeking to show the trade secret, or articles containing the trade secret, to any person not designated by the protective order shall first obtain court approval to do so:

(i)   The court may require that the person receiving the trade secret do so only in the presence of counsel for the party requesting approval.

(ii)   The court may require the person receiving the trade secret to sign a copy of the protective order and to agree to be bound by its terms. The order may include a provision recognizing the owner of the trade secret to be a third-party beneficiary of that agreement.

(iii)   The court may require a party seeking disclosure to an expert to provide that expert's name, employment history, and any other relevant information to the court for examination. The court shall accept that information under seal, and the information shall not be disclosed by any court except upon termination of the action and upon a showing of good cause to believe the secret has been disseminated by a court-approved expert. The court shall evaluate the expert and determine whether the expert poses a discernible risk of disclosure. The court shall withhold approval if the expert's economic interests place the expert in a competitive position with the victim, unless no other experts are available. The court may interview the expert in camera in aid of its ruling. If the court rejects the expert, it shall state its reasons for doing so on the record and a transcript of those reasons shall be prepared and sealed.

(D) That no articles disclosing the trade secret shall be filed or otherwise made a part of the court record available to the public without approval of the court and prior notice to the owner of the secret. The owner of the secret may give either party permission to accept the notice on the owner's behalf.

(E) Other orders as the court deems necessary to protect the integrity of the trade secret.

(c) A ruling granting or denying a motion for a protective order filed pursuant to subdivision (b) shall not be construed as a determination that the alleged trade secret is or is not a trade secret as defined by subdivision (d) of Section 3426.1 of the Civil Code or paragraph (9) of subdivision (a) of Section 499c of the Penal Code. Such a ruling shall not have any effect on any civil litigation.

(d) This section shall have prospective effect only and shall not operate to invalidate previously entered protective orders.

§ 1062. Exclusion of public from criminal proceeding; motion; contents; hearing; determination

(a) Notwithstanding any other provision of law, in a criminal case, the court, upon motion of the owner of a trade secret, or upon motion by the People with the consent of the owner, may exclude the public from any portion of a criminal proceeding where the proponent of closure has demonstrated a substantial probability that the trade secret would otherwise be disclosed to the public during that proceeding and a substantial probability that the disclosure would cause serious harm to the owner of the secret, and where the court finds that there is no overriding public interest in an open proceeding. No evidence, however, shall be excluded during a criminal proceeding pursuant to this section if it would conceal a fraud, work an injustice, or deprive the People or the defendant of a fair trial.

(b) The motion made pursuant to subdivision (a) shall identify, without revealing, the trade secrets which would otherwise be disclosed to the public. A showing made pursuant to subdivision (a) shall be made during an in camera hearing with only the owner of the trade secret, the People's representative, the defendant, and defendant's counsel present. A court reporter shall be present during the hearing. Any transcription of the proceedings at the in camera hearing, as well as any articles presented at that hearing, shall be ordered sealed by the court and only a court may allow access to its contents upon a showing of good cause. The court, in ruling upon the motion made pursuant to subdivision (a), may consider testimony presented or affidavits filed in any proceeding held in that action.

(c) If, after the in camera hearing described in subdivision (b), the court determines that exclusion of trade secret information from the public is appropriate, the court shall close only that portion of the criminal proceeding necessary to prevent disclosure of the trade secret. Before granting the motion, however, the court shall find and state for the record that the moving party has met its burden pursuant to subdivision (b), and that the closure of that portion of the proceeding will not deprive the People or the defendant of a fair trial.

(d)   The owner of the trade secret, the People, or the defendant may seek relief from a ruling denying or granting closure by petitioning a higher court for extraordinary relief.

(e)   Whenever the court closes a portion of a criminal proceeding pursuant to this section, a transcript of that closed proceeding shall be made available to the public as soon as practicable. The court shall redact any information qualifying as a trade secret before making that transcript available.

(f)   The court, subject to Section 867 of the Penal Code, may allow witnesses who are bound by a protective order entered in the criminal proceeding protecting trade secrets, pursuant to Section 1061, to remain within the courtroom during the closed portion of the proceeding.

§ 1063. Sealing of articles protected by protective order; procedures

The following provisions shall govern requests to seal articles which are protected by a protective order entered pursuant to Evidence Code Section 1060 or 1061:

(a)   The People shall request sealing of articles reasonably expected to be filed or admitted into evidence as follows:

(1)   No less than 10 court days before trial, and no less than five court days before any other criminal proceeding, the People shall file with the court a list of all articles which the People reasonably expect to file with the court, or admit into evidence, under seal at that proceeding. That list shall be available to the public. The People may be relieved from providing timely notice upon showing that exigent circumstances prevent that notice.

(2)   The court shall not allow the listed articles to be filed, admitted into evidence, or in any way made a part of the court record otherwise open to the public before holding a hearing to consider any objections to the People's request to seal the articles. The court at that hearing shall allow those objecting to the sealing to state their objections.

(3)   After hearing any objections to sealing, the court shall conduct an in camera hearing with only the owner of the trade secret contained within those articles, the People's representative, defendant, and defendant's counsel present. The court shall review the articles sought to be sealed, evaluate objections to sealing, and determine whether the People have satisfied the constitutional standards governing public access to articles which are part of the judicial record. The court may consider testimony presented or affidavits filed in any proceeding held in that action. The People, defendant, and the owner of the trade secret may file affidavits based on the affiant's personal knowledge to be considered at that hearing. Those affidavits are to be sealed and not released to the public, but shall be made available to the parties. The court may rule on the request to seal without taking testimony. If the court takes testimony, examination of witnesses shall not be used to obtain discovery, but shall be directed solely toward whether sealing is appropriate.

(4)   If the court finds that the movant has satisfied appropriate constitutional standards with respect to sealing particular articles, the

court shall seal those articles if and when they are filed, admitted into evidence, or in any way made a part of the court record otherwise open to the public. The articles shall not be unsealed absent an order of a court upon a showing of good cause. Failure to examine the court file for notice of a request to seal shall not constitute good cause to consider objections to sealing.

(b)   The following procedure shall apply to other articles made a part of the court record:

(1)   Where any articles protected by a protective order entered pursuant to Section 1060 or 1061 are filed, admitted into evidence, or in any way made a part of the court record in such a way as to be otherwise open to the public, the People, a defendant, or the owner of a trade secret contained within those articles may request the court to seal those articles.

(2)   The request to seal shall be made by noticed motion filed with the court. It may also be made orally in court at the time the articles are made a part of the court record. Where the request is made orally, the movant must file within 24 hours a written description of that request, including a list of the articles which are the subject of that request. These motions and lists shall be available to the public.

(3)   The court shall promptly conduct hearings as provided in paragraphs (2), (3), and (4) of subdivision (a). The court shall, pending the hearings, seal those articles which are the subject of the request. Where a request to seal is made orally, the court may conduct hearings at the time the articles are made a part of the court record, but shall reconsider its ruling in light of additional objections made by objectors within two court days after the written record of the request to seal is made available to the public.

(4)   Any articles sealed pursuant to these hearings shall not be unsealed absent an order of a court upon a showing of good cause. Failure to examine the court file for notice of a request to seal shall not constitute good cause to consider objections to sealing.

CHAPTER 5. IMMUNITY OF NEWSMAN FROM CITATION FOR CONTEMPT

§ 1070. Refusal to disclose news source

(a)   A publisher, editor, reporter, or other person connected with or employed upon a newspaper, magazine, or other periodical publication, or by a press association or wire service, or any person who has been so connected or employed, cannot be adjudged in contempt by a judicial, legislative, administrative body, or any other body having the power to issue subpoenas, for refusing to disclose, in any proceeding as defined in Section 901, the source of any information procured while so connected or employed for publication in a newspaper, magazine or other periodical publication, or for refusing to disclose any unpublished information obtained or prepared in gathering, receiving or processing of information for communication to the public.

(b)   Nor can a radio or television news reporter or other person connected with or employed by a radio or television station, or any person who has been so connected or employed, be so adjudged in contempt for refusing to disclose the source of any information procured while so connected or employed for news or news commentary purposes on radio or television, or for refusing to disclose any unpublished information obtained or prepared in gathering, receiving or processing of information for communication to the public.

(c) As used in this section, "unpublished information" includes information not disseminated to the public by the person from whom disclosure is sought, whether or not related information has been disseminated and includes, but is not limited to, all notes, outtakes, photographs, tapes or other data of whatever sort not itself disseminated to the public through a medium of communication, whether or not published information based upon or related to such material has been disseminated.

DIVISION 9. EVIDENCE AFFECTED OR EXCLUDED BY EXTRINSIC POLICIES

CHAPTER 1. EVIDENCE OF CHARACTER, HABIT, OR CUSTOM

§ 1100. Manner of proof of character

Except as otherwise provided by statute, any otherwise admissible evidence (including evidence in the form of an opinion, evidence of reputation, and evidence of specific instances of such person's conduct) is admissible to prove a person's character or a trait of his character.

§ 1101. Evidence of character to prove conduct

(a)   Except as provided in this section and in Sections 1102, 1103, 1108, and 1109, evidence of a person's character or a trait of his or her character (whether in the form of an opinion, evidence of reputation, or evidence of specific instances of his or her conduct) is inadmissible when offered to prove his or her conduct on a specified occasion.

(b)   Nothing in this section prohibits the admission of evidence that a person committed a crime, civil wrong, or other act when relevant to prove some fact (such as motive, opportunity, intent, preparation, plan, knowledge, identity, absence of mistake or accident, or whether a defendant in a prosecution for an unlawful sexual act or attempted unlawful sexual act did not reasonably and in good faith believe that the victim consented) other than his or her disposition to commit such an act.

(c)   Nothing in this section affects the admissibility of evidence offered to support or attack the credibility of a witness.

§ 1102. Opinion and reputation evidence of character of criminal defendant to prove conduct

In a criminal action, evidence of the defendant's character or a trait of his character in the form of an opinion or evidence of his reputation is not made inadmissible by Section 1101 if such evidence is:

(a)   Offered by the defendant to prove his conduct in conformity with such character or trait of character.

(b)   Offered by the prosecution to rebut evidence adduced by the defendant under subdivision (a).

§ 1103. Character evidence of crime victim to prove conduct; evidence of defendant's character or trait for violence; evidence of manner of dress of victim; evidence of complaining witness' sexual conduct

(a)   In a criminal action, evidence of the character or a trait of character (in the form of an opinion, evidence of reputation, or evidence of specific instances of conduct) of the victim of the crime for which the defendant is being prosecuted is not made inadmissible by Section 1101 if the evidence is:

(1)   Offered by the defendant to prove conduct of the victim in conformity with the character or trait of character.

(2)   Offered by the prosecution to rebut evidence adduced by the defendant under paragraph (1).

(b) In a criminal action, evidence of the defendant's character for violence or trait of character for violence (in the form of an opinion, evidence of reputation, or evidence of specific instances of conduct) is not made inadmissible by Section 1101 if the evidence is offered by the prosecution to prove conduct of the defendant in conformity with the character or trait of character and is offered after evidence that the victim had a character for violence or a trait of character tending to show violence has been adduced by the defendant under paragraph (1) of subdivision (a).

(c)(1)   Notwithstanding any other provision of this code to the contrary, and except as provided in this subdivision, in any prosecution under Section 261, 262, or 264.1 of the Penal Code, or under Section 286, 287, or 289 of, or former Section 288a of, the Penal Code, or for assault with intent to commit, attempt to commit, or conspiracy to commit a crime defined in any of those sections, except where the crime is alleged to have occurred in a local detention facility, as defined in Section 6031.4, or in a state prison, as defined in Section 4504, opinion evidence, reputation evidence, and evidence of specific instances of the complaining witness' sexual conduct, or any of that evidence, is not admissible by the defendant in order to prove consent by the complaining witness.

(2) Notwithstanding paragraph (3), evidence of the manner in which the victim was dressed at the time of the commission of the offense shall not be admissible when offered by either party on the issue of consent in any prosecution for an offense specified in paragraph (1), unless the evidence is determined by the court to be relevant and admissible in the interests of justice. The proponent of the evidence shall make an offer of proof outside the hearing of the jury. The court shall then make its determination and at that time, state the reasons for its ruling on the record. For the purposes of this paragraph, "manner of dress" does not include the condition of the victim's clothing before, during, or after the commission of the offense.

(3) Paragraph (1) shall not be applicable to evidence of the complaining witness' sexual conduct with the defendant.

(4) If the prosecutor introduces evidence, including testimony of a witness, or the complaining witness as a witness gives testimony, and that evidence or testimony relates to the complaining witness' sexual conduct, the defendant may cross-examine the witness who gives the testimony and offer relevant evidence limited specifically to the rebuttal of the evidence introduced by the prosecutor or given by the complaining witness.

(5) Nothing in this subdivision shall be construed to make inadmissible any evidence offered to attack the credibility of the complaining witness as provided in Section 782.

(6) As used in this section, "complaining witness" means the alleged victim of the crime charged, the prosecution of which is subject to this subdivision.

§ 1104. Character trait for care or skill

Except as provided in Sections 1102 and 1103, evidence of a trait of a person's character with respect to care or skill is inadmissible to prove the quality of his conduct on a specified occasion.

§ 1105. Habit or custom to prove specific behavior

Any otherwise admissible evidence of habit or custom is admissible to prove conduct on a specified occasion in conformity with the habit or custom.

§ 1106. Sexual harassment, sexual assault, or sexual battery cases; opinion or reputation evidence of plaintiff's sexual conduct; inadmissibility; exception; cross-examination

(a) In any civil action alleging conduct which constitutes sexual harassment, sexual assault, or sexual battery, opinion evidence, reputation evidence, and evidence of specific instances of the plaintiff's sexual conduct, or any of such evidence, is not admissible by the defendant in order to prove consent by the plaintiff or the absence of injury to the plaintiff, unless the injury alleged by the plaintiff is in the nature of loss of consortium.

(b) Subdivision (a) does not apply to evidence of the plaintiff's sexual conduct with the alleged perpetrator.

(c) Notwithstanding subdivision (b), in any civil action brought pursuant to Section 1708.5 of the Civil Code involving a minor and adult as described in Section 1708.5.5 of the Civil Code, evidence of the plaintiff minor's sexual conduct with the defendant adult shall not be admissible to prove consent by the plaintiff or the absence of injury to the plaintiff. Such evidence of the plaintiff's sexual conduct may only be introduced to attack the credibility of the plaintiff in accordance with Section 783 or to prove something other than consent by the plaintiff if, upon a hearing of the court out of the presence of the jury, the defendant proves that the probative value of that evidence outweighs the prejudice to the plaintiff consistent with Section 352.

(d) If the plaintiff introduces evidence, including testimony of a witness, or the plaintiff as a witness gives testimony, and the evidence or testimony relates to the plaintiff's sexual conduct, the defendant may cross-examine the witness who gives the testimony and offer relevant evidence limited specifically to the rebuttal of the evidence introduced by the plaintiff or given by the plaintiff.

(e) This section shall not be construed to make inadmissible any evidence offered to attack the credibility of the plaintiff as provided in Section 783.

§ 1107. Intimate partner battering and its effects; expert testimony in criminal actions; sufficiency of foundation; abuse and domestic violence; applicability to Penal Code; impact on decisional law

(a) In a criminal action, expert testimony is admissible by either the prosecution or the defense regarding intimate partner battering and its effects, including the nature and effect of physical, emotional, or mental abuse on the beliefs, perceptions, or behavior of victims of domestic violence, except when offered against a criminal defendant to prove the occurrence of the act or acts of abuse which form the basis of the criminal charge.

(b) The foundation shall be sufficient for admission of this expert testimony if the proponent of the evidence establishes its relevancy and the proper qualifications of the expert witness. Expert opinion testimony on intimate partner battering and its effects shall not be considered a new scientific technique whose reliability is unproven.

(c)   For purposes of this section, "abuse" is defined in Section 6203 of the Family Code and "domestic violence" is defined in Section 6211 of the Family Code and may include acts defined in Section 242, subdivision (e) of Section 243, Sections 262, 273.5, 273.6, 422 or 653m of the Penal Code.

(d)   This section is intended as a rule of evidence only and no substantive change affecting the Penal Code is intended.

(e)   This section shall be known, and may be cited as, the Expert Witness Testimony on Intimate Partner Battering and its Effects Section of the Evidence Code.

(f)   The changes in this section that become effective on January 1, 2005, are not intended to impact any existing decisional law regarding this section, and that decisional law should apply equally to this section as it refers to "intimate partner battering and its effects" in place of "battered women's syndrome."

§ 1107.5. Expert testimony regarding effects of human trafficking on human trafficking victims; admissibility

(a)   In a criminal action, expert testimony is admissible by either the prosecution or the defense regarding the effects of human trafficking on human trafficking victims, including the nature and effect of physical, emotional, or mental abuse on the beliefs, perceptions, or behavior of human trafficking victims.

(b)   The foundation shall be sufficient for admission of this expert testimony if the proponent of the evidence establishes its relevancy and the proper qualifications of the expert witness.

(c)   For purposes of this section, "human trafficking victim" is defined as a victim of an offense described in Section 236.1 of the Penal Code.

(d)   This section is intended as a rule of evidence only and no substantive change affecting the Penal Code is intended.

§ 1108. Evidence of another sexual offense by defendant; disclosure; construction of section

(a)   In a criminal action in which the defendant is accused of a sexual offense, evidence of the defendant's commission of another sexual offense or offenses is not made inadmissible by Section 1101, if the evidence is not inadmissible pursuant to Section 352.

(b)   In an action in which evidence is to be offered under this section, the people shall disclose the evidence to the defendant, including statements of witnesses or a summary of the substance of any testimony that is expected to be offered in compliance with the requirements of Section 1054.7 of the Penal Code.

(c)   This section does not limit the admission or consideration of evidence under any other section of this code.

(d)   As used in this section, the following definitions shall apply:

(1)   "Sexual offense" means a crime under the law of a state or of the United States that involves any of the following:

(A)   Any conduct proscribed by subdivision (b) or (c) of Section 236.1, Section 243.4, 261, 261.5, 262, 264.1, 266c, 269, 286, 287, 288, 288.2, 288.5, or 289, or subdivision (b), (c), or (d) of Section

311.2 or Section 311.3, 311.4, 311.10, 311.11, 314, or 647.6 of, or former Section 288a of, the Penal Code.

(B)   Any conduct proscribed by Section 220 of the Penal Code, except assault with intent to commit mayhem.

(C)   Contact, without consent, between the genitals or anus of the defendant and any part of another person's body.

(D)   Deriving sexual pleasure or gratification from the infliction of death, bodily injury, or physical pain on another person.

(E)   An attempt or conspiracy to engage in conduct described in this paragraph.

(2)   "Consent" shall have the same meaning as provided in Section 261.6 of the Penal Code, except that it does not include consent which is legally ineffective because of the age, mental disorder, or developmental or physical disability of the victim.

§ 1109. Evidence of defendant's other acts of domestic violence

(a)(1)   Except as provided in subdivision (e) or (f), in a criminal action in which the defendant is accused of an offense involving domestic violence, evidence of the defendant's commission of other domestic violence is not made inadmissible by Section 1101 if the evidence is not inadmissible pursuant to Section 352.

(2)   Except as provided in subdivision (e) or (f), in a criminal action in which the defendant is accused of an offense involving abuse of an elder or dependent person, evidence of the defendant's commission of other abuse of an elder or dependent person is not made inadmissible by Section 1101 if the evidence is not inadmissible pursuant to Section 352.

(3)   Except as provided in subdivision (e) or (f) and subject to a hearing conducted pursuant to Section 352, which shall include consideration of any corroboration and remoteness in time, in a criminal action in which the defendant is accused of an offense involving child abuse, evidence of the defendant's commission of child abuse is not made inadmissible by Section 1101 if the evidence is not inadmissible pursuant to Section 352. Nothing in this paragraph prohibits or limits the admission of evidence pursuant to subdivision (b) of Section 1101.

(b)   In an action in which evidence is to be offered under this section, the people shall disclose the evidence to the defendant, including statements of witnesses or a summary of the substance of any testimony that is expected to be offered, in compliance with the provisions of Section 1054.7 of the Penal Code.

(c)   This section shall not be construed to limit or preclude the admission or consideration of evidence under any other statute or case law.

(d)   As used in this section:

(1)   "Abuse of an elder or dependent person" means physical or sexual abuse, neglect, financial abuse, abandonment, isolation, abduction, or other treatment that results in physical harm, pain, or mental suffering, the deprivation of care by a caregiver, or other deprivation by a custodian or provider of goods or services that are necessary to avoid physical harm or mental suffering.

(2) "Child abuse" means an act proscribed by Section 273d of the Penal Code.

(3) "Domestic violence" has the meaning set forth in Section 13700 of the Penal Code. Subject to a hearing conducted pursuant to Section 352, which shall include consideration of any corroboration and remoteness in time, "domestic violence" has the further meaning as set forth in Section 6211 of the Family Code, if the act occurred no more than five years before the charged offense.

(e) Evidence of acts occurring more than 10 years before the charged offense is inadmissible under this section, unless the court determines that the admission of this evidence is in the interest of justice.

(f) Evidence of the findings and determinations of administrative agencies regulating the conduct of health facilities licensed under Section 1250 of the Health and Safety Code is inadmissible under this section.

CHAPTER 2. MEDIATION

§ 1115. Definitions

For purposes of this chapter:

(a) "Mediation" means a process in which a neutral person or persons facilitate communication between the disputants to assist them in reaching a mutually acceptable agreement.

(b) "Mediator" means a neutral person who conducts a mediation. "Mediator" includes any person designated by a mediator either to assist in the mediation or to communicate with the participants in preparation for a mediation.

(c) "Mediation consultation" means a communication between a person and a mediator for the purpose of initiating, considering, or reconvening a mediation or retaining the mediator.

§ 1116. Effect of chapter

(a) Nothing in this chapter expands or limits a court's authority to order participation in a dispute resolution proceeding. Nothing in this chapter authorizes or affects the enforceability of a contract clause in which parties agree to the use of mediation.

(b) Nothing in this chapter makes admissible evidence that is inadmissible under Section 1152 or any other statute.

§ 1117. Application of chapter

(a) Except as provided in subdivision (b), this chapter applies to a mediation as defined in Section 1115.

(b) This chapter does not apply to either of the following:

(1) A proceeding under Part 1 (commencing with Section 1800) of Division 5 of the Family Code or Chapter 11 (commencing with Section 3160) of Part 2 of Division 8 of the Family Code.

(2) A settlement conference pursuant to Rule 3.1380 of the California Rules of Court.

§ 1118. Oral agreements

An oral agreement "in accordance with Section 1118" means an oral agreement that satisfies all of the following conditions:

(a)   The oral agreement is recorded by a court reporter or reliable means of audio recording.

(b)   The terms of the oral agreement are recited on the record in the presence of the parties and the mediator, and the parties express on the record that they agree to the terms recited.

(c)   The parties to the oral agreement expressly state on the record that the agreement is enforceable or binding, or words to that effect.

(d)   The recording is reduced to writing and the writing is signed by the parties within 72 hours after it is recorded.

§ 1119. Written or oral communications during mediation process; admissibility

Except as otherwise provided in this chapter:

(a)   No evidence of anything said or any admission made for the purpose of, in the course of, or pursuant to, a mediation or a mediation consultation is admissible or subject to discovery, and disclosure of the evidence shall not be compelled, in any arbitration, administrative adjudication, civil action, or other noncriminal proceeding in which, pursuant to law, testimony can be compelled to be given.

(b)   No writing, as defined in Section 250, that is prepared for the purpose of, in the course of, or pursuant to, a mediation or a mediation consultation, is admissible or subject to discovery, and disclosure of the writing shall not be compelled, in any arbitration, administrative adjudication, civil action, or other noncriminal proceeding in which, pursuant to law, testimony can be compelled to be given.

(c)   All communications, negotiations, or settlement discussions by and between participants in the course of a mediation or a mediation consultation shall remain confidential.

§ 1120. Evidence otherwise admissible

(a)   Evidence otherwise admissible or subject to discovery outside of a mediation or a mediation consultation shall not be or become inadmissible or protected from disclosure solely by reason of its introduction or use in a mediation or a mediation consultation.

(b)   This chapter does not limit any of the following:

(1)   The admissibility of an agreement to mediate a dispute.

(2)   The effect of an agreement not to take a default or an agreement to extend the time within which to act or refrain from acting in a pending civil action.

(3)   Disclosure of the mere fact that a mediator has served, is serving, will serve, or was contacted about serving as a mediator in a dispute.

(4)   The admissibility of declarations of disclosure required by Sections 2104 and 2105 of the Family Code, even if prepared for the

purpose of, in the course of, or pursuant to, a mediation or a mediation consultation.

§ 1121. Mediator's reports and findings

Neither a mediator nor anyone else may submit to a court or other adjudicative body, and a court or other adjudicative body may not consider, any report, assessment, evaluation, recommendation, or finding of any kind by the mediator concerning a mediation conducted by the mediator, other than a report that is mandated by court rule or other law and that states only whether an agreement was reached, unless all parties to the mediation expressly agree otherwise in writing, or orally in accordance with Section 1118.

§ 1122. Communications or writings; conditions to admissibility

(a) A communication or a writing, as defined in Section 250, that is made or prepared for the purpose of, or in the course of, or pursuant to, a mediation or a mediation consultation, is not made inadmissible, or protected from disclosure, by provisions of this chapter if any of the following conditions are satisfied:

(1) All persons who conduct or otherwise participate in the mediation expressly agree in writing, or orally in accordance with Section 1118, to disclosure of the communication, document, or writing.

(2) The communication, document, or writing was prepared by or on behalf of fewer than all the mediation participants, those participants expressly agree in writing, or orally in accordance with Section 1118, to its disclosure, and the communication, document, or writing does not disclose anything said or done or any admission made in the course of the mediation.

(3) The communication, document, or writing is related to an attorney's compliance with the requirements described in Section 1129 and does not disclose anything said or done or any admission made in the course of the mediation, in which case the communication, document, or writing may be used in an attorney disciplinary proceeding to determine whether the attorney has complied with Section 1129.

(b) For purposes of subdivision (a), if the neutral person who conducts a mediation expressly agrees to disclosure, that agreement also binds any other person described in subdivision (b) of Section 1115.

§ 1123. Written settlement agreements; conditions to admissibility

A written settlement agreement prepared in the course of, or pursuant to, a mediation, is not made inadmissible, or protected from disclosure, by provisions of this chapter if the agreement is signed by the settling parties and any of the following conditions are satisfied:

(a) The agreement provides that it is admissible or subject to disclosure, or words to that effect.

(b) The agreement provides that it is enforceable or binding or words to that effect.

(c) All parties to the agreement expressly agree in writing, or orally in accordance with Section 1118, to its disclosure.

(d)   The agreement is used to show fraud, duress, or illegality that is relevant to an issue in dispute.

§ 1124. Oral agreements; conditions to admissibility

An oral agreement made in the course of, or pursuant to, a mediation is not made inadmissible, or protected from disclosure, by the provisions of this chapter if any of the following conditions are satisfied:

(a)   The agreement is in accordance with Section 1118.

(b)   The agreement is in accordance with subdivisions (a), (b), and (d) of Section 1118, and all parties to the agreement expressly agree, in writing or orally in accordance with Section 1118, to disclosure of the agreement.

(c)   The agreement is in accordance with subdivisions (a), (b), and (d) of Section 1118, and the agreement is used to show fraud, duress, or illegality that is relevant to an issue in dispute.

§ 1125. End of mediation; satisfaction of conditions

(a)   For purposes of confidentiality under this chapter, a mediation ends when any one of the following conditions is satisfied:

(1)   The parties execute a written settlement agreement that fully resolves the dispute.

(2)   An oral agreement that fully resolves the dispute is reached in accordance with Section 1118.

(3)   The mediator provides the mediation participants with a writing signed by the mediator that states that the mediation is terminated, or words to that effect, which shall be consistent with Section 1121.

(4)   A party provides the mediator and the other mediation participants with a writing stating that the mediation is terminated, or words to that effect, which shall be consistent with Section 1121. In a mediation involving more than two parties, the mediation may continue as to the remaining parties or be terminated in accordance with this section.

(5)   For 10 calendar days, there is no communication between the mediator and any of the parties to the mediation relating to the dispute. The mediator and the parties may shorten or extend this time by agreement.

(b)   For purposes of confidentiality under this chapter, if a mediation partially resolves a dispute, mediation ends when either of the following conditions is satisfied:

(1)   The parties execute a written settlement agreement that partially resolves the dispute.

(2)   An oral agreement that partially resolves the dispute is reached in accordance with Section 1118.

(c)   This section does not preclude a party from ending a mediation without reaching an agreement. This section does not otherwise affect the extent to which a party may terminate a mediation.

§ 1126. Protections before and after mediation ends

Anything said, any admission made, or any writing that is inadmissible, protected from disclosure, and confidential under this chapter before a mediation ends, shall remain inadmissible, protected from disclosure, and confidential to the same extent after the mediation ends.

§ 1127. Attorney's fees and costs

If a person subpoenas or otherwise seeks to compel a mediator to testify or produce a writing, as defined in Section 250, and the court or other adjudicative body determines that the testimony or writing is inadmissible under this chapter, or protected from disclosure under this chapter, the court or adjudicative body making the determination shall award reasonable attorney's fees and costs to the mediator against the person seeking the testimony or writing.

§ 1128. Subsequent trials; references to mediation

Any reference to a mediation during any subsequent trial is an irregularity in the proceedings of the trial for the purposes of Section 657 of the Code of Civil Procedure. Any reference to a mediation during any other subsequent noncriminal proceeding is grounds for vacating or modifying the decision in that proceeding, in whole or in part, and granting a new or further hearing on all or part of the issues, if the reference materially affected the substantial rights of the party requesting relief.

§ 1129. Confidentiality restrictions; client disclosure and acknowledgment requirements; requirements for printed disclosure; form; effect of noncompliance

(a)   Except in the case of a class or representative action, an attorney representing a client participating in a mediation or a mediation consultation shall, as soon as reasonably possible before the client agrees to participate in the mediation or mediation consultation, provide that client with a printed disclosure containing the confidentiality restrictions described in Section 1119 and obtain a printed acknowledgment signed by that client stating that he or she has read and understands the confidentiality restrictions.

(b)   An attorney who is retained after an individual agrees to participate in the mediation or mediation consultation shall, as soon as reasonably possible after being retained, comply with the printed disclosure and acknowledgment requirements described in subdivision (a).

(c)   The printed disclosure required by subdivision (a) shall:

(1)   Be printed in the preferred language of the client in at least 12-point font.

(2)   Be printed on a single page that is not attached to any other document provided to the client.

(3)   Include the names of the attorney and the client and be signed and dated by the attorney and the client.

(d)   If the requirements in subdivision (c) are met, the following disclosure shall be deemed to comply with the requirements of subdivision (a):

Mediation Disclosure Notification and Acknowledgment

To promote communication in mediation, California law generally makes mediation a confidential process. California's mediation confidentiality laws are laid out in Sections 703.5 and 1115 to 1129, inclusive, of the Evidence Code. Those laws establish the confidentiality of mediation and limit the disclosure, admissibility, and a court's consideration of communications, writings, and conduct in connection with a mediation. In general, those laws mean the following:

- All communications, negotiations, or settlement offers in the course of a mediation must remain confidential.

- Statements made and writings prepared in connection with a mediation are not admissible or subject to discovery or compelled disclosure in noncriminal proceedings.

- A mediator's report, opinion, recommendation, or finding about what occurred in a mediation may not be submitted to or considered by a court or another adjudicative body.

- A mediator cannot testify in any subsequent civil proceeding about any communication or conduct occurring at, or in connection with, a mediation.

This means that all communications between you and your attorney made in preparation for a mediation, or during a mediation, are confidential and cannot be disclosed or used (except in extremely limited circumstances), even if you later decide to sue your attorney for malpractice because of something that happens during the mediation.

I, _____ [Name of Client], understand that, unless all participants agree otherwise, no oral or written communication made during a mediation, or in preparation for a mediation, including communications between me and my attorney, can be used as evidence in any subsequent noncriminal legal action including an action against my attorney for malpractice or an ethical violation.

NOTE: This disclosure and signed acknowledgment does not limit your attorney's potential liability to you for professional malpractice, or prevent you from (1) reporting any professional misconduct by your attorney to the State Bar of California or (2) cooperating with any disciplinary investigation or criminal prosecution of your attorney.

[Name of Client] _____ [Date signed] _____

[Name of Attorney] _____ [Date signed] _____

(e) Failure of an attorney to comply with this section is not a basis to set aside an agreement prepared in the course of, or pursuant to, a mediation.

CHAPTER 3. OTHER EVIDENCE AFFECTED OR EXCLUDED BY EXTRINSIC POLICIES

§ 1150. Evidence to test a verdict

(a) Upon an inquiry as to the validity of a verdict, any otherwise admissible evidence may be received as to statements made, or conduct, conditions, or events occurring, either within or without the jury room, of such a character as is likely to have influenced the verdict improperly. No evidence is admissible to show the effect of such statement, conduct, condition, or event upon a juror either in influencing him to assent to or dissent from the verdict or concerning the mental processes by which it was determined.

(b)   Nothing in this code affects the law relating to the competence of a juror to give evidence to impeach or support a verdict.

§ 1151. Subsequent remedial conduct

When, after the occurrence of an event, remedial or precautionary measures are taken, which, if taken previously, would have tended to make the event less likely to occur, evidence of such subsequent measures is inadmissible to prove negligence or culpable conduct in connection with the event.

§ 1152. Offers to compromise

(a)   Evidence that a person has, in compromise or from humanitarian motives, furnished or offered or promised to furnish money or any other thing, act, or service to another who has sustained or will sustain or claims that he or she has sustained or will sustain loss or damage, as well as any conduct or statements made in negotiation thereof, is inadmissible to prove his or her liability for the loss or damage or any part of it.

(b)   In the event that evidence of an offer to compromise is admitted in an action for breach of the covenant of good faith and fair dealing or violation of subdivision (h) of Section 790.03 of the Insurance Code, then at the request of the party against whom the evidence is admitted, or at the request of the party who made the offer to compromise that was admitted, evidence relating to any other offer or counteroffer to compromise the same or substantially the same claimed loss or damage shall also be admissible for the same purpose as the initial evidence regarding settlement. Other than as may be admitted in an action for breach of the covenant of good faith and fair dealing or violation of subdivision (h) of Section 790.03 of the Insurance Code, evidence of settlement offers shall not be admitted in a motion for a new trial, in any proceeding involving an additur or remittitur, or on appeal.

(c)   This section does not affect the admissibility of evidence of any of the following:

(1)   Partial satisfaction of an asserted claim or demand without questioning its validity when such evidence is offered to prove the validity of the claim.

(2)   A debtor's payment or promise to pay all or a part of his or her preexisting debt when such evidence is offered to prove the creation of a new duty on his or her part or a revival of his or her preexisting duty.

§ 1152.5. Repealed by Stats.1997, c. 772 (A.B.939), § 5

§ 1152.6. Repealed by Stats.1997, c. 772 (A.B.939), § 6

§ 1153. Offer to plead guilty or withdrawn plea of guilty by criminal defendant

Evidence of a plea of guilty, later withdrawn, or of an offer to plead guilty to the crime charged or to any other crime, made by the defendant in a criminal action is inadmissible in any action or in any proceeding of any nature, including proceedings before agencies, commissions, boards, and tribunals.

§ 1153.5. Offer for civil resolution of crimes against property

Evidence of an offer for civil resolution of a criminal matter pursuant to the provisions of Section 33 of the Code of Civil Procedure, or admissions made in the course of or negotiations for the offer shall not be admissible in any action.

§ 1154. Offer to discount a claim

Evidence that a person has accepted or offered or promised to accept a sum of money or any other thing, act, or service in satisfaction of a claim, as well as any conduct or statements made in negotiation thereof, is inadmissible to prove the invalidity of the claim or any part of it.

§ 1155. Liability insurance

Evidence that a person was, at the time a harm was suffered by another, insured wholly or partially against loss arising from liability for that harm is inadmissible to prove negligence or other wrongdoing.

§ 1156. Records of medical or dental study of in-hospital staff committee

(a)   In-hospital medical or medical-dental staff committees of a licensed hospital may engage in research and medical or dental study for the purpose of reducing morbidity or mortality, and may make findings and recommendations relating to such purpose. Except as provided in subdivision (b), the written records of interviews, reports, statements, or memoranda of such in-hospital medical or medical-dental staff committees relating to such medical or dental studies are subject to Title 4 (commencing with Section 2016.010) of Part 4 of the Code of Civil Procedure (relating to discovery proceedings) but, subject to subdivisions (c) and (d), shall not be admitted as evidence in any action or before any administrative body, agency, or person.

(b)   The disclosure, with or without the consent of the patient, of information concerning him to such in-hospital medical or medical-dental staff committee does not make unprivileged any information that would otherwise be privileged under Section 994 or 1014; but, notwithstanding Sections 994 and 1014, such information is subject to discovery under subdivision (a) except that the identity of any patient may not be discovered under subdivision (a) unless the patient consents to such disclosure.

(c)   This section does not affect the admissibility in evidence of the original medical or dental records of any patient.

(d)   This section does not exclude evidence which is relevant evidence in a criminal action.

§ 1156.1. Records of medical or psychiatric studies of quality assurance committees

(a)   A committee established in compliance with Sections 4070 and 5624 of the Welfare and Institutions Code may engage in research and medical or psychiatric study for the purpose of reducing morbidity or mortality, and may make findings and recommendations to the county and state relating to such purpose. Except as provided in subdivision (b), the written records of interviews, reports, statements, or memoranda of such committees relating to such medical or psychiatric studies are subject to Title 4 (commencing with Section 2016.010) of Part 4 of the Code of Civil Procedure but, subject to subdivisions (c) and (d), shall not be admitted as evidence in any action or before any administrative body, agency, or person.

(b) The disclosure, with or without the consent of the patient, of information concerning him or her to such committee does not make unprivileged any information that would otherwise be privileged under Section 994 or 1014. However, notwithstanding Sections 994 and 1014, such information is subject to discovery under subdivision (a) except that the identity of any patient may not be discovered under subdivision (a) unless the patient consents to such disclosure.

(c) This section does not affect the admissibility in evidence of the original medical or psychiatric records of any patient.

(d) This section does not exclude evidence which is relevant evidence in a criminal action.

§ 1157. Proceedings and records of organized committees having responsibility of evaluation and improvement of quality of care; exceptions

(a) Neither the proceedings nor the records of organized committees of medical, medical-dental, podiatric, registered dietitian, psychological, marriage and family therapist, licensed clinical social worker, professional clinical counselor or veterinary staffs in hospitals, or of a peer review body, as defined in Section 805 of the Business and Professions Code, having the responsibility of evaluation and improvement of the quality of care rendered in the hospital, or for that peer review body, or medical or dental review or dental hygienist review or chiropractic review or podiatric review or registered dietitian review or veterinary review or acupuncturist review or licensed midwife review committees of local medical, dental, dental hygienist, podiatric, dietetic, pharmacist, veterinary, acupuncture, or chiropractic societies, marriage and family therapist, licensed clinical social worker, professional clinical counselor, or psychological review committees of state or local marriage and family therapist, state or local licensed professional clinical counselor, or state or local psychological associations or societies or licensed midwife associations or societies having the responsibility of evaluation and improvement of the quality of care, shall be subject to discovery.

(b) Except as hereinafter provided, no person in attendance at a meeting of any of those committees shall be required to testify as to what transpired at that meeting.

(c) The prohibition relating to discovery or testimony does not apply to the statements made by any person in attendance at a meeting of any of those committees who is a party to an action or proceeding the subject matter of which was reviewed at that meeting, to any person requesting hospital staff privileges, or in any action against an insurance carrier alleging bad faith by the carrier in refusing to accept a settlement offer within the policy limits.

(d) The prohibitions in this section do not apply to medical, dental, dental hygienist, podiatric, dietetic, psychological, marriage and family therapist, licensed clinical social worker, professional clinical counselor, veterinary, acupuncture, midwifery, or chiropractic society committees that exceed 10 percent of the membership of the society, nor to any of those committees if a person serves upon the committee when his or her own conduct or practice is being reviewed.

(e) The amendments made to this section by Chapter 1081 of the Statutes of 1983, or at the 1985 portion of the 1985–86 Regular Session of the Legislature, at the 1990 portion of the 1989–90 Regular Session of the Legislature, at the 2000 portion of the 1999–2000 Regular Session of the Legislature, at the 2011 portion of the 2011–12 Regular Session of the Legislature, or at the 2015 portion of the 2015–16 Regular Session of the Legislature, do not exclude the discovery or use of relevant evidence in a criminal action.

§ 1157.5. Organized committee of nonprofit medical care foundation or professional standards review organization; proceedings and records

Except in actions involving a claim of a provider of health care services for payment for such services, the prohibition relating to discovery or testimony provided by Section 1157 shall be applicable to the proceedings or records of an organized committee of any nonprofit medical care foundation or professional standards review organization which is organized in a manner which makes available professional competence to review health care services with respect to medical necessity, quality of care, or economic justification of charges or level of care.

§ 1157.6. Proceedings and records of quality assurance committees for county health facilities

Neither the proceedings nor the records of a committee established in compliance with Sections 4070 and 5624 of the Welfare and Institutions Code having the responsibility of evaluation and improvement of the quality of mental health care rendered in county operated and contracted mental health facilities shall be subject to discovery. Except as provided in this section, no person in attendance at a meeting of any such committee shall be required to testify as to what transpired thereat. The prohibition relating to discovery or testimony shall not apply to the statements made by any person in attendance at such a meeting who is a party to an action or proceeding the subject matter of which was reviewed at such meeting, or to any person requesting facility staff privileges.

§ 1157.7. Application of Section 1157 discovery or testimony prohibitions; application of public records and meetings provisions

The prohibition relating to discovery or testimony provided in Section 1157 shall be applicable to proceedings and records of any committee established by a local governmental agency to monitor, evaluate, and report on the necessity, quality, and level of specialty health services, including, but not limited to, trauma care services, provided by a general acute care hospital which has been designated or recognized by that governmental agency as qualified to render specialty health care services. The provisions of Chapter 3.5 (commencing with Section 6250) of Division 7 of Title 1 of the Government Code and Chapter 9 (commencing with Section 54950) of Division 2 of Title 5 of the Government Code shall not be applicable to the committee records and proceedings.

§ 1158. Inspection and copying of patient's records; authorization; failure to comply; costs; authorization form

(a)   For purposes of this section, "medical provider" means physician and surgeon, dentist, registered nurse, dispensing optician, registered physical therapist, podiatrist, licensed psychologist, osteopathic physician and surgeon, chiropractor, clinical laboratory bioanalyst, clinical laboratory technologist, or pharmacist or pharmacy, duly licensed as such under the laws of the state, or a licensed hospital.

(b)   Before the filing of any action or the appearance of a defendant in an action, if an attorney at law or his or her representative presents a written authorization therefor signed by an adult patient, by the guardian or conservator of his or her person or estate, or, in the case of a minor, by a parent or guardian of the minor, or by the personal representative or an heir of a deceased patient, or a copy thereof, to a medical provider, the medical provider shall promptly make all of the patient's records under the medical provider's custody or control available for inspection and copying by the attorney at law or his or her representative.

(c)   Copying of medical records shall not be performed by a medical provider, or by an agent thereof, when the requesting attorney has employed a professional photocopier or anyone identified in Section 22451 of the Business and Professions Code as his or her representative to obtain or review the records on his or her behalf. The presentation of the authorization by the agent on behalf of the attorney shall be sufficient proof that the agent is the attorney's representative.

(d)   Failure to make the records available during business hours, within five days after the presentation of the written authorization, may subject the medical provider having custody or control of the records to liability for all reasonable expenses, including attorney's fees, incurred in any proceeding to enforce this section.

(e)(1)   All reasonable costs incurred by a medical provider in making patient records available pursuant to this section may be charged against the attorney who requested the records.

(2)   "Reasonable cost," as used in this section, shall include, but not be limited to, the following specific costs: ten cents ($0.10) per page for standard reproduction of documents of a size 8 ½ by 14 inches or less; twenty cents ($0.20) per page for copying of documents from microfilm; actual costs for the reproduction of oversize documents or the reproduction of documents requiring special processing which are made in response to an authorization; reasonable clerical costs incurred in locating and making the records available to be billed at the maximum rate of sixteen dollars ($16) per hour per person, computed on the basis of four dollars ($4) per quarter hour or fraction thereof; actual postage charges; and actual costs, if any, charged to the witness by a third person for the retrieval and return of records held by that third person.

(f)   If the records are delivered to the attorney or the attorney's representative for inspection or photocopying at the record custodian's place of business, the only fee for complying with the authorization shall not exceed fifteen dollars ($15), plus actual costs, if any, charged to the record custodian by a third person for retrieval and return of records held offsite by the third person.

(g)   If the records requested pursuant to subdivision (b) are maintained electronically and if the requesting party requests an electronic copy of such information, the medical provider shall provide the requested medical records in the electronic form and format requested by the requesting party, if it is readily producible in such form and format, or, if not, in a readable form and format as agreed to by the medical provider and the requesting party.

(h)   A medical provider shall accept a signed and completed authorization form for the disclosure of health information if both of the following conditions are satisfied:

(1)   The medical provider determines that the form is valid.

(2)   The form is printed in a typeface no smaller than 14-point type and is in substantially the following form:

AUTHORIZATION FOR DISCLOSURE OF HEALTH
INFORMATION PURSUANT TO EVIDENCE
CODE SECTION 1158

The undersigned authorizes the medical provider designated below to disclose specified medical records to a designated recipient. The medical provider shall not condition treatment, payment, enrollment, or eligibility for benefits on the submission of this authorization.

Medical provider:

Patient name:

Medical record number:

Date of birth:

Address:

Telephone number:

Email:

Recipient name:

Recipient address:

Recipient telephone number:

Recipient email:

Health information requested (check all that apply):

_____ Records dated from _____ to _____.

_____ Radiology records:

_____ images or films

reports _____ digital/CD, if available.

_____ Laboratory results dated _____.

_____ Laboratory results regarding specific test(s) only (specify):

_____ All records.

_____ Records related to a specific injury, treatment, or other purpose (specify):

Note: records may include information related to mental health, alcohol or drug use, and HIV or AIDS. However, treatment records from mental health and alcohol or drug departments and results of HIV tests will not be disclosed unless specifically requested (check all that apply):

_____ Mental health records.

_____ Alcohol or drug records.

_____ HIV test results.

Method of delivery of requested records:

_____ Mail

_____ Pick up

_____ Electronic delivery, recipient email:

This authorization is effective for one year from the date of the signature unless a different date is specified here:

This authorization may be revoked upon written request, but any revocation will not apply to information disclosed before receipt of the written request.

A copy of this authorization is as valid as the original. The undersigned has the right to receive a copy of this authorization.

Notice: Once the requested health information is disclosed, any disclosure of the information by the recipient may no longer be protected under the federal Health Insurance Portability and Accountability Act of 1996 (HIPAA).

Patient signature*:

Date:

Print name:

*If not signed by the patient, please indicate relationship to the patient (check one, if applicable):

_____ Parent or guardian of minor patient who could not have consented to health care.

_____ Guardian or conservator of an incompetent patient.

_____ Beneficiary or personal representative of deceased patient.

§ 1159. Animal experimentation in product liability actions

(a)　No evidence pertaining to live animal experimentation, including, but not limited to, injury, impact, or crash experimentation, shall be admissible in any product liability action involving a motor vehicle or vehicles.

(b)　This section shall apply to cases for which a trial has not actually commenced, as described in paragraph (6) of subdivision (a) of Section 581 of the Code of Civil Procedure, on January 1, 1993.

§ 1160. Admissibility of expressions of sympathy or benevolence; definitions

(a)　The portion of statements, writings, or benevolent gestures expressing sympathy or a general sense of benevolence relating to the pain, suffering, or death of a person involved in an accident and made to that person or to the family of that person shall be inadmissible as evidence of an admission of liability in a civil action. A statement of fault, however, which is part of, or in addition to, any of the above shall not be inadmissible pursuant to this section.

(b)　For purposes of this section:

(1)　"Accident" means an occurrence resulting in injury or death to one or more persons which is not the result of willful action by a party.

(2)　"Benevolent gestures" means actions which convey a sense of compassion or commiseration emanating from humane impulses.

(3)　"Family" means the spouse, parent, grandparent, stepmother, stepfather, child, grandchild, brother, sister, half brother, half sister, adopted children of parent, or spouse's parents of an injured party.

§ 1161. Human trafficking; admissibility of evidence of engagement in commercial sexual act by victim or sexual history of victim

(a)　Evidence that a victim of human trafficking, as defined in Section 236.1 of the Penal Code, has engaged in any commercial sexual act as a result of being a victim of human trafficking is inadmissible to prove the victim's criminal liability for the commercial sexual act.

(b)　Evidence of sexual history or history of any commercial sexual act of a victim of human trafficking, as defined in Section 236.1 of the Penal Code, is inadmissible to attack the credibility or impeach the character of the victim in any civil or criminal proceeding.

§ 1162. Evidence that victim or witness to extortion, stalking, or violent felony was engaged in act of prostitution; inadmissibility in separate prostitution prosecution

Evidence that a victim of, or a witness to, extortion as defined in Section 519 of the Penal Code, stalking as defined in Section 646.9 of the Penal Code, or a violent felony as defined in Section 667.5 of the Penal Code, has engaged in an act of prostitution at or around the time he or she was the victim of or witness to the crime is inadmissible in a separate prosecution of that victim or witness to prove his or her criminal liability for the act of prostitution.

DIVISION 10. HEARSAY EVIDENCE

CHAPTER 1. GENERAL PROVISIONS

§ 1200. The hearsay rule

(a) "Hearsay evidence" is evidence of a statement that was made other than by a witness while testifying at the hearing and that is offered to prove the truth of the matter stated.

(b) Except as provided by law, hearsay evidence is inadmissible.

(c) This section shall be known and may be cited as the hearsay rule.

§ 1201. Multiple hearsay

A statement within the scope of an exception to the hearsay rule is not inadmissible on the ground that the evidence of such statement is hearsay evidence if such hearsay evidence consists of one or more statements each of which meets the requirements of an exception to the hearsay rule.

§ 1202. Credibility of hearsay declarant

Evidence of a statement or other conduct by a declarant that is inconsistent with a statement by such declarant received in evidence as hearsay evidence is not inadmissible for the purpose of attacking the credibility of the declarant though he is not given and has not had an opportunity to explain or to deny such inconsistent statement or other conduct. Any other evidence offered to attack or support the credibility of the declarant is admissible if it would have been admissible had the declarant been a witness at the hearing. For the purposes of this section, the deponent of a deposition taken in the action in which it is offered shall be deemed to be a hearsay declarant.

§ 1203. Cross-examination of hearsay declarant

(a) The declarant of a statement that is admitted as hearsay evidence may be called and examined by any adverse party as if under cross-examination concerning the statement.

(b) This section is not applicable if the declarant is (1) a party, (2) a person identified with a party within the meaning of subdivision (d) of Section 776, or (3) a witness who has testified in the action concerning the subject matter of the statement.

(c) This section is not applicable if the statement is one described in Article 1 (commencing with Section 1220), Article 3 (commencing with Section 1235), or Article 10 (commencing with Section 1300) of Chapter 2 of this division.

(d) A statement that is otherwise admissible as hearsay evidence is not made inadmissible by this section because the declarant who made the statement is unavailable for examination pursuant to this section.

§ 1203.1. Hearsay offered at preliminary examination; in application of § 1203

Section 1203 is not applicable if the hearsay statement is offered at a preliminary examination, as provided in Section 872 of the Penal Code.

§ 1204. Hearsay statement offered against criminal defendant

A statement that is otherwise admissible as hearsay evidence is inadmissible against the defendant in a criminal action if the statement was made, either by the defendant or by another, under such circumstances that it is inadmissible against the defendant under the Constitution of the United States or the State of California.

§ 1205. No implied repeal

Nothing in this division shall be construed to repeal by implication any other statute relating to hearsay evidence.

CHAPTER 2. EXCEPTIONS TO THE HEARSAY RULE

ARTICLE 1. CONFESSIONS AND ADMISSIONS

§ 1220. Admission of party

Evidence of a statement is not made inadmissible by the hearsay rule when offered against the declarant in an action to which he is a party in either his individual or representative capacity, regardless of whether the statement was made in his individual or representative capacity.

§ 1221. Adoptive admission

Evidence of a statement offered against a party is not made inadmissible by the hearsay rule if the statement is one of which the party, with knowledge of the content thereof, has by words or other conduct manifested his adoption or his belief in its truth.

§ 1222. Authorized admission

Evidence of a statement offered against a party is not made inadmissible by the hearsay rule if:

(a) The statement was made by a person authorized by the party to make a statement or statements for him concerning the subject matter of the statement; and

(b) The evidence is offered either after admission of evidence sufficient to sustain a finding of such authority or, in the court's discretion as to the order of proof, subject to the admission of such evidence.

§ 1223. Admission of co-conspirator

Evidence of a statement offered against a party is not made inadmissible by the hearsay rule if:

(a) The statement was made by the declarant while participating in a conspiracy to commit a crime or civil wrong and in furtherance of the objective of that conspiracy;

(b) The statement was made prior to or during the time that the party was participating in that conspiracy; and

(c) The evidence is offered either after admission of evidence sufficient to sustain a finding of the facts specified in subdivisions (a) and (b) or, in the court's discretion as to the order of proof, subject to the admission of such evidence.

§ 1224. Statement of declarant whose liability or breach of duty is in issue

When the liability, obligation, or duty of a party to a civil action is based in whole or in part upon the liability, obligation, or duty of the declarant, or when the claim or right asserted by a party to a civil action is barred or diminished by a breach of duty by the declarant, evidence of a statement made by the declarant is as admissible against the party as it would be if offered against the declarant in an action involving that liability, obligation, duty, or breach of duty.

§ 1225. Statement of declarant whose right or title is in issue

When a right, title, or interest in any property or claim asserted by a party to a civil action requires a determination that a right, title, or interest exists or existed in the declarant, evidence of a statement made by the declarant during the time the party now claims the declarant was the holder of the right, title, or interest is as admissible against the party as it would be if offered against the declarant in an action involving that right, title, or interest.

§ 1226. Statement of minor child in parent's action for child's injury

Evidence of a statement by a minor child is not made inadmissible by the hearsay rule if offered against the plaintiff in an action brought under Section 376 of the Code of Civil Procedure for injury to such minor child.

§ 1227. Statement of declarant in action for his wrongful death

Evidence of a statement by the deceased is not made inadmissible by the hearsay rule if offered against the plaintiff in an action for wrongful death brought under Section 377 of the Code of Civil Procedure.

§ 1228. Admissibility of certain out-of-court statements of minors under the age of 12; establishing elements of certain sexually oriented crimes; notice to defendant

Notwithstanding any other provision of law, for the purpose of establishing the elements of the crime in order to admit as evidence the confession of a person accused of violating Section 261, 264.1, 285, 286, 287, 288, 289, or 647a of, or former Section 288a of, the Penal Code, a court, in its discretion, may determine that a statement of the complaining witness is not made inadmissible by the hearsay rule if it finds all of the following:

(a) The statement was made by a minor child under the age of 12, and the contents of the statement were included in a written report of a law enforcement official or an employee of a county welfare department.

(b) The statement describes the minor child as a victim of sexual abuse.

(c) The statement was made prior to the defendant's confession. The court shall view with caution the testimony of a person recounting hearsay where there is evidence of personal bias or prejudice.

(d) There are no circumstances, such as significant inconsistencies between the confession and the statement concerning material facts establishing any element of the crime or the identification of the defendant, that would render the statement unreliable.

(e)   The minor child is found to be unavailable pursuant to paragraph (2) or (3) of subdivision (a) of Section 240 or refuses to testify.

(f)   The confession was memorialized in a trustworthy fashion by a law enforcement official.

If the prosecution intends to offer a statement of the complaining witness pursuant to this section, the prosecution shall serve a written notice upon the defendant at least 10 days prior to the hearing or trial at which the prosecution intends to offer the statement.

If the statement is offered during trial, the court's determination shall be made out of the presence of the jury. If the statement is found to be admissible pursuant to this section, it shall be admitted out of the presence of the jury and solely for the purpose of determining the admissibility of the confession of the defendant.

§ 1228.1. Signature of parent or guardian on child welfare services case plan; acceptance of services; use in court of law; failure to cooperate

(a)   Except as provided in subdivision (b), neither the signature of any parent or legal guardian on a child welfare services case plan nor the acceptance of any services prescribed in the child welfare services case plan by any parent or legal guardian shall constitute an admission of guilt or be used as evidence against the parent or legal guardian in a court of law.

(b)   A parent's or guardian's failure to cooperate, except for good cause, in the provision of services specified in the child welfare services case plan may be used as evidence, if relevant, in any hearing held pursuant to Sections * * * 366.21, 366.22, or 388 of the Welfare and Institutions Code * * * and at any jurisdictional or dispositional hearing held on a petition filed pursuant to Section 300, 342, or 387 of the Welfare and Institutions Code.

ARTICLE 2. DECLARATIONS AGAINST INTEREST

§ 1230. Declarations against interest

Evidence of a statement by a declarant having sufficient knowledge of the subject is not made inadmissible by the hearsay rule if the declarant is unavailable as a witness and the statement, when made, was so far contrary to the declarant's pecuniary or proprietary interest, or so far subjected him to the risk of civil or criminal liability, or so far tended to render invalid a claim by him against another, or created such a risk of making him an object of hatred, ridicule, or social disgrace in the community, that a reasonable man in his position would not have made the statement unless he believed it to be true.

ARTICLE 2.5. SWORN STATEMENTS
REGARDING GANG-RELATED CRIMES

§ 1231. Prior statements of deceased declarant; hearsay exception

Evidence of a prior statement made by a declarant is not made inadmissible by the hearsay rule if the declarant is deceased and the proponent of introducing the statement establishes each of the following:

(a) The statement relates to acts or events relevant to a criminal prosecution under provisions of the California Street Terrorism Enforcement and Prevention Act (Chapter 11 (commencing with Section 186.20) of Title 7 of Part 1 of the Penal Code).

(b) A verbatim transcript, copy, or record of the statement exists. A record may include a statement preserved by means of an audio or video recording or equivalent technology.

(c) The statement relates to acts or events within the personal knowledge of the declarant.

(d) The statement was made under oath or affirmation in an affidavit; or was made at a deposition, preliminary hearing, grand jury hearing, or other proceeding in compliance with law, and was made under penalty of perjury.

(e) The declarant died from other than natural causes.

(f) The statement was made under circumstances that would indicate its trustworthiness and render the declarant's statement particularly worthy of belief. For purposes of this subdivision, circumstances relevant to the issue of trustworthiness include, but are not limited to, all of the following:

(1) Whether the statement was made in contemplation of a pending or anticipated criminal or civil matter, in which the declarant had an interest, other than as a witness.

(2) Whether the declarant had a bias or motive for fabricating the statement, and the extent of any bias or motive.

(3) Whether the statement is corroborated by evidence other than statements that are admissible only pursuant to this section.

Whether the statement was a statement against the declarant's interest.

§ 1231.1. Statements made by deceased declarant; admissibility; notice of statement to adverse party

A statement is admissible pursuant to Section 1231 only if the proponent of the statement makes known to the adverse party the intention to offer the statement and the particulars of the statement sufficiently in advance of the proceedings to provide the adverse party with a fair opportunity to prepare to meet the statement.

§ 1231.2. Administer and certify oaths

A peace officer may administer and certify oaths for purposes of this article.

§ 1231.3. Testimony of law enforcement officer; hearsay

Any law enforcement officer testifying as to any hearsay statement pursuant to this article shall either have five years of law enforcement experience or have completed a training course certified by the Commission on Peace Officer Standards and Training which includes training in the investigation and reporting of cases and testifying at preliminary hearings and trials.

§ 1231.4. Cause of death; deceased declarant

If evidence of a prior statement is introduced pursuant to this article, the jury may not be told that the declarant died from other than natural causes, but shall merely be told that the declarant is unavailable.

ARTICLE 3. PRIOR STATEMENTS OF WITNESSES

§ 1235. Inconsistent statement

Evidence of a statement made by a witness is not made inadmissible by the hearsay rule if the statement is inconsistent with his testimony at the hearing and is offered in compliance with Section 770.

§ 1236. Prior consistent statement

Evidence of a statement previously made by a witness is not made inadmissible by the hearsay rule if the statement is consistent with his testimony at the hearing and is offered in compliance with Section 791.

§ 1237. Past recollection recorded

(a) Evidence of a statement previously made by a witness is not made inadmissible by the hearsay rule if the statement would have been admissible if made by him while testifying, the statement concerns a matter as to which the witness has insufficient present recollection to enable him to testify fully and accurately, and the statement is contained in a writing which:

(1) Was made at a time when the fact recorded in the writing actually occurred or was fresh in the witness' memory;

(2) Was made (i) by the witness himself or under his direction or (ii) by some other person for the purpose of recording the witness' statement at the time it was made;

(3) Is offered after the witness testifies that the statement he made was a true statement of such fact; and

(4) Is offered after the writing is authenticated as an accurate record of the statement.

(b) The writing may be read into evidence, but the writing itself may not be received in evidence unless offered by an adverse party.

§ 1238. Prior identification

Evidence of a statement previously made by a witness is not made inadmissible by the hearsay rule if the statement would have been admissible if made by him while testifying and:

(a) The statement is an identification of a party or another as a person who participated in a crime or other occurrence;

(b)   The statement was made at a time when the crime or other occurrence was fresh in the witness' memory; and

(c)   The evidence of the statement is offered after the witness testifies that he made the identification and that it was a true reflection of his opinion at that time.

ARTICLE 4. SPONTANEOUS, CONTEMPORANEOUS, AND DYING DECLARATIONS

§ 1240. Spontaneous statement

Evidence of a statement is not made inadmissible by the hearsay rule if the statement:

(a)   Purports to narrate, describe, or explain an act, condition, or event perceived by the declarant; and

(b)   Was made spontaneously while the declarant was under the stress of excitement caused by such perception.

§ 1241. Contemporaneous statement

Evidence of a statement is not made inadmissible by the hearsay rule if the statement:

(a)   Is offered to explain, qualify, or make understandable conduct of the declarant; and

(b)   Was made while the declarant was engaged in such conduct.

§ 1242. Dying declaration

Evidence of a statement made by a dying person respecting the cause and circumstances of his death is not made inadmissible by the hearsay rule if the statement was made upon his personal knowledge and under a sense of immediately impending death.

ARTICLE 5. STATEMENTS OF MENTAL OR PHYSICAL STATE

§ 1250. Statement of declarant's then existing mental or physical state

(a)   Subject to Section 1252, evidence of a statement of the declarant's then existing state of mind, emotion, or physical sensation (including a statement of intent, plan, motive, design, mental feeling, pain, or bodily health) is not made inadmissible by the hearsay rule when:

(1)   The evidence is offered to prove the declarant's state of mind, emotion, or physical sensation at that time or at any other time when it is itself an issue in the action; or

(2)   The evidence is offered to prove or explain acts or conduct of the declarant.

(b)   This section does not make admissible evidence of a statement of memory or belief to prove the fact remembered or believed.

§ 1251. Statement of declarant's previously existing mental or physical state

Subject to Section 1252, evidence of a statement of the declarant's state of mind, emotion, or physical sensation (including a statement of intent, plan, motive, design, mental feeling, pain, or bodily health) at a time prior to the statement is not made inadmissible by the hearsay rule if:

(a)   The declarant is unavailable as a witness; and

(b)   The evidence is offered to prove such prior state of mind, emotion, or physical sensation when it is itself an issue in the action and the evidence is not offered to prove any fact other than such state of mind, emotion, or physical sensation.

§ 1252. Restriction on admissibility of statement of mental or physical state

Evidence of a statement is inadmissible under this article if the statement was made under circumstances such as to indicate its lack of trustworthiness.

§ 1253. Statements for purposes of medical diagnosis or treatment; contents of statement; child abuse or neglect; age limitations

Subject to Section 1252, evidence of a statement is not made inadmissible by the hearsay rule if the statement was made for purposes of medical diagnosis or treatment and describes medical history, or past or present symptoms, pain, or sensations, or the inception or general character of the cause or external source thereof insofar as reasonably pertinent to diagnosis or treatment. This section applies only to a statement made by a victim who is a minor at the time of the proceedings, provided the statement was made when the victim was under the age of 12 describing any act, or attempted act, of child abuse or neglect. "Child abuse" and "child neglect," for purposes of this section, have the meanings provided in subdivision (c) of Section 1360. In addition, "child abuse" means any act proscribed by Chapter 5 (commencing with Section 281) of Title 9 of Part 1 of the Penal Code committed against a minor.

ARTICLE 6. STATEMENTS RELATING TO WILLS AND TO CLAIMS AGAINST ESTATES

§ 1260. Statement concerning declarant's will or revocable trust

(a)   Except as provided in subdivision (b), evidence of any of the following statements made by a declarant who is unavailable as a witness is not made inadmissible by the hearsay rule:

(1)   That the declarant has or has not made a will or established or amended a revocable trust.

(2)   That the declarant has or has not revoked his or her will, revocable trust, or an amendment to a revocable trust.

(3)   That identifies the declarant's will, revocable trust, or an amendment to a revocable trust.

(b)   Evidence of a statement is inadmissible under this section if the statement was made under circumstances that indicate its lack of trustworthiness.

§ 1261. Statement of decedent offered in action against his estate

(a)   Evidence of a statement is not made inadmissible by the hearsay rule when offered in an action upon a claim or demand against the estate of the declarant if the statement was made upon the personal knowledge of the declarant at a time when the matter had been recently perceived by him and while his recollection was clear.

(b)   Evidence of a statement is inadmissible under this section if the statement was made under circumstances such as to indicate its lack of trustworthiness.

ARTICLE 7. BUSINESS RECORDS

§ 1270. A business

As used in this article, "a business" includes every kind of business, governmental activity, profession, occupation, calling, or operation of institutions, whether carried on for profit or not.

§ 1271. Admissible writings

Evidence of a writing made as a record of an act, condition, or event is not made inadmissible by the hearsay rule when offered to prove the act, condition, or event if:

(a)   The writing was made in the regular course of a business;

(b)   The writing was made at or near the time of the act, condition, or event;

(c)   The custodian or other qualified witness testifies to its identity and the mode of its preparation; and

(d)   The sources of information and method and time of preparation were such as to indicate its trustworthiness.

§ 1272. Absence of entry in business records

Evidence of the absence from the records of a business of a record of an asserted act, condition, or event is not made inadmissible by the hearsay rule when offered to prove the nonoccurrence of the act or event, or the nonexistence of the condition, if:

(a)   It was the regular course of that business to make records of all such acts, conditions, or events at or near the time of the act, condition, or event and to preserve them; and

(b)   The sources of information and method and time of preparation of the records of that business were such that the absence of a record of an act, condition, or event is a trustworthy indication that the act or event did not occur or the condition did not exist.

ARTICLE 8. OFFICIAL RECORDS AND OTHER OFFICIAL WRITINGS

§ 1280. Record by public employee

Evidence of a writing made as a record of an act, condition, or event is not made inadmissible by the hearsay rule when offered in any civil or criminal proceeding to prove the act, condition, or event if all of the following applies:

(a)   The writing was made by and within the scope of duty of a public employee.

(b)   The writing was made at or near the time of the act, condition, or event.

(c)   The sources of information and method and time of preparation were such as to indicate its trustworthiness.

§ 1281. Vital statistics record

Evidence of a writing made as a record of a birth, fetal death, or marriage is not made inadmissible by the hearsay rule if the maker was required by law to file the writing in a designated public office and the writing was made and filed as required by law.

§ 1282. Finding of presumed death by authorized federal employee

A written finding of presumed death made by an employee of the United States authorized to make such finding pursuant to the Federal Missing Persons Act (56 Stats. 143, 1092, and P.L. 408, Ch. 371, 2d Sess. 78th Cong.; 59 U.S.C. App. 1001–1016), as enacted or as heretofore or hereafter amended, shall be received in any court, office, or other place in this state as evidence of the death of the person therein found to be dead and of the date, circumstances, and place of his disappearance.

§ 1283. Record by federal employee that person is missing, captured, beleaguered, beseiged, detained, or dead

An official written report or record that a person is missing, missing in action, interned in a foreign country, captured by a hostile force, beleaguered by a hostile force, besieged by a hostile force, or detained in a foreign country against his will, or is dead or is alive, made by an employee of the United States authorized by any law of the United States to make such report or record shall be received in any court, office, or other place in this state as evidence that such person is missing, missing in action, interned in a foreign country, captured by a hostile force, beleaguered by a hostile force, besieged by a hostile force, or detained in a foreign country against his will, or is dead or is alive.

§ 1284. Statement of absence of public record

Evidence of a writing made by the public employee who is the official custodian of the records in a public office, reciting diligent search and failure to find a record, is not made inadmissible by the hearsay rule when offered to prove the absence of a record in that office.

ARTICLE 9. FORMER TESTIMONY

§ 1290. Former testimony

As used in this article, "former testimony" means testimony given under oath in:

(a)   Another action or in a former hearing or trial of the same action;

(b)   A proceeding to determine a controversy conducted by or under the supervision of an agency that has the power to determine such a controversy and is an agency of the United States or a public entity in the United States;

(c)   A deposition taken in compliance with law in another action; or

(d)   An arbitration proceeding if the evidence of such former testimony is a verbatim transcript thereof.

§ 1291. Former testimony offered against party to former proceeding

(a)   Evidence of former testimony is not made inadmissible by the hearsay rule if the declarant is unavailable as a witness and:

(1)   The former testimony is offered against a person who offered it in evidence in his own behalf on the former occasion or against the successor in interest of such person; or

(2)   The party against whom the former testimony is offered was a party to the action or proceeding in which the testimony was given and had the right and opportunity to cross-examine the declarant with an interest and motive similar to that which he has at the hearing.

(b)   The admissibility of former testimony under this section is subject to the same limitations and objections as though the declarant were testifying at the hearing, except that former testimony offered under this section is not subject to:

(1)   Objections to the form of the question which were not made at the time the former testimony was given.

(2)   Objections based on competency or privilege which did not exist at the time the former testimony was given.

§ 1292. Former testimony offered against person not a party to former proceeding

(a)   Evidence of former testimony is not made inadmissible by the hearsay rule if:

(1)   The declarant is unavailable as a witness;

(2)   The former testimony is offered in a civil action; and

(3)   The issue is such that the party to the action or proceeding in which the former testimony was given had the right and opportunity to cross-examine the declarant with an interest and motive similar to that which the party against whom the testimony is offered has at the hearing.

(b)   The admissibility of former testimony under this section is subject to the same limitations and objections as though the declarant were testifying at the hearing, except that former testimony offered under this section is not subject to objections based on competency or privilege which did not exist at the time the former testimony was given.

§ 1293. Former testimony by minor child complaining witness at preliminary examination

(a)   Evidence of former testimony made at a preliminary examination by a minor child who was the complaining witness is not made inadmissible by the hearsay rule if:

(1)   The former testimony is offered in a proceeding to declare the minor a dependent child of the court pursuant to Section 300 of the Welfare and Institutions Code.

(2)   The issues are such that a defendant in the preliminary examination in which the former testimony was given had the right and opportunity to cross-examine the minor child with an interest and motive similar to that which the parent or guardian against whom the testimony is offered has at the proceeding to declare the minor a dependent child of the court.

(b)   The admissibility of former testimony under this section is subject to the same limitations and objections as though the minor child were testifying at the proceeding to declare him or her a dependent child of the court.

(c)   The attorney for the parent or guardian against whom the former testimony is offered or, if none, the parent or guardian may make a motion to challenge the admissibility of the former testimony upon a showing that new substantially different issues are present in the proceeding to declare the minor a dependent child than were present in the preliminary examination.

(d)   As used in this section, "complaining witness" means the alleged victim of the crime for which a preliminary examination was held.

(e)   This section shall apply only to testimony made at a preliminary examination on and after January 1, 1990.

§ 1294. Prior inconsistent statements of unavailable witnesses properly admitted in conditional examination, preliminary hearing, or prior proceeding

(a)   The following evidence of prior inconsistent statements of a witness properly admitted in a conditional examination, preliminary hearing, or trial of the same criminal matter pursuant to Section 1235 is not made inadmissible by the hearsay rule if the witness is unavailable and former testimony of the witness is admitted pursuant to Section 1291:

(1)   A video or audio recorded statement introduced at a conditional examination, preliminary hearing, or prior proceeding concerning the same criminal matter.

(2)   A transcript, containing the statements, of the conditional examination, preliminary hearing, or prior proceeding concerning the same criminal matter.

(b)   The party against whom the prior inconsistent statements are offered, at his or her option, may examine or cross-examine any person who testified at the conditional examination, preliminary hearing, or prior proceeding, as to the prior inconsistent statements of the witness.

(c) As used in this section, "conditional examination" has the same meaning as in Chapter 4 (commencing with Section 1335) of Title 10 of Part 2 of the Penal Code.

ARTICLE 10. JUDGMENTS

§ 1300. Judgment of conviction of crime punishable as felony

Evidence of a final judgment adjudging a person guilty of a crime punishable as a felony is not made inadmissible by the hearsay rule when offered in a civil action to prove any fact essential to the judgment whether or not the judgment was based on a plea of nolo contendere.

§ 1301. Judgment against person entitled to indemnity

Evidence of a final judgment is not made inadmissible by the hearsay rule when offered by the judgment debtor to prove any fact which was essential to the judgment in an action in which he seeks to:

(a) Recover partial or total indemnity or exoneration for money paid or liability incurred because of the judgment;

(b) Enforce a warranty to protect the judgment debtor against the liability determined by the judgment; or

(c) Recover damages for breach of warranty substantially the same as the warranty determined by the judgment to have been breached.

§ 1302. Judgment determining liability of third person

When the liability, obligation, or duty of a third person is in issue in a civil action, evidence of a final judgment against that person is not made inadmissible by the hearsay rule when offered to prove such liability, obligation, or duty.

ARTICLE 11. FAMILY HISTORY

§ 1310. Statement concerning declarant's own family history

(a) Subject to subdivision (b), evidence of a statement by a declarant who is unavailable as a witness concerning his own birth, marriage, divorce, a parent and child relationship, relationship by blood or marriage, race, ancestry, or other similar fact of his family history is not made inadmissible by the hearsay rule, even though the declarant had no means of acquiring personal knowledge of the matter declared.

(b) Evidence of a statement is inadmissible under this section if the statement was made under circumstances such as to indicate its lack of trustworthiness.

§ 1311. Statement concerning family history of another

(a) Subject to subdivision (b), evidence of a statement concerning the birth, marriage, divorce, death, parent and child relationship, race, ancestry, relationship by blood or marriage, or other similar fact of the family history of a person other than the declarant is not made inadmissible by the hearsay rule if the declarant is unavailable as a witness and:

(1) The declarant was related to the other by blood or marriage; or

521

(2)   The declarant was otherwise so intimately associated with the other's family as to be likely to have had accurate information concerning the matter declared and made the statement (i) upon information received from the other or from a person related by blood or marriage to the other or (ii) upon repute in the other's family.

(b)   Evidence of a statement is inadmissible under this section if the statement was made under circumstances such as to indicate its lack of trustworthiness.

§ 1312. Entries in family records and the like

Evidence of entries in family Bibles or other family books or charts, engravings on rings, family portraits, engravings on urns, crypts, or tombstones, and the like, is not made inadmissible by the hearsay rule when offered to prove the birth, marriage, divorce, death, parent and child relationship, race, ancestry, relationship by blood or marriage, or other similar fact of the family history of a member of the family by blood or marriage.

§ 1313. Reputation in family concerning family history

Evidence of reputation among members of a family is not made inadmissible by the hearsay rule if the reputation concerns the birth, marriage, divorce, death, parent and child relationship, race, ancestry, relationship by blood or marriage, or other similar fact of the family history of a member of the family by blood or marriage.

§ 1314. Reputation in community concerning family history

Evidence of reputation in a community concerning the date or fact of birth, marriage, divorce, or death of a person resident in the community at the time of the reputation is not made inadmissible by the hearsay rule.

§ 1315. Church records concerning family history

Evidence of a statement concerning a person's birth, marriage, divorce, death, parent and child relationship, race, ancestry, relationship by blood or marriage, or other similar fact of family history which is contained in a writing made as a record of a church, religious denomination, or religious society is not made inadmissible by the hearsay rule if:

(a)   The statement is contained in a writing made as a record of an act, condition, or event that would be admissible as evidence of such act, condition, or event under Section 1271; and

(b)   The statement is of a kind customarily recorded in connection with the act, condition, or event recorded in the writing.

§ 1316. Marriage, baptismal and similar certificates

Evidence of a statement concerning a person's birth, marriage, divorce, death, parent and child relationship, race, ancestry, relationship by blood or marriage, or other similar fact of family history is not made inadmissible by the hearsay rule if the statement is contained in a certificate that the maker thereof performed a marriage or other ceremony or administered a sacrament and:

(a) The maker was a clergyman, civil officer, or other person authorized to perform the acts reported in the certificate by law or by the rules, regulations, or requirements of a church, religious denomination, or religious society; and

(b) The certificate was issued by the maker at the time and place of the ceremony or sacrament or within a reasonable time thereafter.

ARTICLE 12. REPUTATION AND STATEMENTS CONCERNING COMMUNITY HISTORY, PROPERTY INTERESTS, AND CHARACTER

§ 1320. Reputation concerning community history

Evidence of reputation in a community is not made inadmissible by the hearsay rule if the reputation concerns an event of general history of the community or of the state or nation of which the community is a part and the event was of importance to the community.

§ 1321. Reputation concerning public interest in property

Evidence of reputation in a community is not made inadmissible by the hearsay rule if the reputation concerns the interest of the public in property in the community and the reputation arose before controversy.

§ 1322. Reputation concerning boundary or custom affecting land

Evidence of reputation in a community is not made inadmissible by the hearsay rule if the reputation concerns boundaries of, or customs affecting, land in the community and the reputation arose before controversy.

§ 1323. Statement concerning boundary

Evidence of a statement concerning the boundary of land is not made inadmissible by the hearsay rule if the declarant is unavailable as a witness and had sufficient knowledge of the subject, but evidence of a statement is not admissible under this section if the statement was made under circumstances such as to indicate its lack of trustworthiness.

§ 1324. Reputation concerning character

Evidence of a person's general reputation with reference to his character or a trait of his character at a relevant time in the community in which he then resided or in a group with which he then habitually associated is not made inadmissible by the hearsay rule.

ARTICLE 13. DISPOSITIVE INSTRUMENTS AND ANCIENT WRITINGS

§ 1330. Recitals in writings affecting property

Evidence of a statement contained in a deed of conveyance or a will or other writing purporting to affect an interest in real or personal property is not made inadmissible by the hearsay rule if:

(a) The matter stated was relevant to the purpose of the writing;

(b)   The matter stated would be relevant to an issue as to an interest in the property; and

(c)   The dealings with the property since the statement was made have not been inconsistent with the truth of the statement.

§ 1331. Recitals in ancient writings

Evidence of a statement is not made inadmissible by the hearsay rule if the statement is contained in a writing more than 30 years old and the statement has been since generally acted upon as true by persons having an interest in the matter.

ARTICLE 14. COMMERCIAL, SCIENTIFIC, AND SIMILAR PUBLICATIONS

§ 1340. Publications relied upon as accurate in the course of business

Evidence of a statement, other than an opinion, contained in a tabulation, list, directory, register, or other published compilation is not made inadmissible by the hearsay rule if the compilation is generally used and relied upon as accurate in the course of a business as defined in Section 1270.

§ 1341. Publications concerning facts of general notoriety and interests

Historical works, books of science or art, and published maps or charts, made by persons indifferent between the parties, are not made inadmissible by the hearsay rule when offered to prove facts of general notoriety and interest.

ARTICLE 15. DECLARANT UNAVAILABLE AS WITNESS

§ 1350. Unavailable declarant; hearsay rule

(a)   In a criminal proceeding charging a serious felony, evidence of a statement made by a declarant is not made inadmissible by the hearsay rule if the declarant is unavailable as a witness, and all of the following are true:

(1)   There is clear and convincing evidence that the declarant's unavailability was knowingly caused by, aided by, or solicited by the party against whom the statement is offered for the purpose of preventing the arrest or prosecution of the party and is the result of the death by homicide or the kidnapping of the declarant.

(2)   There is no evidence that the unavailability of the declarant was caused by, aided by, solicited by, or procured on behalf of, the party who is offering the statement.

(3)   The statement has been memorialized in a tape recording made by a law enforcement official, or in a written statement prepared by a law enforcement official and signed by the declarant and notarized in the presence of the law enforcement official, prior to the death or kidnapping of the declarant.

(4) The statement was made under circumstances which indicate its trustworthiness and was not the result of promise, inducement, threat, or coercion.

(5) The statement is relevant to the issues to be tried.

(6) The statement is corroborated by other evidence which tends to connect the party against whom the statement is offered with the commission of the serious felony with which the party is charged. The corroboration is not sufficient if it merely shows the commission of the offense or the circumstances thereof.

(b) If the prosecution intends to offer a statement pursuant to this section, the prosecution shall serve a written notice upon the defendant at least 10 days prior to the hearing or trial at which the prosecution intends to offer the statement, unless the prosecution shows good cause for the failure to provide that notice. In the event that good cause is shown, the defendant shall be entitled to a reasonable continuance of the hearing or trial.

(c) If the statement is offered during trial, the court's determination shall be made out of the presence of the jury. If the defendant elects to testify at the hearing on a motion brought pursuant to this section, the court shall exclude from the examination every person except the clerk, the court reporter, the bailiff, the prosecutor, the investigating officer, the defendant and his or her counsel, an investigator for the defendant, and the officer having custody of the defendant. Notwithstanding any other provision of law, the defendant's testimony at the hearing shall not be admissible in any other proceeding except the hearing brought on the motion pursuant to this section. If a transcript is made of the defendant's testimony, it shall be sealed and transmitted to the clerk of the court in which the action is pending.

(d) As used in this section, "serious felony" means any of the felonies listed in subdivision (c) of Section 1192.7 of the Penal Code or any violation of Sections 11351, 11352, 11378, or 11379 of the Health and Safety Code.

(e) If a statement to be admitted pursuant to this section includes hearsay statements made by anyone other than the declarant who is unavailable pursuant to subdivision (a), those hearsay statements are inadmissible unless they meet the requirements of an exception to the hearsay rule.

ARTICLE 16. STATEMENTS BY CHILDREN UNDER THE AGE OF 12 IN CHILD NEGLECT AND ABUSE PROCEEDINGS

§ 1360. Statements describing an act or attempted act of child abuse or neglect; criminal prosecutions; requirements

(a) In a criminal prosecution where the victim is a minor, a statement made by the victim when under the age of 12 describing any act of child abuse or neglect performed with or on the child by another, or describing any attempted act of child abuse or neglect with or on the child by another, is not made inadmissible by the hearsay rule if all of the following apply:

(1) The statement is not otherwise admissible by statute or court rule.

(2) The court finds, in a hearing conducted outside the presence of the jury, that the time, content, and circumstances of the statement provide sufficient indicia of reliability.

(3)   The child either:

(A)   Testifies at the proceedings.

(B)   Is unavailable as a witness, in which case the statement may be admitted only if there is evidence of the child abuse or neglect that corroborates the statement made by the child.

(b)   A statement may not be admitted under this section unless the proponent of the statement makes known to the adverse party the intention to offer the statement and the particulars of the statement sufficiently in advance of the proceedings in order to provide the adverse party with a fair opportunity to prepare to meet the statement.

(c)   For purposes of this section, "child abuse" means an act proscribed by Sections 273a, 273d, or 288.5 of the Penal Code, or any of the acts described in Section 11165.1 of the Penal Code, and "child neglect" means any of the acts described in Section 11165.2 of the Penal Code.

ARTICLE 17.   PHYSICAL ABUSE

§ 1370. Threat of infliction of injury

(a)   Evidence of a statement by a declarant is not made inadmissible by the hearsay rule if all of the following conditions are met:

(1)   The statement purports to narrate, describe, or explain the infliction or threat of physical injury upon the declarant.

(2)   The declarant is unavailable as a witness pursuant to Section 240.

(3)   The statement was made at or near the time of the infliction or threat of physical injury. Evidence of statements made more than five years before the filing of the current action or proceeding shall be inadmissible under this section.

(4)   The statement was made under circumstances that would indicate its trustworthiness.

(5)   The statement was made in writing, was electronically recorded, or made to a physician, nurse, paramedic or to a law enforcement official.

(b)   For purposes of paragraph (4) of subdivision (a), circumstances relevant to the issue of trustworthiness include, but are not limited to, the following:

(1)   Whether the statement was made in contemplation of pending or anticipated litigation in which the declarant was interested.

(2)   Whether the declarant has a bias or motive for fabricating the statement, and the extent of any bias or motive.

(3)   Whether the statement is corroborated by evidence other than statements that are admissible only pursuant to this section.

(c)   A statement is admissible pursuant to this section only if the proponent of the statement makes known to the adverse party the intention to offer the statement and the particulars of the statement sufficiently in advance of the proceedings in order to provide the adverse party with a fair opportunity to prepare to meet the statement.

§ 1380. Elder and dependent adults; statements by victims of abuse

(a) In a criminal proceeding charging a violation, or attempted violation, of *Section 368 of the Penal Code*, evidence of a statement made by a declarant is not made inadmissible by the hearsay rule if the declarant is unavailable as a witness, as defined in subdivisions (a) and (b) of Section 240, and all of the following are true:

(1) The party offering the statement has made a showing of particularized guarantees of trustworthiness regarding the statement, the statement was made under circumstances which indicate its trustworthiness, and the statement was not the result of promise, inducement, threat, or coercion. In making its determination, the court may consider only the circumstances that surround the making of the statement and that render the declarant particularly worthy of belief.

(2) There is no evidence that the unavailability of the declarant was caused by, aided by, solicited by, or procured on behalf of, the party who is offering the statement.

(3) The entire statement has been memorialized in a videotape recording made by a law enforcement official, prior to the death or disabling of the declarant.

(4) The statement was made by the victim of the alleged violation.

(5) The statement is supported by corroborative evidence.

(6) The victim of the alleged violation is an individual who meets both of the following requirements:

(A) Was 65 years of age or older or was a dependent adult when the alleged violation or attempted violation occurred.

(B) At the time of any criminal proceeding, including, but not limited to, a preliminary hearing or trial, regarding the alleged violation or attempted violation, is either deceased or suffers from the infirmities of aging as manifested by advanced age or organic brain damage, or other physical, mental, or emotional dysfunction, to the extent that the ability of the person to provide adequately for the person's own care or protection is impaired.

(b) If the prosecution intends to offer a statement pursuant to this section, the prosecution shall serve a written notice upon the defendant at least 10 days prior to the hearing or trial at which the prosecution intends to offer the statement, unless the prosecution shows good cause for the failure to provide that notice. In the event that good cause is shown, the defendant shall be entitled to a reasonable continuance of the hearing or trial.

(c) If the statement is offered during trial, the court's determination as to the availability of the victim as a witness shall be made out of the presence of the jury. If the defendant elects to testify at the hearing on a motion brought pursuant to this section, the court shall exclude from the examination every person except the clerk, the court reporter, the bailiff, the prosecutor, the investigating officer, the defendant and his or her counsel, an investigator for the defendant, and the officer having custody of the defendant. Notwithstanding any other provision of law, the defendant's testimony at the hearing shall not be admissible in any other proceeding except the hearing brought on the motion pursuant to this section. If a transcript is made of the defendant's testimony, it shall be sealed and transmitted to the clerk of the court in which the action is pending.

§ 1390. Statements against parties involved in causing unavailability of declarant as witness

(a)   Evidence of a statement is not made inadmissible by the hearsay rule if the statement is offered against a party that has engaged, or aided and abetted, in the wrongdoing that was intended to, and did, procure the unavailability of the declarant as a witness.

(b)(1)   The party seeking to introduce a statement pursuant to subdivision (a) shall establish, by a preponderance of the evidence, that the elements of subdivision (a) have been met at a foundational hearing.

(2)   The hearsay evidence that is the subject of the foundational hearing is admissible at the foundational hearing. However, a finding that the elements of subdivision (a) have been met shall not be based solely on the unconfronted hearsay statement of the unavailable declarant, and shall be supported by independent corroborative evidence.

(3)   The foundational hearing shall be conducted outside the presence of the jury. However, if the hearing is conducted after a jury trial has begun, the judge presiding at the hearing may consider evidence already presented to the jury in deciding whether the elements of subdivision (a) have been met.

(4)   In deciding whether or not to admit the statement, the judge may take into account whether it is trustworthy and reliable.

(c)   This section shall apply to any civil, criminal, or juvenile case or proceeding initiated or pending as of January 1, 2011.

DIVISION 11. WRITINGS

CHAPTER 1. AUTHENTICATION AND PROOF OF WRITINGS

ARTICLE 1. REQUIREMENT OF AUTHENTICATION

§ 1400. Authentication

Authentication of a writing means (a) the introduction of evidence sufficient to sustain a finding that it is the writing that the proponent of the evidence claims it is or (b) the establishment of such facts by any other means provided by law.

§ 1401. Authentication required

(a)   Authentication of a writing is required before it may be received in evidence.

(b)   Authentication of a writing is required before secondary evidence of its content may be received in evidence.

§ 1402. Authentication of altered writing

The party producing a writing as genuine which has been altered, or appears to have been altered, after its execution, in a part material to the question in dispute, must account for the alteration or appearance thereof. He may show that the alteration was made by another, without his concurrence, or was made with the consent of the parties affected by it, or otherwise properly or innocently made, or that the alteration did not change the meaning or language of the instrument. If he does that, he may give the writing in evidence, but not otherwise.

ARTICLE 2. MEANS OF AUTHENTICATING AND PROVING WRITINGS

§ 1410. Article not exclusive

Nothing in this article shall be construed to limit the means by which a writing may be authenticated or proved.

§ 1410.5. Graffiti constitutes a writing; admissibility

(a)   For purposes of this chapter, a writing shall include any graffiti consisting of written words, insignia, symbols, or any other markings which convey a particular meaning.

(b)   Any writing described in subdivision (a), or any photograph thereof, may be admitted into evidence in an action for vandalism, for the purpose of proving that the writing was made by the defendant.

(c)   The admissibility of any fact offered to prove that the writing was made by the defendant shall, upon motion of the defendant, be ruled upon outside the presence of the jury, and is subject to the requirements of Sections 1416, 1417, and 1418.

§ 1411. Subscribing witness' testimony unnecessary

Except as provided by statute, the testimony of a subscribing witness is not required to authenticate a writing.

§ 1412. Use of other evidence when subscribing witness' testimony required

If the testimony of a subscribing witness is required by statute to authenticate a writing and the subscribing witness denies or does not recollect the execution of the writing, the writing may be authenticated by other evidence.

§ 1413. Witness to the execution of a writing

A writing may be authenticated by anyone who saw the writing made or executed, including a subscribing witness.

§ 1414. Admission of authenticity; acting upon writing as authentic

A writing may be authenticated by evidence that:

(a)   The party against whom it is offered has at any time admitted its authenticity; or

(b)   The writing has been acted upon as authentic by the party against whom it is offered.

§ 1415. Authentication by handwriting evidence

A writing may be authenticated by evidence of the genuineness of the handwriting of the maker.

§ 1416. Proof of handwriting by person familiar therewith

A witness who is not otherwise qualified to testify as an expert may state his opinion whether a writing is in the handwriting of a supposed writer if the court finds that he has personal knowledge of the handwriting of the supposed writer. Such personal knowledge may be acquired from:

(a)   Having seen the supposed writer write;

(b)   Having seen a writing purporting to be in the handwriting of the supposed writer and upon which the supposed writer has acted or been charged;

(c)   Having received letters in the due course of mail purporting to be from the supposed writer in response to letters duly addressed and mailed by him to the supposed writer; or

(d)   Any other means of obtaining personal knowledge of the handwriting of the supposed writer.

§ 1417. Comparison of handwriting by trier of fact

The genuineness of handwriting, or the lack thereof, may be proved by a comparison made by the trier of fact with handwriting (a) which the court finds was admitted or treated as genuine by the party against whom the evidence is offered or (b) otherwise proved to be genuine to the satisfaction of the court.

§ 1418. Comparison of writing by expert witness

The genuineness of writing, or the lack thereof, may be proved by a comparison made by an expert witness with writing (a) which the court finds was admitted or treated as genuine by the party against whom the evidence is offered or (b) otherwise proved to be genuine to the satisfaction of the court.

§ 1419. Exemplars when writing is 30 years old

Where a writing whose genuineness is sought to be proved is more than 30 years old, the comparison under Sections 1417 or 1418 may be made with writing purporting to be genuine, and generally respected and acted upon as such, by persons having an interest in knowing whether it is genuine.

§ 1420. Authentication by evidence of reply

A writing may be authenticated by evidence that the writing was received in response to a communication sent to the person who is claimed by the proponent of the evidence to be the author of the writing.

§ 1421. Authentication by content

A writing may be authenticated by evidence that the writing refers to or states matters that are unlikely to be known to anyone other than the person who is claimed by the proponent of the evidence to be the author of the writing.

ARTICLE 3. PRESUMPTIONS AFFECTING ACKNOWLEDGED WRITINGS AND OFFICIAL WRITINGS

§ 1450. Classification of presumptions in article

The presumptions established by this article are presumptions affecting the burden of producing evidence.

§ 1451. Acknowledged writings

A certificate of the acknowledgment of a writing other than a will, or a certificate of the proof of such a writing, is prima facie evidence of the facts recited in the certificate and the genuineness of the signature of each person by whom the writing purports to have been signed if the certificate meets the requirements of Article 3 (commencing with Section 1180) of Chapter 4, Title 4, Part 4, Division 2 of the Civil Code.

§ 1452. Official seals

A seal is presumed to be genuine and its use authorized if it purports to be the seal of:

(a) The United States or a department, agency, or public employee of the United States.

(b) A public entity in the United States or a department, agency, or public employee of such public entity.

(c) A nation recognized by the executive power of the United States or a department, agency, or officer of such nation.

(d) A public entity in a nation recognized by the executive power of the United States or a department, agency, or officer of such public entity.

(e) A court of admiralty or maritime jurisdiction.

(f) A notary public within any state of the United States.

§ 1453. Domestic official signatures

A signature is presumed to be genuine and authorized if it purports to be the signature, affixed in his official capacity, of:

(a)   A public employee of the United States.

(b)   A public employee of any public entity in the United States.

(c)   A notary public within any state of the United States.

§ 1454. Foreign official signatures

A signature is presumed to be genuine and authorized if it purports to be the signature, affixed in his official capacity, of an officer, or deputy of an officer, of a nation or public entity in a nation recognized by the executive power of the United States and the writing to which the signature is affixed is accompanied by a final statement certifying the genuineness of the signature and the official position of (a) the person who executed the writing or (b) any foreign official who has certified either the genuineness of the signature and official position of the person executing the writing or the genuineness of the signature and official position of another foreign official who has executed a similar certificate in a chain of such certificates beginning with a certificate of the genuineness of the signature and official position of the person executing the writing. The final statement may be made only by a secretary of an embassy or legation, consul general, consul, vice consul, consular agent, or other officer in the foreign service of the United States stationed in the nation, authenticated by the seal of his office.

CHAPTER 2. SECONDARY EVIDENCE OF WRITINGS

ARTICLE 1. PROOF OF THE CONTENT OF A WRITING

§§ 1500 to 1511.   Repealed by Stats. 1998, c. 100 (S.B.177), § 1, operative Jan. 1, 1999

§ 1520. Content of writing; proof

The content of a writing may be proved by an otherwise admissible original.

§ 1521. Secondary evidence rule

(a)   The content of a writing may be proved by otherwise admissible secondary evidence. The court shall exclude secondary evidence of the content of writing if the court determines either of the following:

(1)   A genuine dispute exists concerning material terms of the writing and justice requires the exclusion.

(2)   Admission of the secondary evidence would be unfair.

(b)   Nothing in this section makes admissible oral testimony to prove the content of a writing if the testimony is inadmissible under Section 1523 (oral testimony of the content of a writing).

(c)   Nothing in this section excuses compliance with Section 1401 (authentication).

(d)   This section shall be known as the "Secondary Evidence Rule."

§ 1522. Additional grounds for exclusion of secondary evidence

(a)   In addition to the grounds for exclusion authorized by Section 1521, in a criminal action the court shall exclude secondary evidence of the content of a writing if the court determines that the original is in the proponent's possession, custody, or control, and the proponent has not made the original reasonably available for inspection at or before trial. This section does not apply to any of the following:

(1)   A duplicate as defined in Section 260.

(2)   A writing that is not closely related to the controlling issues in the action.

(3)   A copy of a writing in the custody of a public entity.

(4)   A copy of a writing that is recorded in the public records, if the record or a certified copy of it is made evidence of the writing by statute.

(b)   In a criminal action, a request to exclude secondary evidence of the content of a writing, under this section or any other law, shall not be made in the presence of the jury.

§ 1523. Oral testimony of the content of a writing; admissibility

(a)   Except as otherwise provided by statute, oral testimony is not admissible to prove the content of a writing.

(b)   Oral testimony of the content of a writing is not made inadmissible by subdivision (a) if the proponent does not have possession or control of a copy of the writing and the original is lost or has been destroyed without fraudulent intent on the part of the proponent of the evidence.

(c)   Oral testimony of the content of a writing is not made inadmissible by subdivision (a) if the proponent does not have possession or control of the original or a copy of the writing and either of the following conditions is satisfied:

(1)   Neither the writing nor a copy of the writing was reasonably procurable by the proponent by use of the court's process or by other available means.

(2)   The writing is not closely related to the controlling issues and it would be inexpedient to require its production.

(d)   Oral testimony of the content of a writing is not made inadmissible by subdivision (a) if the writing consists of numerous accounts or other writings that cannot be examined in court without great loss of time, and the evidence sought from them is only the general result of the whole.

ARTICLE 2. OFFICIAL WRITINGS AND RECORDED WRITINGS

§ 1530. Copy of writing in official custody

(a)   A purported copy of a writing in the custody of a public entity, or of an entry in such a writing, is prima facie evidence of the existence and content of such writing or entry if:

(1)   The copy purports to be published by the authority of the nation or state, or public entity therein in which the writing is kept;

(2)   The office in which the writing is kept is within the United States or within the Panama Canal Zone, the Trust Territory of the

Pacific Islands, or the Ryukyu Islands, and the copy is attested or certified as a correct copy of the writing or entry by a public employee, or a deputy of a public employee, having the legal custody of the writing; or

(3)　The office in which the writing is kept is not within the United States or any other place described in paragraph (2) and the copy is attested as a correct copy of the writing or entry by a person having authority to make attestation. The attestation must be accompanied by a final statement certifying the genuineness of the signature and the official position of (i) the person who attested the copy as a correct copy or (ii) any foreign official who has certified either the genuineness of the signature and official position of the person attesting the copy or the genuineness of the signature and official position of another foreign official who has executed a similar certificate in a chain of such certificates beginning with a certificate of the genuineness of the signature and official position of the person attesting the copy. Except as provided in the next sentence, the final statement may be made only by a secretary of an embassy or legation, consul general, consul, vice consul, or consular agent of the United States, or a diplomatic or consular official of the foreign country assigned or accredited to the United States. Prior to January 1, 1971, the final statement may also be made by a secretary of an embassy or legation, consul general, consul, vice consul, consular agent, or other officer in the foreign service of the United States stationed in the nation in which the writing is kept, authenticated by the seal of his office. If reasonable opportunity has been given to all parties to investigate the authenticity and accuracy of the documents, the court may, for good cause shown, (i) admit an attested copy without the final statement or (ii) permit the writing or entry in foreign custody to be evidenced by an attested summary with or without a final statement.

(b)　The presumptions established by this section are presumptions affecting the burden of producing evidence.

§ 1531. Certification of copy for evidence

For the purpose of evidence, whenever a copy of a writing is attested or certified, the attestation or certificate must state in substance that the copy is a correct copy of the original, or of a specified part thereof, as the case may be.

§ 1532. Official record of recorded writing

(a)　The official record of a writing is prima facie evidence of the existence and content of the original recorded writing if:

(1)　The record is in fact a record of an office of a public entity; and

(2)　A statute authorized such a writing to be recorded in that office.

(b)　The presumption established by this section is a presumption affecting the burden of producing evidence.

ARTICLE 3. PHOTOGRAPHIC COPIES AND PRINTED REPRESENTATIONS OF WRITINGS

§ 1550. Types of evidence as writing admissible as the writing itself

(a)   If made and preserved as a part of the records of a business, as defined in Section 1270, in the regular course of that business, the following types of evidence of a writing are as admissible as the writing itself:

(1)   A nonerasable optical image reproduction or any other reproduction of a public record by a trusted system, as defined in Section 12168.7 of the Government Code, if additions, deletions, or changes to the original document are not permitted by the technology.

(2)   A photostatic copy or reproduction.

(3)   A microfilm, microcard, or miniature photographic copy, reprint, or enlargement.

(4)   Any other photographic copy or reproduction, or an enlargement thereof.

(b)   The introduction of evidence of a writing pursuant to subdivision (a) does not preclude admission of the original writing if it is still in existence. A court may require the introduction of a hard copy printout of the document.

§ 1550.1. Admissibility of reproductions of files, records, writings, photographs, and fingerprints

Reproductions of files, records, writings, photographs, fingerprints or other instruments in the official custody of a criminal justice agency that were microphotographed or otherwise reproduced in a manner that conforms with the provisions of Sections 11106.1, 11106.2, or 11106.3 of the Penal Code shall be admissible to the same extent and under the same circumstances as the original file, record, writing or other instrument would be admissible.

§ 1551. Photographic copies where original destroyed or lost

A print, whether enlarged or not, from a photographic film (including a photographic plate, microphotographic film, photostatic negative, or similar reproduction) of an original writing destroyed or lost after such film was taken or a reproduction from an electronic recording of video images on magnetic surfaces is admissible as the original writing itself if, at the time of the taking of such film or electronic recording, the person under whose direction and control it was taken attached thereto, or to the sealed container in which it was placed and has been kept, or incorporated in the film or electronic recording, a certification complying with the provisions of Section 1531 and stating the date on which, and the fact that, it was so taken under his direction and control.

§ 1552. Printed representation of computer-generated information

(a)   A printed representation of computer information or a computer program is presumed to be an accurate representation of the computer information or computer program that it purports to represent. This presumption is a presumption affecting the burden of producing evidence. If a party to an action introduces evidence that a printed representation of computer information or computer program is inaccurate or unreliable, the party introducing the printed representation into evidence has the burden of proving, by a preponderance of evidence, that the printed representation is an accurate representation of the existence and content of the computer information or computer program that it purports to represent.

(b)　Subdivision (a) applies to the printed representation of computer-generated information stored by an automated traffic enforcement system.

(c)　Subdivision (a) shall not apply to computer-generated official records certified in accordance with Section 452.5 or 1530.

§ 1553. Printed representation of video or digital images

(a)　A printed representation of images stored on a video or digital medium is presumed to be an accurate representation of the images it purports to represent. This presumption is a presumption affecting the burden of producing evidence. If a party to an action introduces evidence that a printed representation of images stored on a video or digital medium is inaccurate or unreliable, the party introducing the printed representation into evidence has the burden of proving, by a preponderance of evidence, that the printed representation is an accurate representation of the existence and content of the images that it purports to represent.

(b)　Subdivision (a) applies to the printed representation of video or photographic images stored by an automatic traffic enforcement system.

ARTICLE 4. PRODUCTION OF BUSINESS RECORDS

§ 1560. Compliance with subpoena duces tecum or search warrant for business records

(a)　As used in this article:

(1)　"Business" includes every kind of business described in Section 1270.

(2)　"Record" includes every kind of record maintained by a business.

(b)　Except as provided in Section 1564, when a subpoena duces tecum is served upon the custodian of records or other qualified witness of a business in an action in which the business is neither a party nor the place where any cause of action is alleged to have arisen, and the subpoena requires the production of all or any part of the records of the business, it is sufficient compliance therewith if the custodian or other qualified witness delivers by mail or otherwise a true, legible, and durable copy of all of the records described in the subpoena to the clerk of the court or to another person described in subdivision (d) of Section 2026.010 of the Code of Civil Procedure, together with the affidavit described in Section 1561, within one of the following time periods:

(1)　In any criminal action, five days after the receipt of the subpoena.

(2)　In any civil action, within 15 days after the receipt of the subpoena.

(3)　Within the time agreed upon by the party who served the subpoena and the custodian or other qualified witness.

(c) The copy of the records shall be separately enclosed in an inner envelope or wrapper, sealed, with the title and number of the action, name of witness, and date of subpoena clearly inscribed thereon; the sealed envelope or wrapper shall then be enclosed in an outer envelope or wrapper, sealed, and directed as follows:

(1) If the subpoena directs attendance in court, to the clerk of the court.

(2) If the subpoena directs attendance at a deposition, to the officer before whom the deposition is to be taken, at the place designated in the subpoena for the taking of the deposition or at the officer's place of business.

(3) In other cases, to the officer, body, or tribunal conducting the hearing, at a like address.

(d) Unless the parties to the proceeding otherwise agree, or unless the sealed envelope or wrapper is returned to a witness who is to appear personally, the copy of the records shall remain sealed and shall be opened only at the time of trial, deposition, or other hearing, upon the direction of the judge, officer, body, or tribunal conducting the proceeding, in the presence of all parties who have appeared in person or by counsel at the trial, deposition, or hearing. Records that are original documents and that are not introduced in evidence or required as part of the record shall be returned to the person or entity from whom received. Records that are copies may be destroyed.

(e) As an alternative to the procedures described in subdivisions (b), (c), and (d), the subpoenaing party in a civil action may direct the witness to make the records available for inspection or copying by the party's attorney, the attorney's representative, or deposition officer as described in Section 2020.420 of the Code of Civil Procedure, at the witness' business address under reasonable conditions during normal business hours. Normal business hours, as used in this subdivision, means those hours that the business of the witness is normally open for business to the public. When provided with at least five business days' advance notice by the party's attorney, attorney's representative, or deposition officer, the witness shall designate a time period of not less than six continuous hours on a date certain for copying of records subject to the subpoena by the party's attorney, attorney's representative, or deposition officer. It shall be the responsibility of the attorney's representative to deliver any copy of the records as directed in the subpoena. Disobedience to the deposition subpoena issued pursuant to this subdivision is punishable as provided in Section 2020.240 of the Code of Civil Procedure.

(f) If a search warrant for business records is served upon the custodian of records or other qualified witness of a business in compliance with Section 1524 of the Penal Code regarding a criminal investigation in which the business is neither a party nor the place where any crime is alleged to have occurred, and the search warrant provides that the warrant will be deemed executed if the business causes the delivery of records described in the warrant to the law enforcement agency ordered to execute the warrant, it is sufficient compliance therewith if the custodian or other qualified witness delivers by mail or otherwise a true, legible, and durable copy of all of the records described in the search warrant to the law enforcement agency ordered to execute the search warrant, together with the affidavit described in Section 1561, within five days after the receipt of the search warrant or within such other time as is set forth in the warrant. This subdivision does not abridge or limit the scope of search warrant procedures set forth in

Chapter 3 (commencing with Section 1523) of Title 12 of Part 2 of the Penal Code or invalidate otherwise duly executed search warrants.

§ 1561. Affidavit accompanying records

(a)   The records shall be accompanied by the affidavit of the custodian or other qualified witness, stating in substance each of the following:

(1)   The affiant is the duly authorized custodian of the records or other qualified witness and has authority to certify the records.

(2)   The copy is a true copy of all the records described in the subpoena duces tecum or search warrant, or pursuant to subdivision (e) of Section 1560 the records were delivered to the attorney, the attorney's representative or deposition officer for copying at the custodian's or witness' place of business, as the case may be.

(3)   The records were prepared by the personnel of the business in the ordinary course of business at or near the time of the act, condition, or event.

(4)   The identity of the records.

(5)   A description of the mode of preparation of the records.

(b)   If the business has none of the records described, or only part thereof, the custodian or other qualified witness shall so state in the affidavit, and deliver the affidavit and those records that are available in one of the manners provided in Section 1560.

(c)   If the records described in the subpoena were delivered to the attorney or his or her representative or deposition officer for copying at the custodian's or witness' place of business, in addition to the affidavit required by subdivision (a), the records shall be accompanied by an affidavit by the attorney or his or her representative or deposition officer stating that the copy is a true copy of all the records delivered to the attorney or his or her representative or deposition officer for copying.

§ 1562. Admissibility of affidavit and copy of records

If the original records would be admissible in evidence if the custodian or other qualified witness had been present and testified to the matters stated in the affidavit, and if the requirements of Section 1271 have been met, the copy of the records is admissible in evidence. The affidavit is admissible as evidence of the matters stated therein pursuant to Section 1561 and the matters so stated are presumed true. When more than one person has knowledge of the facts, more than one affidavit may be made. The presumption established by this section is a presumption affecting the burden of producing evidence.

§ 1563. One witness and mileage fee

(a)   This article does not require tender or payment of more than one witness fee and one mileage fee or other charge, to a witness or witness' business, unless there is an agreement to the contrary between the witness and the requesting party.

(b)   All reasonable costs incurred in a civil proceeding by a witness who is not a party with respect to the production of any part of business records requested pursuant to a subpoena duces tecum shall be charged against the party serving the subpoena duces tecum.

(1)   "Reasonable costs," as used in this section, includes, but is not limited to, the following specific costs: ten cents ($0.10) per page for standard reproduction of documents of a size 8½ by 14 inches or less; twenty cents ($0.20) per page for copying of documents from microfilm; actual costs for the reproduction of oversize documents or the reproduction of documents requiring special processing which are made in response to a subpoena; reasonable clerical costs incurred in locating and making the records available to be billed at the maximum rate of twenty four dollars ($24) per hour per person, computed on the basis of six dollars ($6) per quarter hour or fraction thereof; actual postage charges; and the actual cost, if any, charged to the witness by a third person for the retrieval and return of records held offsite by that third person.

(2)   The requesting party, or the requesting party's deposition officer shall not be required to pay the reasonable costs or any estimate thereof before the records are available for delivery pursuant to the subpoena, but the witness may demand payment of costs pursuant to this section simultaneous with actual delivery of the subpoenaed records, and until such time as payment is made, the witness is under no obligation to deliver the records.

(3)   The witness shall submit an itemized statement for the costs to the requesting party, or the requesting party's deposition officer, setting forth the reproduction and clerical costs incurred by the witness. If the costs exceed those authorized in paragraph (1), or if the witness refuses to produce an itemized statement of costs as required by paragraph (3) upon demand by the requesting party, or the requesting party's deposition officer, the witness shall furnish a statement setting forth the actions taken by the witness in justification of the costs.

(4)   The requesting party may petition the court in which the action is pending to recover from the witness all or a part of the costs paid to the witness, or to reduce all or a part of the costs charged by the witness, pursuant to this subdivision, on the grounds that those costs were excessive. Upon the filing of the petition the court shall issue an order to show cause and from the time the order is served on the witness the court has jurisdiction over the witness. The court may hear testimony on the order to show cause and if it finds that the costs demanded and collected, or charged but not collected, exceed the amount authorized by this subdivision, it shall order the witness to remit to the requesting party, or reduce its charge to the requesting party by an amount equal to, the amount of the excess. If the court finds the costs were excessive and charged in bad faith by the witness, the court shall order the witness to remit the full amount of the costs demanded and collected, or excuse the requesting party from any payment of costs charged but not collected, and the court shall also order the witness to pay the requesting party the amount of the reasonable expenses incurred in obtaining the order including attorney's fees. If the court finds the costs were not excessive, the court shall order the requesting party to pay the witness the amount of the reasonable expenses incurred in defending the petition, including attorney's fees.

(5)   If a subpoena is served to compel the production of business records and is subsequently withdrawn, or is quashed, modified or limited on a motion made other than by the witness, the witness shall be entitled to reimbursement pursuant to paragraph (1) for all reasonable costs incurred in compliance with the subpoena to the time

that the requesting party has notified the witness that the subpoena has been withdrawn or quashed, modified or limited. If the subpoena is withdrawn or quashed, if those costs are not paid within 30 days after demand therefor, the witness may file a motion in the court in which the action is pending for an order requiring payment, and the court shall award the payment of expenses and attorney's fees in the manner set forth in paragraph (4).

(6) If records requested pursuant to a subpoena duces tecum are delivered to the attorney, the attorney's representative or the deposition officer for inspection or photocopying at the witness' place of business, the only fee for complying with the subpoena shall not exceed fifteen dollars ($15), plus the actual cost, if any, charged to the witness by that third person for retrieval and return of records held offsite by the third person. If the records are retrieved from microfilm, the reasonable costs, as defined in paragraph (1), applies.

(c) If the personal attendance of the custodian of a record or other qualified witness is required pursuant to Section 1564, in a civil proceeding, he or she shall be entitled to the same witness fees and mileage permitted in a case where the subpoena requires the witness to attend and testify before a court in which the action or proceeding is pending and to any additional costs incurred as provided by subdivision (b).

§ 1564. Personal attendance of custodian and production of original records

The personal attendance of the custodian or other qualified witness and the production of the original records is not required unless, at the discretion of the requesting party, the subpoena duces tecum contains a clause which reads:

"The personal attendance of the custodian or other qualified witness and the production of the original records are required by this subpoena. The procedure authorized pursuant to subdivision (b) of Section 1560, and Sections 1561 and 1562, of the Evidence Code will not be deemed sufficient compliance with this subpoena."

§ 1565. Service of more than one subpoena duces tecum

If more than one subpoena duces tecum is served upon the custodian of records or other qualified witness and the personal attendance of the custodian or other qualified witness is required pursuant to Section 1564, the witness shall be deemed to be the witness of the party serving the first such subpoena duces tecum.

§ 1566. Applicability of article

This article applies in any proceeding in which testimony can be compelled.

§ 1567. Employee income and benefit information; forms completed by employer; support modification or termination proceedings

A completed form described in Section 3664 of the Family Code for income and benefit information provided by the employer may be admissible in a proceeding for modification or termination of an order for child, family, or spousal support if both of the following requirements are met:

(a)   The completed form complies with Sections 1561 and 1562.

(b)   A copy of the completed form and notice was served on the employee named therein pursuant to Section 3664 of the Family Code.

CHAPTER 3. OFFICIAL WRITINGS AFFECTING PROPERTY

§ 1600. Record of document affecting property interest

(a)   The record of an instrument or other document purporting to establish or affect an interest in property is prima facie evidence of the existence and content of the original recorded document and its execution and delivery by each person by whom it purports to have been executed if:

(1)   The record is in fact a record of an office of a public entity; and

(2)   A statute authorized such a document to be recorded in that office.

(b)   The presumption established by this section is a presumption affecting the burden of proof.

§ 1601. Proof of content of lost official record affecting property

(a)   Subject to subdivisions (b) and (c), when in any action it is desired to prove the contents of the official record of any writing lost or destroyed by conflagration or other public calamity, after proof of such loss or destruction, the following may, without further proof, be admitted in evidence to prove the contents of such record:

(1)   Any abstract of title made and issued and certified as correct prior to such loss or destruction, and purporting to have been prepared and made in the ordinary course of business by any person engaged in the business of preparing and making abstracts of title prior to such loss or destruction; or

(2)   Any abstract of title, or of any instrument affecting title, made, issued, and certified as correct by any person engaged in the business of insuring titles or issuing abstracts of title to real estate, whether the same was made, issued, or certified before or after such loss or destruction and whether the same was made from the original records or from abstract and notes, or either, taken from such records in the preparation and upkeeping of its plant in the ordinary course of its business.

(b)   No proof of the loss of the original writing is required other than the fact that the original is not known to the party desiring to prove its contents to be in existence.

(c)   Any party desiring to use evidence admissible under this section shall give reasonable notice in writing to all other parties to the action who have appeared therein, of his intention to use such evidence at the trial of the action, and shall give all such other parties a reasonable opportunity to inspect the evidence, and also the abstracts, memoranda, or notes from which it was compiled, and to take copies thereof.

§ 1602. Repealed by Stats. 1967, c. 650, p. 2008, § 10

§ 1603. Deed by officer in pursuance of court process

A deed of conveyance of real property, purporting to have been executed by a proper officer in pursuance of legal process of any of the courts of record of this state, acknowledged and recorded in the office of the recorder of the county wherein the real property therein described is situated, or the record of such deed, or a certified copy of such record, is prima facie evidence that the property or interest therein described was thereby conveyed to the grantee named in such deed. The presumption established by this section is a presumption affecting the burden of proof.

§ 1604. Certificate of purchase or of location of lands

A certificate of purchase, or of location, of any lands in this state, issued or made in pursuance of any law of the United States or of this state, is prima facie evidence that the holder or assignee of such certificate is the owner of the land described therein; but this evidence may be overcome by proof that, at the time of the location, or time of filing a preemption claim on which the certificate may have been issued, the land was in the adverse possession of the adverse party, or those under whom he claims, or that the adverse party is holding the land for mining purposes.

§ 1605. Authenticated Spanish title records

Duplicate copies and authenticated translations of original Spanish title papers relating to land claims in this state, derived from the Spanish or Mexican governments, prepared under the supervision of the Keeper of Archives, authenticated by the Surveyor-General or his successor and by the Keeper of Archives, and filed with a county recorder, in accordance with Chapter 281 of the Statutes of 1865–66, are admissible as evidence with like force and effect as the originals and without proving the execution of such originals.

Appendix III

CASE LAW DIVERGENCE FROM THE FEDERAL RULES OF EVIDENCE

By Daniel J. Capra, Philip Reed Professor of Law, Fordham Law School, and Reporter to the Judicial Conference Advisory Committee on Evidence Rules

I. Introduction

Assume that a lawyer is reading one of the Federal Rules of Evidence to determine whether a piece of evidence will be admissible at trial. Obviously, the best place to start is with the text of the Federal Rules of Evidence. But if the lawyer thinks that the text of a particular rule plainly answers the question of admissibility, or simply leaves the question open for argument, that lawyer will often be wrong. That is because the case law has diverged from the text of the Federal Rules on many important points.

The Advisory Committee on Evidence Rules, which this author currently serves as Reporter, has expressed concern that the divergence between case law and the text of the Rule might create a trap for the unwary. *See generally,* Becker and Orenstein, *The Federal Rules of Evidence After Sixteen Years— The Effect of "Plain Meaning" Jurisprudence, the Need for an Advisory Committee on the Rules of Evidence, and Suggestions for Selective Revision of the Rules,* 60 Geo.Wash.L.Rev. 857, 868 (1992) (noting the need to "resolve discrepancies between the plain text of the Federal Rules and the generally shared interpretation of the Rules deriving from preexisting common law traditions"). One way to correct this divergence might be to propose an amendment to the text of any Rule subject to divergent case law. But the Advisory Committee is acutely aware of the costs of amending an evidence rule. Amendments can lead to the disruption of settled expectations, and may create further problems of interpretation and divergence. The Advisory Committee resolved to take a less drastic course—a course that would not require an amendment of any rules and yet would highlight for lawyers and judges the existence of divergent case law. The Committee directed the Reporter to prepare this report in an effort to increase the awareness of counsel practicing in federal courts, as well as judges, about the possibility that case law has diverged from the text of some of the Federal Rules of Evidence. This divergence comes in two forms: 1) where the case law (defined as case law in at least one circuit) is inconsistent with either the text of the Rule, the Advisory Committee Note explaining the text, or both; and 2) where the case law has provided significant development on a point that is not addressed by either the text of the Rule or the Committee Note.

This report highlights the major instances in which case law has diverged from an applicable Rule. Before proceeding to these illustrations, it is important to stress several qualifications on the scope of this report.

First, there is no intent to imply that any of the case law discussed herein is incorrect or "wrongly decided." The goal of this report is to point out the case law divergence from the Federal Rules of Evidence, without commenting on the merits of that divergence. Indeed, commentators have opined that much of the divergent case law is sensible and well-decided. *See, e.g.,* Jonakait, *Text, Texts, or Ad Hoc Determinations: Interpretation of the Federal Rules of Evidence,* 71 Ind.L.J. 551, 571 (1996) ("Sometimes we must look beyond the words of the Rules to understand evidentiary doctrine. We must do so when the Rules are not definitive or ambiguous * * * but sometimes even when the text is clear.").

Second, there is no intent to imply that any of the Rules discussed herein are problematic or need to be amended. The fact that the case law diverges from the Rule might be relevant to the need for an amendment, but it is certainly not dispositive. Whether a particular Rule should be amended is a complex question that is well beyond the scope of this report.

Third, there is no attempt to be comprehensive in the treatment of the case law construing the Evidence Rules discussed herein. Divergent case law is defined as case law in at least one circuit that has diverged from the text of the particular rule. This report does not purport to provide a treatise-like discussion of all the pertinent case law, from all the circuits, construing a particular rule. The goal of this report is to raise "red flags" with lawyers and judges, by providing basic information about areas where case law can be found that diverges from the text of the Federal Rules of Evidence.

II. Examples of Case Law In Conflict With the Text of the Rule and/or Committee Note

1.   Rule 106: Rule 106 sets forth a rule of completeness, providing that when a party introduces a writing or recorded statement, the adversary may "require the introduction, at that time, of any other part—or any other writing or recorded statement—that in fairness ought to be considered at the same time." Rule 106 by its terms permits the adversary to introduce completing statements only where the proponent introduces a *written or recorded* statement. The language of the Rule does not on its face permit completing evidence when the proponent introduces an oral statement, such as a criminal defendant's oral confession. Some courts have found, however, that Rule 106, or at least the principle of completeness embodied therein, applies to require admission of omitted portions of an oral statement when necessary to correct a misimpression. See *United States v. Tarantino,* 846 F.2d 1384 (D.C. Cir. 1988) (prior oral statements of a government witness were properly offered on redirect examination since the defendant had used portions of the statements in cross-examination and the omitted portions placed the statements in context). Compare *United States v. Harvey,* 914 F.2d 966 (7th Cir. 1990) (Rule 106 does not apply to oral statements).

Moreover, some courts have held that Rule 106 can operate as a de facto hearsay exception when the opponent opens the door by creating a misimpression in offering only part of a statement. In other words, completing evidence is found admissible under Rule 106 even if it would otherwise be hearsay. See *United States v. Sutton,* 801 F.2d 1346, 1369 (D.C.Cir. 1986) ("Rule 106 can adequately fulfill its function only by permitting the admission of some otherwise inadmissible evidence when the court finds in fairness that that proffered evidence should be considered contemporaneously"). *See also* C. Wright & K. Graham, *Federal Practice and Procedure: Evidence* § 5078, at 376 (supporting this approach). Such a reading is not apparent from the text or Committee Note. See *United States v. Wilkerson,* 84 F.3d 692 (4th Cir. 1996) (interpreting Rule 106 as purely a timing device, not as a rule permitting the admission of otherwise inadmissible evidence).

CASE LAW DIVERGENCE FROM THE
FEDERAL RULES OF EVIDENCE

2.   ***Rule 403:*** Rule 403 provides that a trial judge may exclude proffered evidence if its probative value is substantially outweighed by a danger of "unfair prejudice, confusing the issues, misleading the jury, undue delay, wasting time, or needlessly presenting cumulative evidence." Of the negative factors listed that would support exclusion, only one refers to the jury directly—the danger of "misleading the jury". This would seem to indicate that other negative factors mentioned in the Rule, specifically the danger of unfair prejudice and confusion of the issues, must be taken into account in a bench trial. Yet courts have held to the contrary, reasoning that unfair prejudice and confusing evidence will not have the same negative impact on the judge as it would have on the jury. *See, e.g., Schultz v. Butcher,* 24 F.3d 626 (4th Cir. 1994) (trial court erred in excluding evidence in a bench trial on the ground of its prejudicial effect); *Gulf States Utils. v. Ecodyne Corp.,* 635 F.2d 517 (5th Cir. 1981) (the portion of Rule 403 referring to prejudicial effect "has no logical application in bench trials").

3.   ***Rule 407:*** Rule 407 prohibits the admission of actions taken after an injury or harm which, if taken previously, would have made the injury or harm less likely to occur, if the remedial measure is offered to prove negligence, culpable conduct, product defect, design defect, or failure to warn. The Rule by its terms would appear to preclude evidence of any action by *anyone* that would have made the injury or harm less likely to occur. Some courts have held, however, that subsequent remedial measures are not excluded by Rule 407 if the measure is taken by someone *other than the defendant,* i.e., if it is a "third party repair." *See, e.g., TLT-Babcock, Inc. v. Emerson Elec. Co.,* 33 F.3d 397 (4th Cir. 1994) (design change not excluded by Rule 407 where the change was made by an entity that was not a party to the case); *Dixon v. International Harvester Co.,* 754 F.2d 573 (5th Cir. 1985) (repair by tractor owner after an accident not excluded when offered against tractor manufacturer).

Also, the Rule states that "impeachment" is a proper purpose for admitting subsequent remedial measures. Taken literally, this would mean that a plaintiff in a product liability case could offer proof of a subsequent remedial measure to "impeach" a defense witness' assertion that the product used by the plaintiff was safely designed. Yet courts have generally limited the use of subsequent remedial measures when offered for impeachment by way of contradiction. The fear is that this exception would swallow the rule of exclusion. *See, e.g., Harrison v. Sears, Roebuck & Co.,* 981 F.2d 25 (1st Cir. 1992) (a desire merely to undercut an expert's credibility cannot be sufficient to trigger the impeachment exception to Rule 407, or else the exception would swallow the rule of exclusion); *Kelly v. Crown Equip. Co.,* 970 F.2d 1273 (3d Cir. 1992) (subsequent remedial measure cannot be offered for simple contradiction of expert's statement that a design was safe). Thus, the "impeachment" permitted by the Rule has been limited to cases where defense witnesses have made extravagant claims of safety. See *Wood v. Morbark Indus.,* 70 F.3d 1202 (11th Cir. 1995) (post-accident design change admissible for impeachment where defense witness testified that the original design was the safest possible design); *Muzyka v. Remington Arms Co.,* 774 F.2d 1309 (5th Cir. 1985) (design change should have been admitted for impeachment where defense witnesses testified that the product was the best and safest product of its kind).

4.   ***Rule 601:*** Rule 601 essentially states that all questions that had been treated previously as matters of competency are now matters of credibility for the factfinder. The Advisory Committee Note, elaborating on the Rule, indicates an intent to prohibit a trial judge from excluding a witness

APPENDIX III

on grounds of incompetence. Yet courts have excluded witnesses who have been found incapable of testifying in a competent fashion. *See, e.g., United States v. Gates,* 10 F.3d 765, 766 (11th Cir. 1993) ("Notwithstanding Rule 601, a court has the power to rule that a witness is incapable of testifying, and in an appropriate case it has the duty to hold a hearing to determine that issue."); *United States v. Gutman,* 725 F.2d 417, 420 (7th Cir. 1984) (trial court retains the power, and sometimes the duty, to hold a hearing "to determine whether a witness should not be allowed to testify because insanity has made him incapable of testifying in a competent fashion.").

5. ***Rule 607:*** The Rule states categorically that a party can impeach any witness it calls. On its face, the Rule permits the following scenario: 1) in a criminal case, a witness would testify at trial that the defendant was not at the scene of the crime, though having stated previously to a police officer that the defendant committed the crime; 2) the prior statement to the police officer could not be admitted as substantive evidence because it is hearsay; 3) but the prosecutor calls the witness, knowing he will give testimony favorable to the defendant, and then "impeaches" the witness with his prior statement to the police officer, on the ground that it is inconsistent with the witness's in-court testimony. Thus, Rule 607 by its terms permits the prosecutor to proffer prior inconsistent statements, not made under oath (and therefore not admissible for their truth under Rule 801(d)(1)(A) in the guise of impeachment. Yet despite the affirmative and permissive language of the Rule, courts have held that a prosecutor cannot call a witness solely to impeach that witness, because to allow this practice would undermine the hearsay rule. *See, e.g., United States v. Hogan,* 763 F.2d 697, 702 (5th Cir. 1985) ("The prosecution, however, may not call a witness it knows to be hostile for the primary purpose of eliciting otherwise inadmissible impeachment testimony, for such a scheme merely serves as a subterfuge to avoid the hearsay rule. The danger in this procedure is obvious."); *United States v. Morlang,* 531 F.2d 183 (4th Cir. 1975) (conviction reversed on the ground that the government should not have been permitted to call a witness for no other purpose than to impeach him). *See generally,* Jonakait, *The Supreme Court, Plain Meaning, and the Changed Rules of Evidence,* 68 Tex. L. Rev. 745 (1990) (noting this and other situations where courts have felt compelled to diverge from the text of an Evidence Rule in order to reach a just result).

6. ***Rule 613(b):*** The Rule and the Advisory Committee Note both indicate that it is not necessary to give a witness an opportunity to examine a prior inconsistent statement before that statement is admitted to impeach the witness. All that is necessary is that the witness be given an opportunity at some point in the trial to explain or deny the statement. The Rule thus rejects the common-law rule from Queen Caroline's case, under which the proponent was required to lay a foundation for the prior inconsistent statement at the time the witness testified. Despite the language of the Rule and Note, however, some courts have reverted to the common-law rule. *See, e.g., United States v. Sutton,* 41 F.3d 1257 (8th Cir. 1994) (trial judge properly excluded testimony as to inconsistent statements by a prosecution witness on the ground that the witness had not been given an opportunity to explain or deny the prior statement while cross-examined by defense counsel); *United States v. Marks,* 816 F.2d 1207, 1211 (7th Cir. 1987) (trial judge is entitled despite the language of Rule 613(b) "to conclude that in particular circumstances the older approach should be used in order to avoid confusing witnesses and juries").

546

CASE LAW DIVERGENCE FROM THE
FEDERAL RULES OF EVIDENCE

7. ***Rule 615:*** The Rule provides that the trial court must, upon request, exclude prospective witnesses from the courtroom until they testify. The rule is grounded in the concern that a prospective witness could tailor his testimony to that of prior witnesses if he was allowed to sit in the courtroom. By its terms the extent of the Rule's coverage is limited to excluding witnesses from the courtroom. But many courts have held that a Rule 615 order also prohibits prospective witnesses from receiving or obtaining trial testimony outside of court. *See, e.g., United States v. Robinson,* 895 F.3d 1206, 1214 (9th Cir. 2018) ("An exclusion order would mean little if a prospective witness could simply read a transcript of prior testimony he was otherwise barred from hearing. Therefore, we join those circuits that have determined there is no difference between reading and hearing testimony for purposes of Rule 615."). *See also United States v. McMahon,* 104 F.3d 638, 642–45 (4th Cir. 1997) (affirming the district court's conclusion that a witness violated a Rule 615 exclusion order by reading daily trial transcripts)

8. ***Rule 702:*** The 2000 amendment to Rule 702, and the accompanying detailed Committee Note, impose requirements for the admissibility of expert testimony. The rule states that the trial court must find, among other things: 1) that the expert's testimony is based on sufficient facts or data; 2) that the expert's testimony is the product of reliable principles and methods; and 3) that the expert has reliably applied the principles and methods to the facts of the case. These three factors must be found by the trial judge by a preponderance of the evidence—by the terms of the Rule and Committee Note they are questions of admissibility, not matters of weight for the jury. Yet despite the text of the Rule and the emphasis in the Note, many courts have held that two of these factors—sufficient facts or data and reliable application—are questions of weight and not admissibility. *See, e.g., Milward v. Acuity Specialty Products Group, Inc.,* 639 F.3d 11, 22 (1st Cir. 2011) ("when the factual underpinning of an expert's opinion is weak it is a matter affecting the weight and credibility of the testimony—a question to be resolved by the jury"); *United States v. Gipson,* 383 F.3d 689, 696 (8th Cir. 2004) (drawing a distinction between "on the one hand, challenges to a scientific methodology, and, on the other hand, challenges to the application of that methodology"; holding that the reliability of the methodology is a question for the judge while the reliability of the application of that methodology is a question for the jury).

9. ***Rule 704(b):*** Rule 704(b) would seem to prohibit all expert witnesses from testifying that a criminal defendant either did or did not have the requisite mental state to commit the crime charged. It states that "an expert witness must not state an opinion about whether the defendant did or did not have a mental state or condition that constitutes an element of the crime charged or of a defense." But some courts have held (and others have implied) that the rule is applicable only to mental health experts, and therefore does not prohibit intent-based testimony from law enforcement personnel such as narcotics agents. *See, e.g., United States v. Gastiaburo,* 16 F.3d 582 (4th Cir. 1994) (stating that Rule 704(b) does not apply to the testimony of an expert law enforcement agent); *United States v. Lipscomb,* 14 F.3d 1236 (7th Cir. 1994) (expressing sympathy with such a position, but finding it unnecessary to decide the matter). Other courts, while technically applying the Rule 704(b) limitation to all expert witnesses, have applied it in such a way as to nullify its impact—permitting, for example, an expert to opine as to the mental state of a hypothetical person whose fact situation mirrors the fact situation in issue. *See, e.g., United States v. Williams,* 980 F.2d 1463 (D.C.Cir. 1992) (permitting a law enforcement agent to testify that a hypothetical person carrying ziplock bags each containing small amounts of drugs was intending to distribute them; the hypothetical matched the facts of the case).

   10. Rule 801(c) (Implied Assertions): Rule 801(c) defines hearsay as an out-of-court statement offered in evidence "to prove the truth of the matter asserted in the statement." The Committee Note states that "verbal conduct which is assertive but offered as a basis for inferring something other than the matter asserted" is excluded from the definition of hearsay "by the language of subdivision (c)". This would mean that a statement would be hearsay only if it were offered for the truth of the express assertion in the statement—offering it for any implied assertion would escape hearsay proscription. So for example, a statement "It is raining cats and dogs" would be admissible to prove it is raining—the statement would not be offered to prove the express assertion that cats and dogs were falling from the sky.

   This highly constricted definition of hearsay generally has been rejected by the courts. The cases generally state that statements are hearsay if 1) they are offered for the truth of a matter *implied* in the statement and 2) the speaker *intended* to communicate that implication. *See, e.g., United States v. Reynolds,* 715 F.2d 99 (3rd Cir. 1983) (rejecting the government's suggestion that only a statement's express assertion should be considered in deciding whether it constitutes hearsay); *Lyle v. Koehler,* 720 F.2d 426, 433 (6th Cir. 1983) (concluding that letters were hearsay because "the inferences they necessarily invite form an integral part of the letters"; the reference to "matters asserted" in Rule 801(c) covers both express and implied assertions); *United States v. Jackson,* 88 F.3d 845, 848 (10th Cir. 1996) (stating that the important question under Rule 801(c) is whether the assertion, express or implied, "is intended"). *See also* Milich, *Re-examining Hearsay Under the Federal Rules: Some Method for the Madness,* 39 Kan. L.Rev. 893 (1991) (arguing for an intent-based test in determining whether implied assertions are hearsay).

   11. Rule 801(d)(2)(D): The rule provides a hearsay exemption for a statement made by a party's agent, when offered against the party, and when the statement concerns a matter within the agent's scope of authority. So for example, a statement by a janitor, "I am sorry the floor was slippery, I should have cleaned up the spill before you slipped in it," can be admitted against the employer in a slip-and-fall case. But what if the party against whom the statement is offered is the government, and the statement is that of a government agent? The Rule provides no relief for statements from government agents, and so it would appear that a statement of a government agent should be admissible against the government in the same way as it would against a private employer. But several courts have held that Rule 801(d)(2)(D) cannot be used against the government. See *United States v. Yildiz,* 355 F.3d 80 (2d Cir. 2003). These courts rely on the common-law rule that refused to hold the government to the statements of its agents. But in principle, the common-law did not survive a Federal Rule of Evidence that is to the contrary.

   12. Rule 803(4): The Rule provides a hearsay exception for statements made for purposes of treatment or diagnosis when the statements deal with the cause of the medical condition. The exception does not, by its terms, provide a hearsay exception for statements attributing fault. The Committee Note states that statements of fault "would not ordinarily qualify" under the exception, and distinguishes a statement "I was hit by a car" (admissible when made to medical personnel) from "I was hit by a car that ran a red light" (inadmissible). Yet in at least some classes of cases, statements attributing fault, when made to medical personnel, are admitted by the courts under Rule 803(4). The most common example is a statement from a child victim of sexual abuse, specifically identifying her attacker. *See, e.g., United States v. Renville,* 779 F.2d 430, 438 (8th Cir. 1985) (child's statement attributing fault is admissible under Rule 803(4) "where the physician makes clear to the victim that the inquiry into the identity of the abuser is important to diagnosis and treatment, and the victim manifests such an understanding"); *United States v. Joe,* 8 F.3d 1488, 1494 (10th Cir. 1993) ("[T]he domestic sexual abuser's identity is admissible under Rule 803(4) where the abuser has such an intimate relationship with the victim that the abuser's identity becomes reasonably pertinent to the victim's proper treatment.").

    13. Rule 803(5): The Rule provides a hearsay exception for past recollection recorded: a record on a matter the witness once knew about but now cannot recall enough to testify fully and accurately. What happens, however, when a person makes a statement to another person, and that other person is the one who writes it down? The exception by its terms does not seem to permit a "two-party voucher" system of proving past recollection recorded, since it states that the record must be shown to have been "made or adopted by the witness." Thus, the Rule does not envision that a person with personal knowledge might make a statement recorded by another, with the record being made admissible by calling both the reporter and the recorder. Despite the language of the Rule, however, cases can be found that permit two-party vouching under Rule 803(5). *See, e.g., United States v. Williams,* 951 F.2d 853 (7th Cir. 1993).

    14. Rule 803(6): The Rule defines a business record as one "made at or near the time by—or from information transmitted by—someone with knowledge if kept in the course of a regularly conducted activity." This language could be read as abrogating the common-law requirement that the person transmitting the information to the recorder must have a business duty to do so. It states only that the transmitting person must have "knowledge," not that the person must be reporting within the business structure. Yet despite the text, the courts have held that all those who report information included in a business record must be under a business duty to do so—or else the hearsay problem created from the report by an outsider must be satisfied in some other way. See *United States v. Turner,* 189 F.3d 712, 719–20 (8th Cir. 1999) ("[W]hen the source of information and the recorder of that information are not the same person, the business record contains hearsay upon hearsay. If both the source and recorder of the information were acting in the regular course of the organization's business, however, the hearsay upon hearsay problem may be excused by the business records exception to the rule against hearsay."); *Bemis v. Edwards,* 45 F.3d 1369 (9th Cir. 1995) (911 call was not admissible as a business record because the caller was not under any business duty to report, and the report did not independently satisfy any hearsay exception); *Cameron v. Otto Bock Orthopedic Indus. Inc.,* 43 F.3d 14 (1st Cir. 1994) (product failure reports submitted to the manufacturer after the plaintiff's accident were inadmissible; the reports were submitted by parties who had no business duty to report accurately to the manufacturer).

    15. Rule 803(8)(A)(ii): Rule 803(8)(A)(ii) provides a hearsay exception for public reports. But the Rule specifically excludes from its coverage public reports setting forth "a matter observed by law-enforcement personnel" if such reports are offered "in a criminal case." Read literally, the Rule would not provide a hearsay exception for a forensic report prepared by the police that concluded that the defendant was innocent. Such a report would be offered by the defendant, but the exclusionary language of Rule 803(8)(A)(ii) covers all police reports offered in criminal cases. Yet some lower courts have refused to be bound by the plain meaning of the rule, reasoning that Congress intended to regulate only police reports that *inculpate* a criminal defendant—in deference to the accused's Sixth Amendment right to confrontation—and that the hearsay exception should therefore be available to public reports offered by the accused. *See, e.g., United States v. Smith*, 521 F.2d 957 (D.C.Cir. 1975) (despite its exclusionary language, Rule 803(8)(A)(ii) should be read in light of Congress' intent to exclude police reports only when offered *against* a criminal defendant). But see *United States v. Sharpe*, 193 F.3d 852, 868 (5th Cir. 1999) (the defendant's reliance on Rule 803(8)(A)(ii) to admit an exculpatory police report was "misplaced" because the Rule does not grant admissibility for any such reports offered in criminal cases).

   16. Rule 803(8)(A)(ii) and (A)(iii): Rule 803(8)(A)(ii) and (A)(iii) both contain language appearing to exclude from the hearsay exception all records prepared by law enforcement personnel, when such records are offered against a criminal defendant. Read literally, these provisions would prevent the government from introducing simple tabulations of non-adversarial information. For example, these subdivisions appear not to grant a hearsay exception for a routine printout from the Customs Service recording license plates of cars that crossed the border on a certain day, when offered in a criminal case to show a person's location. Courts have refused to apply the plain exclusionary language of these subdivisions literally, however. They reason that the language could not have been intended to cover reports that are ministerial in nature and prepared under non-adversarial circumstances; it is only adversarial, evaluative reports (such as crime scene reports) that carry the risk of fabrication that the exclusionary language was designed to regulate. *See, e.g., United States v. Orozco*, 590 F.2d 789 (9th Cir. 1979) (customs records of border crossings are admissible under Rule 803(8) because they are ministerial and not prepared under adversarial circumstances); *United States v. Grady*, 544 F.2d 598 (2d Cir. 1976) (reports concerning firearms' serial numbers were admissible because they were records of routine factual matters prepared in nonadversarial circumstances).

   17. Rule 804(b)(1): The Rule provides a hearsay exception for prior testimony when offered against a party who either 1) had a similar motive and opportunity to develop the testimony at the time it was given, or 2) in civil cases, had a predecessor in interest with such a similar motive and opportunity at the time the testimony was given. Some courts have defined the term "predecessor in interest" in civil cases as *anyone* who had a similar motive and opportunity to develop the testimony, at the time it was given, as the opponent would have at the instant trial; these courts do not require some legal relationship between the prior party and the party against whom the evidence is now offered. This construction collapses the term "predecessor in interest" with the term "similar motive". *See, e.g., Lloyd v. American Export Lines, Inc.*, 580 F.2d 1179 (3rd Cir. 1978) (prior testimony properly admitted against plaintiff, where prior party had a similar motive to develop the testimony as the plaintiff in the instant case would have were the declarant to testify at trial; Judge Stern, concurring, states that such an expansive definition of "predecessor in interest" effectively reads that term out of the Rule); *Horne v. Owens-Corning Fiberglass Corp.*, 4 F.3d 276 (4th Cir. 1993) (prior testimony from a different case properly admitted against the plaintiff, where the previous plaintiff, though not affiliated in any way with the plaintiff, had a similar motive to develop the testimony). Other courts have admitted such evidence not as prior testimony (for want of a predecessor in interest) but as residual hearsay. See *Dartez v. Fibreboard Corp.*, 765 F.2d 456 (5th Cir. 1985).

   18. Rule 804(b)(3): The Rule requires that in a criminal case the proponent of a declaration against penal interest must provide corroborating circumstances clearly indicating that the hearsay statement is trustworthy. The corroborating circumstances requirement does not, by its terms, apply to declarations against penal interest offered in civil cases. Some courts, however, have applied the corroborating circumstances requirement to declarations against penal interest offered in civil cases. *See, e.g., American Automotive Accessories, Inc. v. Fishman*, 175 F.3d 534, 541 (7th Cir. 1999) (reasoning that it is important to have a "unitary standard" for declarations against penal interest, no matter in what case and no matter by whom they are offered). Compare *Linde v. Arab Bank PLC*, 97 F.Supp.3d 287 (E.D.N.Y. 2015) (corroborating circumstances requirement not applicable to a declaration against penal interest when offered in a civil case). The 2010 amendment to the Rule extended the corroborating circumstances requirement to declarations against penal interest offered by the government in a criminal case. The Committee Note to that amendment specifically states that the amendment is not intended to affect the law on admissibility of declarations against penal interest in a civil case.

   19. Rule 806: The Rule states that a hearsay declarant's credibility may be attacked by any evidence that would be admissible if the declarant had testified as a witness. The language raises a problem when the proponent wishes to attack the declarant by proffering specific bad acts to prove the witness's bad character for veracity. Rule 608(b) prohibits extrinsic proof of bad acts when offered to show the witness's character for untruthfulness. Rule 806 could therefore be read literally as prohibiting bad acts impeachment of a hearsay declarant. This is because the extrinsic evidence is likely to be the only way to introduce bad acts when the witness is not there to be asked about them. But some courts have stated that extrinsic evidence of a bad act can be admitted to prove a hearsay declarant's character for veracity, subject to Rule 403. The reasoning is that because the declarant is not available for cross-examination, extrinsic evidence is "the only means of presenting such evidence to the jury." *United States v. Friedman*, 854 F.2d 535, n.8 (2d Cir. 1988). See the extensive discussion of this problem in Cordray, *Evidence Rule 806 and the Problem of the Nontestifying Declarant*, 56 Ohio State L.J. 495 (1995). But see *United States v. Saada*, 212 F.3d 210 (3d Cir. 2000), holding that extrinsic evidence may never be admitted to prove a bad act offered to impeach a hearsay declarant's character for truthfulness. The *Saada* court relied on the "plain language" of Rule 806, which it read as creating exactly the same impeachment rules for hearsay declarants as apply for in-court witnesses, with one exception—impeachment with inconsistent statements (as to which the requirement at trial of confronting the witness with the statement is specifically excused under Rule 806).

   20. Rule 807: Rule 807 provides a "residual exception" to the hearsay rule, granting admissibility to trustworthy statements that are "not specifically covered by" other exceptions. There are at least two ways in which the case law diverges from the text and/or Committee Note to Rule 807. First, the Rule permits the admission of residual hearsay only if that hearsay is "not specifically covered" by another exception. This might seem to indicate that hearsay that "nearly misses" one of the established exceptions should not be admissible as residual hearsay—because it is specifically covered by, and yet not admissible under, another exception. In fact, however, most courts have construed the term "not specifically covered" by another hearsay exception to mean "not admissible under" another hearsay exception. *See, e.g., United States v. Fernandez,* 892 F.2d 976 (11th Cir. 1989) (grand jury statement is "not specifically covered" by another hearsay exception because it is not admissible under any such exception). An amendment to Rule 807, scheduled to take effect on December 1, 2019, clarifies that the residual exception *is* available for "near misses" of the categorical exceptions.

The second divergence between the case law and the text of the residual exception involves the notice requirement. The Rule states that a statement may not be admitted under this exception unless the proponent gives reasonable notice—in advance of trial—of the intent to offer the statement. Most courts have read the notice requirement far more flexibly than its language would seem to indicate. For example, most courts have held that the notice requirement can be satisfied by providing notice *at* trial, so long as the adversary is given sufficient time to prepare. *See, e.g., United States v. Baker,* 985 F.2d 1248 (4th Cir. 1993). Other courts have read a good cause exception into the notice requirement. *See, e.g., United States v. Lyon,* 567 F.2d 777 (8th Cir. 1977). But see *United States v. Ruffin,* 575 F.2d 346 (2d Cir. 1978) (rejecting a good cause exception as not permitted by the text of the Rule). The Advisory Committee on Evidence Rules has proposed a rule amendment that would specifically provide for a good cause exception to the Rule 807 notice requirement. That amendment is scheduled to take effect on December 1, 2019.

21. Rule 1006: Rule 1006 allows admission of summaries in lieu of having the voluminous originals presented at trial. Thus the Rule allows a summary to operate as evidence when admitting the underlying components would be too burdensome. The use of summaries as evidence must be distinguished from the use of charts and summaries only to clarify or amplify argument based on evidence that has already been admitted. *See, e.g., Air Disaster at Lockerbie Scot. on Dec. 21, 1988,* 37 F.3d 804 (2d Cir. 1994) (finding no error where experts gave their opinions on the adequacy of PanAm security measures, relying from time to time on trial transcripts displayed on a projection screen; Rule 1006 objection was misplaced because the trial transcripts were records of testimony at the trial itself). Some courts have considered the "admissibility" of charts and summaries of trial evidence under Rule 1006, but this is a mistake; the Rule is really not applicable because pedagogical summaries are not evidence. *See, e.g., United States v. Sawyer,* 85 F.3d 713 (1st Cir. 1996) (applying Rule 1006 to approve the use of summaries based on evidence that had already been admitted at trial); *United States v. Stephens,* 779 F.2d 232 (5th Cir. 1985) (same).

III. Examples of Case Law Development Where the Rules and Committee Note Are Silent

1. Rule 103: The Rule provides conditions for a party wishing to preserve a claim of evidentiary error for appeal. It states that a party must make a timely objection or motion to strike, stating the specific ground of objection if that ground is not apparent from the context. An amendment to Rule 103 effective December 1, 2000 further provides that if the trial court makes a definitive ruling on the record admitting or excluding evidence, either at or before trial, a party need not renew an objection or offer of proof to preserve a claim of error for appeal. But the Rule does not address the question whether a party can appeal an advance ruling holding evidence admissible, if the evidence is not actually admitted at trial. For example, assume that a criminal defendant moves in advance of trial to preclude the prosecution from impeaching him with his prior convictions. Assume further that the trial court rules definitively that the convictions are admissible impeachment evidence. Can the defendant decide not to testify at trial, and then argue on appeal that the trial court erred in its advance ruling?

While Rule 103 is silent on whether an appeal can be taken from a ruling holding evidence admissible where the evidence is not eventually admitted at trial, there is significant case law on this question. The Supreme Court, in *Luce v. United States*, 469 U.S. 38 (1984), specifically held that an accused must testify at trial in order to preserve a claim of error predicated upon a trial court's decision to admit the accused's prior convictions for impeachment. The *Luce* principle has been extended by many lower courts to other comparable situations. See *United States v. DiMatteo*, 759 F.2d 831 (11th Cir. 1985) (applying *Luce* where the defendant's witness would be impeached with evidence offered under Rule 608). *See also United States v. Goldman*, 41 F.3d 785, 788 (1st Cir. 1994) ("Although *Luce* involved impeachment by conviction under Rule 609, the reasons given by the Supreme Court for requiring the defendant to testify apply with full force to the kind of Rule 403 and 404 objections that are advanced by Goldman in this case."); *Palmieri v. DeFaria*, 88 F.3d 136 (2d Cir. 1996) (where the plaintiff decided to take an adverse judgment rather than challenge an advance ruling by putting on evidence at trial, the *in limine* ruling would not be reviewed on appeal); *United States v. Ortiz*, 857 F.2d 900 (2d Cir. 1988) (where uncharged misconduct is ruled admissible if the defendant pursues a certain defense, the defendant must actually pursue that defense at trial in order to preserve a claim of error on appeal); *United States v. Bond*, 87 F.3d 695 (5th Cir. 1996) (where the trial court rules *in limine* that the defendant would waive his fifth amendment privilege were he to testify, the defendant must take the stand and testify in order to challenge that ruling on appeal).

Rule 103 is also silent on whether a party who objects to evidence that the trial court definitively rules admissible, and who then offers the evidence to "remove the sting" of its anticipated prejudicial effect, thereby waives the right to appeal the trial court's ruling. Lower courts had been in conflict on this question. *See, e.g., Judd v. Rodman*, 105 F.3d 1339 (11th Cir. 1997) (an objection made *in limine* is sufficient to preserve a claim of error when the movant, as a matter of trial strategy, presents the objectionable evidence herself on direct examination to minimize its prejudicial effect); *Gill v. Thomas*, 83 F.3d 537, 540 (1st Cir. 1996) ("by offering the misdemeanor evidence himself, Gill waived his opportunity to object and thus did not preserve the issue for appeal"). The Supreme Court, in *Ohler v. United States*, 529 U.S. 753 (2000), resolved this question by holding that a party who introduces evidence of a prior conviction on direct examination waives any right to appeal an *in limine* ruling holding that the evidence would be admissible at trial. The Court, in an opinion by Chief Justice Rehnquist, recognized that Rule 103 was silent on this question. It refused to depart from the general common-law rule that "a party introducing evidence cannot complain on appeal that the evidence was erroneously admitted."

2.   *Rule 104(a):* This Rule states that preliminary questions "about whether a witness is qualified, a privilege exists, or evidence is admissible are determined by the court." But the Rule is silent on who bears the burden of proof on admissibility questions, and it is also silent on what standard of proof is to be employed. A significant body of case law has been developed to answer these questions. Most importantly, in *Bourjaily v. United States*, 483 U.S. 171 (1987), the Court held that the party seeking to admit the evidence—

the proponent—generally has the burden of proving that the admissibility requirements set forth in the Federal Rules are met. Furthermore, the *Bourjaily* Court held that the burden of proving an admissibility requirement under Rule 104(a) is by a preponderance of the evidence. The specific holding in *Bourjaily* was that for a statement to be admissible under the coconspirator exception to the hearsay rule, the trial court must find that the prosecution has established by a preponderance of the evidence that the defendant and the hearsay declarant were members of the same conspiracy. The reasoning in *Bourjaily* has been extended to most other questions of admissibility under the Federal Rules of Evidence. *See, e.g., Daubert v. Merrell Dow Pharmaceuticals,* 509 U.S. 79 (1993) (proponent of expert testimony has the burden of showing it is more likely than not reliable). So for example, a proponent who proffers a hearsay statement under the excited utterance exception has the burden of showing it more likely than not that the declarant was under the influence of a startling event when he spoke. See *Miller v. Keating,* 754 F.2d 507 (3d Cir. 1985) (proponent must establish admissibility of an excited utterance by a preponderance of the evidence). One important exception arises with privileges. Because privilege rules operate to exclude relevant and reliable evidence, they are not favored. Therefore, the party seeking to *exclude* proffered evidence on the ground that it is privileged bears the burden of showing, by a preponderance of the evidence, that a privilege applies. *See generally, United States v. Zolin,* 491 U.S. 554 (1989).

   3. Rule 301: This Rule provides some guidance on the effect of a presumption. The Rule does not define the term "presumption"; it simply states that unless otherwise provided, "the party against whom a presumption is directed has the burden of producing evidence to rebut the presumption." The Rule specifically leaves it to substantive law to determine when proffered evidence establishes a presumption that a fact exists. Generally speaking, presumptions are based on one or more of the following rationales: (1) one party has superior access to proof; (2) social or economic policies warrant a presumption; (3) experience indicates the high probability of a given conclusion from a given set of facts; (4) a presumption will promote efficiency and convenience. So for example, it has been held that proof that a letter was mailed establishes a presumption that it was received. *Anderson v. United States,* 966 F.2d 487 (9th Cir. 1982) (in a taxpayer's suit for a refund, the Government failed to rebut the common-law presumption of receipt that arose from the taxpayer's proof of mailing her return).

   Rule 301 is also silent on whether a party favored by a presumption is entitled to a peremptory instruction if the party against whom the presumption operates fails to offer any rebuttal evidence. For example, if a party proves that he mailed a letter, and the opponent provides no conflicting evidence, is the mailing party entitled to an instruction to the jury that the letter is to be deemed mailed? Courts have held that such an instruction must be given upon request. *See, e.g., A.C. Aukerman Co., v. R.L. Chaides Constr. Co.,* 960 F.2d 1020, 1037 (Fed.Cir. 1992) (where presumption applies, the presumed fact "must be inferred, absent rebuttal evidence.").

   4. Rule 404(b): Rule 404(b) provides that a person's uncharged acts of misconduct can be offered to prove something other than a person's character, such as intent or motive. Rule 404(b) imposes a notice requirement on the prosecution in criminal cases, which is intended to protect the accused from unfair surprise; it provides that upon request by the accused, the prosecution must give reasonable notice in advance of trial of the general nature of the Rule 404(b) evidence it intends to produce.

CASE LAW DIVERGENCE FROM THE
FEDERAL RULES OF EVIDENCE

What happens if the government gives pretrial notice of its intent to proffer a prior bad act, and then subsequently discovers a *different* bad act that it wants to use as well? Or what if the government responds to a defense request by stating that it does not intend to use Rule 404(b) evidence, and *then* uncovers a bad act committed by the defendant that it does intend to use? The notice requirement of Rule 404(b) does not state whether the prosecution has a continuing obligation to notify the defendant, should it discover Rule 404(b) evidence after an initial response to the defendant's request. But it has been held that the Rule imposes a continuing obligation of notice. *See, e.g., United States v. Barnes,* 49 F.3d 1144, 1148 (6th Cir. 1995) (declaring that Rule 404(b) requires "a continuing obligation on the government to comply with the notice requirement * * * whenever it discovers information that meets the previous defense request"; noting that a contrary reading "would force the defense to make numerous, periodic requests until the trial has been completed—surely a wasteful procedure.").

The notice requirement of Rule 404(b) is conditioned on a request by the accused. The Rule does not state how specific the request must be to trigger the government's notice obligation. For example, is an omnibus motion for discovery sufficient to trigger the notice requirement? Courts have held that an omnibus motion is not sufficient to trigger the government's obligation to notify under the Rule. Rather, a request for notification, "at a minimum, must be sufficiently clear and particular, in an objective sense, fairly to alert the prosecution that the defense is requesting pretrial notification of the general nature of any Rule 404(b) evidence the prosecution intends to introduce." *United States v. Tuesta-Toro,* 29 F.3d 771, 774 (1st Cir. 1994) (notice not required where defense demanded outright pretrial disclosure of statements in any form, referring to the defendant in any way, without regard to their admissibility or the government's intention to introduce them). Compare *United States v. Williams,* 792 F.Supp. 1120, 1133 (S.D.Ind. 1992) (notification required in response to detailed request reciting text of Rule 404(b)); *United States v. Alex,* 791 F.Supp. 723, 728 (N.D.Ill. 1992) (notification required in response to request specifically referencing Rule 404(b)). The Advisory Committee has proposed an amendment that would eliminate the request requirement of Rule 404(b) on the ground that it is a needless procedure that proves only to be a trap for the unwary. That amendment is scheduled to take effect on December 1, 2020.

5. *Rule 410:* Rule 410 provides certain protections to criminal defendants during the process of plea bargaining. Rule 410 is silent, however, on whether its protections can be waived by a criminal defendant. In *United States v. Mezzanatto,* 513 U.S. 196 (1995), during guilty plea negotiations the defendant agreed that he could be impeached with statements made during the negotiations if he ultimately went to trial and testified inconsistently with those statements. The Supreme Court upheld the agreement, finding that the defendant had knowingly and voluntarily waived his right to the protection of Rule 410. The Court refused to hold that the Rule's silence on the matter meant that its protections could not be waived. Instead the Court presumed that any statutory right could be waived in the absence of a specific provision to the contrary, so long as the waiver was knowing and voluntary. The facts of *Mezzanatto* involved a waiver permitting the use for impeachment purposes of statements made during guilty plea negotiations. Neither *Mezzanatto* nor Rule 410 itself says anything explicitly about whether a defendant can waive the protections of the Rule so as to provide that the prosecution can admit his statements during plea negotiations as substantive evidence at trial, *i.e.,* as a party-opponent statement admissible even if the defendant does not testify. Several courts have relied on the rationale of

Mezzanatto to uphold a waiver of Rule 410 protections that permitted the government to use the defendant's statements as substantive evidence in its case-in-chief. *See, e.g., United States v. Burch,* 156 F.3d 1315 (D.C.Cir. 1998).

      6.   Article VI: Article VI governs treatment of testifying witnesses. The Article is silent about many of the common forms of impeachment, such as bias, contradiction, and mental capacity. There is, of course, a significant amount of case law dealing with impeachment matters on which Article VI is silent. Case law generally regulates the forms of impeachment not specifically covered by Article VI by using principles derived from Evidence Rules 402 and 403—such impeachment is permitted unless the probative value of the impeachment evidence is substantially outweighed by the risks of prejudice, confusion and delay. See *United States v. Abel,* 469 U.S. 45 (1984) (impeachment for bias governed by Rule 403 principles). *See generally,* S. Saltzburg, M. Martin and D. Capra, *Federal Rules of Evidence Manual* §§ 607.02, 608.02 (11th ed. 2015). *See also* Imwinkelreid, *The Silence Speaks Volumes: A Brief Reflection on the Question of Whether It Is Necessary To Fill the Seeming Gaps In Article VI of the Federal Rules of Evidence, Governing the Admissibility of Evidence Logically Relevant to the Witness's Credibility,* 1998 Univ. Ill. L.Rev. 1013, 1036 (noting that Article VI is silent about most matters of impeachment, but concluding that "as a general proposition, there is little to be gained and much to be lost by initiating the process of revising Article VI.").

      7.   Rule 803(3): The Rule provides a hearsay exception for statements of a declarant's state of mind. The Rule is silent, however, on whether a declarant's statement of intent can be used to prove the subsequent conduct of someone other than the declarant. When the victim says, "I am going to meet Frank tonight", is the statement admissible to prove that Frank and the victim actually met? Or is the statement admissible only to prove the future conduct of the declarant? The Advisory Committee Note refers to the Rule as allowing "evidence of intention as tending to prove the act intended." The case law is conflicted. Some courts have refused to admit a statement that the declarant intended to meet with a third party as proof that they actually did meet. *See, e.g., Gual Morales v. Hernandez Vega,* 579 F.2d 677 (1st Cir. 1978); *United States v. Jenkins,* 579 F.2d 840 (4th Cir. 1978) (statements of intent can prove only the declarant's subsequent conduct). Other courts hold such statements admissible if the proponent provides corroborating evidence that the meeting took place. *See, e.g., United States v. Delvecchio,* 816 F.2d 59 (2d Cir. 1987).

      8.   Rule 1101: Rule 1101 states that the Federal Rules of Evidence are generally applicable to all federal proceedings. Rule 1101(d) lists certain proceedings to which the Rules are inapplicable, including grand jury and bail proceedings—and other miscellaneous proceedings such as those set forth in Rule 1101(d)(3). Courts have found that the Federal Rules are inapplicable to a number of proceedings that are not specifically mentioned as exempt in Rule 1101(d). Examples include suppression hearings, proceedings to obtain a temporary restraining order, and proceedings seeking release from psychiatric commitment. *See, e.g., United States v. Frazier,* 26 F.3d 110 (11th Cir. 1994) (Evidence Rules inapplicable in supervised release revocation proceedings); *United States v. Schaefer,* 87 F.3d 562 (1st Cir. 1996) (evidence rules inapplicable at suppression hearings); *United States v. Palesky,* 855 F.2d 34 (1st Cir. 1988) (Evidence Rules are not applicable in hearings held to determine whether a person will be committed to or released from a psychiatric facility). The courts establish these exemptions because they are within the spirit of Rule 1101(d)—exempting from the Rules those proceedings that are less formal than a trial and in which the judge is the finder of fact. *See, e.g., Government of Virgin Islands in Interest of A.M.*, 34 F.3d 153, 161 (3rd Cir. 1994) (Evidence Rules do not apply in juvenile transfer proceedings, even though such proceedings are not specifically exempted in Rule 1101(d)(1); a juvenile transfer proceeding "is of a preliminary nature and is consequently not comparable to a civil or criminal trial."). The Restyled Rules, effective December 1, 2011, clarify that the list of exempted proceedings in Rule 1101(d) is not exclusive. *See* Rule 1101(d)(3) (rules not applicable to Miscellaneous Proceedings "such as" . . .).

Appendix IV

BEST PRACTICES FOR AUTHENTICATING DIGITAL EVIDENCE

Hon. Paul W. Grimm[1]

Daniel J. Capra[2]

Gregory P. Joseph, Esq.[3]

I. Introduction

Digital evidence is now commonly offered at trial. Examples include emails, spreadsheets, evidence from websites, digitally-enhanced photographs, PowerPoint presentations, texts, tweets, Facebook posts, and computerized versions of disputed events. Does the fact that an item is electronic raise any special challenges in authenticating that item?

In Federal Courts, authenticity is governed by Rule 901(a), which requires that to establish that an item is authentic, a proponent must produce admissible evidence "sufficient to support a finding that the item is what the proponent claims it is."[4] Rule 901(b) provides many examples of evidence that satisfies the standard of proof for establishing authenticity, including testimony of a witness with knowledge,[5] circumstantial evidence,[6] and evidence describing a process or system that shows that it produces an accurate result.[7] The standards and examples provided by Rule 901(a) and (b) are flexible enough to adapt to all forms of evidence—including electronic evidence.

That does not mean that authenticating digital evidence is automatic. There are a large number of cases dealing with authentication of digital evidence over the last 15 or so years; and such evidence can present challenges in establishing that it has not been altered and that it comes from a certain source. The Judicial Conference Advisory Committee on Evidence Rules, surveying this case law, determined that the Bench and Bar would be well-served by a Best Practices Manual that would provide guidance on factors that should be taken into account for authenticating each of the major new forms of digital evidence that are being offered in the courts.

---

[1] United States District Judge for the District of Maryland; Member, Judicial Conference Advisory Committee on Civil Rules.

[2] Reed Professor of Law, Fordham Law School; Reporter to the Judicial Conference Advisory Committee on Evidence Rules.

[3] Partner, Joseph Hage Aaronsen, New York City; former member of the Judicial Conference Advisory Committee on Evidence Rules.

[4] Evidence proffered to support authenticity of a challenged item must itself be admissible. *See, e.g.*, United States v. Bonds, 608 F.3d 495 (9th Cir. 2010) (records could not be authenticated where the only basis for authentication was a hearsay statement not admissible under any exception).

[5] Fed.R.Evid. 901(b)(1).

[6] Fed.R.Evid. 901(b)(4).

[7] Fed.R.Evid. 901(b)(9).

APPENDIX IV

The idea for a Best Practices Manual grew out of a symposium sponsored by the Advisory Committee on the challenges of electronic evidence. After that Symposium, the Reporter to the Advisory Committee began to work with two noted authorities on electronic evidence—Hon. Paul Grimm and Gregory P. Joseph, Esq. The result is this Best Practices Manual; it is the work of the authors alone.

This Manual begins with an analysis by Judge Grimm of the basic rules on authenticating evidence, with a focus on digital evidence and the interplay between Evidence Rules 104(a) (providing that the judge is to decide admissibility factors by a preponderance of the evidence) and Rule 104(b) (providing that for questions of conditional relevance—such as authenticity— the standard of proof for admissibility is enough evidence to support a finding).

Following Judge Grimm's introduction, Part Two of the Handbook sets forth some guidelines on authentication of the kinds of electronic evidence that are most frequently offered in litigation today: 1) emails; 2) texts; 3) chatroom conversations; 4) web postings; and 5) social media postings.[8] In Part Three, we consider whether and when the proponent might argue that the court can take judicial notice of the authenticity of certain digital evidence. Finally, Part Four provides an extensive discussion of two amendments to the Federal Rules of Evidence—Rules 902(13) and (14)—that went into effect on December 1, 2017, and are designed to ease the burden of authenticating electronic evidence.

At the outset it is important to emphasize that the standard for establishing authenticity of digital evidence is the same mild standard as for traditional forms of evidence. None of the checklists set forth below are going to be required to be met *in toto* before digital evidence is found authentic. They are just relevant factors, and usually satisfying one or two of any of the listed factors will be enough to convince the court that a juror could find the digital evidence to be authentic. But the factors will need to be applied case-by-case.

II. An Introduction to the Principles of Authentication for Electronic Evidence: The Relationship Between Rule 104(a) and 104(b)

This Manual is designed to provide answers to the fundamental evidentiary questions of how to authenticate digital evidence. But before turning to the authentication rules themselves, there are two preliminary rules that must be discussed and understood, because without them, authentication decisions are apt to be erroneous. These rules are Fed.R.Evid. 104(a) (which states the general rule governing preliminary questions about the admissibility of evidence) and Fed.R.Evid. 104(b) (the so-called

---

[8] This Best Practices Handbook covers the relatively new forms of electronic communications. Parties have been authenticating more traditional forms of electronic evidence for many years—examples include telephone conversations, audiotapes, and video recordings. *See, e.g.,* United States v. Taylor, 530 F.2d 639 (5th Cir. 1976). (video evidence from a bank security camera was properly authenticated where testimony revealed the camera was present on the day in question and was facing the events of an armed robbery, and was functioning properly). This pamphlet does not cover such traditional forms of electronic communication. For more on authentication of such information, see Saltzburg, Martin & Capra, Federal Rules of Evidence Manual § 901 (11th ed. 2015), which provides relevant case law and commentary.

BEST PRACTICES FOR AUTHENTICATING
DIGITAL EVIDENCE

"conditional relevance" rule[9]). Understanding these two rules is essential to making correct decisions about the authentication of digital evidence.

We start with Rule 104(a). Its text is deceptively straightforward: "[t]he court must decide any preliminary question about whether a witness is qualified, a privilege exists, *or evidence is admissible*. In so deciding, the court is not bound by evidence rules, except those on privilege." (emphasis added). Most decisions about admissibility of evidence, whether digital or otherwise, are made by the judge alone. They include decisions about whether evidence is relevant, constitutes hearsay (or fits within one of the many hearsay exceptions), or is excessively prejudicial when compared to its probative value, whether experts are qualified and the extent of opinion testimony that will be allowed, and most questions regarding application of the original writing rule. When the judge makes a ruling under Rule 104(a) he or she is the sole decision maker as to whether the evidence may be heard by the jury. If admitted, of course, the jury is free to give the evidence whatever weight (if any) they think it deserves. This is familiar turf to trial judges, but with digital evidence, there is a greater likelihood that the judge alone may not be the final decision maker regarding admissibility. The jury also may have a part to play in the admissibility decision, and this is where Rule 104(b) comes in.

Rule 104(b) qualifies Rule 104(a). It provides "[w]hen the relevance of evidence depends on whether a fact exists, proof must be introduced sufficient to support a finding that the fact does exist. The court may admit the proposed evidence on the condition that the proof be introduced later." Read in isolation, Rule 104(b) seems too abstract to be helpful. But, in the case of disputes over the authenticity of digital evidence, it can be an important qualifier to the general rule of 104(a) that the trial judge decides questions about the admissibility of evidence.

An illustration will help bring things into focus. Imagine the following variations of a common theme. In an employment discrimination case the plaintiff, a woman, alleges that her supervisor, a man, intentionally discriminated against her in deciding to promote a lesser qualified man to a position that the plaintiff sought. As evidence of intentional discrimination, the plaintiff wants to introduce an email that she asserts her supervisor sent to her that says: "Jane, stop bugging me about the sales supervisor position. Your track record compared to the men in our sales group is terrible, and confirms what I always have suspected. Women just don't have the stuff it takes to get out there and sell our products. You should be glad you still have your sales job, and quit trying to be something you can never do well. Bob." The email is from the company email account (Bob@company.com), addressed to the plaintiff (Jane@company.com), apparently signed by the supervisor (Bob), discusses a subject matter about which the supervisor has knowledge, and is dated on a day and time the supervisor was known to be at the office. Plaintiff contends that the email is "smoking gun" evidence of intentional gender discrimination.

Imagine further the following scenarios when the plaintiff offers the email into evidence at trial:

> One: the defense attorney objects to the introduction of the email, the judge asks for the basis of the objection, and the defense attorney says "inadequate foundation".

---

[9] Fed.R.Evid. 104(b) (1972) Advisory Note.

APPENDIX IV

Two: the defense attorney objects, the judge asks for the basis of the objection, and the defense attorney says "Judge, this is an email, there is no evidence that the supervisor was the one who actually wrote it. It was found on a company computer, anyone in the company had access to that computer, including the plaintiff herself, whose office was right next to his, and my client is often away from his desk during the day, and he does not log out of his computer. Plaintiff hasn't shown that someone else didn't send that email pretending to be my client, and everyone knows how easy it is to fake an email."

Three: the defense attorney objects, the judge asks for the basis of the objection, and the defense attorney says "Judge, my client will testify that on the day and time stated on the email he was at a sales meeting with the other supervisors and the president of the company. Five other people saw him there at that day and time and will testify that they did. During those meetings, no one is allowed to use their smart phone or to send or receive emails, on pain of being fired if the president sees them looking at their phones. The location of the meeting was on a different floor from where my client and the plaintiff work. He will testify that he did not send the email, and that when he leaves his office he does not log out, his computer stays on, and anyone can access it without a password and use his office email account. He also will testify that when he came back from the meeting, the plaintiff looked at him in a strange way, and said "I wouldn't look so smug if I were you. You might not be that way for very long."

With these scenarios in mind, what is the interplay between Rule 104(a) and 104(b) in determining whether the email may be admitted at trial and considered by the jury? In the first scenario, no explanation was given by the defense attorney for excluding the email other than the conclusory statement that the plaintiff had not laid a sufficient foundation. Here, the trial judge alone decides, under Rule 104(a), whether an adequate foundation has been established. If the foundation was deficient, the judge will require the plaintiff's lawyer to make a fuller showing, and allow or exclude the email accordingly. Rule 104(b) is not implicated.

In the second scenario, the defense attorney has made a conclusory legal argument that provides no facts showing that the supervisor did not author the email, but rather speculates that it *could have* been written by someone else. The argument invites the trial judge to require the plaintiff's lawyer to "prove a negative"—that no one but the supervisor was the author. But this is not the burden that the plaintiff must meet under Rule 104(a) to establish the admissibility of the email. Rather, all that plaintiff must do is to meet the obligation imposed by Rule 901(a), which is to "produce evidence sufficient to support a finding that the item is what the proponent claims it is." Certainty is not required. All that is needed is evidence sufficient to convince a reasonable juror that, more likely than not, the email is what the plaintiff claims it is—an email her supervisor drafted. And, under the hypothetical facts of the second scenario, the defense counsel is wrong in saying the plaintiff has offered no evidence that the email came from the supervisor. She has shown that the email came from the supervisor's email address, on the company email server, on a day when the supervisor was at the office, discussing a topic about which the supervisor had knowledge, and is signed with his name. Certainly this would be an example of authentication under Rule 901(b)(4), where the "appearance, contents, substance . . . or other distinctive characteristics of the item, taken together with all the circumstances" tend to show that the supervisor authored the email.

BEST PRACTICES FOR AUTHENTICATING
DIGITAL EVIDENCE

The second scenario also raises only Rule 104(a) issues for the trial judge alone to determine admissibility. The facts, under which admissibility must be judged, are undisputed. If the trial judge concludes (as she should under these facts) that a reasonable juror *could* find from the foundation presented that it is more likely than not that the supervisor wrote the email, it is admissible. Defense counsel's speculation about what "could" have happened is reserved for argument to the jury about how much weight (if any) to give to the email. Absent from scenario two is evidence that the supervisor in fact did not author the email, to contradict the undisputed facts introduced by the plaintiff regarding the distinctive characteristics of the email that associate it with the supervisor. Put another way, if "it might have been hacked" or "it might have been photoshopped" were enough to preclude authentication, then no digital evidence could ever be authenticated.[10]

Scenario three does introduce facts contradicting the evidence the plaintiff introduced about the distinctive characteristics of the email tying it to the supervisor. The defense attorney has proffered that he will introduce evidence (the supervisor, the five witnesses who corroborate that he was with them at the time the email was sent, the policy prohibiting use of cell phones during meetings with the company president, the meeting's location on a different floor of the building). Now the trial judge is presented with competing evidence that the supervisor did, and did not, author the email. If the plaintiff's evidence is accepted over that of the defendant, then it is more likely than not that the supervisor is the author, and the email is relevant to show his discriminatory intent. But, if the defendant's version of the facts is accepted over those offered by the plaintiff, then the supervisor did not author the email, and it is irrelevant to prove his state of mind. The relevance of the email turns on whether the plaintiff's version or the defendant's version is accepted, and this falls squarely within the scope of Rule 104(b). The relevance of the email depends on the existence of a disputed fact— authorship of the email. Who decides between the competing versions? If the case is tried before a jury, it is the jury, not the judge, who must resolve the dispute.[11] The judge's role under Rule 104(a) is to evaluate whether a reasonable jury *could* find (more likely than not) either that the supervisor did, or did not, author the email. If either version is plausible, then the judge conditionally admits the email, but at the time it is introduced instructs the jury that if they find that the plaintiff has shown that the supervisor more likely than not authored the email, they may consider it as evidence and give it the weight that they feel it is entitled to. Contrastingly, if they find that the defendant has persuaded them that, more likely than not, he did not author the email, they must disregard it entirely, and give it no weight in

---

[10] *See, e.g.,* United States v. Safavian, 435 F.Supp.2d 36, 41 (D.D.C. 2006) ("The possibility of alteration does not and cannot be the basis for excluding e-mails as unidentified or unauthenticated as a matter of course, any more than it can be the rationale for excluding paper documents (and copies of those documents) . . . . Absent specific evidence showing alteration . . . the Court will not exclude any . . . emails because of the mere possibility that it can be done.").

[11] Fed.R.Evid. 104(b) (1972) Advisory Note ("If preliminary questions of conditional relevancy were determined solely by the judge, as provided in subdivision (a), the functioning of the jury as a trier of fact would be greatly restricted and in some cases virtually destroyed. These are appropriate questions for juries. Accepted treatment, as provided in the rule, is consistent with that given fact questions generally. The judge makes a preliminary determination whether the foundation evidence is sufficient to support a finding of fulfillment of the condition. If so, the item is admitted. If after all the evidence on the issue is in, pro and con, the jury could reasonably conclude that fulfillment of the condition is not established, the issue is for them. If the evidence is not such as to allow a finding, the judge withdraws the matter from their consideration.").

their deliberations. The final decision about whether the email has been admitted (and can be considered by the jury) or excluded (and disregarded by the jury) must await the jury's deliberation on the merits of the case. The judge makes a preliminary assessment of whether the evidence is one-sided or two, and if the latter, submits it to the jury for their decision. The issue of conditional relevance generated by disputed facts regarding the authenticity (and hence, relevance) of evidence is especially prevalent with digital evidence.

It is important for judges to distinguish between which of the scenarios listed above is presented to them when ruling on admissibility of digital evidence. For scenario one situations, the judge alone decides whether the proponent has laid a proper foundation to authenticate the digital evidence. Most often, the judge will consider whether one or more of the illustrations of how to authenticate found at Fed.R.Evid. 901(b)[12] or 902[13] has been shown.

For scenario two situations, the judge alone makes the decision whether to admit or exclude. In doing so, the judge must be careful not to let unparticularized and conclusory argument by the party objecting to the introduction of the digital evidence about what "might" or "could have happened" lead the judge to impose on the proponent of the evidence a burden of proof greater than that ordinarily required by Rule 104(a)—a showing that the evidence more likely than not is what it purports to be. It is a mistake for a judge to require the party introducing digital evidence to prove that no one other than the purported maker could have created the evidence if the introducing party has shown that, more likely than not, it was created by a particular person, unless there is evidence (not argument) that some other person could have done so.[14] Finally, for scenario three situations, where the judge is faced with competing facts plausibly showing that the digital evidence was, and was not, created by the person claimed by the proponent, then she should allow the evidence to be admitted "conditionally" under Rule 104(b). The judge should then instruct the jury that if they find that the evidence that the person claimed to have created the evidence did not do so

---

[12] For digital evidence, the most useful authentication rules within Rule 901(b) are: 901(b)(1) (a witness with personal knowledge that the evidence is what it purports to be); 901(b)(3) (comparison of the evidence with an authenticated specimen by an expert witness or the finder of fact); 901(b)(4) (the appearance, contents, substance, internal patterns or other distinctive characteristics of the item, taken together with all the circumstances); 901(b)(5) (for audio recordings, an opinion identifying a person's voice, whether heard firsthand or through electronic transmission or recording, based on having heard that voice in the past); and 901(b)(9) (evidence describing a process or system of showing that it produces an accurate result).

[13] Fed.R.Evid. 902 provides examples of self-authentication, where no extrinsic evidence or testimony is needed to authenticate. The following self-authentication rules may be helpful for digital evidence; 902(5) (A book, pamphlet, or other publication purporting to be issued by a public authority. Most public authorities have web sites and post publications relating to their fields of jurisdiction.); 902(6) (Printed material purporting to be a newspaper or periodical. Most newspapers and periodicals have "on line editions", and this rule potentially is available to self-authenticate.); 902(11) and (12) (certified copy of domestic and foreign records of regularly conducted activities); proposed Rule 902(13) (certified copy of machine-generated information); and proposed Rule 902(14) (certified copy of computer generated or stored information). Authentication under Rules 902(13) and (14) is discussed in a separate section, infra.

[14] Grimm, et al, *Authentication of Social Media Evidence*, 36 American Journal of Trial Advocacy 433, 459 (2013) ("A trial judge should admit the evidence if there is plausible evidence of authenticity produced by the proponent of the evidence and only speculation or conjecture—not facts—by the opponent of the evidence about how, or by whom, it 'might' have been created.").

is more believable than the evidence that he did, they must disregard it and give it no weight in their deliberations.

Careful attention to the interplay between Rule 104(a) and 104(b), as well as consideration of the abundant authentication tools identified in Rules 901(b) and 902, will go a long way towards removing the mystery about authenticating digital evidence, even when the technology at play is unfamiliar to the judge. In the end, technical expertise is not needed. Rather, an awareness of the fundamental evidence rules governing admissibility and authentication of any evidence, whether digital or not, is all that is needed. And this Manual aims to provide illustrations to make the effort even easier.

III. Relevant Factors for Authenticating Digital Evidence

What follows are general guidelines and lists of relevant factors for authenticating the basic forms of digital evidence that have developed over the last 15–20 years. The lists of relevant factors do not purport to be exclusive. There is no attempt to weigh the factors, or to take a cumulative approach, as the importance of any factor will be case-dependent. And there is no intent to imply that all of the factors listed must be met before the proffered digital evidence can be found authentic.

In evaluating all the factors below, it is important to remember that the threshold for the court's determination of authenticity under Rule 901 is not high: "the court need not find that the evidence is necessarily what the proponent claims, but only that there is sufficient evidence that the jury ultimately might do so."[15] The possibility of alteration "does not and cannot be the basis for excluding ESI as unauthenticated as a matter of course, any more that it can be the rationale for excluding paper documents."[16]

Generally speaking, it will be a rare case in which an item of digital evidence *cannot* be authenticated. The question is whether the proponent is willing and able to expend the resources necessary to do so.[17] The factors set forth below are intended to direct litigants to ways in which resources can be usefully spent on authenticating digital evidence—and on ways to avoid such costs in certain situations.

A. *Emails*

The authentication questions for email most commonly focus on whether the email was sent or received by the person whom the party claims sent or received it. There are a number of factors that will assist the proponent in establishing authenticity for either or both of these purposes. Among them are:

---

[15] United States v. Safavian, 435 F. Supp. 2d 36, 38 (D.D.C. 2006).

[16] *Id.* at 40.

[17] *See* Jeffrey Bellin and Andrew Guthrie Ferguson, *Judicial Notice in the Information Age,* 108 Nw. U. L.Rev. 1137, 1157 (2014) ("Although much is made of [the authentication] hurdle in the Information Age, it is * * * an easy one to surmount. Success generally depends not on legal or factual arguments, but rather the amount of time and resources a litigant devotes to the problem.")

APPENDIX IV

1. A Witness with Personal Knowledge May Testify to Authenticity[18]

Possibilities include:

- The author of the email in question testifies to its authenticity.[19]

- A witness testifies that s/he saw the email in question being authored/received by the by the person who the proponent claims authored/received it.[20]

2. Business Records

The custodian of records of a regularly conducted activity testifies to a foundation, or certifies, in accordance with Fed.R.Evid. 902(11) or (12), that an email satisfies the criteria of Fed.R.Evid. 803(6). It should be noted, however, that emails—even of a business, do not automatically qualify as business records.[21]

3. Jury Comparison with Other Authenticated Emails[22]

The authenticity of an email can be determined by the trier of fact by comparing the email in question with emails already authenticated and in evidence.[23]

4. Production in Discovery

If a document request is sufficiently descriptive, production in response to that request may serve in itself to authenticate the email, as the act of

---

[18] See Fed.R.Evid. 901(b)(1).

[19] *See, e.g.,* Anderson v. United States, 2014 U.S. Dist. LEXIS 166799, at *13 (N.D. Ga. Dec, 2, 2014) (defendant-witness acknowledged that the documents in question contained emails he sent to an undercover agent, the emails were sent from his email address, and the document contained the entirety of his email exchange with the undercover agent; this was a sufficient showing of authenticity). *See also* Citizens Bank & Trust v. LPS Nat'l Flood, LLC, 2014 U.S. Dist. LEXIS 134933, at *12 (N.D. Ala. Sept. 25, 2014) (witness's personal knowledge of email contents and her affidavit authenticating emails as the ones she sent sufficient for admissibility).

[20] United States v. Fluker, 698 F.3d 988 (7th Cir. 2012) (the court, in outlining the variety of ways in which an email could be authenticated, stated that testimony from a witness who purports to have seen the declarant create the email in question was sufficient for authenticity under Rule 901(b)(1)).

[21] *See, e.g.,* United States v. Cone, 714 F.3d 197, 220 (4th Cir. 2013):

While properly authenticated e-mails may be admitted into evidence under the business records exception, it would be insufficient to survive a hearsay challenge simply to say that since a business keeps and receives e-mails, then ergo all those e-mails are business records falling within the ambit of Rule 803(6)(B). "An e-mail created within a business entity does not, for that reason alone, satisfy the business records exception of the hearsay rule." Morisseau v. DLA Piper, 532 F. Supp. 2d 595, 621 n. 163 (S.D.N.Y. 2008).

It is probably fair to state that emails and social media postings will often be prepared too casually and irregularly to be admissible as business records. But this is not inevitably so, and again if the electronic communication does fit the admissibility requirements it is just as admissible as a hardcopy record.

[22] Fed.R.Evid. 901(b)(3).

[23] United States v. Safavian, 435 F. Supp. 2d 36, 40 (D.D.C. 2006) ("Those emails that are not clearly identifiable on their own can be authenticated under Rule 901(b)(3), which states that evidence may be authenticated by the trier of fact with 'specimens which have been authenticated'—in this case those emails that have been independently authenticated.").

production may be a concession that the document is what the party asked for—and thus is what the party says it is. The act of production can constitute a statement of a party-opponent and consequently admissible evidence of authenticity. See Fed.R.Evid. 801(d)(2).[24] Authentication has also been found when an adversary produces in discovery a third party's email received by the producing party in the ordinary course of business, and the email is offered against the adversary.[25] But some production may be so massive and extensive that it cannot be concluded that production *itself* is a concession of authenticity. Moreover, it is possible that a party might knowingly produce inauthentic documents, such as a forged check, and such production could not be found to be tantamount to authentication. Nonetheless, production in discovery is at a minimum relevant to authenticity in the vast majority of cases.[26]

5.   Circumstantial Evidence[27]

Applying Rule 901(b)(4)—covering authentication on the basis of "appearance, contents, substance, internal patterns, or other distinctive characteristics of the item"—requires consideration of the "totality of circumstantial evidence."[28] While any one factor *may* be insufficient to determine admissibility, when weighed together, authenticity may be established. "This rule is one of the most frequently used to authenticate e-mail and other electronic records."[29]

Set forth below are factors that can, alone or in conjunction (depending on the case), establish authenticity. Different circumstantial factors may be relevant depending on whether the authenticity dispute is over whether a person sent or received the email.

a.   Authenticating Authorship Circumstantially

The inclusion of some or all of the following in an email can be sufficient to authenticate the email as having been sent by a particular person:

- the purported author's known email address;[30]

---

[24] *See, e.g.,* AT Engine Controls Ltd. v. Goodrich Pump & Engine Control Sys., Inc., 2014 U.S. Dist. LEXIS 174535 (D. Conn. Dec. 18, 2014) (collecting cases holding that production of emails in discovery constitutes a concession of authenticity); Nola Fine Art, Inc. v. Ducks Unlimited, Inc., 2015 U.S. Dist. LEXIS 17450 (E.D. La. Feb. 12, 2015) ("[Defendant] produced the email to plaintiffs in discovery and therefore cannot seriously dispute the email's authenticity").

[25] Broadspring, Inc. v. Congoo, LLC, 2014 U.S. Dist. LEXIS 177838 (S.D.N.Y. Dec. 29, 2014) (third party emails sent to a party in the ordinary course of business and produced by the party in litigation are sufficiently authenticated by the act of production when offered by an opponent, but hearsay and other admissibility objections as to the third parties' statements must separately be satisfied).

[26] *See, e.g.,* American Federation of Musicians v. Paramount Pictures Corp., 903 F.3d 968 (9th Cir. 2018) (e-mail sent by a studio employee was properly authenticated; it was produced by the studio during discovery, included the employee's e-mail signature, and included the studio's e-mail address).

[27] Fed.R.Evid. 901(b)(4).

[28] United States v. Henry, 164 F.3d 1304, 1305 (10th Cir. 1999).

[29] Lorraine v. Markel Am. Ins. Co., 241 F.R.D. 534, 546 (D. Md. 2007).

[30] *See, e.g.,* United States v. Siddiqui, 235 F.3d 1318, 1322 (11th Cir. 2000) (an email identified as originating from the defendant's email address and that automatically

APPENDIX IV

- the author's electronic signature;

- the author's name;[31]

- the author's nickname;[32]

- the author's screen name;

- the author's initials;

- the author's moniker;[33]

- the author's customary use of emoji or emoticons;

- the author's use of the same email address elsewhere;

- a writing style similar or identical to the purported author's manner of writing;

- reference to facts only the purported author or a small subset of individuals including the purported author would know;[34]

- reference to facts uniquely tied to the author—*e.g.*, contact information for relatives or loved ones; photos of the author or items of importance to the author (*e.g.*, car, pet); the author's personal information, such as a cell phone number, social security number, etc.[35]

Factors outside the content of the email itself can establish authenticity of authorship circumstantially. For example:

- a witness testifies that the author told him to expect an email prior to its arrival;[36]

- the purported author acts in accordance with, and in response to, an email exchange with the witness;

- the author orally repeats the contents soon after the email is sent;

---

included the defendant's address when the reply function was selected was considered sufficiently authenticated).

[31] *See, e.g.,* United States v. Fluker, 698 F.3d 988, 999–1000 (7th Cir. 2012) (emails sent from a "More Than Enough, LLC" (MTE) email address were sufficiently authenticated when the purported author was an MTE board member and "[i]t would be reasonable for one to assume that an MTE Board member would possess an email address bearing the MTE acronym."); *Safavian*, 435 F. Supp. 2d at 40 (email messages held properly authenticated when containing distinctive characteristics, including email addresses and name of the person connected to the address).

[32] United States v. Brinson, 772 F.3d 1314 (10th Cir. 2014) (use of fake name commonly used by defendant).

[33] See United States v. Simpson, 152 F.3d 1241 (10th Cir. 1998) (chatroom log where user "Stavron" identified himself as the defendant and shared his email address was used to authenticate subsequent emails from that email address).

[34] See United States v. Siddiqui, 235 F.3d 1318, 1322 (11th Cir. 2000) (messages that referred to facts only the defendant was familiar with were ruled admissible).

[35] Commonwealth v. Amaral, 78 Mass. App. Ct. 671, 674–675, 941 N.E.2d 1143, 1147 (2011) ("In other e-mails, Jeremy provided his telephone number and photograph. When the trooper called that number, the defendant immediately answered his telephone, and the photograph was a picture of the defendant. These actions served to confirm that the author of the e-mails and the defendant were one and the same") (citing Mass. G. Evid. § 901(b)(6)).

[36] State v. Ruiz, 2014 Mich. App. LEXIS 855 (Mich. Ct. App. May 15, 2014) (interpreting MRE 901) (witness testified to knowing the defendant authored an email because the defendant told him to expect an email relating to arson—the contents of the email subsequently received).

- the author discusses the contents of the email with a third party;

- the author leaves a voicemail with substantially the same content.

Forensic information may be used to support a circumstantial showing that the email was sent by the purported author. Forensic sources include:

- an email's hash values;[37]

- testimony from a forensic witness that an email issued from a particular device at a particular time.[38]

b.   Authenticating Receipt Circumstantially

The following factors can be probative in authenticating an email as having been received by a particular person:

- a reply to the email was received by the sender from the email address of the purported recipient;

- the subsequent conduct of the recipient reflects his or her knowledge of the contents of the sent email;

- subsequent communications from the recipient reflects his or her knowledge of the contents of the sent email;

- the email was received and accessed on a device in the possession and control of the alleged recipient.

In addition to the factors listed above, a court may take judicial notice[39] of an email, or an email chain when the contents of the email are authenticated elsewhere. For example, in *Shurnas v. Owen*, the authors of the emails in question were not in dispute and the contents of the emails were "contained in the certified records of the California Department of Business Oversight."[40] These factors allowed the court to take judicial notice of the emails the defendant sought to introduce.[41]

Finally, while it is true that an email may be sent by anyone who, with a password, gains access to another's email account, similar questions (of

---

[37]   A hash value is "[a] unique numerical identifier that can be assigned to a file, a group of files, or a portion of a file, based on a standard mathematical algorithm applied to the characteristics of the data set. The most commonly used algorithms, known as MD5 and SHA, will generate numerical values so distinctive that the chance that any two data sets will have the same hash value, no matter how similar they appear, is less than one in one billion. 'Hashing' is used to guarantee the authenticity of an original data set and can be used as a digital equivalent of the Bates stamp used in paper document production." Federal Judicial Center, Managing Discovery of Electronic Information: A Pocket Guide for Judges, Federal Judicial Center, 2007 at 24. *See also* Lorraine v. Markel American Ins. Co, 241 F.R.D. 534, 547 (D. Md. 2007) (noting that "[h]ash values can be inserted into original electronic documents when they are created to provide them with distinctive characteristics that will permit their authentication under Rule 901(b)(4).").

[38]   *Lorraine,* 241 F.R.D. 534 at 547–48 (because an electronic message's metadata (including an email's metadata) can reveal when, where, and by whom the message was authored, the court found it could be used to successfully authenticate a document under 901(b)(4)).

[39]   Judicial notice is discussed in more detail in Section III, *infra.*

[40]   2016 U.S. Dist. LEXIS 18640, at *6–8 (E.D. Cal. Feb. 16, 2016).

[41]   *Id.*

possible hacking) could be raised with traditional documents. Therefore, there is no need for separate rules of authenticity for emails. And importantly, the mere fact that hacking, etc., is possible is not enough to exclude an email or any other form of digital evidence. If the mere possibility of electronic alteration were enough to exclude the evidence, then no digital evidence could ever be authenticated.[42]

B. Text Messages

Text messages are not different in kind from email and so the rules and guidelines on authentication are similar. Here are some of the relevant factors for authenticating text messages:[43]

1. A Witness with Personal Knowledge May Testify to Authenticity

Possibilities include:

- The author of the text in question testifies to its authenticity.

- A witness testifies that s/he saw the text in question being authored/received by the person who the proponent claims authored/received it.[44]

2. Jury Comparison with Other Authenticated Texts

3. Production in Discovery

4. Establishing That an Electronic System of Recordation Records Accurately. This process of illustration, authorized by Fed.R.Evid. 901(b)(9), can be useful if the objection to authenticity is that the original text has been altered in some way. For example, in *United States v. Kilpatrick*, 2012 U.S. Dist. LEXIS 110166 (E.D. Mich. Aug. 7, 2012), the government sought to authenticate text messages sent from two SkyTel pages, each belonging to one of the defendants respectively. A SkyTel records-custodian verified that the text messages the government offered had not been and could not be edited in any way because when the messages are sent from the devices belonging to the defendants, they are automatically saved on SkyTel's server with no capacity for editing. The court ruled that this showing was

---

[42] *See, e.g.,* Interest of F.P., 878 A.2d 91 (Pa. Super. 2005) (just as an email can be faked, a "signature can be forged; a letter can be typed on another's typewriter; distinct letterhead stationary can be copied or stolen. We believe that e-mail messages and similar forms of electronic communication can be properly authenticated within the existing framework of Pa. R.E. 901 and Pennsylvania case law.").

[43] The case law cited under the various factors discussed in the section on emails should be equally useful as supportive citations for the similar (or identical) factors supporting authentication of texts.

[44] United States v. Barnes, 803 F.3d 209 (5th Cir. 2015) (government laid a proper foundation to authenticate Facebook and text messages as having been sent by the defendant; the defendant was a quadriplegic, but the witness who received the messages testified she had seen the defendant use Facebook, she recognized his Facebook account, and the Facebook messages matched the defendant's manner of communicating: "[a]lthough she was not certain that Hall [the defendant] authored the messages, conclusive proof of authenticity is not required for admission of disputed evidence"); United States v. Ramirez, 2016 U.S. App. LEXIS 15384, at * 5 (11th Cir.) (admitting photos that were sent by text message because the recipient of the text message testified she received them, an agent testified he was present when the text messages were sent, and the defendant was listed as the owner of the phone number sending the messages).

sufficient, under Fed.R.Evid. 901(b)(9), to establish authenticity over a claim that the messages had been altered.

It should be noted that the showing as to the process or system in *Kilpatrick* will be able to be made by a certificate of the foundation witness— substituting for live testimony—under an amendment to the Evidence Rules that that took effect on December 1, 2017.[45]

5. Circumstantial Evidence

a. Authenticating Authorship Circumstantially

The inclusion of some or all of the following in a text can be sufficient to authenticate the text as having been sent by a particular person:

- the purported author's ownership of the phone or other device from which the text was sent;[46]

- the author's possession of the phone;

- the author's known phone number;

- the author's name;

- the author's nickname;[47]

- the author's initials;

- the author's moniker;

- the author's name as stored on the recipient's phone;

- the author's customary use of emoji or emoticons;

- the author's use of the same phone number on other occasions;[48]

- a writing style similar or identical to the purported author's manner of writing;

- reference to facts only the purported author or a small subset of individuals including the purported author would know;

- reference to facts uniquely tied to the author—*e.g.*, contact information for relatives or loved ones; photos of author or items of importance to author (*e.g.*, car, pet); author's personal information, such as contact information, social security number, etc.; receipt of messages addressed to the author by name or reference.[49]

---

[45] These amendments to Rule 902 are discussed in detail infra.

[46] United States v. Mebrtatu, 543 F. App'x 137, 140–141 (3d Cir. 2013) (phone was in the purported sender's possession; phone contains texts sent to and signed with the purported author's first name, including texts from her boyfriend professing love and other texts whose content links them to her; texts sufficiently authenticated as hers).

[47] United States v. Kilpatrick, 2012 U.S. Dist. LEXIS 110166, at *11 (E.D. Mich. Aug. 7, 2012)(the court outlined a number of distinctive characteristics that established the authenticity of the pager and cellphone text messages at issue; among these factors were the defendants' use of their names (Kilpatrick) and nicknames ("Zeke" or "Zizwe") to sign the messages they sent).

[48] See United States v. Fults, 639 Fed. App'x 366, 373 (6th Cir. 2016) (upholding the admission of text messages when the recipient testified he communicated with the defendant using that phone number many times).

[49] United States v. Benford, 2015 U.S. Dist. LEXIS 17046, at *16–*17 (W.D. Okla. Feb. 12, 2015) (in establishing that text messages from a device were authored by the defendant,

APPENDIX IV

Factors outside the content of the text itself can establish authenticity of authorship circumstantially. For example:

- a witness testifies that the author told him to expect a text message prior to its arrival;

- the purported author acts in accordance with a text exchange;

- the purported author orally repeats the contents soon after the text message is sent or discusses the contents with a third party.

b.   Authenticating Receipt Circumstantially

The following factors can be probative in authenticating a text as having been received by a particular person:

- a reply to the text message was received by the sender from the purported recipient's phone number;

- the subsequent conduct of the recipient reflects his or her knowledge of the sent message's contents;

- subsequent communications from the recipient reflect his or her knowledge of the contents of the sent text message;

- the text message was received and accessed on a device in the possession and control of the alleged recipient.

C.   *Chatroom and Other Social Media Communications*

By definition, chatroom postings and other social media communications are made by third parties, not the owner of the site. Further, chatroom participants usually use screen names (pseudonyms) rather than their real names. Thus the authenticity challenge is to provide enough information for a juror to believe that the chatroom entry or other social media communication is made by a particular person.

Simply to show that a posting appears on a particular user's webpage is insufficient to authenticate the post as one written by the account holder. Third party posts, too, must be authenticated by more than the names of the purported authors reflected on the posts. Evidence sufficient to attribute a social media or chat room posting to a particular individual may include, for example:

- testimony from a witness who identifies the social media account as that of the alleged author, on the basis that the witness on other occasions communicated with the account holder;

- testimony from a participant in the conversation based on firsthand knowledge that the transcript fairly and accurately captures the conversation;[50]

---

the prosecution pointed to evidence that contact information for the defendant's brother and girlfriend were saved on the phone and that incoming messages addressed the defendant by name); United States v. Ellis, 2013 U.S. Dist. LEXIS 73031, at *3–*4 (E.D. Mich. May 23, 2013) (the defendant's possession of a cellphone that received messages addressed to him by name or moniker was, among other circumstantial evidence (such as his possession of the device), sufficient to establish that he was the author of outgoing text messages from the same phone).

   [50] *See, e.g.,* United States v. Lebowitz, 676 F.3d 1000 (11th Cir. 2012) (internet chat authenticated by credible testimony of one participant); United States v. Lundy, 676 F.3d 444 (5th Cir. 2012) (testimony by one party to chat that the chats are as he recorded them

- evidence that the purported author used the same screen name on other occasions;

- evidence that the purported author acted in accordance with the posting (*e.g.*, when a meeting with that person was arranged in a chat room conversation, he or she attended);

- evidence that the purported author identified himself or herself as the individual using the screen name;

- an admission that the computer account containing the chat is that of the purported author;[51]

- use in the conversation of the customary signature, nickname, or emoticon associated with the purported author;

- disclosure in the conversation of particularized information that is either unique to the purported author or known only to a small group including the purported author;

- evidence that the purported author had in his or her possession information given to the person using the screen name;

- evidence from the hard drive of the purported author's computer reflecting that a user of the computer used the screen name in question;

- evidence that the chat appears on the computer or other device of the account owner and purported author;

- evidence that the purported author elsewhere discussed the same subject matter.

Authentication as Business Records?

Note that an attempt to authenticate social media messaging as business records will, of necessity, be limited to the timestamps, metadata, etc. maintained by the owner. The content of the messages themselves will not qualify as business records and accordingly cannot be authenticated as business records under Rule 902(11). For example, in *United States v. Browne,* 834 F.3d 403, 405 (3d Cir. 2016), the government contended that Browne engaged in incriminating conversations over Facebook Messenger. The government sought to authenticate the records with a certificate of a records custodian of Facebook. The custodian certified that the records "were made and kept by the automated systems of Facebook in the course of regularly conducted activity as a regular practice of Facebook." The court held correctly that this showing was insufficient to authenticate the messages as having come from the defendant—whether the defendant made the communications involved another level of hearsay, and the custodian had no personal knowledge of the authorship of the messages. Thus, the certificate

---

is enough to meet the low threshold for authentication); United States v. Barlow, 568 F.3d 215, 220 (5th Cir. 2009) ("English, as the other participant in the year-long 'relationship,' had direct knowledge of the chats. Her testimony could sufficiently authenticate the chat log presented at trial").

[51] United States v. Manley, 787 F.3d 937, 942 (8th Cir. 2014) ("the government presented testimony of a law enforcement officer who helped to execute the search warrant, and the officer testified that the defendant admitted adopting the username 'mem659' for his computer account. The username for his computer account was the same one used in some of the chats.").

could authenticate only the fact of that the message was sent at a certain time from one address to another.

The *Browne* court held, however, that any error in admitting the records with an inadequate authentication was harmless, because there was sufficient extrinsic evidence to authenticate Browne as the author of the messages: the people that he communicated with testified at trial consistently with the communications; Browne "made significant concessions that served to link him to the Facebook conversations"; the content of the conversation indicated facts about the sender that linked to Browne; and the government "supported the accuracy of the chat logs by obtaining them directly from Facebook and introducing a certificate attesting to their maintenance by the company's automated systems."[52]

D. *Internet, Websites, etc.*

Websites present authenticity issues because they are dynamic. If the issue is what is on the website at the time the evidence is being proffered, then there are no authenticity issues because the court and the parties can simply access the site and see what the website says.[53] But proving up historic information on the website raises the issue of whether the information was actually posted as the proponent says it was.[54]

1. Rule 901 Authentication Standards as Applied to Dynamic Website Information

In applying Rule 901 authentication standards to website evidence, there are three questions that must be answered:

- What was actually on the website?

- Does the exhibit or testimony accurately reflect it?

- If so, is it attributable to the owner of the site?

A sufficient showing of authenticity of dynamic website information is usually found if a witness testifies—or certifies in compliance with a statute or rule—that:

- the witness typed in the Internet address reflected on the exhibit on the date and at the time stated;

- the witness logged onto the website and reviewed its contents; and

---

[52] *See also* United States v. Farrad, 895 F.3d 859, 879 (6th Cir. 2018) (error to deem photographs posted on Facebook to be self-authenticating as Facebook business records; but the error was harmless because the postings could be authenticated by circumstantial evidence under Rule 901(b)(4)).

[53] Jeffrey Bellin & Andrew Guthrie Ferguson, *Trial by Google: Judicial Notice in the Information Age*, 108 Nw. U.L.Rev. 1137, 1157 (2014) ("It is hard to imagine many good faith disputes about whether proffered evidence really is a page from Google Maps or WebMD. Malfeasance would be foolish. The opposing party can simply go to the website to verify its authenticity, and if fraud is detected, the consequences for the offering party are dire."). *See also* Wells Fargo Bank, N.A. v. Wrights Mill Holdings, LLC, 2015 U.S. Dist. LEXIS 115610, at*21–22 (S.D.N.Y. Aug. 31, 2015) (confirming that authenticity of existing website information could be determined by conducting a "basic Internet search.").

[54] *See, e.g.,* Adobe Sys. v. Christenson, 2011 U.S. Dist. LEXIS 16977, at *29 (D. Nev. Feb. 7, 2011) ("[a]lthough Defendants can probably determine, with little difficulty, whether a current Google search for the search terms 'software surplus' provides links on the first page [of a website], this would not prove that such a search would have resulted in such a link at a prior point in time.").

- the exhibit fairly and accurately reflects what the witness perceived.[55]

The exhibit should bear the Internet address and the date and time the webpage was accessed and the contents downloaded.[56]

When evaluating the proffer, the court may consider the following factors as circumstantial indications that the information was posted by the owner of the site, under Rule 901(b)(4):

- distinctive website design, logos, photos, or other images associated with the website or its owner;[57]

- the contents of the webpage are of a type ordinarily posted on that website or websites of similar people or entities;

- the owner of the website has elsewhere published the same contents, in whole or in part;

- the contents of the webpage have been republished elsewhere and attributed to the website; and

- the length of time the contents were posted on the website.

Other possible means of authenticating website postings are as follows:

- testimony of a witness who created or is in charge of maintaining the website. That witness may testify on the basis of personal knowledge that the printout of a webpage came from the site.[58]

- a printout obtained from the Internet Archive's "wayback machine." The Internet Archive documents and stores all websites and the "wayback machine" can retrieve website information from

---

[55] *See, e.g.,* Estate of Konell v. Allied Prop. & Cas. Ins. Co., 2014 U.S. Dist. LEXIS 10183 (D. Or. Jan. 28, 2014) ("To authenticate a printout of a web page, the proponent must offer evidence that: (1) the printout accurately reflects the computer image of the web page as of a specified date; (2) the website where the posting appears is owned or controlled by a particular person or entity; and (3) the authorship of the web posting is reasonably attributable to that person or entity"); Buzz Off Insect Shield, LLC v. S.C. Johnson & Son, Inc., 2009 U.S. Dist. LEXIS 17530 (M.D.N.C. Mar. 6, 2009) ("[defendant] could authenticate its printouts of various websites by calling witnesses who could testify that they viewed and printed the information, or supervised others in doing so, and that the printouts were accurate representations of what was displayed on the listed website on the listed day and time"); Rivera v. Inc. Village of Farmingdale, 29 F. Supp. 3d 121 (E.D.N.Y. 2013) (internet postings offered to show community bias in Fair Housing Act case; testimony that witness "personally downloaded all of the postings and confirmed the identities of the key posters . . . [suffices to show] a 'reasonable likelihood' that they were actually posted on the internet by members of an online community comprised of the Village's own residents").

[56] *See, e.g.,* Foreword Magazine, Inc. v. OverDrive Inc., 2011 U.S. Dist. LEXIS 125373, at *8–*11 (W.D. Mich. Oct. 31, 2011) (admitting screenshots from websites, accompanied only by the sworn affidavit of an attorney, given "other indicia of reliability (such as the Internet domain address and the date of printout)").

[57] *See, e.g.,* Metcalf v. Blue Cross Blue Shield of Mich., 2013 U.S. Dist. LEXIS 109641 (D. Or. Aug. 5, 2013). (authenticity of website information of an organization's purported website was established by logos or headers matching those of the organization).

[58] St. Luke's Cataract & Laser Inst., P.A. v. Sanderson, 2006 U.S. Dist. LEXIS 28873 (M.D. Fla. May 12, 2006) (web master's testimony can authenticate a printout).

any particular time.[59] Some courts require a witness from the Internet archive to testify to establish that the "wayback machine" employs a process that produces accurate results under Rule 901(b)(9).[60] Other courts, as discussed infra, take judicial notice of the reliability of the "wayback machine."

The opponent of the evidence is free to challenge authenticity of dynamic website data by adducing facts showing that the exhibit does not accurately reflect the contents of a website, or that those contents are not attributable to the ostensible owner of the site. There may be legitimate questions concerning the ownership of the site or attribution of statements contained on the site to the ostensible owner.

2. Self-Authenticating Website Data

Under Fed.R.Evid. 902, three types of webpage exhibits are self-authenticating—meaning that a presentation of the item itself is sufficient to withstand an authenticity objection from the opponent.[61]

a. Government Websites

Under Rule 902(5) data on governmental websites are self-authenticating.[62] As discussed below, courts regularly take judicial notice of these websites.

---

[59] Another example of a website that allows users to access archival copies of webpages is www.viewcached.com, which allows users to employ one interface to search three different archival services—the Wayback Machine, Google Cache, and Coral Cache.

[60] *See, e.g.,* Telewizja Polska USA, Inc. v. Echostar Satellite Corp., No. 02 C 3293, 2004 WL 2367740, at 6* (N.D. Ill. Oct. 15, 2004) (approving the use of the Internet Archive's "wayback machine" to authenticate websites as they appeared on various dates relevant to the litigation). Compare Open Text S.A. v. Box, Inc., 2015 U.S. Dist. LEXIS 11312 (N.D. Cal. Jan. 30, 2015) (court was unwilling to accept a screenshot from the Wayback Machine into evidence without testimony from a representative of the Internet Archive confirming its authenticity).

Under the newly enacted amendment to the Federal Rules of Evidence, the reliability of the wayback machine process could be established by a certificate of the Internet Archive official, rather than in-court testimony). See Rule 902(13) (allowing proof of authenticity of electronic information produced by a process leading to an accurate result to be established by the certificate of a knowledgeable witness).

[61] The relationship between Rules 901 and 902 is a complicated one. The examples of authenticity provided in Rule 901(b) essentially are given the same effect as the conditions establishing self-authentication under Rule 902, i.e., when met, they satisfy the admissibility standard and the authenticity question becomes a matter of weight for the jury. The only difference between the examples in Rules 901 and 902 is that in the latter, the factors establishing authenticity are found on the face of the evidence—no extrinsic evidence is necessary.

It is not obvious that there should be an evidentiary distinction between establishing authenticity through extrinsic evidence and establishing authenticity on the face of the item. The rules are looking for the same thing—enough evidence to indicate to a reasonable person that the item is what the proponent says it is—and it doesn't seem that the location of that evidence should be important to the court. Put another way, the factors in Rule 902 could have just been added to the list of factors in Rule 901(b) without any loss of utility. That said, the distinction exists in the Evidence Rules, and so this Manual follows that structure.

[62] *See, e.g.,* Williams v. Long, 585 F. Supp. 2d 679, 686–88 & n. 4 (D. Md. 2008) (collecting cases indicating that postings on government websites are self-authenticating).

BEST PRACTICES FOR AUTHENTICATING
DIGITAL EVIDENCE

b. Newspaper and Periodical Websites

Under Rule 902(6) (*Newspapers and Periodicals*), "[p]rinted material purporting to be a newspaper or periodical" is self-authenticating. This includes online newspaper and periodicals, because Rule 101(b)(6) provides that any reference in the Rules to printed material also includes comparable information in electronic form. Thus all newspaper and periodical material is self-authenticating whether or not it ever appeared in hard copy.[63]

c. Websites Certified as Business Records

Rules 902(11) and (12) render self-authenticating business (organizational) records that are certified as satisfying Rule 803(6) by "the custodian or another qualified person." Exhibits extracted from websites that are maintained by, for, and in the ordinary course of, a business or other regularly conducted activity can satisfy this rule.[64] However, if the record is maintained by a provider that does not check postings for accuracy, the posting will not be properly authenticated simply because they are regularly maintained by the provider.[65]

3. Authenticating the Date of Information Posted on a Website

In some cases, a party may need to show not only that a posting was made on a website, but also the date on which the information was generated—this can be a distinct question from establishing what the website looked like at a particular time, which can be shown by the methods discussed above. Assume, for example, that a video is posted on YouTube on January 1, 2016. If the proponent wants to prove that it was posted on that day, this can be done by a person with knowledge, circumstantial evidence, etc. It is a different question if the proponent needs to show that the information itself was *generated* on a certain day. That will not be shown by proving it was posted on a certain date. For example, in *Sublime v. Sublime Remembered*, 2013 U.S. Dist. LEXIS 103813 (C.D. Cal.), the plaintiffs brought suit against the defendant for violating a court order prohibiting defendant from performing songs belonging to the plaintiffs. As evidence, the plaintiffs sought to admit a YouTube video of the defendant performing the prohibited music. The court ruled that the video was not properly authenticated without evidence that it was recorded *after* the court order was issued. The mere fact that it was *posted* after the court order was issued was not enough to establish that the video was what the proponent said it was—performance of the music after the court order was entered.

Establishing that a video (or any other kind of information posted on a website) was *prepared* on—or before or after—a certain date thus presents a

---

[63] *See, e.g.,* White v. City of Birmingham, 2015 U.S. Dist. LEXIS 39187 (N.D. Ala. Mar. 27, 2015) (noting sua sponte that news articles from Huntsville Times website (AL.com) "could be found self-authenticating at trial").

[64] *See, e.g.,* Randazza v. Cox, 2014 U.S. Dist. LEXIS 49762 (D. Nev. April 10, 2014) (videos posted to YouTube "are self-authenticating as a certified domestic record of a regular conducted activity if their proponent satisfies the requirements of the business-records hearsay exception.").

[65] *See, e.g.,* United States v. Browne, 834 F.3d 403, 410 (3rd Cir. 2016) (Facebook postings could not be authenticated as Facebook business records because "Facebook does not purport to verify or rely on the substantive contents of the communications in the course of its business."); United States v. Farrad, 895 F.3d 859, 879 (6th Cir. 2018) (error to deem photographs posted on Facebook to be self-authenticating as Facebook business records; but the error was harmless because the postings could be authenticated by circumstantial evidence under Rule 901(b)(4)).

separate question of authenticity. But it is a question that can be addressed through the same factors discussed above: for example, by a person with personal knowledge, a forensic expert, and/or circumstantial evidence. Illustrative is *United States v. Bloomfield*,[66] in which the defendant was convicted of felon-firearm possession. The government offered a YouTube video which showed the defendant discharging an AR–15 rifle in front of Fowler Firearms. The date that the video was made was obviously critical. If it was made before the defendant was a convicted felon, then it depicted no crime. The government was not required, necessarily, to prove that the video was taken on a specific day, but it was required to establish that the video was taken after the defendant was convicted of a felony. And the date that the video was posted on YouTube was not the relevant date. The court found the date was properly authenticated in the following passage:

- Fowler Firearms's manager testified that Broomfield was a Fowler Firearms member, that on January 21, 2011, Broomfield purchased two boxes of PMC .223 ammunition, and that he had not purchased that ammunition at any other time. Dezendorf stated that the only firearm Fowler Firearms rented to customers at the time that used PMC .223 ammunition was the AR–15 rifle.

- An employee who had worked at Fowler Firearms for ten years testified that he could discern the approximate date the video was taken. He explained that the video showed side deflectors and lights on the gun range, which Fowler Firearms had installed in late 2010 or early 2011. He also testified that Fowler Firearms paints its floors and walls at the beginning of the season, and the freshly-painted floor and walls seen in the video indicated that the footage was filmed close to the start of 2011.

- A witness who operated a maintenance business that provided repair and maintenance to Fowler Firearms testified that he installed the lighted baffles shown in the video, in late September or early October of 2010.

All this was more than enough to indicate that the video was taken around the beginning of 2011—post-dating the defendant's felony status—and so depicted the crime of felon-firearm possession.

E. *Social Media Postings*

"Social media" is defined as "forms of electronic communications (as websites for social networking and microblogging) through which users create online communities to share information, ideas, personal messages, and other content."[67] Parties have increasingly sought to use social media evidence to their advantage at trial. A common example would be a picture or entry posted on a person's Facebook page, that could be relevant to contradict that person's testimony at trial. If the entry is challenged for authenticity, the proponent must present a prima facie case that the evidence is what the party says it is—*e.g.*, that it is in fact a posting on the person's Facebook page. If the goal is to prove that the page or a post is that of a particular person, authenticity standards are not automatically satisfied by the fact that the post or the page is in that person's name, or that the person

---

[66] 591 Fed.Appx. 847, 848–49 (11th Cir. 2014).

[67] Definition of Social Media, Merriam-Webster, http://www.merriam-webster.com/dictionary/social%20media# (last visited January 16, 2016).

is pictured on the post.[68] That is because someone can create a Facebook or other social media page in someone else's name. Moreover, one person may also gain access to another's account.

What more must be done to establish authenticity of a social media page? Most courts have found that it is enough for the proponent to show that the pages and accounts can be tracked through internet protocol addresses associated with the person who purportedly made the post.[69] And there are other alternatives that should satisfy the low standard for establishing authenticity under Rule 901.

Other factors that can be relied upon to support authentication of social media postings include the following:[70]

- testimony from the purported creator of the social network profile and related postings;

- testimony from persons who saw the purported creator establish or post to the page;

- testimony of a witness that she often communicated with the alleged creator of the page through that account;

- expert testimony concerning the results of a search of the social media account holder's computer hard drive;[71]

---

[68] *See, e.g.,* United States v. Vayner, 769 F.3d 125, 132 (2d Cir. 2014), where the court held that a page on the Russian version of Facebook was not sufficiently authenticated simply by the fact that it bore the name and picture of the purported "owner" Zhyltsou:

It is uncontroverted that information about Zhyltsou appeared on the VK page: his name, photograph, and some details about his life consistent with Timku's testimony about him. But there was no evidence that Zhyltsou himself had created the page or was responsible for its contents. Had the government sought to introduce, for instance, a flyer found on the street that contained Zhyltsou's Skype address and was purportedly written or authorized by him, the district court surely would have required some evidence that the flyer did, in fact, emanate from Zhyltsou. Otherwise, how could the statements in the flyer be attributed to him?

Essentially the court in *Vayner* held that a Facebook page is not self-authenticating. Compare United States v. Encarnacion-LaFontaine, 639 Fed. Appx. 710, 713 (2d Cir. 2016) (threatening Facebook posts were properly authenticated where "the Government introduced evidence that (1) the Facebook accounts used to send the messages were accessed from IP addresses connected to computers near Encarnacion's apartment; (2) patterns of access to the accounts show that they were controlled by the same person; (3) in addition to the Goris threats, the accounts were used to send messages to other individuals connected to Encarnacion; (4) Encarnacion had a motive to make the threats, and (5) a limited number of people, including Encarnacion, had information that was contained in the messages.").

[69] United States v. Hassan, 742 F.3d 104, 133 (4th Cir. 2014) (the trial court did not abuse its discretion in admitting Facebook pages purportedly maintained by two of the defendants; the trial court properly determined that the prosecution had satisfied its burden under Rule 901(a) "by tracking the Facebook pages and Facebook accounts to Hassan's and Yaghi's email addresses via internet protocol addresses"); United States v. Brinson, 772 F.3d 1314 (10th Cir. 2014) (Facebook account linked to the defendant's email).

[70] *See generally,* Honorable Paul W. Grimm, *Authentication of Social Media Evidence,* 36 AM. J. TRIAL ADVOC. 433 (2013); Richard Raysman and Peter Brown, Authentication of Social Media Evidence, New York Law Journal, November 11, 2011, p. 3.

[71] Honorable Paul W. Grimm, *Authentication of Social Media Evidence,* 36 AM. J. TRIAL ADVOC. 433, 468 (2013) ("A computer forensic expert can frequently authenticate the maker of social media content. Obviously, you will need to retain the proper expert and ensure that he or she has enough time and information to make the identification. Advance planning is essential, and be mindful of the potentially substantial cost.").

- testimony about the contextual clues and distinctive aspects in the posting tending to reveal the identity of the purported author;[72]
- testimony regarding the account holder's exclusive access to the originating computer and social media account;
- information from the social media network that links the page or post to the purported author;
- testimony directly from the social networking website that connects the establishment of the profile to the person who allegedly created it and also connects the posting sought to be introduced to the person who initiated it;
- expert testimony regarding how social network accounts are accessed and what methods are used to prevent unauthorized access;
- production pursuant to a document request;
- whether the purported author knows the password to the account, and how many others know it as well;
- that the page or post contains some of the factors previously discussed as circumstantial evidence of authenticity of texts, emails, etc., including:
  — nonpublic details of the purported author's life;
  — other items known uniquely to the purported author or a small group including him or her;
  — references or links to, or contact information about, loved ones, relatives, co-workers, others close to the purported author;
  — photos and videos likely to be accessed by the purported author;
  — biographical information, nicknames, not generally accessible;
  — the structure or style of comments that are in the style of the purported author;
  — that the purported author acts in accordance with the contents of the page or post.

Finally, a social media post meeting the foundational requirements of a business record under Fed.R.Evid. 803(6) may be self-authenticating under 902(11). While this may not be enough to authenticate the *identity* of the

---

[72] *See, e.g.,* United States v. Ferrad, 895 F.3d 859 (6th Cir. 2018) (Facebook photos were properly authenticated where the pictures were established as coming from an account maintained by the defendant, and the pictures appeared to show the defendant's tattoos and distinctive features of his deportment, as confirmed by police investigation).

person posting,[73] it will be enough to establish that the records were not altered in any way after they were posted.[74]

IV. Judicial Notice of Digital Evidence

This Best Practices Handbook has discussed the many ways that new forms of digital evidence might be authenticated. Almost all of these methods require expenditure of resources. Courts and parties have begun to realize that some of this new digital evidence has reached the point of being an undisputed means of proving a fact. In these circumstances, judicial notice may be used to alleviate the expenditure of resources toward authentication.

Under Fed.R.Evid. 201(b) a court may judicially notice a fact if it is not subject to reasonable dispute. An example of a court taking judicial notice of a fact obtained through an electronic process is found in *United States v. Brooks,* 715 F.3d 1069, 1078 (8th Cir. 2013). The defendant in a bank robbery prosecution challenged the admissibility of GPS data that was obtained from a GPS tracker that the teller placed in the envelope of stolen money. The trial court took judicial notice of the accuracy and reliability of GPS technology. The court of appeals found no error:

> We cannot conclude that the district court abused its discretion in taking judicial notice of the accuracy and reliability of GPS technology. Commercial GPS units are widely available, and most modern cell phones have GPS tracking capabilities. Courts routinely rely on GPS technology to supervise individuals on probation or supervised release, and, in assessing the Fourth Amendment constraints associated with GPS tracking, courts generally have assumed the technology's accuracy.

Another common example of judicial notice of digital information is that courts take judicial notice of distances, locations, and the physical contours of an area by reference to Google Maps.[75]

---

[73] See United States v. Browne, 834 F.3d 403, 409 (3d Cir. 2016), where the court found that a Rule 902(11) certification by a Facebook custodian concerning Facebook posts was not sufficient authentication that the post was made by a certain individual:

> Facebook does not purport to verify or rely on the substantive contents of the communications in the course of its business. At most, the records custodian employed by the social media platform can attest to the accuracy of only certain aspects of the communications exchanged over that platform, that is, confirmation that the depicted communications took place between certain Facebook accounts, on particular dates, or at particular times. This is no more sufficient to confirm the accuracy or reliability of the contents of the Facebook chats than a postal receipt would be to attest to the accuracy or reliability of the contents of the enclosed mailed letter.

[74] See, e.g., United States v. Hassan, 742 F.3d 104, 134 (4th Cir. 2014):

> The government presented the certifications of records custodians of Facebook and Google, verifying that the Facebook pages and YouTube videos had been maintained as business records in the course of regularly conducted business activities. According to those certifications, Facebook and Google create and retain such pages and videos when (or soon after) their users post them through use of the Facebook or Google servers.

[75] See, e.g., United States v. Burroughs, 810 F.3d 833, 835, n.1 (D.C.Cir. 2016) ("We grant the government's motion to take judicial notice of a Google Map. It is a 'source whose accuracy cannot be reasonably questioned,' at least for the purpose of identifying the area where Burroughs was arrested and the general layout of the block."); McCormack v. Hiedeman, 694 F.3d 1004, 1008 (9th Cir. 2012) (relying on Google Maps to determine the distance between two cities; the court held that Google Maps was a website whose accuracy could not reasonably be questioned under Fed.R.Evid. 201(b)(2).). See also Cline v. City of Mansfield, 745 F. Supp. 2d 773, 800 n.23 (N.D. Ohio 2010) (the court took judicial notice that the sun set at 7:47 pm on a particular date according to www.timeanddate.com).

APPENDIX IV

What follows are some examples of judicial notice of digital information.

1. Government Websites

Judicial notice may be taken of postings on government websites,[76] including:

- Federal, state, and local court websites.[77]
- Federal, state, and local agency, department and other entities' websites.[78]
- Foreign government websites.[79]
- International organization websites.[80]

2. Non-Government Websites

Generally, courts are reluctant to take judicial notice of non-governmental websites because the Internet "is an open source" permitting anyone to "purchas[e] an internet address and create a website" and so the information recorded is subject to dispute.[81] A few websites, however, as discussed above, have become a part of daily life—their accuracy is both objectively verifiable and actually verified millions of times a day. Other websites are the online versions of sources that courts have taken judicial notice of for years, and the courts find little reason to distinguish a reputable web equivalent from a reputable hard copy edition.

Examples of Information Found Authentic on Non-Governmental Websites Through Judicial Notice:

- Internet maps (*e.g.*, Google Maps, MapQuest).
- Calendar information.[82]
- Newspaper and periodical articles.[83]

---

[76] *See, e.g.,* United States v. Head, 2013 U.S. Dist. LEXIS 151805, at *7 n.2 (E.D. Cal. Oct. 22, 2013) ("The court may take judicial notice of information posted on government websites as it can be 'accurately and readily determined from sources whose accuracy cannot reasonably be questioned.' "); Puerto Rico v. Shell Oil Co. (In re MTBE Prods. Liab. Litig.), 2013 U.S. Dist. LEXIS 181837, at *16 (S.D.N.Y. 2013) ("Courts routinely take judicial notice of data on government websites because it is presumed authentic and reliable").

[77] *See, e.g.,* Feingold v. Graff, 516 Fed. App'x 223, 226 (3d Cir. 2013).

[78] *See, e.g.,* United States v. Iverson, 818 F.3d 1015, 1022 (9th Cir. 2016) (noting that "courts have considered the FDIC website so reliable that they have taken judicial notice of information on it"; citing cases); Lawrence v. Fed. Home Loan Mortg. Corp., 2015 U.S. Dist. LEXIS 40012 (W.D. Tex. Mar. 30, 2015) (federal government's agreement with national bank as posted on government website); Flores v. City of Baldwin Park, 2015 U.S. Dist. LEXIS 22149 (C.D. Cal. Feb. 23, 2015) (municipal police department website).

[79] *See, e.g.,* United States v. Broxmeyer, 699 F.3d 265, 296 (2d Cir. 2012) (websites of governments of Vietnam and Brazil).

[80] *See, e.g.,* Kirtsaeng v. John Wiley & Sons, Inc., 133 S.Ct. 1351, 1367 (2013) (World Bank website).

[81] United States v. Kane, 2013 U.S. Dist. LEXIS 154248 (D. Nev. Oct. 28, 2013).

[82] *See, e.g.,* Tyler v. United States, 2012 U.S. Dist. LEXIS 184007, at *9–*10 n.6 (N.D. Ga. Dec. 6, 2012); Local 282, Int'l Bhd. of Teamsters v. Pile Found. Constr. Co., 2011 U.S. Dist. LEXIS 86644, at *17–*18 n.5 (E.D.N.Y. Aug. 5, 2011).

[83] *See, e.g.,* Ford v. Artiga, 2013 U.S. Dist. LEXIS 106805, at *19 n.5 (E.D. Cal. July 30, 2013); HB v. Monroe Woodbury Cent. Sch. Dist., 2012 U.S. Dist. LEXIS 141252 (S.D.N.Y. Sept. 27, 2012).

- Online versions of textbooks, dictionaries, rules, charters.[84]

Most non-Governmental websites, even if familiar, are of debatable authenticity and therefore not appropriately the object of judicial notice. Wikipedia is a prime example. Courts have declined requests to take judicial notice of the contents of Wikipedia entries,[85] except for the fact that the contents appear on the site as of a certain date of access.[86]

3. Wayback Machine

Archived versions of websites as displayed on the "wayback machine" (www.archive.org) are frequently the subject of judicial notice,[87] but this is not always the case.[88] Note that it is only the contents of the archived pages that may warrant judicial notice—the dates assigned to archived pages may not apply to images linked to them, and more generally, links on archived pages may direct to the live web if the object of the old link is no longer available.

V. Authenticating Electronic Evidence by Way of Certification—New Amendments to the Federal Rules of Evidence

As of December 1, 2017, two subdivisions to Rule 902, the rule on self-authentication, have been added with the goal of reducing the costs of authenticating digital evidence. The first provision, Rule 902(13), allows self-authentication of machine-generated information, upon a submission of a certification prepared by a qualified person. The second Rule provides a similar certification procedure for a copy of data taken from an electronic device, medium or file. These proposals are analogous to Rules 902(11) and (12) of the Federal Rules of Evidence, which permit a foundation witness to establish the authenticity of business records by way of certification.

The proposals have a common goal of making authentication easier for certain kinds of electronic evidence that are, under current law, likely to be

---

[84] *See, e.g.,* United States v. Mosley, 672 F.3d 586, 591 (8th Cir. 2012) (PHYSICIANS' DESK REFERENCE); Shuler v. Garrett, 2014 U.S. App. LEXIS 2772, at *7 (6th Cir. Feb. 14, 2014) (OXFORD ENGLISH DICTIONARY); Dealer Computer Servs. v. Monarch Ford, 2013 U.S. Dist. LEXIS 11237, at *11 & n.3 (E.D. Cal. Jan. 25, 2013) (American Arbitration Association rules); Morgan Stanley Smith Barney LLC v. Monaco, 2014 U.S. Dist. LEXIS 149419 (D. Colo. Aug. 26, 2014) (FINRA rules); Famous Music Corp. v. 716 Elmwood, Inc., 2007 U.S. Dist. LEXIS 96789, at *12–*13 n.7 (W.D.N.Y. Dec. 28, 2007) (Articles of Association of ASCAP).

[85] *See, e.g.,* Blanks v. Cate, 2013 U.S. Dist. LEXIS 11233, at *8 n.4 (E.D. Cal Jan. 28, 2013) (refusing to take judicial notice of a Wikipedia entry "as such information is not sufficiently reliable"); Stein v. Bennett, 2013 U.S. Dist. LEXIS 126667, at *20–21 n.10 (M.D. Ala. Sept. 5, 2013) ("Wikipedia is not a source that warrants judicial notice"); Gonzales v. Unum Life Ins. Co. of Am., 861 F. Supp. 2d 1099, 1104 n.4 (S.D. Cal. 2012) ("The Court declines Plaintiff's request to take judicial notice of the Wikipedia definition of Parkinson's Disease because the internet is not typically a reliable source of information").

[86] *See, e.g.,* McCrary v. Elations Co., LLC, 2014 U.S. Dist. LEXIS 8443, at *4–5 n.3 (C.D. Cal. Jan. 13, 2014) ("While the court may take judicial notice of the fact that the internet, Wikipedia, and journal articles are available to the public, it may not take judicial notice of the truth of the matters asserted therein").

[87] *See, e.g.,* Under a Foot Plant Co. v. Exterior Design, Inc., 2015 U.S. Dist. LEXIS 38190 (D. Md. Mar. 25, 2015) ("District courts have routinely taken judicial notice of content from The Internet Archive").

[88] *See, e.g.,* Open Text S.A. v. Box, Inc., 2015 U.S. Dist. LEXIS 11312 (N.D. Cal. Jan. 30, 2015) (proffered Wayback Machine printouts not authenticated absent certification from representative of InternetArchive.org).

authenticated under Rule 901 but only by calling a witness to testify to authenticity. The Advisory Committee concluded that the types of electronic evidence covered by the two proposed rules are rarely the subject of a legitimate authenticity dispute, but it has often been the case that the proponent is nonetheless forced to produce an authentication witness, incurring expense and inconvenience—and often, at the last minute, opposing counsel ends up stipulating to authenticity in any event.

The self-authentication proposals, by following the approach taken in Rule 902(11) and (12) regarding business records, essentially leave the burden of going forward on authenticity questions to the opponent of the evidence. Under those rules a business record is authenticated by a certificate, but the opponent is given "a fair opportunity" to challenge both the certificate and the underlying record. New Rules 902(13) and 902(14) have the same effect of shifting to the opponent the burden of going forward (not the burden of proof) on authenticity disputes regarding the described electronic evidence.

These new amendments do not change the *standards* for authentication of electronic evidence. Rather, they change the *manner* in which the proponent's submission on authenticity can be made. Instead of calling a witness, the proponent can provide a certificate prepared by the witness of the submission that he would have made if required to testify. Of course, if that submission would be insufficient if he *had* testified, these new amendments will be of no use. An insufficient showing of authenticity does not somehow become better by way of a certificate in lieu of testimony.

It should be remembered that while these new rules allow the party to present a certificate in lieu of authenticating testimony, a party may well choose to call an authenticating witness to trial, especially if the process by which the electronic information is obtained would be difficult for a jury to understand. A live witness may be useful to explain the particulars, and will also show the jury that the proponent is not trying to hide anything about the procedure in a certificate.

Applications of Rules 902(13) and (14)

In order to assist the Bench and the Bar in evaluating how these new self-authentication rules can be used, the Reporter to the Advisory Committee, with the assistance of John Haried, an attorney from the Justice Department, prepared the following illustrative examples:

Examples of how Rule 902(13) can be used:

1. **Proving that a USB device was connected to (i.e., plugged into) a computer:** In a hypothetical civil or criminal case in Chicago, a disputed issue is whether Devera Hall used her computer to access files stored on a USB thumb drive owned by a co-worker. Ms. Hall's computer uses the Windows operating system, which automatically records information about every USB device connected to her computer in a database known as the "Windows registry." The Windows registry database is maintained on the computer by the Windows operating system in order to facilitate the computer's operations. A forensic technician, located in Dallas, Texas, has provided a printout from the Windows registry that indicates that a USB thumb drive, identified by manufacturer, model, and serial number, was last connected to Ms. Hall's computer at a specific date and time.

BEST PRACTICES FOR AUTHENTICATING
DIGITAL EVIDENCE

Without Rule 902(13): Without Rule 902(13), the proponent of the evidence would need to call the forensic technician who obtained the printout as a witness, in order to establish the authenticity of the evidence. During his or her testimony, the forensic technician would typically be asked to testify about his or her background and qualifications; the process by which digital forensic examinations are conducted in general; the steps taken by the forensic technician during the examination of Ms. Hall's computer in particular; the process by which the Windows operating system maintains information in the Windows registry, including information about USB devices connected to the computer; and the steps taken by the forensic examiner to examine the Windows registry and to produce the printout identifying the USB device.

Impact of Rule 902(13): With Rule 902(13), the proponent of the evidence could obtain a written certification from the forensic technician, stating that the Windows operating system regularly records information in the Windows registry about USB devices connected to a computer; that the process by which such information is recorded produces an accurate result; and that the printout accurately reflected information stored in the Windows registry of Ms. Hall's computer. The proponent would be required to provide reasonable written notice of its intent to offer the printout as an exhibit and to make the written certification and proposed exhibit available for inspection. If the opposing party did not dispute the accuracy or reliability of the process that produced the exhibit, the proponent would not need to call the forensic technician as a witness to establish the authenticity of the exhibit. (There are many other examples of the same types of machine-generated information on computers, for example, internet browser histories and wifi access logs.)

2.   **Proving that a server was used to connect to a particular webpage:** Hypothetically, a malicious hacker executed a denial-of-service attack against Acme's website. Acme's server maintained an Internet Information Services (IIS) log that automatically records information about every internet connection routed to the web server to view a web page, including the IP address, webpage, user agent string and what was requested from the website. The IIS logs reflected repeated access to Acme's website from an IP address known to be used by the hacker. The proponent wants to introduce the IIS log to prove that the hacker's IP address was an instrument of the attack.

Without Rule 902(13): The proponent would have to call a website expert to testify about the mechanics of the server's operating system; his search of the IIS log; how the IIS log works; and that the exhibit is an accurate record of the IIS log.

With Rule 902(13): The proponent would obtain the website expert's certification of the facts establishing authenticity of the exhibit and provide the certification and exhibit to the opposing party with reasonable notice that it intends to offer the exhibit at trial. If the opposing party does not timely dispute the reliability of the process that produced the registry key, then the proponent would not need to call the website expert to establish authenticity.

3.   **Proving that a person was or was not near the scene of an event:** Hypothetically, Robert Jackson is a defendant in a civil (or criminal) action alleging that he was the driver in a hit-and-run collision with a U.S.

APPENDIX IV

Postal Service mail carrier in Atlanta at 2:15 p.m. on March 6, 2015. Mr. Jackson owns an iPhone, which has software that records machine-generated dates, times, and GPS coordinates of each picture he takes with his iPhone. Mr. Jackson's iPhone contains two pictures of his home in an Atlanta suburb at about 1 p.m. on March 6. He wants to introduce into evidence the photos together with the metadata, including the date, time, and GPS coordinates, recovered forensically from his iPhone to corroborate his alibi that he was at home several miles from the scene at the time of the collision.

Without Rule 902(13): The proponent would have to call the forensic technician to testify about Mr. Jackson's iPhone's operating system; his search of the phone; how the metadata was created and stored with each photograph; and that the exhibit is an accurate record of the photographs.

With Rule 902(13): The proponent would obtain the forensic technician's certification of the facts establishing authenticity of the exhibits and provide the certification and exhibit to the opposing party with reasonable notice that it intends to offer the exhibit at trial. If the opposing party does not timely dispute the reliability of the process that produced the iPhone's logs, then the proponent would not have to call the technician to establish authenticity.

4. **Proving association and activity between alleged co-conspirators:** Hypothetically, Ian Nichols is charged with conspiracy to commit the robbery of First National Bank that occurred in San Diego on January 30, 2015. Two robbers drove away in a silver Ford Taurus. The alleged co-conspirator was Dain Miller. Dain was arrested on an outstanding warrant on February 1, 2015, and in his pocket was his Samsung Galaxy phone. The Samsung phone's software automatically maintains a log of text messages that includes the text content, date, time, and number of the other phone involved. Pursuant to a warrant, forensic technicians examined Dain's phone and located four text messages to Ian's phone from January 29: "Meet my house @9"; "Is Taurus the Bull out of shop?"; "Sheri says you have some blow"; and "see ya tomorrow." In the separate trial of Ian, the government wants to offer the four text messages to prove the conspiracy.

Without Rule 902(13): The proponent would have to call the forensic technician to testify about Dain's phone's operating system; his search of the phone's text message log; how logs are created; and that the exhibit is an accurate record of the iPhone's logs.

With Rule 902(13): The proponent would obtain the forensic technician's certification of the facts establishing authenticity of the exhibit and provide the certification and exhibit to the opposing party with reasonable notice that it intends to offer the exhibit at trial. If the opposing party does not timely dispute the reliability of the process that produced the iPhone's logs, then the court would make the Rule 104 threshold authenticity finding and admit the exhibits, absent other proper objection.

Hearsay Objection Retained: Under Rule 902(13), the opponent—here, criminal defendant Ian—would retain his hearsay objections to the text messages found on Dain's phone. For example, the judge would evaluate the text "Sheri says you have some blow" under F.R.E. 801(d)(2)(E) to determine whether it was a coconspirator's statement during and in furtherance of a conspiracy, and under F.R.E. 805, to assess the hearsay within hearsay. The court might exclude the text "Sheri says you have some blow" under either rule or both.

BEST PRACTICES FOR AUTHENTICATING
DIGITAL EVIDENCE

Example of how Rule 902(14) can be used:

In the armed robbery hypothetical, above, forensic technician Smith made a forensic copy of Dain's Samsung Galaxy phone in the field. Smith verified that the forensic copy was identical to the original phone's text logs using an industry standard methodology (*e.g.,* hash value or other means). Smith gave the copy to forensic technician Jones, who performed his examination at his lab. Jones used the copy to conduct his entire forensic examination so that he would not inadvertently alter the data on the phone. Jones found the text messages. The government wants to offer the copy into evidence as part of the basis of Jones's testimony about the text messages he found.

Without Rule 902(14): The government would have to call two witnesses. First, forensic technician Smith would need to testify about making the forensic copy of information from Dain's phone, and about the methodology that he used to verify that the copy was an exact copy of information inside the phone. Second, the government would have to call Jones to testify about his examination.

With Rule 902(14): The proponent would obtain Smith's certification of the facts establishing how he copied the phone's information and then verified the copy was true and accurate. Before trial the government would provide the certification and exhibit to the opposing party—here defendant Ian—with reasonable notice that it intends to offer the exhibit at trial. If Ian's attorney does not timely dispute the reliability of the process that produced the Samsung Galaxy's text message logs, then the proponent would only call Jones.

The Committee Note for the new rules, written by the Advisory Committee, emphasizes that the goal of the amendment is a narrow one: to allow authentication of electronic information that would otherwise be established by a witness, instead to be established through a certification by that same witness. The Note makes clear that these are authentication-only rules and that the opponent retains all objections to the item other than authenticity—most importantly that the item is hearsay or that admitting the item would violate a criminal defendant's right to confrontation.

What follows is the text of the new rules and the Committee Notes:

Rule 902.   Evidence That Is Self-Authenticating

The following items of evidence are self-authenticating; they require no extrinsic evidence of authenticity in order to be admitted:

* * *

(13) *Certified Records Generated by an Electronic Process or System.* A record generated by an electronic process or system that produces an accurate result, as shown by a certification of a qualified person that complies with the certification requirements of Rule 902(11) or (12). The proponent must also meet the notice requirements of Rule 902(11).

APPENDIX IV

COMMITTEE NOTE

The amendment sets forth a procedure by which parties can authenticate certain electronic evidence other than through the testimony of a foundation witness. As with the provisions on business records in Rules 902(11) and (12), the Committee has found that the expense and inconvenience of producing a witness to authenticate an item of electronic evidence is often unnecessary. It is often the case that a party goes to the expense of producing an authentication witness and then the adversary either stipulates authenticity before the witness is called or fails to challenge the authentication testimony once it is presented. The amendment provides a procedure under which the parties can determine in advance of trial whether a real challenge to authenticity will be made, and can then plan accordingly.

Nothing in the amendment is intended to limit a party from establishing authenticity of electronic evidence on any ground provided in these Rules, including through judicial notice where appropriate.

A proponent establishing authenticity under this Rule must present a certification containing information that would be sufficient to establish authenticity were that information provided by a witness at trial. If the certification provides information that would be insufficient to authenticate the record if the certifying person testified, then authenticity is not established under this Rule. The Rule specifically allows the authenticity foundation that satisfies Rule 901(b)(9) to be established by a certification rather than the testimony of a live witness.

The reference to the "certification requirements of Rule 902(11) or (12)" is only to the procedural requirements for a valid certification. There is no intent to require, or permit, a certification under this rule to prove the requirements of Rule 803(6). Rule 902(13) is solely limited to authentication and any attempt to satisfy a hearsay exception must be made independently.

A certification under this Rule can establish only that the proffered item has satisfied the admissibility requirements for authenticity. The opponent remains free to object to admissibility of the proffered item on other grounds—including hearsay, relevance, or in criminal cases the right to confrontation. For example, assume that a plaintiff in a defamation case offers what purports to be a printout of a webpage on which a defamatory statement was made. Plaintiff offers a certification under this Rule in which a qualified person describes the process by which the webpage was retrieved. Even if that certification sufficiently establishes that the webpage is authentic, defendant remains free to object that the statement on the webpage was not placed there by defendant. Similarly, a certification authenticating a computer output, such as a spreadsheet, does not preclude an objection that the information produced is unreliable—the authentication establishes only that the output came from the computer.

A challenge to the authenticity of electronic evidence may require technical information about the system or process at issue, including possibly retaining a forensic technical expert; such factors will effect whether the opponent has a fair opportunity to challenge the evidence given the notice provided.

The reference to Rule 902(12) is intended to cover certifications that are made in a foreign country.

* * *

BEST PRACTICES FOR AUTHENTICATING
DIGITAL EVIDENCE

(14) *Certified Data Copied from an Electronic Device, Storage Medium, or File.* Data copied from an electronic device, storage medium, or file, if authenticated by a process of digital identification, as shown by a certification of a qualified person that complies with the certification requirements of Rule 902(11) or (12). The proponent also must meet the notice requirements of Rule 902(11).

Committee Note

The amendment sets forth a procedure by which parties can authenticate data copied from an electronic device, storage medium, or an electronic file, other than through the testimony of a foundation witness. As with the provisions on business records in Rules 902(11) and (12), the Committee has found that the expense and inconvenience of producing an authenticating witness for this evidence is often unnecessary. It is often the case that a party goes to the expense of producing an authentication witness, and then the adversary either stipulates authenticity before the witness is called or fails to challenge the authentication testimony once it is presented. The amendment provides a procedure in which the parties can determine in advance of trial whether a real challenge to authenticity will be made, and can then plan accordingly.

Today, data copied from electronic devices, storage media, and electronic files are ordinarily authenticated by "hash value." A hash value is a number that is often represented as a sequence of characters and is produced by an algorithm based upon the digital contents of a drive, medium, or file. If the hash values for the original and copy are different, then the copy is not identical to the original. If the hash values for the original and copy are the same, it is highly improbable that the original and copy are not identical. Thus, identical hash values for the original and copy reliably attest to the fact that they are exact duplicates. This amendment allows self-authentication by a certification of a qualified person that she checked the hash value of the proffered item and that it was identical to the original. The rule is flexible enough to allow certifications through processes other than comparison of hash value, including by other reliable means of identification provided by future technology.

Nothing in the amendment is intended to limit a party from establishing authenticity of electronic evidence on any ground provided in these Rules, including through judicial notice where appropriate.

A proponent establishing authenticity under this Rule must present a certification containing information that would be sufficient to establish authenticity were that information provided by a witness at trial. If the certification provides information that would be insufficient to authenticate the record if the certifying person testified, then authenticity is not established under this Rule.

The reference to the "certification requirements of Rule 902(11) or (12)" is only to the procedural requirements for a valid certification. There is no intent to require, or permit, a certification under this rule to prove the requirements of Rule 803(6). Rule 902(14) is solely limited to authentication and any attempt to satisfy a hearsay exception must be made independently.

A certification under this Rule can only establish that the proffered item is authentic. The opponent remains free to object to admissibility of the proffered item on other grounds—including hearsay, relevance, or in criminal cases the right to confrontation. For example, in a criminal case in which data

APPENDIX IV

copied from a hard drive is proffered, the defendant can still challenge hearsay found in the hard drive, and can still challenge whether the information on the hard drive was placed there by the defendant.

A challenge to the authenticity of electronic evidence may require technical information about the system or process at issue, including possibly retaining a forensic technical expert; such factors will effect whether the opponent has a fair opportunity to challenge the evidence given the notice provided.

The reference to Rule 902(12) is intended to cover certifications that are made in a foreign country.

CONCLUSION

Determining whether digital evidence is authentic can be a difficult task, but it is not a task that is different in kind from authenticating hardcopy items. The admissibility standard for authenticity is relatively low, and compiling circumstantial evidence tied to the purported source of the electronic evidence will go a long way toward meeting that standard.

But expenditure of resources is a concern, especially if that expenditure is required to meet broad objections like "my webpage might have been hacked." The Advisory Committee has been working to ameliorate some of those costs; and a proper knowledge of the relationship between Rule 104(a) and (b) will go a long way toward streamlining the admissibility decision for the judge and overcoming such blunderbuss arguments. This Manual hopefully reduces the burden of authenticating evidence further by providing guidelines on how to authenticate the basic forms of digital evidence used in trials today.